COLIN WILSON, renowned criminologist, TV and radio personality, is one of the most popular and respected writers on both criminology and psychology. His many books include *The Mammoth Book of True Crime* and *A Plague of Murder*.

DAMON WILSON is author of over a dozen books, most notably *Murder Most Foul*, *The Encyclopaedia of Unsolved Mysteries* and *The Mammoth Book of Prophecy*.

WRITTEN IN BLOOD

A HISTORY OF FORENSIC DETECTION

COLIN WILSON & DAMON WILSON

ROBINSON

London

Constable & Robinson Ltd
3 The Lanchesters
162 Fulham Palace Road
London W6 9ER
www.constablerobinson.com

First published by Thorsons Publishing Group Limited 1989

This revised paperback edition published by Robinson,
an imprint of Constable & Robinson Ltd 2003

A copy of the British Library Cataloguing in
Publication data is available from the British Library

ISBN 1-84119-807-2

Printed and bound in the EU

10 9 8 7 6 5 4 3 2 1

Analytical Table of Contents

6   Every Bullet Has a Fingerprint

7   The Microscope As Detective

Angeles Jack the Ripper. The Black Dahlia. The Christie case. Was Evans guilty? The rise of motiveless murder – the case of Pastré-Beaussier. Penny Bjorkland. Robert Smith. The Moors murder case. Charles Manson. Graham Young, the thallium poisoner. Peter Sutcliffe, the Yorkshire Ripper. The five-man investigation team. The capture of the Ripper. The Railway Rapist. Duffy captured by computer.

Allan Pinkerton captures a gang of comers. The Pinkerton detective agency. The case of the murdered bank teller. The downfall of the Reno gang. The murder of Jesse James. The last Western bad man: Marion Hedgepeth. Hedgepeth and H. H. Holmes. The death of Benjamin Pitezel. Capture of America's worst mass murderer. The Muswell Hill murder. Improvements in detection. A spectacular failure: the case of Jeanne Weber. Thoinot's stupidity costs more lives. The Landru case. Kidnapping in America: the Charlie Ross case. The murder of Marion Parker. The Lindbergh kidnapping. Was Hauptmann guilty? The kidnapping of Brooke Hart. The lynching of the kidnappers. The kidnapping of Charles Urschel. The capture of Machine Gun Kelly. Belin and the case of Eugen Weidmann. Oregon's 'Sleeping Beauty' case. Fabian traces a demob suit. Japan's teacup bank robbery. The case of Ronald Harries.

The case of New York's Mad Bomber. Brussel's 'psychological portrait'. Lombroso and the science of criminology. The Jukes family. Lacassagne: 'Society gets the criminals it deserves.' The theories of Charles Goring: the inadequate criminal. The crimes of Carl Panzram. Fredric Wertham and the Oedipus murder case. Yochelson and Samenow are converted from 'liberalism'. Dan MacDougald and the 'faulty blocking mechanism'. The FBI Psychological Profiling team. The psychology of a sex killer. The Boston Strangler. Son of Sam. The case of Gerald Stano. Lombroso invents the lie detector. August Vollmer is appointed Marshall of Berkeley. Larson and the lie detector. The kidnapping of Father Heslin. Gerald Thompson fools the lie detector. Chris Gugas and the actor accused of indecent exposure. The Petroklos murder case. Hypnosis as a tool of detection. The murder of

Ruth Downing. Avery and Aurbeck learn hypnosis. Can a man be hynotized to kill?: the Hardrup case. The murders of Carl Gregory. The new menace: the 'random killer'. Dean Corll. The Freeway Killer. John Wayne Gacy. Pedro Lopez, Ecuador's mass murderer of girls. Dennis Nilsen, the Muswell Hill murderer. Daniel Barbosa. The case of Henry Lee Lucas. Lucas murders his mother. Released from jail. His career as a serial killer. Joel Norris on serial killers. The case of Ted Bundy. The vanishing girls. Bundy's escape. The Tallahassee killings. Bundy is convicted. What turned Bundy into a killer? 'The hunchback.' A new criminology. Van Vogt's 'Right Man' theory. 'The decision to be out of control.' All serial killers have Right Man characteristics. Charles Manson. The case of Leonard Lake. 'Sex slaves.' Maslow on 'dominance'. The Moors Murder case – Brady and Hindley. The 'criminal history of mankind'. Wells on 'jostling crowds'. Murderous tyrants. The 'golden age of crime detection'. The solution of the problem of serial killers? 'A diagnostic or prediction instrument.' VICAP – the Violent Criminal Apprehension Programme. Use of genetic fingerprinting. Conclusions.

Acknowledgements

This book owes an immense debt of gratitude to two friends: John Kennedy Melling and Stuart Kind, both of whom have provided me with so much material that they are virtually the co-authors. I was also fortunate enough to secure the co-operation of many other experts in various fields, including Dr Mike Sayce, Dr Alf Faragher, Dr Denis Hocking, and Candice Skrapec, one of America's leading authorities on serial killers. Other American friends who provided information are June O'Shea, Stephen Spickard, Dennis Stacy, Denis Rickard, Michael Flanagin, and Ann Rule. As usual, access to the immense library of my friend Joe Gaute was invaluable, as was the help of the crime-specialist bookseller Camille Wolfe. Two skilled crime writers, Brian Marriner and John Dunning, also provided invaluable information on many cases. Others to whom I owe a debt of gratitude are Paul Williams, Donald Rumbelow (both of the Metropolitan Police), Robin Odell, James Rentoul, D. J. Werrett, and Ian Kimber.

– Colin Wilson

Introduction

In November 1986, at a reception in Tokyo, I was introduced to Mr Soji Yamazaki, an executive editor on the *Mainichi Daily News*, who proceeded to fascinate me by telling me stories about a real-life Sherlock Holmes called Asaka Fukuda. Inspector Fukuda could predict outbreaks of arson simply by studying the evening newspaper and noting when low atmospheric pressure was forecast. This, he knew, affected people with sinus problems and made it hard for them to breathe. And some of these sufferers remedied the problems by starting fires, because the image of roaring flames somehow relieved the sense of suffocation and caused the nose to clear. Some of them would set many small fires in dustbins – perhaps as many as 20 in one day. Others would prefer one single spectacular blaze. Mr Yamazaki told me of one schoolboy who, at the end of an examination in which he felt he had done badly, set fire to the whole school. When Inspector Fukuda came to question this boy, his intuition told him that this could be the culprit. So instead of asking: 'Did you set fire to the school?', he asked: 'How long did the image of the fire remain in your brain?' And the schoolboy answered instantly: 'For more than two weeks!', his eyes still shining at the memory.

Mr Yamazaki went on to tell me of other cases of Fukuda's 'psychological method'. He was called to a country farmhouse to investigate what looked like a case of family suicide. In Japan there are many such cases: the parents decide to kill themselves, but are worried about what will happen to the children, and so kill them first. In this case, the children had been hacked to death with an axe before the parents had gassed themselves. But Fukuda observed that the children had been killed with heavy and determined blows with the blade of the axe. And it was his experience that when parents kill those they love, they prefer to knock them unconscious with the back of the axe, feeling that this will cause less pain. Fukuda accordingly declined to accept that this was a case of family suicide, and began to look for someone who had a motive to want them all dead. Soon he found a neighbour with whom the father was quarrelling about some land, and further investigation revealed that the neighbour was the killer.

Fukuda was an expert in distinguishing between suicide and murder. In the case of the 'suicide' of a night-club hostess, who had apparently hanged herself, he noted scratches on the neck, and the woman's own skin under her fingernails. To Fukuda this denoted murder – she had scratched herself trying to tear loose the fingers of the man – her lover – who had strangled her, then tried to make it look like suicide. These characteristic scratches were first noted by a pathologist named Yoshikawa, with the result that they have been called 'Yoshikawa lines'.

When we discussed the suicide of the Japanese novelist Mishima, Mr Yamazaki told me another interesting fact. Mishima had killed himself by the now old-fashioned method of ritual disembowelment, driving the knife into his abdomen, then ripping it sideways to expose the intestines. Again, Fukuda had encountered a number of cases in which a murderer had tried to conceal the crime by making it look like seppuku, but had been exposed because he had made a small mistake. In nearly all cases of seppuku, the suicide first of all tries pricking himself with the knife or sword-in the same way that, in the West, most people who cut their own throat first of all make a 'practice cut'. In cases that lacked this 'hesitation injury', Fukuda always assumed murder and began to look for the killer.

I was so fascinated by all this that I persuaded Mr Yamazaki to come and have lunch with me in my hotel, and allow me to tape some of his reminiscences of his days as a crime reporter: the result was over two hours of tape, of which I have quoted only a small fraction. I told him that I was thinking of writing a book about forensic medicine, and that when I did, I would include some of his stories of Fukuda, and would make quite sure that he received a copy. Six months later, I heard from a friend in Tokyo that Mr Yamazaki had died of a heart attack while playing golf. But his tales of Fukuda had set me thinking actively again about the book on forensic medicine.

It was an odd coincidence that, soon after this, my publisher asked me whether I would be interested in writing a history of crime detection. Now it so happens that, over the past 30 years, I have accumulated a considerable library of books on crime, as well as hundreds of *True Detective* magazines. But I have to admit that, after spending a morning browsing through these, some of my enthusiasm had evaporated. What I had forgotten was that it had already been done. In Seattle in 1967, I had bought two volumes by Jürgen Thorwald called *The Century of the Detective* and *Crime and Science: The New Frontier in Criminology.* (In England these were published in five volumes.) And as I re-read these, I realized just how comprehensive they are. And it was at this point, when I was more than half-persuaded to abandon the project, that chance gave it a new impetus. I had written a review of Dan Farson's *Soho in the Fifties* in the *Literary Review,* and it so happened that my own piece was followed by a review of a book called *The Scientific Investigation of Crime* by Stuart S. Kind. It was this that made me aware of how much the science of forensic medicine had progressed in the past quarter of a century. I immediately rang Lewis's Medical Library in Gower Street to ask them if they could get me a copy; they rang back later to say that it had been published in America, and they would order it for me. It looked like being a long wait, so I wrote to the University Bookstore in Seattle, asking if they could locate it and airmail me a copy. They wrote back to say that they could find no trace of it. I began to experience a feeling of smouldering rage and frustration; further enquiries at various English bookshops produced no better result. And at this point, an old friend who also has a passion for crime detection, John Kennedy Melling, told me that he thought Stuart Kind lived in Yorkshire, and offered to find me the address. When it arrived, I immediately wrote Stuart Kind a letter that began: 'Thank heavens I've finally tracked you down', and asked him if I could buy a copy of his book. By return post, an inscribed presentation copy arrived – a gesture that I have since found typical of the author's immense kindness and helpfulnes – and I learned that its publisher, far from being in America, is located in Harrogate.

I read *The Scientific Investigation of Crime* in a single sitting, and it convinced me that, in spite of Thorwald's excellence, there was still room for a comprehensive history of forensic detection. Almost everything in Kind's 420-page book is new, and even so, there is nothing on such recent techniques as genetic fingerprinting and 'psychological profiling'. There was obviously room for a large volume simply on the advances in crime detection since Thorwald was writing in the early 1960s.

But of course, that was not the book I wanted to write. I wanted to begin at the beginning. And as far as I could see, this would involve wholesale theft from Thorwald. But as soon as I settled down to research – availing myself of the vast crime library of my friend Joe Gaute – I began to see that this was not true either. The amount written about individual subjects such as toxicology, fingerprints, ballistics, blood serology – is so enormous that a really comprehensive history of crime detection would be 10,000 pages long; the problem is not what to put in but what to leave out. It became a kind of game finding cases that Thorwald had overlooked. Of course, there are certain landmarks in the history of crime detection that cannot be avoided: the Marie Lafarge case, the Gouffé case, the Tessnow case, the Crippen case, the Blackburn fingerprinting case. My general rule was, where possible, to go back to the original sources, and where this was not possible, to at least try to find as many other accounts as possible.

When finally embarked on the research, I never ceased to be surprised by the kindness and helpfulness of forensic scientists, police officers, and newspaper librarians. Whenever the book has come to a halt for want of a vital piece of information, I have usually been able to obtain it by ringing a Home Office forensic laboratory, a police station, or a reference library. In writing the case of Orrock's chisel, for example, I discovered some baffling gaps in the account given by Major Arthur Griffiths. I tried ringing the Hackney Reference Library, and at first the result was pure frustration; they were unable to find any mention of the case in the *Hackney Gazette* for 1882, or any account of the trial. But 10 days later, a large packet of duplicated newspaper cuttings appeared in the post, containing all the details I needed, and revealing, incidentally, that Griffiths had got much of it wrong – he obviously told the story from memory. Again, when it came to writing up a case that had been presented by Ludovic Kennedy on television, I realized that, for reasons best known to themselves, the BBC had decided to change the names of everyone involved. But Stuart Kind was able to put me on to the forensic scientist who had solved the case, Dr Mike Sayce, who in turn provided me with a mass of details that had not emerged in the television presentation. Again, when I needed information about genetic fingerprinting, I wrote direct to Alec Jeffreys at the University of Leicester, and he immediately sent me the material that is now included in Chapter 5.

Serendipity also played an important part; vital pieces of information occasionally seemed to drop from the sky. For example, my researches revealed only a small amount of information on the techniques of 'psychological profiling' of sex criminals; no one seemed to know much about it. At that point, a Los Angeles television production company asked me if I would be willing to take part in a programme for the Jack the Ripper centenary, and mentioned that members of the FBI 'profiling' team would be providing a psychological portrait of the Ripper. When I asked if they could let me have any information on the techniques they immediately sent me a dozen articles from technical journals that contained – to my immense gratitude – everything I needed.

The result is that the book, in spite of its gruesome subject (a reviewer of one of my earlier books on murder complained that it gave him a sensation of 'wading through mud'), has been a continuous pleasure to write. I can only hope it conveys a fraction of the same feeling to the reader.

CW

1

The Science of Detection

1

The case had all the makings of a classic murder mystery.

The body of Nancy Titterton was found by two furniture removal men; she was lying face downward in an empty bath, naked except for a pair of silk stockings, and for the pyjama jacket knotted round her throat. Torn underclothes on the bedroom floor indicated that the motive had been a sexual attack. When the two men had arrived at four o'clock on that Good Friday afternoon – returning a love seat that had been under repair – they found the front door of the apartment standing open. The elder of the two, Theodore Kruger, had called Mrs Titterton's name, and then, hearing the sound of a shower, glanced in through the open bathroom door; moments later, his young assistant, Johnny Fiorenza, was telephoning the police.

Beekman Place, where the Tittertons lived, was traditionally the home of New York artists and intellectuals. Lewis Titterton was an executive at the National Broadcasting Company, and his 33-year-old wife was a writer of exceptional promise. They had been married for seven years, and were known to be devoted to each other. Most of their small circle of friends were, like themselves, interested in the arts and literature. Neither of them was fond of socializing – Nancy Titterton was shy and introverted. Yet she had opened her door to her killer and let him into the apartment, which argued that she knew him.

It was the kind of case that would have driven a nineteenth-century detective to despair; a preliminary search of the apartment revealed no clues. But this was 1936, and the New York police had an impressive armoury of scientific and forensic aids. At the beginning of the twentieth century, the great criminologist Edmond Locard had formulated the basic principle of scientific crime detection: 'Every contact leaves a trace.' The criminal *must,* of necessity, leave behind something at the scene of the crime, and take something away with him. A single fibre from his clothing could be identified under the microscope; so could dust or mud from his shoes. A new process involving silver nitrate could raise fingerprints on fabric. Even the rapist's blood grouping could be determined from his seminal stains. This is why, as he surveyed the Titterton's flat, Assistant Chief Inspector John A. Lyons was not unduly discouraged.

In fact, a clue came to light as soon as the body was lifted from the bath: a 13-inch length of cord, which had been severed by a sharp knife. Marks on Nancy Titterton's wrists indicated that the killer had bound them before he raped her. He had cut them free when she lay, face downward, in the bath, and taken the cord with him; but in his haste he had overlooked the short piece that slipped under the body. This suggested that he knew the cord could provide a clue to his identity. Lyons ordered his men to check with every manufacturer in the New York area, to try to trace its source.

The mud samples on the carpet were disappointing. Microscopic examination revealed minute traces of lint, such as is found in upholstery establishments; that meant it had been brought into the apartment on the shoes of fhe two men who delivered the love seat.

A minute smear of green paint on the counterpane suggested another lead. The building was in the process of being painted in that precise shade of green. It looked as if the killer had brushed against the wet paint and left some on the bed. It also suggested that he might be one of the four painters. But a check revealed that only one of them had been working there on the day of the murder, and the other tenants were able to confirm that he had been working on another floor between 11 o'clock and midday – estimated by the medical examiner as the time Nancy Titterton had been killed.

A maid in the apartment below offered an interesting piece of information; she had been preparing lunch when she heard a woman's voice call: 'Dudley, oh Dudley!' The name of the janitor was Dudley Mings, and he was unable to offer a verifiable alibi. His story was that he had been working alone in his basement throughout the morning. But a search of his apartment revealed nothing to connect him with the murder, and he seemed to be a man of good character. On the whole, it was probable that his alibi was true.

The search for the origin of the cord seemed hopeless. It was of the kind used on venetian blinds, and was therefore commonplace. And the sharp kitchen knife that had probably been used to cut it from her wrists contained no fingerprints.

Now the general picture of the crime was beginning to emerge. The killer had entered 22 Beekman Place through the front door, either ringing the bell to request the tenant to release the catch, or by manipulating its defective lock. Again, this argued that he was known to the victim. Once inside, he had clamped a hand over her mouth to prevent her from screaming, then stuffed a piece of cloth between her teeth. He had tied her hands behind her with the cord he had brought with him, then carried or dragged her (she weighed only 100 lb) into the bedroom. He had removed her blouse and skirt, then thrown her on to one of the two single beds and torn off her brassiere and panties – both were torn. After raping her, he had knotted a pyjama jacket round her throat, as well as a red blouse. He had carried her into the bathroom and cut the cord from her wrist, after which he had turned on the shower. Then he had hurried out of the apartment, leaving the door open behind him.

All this suggested a crime that was deliberately planned, not one committed on the spur of the moment. He had brought the cord with him and taken it away again; he had wiped his fingerprints off the knife he had used to cut it. Yet he had also placed her in the shower – presumably in an attempt to revive her. That suggested a man who was emotionally involved with her – perhaps a rejected lover – rather than some casual rapist. But as Lyons interviewed every known friend of the couple, he became increasingly convinced that Nancy Titterton had not been the type to engage in a secret love affair.

The break came, as Lyons had hoped, from the crime laboratory. Dr Alexander O. Gettler, the city toxicologist, discovered a puzzling clue when he was examining the bedclothes in his laboratory at the Bellevue Hospital. Studying the candlewick counterpane under a magnifying glass, he found a piece of white hair, less than half an inch long. It was stiffer than human hair, and the microscope revealed it to be horsehair, of the type used for stuffing furniture. In fact, it was of the same type used to stuff the love seat that had been returned on the day of the murder. Since it was too heavy in texture to have been blown into the bedroom on a gust of air, it must have been carried there on someone's clothing. That some-one, Lyons reasoned, could only have been one of the two furniture men. Yet both claimed that they had not entered the bedroom. And since they had been together in the apartment until the police arrived, the only alter-native was that one of them had come to the apartment earlier in the day.

Kruger's upholstery shop was on Second Avenue; Lyons found the proprietor there alone. Asked where he had been on the morning of Good Friday, Theodore replied that he had spent the morning working in the shop.

'And your assistant?'

'Johnny was out until after lunch – he had to report to the parole officer in the morning.'

'He has a criminal record?'

'Only for taking a car. Now he's turned over a new leaf – he's a good boy.'

Outside, Lyons told his assistant: 'Johnny Fiorenza claims he went to see his probation officer on Friday morning. But the office is closed on Good Friday. Keep a tail on him until further notice.'

Back at headquarters, Lyons checked on Johnny Fiorenza's record; he had been arrested four times for theft, and spent two years in Elmira for car stealing. A psychiatrist who had examined him at the time of his first arrest had reported that he was a highly emotional individual. Fiorenza had been up to the Titterton's apartment on two previous occasions, each time with his employer, so Nancy Titterton would know and trust him.

Then came the evidence Lyons needed. The piece of venetian blind cord had been manufactured by the Hanover Cordage Company of York, Pennsylvania, and a New York wholesaler had sold a roll of it to Theodore Kruger's upholstery shop.

Lyons ordered Johnny Fiorenza to be brought in to the office. For four and a half hours, the suspect was questioned, and continued to insist that he had not been near the Titterton's apartment on the morning of Good Friday. Then the detective took out the length of venetian blind cord and dangled it in front of his eyes. 'This is what convinced us you were in the apartment on Friday morning. We've traced it back to the furniture shop.'

Fiorenza began to sweat; then he allowed his head to slump into his hands. 'All right. I guess I may as well tell you about it.' His story bore out what Lyons had already guessed. When Fiorenza first called at the apartment, two months before, he had become instantly infatuated with the attractive authoress; with her charm and social poise, she seemed to be everything he had always wanted – and could never hope to attain. And when he and Kruger called to collect the love seat, on the day before Good Friday, he had decided that he had to possess her at all costs. The next morning, he had telephoned his employer to say that he had to see his probation officer. Instead he had gone to Beekman Place. When Nancy Titterton called: 'Who is it?' he answered: 'The man about the love seat', and she let him in. As he had grabbed her, she shouted: 'Dudley, oh Dudley!', but only the maid in the downstairs apartment heard her. Fiorenza had rammed a handkerchief into her mouth, tied her hands with cord, and pushed her into the bedroom . . .

The jury took very little time to arrive at a guilty verdict; a few weeks later, Johnny Fiorenza went to the electric chair in Sing Sing.

One mystery remains: why did he carry her into the shower? His story was that he was shocked to find that she had died of suffocation, and tried to revive her. But in that case, she would have identified him as the rapist, and he would have been sentenced to a long term in prison. It seems unlikely that he was prepared to allow this to happen, and the only alternative is that he went to the apartment with every intention of killing Nancy Titterton. Then why place her in the bath? There can be only one explanation: it was intended as an insurance policy against getting caught. It would support his story that her death was an accident, and help to convince a jury that he was guilty of manslaughter rather than murder. Johnny Fiorenza was clearly an exceptionally cunning and far-sighted criminal, and there seems no doubt that if he had not been betrayed by a horsehair, he would certainly, as Sherlock Holmes might have said, have gone far in his chosen profession.

2

The Titterton case has a certain classic simplicity that makes it sound like detective fiction; it would undoubtedly have aroused the enthusiasm of Edgar Allan Poe. In fact, Poe himself attempted to apply the same principles of scientific logic to a similar murder case, which had caused an unprecedented sensation in New York almost a century earlier.

On Wednesday 28 July 1841, the body of a young woman was found floating in the Hudson River. She was fully clothed except for her petticoat, and a strip of lace was tied round her throat so tightly that it was almost invisible in the flesh. She was quickly identified as Mary Cecilia Rogers, a 21-year-old salesgirl who had worked in a cigar store on Broadway. In those days, female shop assistants were rare, and the pretty brunette had become a minor celebrity in New York.

She had vanished from her home – a boarding-house in Nassau Street, run by her mother – on the previous Sunday. At 10 o'clock in the morning, she had knocked on the door of her fiancé, Daniel Payne, and told him that she intended to spend the day with her aunt, who lived in Bleecker Street. Payne said he would call for her that evening. But a violent thunderstorm convinced him that she would prefer to spend the night with her aunt. When he came home from work the next evening, Mary had still not returned, so Payne called on the aunt, a Mrs Downing, and learned to his surprise that Mary had not been there.

Two days later, her body was found floating near Castle Point, Hoboken, on the New Jersey side of the river. According to a medical examination, she had been 'horribly outraged'. But the body was already in such a state of decomposition that no further autopsy was performed, and she was buried immediately.

The next day, the coroner received an anonymous letter, postmarked Hoboken, declaring that the writer had seen Mary stepping ashore from a boat with six 'rough-looking characters', and that she had gone with them into the woods. She had been laughing, and was apparently under no kind of constraint. Subsequently, two men who had been walking along the shore in Hoboken confirmed that they had seen a girl resembling Mary entering the woods with six rough-looking men.

In spite of the corroboration, this sounded an unlikely story. Would an attractive young girl, well known for her refusal to tolerate undue familiarity, go for a boat trip with six roughs, and then accompany them into the woods? In fact, a few weeks later, another witness, a stage-driver, declared that he had seen Mary step off the ferry with a tall, well-dressed man of dark complexion, and go with him to a nearby tavern named Nick Mullen's. The tavern keeper, a Mrs Loss, recalled that a man and woman of the correct description had 'partaken of refreshment' at her hostelry, and then gone off into the woods. Soon after, she heard a woman's scream from the woods, but paid little attention.

In September – two months later – Mrs Loss's children found a white silk petticoat in the woods, together with a parasol, a silk scarf, and a handkerchief with the initials M.R. The shrubbery in the area looked torn and trampled, as if it had been the scene of a 'terrific struggle'. Not long after, Mary's fiancé committed suicide at this spot, giving rise to a rumour that he had murdered Mary and killed himself out of remorse. In fact, Payne had been able to account for all his movements on the day of her disappearance.

Earlier that year, Poe had created his detective – the first in fiction – Auguste Dupin, in a story called 'The Murders in the Rue Morgué. Dupin prefers to spend his days indoors, behind 'massive shutters', and to conduct his investigations from a comfortable armchair, to the rapt admiration of a disciple who is also the narrator. Poe's morbid interest in the death of beautiful women ensured that he would be fascinated by the case of Mary Rogers, and in the following year, he revived the Chevalier Auguste Dupin, and set him to solving the enigma in a story called 'The Mystery of Marie Roget', in which the scene of the crime is transferred to Paris. To call it a story is not entirely accurate; it is a 50-page monologue in which Poe's hero discusses the various theories in stupefying detail, with frequent use of polysyllables like 'ratiocination' and 'animadversion'. Poe told an editor to whom he was attempting to sell the story:

No point is omitted. I examine, each by each, the opinions and arguments of the press upon the subject, and show that this subject has been hitherto unapproached. In fact I believe not only that I have demonstrated the fallacy of the general idea – that the girl was the victim of a gang of ruffians – but have *indicated the assassin* in a manner which will give renewed impetus to investigation.

Poe's central point is that Mary could not have been killed by a gang; who battered state of her face suggests that she fought violently, which argued a lone man, not a gang who could easily have overpowered her. Moreover, says Dupin, a strip of lace found tied round the waist was probably a handle for carrying the body, again suggesting a lone man. But who was this man? Poe seizes upon a curious event that had occurred six months before Mary's disappearance. In January 1841 she had vanished from the cigar store, and the police were searching for her when she reappeared, six days later, looking tired and ill, and explained that she had been visiting relatives in the country. There were some rumours that she had been seen during this time with a handsome naval officer, and these led Mary to give up her job in the cigar store; soon after, she became engaged to the clerk Daniel Payne.

This naval officer is Poe's chief suspect. He believes that, after persuading Mary to elope with him, he abandoned her. Six months later, he had again persuaded her to run away with him – possibly because she was pregnant – and had murdered her. The naval officer was the man of dark complexion with whom she was seen on the ferry.

Poe suggests that, after killing her in the woods, he rowed her body into the middle of the river, and threw it from the boat. Then he rowed across to some wharf on the New York waterfront and allowed the boat to drift away, in case it provided the police with a clue. What convinces Poe that the murderer used a boat is that the body was not weighed down; he argues that the murderer must have forgotten to put a weight on board before he pushed off. If the body had been thrown in from the shore, he would have taken the trouble to find a heavy stone . . . Find the missing boat, says Dupin, and it will probably lead to the murderer.

This ingenious theory demonstrates the danger of trying to solve a crime from an armchair. According to an account of the case in Thomas Duke's *Celebrated Criminal Cases of America* (1910), the body was, in fact, weighed down by a stone. And since it was also found close to the shore, it seems logical to assume that it was thrown in from the shore, and not from a boat. So the central argument of Poe's story collapses, as does his conviction that he has 'indicated the assassin'.

In fact, by the time the story was about to reappear in *The Ladies' Companion,* Poe had heard rumour of a rather more convincing theory about Mary's death – that it was simply the result of an abortion that had gone wrong. (Poe had been living in Philadelphia, which explains why it had taken so long to reach his ears.) He hastily inserted several phrases about a 'fatal accident under the roof of Madame Deluc' (i.e., Mrs Loss) which make no sense whatever in the light of his other speculations.

In 1891, half a century after Mary's death, an interesting piece of evidence came to light in the form of a testimony submitted to the Supreme Court of New York. It concerned Mary's employer in the cigar store, John Anderson. Anderson's family were contesting his will, on the grounds that he had been mentally incompetent when he made it. As evidence for this assertion, Anderson's daughter alleged that he had been deeply disturbed by Mary's death, so that he 'had had many, *very* many unhappy days and nights in regard to her', and had even gone to the length of establishing contact with Mary's ghost, presumably through a 'spirit medium'. The case was settled out of court, and the record destroyed. But several years later, the Supreme Court copy had been tracked down by Poe scholar Samuel Copp Worthen, who published an account of it in *American Literature* in 1948. Worthen revealed that Anderson knew rather more about Mary's death than anyone had suspected. He had been arrested and questioned in 1841, but subsequently released without publicity; even so, his fear that this might become known had prevented him from standing for mayor of New York. Moreover, Anderson had admitted that it was he who had paid for an abortion in the January of 1841, and had 'got into some trouble over it'. But, he insisted, apart from that earlier episode, he had not had 'anything, *directly, himself*' to do with Mary's later problems. The phrasing here obviously suggests that, in that earlier episode, he *had* been responsible for her pregnancy, while the words 'directly, himself' hint that he felt that he was indirectly responsible for her later problems. Worthen is inclined to believe that, when she found herself pregnant again (presumably by Daniel Payne), Mary approached Anderson for help, and he arranged a second abortion, to take place under the roof of Mrs Loss. The 'dark complexioned' man on the boat was probably the abortionist. The abortion went wrong, and Mrs Loss found herself an accessory after the fact of manslaughter. With the help of the abortionist and members of her family, she consigned the body to the river. Both she and the abortionist must have been immensely relieved to learn that the doctor who examined the body had pronounced that Mary had been the victim of a sex crime.

In the light of the known facts, it becomes possible to reconstruct the likeliest scenario behind the death of Mary Rogers. When she became a shop assistant in Anderson's shop, she also became his mistress. In due course, Anderson had to pay for an abortion, and 'got into some trouble over it' – presumably from Mary's mother and relatives, or from his own wife. To divert the obvious suspicions, he may have started the rumour about the handsome naval officer. To avoid further scandal, Mary left the cigar store and became engaged to Daniel Payne.

When she became pregnant a second time, she again appealed to Anderson, who felt that her difficulties were indirectly his own fault for having seduced her. He therefore arranged another abortion under the roof of Mrs Loss. When it went wrong, and Mary's body was found floating in the Hudson, he realized that he faced scandal and ruin if his role was discovered. But when the police began looking for a rapist, he knew he was probably safe. Mrs Loss was also quick to take advantage of the mistake; she was responsible for the anonymous letter describing how Mary had been seen going into the woods with six ruffians. (The story was probably inspired by an incident that had recently taken place in Hoboken; a young girl on an outing with her parents had returned to the boat to fetch her parasol; she was seized by six young men, who rowed her out into the centre of the river and sexually assaulted her before setting her ashore.) And by way of further corroboration, Mrs Loss persuaded two more 'gentlemen friends' to state that they had also seen a woman of Mary's description stepping ashore with six ruffians.

Everything seemed to be going well when, a few weeks later, the stage-driver came forward to reveal that he had seen Mary stepping off the ferry and going to Mrs Loss's tavern with a dark complexioned man. Mrs Loss now hastened to recollect that two such people *had* been in her tavern on the afternoon in question, and that later she had heard a scream from the woods. So now the search was diverted towards a solitary assassin. In fact, Mrs Loss had already left Mary's petticoat and handkerchief in the woods; the bushes were broken to suggest a violent struggle. To her disgust, they remained undiscovered for two months, when she had to arrange for her own children to find them.

Anderson, who felt responsible for Mary's death, brooded on his guilty secret; it was still tormenting him 40 years later, when he died, a millionaire, in Paris. But at least he felt he had obtained forgiveness from Mary's spirit. Daniel Payne, who felt equally guilty, committed suicide at the spot where the petticoat had been found.

Even without the virtue of hindsight, we can see that Poe had more than enough clues to point him to the right solution of the case. His greatest blunder was in assuming that Mary had eloped for a second time with the 'blackguard' who had been responsible for her first disappearance. But why should the man persuade her to elope a second time? If she was pregnant, all he had to do was abandon her again. And if he murdered her, why did he increase his risk of being caught by dumping her body in the river, instead of leaving it where it was – as he left her clothes? The fact that it was Mrs Loss's children who found the clothes should have alerted Poe's suspicions. So should the fact that Mrs Loss reported hearing only one scream, when, if there had been a violent struggle, she should have heard a whole series of screams. The truth is that Poe was too excited by what he regarded as his own major insight – that Mary could not possibly have been murdered by a gang – to look more closely at the 'lone blackguard' theory. Again, to the modern reader, the most significant clue is that Mary looked pale and ill after her first disappearance. Poe, too chivalrous or too romantic to jump to the obvious conclusion, preferred to believe that she had been seduced and abandoned, and so failed to glimpse the true solution until too late.

So, for all the brilliance of his reasoning, Poe proves to be an unreliable guide in the realm of criminal actuality. But this should surprise no one. For, as incredible as it sounds, at the time Poe wrote 'Marie Roget', there was not a police officer in the world who would have thought of trying to solve a crime by the use of scientific logic. Then, as now, most murders were solved by common sense and a certain amount of luck. This is because, in most murder cases, there is an obvious link between the murder victim and the suspect. In the decade before the Mary Rogers case, the most famous New York murder was that of an attractive but rather wayward young lady called Helen Jewett who, during the night of 11 April 1836, was killed in her bed by a blow from a hatchet. A woman in the next apartment heard a long moan and looked out of her door in time to see a man in a Spanish cloak hurrying off down the corridor, then smelt smoke and found that Helen's room was in flames. The murderer was subsequently seen scaling a whitewashed fence. The obvious suspect was Helen's lover, a youth named Richard Robinson, and when the police woke him up in bed an hour or so later, they found whitewash on his trousers. Moreover, the Spanish cloak, which had been abandoned near the whitewashed fence, was identified as Robinson's. He also had a motive for murder – he had become engaged to a wealthy young lady, and Helen was threatening to make trouble. Yet all this weight of evidence was not sufficient for the jury, who decided that the case against Robinson was purely circumstantial, and acquitted him. (The Victorian prejudice against 'fallen women' also undoubtedly played its part in the verdict.) This was the straightforward reality of crime detection in the nineteenth century, so it is hardly surprising that Dupin's methods failed to inspire the New York police force.

That they finally became accepted as the basic principle of criminal investigation was due largely to an accident of literary history. Forty years after the death of Mary Rogers, a 21-year-old medical student at Edinburgh confided to a fellow student named George Hamilton that he was fascinated by Poe's Dupin stories, but realized that they were 'caviare to the general'; he was brooding on the idea of inventing a detective 'according to the system of Poe, but greatly simplified and brought down to the level of ordinary people'. Most such projects remain in the realm of good intentions. But when, two years later, Dr Doyle set up his medical practice in Southsea, and failed to attract a single patient, he whiled away the time trying to write fiction. And after selling a number of stories at three guineas each, he embarked upon a murder story in which the detective is blatantly lifted from Poe. But when Conan Doyle's detective burst upon the world in *Beeton's Christmas Annual*, he lost no time in demonstrating that he was no mere armchair reasoner:

. . . he whipped a tape measure and a large round magnifying glass from his pocket. With these two implements he trotted noiselessly about the room, sometimes stopping, occasionally kneeling, and once lying flat upon his face. So engrossed was he with his occupation that he appeared to have forgotten our presence, for he chattered away to himself under his breath the whole time, keeping up a running fire of exclamations, and little cries suggestive of encouragement and of hope. As I watched him I was irresistibly reminded of a pure-blooded, well-trained foxhound as it dashes backwards and forwards through the covert, whining in its eagerness, until it comes across the lost scent. For twenty minutes or more he continued his researches, measuring with the most exact care the distance between marks which were entirely invisible to me, and occasionally applying his tape to the walls in an equally incomprehensible manner. In one place he gathered up very carefully a little pile of grey dust from the floor, and packed it away in an envelope . . .

'They say that genius is an infinite capacity for taking pains,' he remarked with a smile. 'It's a very bad definition, but it does apply to detective work.'

Now this strikes the modern reader as completely authentic – the kind of careful study of the scene of crime that the forensic experts would bring to the Nancy Titterton case. But this again is a mistake. In 1887, the year of *A Study in Scarlet,* scientific crime detection was still virtually non-existent. It is true that in Paris, a persistent young clerk named Alphonse Bertillon had just been permitted, in the face of official indifference, to set up his own complicated system of criminal identification, known as anthropometry; but it had yet to become widely known. In London, Francis Galton had realized that every fingerprint is different, but was still baffled by the problem of how to classify them. In Austria, a magistrate named Hans Gross was making notes for a modest handbook for his fellow magistrates which would one day become known as the Bible of crime detection. But the ordinary overworked copper went about his task in exactly the same manner as in 1841 – or, for that matter, 1741, or 1641. In difficult cases, the essence of this system was elimination and sheer persistence – what might be called the 'needle-in-the-haystack' method. The detective had to be prepared to dismantle the haystack, straw by straw, to discover the lost needle. One of its most remarkable exponents was

Chief Inspector Louis Canler, of the Paris Sûreté, and he had demonstrated its value in tracking down one of the most ruthless and
intelligent of French criminals.

3

On 16 December 1834, a neighbour of the Widow Chardon, who lived
at 271 rue St Martin, noticed a red stain that had seeped under the door,
and when his knocks brought no reply, he went to summon the police.
They discovered the corpse of a man lying in a pool of blood, his head
split open by a hatchet, which lay next to the body. In the next room
they found the body of an old woman, covered with stab wounds. She
was the mother of the murdered man, who was a homosexual begging
letter writer, nicknamed 'Auntie'. 'It was on abject creatures known to
share his tastes,' says the disapproving Canler, 'that suspicion first fell.
Several of these filthy fellows were arrested and then released for want
of proof.' And, for the time being, the police investigation met an
impasse.

Two weeks later, on New Year's Eve, Chief Inspector Canler was
summoned to investigate an attempted murder. A young bank
messenger named Genevey had been asked to call at 66 rue
Montorgueil to collect money from a gentleman named Mahossier. On
the fourth floor, the clerk found a room with 'Mahossier' chalked on
the door and knocked. As he entered the room, the door was closed
behind him, and some sharp instrument was driven into his back. At the
same time, a man tried to grasp him by the throat; he was clumsy, and
his hand went into the clerk's mouth. Genevey was a robust young
man; he struggled violently and shouted. His assailants became
alarmed and ran away. Genevey staggered into the arms of neighbours
who came to investigate.

At this time, the Sûreté – Paris's equivalent of Scotland Yard – was
a modest organization, with a mere 27 men: it had been founded a few
decades earlier by a crook-turned-thief-catcher named Vidocq. Now its
chief was a man named Pierre Allard, and he lost no time in appointing
Canler to investigate both cases. He began by getting a good description of one of the assailants: a well-dressed man with a high forehead
and a silky moustache; his manner, apparently, was polished and
courteous. Significantly, he had been carrying a copy of Rousseau's
Social Contract, the book that had virtually caused the French

Revolution. The landlord at rue Montorgueil had not noticed the other man.

Now Canler proceeded to apply the needle-in-the-haystack method. It involved, quite simply, paying a visit to every cheap hotel and doss house in the Paris area, and asking to see the register that they were obliged to keep. Of course, it was obvious that 'Mahossier' was not the man's real name, but Canler's knowledge of the criminal classes told him that they often used the same alias many times. And eventually, after trying every lodging-house in Montmartre, Île de la Cité, and the Temple area, he found what he wanted in rue du Faubourg du Temple: the name 'Mahossier' in the hotel register. The proprietor shook his head; he had no memory of Mahossier. 'How about this name underneath – Fizellier?' The proprietor, a man named Pageot, called his wife, and she was able to tell Canler that Fizellier was a big, red-haired man. Canler could sense that Pageot was not pleased by his wife's helpfulness; he didn't believe in helping the police more than necessary. So Canler thanked them and took his leave.

The description of Fizellier had rung a bell. A big, red-haired man had recently been arrested on a fraud charge, and he was at present in the central police station. Canler's expression was guileless as he entered his cell, notebook in hand, and pretended to search for a name:

'François, you tell me you're innocent of this fraud?'

'That's so.'

'All right, then why did you call yourself Fizellier when you stayed at Mother Pageot's?'

'Because there was a warrant out for me, and I'd have been stupid to use my real name.'

With quiet satisfaction, Canler went back to his office and made out a report stating that François was one of the two men in the bank messenger case. Then he returned to Mother Pageot's. This time he found her alone, and willing to tell what she knew. Mahossier, it seemed, had a high forehead and silky moustache, and he had stayed there before under the name of Bâton.

There *was* a crook called Bâton, a homosexual thief. 'Fizellier' and 'Mahossier' had shared a bed, so this might be the man. Canler ordered his arrest. But as soon as he saw him, he knew this was not Mahossier; Bâton was anything but distinguished or courteous. But again, Canler used his knowledge of criminal psychology. If Mahossier had borrowed Bâton's name, then he probably knew him. So, leaving Baton in custody, Canler made a round of his haunts, and questioned his friends about a distinguished man with a silky moustache. A number of them agreed that this sounded like a person named Gaillard, with whom Bâton had been in prison. Back went Canler to Bâton, told him he was free to go, then asked him in a casual, friendly way about his friend Gaillard. Baton's description left no doubt that Gaillard and Mahossier were the same person. But where was Gaillard? As soon as Canler began his enquiries, he encountered a difficulty; there were several suspicious characters called Gaillard, and it might be any of them. So, with infinite patience, Canler went back to searching the registers of doss houses. It took him two days to find the signature he wanted, in a hotel in the rue Marivaux-des-Lombards. The proprietress remembered M. Gaillard, a tall man with a high forehead. He had been visited occasionally by a lady. And he had left behind a bundle of Republican songs in his room. She still had them. And they made Canler aware of an interesting aspect of his suspect's character – he was a poet, and not entirely without talent. A letter in the form of a satirical poem made some libellous aspersions about the previous prefect of police. And the handwriting was unmistakably that of Mahossier.

Canler was now told that a prisoner named Avril wanted to talk to him. Avril had heard on the grapevine that Canler wanted to interview Gaillard. He offered to do a deal. If Canler would like to release him, then have him discreetly followed, he would wander around Gaillard's old resorts and see if he could locate him. Canler agreed, and for the next week, Avril was shadowed as he wandered from bar to bar. But when, at the end of that time, there was still no sign of Gaillard, Canler decided he was wasting police expenses, and had Avril put back in jail.

Meanwhile, red-headed François had been convicted, and was doing time in the Sainte-Pélagie prison. Canler decided it was time to renew the pressure. But as he sat beside the prisoner in the cabriolet taking them back to Canler's office, François decided to speak of his own accord. He told Canler that he could give him information about the murder of the Chardons. He had spent an evening drinking with a man who told him that he had murdered the Chardons, while one of his acquaintances kept watch. The man's name? Gaillard . . .

And now, for the first time, Canler realized that his two cases were connected. Mahossier had murdered the Chardons, and attempted to murder and rob the bank messenger. In each crime he had had a different accomplice. In the bank messenger case it had been red-headed François. And in the murder case, Canler had a hunch that the accomplice had been

Avril. Now he questioned Avril further, and obtained a new piece of information. 'Gaillard' had an aunt, old and quite rich, who lived in the rue Bar-du-Bec; he was even able to tell Canler the number. Canler's chief, Allard, was now so interested in the case that he went with him to visit the old lady. When they rang the bell of her apartment, a panel slid open, and a woman asked them what they wanted. 'To speak to Madame Gaillard about her nephew. We are police officers.'

In her apartment, Mme Gaillard explained apologetically that she did not trust her nephew, which was why she had had the grill put in the door – he was perfectly capable of murdering her. What, asked Allard, was her nephew's real name? 'Pierre-François Lacenaire.' It was the first time that Canler had heard the name of the criminal he was hunting for the past three weeks.

A general alert went out. There was no sign of Lacenaire in Paris. But a few days later, on 2 February 1835, the District Attorney in Beaune wrote a letter announcing the arrest of Lacenaire on a charge of passing a forged bill of exchange. He was brought back to Paris in chains. The man Canler and Allard confronted in his cell did not look like a master criminal – more like a gentleman down on his luck. When accused of the attempted robbery of the bank messenger, he admitted it without emotion; like many villains, he felt that it was simply a 'job' that had turned out badly, like any unfortunate business venture. Asked the name of his accomplice, he replied: 'Gentleman, we villains have our code. We do not denounce our accomplices.' Canler replied that his accomplices were not bound by a similar code; François had already betrayed him. Lacenaire merely smiled politely; he knew the police were capable of bluffing. All he would say was: 'I shall make enquiries.' He looked slightly more disturbed when Canler told him that Avril had done his best to betray him, but made the same response. Lacenaire was then transferred to La Force prison.

There his 'enquiries' led to his being savagely beaten up by friends of François, so that he had to spend some weeks in the prison hospital. When he next saw Canler, he was ready to obtain his revenge. He made a full confession of both crimes, implicating Avril in the murder of the Chardons, and François in the attack on the bank messenger.

In prison, Lacenaire became a celebrity. The idea of a poetic murderer appealed to the Parisian public; he received many visitors, and discoursed to them on the injustice of the social system – to which he attributed his choice of a life of crime. In the period of the unpopular July Monarchy, with its repressive laws, this kind of thing appealed to

Republican intellectuals. Lacenaire revelled in the limelight – it was what he had always craved. The poet Theophile Gautier called him 'the Manfred of the gutter' (referring to Byron's noble rebel) and the nickname seemed appropriate. (Pictures of Lacenaire make him look rather like Poe.) In November 1835, Lacenaire, François, and Avril went on trial; Lacenaire and Avril were sentenced to death, François to life imprisonment. Lacenaire admitted frankly that his motive in giving evidence against his accomplices was revenge; he evidently took pleasure in making them aware that if they had observed the code of honour among thieves, none of them would have been in this predicament.

In prison, Lacenaire wrote his *Memoirs,* which were intended to be his justification. He is intent on proving that he is less a criminal than an 'Outsider'. 'A victim of injustice since infancy . . . I had created a view of life very different from other men's. I know only one virtue, which is worth all the rest: it is Sensibility.' In fact, the book is full of the emotional, upside-down logic of the typical criminal, a logic based upon self-pity. He loathed his father, and was upset because his parents preferred his elder brother; convinced at the age of 16 that he would die on the guillotine (to which he liked to refer as his 'mistress') he decided to 'have the blood of society'. But it soon becomes clear that his real trouble was not his philosophy of revolt, but his weakness; when things went well, he was a law-abiding citizen; as soon as they went wrong, he was thrown into a passion of indignation against fate, and tried to take the easy way out by looking around for something to steal. He lacked the ability to face adversity. It is worth commenting on this aspect of Lacenaire's psychology, for we shall encounter it many times in the course of this book.

The execution was carried out, unannounced, on a cold and foggy January morning. Lacenaire watched Avril's head fall into the basket without flinching; but when he himself knelt under the blade, there was an accident that would have broken another man's nerve; as the blade fell, it stuck half-way, and had to be hauled up again; Lacenaire was looking up at it as it dropped and severed his head.

4

The tracking-down of Lacenaire was an outstanding example of the needle-in-the-haystack method, as employed in the days before the arrival of scientific crime detection. Even more remarkable was the tracking of John Todd, a distiller who fled to America with £10,000 of his creditors' money, by the Bow Street Runner Henry Goddard, in 1853. Logically speaking, it should have been impossible for Goddard to find a man who might have vanished to any corner of America without leaving a trace behind. In fact, two days of searching through New York hotel registers yielded no result whatever. Reasoning that any fugitive would head out west, Goddard took a boat up the Hudson, and went from Buffalo to Detroit, then to Chicago and Milwaukee, enquiring at bankers and land agents along the way, still without trace of the quarry. In Milwaukee he enquired the name of the next large town, and was told Janesville; he decided to go there on the off-chance. In a hotel bar, he saw the register lying on the counter, opened it casually, and found John Todd's signature. Chance – and detective instinct – had led him straight to his quarry. The judge to whom he applied for help was deeply impressed by his persistence, which he compared to searching for 'a small needle placed point upward in the middle of a forest'. (Unfortunately, the outcome in this case was less than satisfactory; America had no bankruptcy laws, so the fugitive escaped arrest.)

Goddard and Canler were the exceptions, men with the instinct of bloodhounds. What is so remarkable about the John Todd case is that Goddard undertook his apparently impossible task in a spirit of optimism, a certainty that it would be accomplished. And this in itself was a new attitude towards crime. In earlier centuries it is difficult to find any attempt at intelligent detection. The horrible tortures inflicted on suspects, and the even more horrible torments visited on the condemned, seem to reflect a spirit of hopeless frustration. A crime had been committed; *somebody* had to be responsible. But how could that somebody be made to confess? The answer was to subject the suspect to torture – thumbscrews, red-hot tongs, the iron boot. If he confessed but still refused to plead guilty – which meant he could not be tried – he could be subjected to the *peine forte et dure;* this meant that a man was stripped naked and laid on his back, then successive 50-lb weights were placed on his body until he could bear no more. In many cases, the prisoner was 'pressed' to death. But what if a man was innocent, and pleaded guilty only because he was unable to bear any more pain? The law refused even to contemplate that possibility; it would have deepened the frustration too much. The most amazing illustration of this attitude can be found in the case of a Maltese judge named Cambo, preserved in the records of the Knights of Malta. During the early part of the eighteenth century, a criminal who had been condemned to death decided to unburden his soul of another offence – a murder for which another man had been executed, after having been sentenced by Judge Cambo. The Grand Master of the Knights of Malta was incredulous, and appealed to the judge to deny it; to his amazement, the judge admitted the charge, and insisted that he was justified in condemning an innocent man.

What had happened, it seemed, was that the judge had heard an affray beneath his window one morning, and had been in time to see one man stab another in the back as he tried to run away. The murderer's cap fell off so the judge was able to see his face; at the same moment, the murderer saw the judge looking down at him, and fled, leaving behind the sheath of the knife. A few moments later, a baker carrying a tray of hot loaves came along the street, saw the sheath, and picked it up. Then he saw the dead man, and ran away. A patrol of police saw him fleeing, and stopped him. The sheath in his pocket was found to fit the stiletto, which lay beside the corpse. The baker was taken into custody, and in due course appeared before Judge Cambo.

As the judge later explained to the Grand Master, he felt he had no right to act upon his private knowledge. As a judge, he was a servant of the law, and had to apply it with total impartiality. So he listened to the circumstantial evidence against the baker, and when it was clear this was insufficient, ordered him to be 'put to the question'. Under torture, the baker confessed, and was duly executed.

The Grand Master was outraged by the injustice, but the judge stubbornly defended his position. The Grand Master disagreed, and relieved the judge of his office, at the same time ordering him to pay compensation to the victim's family.

Major Arthur Griffiths, who retells the story in *Mysteries of Police and Crime,* tries to explain the judge's conduct by declaring that he was a dull and stupid man. But he is missing the point – trying to see the world of an eighteenth-century Catholic through the eyes of a nineteenth-century liberal. Cambo was probably the kind of man who feels that the Church has brought a ray of light into our dark and chaotic universe, and that he himself was responsible for preserving this order in his own tiny corner of the universe. We must remember that Saint Augustine took the same attitude in his *City of God,* urging Christians to shun science and intellectual enquiry as a danger to their souls, and that five centuries later, Roger Bacon was thrown into prison for daring to suggest that man should trust the power of his own reason. Judge Cambo would have conceded, of course, that the affair of the baker was an extreme case. But if he should once concede that a judge should begin to rely on his private feelings, who knows where it might end? Judges would acquit defendants they liked and condemn those they disliked . . .

It would be a long time before man would learn to trust his own reason, and even in the 'Age of Reason', there were still appalling miscarriages of justice. In Paris in the age of Voltaire, two aristocratic families shared the same house in the rue Royale: that of the Marquis d'Anglade and that of the Comte de Montgomerie. One day, the comte returned from a stay in the country to find that his strongbox had been opened with a duplicate key, and that thousands of francs were missing. When some of the money was found in the garret, the Lieutenant-General of Police jumped to what seemed to be the logical conclusion. This was an 'inside job', and since the only other person in the house was the Marquis d'Anglade, he *had* to be guilty. So convinced was the officer that he ordered the marquis to be tortured. The man insisted on his innocence, but – since French law was different from that of England – he was still tried and found guilty. Sentenced to the galleys, he died of his ill treatment. His wife, assumed to an accomplice, was confined in a damp underground dungeon. But at this point, a repentant thief revealed the truth; he was a member of a gang, led by a priest named Gaynard, who was the almoner of the Marquis de Montgomerie, and who had taken impressions of his keys; this had enabled him to enter the house and rob the strongbox at his leisure. Gaynard was tortured, and quickly confessed; a necklace found in the possession of an associate proved his guilt. D'Anglade's wife was released and given £4,000 compensation for the injustice she had suffered. But the police chief whose pig-headedness had caused the tragedy was not called to account; like Cambo, he felt he was merely applying the law.

Yet even when clues pointed unmistakably in the right direction, the police frequently failed to appreciate their significance. An early sixteenth-century case, the murder of Lady Mazel, provides a tragic illustration – as well as being one of the earliest examples of that classic detective puzzle, the locked room mystery. Lady Mazel and her household occupied a large mansion in Paris. Every night, when she retired to bed, she closed her bedroom door behind her, and, since it worked on a spring lock (the equivalent of our Yale), she was inaccessible until she herself opened it in the morning. One morning, when she failed to ring for breakfast, and made no answer to repeated knocking, the servants called a locksmith to break into her bedroom; they found her lying dead, with multiple stab wounds. The weapon, a clasp knife, was found among the ashes of the fire. Money was missing from the strongbox, and a gold watch.

Among the bedclothes, the police found a cheap lace cravat, and a napkin – bearing the family crest – which had been twisted into a nightcap. Unfortunately, this improvised nightcap was found to fit the valet Le Brun, and he immediately became the chief suspect. Suspicion was redoubled when Le Brun described how, late the previous evening, he had fallen asleep in the kitchen, and awakened to find the back door open. He had assumed that some careless servant was responsible, and closed it and gone to bed.

There was no blood on any of Le Brun's clothing, so it seemed clear that he had not been the one who had wielded the knife. The police reasoned that he had let an accomplice into the house late at night. But how had the accomplice been admitted to a locked bedroom? This question was apparently answered when Le Brun was found to be in possession of a skeleton key, which fitted most locks in the house, including that of the rear door of Lady Mazel's bedroom.

In the attic, the police found a nightshirt stained with blood. But it did not fit Le Brun. As to the coarse cravat, a housemaid identified it as one she had once washed for a former footman named Berry, since dismissed . . .

Any modern reader of detective stories will have already solved the mystery, since all the clues have now been provided. But the police, convinced that Le Brun was their man, ignored the clues and put him to the 'question'. When he insisted on his innocence, the 'question extraordinary' was applied, and he died under the torture.

A month later, the police in Sens arrested the ex-footman, now a horse dealer, on some minor charge, and found in his possession Lady Mazel's missing gold watch. When tortured, Berry told the whole story. After his dismissal, he had determined to kill Lady Mazel for revenge. He had managed to slip into the house on a Friday morning, when no servants were about, and had hidden in the attic. There he had lain hidden throughout Saturday and Saturday night, living on bread and apples. On Sunday morning, when everyone was at church, he had gone downstairs and hidden under Lady Mazel's bed. That night he woke her up and demanded money; when she tried to raise the alarm, he stabbed her repeatedly. Then he took the money and the watch, returned the bloodstained shirt to the attic (in case he was caught with it in his possession) and let himself out . . .

The police were in possession of all the clues; they merely had to apply logic. If Le Brun had let an accomplice into the bedroom, why had he himself gone in wearing a nightcap and, moreover, an improvised nightcap? He must have had plenty of ordinary nightcaps. The cheap cravat pointed straight to the former footman. The bloodstained nightshirt in the attic confirmed the evidence of the improvised nightcap – that someone had slept there overnight. A careful search of the attic would undoubtedly have revealed other traces of Berry's presence – such as breadcrumbs and apple cores. To the modern reader, the only incomprehensible feature of the crime is that the murderer should feel uncomfortable without his nightcap, and feel forced to improvise one from a napkin; but habit disregards the rules of logic. And the police themselves disregarded the rules of logic when they failed to analyse the evidence that was staring them in the face. The murderer was broken on the wheel, with the usual barbarity of those days, but this must have been small consolation to Le Brun's wife.

5

This strangely defeatist attitude towards clues seems to characterize most of the early murder mysteries whose records we possess. Men, after all, are animals, and it is not natural for animals to apply logic. It has taken man millions of years of evolution to confront problems instead of trying to side-step them. But it is only in the past two and a half thousand years that a few intelligent men have turned problem-solving into an art, or rather, a science. And it is only in the fairly recent past that this science has been applied systematically to the solution of crimes. Even in the nineteenth century, the rate of detection remained appallingly low because the authorities seemed to be afflicted with a strange blindness to the nature of clues. Henry Goddard, the Bow Street Runner whose acquaintance we have already made, can hardly contain his impatience when he describes some of the incompetence that allowed guilty men to go free. When an old lady named Elizabeth Longfoot was found battered and strangled in 1838, the magistrates of Stamford, in Lincolnshire, sent for Goddard, who discovered three sets of footprints near the back door. One was particularly large, and Goddard's enquiries soon pointed to a man named Stancer, a thoroughly bad character who had big feet, and who lived close to Easton, the scene of the crime. Goddard applied his usual 'needle-in-the-haystack' method, enquiring at village after village until he tracked down Stancer in Uppingham. Accused of the murder, Stancer accused two associates called Woodward and Archer. More painstaking tracking led to the arrest of the other two, and Woodward also tried to throw the blame for the murder on his associates. With such straightforward evidence, their guilt seemed obvious. Yet the authorities took so long to bring the case to trial that one vital witness died, and the other evidence was presented so badly that a disgruntled jury acquitted all three defendants.

Similar frustration awaited him in his search for the murderers of a steward named Richardson. Richardson's death holds some interest for investigators of the paranormal, in that there is strong evidence that he dreamed of his murder the night before it happened, and told the dream to a number of witnesses. On the night of 25 March 1834, he woke from a nightmare and told his wife that he had dreamed of being shot on his way home from the Epsom market. The next day, on his way to the market, he also told a toll keeper of his dream, and in the local pub at midday, recounted it to a group of farmers, who cheered him up by saying that dreams go by opposites. But on his way back to Bletchingley, driving a chaise, he was held up by two men and shot through the head. The men robbed him of about £30 (a huge sum in days when a labourer's wage was five shillings a week) and fled across the fields, where they almost ran into the arms of some bell-ringers. Summoned to the scene of the crime, Goddard made his usual painstaking enquiries, but without success. Then an anonymous letter pointed out that two brothers named Childs had been behaving in a suspicious way since the murder. Goddard was sent to arrest them, but since the magistrates declined to furnish him with a warrant, the attempt was unsuccessful – the brothers pointed out that they were just on their way to market with a load of produce, and would lose a great deal of money if they accompanied Goddard to the magistrates. It obviously gave Goddard considerable satisfaction to let them go.

Eventually, the Childs brothers were arrested by two constables who had been near Bletchingley on the day of the murder, and questioned two suspicious characters who were hiding in a ditch. They now identified the Childs brothers as the two men. Witnesses who had seen the murderers fleeing from the scene of the crime also identified the brothers. The prisoners told a number of lies about their whereabouts on the day of the murder, and insisted they had never been to Epsom in their lives; when these statements were proved false, it began to look as if there was little doubt of their guilt. Yet once again, the evidence was presented so badly in court that the magistrates decided there was no real case against them, and discharged them. When Goddard wrote his account 40 years later, he took care to avoid criticism of the authorities, but a certain irony leaves no doubt about his feelings.

It is, of course, pleasant to read of suspects being acquitted rather than tortured until they confessed; but it seems a pity that the alternative to the innocent being tortured to death is for the guilty to escape. But this is what happened with increasing frequency when the law became humane enough to allow a suspect the full benefit of the doubt. The blame cannot be laid entirely on the inadequacy of the police. Magistrates and juries were often reluctant to convict simply because they mistrusted 'circumstantial evidence' – for exactly the same reason that they mistrusted experts: because they felt it was all a little too abstract and logical. In 1832, the chemist James Marsh proved beyond all doubt that a farmer had been poisoned by arsenic, yet a British jury acquitted the accused man. Ten years later, the man confessed to the murder, by which time, Marsh's test for arsenic was in use all over Europe . . .

An interesting case of 1835 establishes Henry Goddard himself as one of the founders of the new method of scientific detection. In January of that year, Goddard was summoned to Southampton to try and track down a gang of burglars. The butler described how he had been awakened in the early hours of the morning when his bedroom door was opened by a man carrying a bull's-eye lantern, which cast the shadow of a man before it; he could also see another man standing behind the intruder. The men backed out of the bedroom, but just as the butler was reaching out for his own pistol, there was a loud report from outside, and a bullet whizzed past his ear and went through the backboard of the bed. 'Had it not been for my turning round to reach my pistol they would have left me a corpse, for as I lay the bullet must have entered my chin and lodged in the gullet.' He then rushed into the corridor, shouting at the top of his lungs, and struggled with two men in masks, who fled, leaving their loot behind.

Goddard examined the door through which the burglars had effected their entrance, and found marks of a jemmy. But these marks puzzled him. A jemmy (a small crow-bar with a flattened end) would have been forced past the edge of the door and used as a lever to break it open;

this would leave a mark on the outside of the door, and another mark on the inside of the door jamb. But these two marks did not correspond. And the same was true of the marks on the closet that contained the valuable plate.

His suspicions alerted, Goddard asked to see the butler's pistol, and the mould in which he cast his lead bullets. He also asked the butler if he had the bullet that had been fired at him by the burglars. It was slightly flattened by its impact with the bed board, but to Goddard's eye, it looked identical with the bullets from the butler's gun. His opinion was confirmed when he observed a tiny pimple on all the bullets, and saw that this was due to a hole, the size of a pinhead, in the mould. Goddard took all the bullets to the local gunsmith who had supplied the pistol, and the man confirmed that the flattened bullet had been cast in the same mould as the others.

When the butler was confronted with this evidence, and was hauled off before the magistrates, he made a full confession. He had made the jemmy marks on the doors, and fired his own pistol at the bed board. The burglary had been faked to gain the favour of his mistress, and in hope of a handsome reward for his bravery. The lady of the house had been taken in by his story, as had the local watchmen. But Goddard had been alerted by the man's description of the bull's-eye lantern which had cast a shadow *before* it, then by the inconsistency of the marks on the doors. (The butler admitted he had made these at different times, and had made one set of impressions in the dark, so he could not see what he was doing.) Since no criminal offence had been committed, the magistrates discharged the butler with a warning; presumably he was dismissed from his post.

So half a century before the creation of Sherlock Holmes, Goddard was applying his methods and, incidentally, earning himself a place in the history of crime detection as the first man to solve a case through the use of ballistic evidence.

6

It sounds incredible that Europe had to wait until the nineteenth century before the police began to apply reason and common sense to the solution of crimes. But that is only because we fail to understand the kind of bloodthirsty anarchy that existed in earlier centuries. From the late Middle Ages onward, robber bands wandered around with impunity, sometimes besieging houses and carrying off the inhabitants for ransom. Master Hans Schmidt, the Nuremberg executioner from 1573 to 1617 records hundreds of hangings and beheadings, many accompanied by torture. These entries in his diary are typical:

> . . . three thieves and robbers who attacked people at night in their house, and in lonely farms, bound them, tortured them and did violence to them . . . All three hanged at Nuremberg.
>
> Frederick Werner of Nuremberg . . . a murderer and a robber who committed three murders and twelve robberies . . . Drawn to execution in a tumbril, twice nipped with red-hot tongs, and afterwards broken on the wheel.
>
> Nicklauss Stuller, of Aydtsfeld . . . a murderer . . . First he shot a horse-soldier; secondly he cut open a pregnant woman alive . . . Fourthly he once more cut open a pregnant woman in whom there were two male children . . . Drawn out on a sledge at Bamberg, his body torn with red tongs, and then he was executed on the wheel . . .

It would be a mistake to think that this kind of thing happened only on the continent of Europe; England was just as bad. In the fourteenth century, robber gangs sometimes took over a whole town and set it on fire when they left; one robber chief invaded the city of Bristol, and was dislodged only when the king sent an army. Even in the age of Dr Johnson, bands of robbers besieged houses in the country; one gang of four were torturing a farmer against the fire – he was naked – when rescuers arrived and drove them away. Footpads (or what we would call muggers) operated by daylight in the streets of London; Horace Walpole saw a highwayman rob a coach in Piccadilly, and was himself shot in the face by a robber in Hyde Park. The poet Shenstone described how gangs armed with bludgeons and big knives attacked whole parties in Covent Garden.

And what were the police doing while all this was going on? The answer is that there were no police. In the countries of Europe, the army kept some kind of order – that is why French policemen were later calls *gens d'armes* or gendarmes – men at arms. But England had no standing army, for it had not been invaded since William the Conqueror. And the British were deeply suspicious of the idea of a police force, believing it would erode their freedom. So in villages, there were local watchmen, and a parish constable – who was a local tradesman who did the job in his spare time. And, as Patrick Pringle points out in his introduction to Goddard's *Memoirs of a Bow Street Runner,* this system worked well enough in the country, but tended to break down in large towns. If a citizen was robbed, he himself had to pursue the robber, setting up a 'hue and cry', and if he caught him, had to prosecute him at his own expense. The government tried to make up for the lack of law and order by the barbarity of punishments, so that as many as a dozen men at a time might be hanged at Tyburn (and on several occasions, as many as 20). The *Gentleman's Magazine* for 1750 recorded: 'Executed at Tyburn, July 6, Elizabeth Banks, for stripping a child; Catherine Conway, for forging a seaman's ticket; and Margaret Harvey for robbing her master. They were all drunk.'* As late as 1801, a boy of 13 was hanged for breaking into a house and stealing a spoon; two sisters, aged 8 and 11, were hanged at Lynn in 1808. In 1831, a boy of 9 was hanged for setting fire to a house, and two years later, another boy of 9 was hanged for pushing a stick through a cracked shop window and stealing two pennyworth of printer's colour.†

When better-off people left London in the mid-eighteenth century to go to the country, they locked up their houses and took their valuables with them, for they expected the houses to be broken into and robbed. And when someone wanted to recover stolen property, they went along to some dubious characters who knew the underworld, and offered a reward. In the previous century, a retired highwaywoman named Mary Frith, or Moll Cutpurse, set up a shop in Fleet Street to sell the goods stolen by her gang of pickpockets, and her best customers were the victims themselves; she was so successful that she drove every other fence out of the business. Moll died, rich and respected, in 1659, in her mid-70s. A century later, Jonathan Wild set himself up in the same business, and soon achieved a success far beyond that of Moll Cutpurse. He became a kind of eighteenth-century Al Capone, who divided London into districts, with a gang to each; any thief or highwayman who preferred to operate alone was hunted down and hanged on evidence supplied by Wild. He owned a London house and a country mansion, as well as a ship for taking stolen goods overseas; at one point, he even had the effrontery to ask the Mayor of London for freedom of the city in consideration of his great public services. When a law was passed making it illegal to take money for restoring stolen goods to their owners, he found ways around it, and became richer than

*Quoted by Christopher Hibbert in *The Roots of Evil*, p. 42.
†Ibid., pp. 62, 67.

ever. Eventually, the law caught up with him, and he was hanged in 1725. And within a year or so, London was in the grip of a crime wave that made it dangerous to walk in Covent Garden in broad daylight.

What caused it? One of the basic causes was undoubtedly the availability of a new drink called Geneva, or gin. Invented around 1650 by a Dutchman named Sylvius – who made it by distilling fermented juniper ('geneva') berries – it arrived in England in 1689 with the new king, William of Orange. The Elizabethans had drunk wine, beer, and sherry – Falstaff's sack – and by 1689, the taxes imposed by various monarchs made them too expensive for the working man. Gin was easy to make, cheap, and very powerful, and the government encouraged its production because, unlike wine and sherry, it could be made in England, and so save imports. Gin took about 30 years to become the mainstay of the working classes, but by 1720, there were 6,000 gin shops in London – one house in every ten. It was to increase to one in six. One observer who stood outside a gin shop on Holborn Hill for three hours one evening counted over 1,400 people going in and out, excluding children. A famous advertisement stated: 'Drunk for a penny, dead drunk for tuppence.' Gin was the easiest way for the poor to endure their misery; mothers fed it to their babies to keep them quiet. The effect was precisely the same as that of the heroin trade in modern cities: rising crime.

Gin was not the only cause. Others attributed it to the increasing number of sailors who flooded into London as Britain's trade with the rest of the world increased. But the novelist Henry Fielding came closest to the heart of the matter in a pamphlet enquiring into 'the late increase of robbers' when he blamed 'the vast torrent of luxury which of late years hath poured itself into this nation'. England was becoming the richest country in the world, but its wealth existed side by side with appalling poverty. Naturally, the poor tried to divert a little of the wealth into their own pockets. The same thing had happened in ancient Rome and every other civilization that achieved wealth and success . . .

London went on a crime rampage, and it was not confined to the poor. The Mohocks, a society whose members were dedicated to the ambition of 'doing all possible hurt to their fellow creatures', were mostly gentlemen. They employed their ample leisure in forcing prostitutes and old women to stand on their heads in tar barrels so that they could prick their legs with their swords; or in making them jump up and down to avoid the swinging blades; in disfiguring their victims by boring out their eyes or flattening their noses; in waylaying servants and, as in the case of Lady Winchelsea's maid, beating them and slashing their faces. To work themselves up to the necessary pitch of enthusiasm for their ferocious games, they first drank so much that they were 'quite beyond the possibility of attending to any notions of reason or humanity'. Some of the Mohocks seem to have been members of the Bold Bucks who, apparently, had formally to deny the existence of God and eat every Sunday a dish known as Holy Ghost Pie. The ravages of the Bold Bucks were more specifically sexual than those of the Mohocks and consequently, as it was practically impossible to obtain a conviction for rape and as the age of consent was 12, they were more openly conducted. An expectation of inviolability was, indeed, shared by many, if not most young men of this class. One evening in the 1770s, Richard Savage, who claimed to be a son of the Countess of Macclesfield, quarrelled with some people playing cards in Robinson's coffee-house, lost his temper, and ran one of them through with his sword. He was tried for murder but he was subsequently pardoned. And when a young gentleman named Plunket called at a shop to collect a wig he had ordered he did not hesitate to pick up a razor from the counter and slit the wig-maker's throat from ear to ear, because he would not reduce the price by more than one guinea. Senseless murders such as this were as common as riots . . .'*

Things began to change for the better in 1729 when a half-pay captain named Thomas De Veil was appointed magistrate for Westminster and Middlesex. A decade earlier, De Veil had been well on the road to ruination with his taste for wine, women and song, which ran him up enormous debts. But he had the sense to retire to a country village and live cheaply before returning to London and setting up as a kind of scrivener, drafting petitions to the government. De Veil made no secret of the fact that he accepted his post as a magistrate because it offered him the opportunity to take bribes and indulge his immense sexual appetite with young ladies who had no other means to bribe him. He had 25 legitimate children and an unknown number of bastards, and next door to his office he kept a private room to which he could quickly retire with any attractive woman who appeared before him and was willing to buy her freedom on the couch. But in spite of being virtually a sex maniac, De Veil was also an efficient and hard-working magistrate. Ten years after the execution of Jonathan Wild, one of London's largest and most desperate robber gangs decided to kill him

*Christopher Hibbert: ibid.

when they heard that he was collecting evidence against them, and well-armed groups of them waited for night after night around Leicester Fields (the present Leicester Square), where De Veil had his office. De Veil seems to have got wind of the plot, and all the waiting finally preyed on the nerves of one of the thugs, who secretly betrayed his companions to the magistrate. So one of London's most dangerous gangs was broken up.

De Veil's greatest triumphs came after he transferred his office to a house in Bow Street, in 1739. Already in his mid-50s (and therefore, in eighteenth-century terms, an old man), De Veil began to build up a reputation as a detective. When an eating house in Chancery Lane was burgled, he found himself interrogating a suspect who professed total innocence of the crime. On a 'hunch', De Veil asked the man casually for a loan of his knife, and he noted that the suspect's pocket knife had a missing point. He sent a constable round to the eating house with instructions to look in the lock; the missing point was found there, and the man convicted. As with most good detectives, De Veil's success rested upon this keen instinct about criminal behaviour.

It was demonstrated again in June 1741, in a case of suspected murder. A certain Mr Wooton told De Veil that his uncle Mr Penny, Principal of Clement's Inn (one of the Inns of Chancery – virtually a school for student barristers), had disappeared. His servant, James Hall, insisted that he had gone somewhere by water', and failed to return, but after making various enquiries, Wooton began to suspect that his uncle had been murdered, probably by Hall. He had Hall taken into custody, and brought before De Veil, now Sir Thomas, who proceeded to cross-question him minutely. Hall soon involved himself in contradictions, then became sullen, and refused to answer. Again De Veil's instinct told him that the man was guilty; but if he had murdered his master, where could he have concealed the body? He ordered a thorough search of Clement's Inn; the Principal's corpse was found stuffed down the outside privy, feet uppermost. Hall thereupon proceeded to make a gruesome confession. Finding himself heavily in debt, he had decided to kill Mr Penny; after helping him undress for bed, he had knocked him unconscious with a blow from a bludgeon, then battered him to death. The chamber was covered in blood, and Hall realized that he was going to have difficulty disposing of the corpse without leaving a trail of blood along the corridor. So he stripped himself naked – to avoid getting more blood on his clothes – and used a fruit knife to cut the throat of the corpse over a chamber pot, which he had to empty down the sink five times. Then, still naked, he carried the body down to the lavatory. This would have been above a sewer that led down to the Thames, and Hall must have hoped that the stench of a London sewer would drown the smell of a decomposing body. Then he made a second journey to dispose of bloody clothes, and the rags he had used to mop up the blood.

Hall displayed a cool nerve. If he had fled, the crime would have been quickly discovered. Instead, he stayed in the chambers, and reported to Penny's nephew that his uncle had failed to return from a trip down the river. Every day he returned to ask Wooton if there was any news of his uncle. Eventually, Wooton reported the matter to De Veil. If it had not been for De Veil's nose for murder, and his skill in examination, Hall might have escaped detection; as it was, he was hanged three months later, and allowed to rot in chains at Shepherd's Bush as a warning to other disaffected servants. Cases like this so enhanced De Veil's reputation that his advice was frequently sought in the solution of crimes outside Westminster, and he became England's first 'consulting detective' a century and a half before Sherlock Holmes claimed that distinction.

After the death of De Veil in 1746, his position and his house in Bow Street were taken over by the novelist and playwright Henry Fielding, who had made the discovery that literature and poverty are almost synonymous. Fielding had made a living as a political playwright, until the Prime Minister, Sir Robert Walpole, grew tired of being satirized, and introduced a bill that required every play to be licensed by an official called the Lord Chamberlain – an office that aroused the fury of generations of playwrights until it was abolished in 1968. That put an end to Fielding's career as a dramatist, and novels like *Joseph Andrews* and *Jonathan Wild* failed to make up for the loss of income. So, with some reluctance, Fielding decided to accept the post of Justice of the Peace. His enemies set up a chorus of derision about the idealistic playwright who had become a 'trading justice'. But Fielding had no intention of lining his own pocket. In his few brief years of office (he was already ill in 1748, and died six years later) he became the most formidable enemy of crime that London had ever known.

His problem was simple: for every thief and highwayman who was sent to jail, there were a hundred more left on the street. With no police force except part-time parish constables, the London criminal had never known any organized opposition. Yet De Veil had shown that gangs could be destroyed by a determined magistrate. With half a dozen public-spirited friends, Fielding began to organize a group of 'thief takers', all ex-parish constables who knew the villains by sight. To us, the system sounds hopelessly amateurish. Victims of robberies were urged to hurry to Fielding's house in Bow Street, whereupon the thief takers would set out in hot pursuit – which is why they soon became known as the Bow Street Runners. And since London's robbers were accustomed to immunity, and seldom bothered to leave their habitual haunts, they were captured in droves. Fielding described his satisfaction as he read the London newspapers, and saw reports of robberies diminishing day by day, until eventually they ceased altogether. He had been granted £600 by the government, and in putting a stop to London's crime wave, he used only half of it.

The next problem was the number of highwaymen and burglars who infested the roads around London. Again, it proved unexpectedly easy to solve. As soon as a few heavily armed constables patrolled the roads, the thieves became nervous, and moved elsewhere. One highwayman had become so accustomed to immunity that he returned regularly to rob the same coach just outside London. Finally, the coachman took a Bow Street Runner with him and when the robber rode up waving his pistol, the Runner fired and blew away half his jaw. The highwayman also fired, but missed; he was taken off to hospital, and thence to jail. This episode took place under the magistracy of Fielding's blind brother John, who continued to be the scourge of London's underworld for more than a quarter of a century after the novelist's death.

It was six years after Sir John Fielding's death in 1780 that the first recorded example of 'scientific detection' took place in Scotland. The name of the victim has not been recorded, but she was a young woman who lived in a lonely farm cottage in Kirkcudbright. Her parents returned from harvesting to find her lying with her throat cut. Doctors who examined the corpse ruled out suicide, and concluded that, since the cut was from the right to left, the murderer must have been left-handed.

Since it was midsummer, the ground around the cottage was hard and showed no footprints; but on some boggy ground nearby, a trail of footprints was found, and the depth of the impressions of the toes showed that the man had been running. At one point he had slipped and been immersed up to the knee. A few blood drops were also noted, and a bloody handprint was found on a stile. This and the footprints were the only clue to the author of the crime, and plaster casts of the footprints were made. It was clear that the shoes were shod with iron nails and had been recently mended. An autopsy on the dead girl revealed that she was pregnant, and so provided a possible motive for the crime. But she seems to have been so discreet about her lover that no one knew his identity.

In such a sparsely populated area, most people would attend the funeral. It struck the investigators that the murderer would hardly dare to absent himself for fear of arousing comment. So after the funeral, all the males had to submit to having their footwear measured. When the schoolmaster's shoes were found to be of the correct size, it looked as if they might have found the culprit; but the schoolmaster's toes were pointed, and those of the murderer were round.

Finally, they found a shoe that fitted the impression. It belonged to a labourer named Richardson, who was also left-handed. He insisted that some scratches on his cheek had been made by branches when he had been gathering nuts in a wood. And he seemed to have a sound alibi for the time of the murder – he had been at work with two other men. But now they were closely questioned, his two companions recalled that they had all been in a cart, which had paused not far from the girl's cottage. Richardson had asked them to wait while he went to the blacksmith's. He was longer than expected – about half and hour – and when he returned, had a scratch on his cheek, and muddy stockings. He told them that he had been in the wood gathering nuts.

A search of Richardson's cottage revealed the stockings hidden in the thatch, and they were found to be bloodstained. But perhaps the most impressive observation, from the scientific point of view, was that the mud in which they were soaked was found to be identical with mud in a puddle near the cottage – a mud that contained sand, and was not to be found elsewhere in the area. When it was established that Richardson had been the girl's secret lover, the evidence was complete, and he was condemned to death. Before his execution, he confessed to the crime. It had been carefully planned, at a time he knew the girl would be alone, and if it had not been for the cast of the footprints, he would probably have remained undetected.

We can see that the solution of the crime depended on the fact that it took place in a remote country district, where everyone knew everyone else, and where it was therefore certain that the murderer was a local. This is why the investigators felt it was worthwhile to study the clues so carefully. In a large town, it would have seemed a pointless exercise.

7

Meanwhile, in London, even the success of the Bow Street Runners had failed to convince the British Parliament of the need for an official police force; the English continued to believe that it would spell the end of their liberty. It was not until 1829 that the Home Secretary Sir Robert Peel succeeded in steering a bill through Parliament that established the first police force; he deliberately made it so vague that many MPs thought it simply referred to night-watchmen. For many years the public remained deeply suspicious of the 'Bobbies' (as they were called after their founder), convinced that they were there to smell out offences and put the culprit in jail – an opinion that was reinforced when the police were issued with steel-lined top hats, not to protect them from blows, but so they could stand on them to peer over walls. When a policeman was kicked to death by two drunken Irishmen in 1830, no one attempted to stop them as they ran away; most Londoners would have liked to see the same thing happen to every policeman in the force.

When, 20 years later, Charles Dickens interviewed a group of Scotland Yard officers for his magazine *Household Words,* things had changed for the better; the British public was learning to think of the Bobby as its protector. The article was called 'The Detective Police', and it seems to have introduced the word 'detective' into literature. The policemen included Inspector Walker and Inspector Charles F. Field; the latter was to become Dickens's guide around London's dockland, and the subject of four more articles in *Household Words* which offer some fascinating insights into the life of a mid-Victorian policeman. Field was also to become the model for the first detective in fiction, Inspector Bucket of *Bleak House.* He is introduced by the lawyer Tulkinghorn as a 'detective officer' (again, the first use of the word in fiction) and is eventually called upon to solve the murder of Tulkinghorn, which he pins upon the French maid Hortense. This is not as a result of careful detective work, but of pure inspiration: 'By the living Lord, it flashed upon me, as I sat opposite her at the table and saw her with a knife in her hand, that she had done it.' (Since Tulkinghorn was shot, the logic is not quite clear.)

The main interest of this scene lies in the fact that Hortense was based upon a real murderess, Maria Manning, who was actually a Swiss lady's maid. The case, which aroused widespread excitement, is an interesting example of mid-Victorian detective work. She was married to a railway guard named Frederick Manning, but continued to be the mistress of a rich Irishman named Patrick O'Connor. When Manning was dismissed on suspicion of being implicated in a bullion robbery, he and his wife opened a beer shop in the Hackney Road. O'Connor was a frequent visitor, and one day, Mrs Manning eloped with him. With the aid of a cabman, Frederick Manning succeeded in finding them, and persuaded her to return home; but her condition for doing so seems to have been that her lover could come too. Manning was too infatuated to leave her, and so was O'Connor. But when she discovered that O'Connor had a fortune of £20,000, and succeeded in persuading him to make a will in her favour, his fate was sealed. Manning bought a crow-bar, a spade and a bag of quicklime. On 9 August 1849, O'Connor was invited for dinner. As he sat at table alone, Mrs Manning came in quietly, and shot him in the head with a pistol. Then Frederick Manning came in, and found the Irishman moaning. 'I never liked him much', he later told the police, 'and battered in his head with a ripping chisel.'

Mrs Manning went to O'Connor's lodgings, with which she was thoroughly familiar, and made off with thousands of pounds' worth of stocks and bonds. While her husband was out selling some of these, she decamped with the remainder and went to Edinburgh. Her husband's nerve broke, and he fled to St Helier, Jersey, where he proceeded to consume large quantities of brandy.

Five days after his disappearance, relatives of O'Connor went to the police. A constable called at the empty house, climbed in through the window, and found nothing suspicious. But a few days later, the police decided on a more thorough search. Nowadays it would be conducted by a team of experienced detectives; in 1849, two ordinary constables were considered sufficent. Fortunately, PC Barnes was a highly observant officer. In the back kitchen, there was an open portmanteau of women's clothes. When this was moved, he noticed that the cement around the flagstones was damp. He scratched it with his knife and found that it was wet. Then he and his companion went and borrowed a crow-bar and a shovel. Under the flagstones they found O'Connor lying in quicklime.

The only problem now was to locate the Mannings. Maria felt she had been marvellously cunning; she had taken a cab to London Bridge station and left two trunks there, labelled 'Smith'. She had then taken a third trunk to Euston, and bought a ticket for Edinburgh. As soon as the news of the murder appeared in the newspapers, the cab-driver came forward and led the police to London Bridge station. The trunks proved to contain Maria Manning's clothing, and some of O'Connor's possessions. Then the cab-driver led them to Euston, where they traced Mrs Manning and her third trunk to the Edinburgh train. They wired the Edinburgh police, and by the time they arrived back at Scotland Yard, had a wire in return saying Mrs Manning was under arrest. She had made the mistake of introducing herself to a firm of stockbrokers as a Scotswoman, and when they had been notified that a foreign woman was wanted for murder and stealing bonds, they alerted the police.

Manning was just as easy to capture; he had been seen on the Channel Islands steamboat by a woman acquaintance, and when she heard of the murder, she went to the police. A Scotland Yard detective sergeant had only to go to Jersey to hear the gossip about the secretive man who spent his days in a lonely cottage drinking himself into a stupor. When arrested, Manning asked eagerly 'Is the wretch taken?', meaning his wife, on whom he tried to lay all the blame. At the trial, Mrs Manning reciprocated. But both were condemned to death, and the hanging took place in public in front of Horsemonger Lane jail. Mrs Manning chose to die in a black satin dress, trimmed with black lace, and a black veil; the result was that black satin abruptly went out of fashion among Victorian womenfolk. Charles Dickens went along to see the execution, and was indignant to observe that the crowd treated it all as a public holiday, and made noisy jokes – he wrote a letter to *The Times* to that effect. And three years later, Maria Manning served as a model for the attractive but murderous Hortense in *Bleak House*.

8

Fifty years earlier, the Mannings would probably have escaped, for by the time she had been traced to Edinburgh, she would have been on the Continent, while her husband would probably have drunk himself quietly to death on Jersey. What the Mannings left out of account was the new swiftness of Victorian communications, which made Edinburgh and Jersey no safer than London. (Sixty years later, Crippen was to make the same disastrous mistake.)

But then, the Manning affair fell into that group of cases, fortunately in the majority, in which there is a link between the victim and the murderer. It is when such a link is missing that the case presents real difficulties. This is what happened when Sarah Millson was murdered in the City of London in 1866. Mrs Millson was an attractive widow who lived on the top floor of a Cannon Street warehouse; her only companion was her cook. In the evenings she often had a mysterious caller, who announced his presence by blowing down the speaking tube – the Victorian equivalent of an intercom. When this happened, she would go downstairs, and remain there for perhaps a quarter of an hour. But one evening, after two hours, the cook went down to see where she was, and found her lying with her head battered in at the foot of the stairs. The motive was not robbery (her purse lay unopened by her side) and since she had never dropped any hint about the nature of her mysterious caller, the police had no leads. A few decades later, an investigator like Edmond Locard might have found a dozen clues; as it was, the murder remained unsolved.

Inspector Field had encountered much the same problem two decades earlier in a south London murder case, and his attempts to solve it were described by Dickens in *Household Words*. The victim was an attractive young woman called Elizabeth Grimwood, known because of her dignified carriage as 'The Countess'. Dickens does not say so, since it would have shocked his readers, but we may assume that her profession involved receiving male visitors. She was found with her throat cut, lying on the floor of her bedroom, in Waterloo Road, and when Field turned back the bedclothes, he found a pair of gentlemen's dress gloves, very dirty, with the letters 'Tr' marked inside them. When Field sniffed them, he noted the smell of sulphur, which indicated that they had at some point been cleaned. (Sulphur dioxide is a bleach.) The problem, then, was to find their owner. Field began by calling on a friend who worked as a glove cleaner in Kennington, who confirmed that the gloves had been cleaned. He also pointed out that there were only eight or nine more glove cleaners in London, and gave Field their addresses. Like Canler in the Lacenaire case, Field proceeded to apply the 'needle-in-the-haystack' method. It took him three days to track down all the glove cleaners on the list, and at each one he drew a blank. Finally, in a state of discouragement, he decided to relax for an hour or so in the Lyceum Theatre, near the Strand. At this point, luck came to his aid; he found himself sitting next to a young man, with whom he fell into conversation. When the show was over, they adjourned to the pub next door for a pint of beer. The young man explained that he could not stay long, because he had to work all night.

'Are you a baker?', asked Field.

'No, a glove cleaner', the man replied.

Field produced the gloves. 'Any idea who cleaned these?'

The young man glanced at the 'Tr' inside them, and answered 'Yes, my father.'

The father lived nearby, in Exeter Street, and he was able to tell Field that the gloves belonged to a Mr Trinkle, an upholsterer in Cheapside. When Trinkle wanted gloves cleaned, he sent them to a Mr Phibbs, a haberdasher, who lived across the road, and the haberdasher brought them to the glove cleaner's.

The inspector felt that the end of the case was in sight. This was a Saturday, and he had to wait until Monday morning before he could call on Mr Phibbs. The haberdasher confirmed that the gloves belonged to Trinkle jun., and pointed out the young man in the shop across the road. Field then revealed that he was investigating the murder of Eliza Grimwood, and would have to place Trinkle jun. under arrest. The haberdasher was upset. 'It would be the ruin of him.' Finally, Field agreed to let the haberdasher call the young man over, so that his father would not see him arrested. Phibbs beckoned, and the young man came over. Field introduced himself, showed him the gloves, and asked if he was acquainted with Eliza Grimwood, of the Waterloo Road. The young man looked blank and said he had never heard of her. Field was convinced by his manner that he was innocent, but asked him never-theless to accompany him before the magistrate who was in charge of the case.

Under close questioning, it emerged that Trinkle was acquainted with the murdered girl's cousin. And when the cousin was questioned, she was able to explain how the gloves had come to be found in Eliza Grimwood's bed. Trinkle had left his gloves behind when he called on the cousin. Eliza Grimwood had seen them there shortly before her murder, decided they were too dirty to be of any use to their owner, and taken them home for her maid to clean the stove with. And when Eliza was about to receive her murderer, she had probably seen the gloves lying on the table or the mantelpiece, and thrust them under the pillow, where Field had discovered them; And so the murder of Eliza Grimwood remained unsolved – or at least, we may assume so, from the fact that Field told Dickens the story a few years later and said nothing about the solution of the case. It is an unsatisfying end to the tale, but one the Victorian police encountered with frustrating frequency.

The credit for writing the first – and many feel, the best-detective novel goes to Dickens's friend Wilkie Collins. *The Moonstone,* which appeared in 1868, tells the story of the disappearance of a famous jewel, and of the efforts of Sergeant Cuff of Scotland Yard to discover the thief. Much of the plot turns upon a paint-stained nightshirt, which Cuff is convinced was worn by the thief, but his efforts to find it lead nowhere. Eventually, the hero discovers, to his embarrassment, that the paint-stained nightshirt is his own, and that he had removed the moonstone while sleep-walking, in an unconscious attempt to protect the heroine from some sinister Hindus who are trying to recover the stone . . .

It sounds an absurd farrago, but in some respects, it is closer to reality than the adventures of Inspector Bucket in *Bleak House*. For Sergeant Cuff was based upon one of Inspector Field's colleagues, Inspector Jonathan Whicher of Scotland Yard, and Whicher's most celebrated case turned upon a disappearing nightdress, although the stains on it were not of paint but of blood.

9

On the morning of Saturday 30 June 1860, a three-year-old boy, Francis Savill Kent, was found to be missing from his cot. The police were informed, and a search revealed the child's body in the outside lavatory; he had a wound in his side, and his throat had been so deeply slashed that his head was almost severed.

Road Hill House, where the murder took place, was a mansion on the Wiltshire-Somerset border, 10 miles south-east of Bath. Its owner, Samuel Kent, was a factory inspector, and the dead child was the son of his second wife, by whom he had three children. Constance and William, his children by his first wife, disliked their new mother intensely. They knew she had been their father's mistress in the days when she was their governess, and they had once tried to run away from home, with the tomboy Constance dressed in male clothes.

There had been other cut-throat murders in the area in recent years, and Mr Kent was convinced that his son was the victim of some intruder. Superintendent Foley, from nearby Trowbridge, was by no means so certain; but he was, in any case, out of his depth in this strange case. But a Dr Parsons, who assisted him, was rather puzzled that the nightdress belonging to 16-year-old Constance was so clean, when she had apparently been wearing it for several days. This seems to have been overlooked in the excitement of another discovery: a bloodstained chemise hidden in the kitchen flu. But the stains on this were obviously of menstrual blood, and it seems certain that it was concealed there by some innocent but nervous housemaid who was afraid that she might become a suspect.

Down the lavatory where the child's body had been found Foley had discovered a 'chest flannel', a garment intended for keeping the chest warm. When this proved to fit the nurse, Elizabeth Gough, she was taken into custody as a suspect; but since there was no evidence against her, she was soon released. But while in custody, she told a policeman's wife that one of Miss Constance's nightdresses was missing, and that this nightdress would lead to the murderer . . .

Two weeks after the murder, Inspector Jonathan Whicher arrived from Scotland Yard. As soon as he learned of the incident, four years earlier, when Constance and William had tried to run away to sea, his suspicions fixed on Constance. And when he saw a list of garments that Constance had brought with her from school, and discovered that she had three nightdresses, he became more suspicious than ever, for Constance claimed she had only two – she explained that the third had been lost in the wash. Whicher did not believe that for a moment. He became convinced that Constance had destroyed her bloodstained nightdress after killing her brother, and had at some point extracted her previously worn nightdress from the laundry basket. She had then exchanged this for the clean nightdress that Dr Parsons had seen, realizing that its obviously unworn state would make her a suspect. A few days after his arrival, Whicher arrested Constance and charged her with the murder of her half-brother.

In due course, Constance appeared before local magistrates in the Temperance Hall. But they decided (rightly, under the circumstances) that the evidence against her was too flimsy, and she was discharged. The spectators cheered, failing to realize that she had not been found not guilty, but only released for lack of evidence.

Whicher was heavily criticized in the Press for his attempt to pin such a crime on an innocent girl. Elizabeth Gough was again arrested and again released. A year after the murder, Mr Kent and his family moved to Wrexham, in North Wales, and Constance was sent to a convent in France. There she seems to have undergone a religious conversion, and in 1865, she finally confessed to the murder of Francis Savill Kent. Her motive, she admitted, was hatred of her stepmother. Constance was sentenced to death, but the sentence was commuted to life imprisonment, and she spent 20 years in Millbank prison. In his book *Cruelly Murdered,* Bernard Taylor presents convincing evidence that she then went to Australia, where she became matron of a nursing home, and died at the age of 100 in 1944.

The Kent case continues to arouse controversy. One writer, Yseult Bridges, has argued that the real murderer was Constance's father, who was sleeping with the nurse when his 3-year-old son wandered into the room; clapping his hands over his child's mouth to prevent him from waking Mrs Kent, he accidentally suffocated him, then had to fake the murder to save his own skin. Constance then confessed to protect her father, although there was obviously no need to do so five years after the murder. This unlikely theory is put forward in a book called *Saint With Red Hands.* Bernard Taylor rejects it in favour of his own theory: that Constance murdered the child by stabbing him in the side with a knife; her father, who was sleeping with the nurse, found the body shortly afterwards, and cut the throat to mislead the police into assuming that the murder was one of a series committed in the area with a cut-throat razor. This theory has one convincing piece of evidence in its favour: Constance claimed that she had made the stab wound in the baby's side with a razor, which would have been virtually impossible. But there is also one powerful argument against this account of the murder: a father who decided to fake the murder of his favourite child would not have slashed the throat with such force that he almost severed the head. Whoever cut the throat of Francis Savill Kent was driven by almost insane hatred. As Whicher recognized, Constance Kent alone could have been responsible.

And when, in 1878, the Criminal Investigation Department was created at Scotland Yard, it was one of Whicher's protégés, Superintendent Adoiphus Williamson, who was chosen to head it.

10

By modern standards, it seems appallingly unfair that Constance Kent should have been sentenced to death for a crime she committed at the age of 16, then made to serve 20 years of a life sentence. Yet when we consider that it was only a century and a half since Judge Cambo of Malta sentenced an innocent man to torture and execution in order to observe a legal formality, we can see what enormous changes had occurred in society's attitude to justice. These changes were not due simply to Victorian humanitarianism. The real cause lay in man's changing attitude to himself. The rise of the novel taught European man to use his imagination and extend his sympathies. Advances in science and engineering taught him to span great rivers with his bridges and continents with his railways. As the nineteenth century drew to a close, he was also learning that crime can be fought with the same efficiency as disease or ignorance. Judge Cambo's attitude was an admission of defeat; the Victorian attitude was based upon boundless optimism about the future of humanity. The new science of crime detection was an outgrowth of this optimism.

The magnitude of the change can be measured by a case that made legal history in America in 1924. On a freezing February evening, the local priest, Father Hubert Dahme, was shot down on the main street of Bridgeport, Connecticut, and died instantly. Startled passers-by saw a dark figure running into an alleyway. The murder made headlines in the newspapers, and two weeks later, a hitch-hiker was questioned by police in nearby Norwalk. A search of his pockets revealed a .32 revolver – the calibre that had killed the priest. The suspect, an alcoholic ex-soldier named Harold Israel, was taken back to Bridgeport for questioning.

The next morning, the newspapers announced that the mystery was solved. Under police questioning, Israel had finally broken down and admitted that he had murdered the priest. He said that he had no motive except sudden hatred and despair. He had been walking around the city in the freezing wind, without money for food and drink, when he saw the priest and shot him . . .

The prosecution was to be conducted by a young State's Attorney named Homer Cummings. He saw immediately that he had a watertight case. A number of witnesses had described the gunman as a young man (Israel was 28) wearing a peaked cap and a long overcoat with a velvet collar, which fitted Israel precisely. A girl working behind the counter in the hamburger bar where Israel had taken his meals stated that she had seen Israel walk past the window at about the time of the murder, and had waved to him. An expert on guns said that the bullet that killed Father Dahme had been fired from Israel's .32. In the lodging-house where Israel had been staying, the police found the shell of a .32 cartridge – evidence, if any was needed, that he had been in possession of the gun when he was in Bridgeport. And, of course, most convincing of all, Israel had confessed. It was true that he had retracted the confession the next morning, but that was an understandable reaction of a man wanting to save his own skin.

Yet in spite of all this evidence, the State's Attorney was unhappy. There was something about the case that struck him as oddly wrong. To begin with, Israel said he was starving, yet he possessed a revolver that could be sold for the price of many meals. He said he had shot the priest in a burst of rage and despair; but in that case, he would surely have shot him in the face? Whoever killed Father Dahme crept up behind him. The ballistic evidence, which nowadays would be conclusive, was less convincing than it sounded. When Cummings looked into it, he discovered that the police had not just found one bullet case, but dozens – from three .32 revolvers. Israel had shared a lodging with two other ex-soldiers, and all three had owned a .32, and used it for target practice out of the window. In fact, the .32 was the most popular hand-gun in America, and there were probably millions of them around. As to the evidence that Israel's gun had fired the bullet, it was simply unacceptable in 1924, at a time when Charles E. Waite, the founder of forensic ballistics, was still learning how to tell whether a bullet had been fired from a rifle or a revolver of the same calibre.

When Cummings had interviewed the accused man, he was less happy than ever. Israel had been kept awake most of the night, under glaring lights, questioned relentlessly, until his weakened nerves could stand it no longer. 'I'd have signed anything, just so I could get some sleep.'

One thing still puzzled Cummings. Israel's original alibi, to which he returned later, was that he had been in a cinema, watching a film called *The Leather Pushers,* at the time Father Dahme was shot. Yet he could remember virtually nothing of the plot of the film, except that it was about boxers, which was obvious from the title. Back in his office, Cummings asked if anyone had seen *The Leather Pushers;* seven of them said they had. Asked to give a summary of its plot, they were all equally vague; apparently, like so many early films, *The Leather Pushers* lacked a memorable story line.

Cummings went back to the scene of the murder, choosing a bleak evening at about eight o'clock – the time it had occurred. With Cummings watching, his assistants re-enacted the crime, with other assistants standing where witnesses claimed to have been. The nearest streetlamp was 50 yards away, and at that distance, the 'murderer' was just a blurred figure. It was impossible to see what kind of hat or coat he was wearing. Cummings recalled that the witnesses had added various details after the newspapers had published descriptions of Israel; he drew his own conclusions.

Next they went to the nearby hamburger joint to talk to the waitress. The first things Cummings noticed was that the window was covered with a layer of condensation – inevitable on such a cold evening. He asked the girl where she had been standing when she had waved to Israel, then joined her behind the counter, and asked his assistants to walk up and down outside. Through the steamy glass it was impossible to recognize any of them. When he wiped the window clean, the lights outside dazzled him, and he was still unable to see them.

The girl resented his questions, and insisted that she *had* recognized Israel and waved to him. 'All right,' said Cummings, 'I'll walk up and down outside. I want you to wave to me.' In the next five minutes, the girl waved to two strangers and two of the assistants; but Cummings walked past three times without being recognized.

Back inside he asked her: 'Have you by any chance applied for the reward?'

The girl blushed. 'Well, a lawyer friend of mine said I ought to let him do it for me . . .

In court on 27 May 1924, Cummings produced a stunned silence when he announced that he would enter a plea of *nolle prosequi*. He told the court: 'A State's Attorney has two duties. One is to convict the guilty. The other is to protect the innocent.' As he spoke, the accused man burst intd tears. His subsequent history demonstrated that his brush with death had jarred him out of his alcoholic defeatism; he married happily and became a prosperous timber merchant. Homer Cummings, who had suspected that his decision not to prosecute would damage his career, found that he had become a celebrity (the story was subsequently filmed by Hollywood) and under Roosevelt he became the youngest-ever Attorney-General.

Yet it is important to recognize that Homer Cummings did *not* prove that Harold Israel was innocent; he only proved that the evidence was not strong enough to convict him. In fact, as we re-examine the evidence, we have to admit that it *is* conceivable that Israel murdered Father Dahme in a fit of rage and despair, just as he said he did. Judge Cambo would certainly have convicted Israel on the evidence, and even the Grand Master would have approved of the verdict. But the real difference between Cambo and Homer Cummings is not that one was a die-hard conservative and the other a democractic liberal. It is that Cummings believed that a crime can be reconstructed from the evidence, and that Cambo would have totally rejected such a notion. Cambo took it for granted that once a crime has been committed, the only way to discover the truth is by extracting a confession. Cummings had learned the lesson of the new science of forensic detection: that at the scene of every crime, there are a host of silent witnesses, and that if the right techniques are used, they can all be persuaded to tell their story.

2

The Power of Poison

For more than 2,000 years, poison was the favourite weapon of the assassin. The reason was simple: it was practically undetectable. There was not a single doctor in the ancient world who could have distinguished between sudden death due to poison and sudden death due to heart attack or stroke. In Rome at the time of Jesus, death from strychnine, aconite, belladonna, arsenic, mercury, lead, and poisonous fungi was as common as death by gunshot wounds in Al Capone's Chicago.

The most notorious *cause célèbre* to come down to us from the ancient world was a case involving multiple poisoning, as well as various other forms of murder, and it provides a remarkable insight into the depravity that prevailed even in the Rome of Julius Caesar, before Tiberius, Caligula, Nero and the rest embarked on their careers of mass murder.

The accused was a man named Cluentius, who was suspected of killing his stepfather by poison. But the reason he was on trial, in 66 BC, was that he was accused of his stepfather's 'judicial murder'. Eight years earlier, Cluentius had accused his stepfather, a man called Oppianicus, of trying to have him poisoned. The resulting trial was particularly disgraceful because it was widely rumoured that the judges had been bribed – probably by both sides. At all events, Oppianicus had been found guilty, and sentenced to exile. And it was while in exile that he had died with an unexpectedness that gave rise to suspicions of poisoning.

The great Roman orator Cicero was engaged to defend Cluentius. Cicero was weak, vain, and boastful, but his brilliance in public argument was unparalleled. He made no attempt to prove his client innocent, or even to prove Oppianicus guilty; instead, he poured out a list of Oppianicus's supposed crimes that left the judges stunned and shattered. If even a half of it is true, then Oppianicus deserves to rank with the most notorious mass murderers in history.

Oppianicus lived in the small town of Larinum, about 125 miles from Rome, and around 80 BC he decided to marry a rich matron named Sassia. This lady was apparently a nymphomaniac who had seduced her own daughter's husband, Melinus, then persuaded him to divorce the daughter and marry herself. So Oppianicus found himself confronting a preliminary obstacle in the form of Sassia's young husband. He overcame this by having Melinus poisoned, after which he lost no time in proposing to the rich widow. But Sassia was unhappy – not about the death of her husband, but about the fact that Oppianicus already had two young children by two recent wives. (One wife had died, and he had divorced the other.) If she married him, part of her own fortune would descend to these children. Oppianicus also, according to Cicero, solved this problem with characteristic simplicity. He invited the son of his divorced wife to come and stay with him; within an hour of arriving, the boy was dead. Ten days later, the other child – a baby – was also dead. In ancient Rome, such deaths, due to cholera or the plague, were common. Sassia now saw no obstacle to the marriage, so she and Oppianicus quickly became husband and wife.

Her motives may have been fear as well as self-interest. Oppianicus was not a man to be crossed with impunity, as he had shown a few years earlier. His mother-in-law in those days was a woman called Dinaea, who had lost all her three sons – which meant, of course, that her fortune would in due course descend to her daughter, Oppianicus's wife. Then, suddenly, Dinaea heard that one of her sons was still alive; he had not been killed in battle, as she thought, but was being held prisoner of war. She begged her relatives to try and find him, and Oppianicus was among those who agreed to help. But he had no intention of keeping his promise; an additional heir would prevent his wife inheriting. Dinaea died suddenly and unexpectedly; and when the other relatives tried to locate the missing heir, he had vanished. Oppianicus had arranged to have him kidnapped and murdered. The relatives denounced Oppianicus as a murderer; the citizens of Larinum rose up against him, and Oppianicus had to flee for his life. But he had no intention of staying in exile The whole country was in ferment, due to civil war, and Oppianicus had no difficulty raising an army of mercenaries. He descended on Larinum, deposed its rulers, and proceeded to execute all his enemies, claiming that the victorious General Sulla (later dictator) had authorized him to do so.

According to Cicero, Oppianicus had poisoned at least one of his previous wives, as well as his brother Gaius and his brother's wife, who was pregnant at the time. But his career of crime began to falter when he murdered a rich young man called Asuvius. It was a brilliantly ingenious plot. Asuvius had decided to go to Rome for a week of debauchery. Oppianicus invited himself along too, taking also a local scoundrel named Avillius. And one night, when Asuvius was safely in bed with a prostitute, Oppianicus rushed around to various acquaintances and claimed that his friend Asuvius was seriously ill, and wanted to make his will. In fact, the man who was lying in bed and pretending to be ill was the scoundrel Avillius. And when the fake Asuvius had made his will, and it had been duly signed and witnessed, the real Asuvius was taken for a walk and murdered; his body was then buried in a sandpit.

It looked like the perfect crime; Oppianicus only had to wait for the statutory time, then claim the dead man's fortune. But things began to go wrong. Friends of the dead man made enquiries, and found that he had last been seen in company with Avillius. Dragged in front of the commissioner of police, Avillius broke down and confessed. Oppianicus was promptly arrested. But his power was great, and his fortune even greater. The commissioner of police was well bribed, and the case abandoned 'for lack of evidence'.

But now the master villain finally overreached himself. He decided that his next victim should be his stepson Cluentius who, ever since the scandal of the seduced son-in-law, had not been on speaking terms with his mother, Sassia. Cluentius was unwell, and was being treated by a doctor. The doctor's slave, Diogenes, was approached and asked to slip poison into Cluentius's medicine. The slave said he would think about it, and went and told his master. The doctor passed on the information to Cluentius, who immediately realized that fate was offering him the opportunity to bring his stepfather to justice. But he had to act with extreme caution. His first step was to buy the slave Diogenes, so he could be relied upon to co-operate. Next, Diogenes had to apparently agree to the murder plot. The intermediary – the man who had tried to bribe Diogenes – was a swindler and confidence man named Fabricius. When Diogenes told him he was willing to co-operate, the trap was set. The poison and the money were to be handed over to Diogenes by a servant called Scamander. And at the crucial moment, a group of Cluentius's friends leapt out of hiding and seized Scamander, as well as the poison and the money.

Even now, Cluentius had to proceed with caution. Unless Scamander implicated Fabricius, and Fabricius implicated Oppianicus, then he was no better off than before. So first he prosecuted Scamander and, when the court found Scamander guilty, went on to prosecute Fabricius, who was obviously responsible for his servant's actions. Only when Fabricius was also found guilty of attempted poisoning did he go on to prosecute Oppianicus for being behind the whole plot. And, as we have already seen, the judges sentenced Oppianicus to exile, where, two years later, he suddenly died . . .

It sounds as if justice had finally triumphed. But this would undoubtedly be a naïve assumption. There can be little doubt that Oppianicus was a multiple murderer; but it is doubtful whether Cluentius was as innocent as Cicero insisted. It seems highly likely that he had his stepfather poisoned. Cicero dismisses this with the comment that Cluentius had no reason to hate Oppianicus, for Oppianicus was already a ruined man, 'whose lot was so wretched that death would have been a happy release'. This is obvious nonsense. Oppianicus was a wealthy man and his wife was a wealthy woman; in exile or not, he could still plot revenge.

Oppianicus died in 72 BC. His son, Oppianicus jun., brought the case against Cluentius six years later. Why such a long wait? The answer can be found in Cicero's defence speech. Cluentius was also accused of trying to poison Oppianicus jun. It happened at the wedding of Oppianicus jun., when someone passed him a cup of honeyed wine. It was intercepted by one of his friends, who drank it and fell down dead. Again, Cicero dismisses the accusation as absurd; why, he asks, should Cluentius want to poison his half-brother? But the answer is obvious: because their mother Sassia was a highly dangerous woman, who would never cease to urge Oppianicus jun. to avenge his father's death. This is, of course, precisely what happened when Oppianicus jun. accused Cluentius of judicial murder. So, far from being innocent, it seems reasonably certain that Cluentius was guilty of murder and attempted murder, as well as of bribing the judges.

Cicero himself emerges from the case without much credit. He later boasted that he had pulled the wool over the eyes of the judges. What he meant is not clear, but the likeliest assumption is that he knew Cluentius was guilty of murder, attempted murder, and bribery. He also had to explain why he himself had been, at one time, the tool of the mass murderer Oppianicus. When the servant Scamander was accused of attempting to murder Cluentius, it was Cicero who appeared in

Scamander's defence. He insisted, with shocked sincerity, that he had
no idea of the strength of the evidence against Scamander. But it is
unlikely that a lawyer as experienced as Cicero took on a case without
knowing exactly what he was doing. The truth is that Cicero was a
brilliant weakling, who changed his allegiance as often as it suited him.
It is satisfying to record that he finally changed it once too often. When
his old friend Julius Caesar was murdered, Cicero took the side of the
murderers. When the assassins were defeated, Mark Antony ordered
Cicero's death; the executioner caught up with him at his villa at
Capetae, and cut off his hands and his head.

2

It seems strange that a criminal as enterprising as Oppianicus should
not have achieved greater notoriety in the annals of mass murder. The
answer is that he was far from unique. In the first century BC, Rome
was full of poisoners and assassins. There were undoubtedly dozens of
other cases that have been forgotten because the advocate was less
celebrated than Cicero. Yet Rome was not always a criminals'
paradise. As Michael Grant notes in his introduction to Cicero's
murder trials: 'Murder first became a conspicuous feature of the public
life of Rome in 133 BC, when the aristocratic but radical and reformist
(popularis) tribune of the people Tiberius Sempronius Gracchus was
clubbed to death by the senators he had defied, and by their friends.'
Before that time, Rome seems to have been a fairly law-abiding place.
It was the murder of Gracchus that unleashed a tide of criminality, so
that Rome in 70 BC had much the same problem as London in AD 1770.
   The cause was also much the same. As Henry Fielding pointed out,
London's 'crime explosion' was due to the extreme misery of the poor
and the conspicuous consumption of the rich. Rome had been familiar
with the problem for centuries – the first strike in history occurred in
494 BC, when the poor (or plebeians) all marched out of Rome, and
threatened to go and found their own city unless they were given their
rights. The patricians were forced to concede them their own represen-
tatives (tribunes), and from then on, Rome became a textbook example
of Karl Marx's class struggle. But the struggle turned into a landslide
of murder only after the killing of Tiberius Gracchus in 133 BC, and of
his brother Gaius 11 years later. Tiberius was stunned by a blow from
the leg of a bench dealt by a fellow senator, then beaten to death by

others. Three hundred of his friends and followers were also murdered. A few years later, the class struggle surfaced again, in the bloody confrontation between the left-wing Marius and the right-wing Sulla. Each retained power for a time; each murdered his enemies by the dozen. Once murder has been justified as a political expedient, it can turn into a habit, then a disease. For the next five centuries, the history of ancient Rome is a story of continuous murder.

During that time, poisoning developed into a fine art; experts in its use could prepare poisons that would kill instantly, or take months. The Roman historian Tacitus tells us about a professional poisoner called Locusta, who had been condemned to death, then reprieved to work for the rich, and how she prepared a poison for the emperor Claudius, which was administered in a dish of mushrooms. When it took too long to work, the emperor's physician Xenophon persuaded him that he needed to vomit, and inserted a poisoned feather down his throat, whereupon Claudius finally succumbed. His successor Nero was so delighted that he often used to make a joke about mushrooms being a dish fit for the gods (Claudius having been proclaimed a god). He also made use of Locusta to get rid of Claudius's son Britannicus. His first attempt was a failure – the poison only gave the 14-year-old youth diarrhoea – so Nero made Locusta prepare the poison in front of his own eyes. When she finally made a poison that killed a pig on the spot, he hastened off to the dining-room, where the boy was eating. A taster had to try every mouthful of food and drink before Britannicus tasted it, but the boy was handed a drink so hot that it scalded his mouth. Thereupon he took a drink from a glass of cold water, which contained the poison, and fell down dead. Nero shook his head sadly, and remarked that such attacks often carried off epileptics. The other guests decided that it was better to show no surprise, and resumed their dinner.

The skill of the Italians in the art of poisoning became a legend; but, like most legends, it lacked a solid foundation. During the Middle Ages and the Renaissance, there were incredible stories of poisons that could be smeared on a letter or the pages of a book, and that would kill the reader through the pores of the skin; in fact, no such poison was known. The same is true of the 'venom' that the Borgias are supposed to have concealed in a spiked ring, so they could kill by merely shaking hands. No such deadly venom existed – most snakes have to inject a fairly large quantity of poison to kill their prey. It is also one of the disappointing facts of history that Lucrezia Borgia, whose name has become synonymous with poison, never killed anyone in her life (she was a mild, gentle girl) by 'venom' or any other means. Her murderous brother Cesare, who undoubtedly had dozens of killings to his credit, usually preferred stabbing or strangling.

But by the beginning of the sixteenth century, the virtues of poison as an easy and undetectable way of removing enemies had become widely recognized in Europe, particularly in Rome and Venice. The most powerful men in Venice belonged to the secret Council of Ten, which dealt with conspiracy, treason and offences against morals, and there is a record of their proceedings dealing with various proposed assassinations, with the word 'Factum' written at the side of assassinations that had been carried out. On 15 December 1543, a Franciscan monk called John of Ragusa offered the council a selection of poisons, and stated his terms for killing various eminent personages: 500 ducats for the Great Sultan, 150 for the King of Spain, 60 for the Duke of Milan, 50 for the Marquis of Mantua and 100 for the Pope. In the following year this offer was accepted, but the records do not detail the results.

The first member of this 'Italian school of poisoners' whose name has come down to us is a Sicilian woman called Tofania di Adamo, born about 1640, who moved to Naples in 1659 and marketed a brand of poison that became known as Acqua Tofana. It seems to have been a clear liquid compounded mainly from arsenic and, since this can be used for the complexion, it was sold quite openly, sometimes under the name of 'Elixir of St Nicholas of Ban' (Ban being a town whose water had healing qualities). The chronicles indicate that Tofania became a kind of consultant poisoner – like certain of her Parisian contemporaries who became notorious in the 'Affair of the Poisons'. She also, apparently, achieved enough influence to become a successful actress. Eventually, alerted by large numbers of sudden deaths, the police decided to arrest her, whereupon she fled and took refuge in a convent. Her pursuers tried psychological warfare, and spread rumours that she had poisoned the city's water supply; this alarmed the nuns, who allowed her arrest. Under torture, she confessed to being responsible for about 600 deaths, including two popes. In 1709 she was strangled and thrown into the courtyard of the convent in which she had taken refuge.

There are also records of a secret society of poisoners, consisting mainly of bored wives, that flourished in Rome during the pontificate of Alexander VII in the 1660s. They gathered about a fortune-teller named Hieronyma Spara, who trained them in the art of poisoning. She was eventually arrested by the Papal police and tortured on the rack. She refused to confess, but one of her acolytes showed less endurance. La Spara and a dozen other women were hanged, and many others whipped through the streets.

A curious glimpse of the state of medical knowledge about poisons can be obtained from an account of the inquest on the Earl of Atholl in 1579. Atholl died after attending a banquet given by the unpopular regent Morton, and poison was suspected. Six doctors were present when the body was opened, and most seemed to agree that he had died from 'venom'. But the only one who made any attempt to test the verdict was a doctor who dipped his finger into the contents of the stomach, and then tasted it. A contemporary account says he became ill within an hour or so. In 1611, a similar method was used at the inquest on George Home, Earl of Dunbar; it was suspected that a poison had been administered to him in tablets of sugar by Queen Elizabeth's chief minister Robert Cecil. The doctor named Martin Souqir tried a popular method of testing for poison – laying his finger on the dead man's heart, then touching the finger to his tongue. The record stated that Souqir died within a few days, but it seems clear that, if this was so, it was certainly not as a result of the poison administered to Dunbar.

By 1530, the poison legend had taken root in England. When a cook named Rose, a member of the household of the Bishop of Rochester, was accused of poisoning a saucepan of porridge and causing two deaths, an Act of Poisoning was hastily passed, on the grounds that 'unless it was severely punished, no man would in the future have any security against death by such means'. The penalty was to be boiled to death, and this was the punishment that was meted out to the cook in Smithfield. Sixty-four years later, Queen Elizabeth's physician, Dr Ruy Lopez, was castrated, disembowelled and quartered on a mere suspicion (which we now know to be unfounded) that he was plotting to poison the queen. And a yeoman named Edward Squyer suffered the same fate after he had placed his hand on the pommel of the queen's saddle, crying 'God save the queen!' The charge was that he had used this opportunity to smear a deadly poison, obtained from Spain, on the saddle, a poison of such a strength that the queen would have died if she had merely touched it. Squyer may have been guilty as charged – at this distance in time there is no way to assess the evidence – but one thing is certain: that at that time, there was no poison that could kill from mere skin contact.

By this time, chemistry was beginning to develop into a science. For centuries it had been merely another name for alchemy: the search for the Philosopher's Stone that would turn base metals into gold and prolong life. But an increasing number of doctors began to study chemistry simply to discover the secrets of healing. Most of them still accepted the notion (derived from Aristotle) that everything was composed of the four elements – earth, air, fire, and water. In the sixteenth century the great Paracelsus had caused a revolution by rejecting that notion – but in favour of the equally dubious idea that the basic elements are mercury, sulphur, and salt. The greatest seventeenth-century chemist Van Helmont rejected the three elements of Paracelsus in favour of water and air. But in spite of this muddle, chemists were becoming skilled in the practical business of learning the medical properhes of various chemicals – so the German Glauber gave his name to a powerful laxative called Glauber's Salt (sodium sulphate), which he preferred to call miracle salt (sal-mirabile). And Franciscus Sylvius, as we have already seen, made the even more interesting discovery of the spirit called Geneva or gin.

In the first decade of the seventeenth century there lived in London an undistinguished apothecary named James Franklin and, towards the end of April 1613, he was approached by a brothel-keeper named Mother Turner with a request for undetectable poisons. (A few poisons caused obvious effects, such as turning the eyeballs yellow, causing the hair to fall out, and so on.) Its purpose was to do away with a brilliant homosexual poet and courtier, Sir Thomas Overbury, who had been thrown into the Tower of London on the orders of the king, James I. Overbury was a victim of a plot hatched by his former lover Robert Carr, and Carr's vindictive mistress Frances, a girl with the face of a juvenile delinquent and the temperament of a young Lady Macbeth. Carr had become the king's favourite, and Overbury was his secretary. But Overbury had made no secret of his detestation of Carr's concubine, Lady Frances Howard, and did his unsuccessful best to dissuade him from marriage. Carr himself was getting tired of Overbury's sulks and tempers, and had no difficulty in persuading the king that a few months in the Tower would improve his manners. But Lady Frances had an even better idea – that Overbury should waste away gently in the Tower, so his death would be ascribed to the dampness of the dungeons.

James Franklin had no difficulty recommending a number of slow poisons. Overbury was in an ideal situation for a poisoner, at the mercy of a jailer – Lady Frances had contrived the dismissal of the governor of the Tower, Sir William Wood, and his replacement by one of her own friends, Sir Gervase Elwes. Another servant of the countess, Richard Weston, was appointed Overbury's personal attendant – and poisoner. Mother Turner handed Weston phials of white arsenic, corrosive sublimate (mercuric chloride), powdered diamonds (probably powdered glass for which Franklin charged the price of diamonds), cantharides (Spanish fly) and something called Great Spiders, and for the next three months, Overbury ingested these regularly with his meals, until he was hardly more than a skeleton. In September, he died of exhaustion. A jury declared that his death was due to natural causes (mercuric chloride produces the symptoms of syphilis) and he was hastily buried.

Carr and Lady Frances now went ahead with their marriage. All seemed well until, two years later, the chemist's assistant who had prepared the poisons for James Franklin lay on his deathbed, and confessed to a priest. If Carr (now the Earl of Rochester) had still been the king's favourite, the confession would undoubtedly have been ignored. But the king had found a new lover, George Villiers, and Carr was making scenes. James ordered the affair to be investigated: the result was the arrest of everyone concerned: Robert and Frances Carr, Mother Turner, Richard Weston, Sir Gervase Elwes, and James Franklin. All were sentenced to death, but the king had promised Carr that he would not be executed; instead, he and Lady Frances – who now hated one another – spent six years in the Tower. They were then allowed to retire to their country home, where Lady Frances died of cancer of the womb at the age of 39.

3

A few decades later, another chemist, rather more eminent than Franklin, found himself in a court of law charged with providing poisons. He was Christoph Glaser, a Swiss from Basle, and he was famous in his time for his method of making 'glaserite' (potassium sulphate) much used as a fertilizer, as well as for his celebrated treatise on chemistry. Glaser was thrown into the Bastille after being charged with aiding the infamous Marquise de Brinvilliers, the most notorious poisoner of her day.

The Marquis – born Marie Madeleine d'Aubray in July 1630 – was not beautiful, but since she was petite, with blue eyes and blonde hair, she was exceedingly attractive. She was also a nymphomaniac; in her later confession she admits that sexual experimentation with her brothers began at the age of 7 and included sodomy. At the age of 21, Marie married a gambler and womanizer, the Marquis de Brinvilliers, the colonel of a regiment. Around 1660, he became acquainted with a handsome young captain, the Chevalier Godin de Sainte-Croix, whom he liked so much that he introduced him into his home, and Ste-Croix and the lively marquise were soon lovers. The husband, apparently, found nothing disagreeable in this situation, since most ladies of the aristocracy had their *cavalier,* but her father took an altogether less relaxed view, and induced the king, Louis XIV, to grant him a *lettre de cachet,* enabling him to have the cavalier arrested and thrown in the Bastille. This act was to have unfortunate consequences for the Viscount d'Aubray and his family, for Ste-Croix found himself sharing a cell with a well-known poisoner named Exili, whose first name seems to be unrecorded. Exili had apparently learned his craft in Italy – one chronicler makes him a pupil of a La Toffana – and had worked for Olimpia Maidalchina, sister-in-law of Pope Innocent the Tenth and unofficial queen of Rome. Queen Christina of Sweden had met the poisoner in Rome, and he is supposed to have entered her service. When he arrived in France, after her abdication, his reputation was so unsavoury that he was thrown into the Bastille. Exili recognized Ste-Croix's value as a patron, and proceeded to teach him the fundamentals of the art of making poison. We are told that one of these was *venin de crapaud* – toad venom, made by injecting a toad with arsenic, allowing it to decay, and distilling the flesh. But this notion sounds as preposterous as a formula attributed to the Borgias – poisoning a bear with arsenic, suspending it upside down, and collecting the froth that dribbles from its mouth. It is far more probable that Exili taught Ste-Croix how to administer poisons like arsenic and mercuric chloride in quantities that could not be detected.

When Ste-Croix came out of prison, after seven weeks, he succeeded in procuring the release of Exili. The latter was promptly deported to London, but soon succeeded in slipping back into France, and went to live in Ste-Croix's house, where the lessons in toxicology continued.

Yet when Ste-Croix and his mistress decided to poison her father, in order to expedite her inheritance, they decided against using one of Exili's concoctions; instead they turned to Christoph Glaser, the king's Apothecary-in-Ordinary. It was Glaser who provided them with a poison that was guaranteed undetectable. They began by trying it out on the maidservant Françoise in a dish of gooseberries. It gave her severe stomach pains and permanently impaired her health, but she recovered; Marie and her lover therefore requested a stronger brew from Glaser.

It was now three years since Ste-Croix had been in prison, and the Viscount d'Aubray was reconciled to his daughter, believing that she had broken off relations with her lover. In Whitsun 1666, he invited her and her children to visit him at his estate at Offémont. There, after eating a bowl of soup, he began to suffer stomach pains. His daughter insisted on sending for a doctor, who diagnosed indigestion. She nursed her father devotedly throughout a six-month illness, during which he had many recoveries and many relapses; finally, in September 1666, he died.

Marie now proceeded to take a series of lovers, including her husband's cousin, the Marquis de Nadaillac, and her own cousin, by whom she had a child. (She had two children by Ste-Croix.) She also seduced the tutor of her children, a young man named Briancourt. But by 1670, both she and her husband were urgently in need of money. The greater part of her father's fortune had been inherited by her two brothers. The solution was obvious . . .

But first, it was necessary to conduct further experiments to make sure the poison was undetectable. Marie began to pay visits to a hospital run by Sisters of Mercy, the Hôtel-Dieu, carrying biscuits and preserved fruits. The doctors were puzzled when some of their patients began to suffer from an unknown disease whose chief symptom was fatigue, followed by a gradual wasting away. Marie called several times to follow the progress of these unfortunates, and showed the appropriate distress when they finally expired. (It is only fair to add that Voltaire, in his book on Louis XIV, dismisses this whole story as the invention of a sensational chronicler.)

Marie's two brothers were, respectively, a Civil Lieutenant and a Court Councillor; the elder, Antoine d'Aubray d'Offémont, was married; the younger brother, who was unmarried, lived with them. Impatient at the slowness of poison, Marie hired two assassins to stab one brother to death when he was on the road, but they bungled it. After that failure, she reverted to the more reliable method. A valet called Jean Hamelin, known as La Chausée, was hired, and accompanied Marie on a visit to her brothers. The elder brother became suspicious one day when some wine tasted too acidic and smelt of vitriol; but La Chausée explained apologetically that he had left some medicine in the bottom of the glass, and this was accepted. Three months later, in April 1670, La Chausée accompanied the brothers to Villequoy, in Beauce. After a meal of pigeon pie, seven people were overcome with vomiting. Five days later, the brothers returned to Paris, where the illness of the elder puzzled the doctors. He died on 17 June 1670. In September, the younger brother died of the same illness. Doctors who performed a post-mortem suspected poison, but were not sufficiently certain to pursue the charge. La Chausée received a bequest of 100 crowns for his devoted service.

Ste-Croix and La Chausée now began to blackmail her, and part of the servant's price was Marie's sexual favours – a secretary calling one day found them in a compromising position. And, incredibly, Marie told her young lover Briancourt about the poisoning of her brothers. When Ste-Croix tried to force her to disgorge the 55,000 livres she had promised to pay for his help, she made a scene and took poison. Warm milk made her vomit and counteracted the poison, but she was ill for several months. And Ste-Croix continued to blackmail her, threatening her with a certain box that he kept in his laboratory, which contained some compromising letters. It seems that she decided that one solution would be to poison her husband and marry Ste-Croix, and proceeded to administer small quantities of poison to the penniless gambler. Ste-Croix had no wish to marry her, and is said to have administered antidotes, so the unfortunate man's health swung like a pendulum between extremes. For whatever reasons, the baron survived her.

Constant need for money led her to decide to poison the two remaining relatives who stood in the way of the family inheritance: her sister-in-law, Marie Thérèse Mangot, and her sister, a nun, also called Thérèse. And she continued to confide her designs to her young lover Briancourt, who was horrified and tried to dissuade her. When she ignored him, he even sent a message to Mme Mangot, warning her to beware of poison. Marie de Brinvilliers was infuriated, and sent a relative of La Chausée to minister to his needs; Briancourt gave the man a beating and sent him away. Then Ste-Croix tried, entering Briancourt's bedroom at night, only to find him awake and fully dressed. Two days later, while passing the Church of St Paul, Briancourt had a narrow escape when a bullet pierced his coat. In a rage, he went to Ste-Croix's house and denounced him as a scoundrel who would come to a bad end. Soon afterwards, he became a teacher in a religious house at Aubervilliers.

Then, in July 1672, Ste-Croix died. There are two accounts of his death, one of which states that he was bending over a bubbling retort in his laboratory in the rue des Bernadins when he inhaled a deadly poison and collapsed; the other, less dramatic but more plausible, is that he died after an illness lasting five months. He had left instructions that a small box, about 18 inches square and covered with red calfskin, should be handed over to Marie de Brinvilliers. But Ste-Croix's wife, from whom he was separated, insisted that it should be opened in the presence of some officials.

Marie heard the news and rushed from her country home to Paris; she was too late. The box had been opened. and its contents were being discussed all over Paris. There was Ste-Croix's will, demanding that the box should be handed over to Marie de Brinvilliers, and two promissory notes: one from Marie, promising to pay 30,000 francs, and the second, from a wealthy man named Reich de Pennautier, promising to pay 10,000 francs. Pennautier was an old friend of Ste-Croix, and had risen suddenly in the world, owing his present position of Receiver-General to the sudden death of a man called Saint-Laurent. The box also proved to contain various packets of poison, listed as corrosive sublimate, Roman vitriol, powdered vitriol, opium, and antimony, as well as a phial of clear liquid with a white powder at the bottom. Animals and birds to whom this was fed died quickly, but showed no trace of poison on being dissected.

La Chausée was found wandering around Paris and arrested; he was found to be in possession of a packet of 'powdered vitriol'. Under torture, he finally confessed that he had poisoned the two d'Aubray brothers on the orders of Ste-Croix. La Chausée was sentenced to be broken on the wheel.

Marie fled, first to Germany, then to a convent in Liege, where she took refuge. A police agent named François Desgrais was sent to entrap her. He had a gentlemanly manner, and posed as an abbé. Marie received him without suspicion; by now she was bored and undoubtedly sex-starved after almost three years 'on the run'. So she had no hesitation in accepting the charming abbés proposal that they should meet for a drive outside the convent. At a signal from Desgrais, archers rushed out of hiding, and Marie was informed that she was under arrest. In her room in the convent Desgrais found a box containing a confession. This acknowledged that she had commenced her career of 'vicious indulgence' at the age of seven, and gave details of poisoning of her father and brothers – mostly with 'toad venom' – as well as an indecisive attempt to poison one of her daughters, whom she regarded as a 'ninny'.

The trial lasted from 29 April to 16 July 1676; one of the chief witnesses against her was her lover Briancourt, whom she taunted with being a weakling. But on the whole, she bore herself with dignity that gained her many sympathizers – even when she was being subjected to the 'water torture', which involved being stripped naked and bent backwards over a trestle, which strained her body into a arc, while gallons of water were poured into her mouth through a funnel. When she became unconscious, her confessor was sent for – he seems to have provided her with much spiritual comfort at the end. Finally, dressed only in a shift, she was taken in a cart, with a rope around her neck, to the Place de la Grève, where she was decapitated by a single blow of the headman's sword. The blow was delivered with such precision that her doctor, who was watching, thought for a moment that the executioner had missed; then the head toppled and rolled backwards. The executioner picked up the body under one arm – she was a small woman – and the head in his other hand, and threw them on to a pile of faggots beside the scaffold; an hour later, nothing of them remained.

It is reported that her last words were that it seemed unfair that she should suffer the penalty of the law when most people of quality were making free use of poison . . .

Pennautier was also tried, charged with having poisoned Saint-Laurent; but he was a great deal richer than Marie, and had no trouble persuading his judges that he was innocent. As to the eminent apothecary Christoph Glaser, he spent some time in the Bastille in 1676, but was soon released; he died two years later, rumour attributing the cause of death to rage and indignation.

4

The police chief, Nicholas de La Reynie, had good reason to know that Marie's last words were no exaggeration. His predecessor – another Daubray – had been poisoned by his wife. And in the year after Ste-Croix's death, La Reynie began to hear rumours of a large-scale poisoning; two priests informed him that many penitents were asking absolution for murdering their spouses. A young lawyer who was having a meal with a fortune-teller known as La Vigoreux, wife of a tailor, was startled to hear another fortune-teller, Marie Bosse, declare 'What a marvellous trade! Duchesses, marquises, princes! Three more poisonings and I'll be able to retire.' The lawyer passed

on this information to Desgrais, who sent the wife of one of his officers along to ask Marie Bosse's advice about her husband's cruelty.
On the second visit, Mme Bosse handed over a phial of a colourless
poison, together with precise instructions for using it. And finally, on
4 January 1669, the police descended on Marie Bosse in the early
hours of the morning and placed her under arrest. La Reynie was
shocked to be told that Marie had been found sharing a huge bed
with her two sons and her daughters, for it was believed that magical
powers could be passed from one member of a family to another by
incest. La Vigoreux was also arrested, and she and Bosse proved
more than willing to talk. At first, La Reynie thought he was dealing
with a harmless matter of witchcraft – love potions and magic spells
– for although belief in magic was still common among the unedu-
cated class, the aristocracy of the Age of Reason was already
inclined to dismiss it as pure imagination. But as La Reynie listened
to the confessions, he realized with alarm that Marie Bosse had not
been exaggerating when she talked about her clients: this affair
involved the 'highest in the land'. Moreover, Bosse and La Vigoreux
were associated with an eminent fortune-teller called Catherine
Deshayes, known as La Voisin, whose wealthy and aristocratic
clients included members of the court. One client, Mme de
Poulaillon, was the wife of the Master of Forests and Waterways in
Champagne, while another two, Mme Leféron and Mme Dreux, were
the wives of Paris magistrates who would probably be called to try
these 'witches'. Finally, with astonishment, La Reynie heard the
names of two of the king's mistresses, Louise de la Vallière and
Mme de Montespan, and at that point he knew that the king himself
must be informed. And when the king heard the details, he decided
immediately that this could not be tried in open court; all this talk of
poisons and love potions could only bring the monarchy into
discredit. La Vigoreux was tortured – she died under torture – and
so were Marie Bosse and La Voisin. They told amazing stories of
poison and magic spells. The pretty Mme Poulaillon, burdened with
an ageing husband and a demanding lover, had been given shirts
treated with arsenic, which would cause her husband to scratch
himself, and a 'healing ointment' that would kill him in ten weeks.
But her husband had come to suspect her designs, and had her
confined in a convent. And Mme de Montespan, for ten years the
king's favourite mistress, had called on the sorceresses whenever the
king's affections had seemed to be diminishing, and had been

supplied with love potions and aphrodisiacs, including Spanish Fly, mashed blister beetles, cocks' combs and cocks' testicles. And there was worse to come. Montespan had raised the question of whether the queen and Louise de la Vallière might be killed by witchcraft. This was beyond the powers of the fortune-tellers; they sent her instead to the 'high priest of devil worship', an evil old man called Abbé Guibourg. The essence of the black masses performed by Guibourg was the sacrifice of a newborn baby. Mme de Montespan was made to lie naked on a bed, her feet dangling on the floor, with the sacred chalice on her groin. La Voisin brought in a baby, and Guibourg slit its throat over the chalice, into which he drained its blood, reciting the names of Mme de Montespan and the king. The child's entrails were removed, and its body burned in a furnace; the entrails were used for distilling a magic potion – which included the Host used in the black mass – and this was given to Mme de Montespan to administer to the king.

La Voisin's daughter, who described all this, also told how a lady of the court named Mme des Oeillets had come for a magic potion, accompanied by a man; Guibourg had explained that he would need to mix the sexual discharges of both into the potion. But since Mme des Oeillets was menstruating, he accepted instead some of her menstrual blood, which he mixed with the sperm which the man had produced by masturbating into the chalice.

The king was horrified. If this became known, he would be the laughing stock of Europe. He therefore gave orders that the case should be tried in private. The trial began in April 1679, and dragged on until July 1683; 104 defendants appeared before a selected panel of 12 judges in a chamber of the old Paris Arsenal; since this was lit by candles and torches it became known as the Chambre Ardente (lighted chamber). Many other priests were found to be involved, and the king was shocked to discover the astonishing extent of black magic in France. Thirty-six death sentences were handed out, and four life sentences to the galleys; another 34 prisoners were sentenced to banishment or heavy fines. No word of the proceedings leaked outside the walls of the 'Poison Chamber', but the long and grim series of executions left the public in no doubt of the seriousness of the crimes involved. The name of Mme de Montespan was never mentioned; she had been replaced by a new favourite, Mme de Maintenon – who had been her protégé – and retired to a convent. In 1709, the king ordered that all papers relating to the case should be destroyed; but by some error, the minute-book of the clerk of the court was overlooked; it was finally published in the second half of the nineteenth century, revealing for the first time one of the most incredible stories of murder and black magic in the recorded annals of crime.

5

The first poisoning case in which medical evidence played the decisive role was the trial, in 1751, of Mary Blandy, charged with poisoning her father with arsenic. In 1746, at the age of 26, Mary was still unmarried, although she was an heiress to a fortune of £10,000; her father, a prosperous lawyer of Henley-on-Thames, took exception to most of the young men who showed signs of interest in his plain but good-natured daughter. But in that year, Mary made the acquaintance of a Scottish captain, the Hon. William Henry Cranstoun, who immediately began to pay her attentions. Cranstoun had many disadvantages; he was small, pock-marked, cross-eyed, and already married; none of this prevented him from deciding to win Mary's hand. The first step was to rid himself of his wife, who was being supported by her relatives in Scotland. He wrote to her explaining that his chances of advancement in the army were poor while he was married, and begging her to write him a letter stating that she had merely been his mistress. She was finally persuaded to do this, whereupon Cranstoun circulated copies to his and her relatives, and instituted divorce proceedings. His wife opposed it and proved that their marriage was legal. And Mr Blandy, who had been prepared to accept Cranstoun as a son-in-law – after all, he was the brother of a Scottish peer – indignantly reproached the ugly little Scot and indicated that the engagement was at an end. Cranstoun nevertheless continued to call, and he and Mary continued to regard themselves as secretly engaged, although she declined his suggestion that they should run away and marry. Mrs Blandy became the captain's ardent ally after he had given her £40 to pay a debt she had contracted on a visit to London. Soon after this visit, in September 1749, Mrs Blandy became suddenly ill and died, begging her husband to allow Mary to marry Cranstoun. When Cranstoun wrote to Mary, telling her that he was besieged by the bailiffs, and needed his £40, she borrowed the money and sent it to him.

From this point on, we must accept either the version of those who believe Mary guilty, or those who are convinced she was an innocent dupe. Cranstoun explained to her that he knew a fortune-teller called Mrs Morgan, whose magic potions could be relied upon to make her father change his mind. And on a visit to the Blandy household in 1750, Cranstoun apparently demonstrated the efficacy of a magic powder by slipping some of it into the old gentleman's tea. He had been in the worst of tempers at breakfast, yet overflowing with benevolence at dinner. Mary allowed herself to be persuaded to continue the doses. And in April 1751, Cranstoun sent Mary some 'Scotch pebbles' – a fashionable ornament at the time – together with a white powder for cleaning them. Mary began to administer the powder to her father in small doses. And the fact that Francis Blandy began to suffer acute stomach pains must have made her aware that the potion was less harmless than her lover claimed. And when the servant, Susan Gunnel, tasted some of the gruel that Mr Blandy was about to eat, she also became ill. After that, Susan poured out the gruel from the pan and noticed a gritty white powder in the bottom; she took this to a neighbour, who sent it to an apothecary. But since no reliable chemical test was known for arsenic, no immediate analysis was attempted. Nevertheless, Susan went to Mr Blandy and warned him that she thought he was being poisoned by his own daughter. And when Blandy asked Mary if she had put anything into his tea, she became pale, and hurried from the room.

Incredibly, Mr Blandy took no steps to prevent Mary from meddling with his food. And when he was shown a letter Mary had written to Cranstoun, begging him to take care of what he wrote, he only smiled and said: 'Poor lovesick girl! What a woman will do for the man she loves.' Then he continued to sink. And when Mary, now in a panic, threw some letters and powder into the kitchen fire, the cook rescued the powder as soon as she left the room. Mr Blandy asked to see Mary, who fell on her knees and begged him not to curse her; he told her that he blessed her, and hoped God would forgive her. Two days later, he died.

That same afternoon, Mary begged the footman to accompany her to France, and offered him £500, which he refused. The following morning, she ran out of the house and tried to escape, but was soon surrounded by an angry crowd. Her lover was more successful; when he heard news of her arrest, he fled to France.

When Mary was tried, on 3 March 1752, the main witnesses against her were four doctors. They agreed that the condition of Mr Blandy's inner organs suggested arsenic poisoning, and that the white powder they had analysed was arsenic. But the only test they had been able to apply involved touching a red-hot iron to the powder, and sniffing the vapour, which they declared to be that of arsenic. In later years such evidence would have been unhesitatingly rejected. On the other hand, servants were able to state, in considerable detail, when and how Mary had administered poison to her father – to such an extent that it now seems astonishing that Mr Blandy was not warned in time. Mary made a passionate speech in which she flatly denied administering poison although she admitted that she *had* put a powder into her father's food 'which had been given me with another intent'. She gave her father the powder, she said, to make him fond of Cranstoun. The prosecution rejected this with contempt, pointing out that she had attempted to destroy the powder as soon as she knew she was suspected. And after 13 hours, the jury took only five minutes to find Mary guilty.

Six weeks later, her hands bound with black ribbon, she mounted the gallows outside Newgate, insisting to the end that she had no intention of killing her father. Her last words were to ask the hangman not to hang her too high 'for the sake of decency'. Cranstoun survived her by only six months, dying 'in considerable agony' at Fumes, in Flanders, in his fortieth year.

Where Cranstoun was concerned, it was the old gentleman who had the last laugh. While Mary was awaiting her trial she was told that her father's estate amounted to less than £4,000. The fortune of £10,000 – which had attracted Cranstoun – had either never existed, or been long spent. This was almost certainly the reason that Frances Blandy had set his face against so many aspiring suitors – because he was unable to provide the promised dowry. The irony of the situation must have come home to him on his deathbed; he had wronged his daughter by withholding the truth, and now she had poisoned him to obtain a non-existent fortune. This would seem to explain why he asked the weeping girl: 'How canst thou think I could curse thee?'; after all, he had only himself to blame.

6

It was at about the time of the Blandy case that Henry Fielding had to interrogate a woman who was accused of causing the death of her husband by poison. No poison was found in her house, and there was no evidence that she had ever purchased poison. And when Fielding applied to doctors to know whether there was any method of detecting poison in the human body, he was told that such a method did not exist. This led Fielding to deplore the absence of some way of 'making poison visible'. In fact, the only fairly reliable method of testing for poison was one employed in the Brinvilliers case – to feed some of the substance to an animal, and see if it died.

Fielding died in 1754, unaware that a generation of men who would transform the science of chemistry had been born within his lifetime: Joseph Priestley in 1728, Henry Cavendish in 1731, Karl Wilhelm Scheele in 1742, and Antoine Lavoisier in 1743. These men, and others like them represent the true dividing line between the alchemy of Paracelsus and the chemistry of Dalton and Mendeleeff. They discovered, to begin with, that air was not an 'element', as all chemists so far had believed, but a mixture of different gases. Cavendish made hydrogen by dissolving zinc in sulphuric acid. Priestley made oxygen by heating red oxide of mercury. Lavoisier took the all-important step of realizing that oxide of mercury is a combination of oxygen and mercury. And in 1775, Scheele, who had already discovered seven or eight acids, discovered that he could make an acid from arsenic by dissolving the oxide ('white arsenic') in nitric acid or water containing chlorine. And when zinc was dropped into arsenic acid, a dangerous gas that smelt of garlic was given off – arseniuretted hydrogen, or arsine. So clearly, if someone's stomach contents contained oxide, it could be made to reveal its presence as a distinctive gas by a few simple steps.

A decade later, Samuel Hahnemann took this process a significant stage further when he discovered that when sulphuretted hydrogen (the gas that smells like rotten eggs) is bubbled into arsenic acid, the result is a yellow deposit – yellow sulphate of arsenic (which the ancients knew as orpiment, and used as a caustic and depilatory). And this, in turn, when heated produces 'white arsenic'. So a mixture containing suspected arsenic could again be identified by three simple steps: dissolving in nitric acid, mixing with sulphuretted hydrogen, and heating – alone or with charcoal – to produce white arsenic.

It was only one step from this to the discovery by Johann Metzger that if substances containing arsenic were heated, and a cold plate was held overhead, a white layer of arsenious oxide would form on the plate. And if the arsenic was heated with charcoal to the point of red heat, metallic arsenic would be deposited on a cold plate, or in the cooler part of the test tube – the so-called arsenic mirror.

All this was useful if a chemist was faced with the problem of whether a substance, or the contents of someone's stomach, contained arsenic. But what if the arsenic had already been absorbed into the body? In 1806, Dr Valentine Rose, of the Berlin Medical Faculty, solved this problem when he cut up the stomach of a possible poison victim and boiled it in water. After many filterings, the liquid was treated with nitric acid, which had the simultaneous effect of getting rid of the remains of the flesh, and of converting any arsenic into arsenic acid, which could then be detected by any of the methods described above. (Rose converted the acid to the carbonate and hydroxide of arsenic with potassium carbonate and calcium hydroxide, then obtained an 'arsenic mirror' by heating with charcoal.)

Three years later, all Germany was thrown into a state of shock by the revelations at the trial of a mass murderess, Anna Zwanziger, the most sensational case of its kind since the Marquise de Brinvilliers. But at least Brinvilliers had poisoned for an understandable motive – money. Zwanziger seems to have killed her victims for the sadistic joy of watching them suffer. The German jurist Anselm Ritter von Feuerbach said that she trembled with joy when she looked on the white powder, and quotes her as saying that arsenic was 'her truest friend'.

The daughter of a Nuremberg innkeeper, Anna Maria Schonleben married a solicitor named Zwanziger who was also an alcoholic, and left her in penury. The constant reading of Goethe's gloomy novel *The Sorrows of Young Werther* led her to attempt suicide on two occasions, and she drifted from place to place, working as a domestic. In Weimar she fled with a diamond ring belonging to her employers, and a public advertisement of the theft came to the attention of her son-in-law, who ordered her out of his home. She found a job as a housekeeper with a judge named Glaser, in Rosendorf, Bavaria. It seems to have struck her that Glaser would make an excellent husband, but there was one impediment: Glaser's wife, from whom he was separated. Anna set about reconciling the two, and was soon able to welcome Frau Glaser back into her home with flowers strewn on the floor. Within a few weeks, Frau Glaser had died in agony. But Judge Glaser showed no sign of wanting to transfer his affection to his housekeeper, who was thin, sallow and 50 years old. Perhaps he was alerted by the stomach ailments suffered by guests after they had eaten meals prepared by Anna; at all events, she decided to move to the house of another judge at Sanspareil, a younger man named Grohmann, who was unmarried but suffered from gout. Regrettably, he had a fiancée, and Anna became increasingly jealous. When the marriage banns were published, Judge Grohmann died suddenly; his doctor attributed the death to natural causes.

Once more Anna found herself a job as a housekeeper to a member of the legal profession, a magistrate named Gebhard. He was also married, and his wife was pregnant; but her health was poor. When she died, accusing the housekeeper of poisoning her, no one took the accusations seriously. But Gebhard, like the others showed no sign of wanting to marry Anna. Moreover, as his servants expressed intense dislike of the skinny widow, and told stories of violent colics suffered by those who incurred her displeasure, he finally decided to dismiss her. Half an hour or so after she had left in a carriage for Bayreuth, most people in the household became ill – including the baby, to whom Anna had given a biscuit soaked in milk. It was recalled that Anna had refilled the salt box before she had left, and its contents were submitted for analysis. As we have seen, this was now a simple matter; there were at least three reliable tests for white arsenic. And this is what proved to have been mixed with the salt.

It took the law some time to catch up with her. She lived in Bayreuth a month, then went back to Nuremberg, then tried to persuade her son-in-law in Mainfernheim to take her in. But he was no longer her son-in-law, having divorced the daughter after she had been imprisoned for theft and swindling. Anna went back to Nuremberg, and was arrested on 18 October 1809. In her pockets were found a packet of tartar emetic and a packet of white arsenic.

For six months Anna Zwanziger simply denied everything. But at this point, Frau Glaser's body was exhumed, and the method of Valentine Rose, invented only four years previously, revealed arsenic in the vital organs – arsenic lingers on in the human body (including the hair) for a very long time. When told about this discovery, Zwanziger knew she was trapped; she fell to the floor in convulsions and had to be carried out of court. And a long and detailed confession followed – including the attempted poisoning of fellow servants and guests of her employers, apparently merely for her own entertainment. Sentenced to death, she remarked that it was probably just as well, since it would have been impossible for her to stop poisoning. She was beheaded, by sword, in 1811, more than two years after her arrest.

In the year Anna Zwanziger was executed, there finally occurred the major turning point in the history of poisons: at the Paris School of Medicine, a young Spaniard named Orfila obtained his medical degree. It would hardly be an exaggeration to describe Orfila as the Isaac Newton of toxicology; after the publication of his great *Treatise on Poisons* in 1813, the murderer who killed by poison took the same risk as the murderer who killed with a knife or gun.

Mathieu Joseph Bonaventure Orfila was born in Mahon, on the east coast of Minorca, on 24 April 1787. The tiny island was, to put it mildly, a backwater; Mahon did not even have a school. But Mathieu learned to read early, and had soon read all the books in his father's library. In the dazzling sunlight of the Mediterranean, he devoured everything he could find about ancient Greece and Rome. His tutors were a series of priests, and it was probably from one of these – a native of Languedoc who had fled from the Revolution – that he first heard the name of the great chemist Lavoisier, who had been guillotined during the Terror. By the age of 14 he could speak five languages, including Latin and Greek, and had written a Latin thesis on philosophy

The first ambition of the young prodigy was to become a sailor – understandably, since a youth of his brilliance must have found the island, where life was dominated by the Catholic Church, boring and stifling. But on his first voyage to Alexandria, at the age of 15, he discovered that travel bored him, and preferred to stay in his cabin reading. Sea sickness, terrifying storms, and a close encounter with pirates confirmed his lack of aptitude for the life of a seaman. Back at home a meeting with a German professor named Cook convinced him that his true vocation was medicine; at the age of 16, he enrolled in the chemistry class in Valencia.

Irritated by the old-fashioned doctrines – which regarded air and water as elements – he began to buy more up-to-date works by Lavoisier and Vauquelin, and was soon so excited by them that he slept for only two hours a night. At 18, his exam results were so brilliant that he was chosen for a scholarship to the University of Barcelona. There his successes were also spectacular, and the university decided to send him on to Paris to complete his education: he was then to return to Barcelona, to occupy a chair of chemistry that would be created for him. But fate had other plans.

In Paris, he lived the life of a penniless student; poverty only spurred his ambition. On the day he received his medical degree he had only six francs in his pocket. Friends came to his aid; one of them lent him a large room in which he could give lectures on chemistry, and within a few weeks, Orfila had 40 enthusiastic students, each paying 40 francs for the course. Soon he was able to set up his own laboratory, in which he also gave a course in botany.

The revelation that turned him into Europe's greatest toxicologist occurred one day in April 1813, when he had a particularly large audience for his chemistry lecture. He was speaking about arsenious acid, and explaining that when it was mixed with various liquids – wine, coffee, broth – there would always be a white, chalk-like precipitate. Whereupon he took some coffee from a cup on his chair and mixed it with the acid. And instead of a white precipitate, there was a murky grey one. He tried the same experiment with ammoniated copper sulphate, and was again embarrassed to obtain a blackish-green colouring with a bright green precipitate. Blushing with vexation, Orfila told his students that there must be some organic matter in the acid which explained the unexpected result.

Orfila was not the kind of person who liked to be proved wrong in public. Immediately after his lecture, he took samples of broth, wine, tea, milk, and other natural substances, and mixed them with various poisons. Then he performed the standard chemical tests to detect these poisons. And in more than half these tests, he failed to detect them.

That stunned him. For it meant that if a professor of chemistry was called upon to try and detect a poison in soup or wine or coffee – or the organs of the body – he would probably fail. He looked up all the volumes of chemistry he could find in the university library, and various books on forensic medicine. None of them seemed to be aware of this problem. 'The central fact that had struck me had never been perceived by anyone else. My first words were these: *toxicology does not yet exist*.' In 19 cases out of 20, the forensic pathologist who was investigating a suspected poisoning would find himself in a state of total confusion.

The challenge was obvious. Could Orfila turn toxicology into a science? His driving ambition told him that here was a chance to become a famous man. And, typically, his first step was to go to a bookseller (in those days most of them were also publishers) and ask if he was willing to bring out a book on poisons in two volumes. An hour later, the contract was signed. Then Orfila went back to his laboratory and settled down to work. And he worked so fast that the first volume of his *Treatise on Poison, or General Toxicology,* was soon published at six francs a copy. Its impact was immediate and tremendous. After all, the 'Italian school of poisoners' still flourished in many parts of Europe, and old hags prepared solid or liquid poisons according to the formulas attributed to the Borgias – poisoning an animal, rubbing arsenic or strychnine into its flesh, and collecting the liquid that dripped from it as it decayed. And now Orfila had created a science of toxicology that should enable a doctor employed by the police to detect any poison, no matter how it had been prepared. And in an age when poison was one of the most popular means of murder, this was virtually a revolution in criminology. It was also the kind of revolution that appealed to the general public; Orfila was a scientist who was also a detective. To his astonishment, the 26-year-old chemistry teacher suddenly found himself in demand in the salons. In 1815, he made an 'advantageous marriage' to the daughter of a successful sculptor, and their honeymoon trip to Minorca was a triumphal procession. Back in Paris, Orfila followed up his success with a volume on medical chemistry, and in 1818, at the age of 31, was rewarded with a professorship at the Medical Faculty of Paris – a chair of 'mental maladies' specially created for him.

The first case of suspected poisoning in which he was consulted took place in 1824. In Montmorency, a woman named Laurent had been married only ten days when her husband died suddenly; an autopsy was carried out, and the local doctor stated that he had found arsenic. A few years earlier, this might have amounted to a death sentence; but since Paris was now famous for its professors of legal medicine, the contents of the dead man's stomach were sent to the Faculty of Medicine. In August 1824, Orfila was asked to carry out tests: he stated with confidence that he could find no trace of poison. And the widow Laurent was acquitted.

In other cases, Orfila became a kind of court of last appeal. In December 1838, Nicholas Mercier, the idiot son of Louis Mercier, of Villey-sur-Tille, near Dijon, died of severe stomach pains. His father had recently married for the second time, and his new wife had objected strenuously to the presence of the idiot in the house. The father had given way and sent his son to live elsewhere for a while, then allowed the boy to return home. The bitter disputes began again. One day Mercier remarked to his wife: 'Don't worry, it will soon be over', and bought an ounce of arsenic. A week later, after severe vomiting, the son died after drinking broth and sugared wine given to him by his father. Two weeks after the funeral, an exhumation was ordered, and three experts performed an autopsy, and testified that Nicholas Mercier had died as a result of poisoning by a metallic substance. But a few days later, two more experts performed another autopsy, and decided that the youth had not been poisoned, by arsenic or any other substance. Finally, Orfila led another group of experts, who examined the remains for the third time; Orfila pronounced that the body undoubtedly contained traces of arsenic. At the trial of the husband and wife at Dijon, another celebrated expert, Raspail, appeared for the defence, and he and Orfila had a spectacular clash in court. But it was Orfila's opinion that prevailed, and Mercier was found guilty and condemned to hard labour for life – he escaped the death sentence because the court found extenuating circumstances. (The wife was acquitted.)

It was this case that led Orfila to investigate another interesting problem. Arsenic, of course, comes from the earth, occurring in an ore called realgar, and in orpiment. And if these happen to occur in the area of cemeteries, then is it not possible that a body that has been buried for several months may absorb arsenic from the soil? With the usual thoroughness, Orfila proceeded to analyse samples of earth from various cemeteries, and was able to state that the soil in certain areas contained traces of arsenic, while others were free from it. But the quantities involved would usually be too small to confuse a medical expert.

Three years earlier, in 1836, such delicate tests for arsenic would have been impossible, for there was no known method of detecting the poison in extremely small quantities. But in October 1836, an article in the *Edinburgh Philosophical Journal* described a method that could detect as little as a thousandth of a milligram of arsenic. Its author was a poverty-stricken English chemist named James Marsh.

8

The man who revolutionized crime detection was no brilliant scientific rebel, but a middle-aged alcoholic who worked in London's Woolwich Arsenal and who stumbled into the business of crime detection by chance. Born in 1794, Marsh at first showed signs of being a scientific prodigy, like the great Michael Faraday, whose assistant he became in 1829. Faraday had started life as a half-starved errand boy, and achieved success with the aid of Sir Humphry Davy. Marsh had no such luck. All his life he earned a mere 30 shillings a week at the Royal Military Academy, and when he died at the age of 52, he left his wife and children destitute.

Yet he had his minor triumphs. In nearby Plumstead, in 1832, a farmer named George Bodle drank his breakfast coffee, and began to suffer from stomach cramps and vomiting. The old man was much disliked by his family, with whom he played the tyrant, and no one was greatly distressed when he died. A Justice of the Peace called Slace decided to investigate rumours that Bodle's grandson John had expressed the wish that the old man would hurry up and die. For John was a wastrel, and on the day the old man had died, John had taken the kettle out to the well to fill it, an uncharacteristic gesture that had startled the maid. The symptoms sounded very much like poisoning. But who in London was competent to analyse the contents of the coffee pot? Judge Slace heard of the assistant at the Royal Military Academy, and asked him if he knew how to test for poison.

A chemist of Marsh's brilliance found this no challenge. Scheele's test, invented more than half a century before revealed the presence of arsenic when the coffee gave off the typical garlic smell of arseni-uretted hydrogen. And when the coffee was subjected to Hahnemann's test, it produced the easily identified yellow precipitate of sulphide of arsenic. Young John's neck seemed destined for the noose. But Marsh had reckoned without a British jury, with its characteristic distaste for abstraction. At the trial in Maidstone that December, John Bodle was found not guilty, and was cheered in court. Ten years later, after being deported for fraud, he confessed to the murder of his grandfather.

Thoroughly irritated – and also, perhaps, fascinated by this glimpse of forensic toxicology, which was certainly more interesting than his work on naval cannons – Marsh decided to continue where Scheele had left off, and try to devise a test that would actually reveal the arsenic to the eyes of the stupidest jury. The most conclusive test would be to show them the arsenic. And Metzger had already shown how to do this: that when arsine gas is heated, it turns into a mixture of hydrogen and metallic arsenic, and the arsenic can be collected by holding a cold dish above the hot charcoal. Marsh saw instantly that the trouble with this test is that most of the gas probably escapes past the dish, and if only a tiny quantity of arsenic is involved, then it has escaped for ever. So he simply devised a sealed apparatus, in which the gas can escape only through a tiny pointed nozzle. First the suspected arsenic compound is dropped into a flask containing zinc and sulphuric acid (which produces hydrogen). The resulting arsine gas, if any, is then heated as it passes along a glass tube; this decomposes it, and the arsenic forms a black 'mirror' as soon as it reaches a cold part of the tube. Or, if the gas is burned as it issues from the nozzle, it forms the mirror on a cold dish or plate. It was simple and obvious, and also incredibly sensitive, making it possible to detect as little as a fiftieth of a milligram of arsenic. When he published his result in 1836, the Society of Arts awarded him their gold medal. Poor Marsh would undoubtedly have preferred an appreciation in cash, like the £30 he received from the Board of Ordnance for a percussion quill for naval guns. When he died in 1846, his achievement was promptly forgotten, so that it is nowadays practically impossible to find his name in a work of reference.

It was the sensitivity of his test that enabled Orfila to test the earth in various cemeteries, and to measure precisely how much arsenic it contained. In fact, the sheer sensitivity of the Marsh test led to a certain alarm when it was found that substances that contained no arsenic could be made to deposit that characteristic arsenic mirror. It was then discovered that the zinc and sulphuric acid used in the tests contained minute traces of arsenic, and that this possibility had to be eliminated before the test . . . As to the problem of arsenic in cemeteries, Orfila demonstrated to his own satisfaction that arsenic could not enter corpses provided the coffin remained intact. It was not a completely satisfactory solution, but it had to serve for the time being.

Meanwhile, Orfila's name continued to be associated with crimes that excited widespread attention, so that he achieved the kind of acclaim that Sir Bernard Spilsbury would receive a century later. In 1839, the year of the Mercier trial, the French equivalent of the Mary Blandy case caused a sensation. A hotelier named Cumon retired in the village of Montignac. When a gendarme named Dupont requested the hand of his daughter Victorine in marriage, he exploded with indignation: the fact that Victorine was eager to accept failed to dislodge his prejudice against an underpaid policeman. As Victorine and Dupont continued to meet, there were violent family quarrels. Victorine confided her misery to her maid Nini. And then, suddenly, old Cumon fell ill with an internal complaint; within a month he was dead. Victorine disdained any hypocritical show of sorrow; declaring that 'What God does must be well done', she lost no time in marrying her gendarme.

One day, a condemned man on his way to hard labour – probably in the hulks – passed through the village, and was 'exhibited', as was the custom, on the village green, as a salutory warning to other potential miscreants. With tears in his eyes he begged his audience to conduct themselves irreproachably, adding with a certain smugness the comment that no doubt many of them had consciences as bad as his own. Nini heard all this only at second hand, but it was enough to release in her a flood of repentance. She now confessed that she had purchased the arsenic, opium, vitriol, and other toxic substances which Victorine had administered to her father. Cumon's body was exhumed, and a panel of experts declared that they suspected poisoning by arsenic. Orfila was called in, and with the aid of the Marsh test, he was able to turn suspicion into certainty. There was a dramatic clash in court in Péngueux between Orfila and the local doctor, who insisted that Cumon's symptoms indicated death by natural causes, but Orfila's expertise prevailed. Victorine was sentenced to life imprisonment with hard labour, and the maid's sensitive conscience was rewarded with 18 years of the same punishment.

But it was in the following year, 1840, that Orfila reached the apex of his fame as a forensic expert. It was in the autumn of that year that he made his sensational intervention in the most notorious poison trial of the period: the case of Marie Lafarge.

9

On 16 January 1840, a 29-year-old ironmaster, Charles Pouch Lafarge, died of a gastric ailment at his farm at Le Glandier, near Limoges. He had been ill ever since he had eaten a slice of cake sent to him in Paris by his newly wedded wife Marie. Not long before Lafarge's painful death, a maidservant had seen Marie stirring a white powder into a glass of milk she was about to take to her husband. She asked what it was, and Marie replied that it was orange blossom sugar. Later, the servant noticed white flakes on the surface of the half-finished glass of milk, and showed it to a doctor. When the doctor tasted one with the tip of his tongue, he found it bitter. And after seeing Marie surreptitiously stirring white powder into her husband's soup, the maid warned the rest of the family that she suspected Marie of poisoning Lafarge. Even before Lafarge's death, a local doctor had been convinced that he was being poisoned with arsenic. This is why, nine days after her husband's death, Marie Lafarge was arrested and charged with murder. As soon as the arrest was reported in the Paris newspapers, Marie's case became a *cause célèbre,* for she had aristocratic connections – she was even illegitimately related to the reigning Royal Family.

Marie Lafarge was a romantic dreamer, of the kind that Gustave Flaubert was to portray in *Madame Bovary*; she was also neurotic and hysterical. Born Marie Capelle, daughter of an artillery officer, in 1816, she was an orphan by the time she was 18. She went to live with a wealthy aunt, who regarded her as a burden, and who began to look around for possible suitors who might take Marie off her hands. A respectable subprefect made a proposal, but Marie indignantly turned him down; she was dreaming of handsome aristocrats and of magnificent country estates in which she could play lady of the manor. Her wealthy cousin, Marie de Nicolai, had married a viscount named Léautaud. During a visit to their château, there was an embarrassing incident; a *parure* of diamonds (a necklace with matching ear-rings) vanished, and Inspector Allard of the Sûreté reached the conclusion that Marie Capelle was probably the thief. Embarrassed at the idea of a scandal involving his bride's best friend, the viscount decided to drop the investigation. Marie was allowed to leave unsearched.

Soon after this, her aunt announced that she had found Marie a husband, a wealthy young ironmaster who lived in an old Carthusian monastery in the Limousin district. What she did not tell her niece was that the suitor had been found through a matrimonial agency, and that he was a widower. Charles Lafarge was fat, coarse and cunning; he had told the matrimonial agency that he had a property worth 200,000 francs and an income of 30,000 francs a year. In fact, his forge had gone bankrupt, and he was looking around for a rich wife. By Lafarge's standards, Marie was rich – to begin with, she had a dowry of 90,000 francs.

· In August 1839, much against her will, Marie Capelle became Marie Lafarge. And when they arrived at Le Glandier, her few remaining daydreams were shattered. The place was unutterably dreary and provincial, and the monastery was little more than a decaying farmhouse. Her mother-in-law and sister-in-law seemed to her to be peasants. The shock was so great that she locked herself in her room and wrote her husband a long, passionate letter declaring that she was in love with someone else, and that if he would not release her, she would kill herself with arsenic. Charles was deeply upset by the document – Marie was still innocent enough to think that this was because he adored her – and promised not to demand his marital rights until he had refurbished the house and borrowed enough money in Paris to re-finance the ironworks. He had developed a new smelting process which he intended to patent.

For the next few months, Marie lived in a rather gloomy day-dream. Her husband had improvements made to the house, took out subscriptions to newspapers, and made his wife a member of a lending library. But she took care not to reveal her misery in her letters to relatives, for the born day-dreamer hates to admit being brought low. There were bitter conflicts with her mother-in-law when she insisted on dismissing old servants, and hiring young girls who were willing to work under the servants Marie had brought from Paris; but eventually, an uneasy peace reigned in the household. On a three-week visit to the town of Tulle, she met a handsome young advocate with whom, under the right circumstances, she would have started a love affair; but she had to return to Glandier. She had a close confidante in the 17-year-old daughter of a local doctor, and when her husband went off to Paris to patent his invention and try to raise money, she actually began to feel happy.

Not long before Christmas 1839, Charles Lafarge received a letter telling him to expect some cakes baked specially for him, at Marie's request, by his mother. What actually arrived was one large cake. He broke off a piece and ate it before he went out to a business appointment; when he returned, he was violently ill.

Back at Glandier, Marie was beginning to suspect the true reason that her husband had married her. Her will vanished from her desk, and when her mother-in-law finally produced it, Marie discovered that it had been changed; legacies to relatives had been cut out, and all her money – and some land she owned – had been left to her husband. The mother-in-law fell on her knees and begged forgiveness, swearing that her son knew nothing of the alterations; finally, Marie agreed to keep silent.

Charles returned home, looking pale and ill; Marie shared some chicken and truffles with him, and he became even sicker. A doctor who was called in diagnosed indigestion. Marie seemed genuinely solicitous, and had him installed in her own bedchamber, which had been decorated according to her Parisian taste. She frequently fed him with her own hand. When someone saw her stirring a white powder into an eggnog, Marie insisted that it was gum arabic, which was good for intestinal complaints. But the family sent some of the eggnog to a local chemist, who declared that the Hahnemann test revealed arsenic.

The servant, Anna Brun, had seen her stirring a white powder – taken from a malachite box – into Charles Lafarge's milk. It was she who warned old Mme Lafarge that she suspected Marie of trying to poison the master. But by now it was too late anyway. Charles Lafarge died, and Marie's 17-year-old confidante, Emma Pontier, exclaimed: 'Oh Marie, if you made some fatal mistake . . .' Marie replied indignantly that she was innocent, and went on to demand an inquest on the body.

When the investigating magistrate learned that she had purchased arsenic – 'for poisoning rats' – a few days before the cake was sent off to Paris, he had no alternative but to order her arrest. And when the police searched her room, they found the missing diamond *parure* of her best friend. If Marie was not a murderess, it seemed certain that she was a thief.

At least Marie had achieved what she had always wanted: national – even international – celebrity. Her aristocratic relatives all took the view that she was innocent, and their position in society made them a powerful influence on the Parisian press. The middle classes took it for granted that she was guilty. From the day of her arrest, column after column was devoted to the affair, and the interest soon spread to foreign newspapers. But the Vicomte de Léautaud revealed a vindictive spirit when he announced that he would prosecute Marie for the theft of the diamonds even before her trial for murder; this aroused much sympathy on her behalf. He also accused her of being a lifelong kleptomaniac. Charles Lachaud, the handsome young attorney from Tulle, had become Marie's advocate. When he begged her to tell the truth about the diamonds, she declared that Marie de Nicolai, the viscount's wife, had given them to her to sell. Just before her marriage, Marie de Nicolai had become involved with a handsome but penniless young Spaniard named Felix Clavé, who became frantic when he learned she was about to discard him. Terrified that he would divulge the affair to her husband, the countess begged her closest friend to sell her diamonds and give the money to Clavé . . . Approached by Marie's defence lawyer, Mme de Léautaud indignantly denied Marie's story, declaring that the relationship with Clavé had been no more than a schoolgirl flirtation, encouraged by Marie herself. The Vicomte de Léautaud became even more determined to pursue the case. And Marie Lafarge received thousands of letters of sympathy. But at her trial for theft in Brives, she offered no defence, and was given a two-year sentence, suspended until after her trial for murder.

By British standards, the murder trial, which opened in Tulle on

3 September 1840, was a travesty of justice. From the beginning, the prosecutor branded Marie a monster who had carefully planned her husband's murder, then watched him die in agony; every device of melodrama was used to sway the jury. Many of the witnesses had only hearsay evidence to offer – gossip and rumour. Through all this, Marie bore herself with a grace and dignity that impressed even her enemies. Yet the case against her certainly looked black. It was proved that she had purchased arsenic on two occasions, and that she had been seen stirring powder into her husband's drink and scattering it on his food. The powder in the malachite box had proved to be arsenic, not gum arabic. The local chemist had detected the presence of arsenic in the milk and eggnog, and also in the dead man's vomit and stomach contents.

Now it so happened that Marie's defence lawyer, *maître* Paillet, was an old friend of Orfila. He hurried to Paris to consult the great toxicologist, and showed him the report of the chemists. Orfila was contemptuous. The report demonstrated a lamentable carelessness. They had obtained yellow precipitates that were soluble in ammonia, but there are dozens of yellow precipitates that contain no arsenic. And they had performed the Rose test so carelessly that the apparatus had exploded; therefore there was no proof that the – 'mirror' was arsenic.

Back in court, Paillet had a field day; with urbane ruthlessness he exposed the incompetence of the local chemists, pointing out that they had not even heard of the Marsh test. But the prosecution called his bluff. They were perfectly willing to allow the contents of the dead man's stomach to be subjected to a Marsh test . . . Paillet protested. Provincial 'science has already revealed its incompetence; let them send for his friend Orfila. But the prosecution prevailed. The materials were handed over to the chemists, who were instructed to carry out a Marsh test. And, to Paillet's delight, they admitted that the new tests had failed to reveal unmistakable signs of arsenic. Suddenly, the Lafarge supporters began to smile. Marie beamed at her defence attorney, who was unable to restrain tears of joy. The news quickly spread over the town: Marie Lafarge had been proved innocent . . . At this stage, everyone forgot the result of the tests on the milk and eggnog.

But the question was raised again that afternoon. The experts repeated their tests on the eggnog, the malachite box, and other items from Glandier, and this time the tests revealed large quantities of arsenic – enough to kill 10 men. The prosecution lawyer leapt to his feet. Since Paillet had asked for Orfila, let Orfila be brought from Paris; let the great toxicologist himself examine the contents of the dead man's stomach. Paillet was forced to agree.

A telegram was despatched to Paris, and a week later, on 13 September, he arrived in the stage-coach. He demanded that the local chemists should witness his experiments, and for the remainder of that day, and most of the following night, he performed his experiments in a room in the courthouse. The following afternoon, the chemists and doctors followed him into the courtroom. The lean, black-coated man with a hawk-like nose and grey whiskers cleared his throat. 'I shall prove that there is arsenic in the body of Lafarge, and that this arsenic cannot have found its way there from the soil . . .'

Paillet was stunned. Marie Lafarge rose to her feet, her hand on her heart. Her supporters sighed with dismay. Orfila seemed oblivious of the effect he was producing. In a dry, detached manner he detailed his tests on the stomach, the liver, the thorax, the heart, the brain, and the intestinal canal; in all these, he said, arsenic had been discovered, though admittedly in small quantities. But, he added, no arsenic had been found in the flesh, so it was just possible that the poison had been placed in the body after death. But as he left the box, Marie Lafarge buried her face in her hands. Outside the courtroom, a storm was raging, but few people noticed it until Orfila had stopped speaking.

Paillet surpassed himself in his final address to the jury, but it was all to no effect. On 19 September 1840, Marie Lafarge was found guilty, and condemned to hard labour for life, and to be exposed at the market-place at Tulle.

The sentence was, in fact, commuted to one of imprisonment without hard labour. Marie spent ten years in the prison at Montpellier, from 1841 until 1851; a few months after her release, she died of tuberculosis. Her Memoirs, in which she continues to maintain her innocence, reveal considerable literary talent. If Marie had reconciled herself to life at Le Glandier and directed her romantic imagination into the composition of novels, she might well have achieved a success comparable to that of her heroine George Sand.

Was Marie guilty? In retrospect there seems little doubt of it. One of the best books about her, *The Lady and the Arsenic* by Joseph Shearing (1944), points out that in a modern British or American court she could certainly have been acquitted. Shearing also comes close to convincing the reader that Lafarge deserved to be poisoned; from the beginning, he was determined to lay his hands on Marie's fortune. He obtained bank loans by forging her signature, which she was forced to repay, and he was fairly certainly a party to the swindle involving her will. Yet even Shearing's skilful advocacy leaves the reader in no doubt that Marie poisoned her husband. It is true that he also throws suspicion on Lafarge's assistant manager, Denis Barbier, who hated Marie, and who was a party to the various forgeries. Barbier vanished before the trial, which suggests a guilty conscience. Shearing speculates that he might have known that Marie was introducing small quantities of poison into her husband's food, and decided to strengthen the case against her by planting large quantities of powdered arsenic in her room and in the death chamber. Yet even if this could be proved, it would still fail to acquit Marie of the charge of murdering her husband; Barbier could have had no possible motive to kill his employer.

Why, then, did she do it? Few writers on the case have seized upon the obvious clue: Marie's insistence that the marriage was never consummated. Yet when asked why her relations with her husband had improved in the weeks before he left for Paris, she explained that he had made many attempts to win her affection. 'That touched me. I was not able to do otherwise than . . .' (here she hesitated), 'than to fulfil my duties, to make life happier for Monsieur Lafarge.' She even admitted that at one point she thought she might be pregnant; then she hastened to declare that she considered this some kind of immaculate conception. It sounds as if Marie allowed Lafarge into her bed, perhaps once, perhaps more often. Having yielded, it would seem logical that sexual relations would continue after his return from Paris, and that, in due course, she would find herself pregnant. This may have been the prospect that, in his absence, made Marie determine that she would never again yield her body to the boorish oaf. If this was, in fact, her motive in sending Lafarge the poisoned cake, then it becomes possible to understand why she was so insistent that the marriage had never been consummated; provided this was believed, her motive would remain unsuspected.

10

After the Affair of the Poisons, Louis XIV issued a decree forbidding apothecaries to sell poison – particularly arsenic – to persons who were unknown to them. He also introduced the law that made it necessary for the purchaser to sign the 'poisons book'. Other countries soon adopted the same rule. In spite of which, arsenic remained the easiest of poisons to purchase, even in the nineteenth century. In Great Britain, it could easily be obtained in the form of rat poison – although in that case it was mixed with soot or indigo so that it was visible in food – or on fly papers which could be soaked in water. A Breton peasant woman named Hélène Jegado, who shared Anna Zwanziger's sadistic enthusiasm for poison, managed to acquire a fairly large quantity of arsenic at an early stage in her career as a servant, and used it to devasting effect over a 20-year period, enjoying the sense of power that it gave her. In one household where she worked, seven people – including her own sister – died in agony during a three-month period. At least another 16 victims had died by 1851, when she took a job in the house of Professor Théophile Bidard, of the University of Rennes. When a servant named Rosalie Sarrazin, of whom she was jealous, died in agony that July, an investigating magistrate accompanied police officers to the house. 'I am innocent!' declared Hélène without preamble. 'Of what?' asked the magistrate, 'No one has accused you.' And an investigation into Jegado's background revealed a toll of deaths even longer than in the Zwanziger case. She was executed in 1852.

In Glasgow in 1855, an attractive but bored 19-year-old girl named Madeleine Smith, daughter of a well-to-do architect, was introduced in the street to Pierre L'Angelier, a young Frenchman from Jersey, who had gone to considerable trouble to engineer the introduction. Soon afterwards, Madeleine received a letter from L'Angelier declaring his love; she replied encouragingly, using the maid as a go-between. The course of true love was far from smooth; when her parents found out, they ordered her never to communicate with him again. But the lovers continued to snatch brief and frustrating meetings, during which they exchanged hasty kisses and caresses. By December she was addressing him as 'My own darling husband'. But no real intimacy was possible between them until the following summer, when the Smiths went to their country house at Row; here Madeleine had a chance to take unchaperoned country walks. A letter to L'Angelier in June 1856 begins: 'If we did wrong last night, it was in the excitement of our love', and went on to note prosaically: 'I did not bleed in the least but I had a good deal of pain during the night.'

But later that summer, disillusionment – or perhaps merely satiety – began to set in. This may have had something to do with the attentions of a wealthy bachelor named William Minnoch, a close friend of her father's, who eventually proposed. Madeleine accepted. And at this point, L'Angelier played into her hands with a fit of petulance that led him to return one of her letters; she promptly replied that their engagement was at an end. 'My love for you has ceased.' L'Angelier's response was to threaten to write to her father revealing all. Madeleine hastily agreed to meet him again; again her letters address him as 'dearest pet' and 'sweet love'; but no longer as 'My darling husband'. For the truth was that she loathed the ungentlemanly blackmailer with her whole heart. They had two more meetings, each in the basement of Madeleine's house, and on each occasion he drank a cup of cocoa prepared by Madeleine. After the first meeting, L'Angelier was ill; after the second, in March 1857, he returned home in agony, bent over and clutching his stomach; by 11 o'clock the next morning he was dead. His doctor insisted on a post-mortem, and 87 grains of arsenic were found in his stomach – the lethal dose being three grains.

Madeleine's letters were found; she immediately became the chief suspect, and was arrested on 31 March. But although the case aroused the same excitement as the Lafarge poisoning, Madeleine had no defenders; the notion of a young girl becoming the mistress of a Frenchman horrified Scottish public opinion. Her guilt seemed obvious. Yet although it was proved that she had purchased three lots of arsenic, as rat poison, they had been mixed with soot or indigo. And no signs of soot or indigo were found in the dead man's stomach – but one medical witness commented that the grains of indigo could easily be washed from the arsenic with cold water. Madeleine insisted that her lover was in a habit of taking small quantities of arsenic for health reasons (arsenic is a stimulant and improves the complexion), but the defence offered no proof of this assertion. The jury eventually brought in a verdict of 'not proven' – peculiar to Scotland – which implied that they regarded her as guilty, but found the proof insufficient. The crowd in court cheered, evidently feeling that L'Angelier deserved what he got.

Madeleine did not marry William Minnoch. Instead, she went to London, where she married a man named Hora, and became a successful hostess.

The artist George du Maurier is said to have attended a Hora soirée and, unaware of the identity of his hostess, remarked 'Madeleine Smith's beauty shouldn't have saved her from the scaffold.' She later married an artist, George Wardle, who became manager of William Morris' silk weaving firm, and she developed an interest in socialism; Bernard Shaw once ate at her table. She died in America at the age of 92.

11

Although arsenic was the most widely used poison in the nineteenth century, there were dozens of others; antimony, aconitine, prussic acid, belladonna, mercury, lead, strychnine, opium, phosphorus, quinine, chloroform, brucine, codeine, and nicotine. In the early years of the century, new poisons were discovered at such a pace that the chemists were unable to keep up: morphine in 1803, strychnine in 1818, brucine in 1819, quinine in 1820, conium (extracted from hemlock) in 1826, nicotine in 1828, chloroform in 1831, codeine in 1832, and aconite and belladonna (from deadly nightshade) in 1833. Many of these, it will be noticed, are often regarded as medicines or useful drugs: codeine, quinine, nicotine, morphine; yet all, including caffeine, can cause death in sufficient quantities.

Yet although most metallic poisons were easy enough to detect (antimony, for example, could be measured precisely by the Marsh test), the vegetable poisons or alkaloids were a different matter – opium, for example, could vanish and leave no trace within hours. In Edinburgh in 1877, an alcoholic teacher named Eugène Marie Chantrelle poisoned his wife with opium, after insuring her life, and tried to make the death appear accidental by filling the bedroom with coal gas. No opium whatever was found in the body, but Chantrelle was convicted on the evidence of opium found in vomit on the bedclothes. Half a century earlier, the situation was considerably worse in that no chemical tests could reveal the presence of any alkaloid poisons in the body. In 1823, a Paris doctor named Edmé Castaing agreed to help a friend named Auguste Ballet to murder his elder brother Hyppolyte, who was dying of tuberculosis. Hyppolyte was wealthy, and Auguste had learned, to his indignation, that he had been excluded from his brother's will; he asked Castaing's help in destroying the will. When Hyppolyte died suddenly, with Castaing in attendance, the physician suddenly paid off all his debts. But success made Castaing greedy, and he persuaded Auguste to make a will in his favour. He consulted a lawyer to make sure such a will was valid and, having been reassured on this point, invited Auguste to drive with him into the country to inspect some property. That night, Auguste died in a

St-Cloud hotel, after drinking mulled wine which had been 'sugared' by Castaing. But although Auguste Ballet showed symptoms of morphine poisoning (contraction of the pupils, inflammation of the lungs), it was impossible in 1823 to detect morphine in the body – which is undoubtedly why Castaing chose it. Even the great Orfila had to confess his helplessness at the trial. But the circumstantial evidence against Castaing was strong enough to secure a guilty verdict, and his subsequent execution. As late as 1847, Orfila admitted that it was possible that the vegetable poisons might remain for ever undetectable in the body.

Fortunately, it was a mere four years before a young Belgian chemist proved him wrong. The James Marsh of vegetable poisons was Jean Servais Stas, a professor of chemistry at the École Royale Militaire in Brussels.

On 20 November 1850, a man named Gustave Fougnies died on the dining-room floor of Château Bitremont, near the village of Bury, in Belgium. Gustave Fougnies had been a sick man for many years, and the amputation of a leg seemed likely to hasten his death. This prospect was by no means entirely disagreeable to his sister Lydie, who was married to the Count Hyppolyte de Bocarmé. Bocarmé had married Lydie for her money – she was the daughter of a well-to-do apothecary – and then discovered that she had less than he had hoped. The two were deeply in debt. Gustave's death would solve their money problems. Then Gustave had announced that he had decided to marry; he had purchased a château, fallen in love with its previous owner, and been accepted. The Bocarmés were shattered. On 20 November, they had invited Gustave to lunch. But the children were sent off to eat in the nursery, and the countess herself served the meal.

In the late afternoon, the servants heard a thud from the dining-room, and the countess calling for help. Gustave was lying on the floor, obviously dead – the countess said she thought it was a stroke. The count ordered a servant to fetch vinegar, then poured a large quantity into the dead man's mouth, apparently in the belief that it would revive him. He then ordered the servant to undress the dead man and wash his body with vinegar. The countess took her brother's clothes and took them to the laundry, where she threw them in boiling water. Then she and the count scrubbed the floor of the dining-room and even scraped it with a knife. When an examining magistrate finally arrived, Gustave Fougnies was lying, naked, on bed in a servant's room; his cheeks were cut and his mouth and throat were scarred with burns.

A post-mortem was carried out; the doctors reported that the death was not due to a stroke, but to drinking some corrosive substance, possibly acid. But vinegar would not, of course, be strong enough to cause burns.

It all looked extremely suspicious. The Bocarmés were placed under arrest, and the contents of the dead man's stomach were sent to the military school in Brussels, to be examined by Stas, a pupil of Orfila.

Stas immediately noted the smell of vinegar in the unpleasant greenish-black mess that had been delivered to him. When told that this had been poured down the dead man's throat, and that the body had also been washed in vinegar, he immediately suspected that this had been intended to mask some other smell.

The stomach contents were preserved in alcohol. Stas' first step was to mix some of them with water, and filter and distil the result. His reasoning was body substances are soluble in alcohol or water, but not in both, so that body substances that passed through the filter with alcohol would be caught by water, and vice versa. The result should be a fairly pure solution of any poison that had been used. When Stas distilled the result repeatedly he thought he could detect a smell like mouse urine – the typical smell of conine, the hemlock derivative. But more washing and filtering produced a stronger smell – that of tobacco.

Nicotine is, in fact, one of the strongest of poisons – Taylor's *Medical Jurisprudence* compares it to prussic acid. Cases had been known of children dying from sucking at old pipes, with their brown deposit, while a rabbit could be killed within minutes from a single drop of nicotine.

The problem now was how to separate the poison from the liquid distillate. Stas had an inspiration. He mixed the liquid with ether – first discovered by the alchemist Raymond Lull, and rediscovered in 1792 by Frobenius – which was lighter than water. After a while, the ether separated out on top of the water, taking with it the brownish colouring. Stas carefully poured off the ether, and left it in an open dish to evaporate. And when it had done so, it left a quantity of a colourless, oily liquid with a strong smell of tobacco. It burned his tongue and filled his mouth with an unpleasant taste. Now Stas only had to prove that it was nicotine by chemical tests with tannic acid, mercuric iodide of potassium, bichromate of potassium, and so on. Each test was positive.

By the time Stas had removed all the nicotine from the stomach's contents, he had enough to fill a small flask – that is, enough to kill several men.

Bocarmé's murder plot had been truly ingenious. The château possessed a laboratory, for Bocarmé was interested in the scientific side of agriculture. Bocarmé had heard of the deadly qualities of pure nicotine, and he also knew that vegetable poisons were undetectable. So he had grown tobacco leaves, and then distilled from them a quantity of the colourless liquid. He had told his feeble-minded gardener that he was making eau-de-Cologne. The police were able to trace a professor of chemistry in Ghent with whom Bocarmé had discussed the problems of extracting nicotine from tobacco leaves (Bocarmé had given the professor a false name).

Gustave had been seized from behind and thrown to the floor; then, as he was held down by Bocarmé, the poison had been poured into his mouth by his sister. When he lost consciousness, more of it was poured down his throat – the inevitable result being that much of it splashed on to the floor. (In fact, in spite of all the scrubbing and scraping, Stas was able to find traces of nicotine on the floorboards.)

Then the count made the mistake that cost him his life and brought Stas immortality. He poured vinegar into the dead man's mouth to mask the smell. But the vinegar combined with the nicotine to produce the burns that had made the police suspicious. (Stas experimented with two dogs, poisoning both with nicotine, and then pouring vinegar into the mouth of one of them. Only this dog developed acid burns.) Moreover, the vinegar then mixed with the alcohol in which the stomach contents were preserved, and this acidified alcohol happened to be exactly the right solution for dissolving certain bodily substances such as sugar and mucus, while other substances dissolved in acidified water.

At the trial, the countess insisted that her husband had used force to make her agree to the murder plot; she was acquitted. But Bocarmé was executed on 19 July 1851, in Mons. And the method of detecting vegetable poisons – on which he had inadvertently collaborated with Stas – is still in use to this day.

12

By the middle of the nineteenth century, forensic medicine had become a science in its own right. The Scots deserve the credit for recognizing its importance. It was Andrew Duncan, Professor of Physiology at the University of Edinburgh from 1789, who succeeded in persuading the government to create the first chair of forensic medicine at the university in 1807, and his son, another Andrew Duncan, became its first incumbent. The senate of the university intensely disliked this innovation, but in due course, universities all over Europe followed suit – including, of course, Paris, which appointed Orfila.

In 1834, at the age of 28, Alfred Swaine Taylor became Professor of Medical Jurisprudence (as the subject was then called) at Guy's Hospital Medical School, and he went on to become perhaps the most influential forensic scientist, with the exception of Orfila, of the century. The first edition of his classic *Principles and Practice of Medical Jurisprudence* appeared two years later – and in updated editions, is still in use today. Taylor had spent some time studying with Orfila, and he was in Paris during the revolution of 1830, which gave him the opportunity to make a close study of gunshot wounds.

It must nevertheless be admitted that none of the major poisoning cases in which he was involved can be regarded as triumphs of toxicology. The first concerned a Quaker, John Tawell, who was accused of poisoning his mistress with cyanide. Tawell, who began life as a druggist, was transported to Australia for forgery in 1814, but by the time he returned to England, had amassed a fortune of £30,000. His wife fell ill and died, and during her illness, Tawell began a liaison with the attractive girl who nursed her, Sarah Hadler. She later bore him two children, and Tawell moved her to a cottage at Salthill, near Slough. Meanwhile, he married a second time, a Miss Catforth, from whom he took care to conceal the liaison. He paid Sarah Hadler (now known as Hart) £1 a week. After Tawell paid Sarah a visit in September 1844, she fell ill and vomited, but recovered from the attack.

On New Year's Day, 1845, Tawell went down to Salthill from his home in Berkhamsted; a neighbour saw him arrive, and a little later, met Sarah on her way to buy stout, and remarked how happy she looked. Soon after dusk, the neighbour heard Sarah scream, and went to her door with a lighted candle; she met Tawell, hurrying away, and found Sarah writhing on the floor in agony. Before the arrival of the doctor, she was dead.

A telegraph line – one of the first – had recently been constructed from Slough to Paddington, and a message was sent, asking the police to look out for a man in Quaker dress. When Tawell arrived at Paddington, he was followed to the lodging he had taken for the night, and arrested the next morning. He immediately made his first mistake by denying that he had left London the previous day.

Meanwhile, Sarah Hadler's body had been opened, and the bitter smell of prussic acid had been noted. The analyst, Mr Cooper, mixed the stomach contents with potassium ferrosulphate, and obtained the deep Prussian blue colour of potassium ferrocyanide. His conclusion was that Sarah Hadler had been poisoned by prussic acid, probably administered in stout. When it was proved that Tawell had bought the acid at a chemist shop in Bishopsgate, the case against him looked black.

The defending counsel, Fitzroy Kelly, advanced an ingenious defence, probably based on Taylor's suggestion: that apple pips contain prussic acid, and that there had been a barrel of apples in the room in which Sarah Hadler had died. At this, both sets of medical experts proceeded to distil apple pips to see how much cyanide they could obtain. The prosecution said that the amount distilled from 15 apples was not even dangerous; the defence replied that they had succeeded in distilling two-thirds of a grain of pure hydrocyanic acid from 15 apples, and that such a dose could be toxic.

The jury took the view that all this was irrelevant, and sentenced Tawell to death. Shortly before his execution, he confessed to the murder, and to an attempt to poison Sarah Hadler with morphine the previous September. His motive had been financial – his Australian investments had dropped in value, and he wanted to save the £1 a week he paid his mistress. Tawell was hanged in April 1845, and is now remembered mainly as the first murderer to be trapped by the electric telegraph. The defence lawyer became known forever afterwards as 'Apple Pip Kelly'.

The next major poisoning case in which Taylor was involved became one of the most famous in British criminal history. Dr William Palmer, of Rugeley, Staffordshire, was accused of poisoning a friend named Cook with strychnine. Palmer, an inveterate gambler on horses, was known to be heavily in debt. On 13 November 1855, Palmer and John Parsons Cook attended the races at Shrewsbury, and Cook's mare, Polestar, won. Back in a hotel in Rugeley, where they were celebrating, Cook took a swallow of his brandy and jumped to his feet crying: 'Good God, there's something in that that burns my throat.' Palmer retorted 'Nonsense', and drained the rest of the brandy. But Cook became increasingly ill. And after taking some pills offered to him by Palmer, his body convulsed so violently that his head touched his heels, and he died a few minutes later. Palmer was not slow to claim that the dead man had negotiated £4,000 for his benefit, and produced a document to prove it.

It was some days before Cook's stepfather became suspicious and demanded an autopsy. Palmer was arrested on a moneylender's writ. Yet, incredibly, he was not only permitted to be present at the autopsy, but to sneak out of the room with the jar containing Cook's stomach – he was caught only just in time.

Now it was recalled that Palmer had been associated with a long series of sudden deaths, and with many dubious financial transactions. As a trainee doctor he had fathered no fewer than 14 illegitimate children, and one of these had died unexpectedly after a visit to Palmer. An acquaintance named Abbey had died in the Staffordshire Infirmary after drinking a glass of brandy with Palmer.

Back in Rugeley with his medical diploma, Palmer had married an heiress, the illegitimate daughter of an Indian army officer; but apparently she was not as rich as he had hoped. Three years later, he invited his mother-in-law to stay with them, and she died suddenly during the visit. Her money passed to her daughter – and in turn to Palmer. In the following year, a bookmaker named Bladon died with equal suddenness when staying with Palmer. A large sum of money disappeared, and so did Bladon's betting book, in which Palmer figured as a heavy loser. His wife was heard to enquire wearily: 'Where will it end?' – her own sudden death would occur three years later. But in the meantime, sudden deaths continued to occur with suspicious frequency – a creditor named Bly, an uncle named 'Beau' Bentley, and four of Palmer's children, who died in convulsions. Then, in 1853, Palmer insured his wife for £13,000, and she died soon afterwards. The ease with which he had acquired this money – and staved off bankruptcy – evidently decided Palmer to insure the life of his brother Walter for £82,000. But when Walter died suddenly, after a drinking bout, the company was suspicious, and refused to pay. Palmer succeeded in insuring a friend called George Bates for £25,000, who also died unexpectedly; but when a detective employed by the company learned from a boot boy that he had seen Palmer pouring something into Bates's drink, they once again refused to pay. Palmer then had a drinking session with the boot boy, who was severely ill after it.

It was after these setbacks that Palmer attended the Shrewsbury races with Cook, who died in agony a week later.

The bodies of Palmer's wife and brother were now exhumed; and a considerable quantity of antimony was found in Anne Palmer. There was no poison in Walter Palmer, but Taylor pointed out that prussic acid would escape from the body after death in the form of gases.

Cook's stomach had been sent to Professor Taylor for analysis. It had been turned inside out before it had been thrown in the jar, and Palmer had then succeeded in taking the jar out of the room before anyone noticed; when it was returned, there were two slits in its parchment cap. Taylor was able to find a small quantity of antimony in the stomach – not enough to kill a man – but no strychnine. Palmer was still at large when Taylor's letter, containing his results, arrived in Rugeley, and he suceeded in intercepting the letter, and sending the coroner a present of game, pointing out that no strychnine had been found.

If the case had depended solely on Taylor's evidence, there can be no doubt that Palmer would have been acquitted. But the circumstantial evidence was overwhelming. It was proved that he had forged Cook's signature on a cheque for £350 while his friend lay ill, and also forged the document showing that Cook owed him £4,000. So although Taylor's evidence came in for some derision, there was never any doubt about the verdict, and Palmer's guilt. He was hanged at Stafford on 14 June 1856.

Where Taylor was concerned, the case of Dr Thomas Smethurst was also a fiasco. In 1853, the 48-year-old doctor had retired to a boarding-house in Bayswater with his 68-year-old wife. There he met Miss Isabella Bankes, who was six years his junior, and the acquaintance soon ripened into an intimacy that led the landlady to give him notice. Thereupon, Dr Smethurst and Miss Bankes moved to Richmond, and he married her bigamously. The following March, 1859, Miss Bankes became ill, with vomiting and stomach pains, and two doctors called in by Smethurst thought the symptoms looked like poisoning. They went to a local magistrate, and when it was learned that Smethurst would gain £1,750 from her will, he was arrested. Miss Bankes died the next day. Some of her excreta was sent to Professor Taylor, who detected arsenic. A bottle of colourless liquid, found in Smethurst's room, was also sent to Taylor, who subjected it to the Reinsch test for arsenic. In this test, the suspected arsenic is mixed with hydrochloric acid, and then a piece of copper gauze is steeped in the acid; if arsenic is present, the gauze becomes black with a deposit of metallic arsenic. In later editions of his famous textbook, Taylor emphasizes that it is important to use copper of a high degree of purity, since ordinary commercial copper contains a small quantity of arsenic. And this, it seems, explains why Taylor believed he had found arsenic in the colourless liquid. In fact, it later proved to be a solution of potassium chlorate. Before the trial began, Taylor was forced to write to the prosecution and defence admitting his mistake. His analysis of the excreta was now obviously suspect.

At the trial, three doctors insisted that the death revealed all the symptoms of irritant poisoning; but Taylor's mistake crippled the prosecution case. The result was that although Smethurst was found guilty, the controversy surrounding the case led the Home Secretary to submit all the evidence to a surgeon, Sir Benjamin Collins-Brodie. Brodie reported that although the case against Smethurst was full of suspicious circumstances, 'there was no absolute and convincing proof of his guilt'. Accordingly, Smethurst was granted a free pardon.

One interesting piece of evidence was discovered later. Smethurst had written a letter in the *Lancet* in 1844 on the extraction of teeth, and on the opposite page there was a letter from the well-known chemist Frisenius stating that the Reinsch test for arsenic would fail in the presence of potassium chlorate. This has given rise to the speculation that Smethurst may have disguised the poisoning of Miss Bankes by also giving her potassium chlorate. On the other hand, the doctors who attended Miss Bankes were unaware that she was pregnant, or they might have reached the conclusion that her vomiting was due to pregnancy complicated by dysentery. This contradictory evidence helps to explain why the guilt or innocence of Thomas Smethurst has remained a matter of controversy ever since.

The same ambiguity surrounds the case of Dr Alfred Warder, one of the forensic experts who gave evidence at the trial of William Palmer. In 1866, Dr Warder and his third wife, Ethel, moved to Brighton. Her health had so far been good, but now she fell ill with symptoms that were curiously similar to those that had preceded the death of Warder's previous wife. A Dr Taafe, who was called in on the insistence of Warder's brother-in-law, found her to be suffering from bladder pains. Warder said he had prescribed Fleming's Tincture of Aconite. Taafe pointed out that this was supposed to be for external application only, and insisted on substituting a mixture of henbane and opium. He was greatly puzzled that Mrs Warder failed to improve; Warder told him that his wife had got tired of the medicine and would not take it. Soon after, Mrs Warder died. Because of the suspicious circumstances, an inquest was held, and her viscera were sent to Professor Taylor for analysis.

He performed a series of tests for metallic poisons – arsenic, antimony, and so on, but all were negative. So were his tests for vegetable poisons, using the Stas method and various colour tests. (By then, many reagents had been developed that would reveal the presence of various vegetable poisons – morphine, atrophine, hyoscine, and others – by changing colour in the presence of sulphuric acid.) He was not even able to detect aconite, which *had* been administered by Warder. He concluded, nevertheless, that the symptoms observed by the doctors were consistent with slow aconite poisoning. And at the inquest on Mrs Warder, Dr Taafe expressed the same opinion.

However, before the jury could return a verdict, Dr Warder poisoned himself with cyanide. This looked like an admission of guilt, so the jury reached the decision that Mrs Warder had died of aconite administered by her husband. Yet the unsatisfactory nature of Taylor's conclusions suggests that if Warder had been tried for murder, he would have been acquitted. It is possible that he committed suicide because he realized that he would never escape the suspicion of being a wife-murderer.

It seems clear, on the whole, that as a toxicologist, Taylor was lacking in the brilliance that characterized Orfila and Stas. Yet this in itself is hardly a condemnation; it only underlines the incredible difficulties that face a doctor who has been sent a mass of decaying intestines and half-digested food, and asked to make up his mind whether one of dozens of poison has been the cause of death. In many of the famous poisoning cases, success has been the result either of luck or of some incredible inspiration on the part of the pathologist. Or, of course, of some fatal oversight on the part of the poisoner . . .

13

And what if no chemical test exists to identify a poison – as, for example, in the case of aconite and digitalis? This was the problem that, in 1863, confronted one of France's foremost experts on forensic medicine, Dr Ambroise Tardieu.

The death that concerned him was that of a young widow named Mme de Pauw; the suspect was her ex-lover, a doctor named Couty de la Pommerais. If the evidence that was beginning to emerge was correct, he was one of the most calculating and heartless murderers in medical history. But if Mme de Pauw *had* died of poison, then he had used his medical knowledge to choose a poison for which there was no known chemical test.

Pommerais had been in Paris since 1859 when, at the age of 24, he had come from Orleans. His charm and good looks ensured his success among the aristocracy, and he himself claimed to be a count (a title to which, in fact, he had no right). One of his patients was an artist named de Pauw, and when he died he left behind a pretty widow and three small children. Pommerais was susceptible, and she soon became his mistress. Unfortunately, Pommerais was a gambler, and he needed money. The solution seemed to be to marry some rich patient. His choice fell upon the daughter of a wealthy widow named Dabizy. The widow was doubtful about the match, no doubt suspecting the doctor's motive, so she took the precaution of making sure that her daughter's money should be placed legally beyond her husband's reach. But a mere two months after the marriage, the widow Dabizy died after dining with her daughter and son-in-law, and Pommerais certified the death as Asiatic cholera – after all, she was his patient.

Without a husband and without a lover, Mme de Pauw was finding it hard to make ends meet, and her children were suffering from under-nourishment. It seems possible it was she who approached her ex-lover for help; at all events, in March 1863, they renewed their acquaintance. And eight months later, on the night of 17 November, Mme de Pauw died, apparently of cholera. She was buried soon after.

The police had no reason to suspect the personable young doctor. Then Chief Inspector Claude, of the Sûreté, received an anonymous letter suggesting that he ought to look into the question of whether Pommerais would benefit financially from the death of Mme de Pauw. When he did so, he learned that Pommerais had insured Mme de Pauw's life for 500,000 francs, and that the insurance company was even now preparing to pay him.

The author of the anonymous letter was almost certainly the dead woman's sister, Mme Ritter. Five days after Mme de Pauw's death she called on Claude, and told him an amazing story. Hearing that her sister had had a fall on the stairs, and was confined to her bed, she had gone to call on her. Mme de Pauw had sworn her to silence, then explained that the fall was all part of an ingenious plot devised by Pommerais, the aim of which was to give her an income for life. The sound of the fall downstairs, which had been heard by neighbours was, in fact, a stuffed sack. The next task, Pommerais had explained, was to convince the insurance company that her life was in danger, so that when she proposed that her life insurance should be exchanged for a small annuity of 5,000 francs a year they would seize the opportunity to save themselves a far larger sum . . .

Mme Ritter told Claude that she had warned her sister against involving herself in such a plot; but Mme de Pauw needed the money to support three children. And now she was dead.

Clearly, Pommerais had given Mme de Pauw some drug that produced symptoms like cholera. And instead of allowing her to live when the insurance company agreed to the annuity, he had increased the dose and killed her.

Claude lost no time in having Mme de Pauw's body exhumed, and sent to Professor Tardieu. The police called at the doctor's surgery and took away various bottles of poison, as well as some letters from Mme de Pauw. And Tardieu settled down to trying to determine whether Mme de Pauw had died of poison. One thing was clear: it had not been from cholera, or any other natural cause. Neither had it been from any metallic poison like arsenic, antimony or mercury. The alternative was a vegetable poison. But which? Patiently, Tardieu and his assistants applied Stas's method to the contents of the stomach, discouraged by the knowledge that many of the poisons would have disappeared from the system and left no trace. And even if there *were* traces, the poison might be one of those to which no reaction had been found.

On the other hand, the concentrated extract that was now contained in a sealed flask probably contained the poison. And there was at least an obvious way of testing this hypothesis. Tardieu injected it into a dog. And after six and a half hours, the dog's heartbeat slowed to half its normal rate, and it lay gasping on the floor. Then, slowly, it recovered. Tardieu was triumphant. The liquid from Mme de Pauw's stomach contained a poison; the problem was to identify it.

And now the clue came from the material turned over to Tardieu by the police. One of the letters went out of its way to mention the drug digitalis, with which Pommerais was treating her. Digitalis is an extract of foxglove, and is used to treat heart disease. In large doses, it causes fluctuations in the heartbeat, and a slowing of the heart that can lead to death. Moreover, the bottle containing digitalis, taken from Pommerais's surgery, was almost empty, although the records showed that he had bought three grains of it recently. Injected into a large dog, Pommerais's digitalis caused wild fluctuations of heartbeat; within a few hours, it was dead.

Tardieu now tried his stomach extract on a frog, opening its chest so as to observe the heart. An injection of the stomach extract produced precisely the same effect as an injection of digitalis; the heart beat slower and slower, then stopped.

The body of Pommerais's mother-in-law was also exhumed. It had been buried too long to reveal a vegetable poison, but the symptoms of her short illness were undoubtedly those of digitalis poisoning.

In court, the defence – predictably – challenged Tardieu's medical evidence, arguing that he had failed to demonstrate the presence of digitalis by chemical means. Tardieu's evidence was not the factor that ultimately swayed the jury. They were overwhelmed by the circumstantial evidence, particularly by the method by which Pommerais had almost obtained 500,000 francs from the insurance company. He had not insured Mme de Pauw's life in his own name – which would obviously arouse suspicion – but had persuaded her to do it, providing her with the premium. But if she died, the insurance money would be paid to her children. To prevent this, Pommerais had visited a lawyer and explained that a close woman friend, now married, owed him 100,000 francs. She lacked the money to pay, but had insured her life for that amount. Would it be legally binding if she signed a document agreeing that she owed him the money? The lawyer assured him that it would be, and drew up the document. Pommerais then changed the amount to 500,000 francs, and persuaded Mme de Pauw to sign it. It would, he said, be further evidence that she was convinced she was close to death, and that she relied on him to look after her children. But if Pommerais did not intend to kill her, then he could have no possible motive to get her to sign such a document . . .

So Pommerais was found guilty, and executed in June 1864. And Tardieu's method of testing for digitalis – with the aid of a frog – is still to be found in every modern textbook of toxicology.

14

The science of toxicology has undoubtedly made greater advances in the past century than any other branch of forensic medicine. And this has been largely a matter of necessity. If the number of known poisons had remained the same as in the days of ancient Rome, or the court of Louis XIV, the modern toxicologist would have no problems, for arsenic, mercury, conium, belladonna and the rest are relatively easy to detect. But medical science has devoted itself to the discovery of new drugs, and most of these drugs are also poisons. The sheer number of synthetic alkaloids developed since the Second World War – Clarke's standard *Isolation and Identification of Drugs* mentions more than

2,000 of them – means that the modern toxicologist is faced with an apparently impossible task.

It is not, of course, quite impossible, since science has also developed a number of important short cuts. Many alkaloids form distinctive crystals that can easily be recognized under the microscope. Each crystal has its own melting point. In the early days, in the first decade of the century, this test required a fairly large amount of the suspected alkaloid, but by the early 1950s, microscopic amounts could be tested. The discovery of X-rays by Röntgen in 1895 resulted in the new science of X-ray crystallography: when X-rays pass through a crystal, they are diffracted as light is refracted by a prism, and the unique pattern of diffraction can be captured on a photographic plate.

Even more important was the discovery of column chromatography. If a dye solution is poured into an upright glass tube containing fine chalk, the colour is filtered out near the top of the tube, and only pure water runs out of the bottom. If more water is poured in at the top, the area of colour will descend down the tube, meanwhile splitting into different layers representing the different dyes or components. This discovery was made in 1906 by a Russian, Tsvett, and rediscovered in the early 1930s. When filter paper was substituted for the chalk, it could be flattened out, and its various layers examined and tested separately. If one of these contained even a small quantity of an alkaloid poison, it could be revealed by the appropriate reagent.

Another ingenious way of determining the composition of an unknown substance is the spectroscope. When any substance is heated, its atoms vibrate and give off a characteristic light, and if this light is passed through a prism or a narrow slit, the dark background is crossed by a number of bright 'emission' lines – they were first carefully studied by Bunsen and Kirchhoff in 1859. Each element has its own characteristic lines, so that it is even possible to tell what elements are present in a star by passing its light through a prism. The intensity of the lines depends upon the quantity of the heated substance in the sample. So if a known poison is sprayed into a flame, the exact amount of poison can be determined by a light meter attached to the spectroscope. Metallic poisons like arsenic could also be measured by electrolysis. When an electric current is passed through a metal salt dissolved in water, the salt is split into its positive and negative constituents (ions), and the positive metal ions move to the negative electric pole (the cathode). So if the cathode is weighed before and after the experiment, it is possible to determine just how much arsenic or antimony or mercury has been deposited.

In the 1950s, an even more ingenious method for detecting arsenic was developed by nuclear physicists. When bombarded with neutrons in a nuclear reactor, arsenic becomes radioactive, and the radioactivity can be measured by a Geiger counter. So a hair that had absorbed arsenic could be made radioactive, and then the exact quantity of arsenic measured. And since the amount of arsenic in a hair is proportional to the amount in the whole body of a poison victim, it could easily be determined whether a fatal dose had been administered.

In spite of these sensitive methods of detecting and measuring poison, there were many setbacks. In the 1870s, an Italian professor of chemistry, Francesco Anselmo, discovered the 'cadaveric alkaloids', certain alkaloids that form naturally in corpses, and which can be mistaken for poisons administered with malice. Anselmo had investigated cases in which poisoning by morphine and delphinine were suspected, and in which the 'poison' turned out to be alkaloids that had developed naturally in corpses. This discovery caused alarm among experts in forensic medicine, for it complicated the already impossibly complicated problem of detecting vegetable poisons. In 1882, the question of cadaveric alkaloids was raised in a British court of law during the trial of Dr George Lamson, accused of poisoning his schoolboy brother-in-law with aconite, the poison extracted from monkshood (or wolfbane). For this poison there is – as already noted – no straightforward colour reaction test, as there is for morphine, heroin, atropine, hyoscine, and so on. Lamson undoubtedly knew this, and decided to solve his serious financial problems, which included writing dud cheques, with the poison. Another brother-in-law, Herbert, had already died at a convenient moment – later giving rise to the suspicion that Lamson had poisoned him – and the doctor had benefited by £700.

Eighteen-year-old Percy John suffered from curvature of the spine, and was a pupil at a private school in Wimbledon. On 3 December 1881, Lamson called on him there and saw him in the presence of the headmaster. He then went through a pantomine that seems typical of a certain type of murderer, involving an excess of ingenuity. The headmaster offered him sherry, and Lamson said he would like to put some sugar in it; a basin was brought, and Lamson spooned some into his sherry. Then he took out a Dundee cake, cut three slices, and handed one to the headmaster, one to Percy, and ate one himself. The poison had undoubtedly been inserted in Percy's slice of cake before it was baked. After they had eaten, he told the headmaster that he had brought some empty pill capsules from America, which would make it easier for pupils to be persuaded to take medicines. Lamson spooned some sugar into one capsule, and handed it to Percy with the words: 'Here, Percy, you are a champion pill-taker.' The boy took the 'pill', and Lamson left. Within two hours, Percy was dead. Lamson went to Paris, but voluntarily gave himself up on his return, and was arrested.

His excessive ingenuity was his undoing. The pathologist, Dr Thomas Stevenson (Alfred Swain Taylor's successor at Guy's) applied every possible test to the dead boy's vomit, and from the lack of result, concluded that the poison could only be aconite. And when Lamson was proved to have purchased aconite, the case against him was very strong indeed. Experiments with mice left Stevenson in no doubt that the liquid distilled from the dead youth's organs was a poison.

At the trial, the defence made much of the problem of cadaveric alkaloids, about which Stevenson proved to ignorant. For a while, it looked as if he had introduced serious doubts into the minds of the jury. But when the verdict came, it meant a sentence of death for Lamson. It emerged later that the verdict had been based on the other evidence – all of which pointed very clearly to a murder plot that was too ingenious and complicated by half. Before his execution on 28 April 1882, Lamson confessed to murdering Percy John, although he continued to deny murdering his other brother-in-law Herbert to the end.

Nevertheless, it was some 40 years before forensic science could assert with confidence that there was no chance of confusing cadaveric alkaloids with vegetable poison.

In a case of the late 1940s, even Orfila's well-established conclusion that arsenic could not enter the body from the surrounding soil came under attack. The accused was a Frenchwoman named Marie Besnard, who came under suspicion after the sudden death of her husband in October 1947. Before he died, he had time to whisper to the local postmistress that he thought his wife was poisoning him. She seemed to have a motive, in that she was suspected of having an affair with the hired man. Her husband was exhumed and found to contain a large quantity of arsenic. Then many other mysterious and sudden deaths were recalled – 11 in all – beginning with that of her first husband in 1929. His body was also exhumed and found to contain arsenic. And the same was true of body after body. It looked as if there could not be the slightest doubt of Marie Besnard's guilt. But the defence counsel, Albert Gautrat, thought otherwise. He unearthed recent scientific publications which revealed that certain bacteria in the soil can interact with natural arsenic, causing it to become far more soluble than it is normally. Moreover, when these 'anaerobic microbes' extracted hydrogen from sulphur compounds in human hair, they allowed the sulphur to be replaced by arsenic. Tests of these claims took seven years to investigate, and even so, were indecisive. In 1961, 14 years after her arrest, Marie Besnard was acquitted for lack of proof.

Yet, oddly enough, it is these continual doubts and uncertainties, the apparently endless proliferation of new and more subtle problems, that has made forensic toxicology the most brilliantly successful of all branches of legal medicine.

3

The Discovery of Fingerprints

1

At the age of 34, Eugène-François Vidocq was a short, powerfully built man with a scarred face and a jaw like a lion. Born in Arras on 24 July 1775, he had been in trouble most of his life; never serious trouble, but Vidocq had a quick temper and a powerful will, qualities that had led to a number of personal combats and jail sentences. Injustice enraged him, and his attempts to escape from jail had been determined and desperate. By 1808, when he found himself in Paris, the list of his offences was enough to ensure a lifetime in the galleys. He asked to see M. Henry, head of the criminal department of the Paris police, and made him an offer. If he could be guaranteed immunity, he would act as informer against a number of men that the police wanted far more than they wanted Vidocq.

Henry knew he had a bargain, but he felt it could be improved. He allowed Vidocq to go. And when, a few weeks later, Vidocq was denounced by criminal associates and appeared again in front of the chief of police, M. Henry drove a very hard bargain indeed. Vidocq was to become a police spy in one of Paris's toughest prisons, the Bicetre. If Vidocq was even suspected of being a police informer, he would be found dead the next morning. But, as M. Henry knew, he had no alternative.

Vidocq's task was to obtain evidence against a burglar named Barthélemy Lacour, known to the police as Coco. He had stolen a quantity of silver from a police official. Now he was about to come up for trial, and the police had no evidence. Vidocq's task was to obtain that evidence.

It proved unexpectedly easy. Because of his reputation as an escaper, Vidocq was something of a hero to the other prisoners, and soon became a kind of unofficial lawgiver. One of the first 'cases' brought before him in this capacity was, oddly enough, Coco himself, who was suspected of being a police informer. Vidocq saved Coco's life, and so became his trusted intimate. And soon Coco had confided in him that the police would never convict him, for the only witness was a street porter whom the police had failed to question. Coco did not tell Vidocq the porter's name, but he mentioned the street he lived in. Vidocq passed on this information to Henry, and the man was soon traced. Coco never knew how they obtained the evidence that convicted him . . .

For the next two years, Vidocq continued his career of betrayal. Then Henry kept his side of the bargain and allowed him to 'escape' on his way to court – the other prisoners were delighted with Vidocq's latest exploit. After that, the great escaper apparently returned to his old habits, spending his days in low wine shops. But the criminals were baffled that the police seemed to know of their best laid plans in advance. No one suspected that the culprit might be the great escaper.

In due course, Vidocq's successes became so great that, in 1810, he was given his own police department; it was called the Sûreté. His priority was to establish a network of informers or 'grasses' – a method most police forces now take for granted, but which was established by Vidocq. And from 1810 until he retired in 1833, he scored a remarkable series of successes.

One example will suffice to illustrate his methods. In 1821, a butcher named Fontaine stopped at a roadside inn, and fell into conversation with two respectable-looking travellers; the butcher was delighted when they said they were on their way to a fair at Corbeil, and asked if he could join them. He was carrying a large sum of money, and was worried about robbers. At a lonely spot a few miles further on, they beat him unconscious, stabbed him, and took his money, leaving him for dead. But the butcher survived, and was able to describe his assailants. At the scene of the crime, the police found a fragment of an envelope with part of an address, including 'M. Raoul' and 'Roche . . .' Vidocq knew a M. Raoul who kept a bar at the Barriere Rochechouart, and whose reputation was sinister.

The butcher had succeeded in delivering a powerful kick at the knee of one of the men, so Vidocq assumed he was looking for a man with a limp. His men kept the bar under surveillance, and soon observed a man with a limp who fitted the butcher's description of one of the robbers. When Vidocq saw him, he recognized a criminal named Court, whom he had arrested some time before for armed robbery. At dawn the next morning he went to Court's room. He told Court he had been accused of smuggling, and observed the expression of relief that crossed the robber's face. Court invited him to search the room, and Vidocq took possession of some weapons, then took Court to the nearest gendarme post.

Now Vidocq used the same technique on Raoul. He explained that Raoul had been denounced for holding anti-Government meetings and distributing seditious pamphlets. Raoul invited him to search the place. There was, as Vidocq expected, nothing. But Raoul had another apartment in Paris. And there, in a bureau, Vidocq found the other half of the envelope. He arrested Raoul and lodged him in prison.

Vidocq proceeded to question Court, carefully failing to mention the attack on the butcher; eventually, Court divulged that he had been concerned in the murder of a poultry dealer, who had been robbed of four louis. Now, at last, Vidocq revealed that the crime he was investigating was the attempted murder of the butcher. By now demoralized, Court also confessed to this, but accused Raoul of the stabbing. Faced with his confederate's admissions, Raoul also confessed. Both men were condemned to the guillotine. Yet it is typical of the close relationship that Vidocq was able to form with criminals that he went to enormous lengths to make their last days comfortable, and that when they knelt at the block, they regarded Vidocq as a friend.

At the age of 58, Vidocq declined to retire into civilian life, and became the first private detective in Europe. He wrote his memoirs, and became a close friend of the novelist Balzac, who immortalized Vidocq as the sinister but extraordinary criminal Vautrin; in return, Balzac helped Vidocq to write novels based on his early life.

2

After Vidocq's retirement, the next head of the Sûreté was Pierre Allard, whose subordinate, Chief Inspector Louis Canler, tracked down Lacenaire in 1834. And not long after the execution of Lacenaire, Canler again demonstrated the value of the 'needle-in-the-haystack' method of tracking down a criminal. A widow named Senepart was the victim of murder and robbery; her assailant had smashed her skull with some heavy instrument after strangling her into insensibility. Mme Senepart's son was able to tell the police that a few days before the murder, a young man from Toulouse had called on his mother, bringing her news of Senepart cousins in that city. It sounded as if this young man was a likely suspect. But the son was not even sure of his name; it could be Pagés or Magés.

Canler made his usual careful search through hotel registers for a Pagés or Magés; eventually, he tracked down a man of that name in a Paris hotel. But it was not the man he was looking for.

The only other clue was that the young man had arrived by coach from Toulouse. Canler examined the lists of passengers for the days before the murder, and set out to track down as many as possible, hoping that one of them might have struck up an acquaintance with the young man. Eventually, he found a Colonel Graves of Toulouse, who knew the victim's relative, Colonel Senepart. He vaguely recalled the young man who had travelled in the same coach, but had not spoken to him.

Canler tried another tack: did Colonel Senepart have any more friends or relatives living in Paris? Here Graves was able to be more helpful – he mentioned a Mme Gibou, who lived in the rue d'Orléans.

If the telephone or telegraph had existed in the 1830s, Canler could have contacted Colonel Senepart and asked for the lady's address. Or, of course, he could have taken the coach to Toulouse and put the question. Instead, he preferred to enquire at every house in the rue d'Orléans. He was unsuccessful. Eventually he tracked down Mme Gibou in the rue d'Orléans du Marais. And she recognized his description as that of a young man who had called on her and brought her a letter from the Seneparts. He had gone off without leaving his name or address, but had asked permission to call again . . . Canler warned the lady that the young man was wanted for robbery and murder, and asked her to give a signal – open a certain window overlooking the street – if he returned. Two days later, police keeping watch on the apartment saw Mme Gibou open the window; they rushed in, and arrested her visitor, whose name proved to be Pagés. He was identified by the son of the murdered woman, found guilty of killing her, and executed.

The case makes it clear that one of the chief problems in France in the 1830s was quite simply one of communication. It was easier for Canler to spend days in house-to-house enquiries than to travel the 400 miles to Toulouse in a bumpy diligence. By the 1840s, all this was changing, and the coming of the railway made long-distance travel fast and relatively comfortable. Samuel Morse obtained a patent for the telegraph in 1840, and in 1845, the Quaker John Tawell became the first murderer to be arrested through the new invention. The very word 'scientist' was coined in the 1840s by the scholar William Whewell. But another new invention, photography, was still too crude to be of use in identifying criminals, since it required the subject to sit perfectly still for a quarter of an hour or so. (There is an amusing American photograph of the 1890s showing police attempting to photograph an accused man, with one policeman grabbing his hair and three more trying to hold his arms and legs still.)

Most of the murders that took place in France – and in Paris alone there were still about 200 a year – were associated with robbery, and for the next few decades, Allard, Canler and their successors had to hunt their prey without the aid of science. But then, the criminals often behaved with such stupidity that little detective skill was required. In 1869, a 20-year-old youth named Jean Baptiste Troppmann decided to become rich by murdering a family of eight people, then fleeing to America. The husband, Jean Kinck, was poisoned over a meal, and his body buried; next, the eldest son Gustave was lured to Paris and murdered. Before his death he had been persuaded to write a letter to his mother, asking her to come to Paris. Troppmann met them, took them to Pantin Common, and hacked them to death with a spade, disembowelling the 2-year-old daughter. The crime was discovered the next morning when a labourer noticed pools of blood and saw the freshly dug grave. A manufacturer's label in the coat of one of the children enabled the family to be identified as the Kincks from Roubaix. Troppmann was sitting in a bar in Le Havre when a policeman asked to see his papers – he thought Troppmann might be a harbour sneakthief. Troppmann ran away and leapt into the harbour. Pulled out and searched, he was identified through the Kinck family papers. He was beheaded in January 1870.

The case of Henri Pranzini reveals the shortcomings of the 'needle-in-the-haystack' method. On 17 March 1887, police forced their way into the apartment of Mme de Montille, a highly successful courtesan, and found the place deluged in blood; someone had cut the throats of Mme de Montille, her maidservant, and the servant's little daughter. Jewellery was missing, but the killer had not succeeded in forcing the safe. Two shirt-cuffs and a belt, all bearing the name 'Geissler', were found in the apartment. It was discovered that a man named Geissler had disappeared from his hotel room near the Gare du Nord, and Inspector Goron of the Sûreté set out to find him, utilizing clues found in the room. Goron revealed the same incredible persistence that the Bow Street Runner Henry Goddard had shown in hunting down John Todd across America.

He followed Geissler's trail first to Brussels, then Cologne, then Berlin. It was finally in Breslau that he learned that the man he sought had been in the Mazas prison in Paris all the time – charged with attempted suicide – and that he had nothing whatsoever to do with the crime. The belt and cuffs had been a deliberate false lead.

But the real murderer was also under arrest by now. An adventurer who called himself Dr Henry Pranzini, and who had been living off women most of his life, visited a Marseilles brothel five days after the murder, and tried to sell small items of jewellery to the prostitutes; one bought a gold watch, and he presented her with a pair of ear-rings. The Madame was suspicious and contacted the police; by good fortune, they were able to find the cab-driver who had taken Pranzini to the brothel, and who was now waiting for his fare outside the Grand Theatre, where Pranzini was enjoying *The Barber of Seville*. Pranzini was arrested at the end of the first act. He made the mistake of denying that he was the man who had sold the prostitute the gold watch – a convincing story might have obtained his release – and the following morning, the police received a letter from Paris which described in detail the missing jewellery of the murdered woman. Pranzini was returned to Paris, and was executed five months later.

The sensation of the following year was the trial of another adventurer called Prado (whose first name seems to be unknown). Prado kept two mistresses, and this proved to be his undoing. He had given both women some jewellery which he had stolen in Bordeaux, and the police tracked down the jewellery, and placed both women together in the same cell. Jealousy was forgotten in their irritation with the lover who was responsible for their plight, and the old mistress, Eugénie Forestier, told the new one, Mauricette Couronneau, how her lover had returned to her bed in the middle of the night and confessed that he had just cut a woman's throat. That had been two years earlier, in January 1886.

Now it so happened that Prado was already in custody, and likely to remain so for a long time. In November 1887, he was interrupted while burgling a bedroom of a diamond merchant. Pursued by a hotel servant and two policemen, he had seriously wounded one of the policemen with a revolver before being overpowered. Now he was awaiting trial for attempted murder. And when the indignant mistresses mentioned his confession to the examining magistrate, the police recollected an unsolved murder of the previous January – that of a courtesan called Marie Agaetan, who had been killed in her rue Caumartin apartment, her head almost severed from her body. Again, they were favoured by chance. After a quarrel with Prado, Eugenie had taken possession of a portion of a receipt that had fallen from his pocket; it contained the address of a goldsmith in Madrid. And the goldsmith proved to have purchased some of the jewels stolen from Marie Agaetan.

In court, Prado chose to be his own advocate, and proved to be highly articulate – in fact, downright voluble. Nietzsche was impressed by his wit and bravado, and thought that Prado belonged to a type of criminal who was 'too strong for his particular social environment' and whose crime was an expression of individual revolt – that is, an 'Outsider'. But all Prado's self-justifications and evasions failed to influence the jury, and he was condemned to death.

One of the most sensational, and certainly most pointless, crimes of the period was committed by two young men named Aimé Barré and Paul Lebiez. They had been fellow students at the Lycée at Angers, but had decided that fame and fortune were to be found in Paris. Barré set up as a 'financial agent', but was soon heavily in debt. Lebiez had abandoned medicine for schoolteaching, but lost his job due to unpunctuality. The two actually discussed committing suicide together, then decided that murder might be a more attractive alternative. Opposite Barré's apartment in the rue d'Hautville lived an old milkseller named Mme Gillet, who worked during the day as a charlady. She was believed by her neighbours to possess savings amounting to 5,000 francs. Barré offered to double her fortune if she would entrust him with the management of her financial affairs, but she declined. So the two men decided to kill her.

Their first idea was to administer poison – enough to make her sick enough to be taken into hospital; then Barré would burgle her attic and steal her money. But if she recovered, she would guess who had robbed her. And if she died, the poison would undoubtedly be detected by the latest forensic methods. On the whole, it seemed simplest to kill her with a blow on the head.

Since Barré was known – and to some extent trusted – by the old lady, he was chosen to commit the murder. The plan was for him to go up to her attic and knock her unconscious. But Barré's nerve failed him. Three times he mounted to the attic with a hammer concealed in a briefcase, and three times changed his mind. Lebiez, who possessed a certain brutal courage, was contemptuous. Finally, on the morning of 23 March 1878, Barré went and awoke Lebiez, who was in bed with his mistress. 'It's coming off today' he explained enigmatically. They hurried back to Barré's apartment in the rue d'Hautville. The old woman had been asked to call with the milk. When she appeared at the door, Barré said with smiling courtesy: 'Please come in, Madame Gillet.' And as she stepped into the dining-room, she was struck down by a violent blow on the back of the head. Then Lebiez stabbed her through the heart.

While Barré hurried off to the old lady's attic, Lebiez proceeded to dismember the body, a task for which his medical training had equipped him. Barré was able to find only about 2,000 francs, less than half the expected sum – he needed more than that to pay off his most pressing debts. When the conspirators met again, Lebiez agreed to accept a mere 30 francs as his share.

That evening, Barré went to the rue Poliveau, near the medical school, and rented a room, giving his name as Émile Gérard, a medical student. Early the next morning, he and Lebiez took two parcels to the room, and left them in a cupboard. They contained Mme Gillet's arms and thighs. The rest of the body was packed in a portmanteau and despatched to Mans by rail. At this stage, it looked as if they had got away with the murder.

When her lodger failed to reappear, the landlady re-let the room in the rue Poliveau, and the parcels containing the remains were soon discovered. At first the police were inclined to treat the affair as a practical joke played by a medical student – which is exactly what Barré had wanted them to think – but when the remains were identified as those of a woman, they began to consider the possibility that they might be those of the missing Mme Gillet. Everyone who had had business dealings with Mme Gillet was summoned before an examining magistrate. Among them were Aimé Barré, who was soon allowed to leave. But the magistrate was struck by Barré's resemblance to the landlady's description of 'Émile Gérard', the medical student who had rented her room. Barré was summoned back and confronted by the landlady, who declared that there was a strong resemblance, except that Émile Gérard had been bearded. When Barré admitted that he had recently shaved off his beard, he immediately became a leading suspect. In Barré's room, police found a number of women's blouses similar to those in which the remains had been wrapped – they had belonged to his mistress, from whom he was now separated. This had been the first of Barrés major mistakes. The second was his failure to take from Mme Gillet's attic her list of her securities. The police found it, and were able to trace the securities through various brokers. All had been negotiated by Barré.

Faced with this evidence, Barré broke down and confessed, incriminating Paul Lebiez. The portmanteau containing the rest of the old lady's body was traced to Mans; purchase of the portmanteau was traced to Barré. The trial of Barré and Lebiez lasted a mere three days; each did his best to throw the blame on the other. They were guillotined together, Lebiez meeting death with indifference, Barré with abject terror.

It can be seen that cases like these hardly required the application of the principles of scientific detection; the criminals fell into the hands of the police like ripe plums. But a murder mystery of 1876 demanded a combination of the old 'needle-in-the-haystack' method with the new scientific approach. Two children playing by the Seine noticed a bundle that had become stuck against some timbers and tried to pull it ashore. Some passers-by came to their aid and opened the bundle; it proved to contain a woman's head and part of her body.

The problems of tracing the victim's identity were immense – hundreds of women disappeared in the area of Paris and its surroundings every year. But at least the head was in a good state of preservation. A decision was taken to photograph it, and to sell the photographs in newsagents and tobacco kiosks – the morbidity of the Paris public should ensure a good sale. In fact, hundreds of copies were sold, and the police received no fewer than 183 identifications, all false. Dozens of missing women were located by the police search, but the investigations brought them no nearer to finding the dead woman's identity.

The solution came, as the police had hoped, by chance. Someone was handing around a copy of the photograph in a café on the boulevard Ornano when a man said: 'I know who that is. It's the wife of that old soldier with the decoration.' He was an *habitué* of the café. He was traced to a lodging in the rue des Trois Frères; his name was Billoir.

Billoir was indignant. It was true that his wife was missing, but she had left him. The police were more than half convinced by his protestations, and prepared to release him. But at this point, police searching his lodging discovered signs that a human body had been dismembered there.

Billoir now confessed to dismembering his wife, but insisted he had not murdered her. He had kicked her during a drunken quarrel, and she had collapsed and died. Thereupon he had decided to dismember her and throw the pieces in the river.

But the medical evidence disproved his story. There was no sign on the body of a bruise that would be caused by a kick hard enough to kill her. Moreover, the small amount of blood in the remains indicated that her heart had been beating when Billoir had started to dismember her; she had been unconscious, not dead. It was this medical evidence that brought Billoir to the guillotine in 1876. He remarked gloomily and accurately: 'The doctors have done for me.'

3

In the nineteenth century, all the major cities of Europe expanded; inevitably, their crime rates rose in proportion. Looking back on the period from our age of pointless brutality, it is possible to feel a kind of nostalgia about crime in that less complicated century. Most of it was committed by the poor, and the motive was, quite simply, economic. In 1826, two Edinburgh cobblers named William Burke and William Hare sold the corpse of one of their lodgers, who had died of natural causes, to the medical school, and were delighted to receive £7. 10s, a vast sum that would nowadays be worth over £100. They decided that if the medical school was so anxious to buy corpses, they would make it their business to supply them. Their method was to lure derelicts to their room, make them drunk, then suffocate them, and they had despatched more than a dozen in this way before they were caught. In France in the 1850s, a peasant named Martin Dumollard would pick up servant girls looking for work and offer them a job on his farm. The girls never arrived; they were strangled or battered to death in some lonely place, and their bodies stripped of clothing. Then Dumollard would make his way back home with the girl's trunk on his back and announce to his grim-faced wife: 'I've just killed another girl. I must go and bury her.' Inevitably, a girl finally escaped and identified her assailant, who had a tumour on his face and a scarred lip. The clothes of ten girls were found in Dumollard's cottage, and he was able to lead the police to some of their graves – one had been buried alive. Dumollard was guillotined in 1862, while his wife was sentenced to hard labour for life. Few of the victims had any money, so the murders were committed for their few possessions.

When the prosperous middle classes committed murder in the nineteenth century, it was usually by way of preserving their domestic security, as when John Tawell rid himself of his unwanted mistress, or Madeleine Smith poisoned her importunate lover. Although such crimes strike us as 'typically Victorian', they were, in fact, so rare as to be completely untypical. Most murders were committed for the sake of a few shillings.

Inevitably, then, the chief problem confronting the police was simply how to identify habitual thieves. A man arrested in Lyon might be wanted for burglary in Toulouse, Lille and Strasbourg, but unless he had some marked peculiarity, like Dumollard's tumour and scarred lip, there was no way of finding out. The railways made increasingly large areas accessible to the travelling criminal, but the police had no corresponding method of keeping track of them. In Brussels in the 1840s, photographs began to be used, and the Sûreté soon adopted the same method, building up a library of more than 80,000 photographs. But this tended to be self-defeating, since there was no simple way of classifying them, and it would have taken days to compare 80,000 blurred and unsatisfactory pictures of scowling bearded faces with the photograph of a captured burglar who had probably shaved off his beard and moustache.

Now if the police had been interested, they might have found some stimulating hints in a work called *On Man*, by the Belgian astronomer Lambert Quételet, published in 1835. Quételet was a statistician – he has been called the father of modern statistics – and he was struck by 'the frightening regularity of the recurrence of suicides', and the same regularity in crime. His book is an attempt to apply the statistical method to the development of man's physical and intellectual faculties. (He has the dubious distinction of having coined the term 'average man' – *homme moyen*.) In fact, it caused a great deal of excited discussion – but only among philosophers, who felt that his observations were a denial of free will.

But one of Quételet's enthusiastic readers was an impecunious young medical student called Louis-Adolphe Bertillon, and he was immensely excited by what Quetelet called 'social physics' – the attempt to discover by scientific methods 'what makes people tick'. During the revolution of 1848, the young doctor found himself in prison for six months with one of his professors, Achille Guillard, whose interest in 'what makes people tick' caused him to be regarded as a dangerous liberal. When they were released, Bertillon became a regular caller at Guillard's house, and soon married his pretty daughter Zoé. And together, he and his father-in-law founded the School of Anthropology, thus inventing a new science. Guillard was also the inventor of demography, the study of regional groups and races.

It is not surprising that when, in 1853, Zoé Bertillon produced a second son, who was christened Alphonse, he should have shown early signs of genius; from the time he could crawl he was moving among men of science. And, considering the liberal opinions of his father and grandfather, it is also hardly surprising that he should have been a born rebel, who was removed from his first school because he made the other pupils unmanageable. A German tutor found him impossible, and soon left. And throughout his schooldays, Alphonse Bertillon remained an *enfant terrible*. He was dismissed from a boarding school in Versailles for cooking inside the lid of his desk with a spirit lamp, and causing a fire. The death of his mother in 1866 made him even more of a 'loner'.

The trouble with all this rebellion was that it made him practically unemployable, and when he left school, he drifted to England and became a badly paid private schoolmaster. A period of military conscription was equally inglorious. And finally, at the absurdly late age of 26, the rebel genius accepted a clerical job that had become vacant at the department of the Préfecture of Police. He only obtained this through the influence of his father. His daily work was simply to copy out forms, a task that is now performed by a duplicator. It drove him almost insane with boredom.

But it was too late now for further revolt. He revealed his common sense by deciding to make the best of it, and attempting to apply his scientific intelligence to the problems of police work. The forms mostly contained 'descriptions' of criminals, descriptions that were virtually useless, even when accompanied by a blurry photograph. Bertillon saw immediately that this futility was due to a lack of system of identification. Police officers were posted at the door to greet convicted felons as if they were old friends, in the hope of leading them to admit previous convictions. Every time a policeman was successful, he was rewarded with five francs. Bertillon soon learned that many prisoners were persuaded to admit to previous felonies by the offer of a share of the five francs.

But Bertillon was the son of the man who had helped to found the science of anthropology, and he had also read Quételet's later work *Anthropometry, or the Measurement of Different Faculties in Man* (1871). And if human faculties could be measured, then surely man's physical characteristics should present no difficulty?

Bertillon began by attempting to invent what would later be called 'photofit pictures'. He sliced up photographs, stuck them on bits of cardboard like pieces of a jigsaw puzzle, and tried making different arrangements of ears, noses and mouths. Three years earlier, the Italian criminologist Cesare Lombroso had caused a European controversy with his book *Criminal Man (L'Uomo delinquente)* in which he had suggested that criminals are a throwback to primitive atavistic types, and that they can often be recognized by 'degenerative characteristics' – receding chins, sloping foreheads, and so on. So Bertillon's attempt was not quite as insane as some of his colleagues thought it.

But Bertillon's optimism about 'anthropometry' was based on a discovery made by Quételet and confirmed by his own father: that measurements of human characteristics tend to fall into statistical groups – as all tailors and hatters know – but that no two human beings have exactly the same set of measurements. His idea was that if he could devise a series of simple measurements – length of the head, width of the head, length of middle finger, length of forearm, and so on – he could use these as a system of criminal classification that would enable a policeman to check whether a suspect had a criminal record or was using a false name. If, for example, a suspect's head was 190 millimetres wide, then his form would be filed under 190. If the width was 160 millimetres, then the clerk would find this subdivision under 160. And so on. It would be rather complicated at first, but, like a foreign language, easy enough once it had been properly learned.

Bertillon wrote out his ideas in his best handwriting, and submitted the report to his chief, M. Louis Andrieux, the prefect. M. Andrieux ignored it. Bertillon wrote a second report, even more detailed. This time Andrieux sent for him and asked irritably if it was a practical joke. Bertillon assured him it was not. But when Andrieux asked him to explain in words of one syllable, he began to stammer; Bertillon was not a highly articulate man – his genius was that of intuition. When the clerk told the prefect that the present system was useless, Andrieux lost his temper and sent him back to his desk. Moreover, he wrote an angry letter to Bertillon's father, intimating that he thought his son was mad. Dr Bertillon was plunged into gloom – it looked as if his scapegrace son was intent on proving that he was unemployable. But when Alphonse asked him to read his report, he agreed. An hour later, when Alphonse returned, his father was looking thoughtful. 'I have to apologize, Alphonse. This is a very important idea.'

Alphonse who, like his father, was a restrained man, smiled with embarrassment. 'I only wanted to improve things in the department.'

'You will do far more than that.' Dr Bertillon could no longer hide his emotion. 'If this works, it will prove what I have spent my life trying to demonstrate – that every human being is unique.' And Dr Bertillon embraced his son and kissed his bearded cheek. There were tears in his eyes. For the first time, Alphonse Bertillon had a glimpse of the triumph that might be awaiting him.

But M. Andrieux proved harder to convince. He was not an intelligent man, and may have felt some obscure resentment of his clerk's intelligence, and of his intellectual family background. For the time being, he refused to allow even Dr Bertillon to persuade him to reconsider his refusal. Alphonse was forced to return to copying forms, and he did it with a bad grace. He was not much liked by his colleagues, who found him aloof; now he occasionally caught their sarcastic smiles, and flushed with fury. Patience was not among his gifts.

Meanwhile, his father counselled hard work. Whether Andrieux agreed or not, there was nothing to stop Alphonse from testing his system by taking measurements of anyone who would allow it. And one of these days, Andrieux would be replaced. In the meantime, Alphonse made a more conventional bid for recognition by writing a book called *The Savage Races*. It was published in 1892, but excited little interest. Meanwhile, Alphonse had received promotion to a slightly higher grade. And finally, the long-awaited change came about. M. Andrieux was removed, and his place taken by M. Jean Camecasse. Dr Bertillon now exerted all his influence to persuade the new prefect to consider his son's method of criminal identification. Dr Bertillon was dangerously ill, and knew he had not long to live. Even so, such is the inertia of bureaucracy that it took a full year for his efforts to bear fruit. Then, finally, a lawyer named Edgar Demange persuaded Camecasse to listen to his copying clerk. One morning in November 1882, Camecasse sent for Bertillon and asked him to explain his idea. Once again, Bertillon went into tiresome and complicated explanations of the kind that had drained Andrieux's patience. But Camecasse had promised Demange that he would try it. Suppressing his misgivings, he said: 'Very well, I'll give you three months to try out your method. If during that time you can identify one habitual criminal, we'll continue the experiment.'

As Bertillon rushed home to tell his father and his fiancée – an Austrian girl called Amélie, whose acquaintance he had made when she asked him to help her across the street – his enthusiasm was tempered by doubt. How likely was it that a criminal would be re-arrested within three months? However, there was no point in complaining. The next day he began work, with the aid of two clerks assigned to him by the Préfecture. He had had two years to perfect his method. It involved taking 11 basic measurements, including length and width of head, the right ear, forearm, middle and ring fingers, left foot, height, length of trunk, and so. The chances of two men having all 11 identical measurements was more than four million to one. Bertillon also insisted on two photographs; one full-face and one in profile. Finally, he added what he called a *portrait parlé,* a spoken portrait that mentioned any special marks, and anything else that might help a policeman to identify a face. These measurements were copied down on filing cards, which in turn were stored in a cabinet with 81 drawers. The three basic divisions were for length of head – large, medium, or small – and these were subdivided into large, medium, and small width of head. Next came middle fingers, then left little fingers. On these four measurements, Bertillon would rely for identifying his criminal – they gave odds of 276 to 1. Of course, each card also contained seven other measurements, which would, with luck, finally pin down the recidivist. But it was hardly practical to have over four million drawers, so Bertillon entrusted his luck to the much smaller odds.

Throughout December 1882 and January 1883, Bertillon measured, photographed and dictated his *portraits parlés* to his clerks. As the number of cards grew, so did his nervousness, and the more he wondered whether the prefect might be persuaded to extend the three-month deadline. His fellow clerks watched the experiment with malicious irony, while the great Gustave Macé, one of the Sûretés most brilliant exponents of the 'needle-in-the-haystack' method (in a later chapter we shall study the manner in which he trapped the murderer Voirbo) grumbled at the appalling waste of money.

Towards the end of a dark February afternoon, Bertillon was feeling exhausted and discouraged. He had almost finished his day's work, which had included, by chance, no fewer than five criminals named Dupont. If Bertillon had been a student of the laws of chance, he might have hazarded a guess that fate had some interesting synchronicity in store. Just before it was time to leave, he found himself confronting a sixth criminal named Dupont. This man had a mole near the left eyebrow and the face seemed familiar. But had he seen it in the course of his work, or outside in the street? He measured the length of the head, then the width, then the two fingers. Those who were with him on that day declared that when he went to the filing cabinet, he was trembling. The section he had to search contained 50 cards under the heading 'medium heads'. He searched through for the other measurement, and found it. The two fingers were correct too. The man was called Martin, and he had been arrested on 15 December 1882, charged with stealing empty bottles. The *portrait parlé* mentioned the mole. Bertillon took the photograph back into the other room, where the man was in the charge of an inspector. 'You were arrested last December under the name of Martin.' Dupont denied it. Bertillon showed him the photograph, then showed it to the inspector. 'Look, you can see that mole clearly.' At this point, Dupont shrugged. 'All right, I might as well admit it . . .'

That evening, hardly able to believe that three months of suspense were at an end, Bertillon hired a *fiacre* to go and tell Amélie about his triumph – he had to repeat the story several times. Then he went to tell his father, who was now totally bedridden. The old man rallied at the news; for a few days, it began to look as if he might recover. Then, suddenly, he had a relapse. His family were around him when he died. But he had had the supreme satisfaction of knowing of his son's first triumph. And Alphonse had the satisfaction of knowing that he had enabled his father to die happy.

4

Now the successes came in increasing numbers. In the following month, the system identified another habitual criminal, six more during the next three months, 15 in the next three, and 26 in the last quarter. The most old-fashioned adherent of the needle-in-the-haystack method had to admit that Bertillon had, single-handed, brought about the greatest advance in law enforcement of the nineteenth century.

Let us pause for a moment to reiterate an observation made in the first chapter. Criminology had failed to develop into a science because no one could be *bothered* to attempt it. The problem was that men failed to trust in their powers of reason. Poe's Dupin was obviously correct: a crime should be soluble by reason. But no policeman actually believed it; they instinctively preferred the rule-of-thumb method. Yet the extraordinary story of human evolution in the past half million years has been the story of man's slowly increasing trust in his own reason. It took a man who was the son and grandson of a scientist to bring this revolution into the realm of crime detection. And he had to do it in the face of entrenched official stupidity. It was not that the police did not want to catch criminals just as much as Bertillon did. But they did not believe that anything as complicated as taking 11 measurements and filing them in 81 drawers would bring them closer to their objective. Bertillon, who happened to be a man of genius, knew better.

In the same year, 1893, Bertillon married his Austrian 'secretary', and their working relationship was long and successful. But she was not his first choice. His biographer H. T. F. Rhodes discovered that Bertillon had fallen in love with a Swedish girl whom he met in 1879, the year he began to work at the Préfecture. Rhodes speculates that she was a professor's daughter whom he met at the Society of Anthropology, and that she returned to Sweden, and was responsible for an academic honour, the Order of Vasa, that he received in 1893. He seems to have kept her photograph all his life; it was probably destroyed, together with other documents relating to her, by Amélie after Bertillon's death – an event which caused Amélie to lose her mind.

Amélie had every reason to be proud of her husband. Within a year or two, the word *bertillonage* had passed not only into the French language, but into many others. The method proved its value not only with the identification of the living, but also of the dead. At the time when Bertillon's method was still regarded with amused hostility by his police colleagues, an inspector invited Bertillon to try out his method on a corpse that had been pulled out of the river; the man had been shot. The inspector may have intended the challenge as a joke, hoping to see the aloof Bertillon retching as he tried to measure a two-month-old corpse. He was disappointed. Bertillon measured the length and width of the head, the middle finger, the height and the length of forearm – other measurements were impossible, but these were enough. Within minutes, Bertillon had found the five measurements on a file card; the man had been arrested 12 months earlier for violent assault. And now the inspector knew his identity, he was able to trace his associates – and arrest the man who had shot him and thrown him into the river after a quarrel about a debt.

By 1888, Bertillon's method had proved itself so successful that a new Department of Judicial Identity was founded at the Préfecture. Bertillon, naturally, was its head. It might have been founded earlier if Bertillon had been a more popular man. But he was irritable and despotic. The truth was that he was by temperament a scientist; he would have been happier in a laboratory or a research institute rather than a police headquarters; police work bored him, and he adjusted himself to it by a formidable effort of will. His increasing fame was a compensation, but he never reconciled himself to being a mere hunter of criminals.

It was in the year 1892, nine years after his first success, that his name became known throughout France. The case was that of a notorious anarchist named Ravachol, perhaps the most celebrated French criminal since Lacenaire.

The anarchists were idealists who believed that the perfect society could be achieved simply by abolishing all authority, and allowing everyone to do as they liked; they believed implicitly in the fundamental goodness of human nature; their prophets were Pierre Proudhon, Michael Bakunin, and Prince Peter Kropotkin, who had written a book arguing, in the face of all the zoological evidence, that animals live by 'mutual aid', and that if human beings could get rid of their law-givers and soldiers and policemen, human beings could do the same. Understandably, every law-giver, soldier and policeman regarded this as a piece of outrageous nonsense. Proudhon believed that the millennium would come about simply through reason – men of good will would *see* that a 'stateless society' was the answer. Karl Marx and his disciples disagreed; they believed that the revolution would come about when the industrial proletariat recognized its own power and decided to take over. Marx's ideas prevailed in the Paris Commune of 1871, which ended in the death of thousands of 'idealists' at the hands of the police and the military. Then came the Third Republic and a new age of prosperity, the age of Offenbach and Maupassant and Mallarmé, symbolized by the sunlit canvases of the Impressionists; the French, as a nation, rejected these political ideas with horror. Their views were confirmed when, in 1881, Tsar Alexander II of Russia, the man who had tried to liberalize his backward country, was blown up by an anarchist's bomb. In Chicago in May 1886, an anarchist bomb killed seven policemen; eight anarchists were condemned to death. The bourgeoisie might be contented with the age of the cancan, but the overcrowded and underfed poor dreamed of social justice. Anarchist leaders like Reclus and Malatesta were continually in and out of prison.

On May Day 1891, an anarchist demonstration at Clichy was charged by the police. Three anarchist leaders were arrested and beaten up, and two of them were sentenced to terms of imprisonment. Six months later, the home of the presiding judge was wrecked by a bomb, and soon after that, the home of the prosecuting counsel (who had demanded the death sentence). A police spy reported that the man behind the bombings was a teacher at the Technical School in St-Denis called Chaumartin. When arrested, he confessed to planning the bombings, but said they had been carried out by a fanatical anarchist named Léger. Further investigation revealed that Léger was a wanted revolutionary called Ravachol, who was described as a muscular man in his 20s with a sallow, bony face and a consumptive look. A massive police hunt began. Ravachol's real name was François Koenigstein, and he had been arrested in 1891, suspected of the murder of an old miser and his housekeeper in the Forez Mountains, but he had broken away from his captors. In July 1891, two women who ran a hardware store in St-Étienne had been killed with a hammer in the course of robbery; Ravachol was again suspected.

On the evening of the explosion at the house of the prosecuting attorney, a sallow young man with a scar on his left hand dined at the Restaurant Véry in the boulevard Magenta, and talked to a waiter named Lhérot about the explosion, which had taken place only a short time earlier; he also expressed anarchist opinions. When the same young man returned two days later, the waiter noticed the scar – which had been mentioned in police descriptions of Ravachol – and told the proprietor, who notified the police. Ravachol fought like a man possessed. He was eventually subdued – with a certain brutality – and taken to the Préfecture, where Bertillon was summoned to take his 'measurements'. When Bertillon announced that he had to begin by photographing him, Ravachol replied with the French equivalent of 'over my dead body'.

'Why?' asked Bertillon, 'It's only my job.'

'With a face like this?' It was true that, with his swollen lips and bruised and torn cheek, he was scarcely recognizable. Bertillon said courteously:

'You are right. We will put it off until later.'

A few days later, Ravachol sat perfectly still and allowed himself to be measured and photographed. And Bertillon sent him a mounted copy of the picture. Ravachol, who hated everything to do with the law, later remarked:

'That Bertillon is a gentleman.'

But, gentleman or not, Bertillon was certainly bad news for Ravachol. His records revealed that Ravachol had been arrested earlier for smuggling and burglary, under the name of Koenigstein. That meant that he was probably the Koenigstein wanted for the murder of the old miser and the two women, as well as forcing his way into a funeral vault and robbing the corpse. Ravachol indignantly denied this before his Paris judges, and read aloud a statement about his anarchist ideals; recalling the previous bombings, the court treated him with nervous respect. But when Ravachol appeared in Montbrison, charged with the grave robbery and murders, the judge was unimpressed, and sentenced him to death. And, to the dismay of the anarchist movement, Ravachol confessed that he was Koenigstein and that he had committed the crimes he was charged with. The idealistic anarchist was a grave-robber and murderer of helpless old people. Kropotkin and Malatasta denounced Ravachol as an *'opéra-bouffe* revolutionary'. There had been some general sympathy for Ravachol when it had been learned that he had taken to crime in order to feed his family, after he and his brother had been dismissed from their jobs for their political opinions; this sympathy now evaporated. When Ravachol went to his death crying: 'Goodbye, you pigs! Long live anarchy!', there was general relief. In the meantime, the restaurant where he had been arrested had been blown up by a bomb, and the proprietor and one of the customers killed . . .

Only Bertillon came out of the affair with credit. He had shown no bourgeois antipathy for the revolutionary, yet in the course of doing his job, he had revealed him to be an ordinary criminal. The case made Bertillon's name famous all over France.

5

Yet, at the moment of his greatest triumph, Bertillon's achievement was about to be undermined. The cause: the rise of a more efficient system of identification known as fingerprinting. As long ago as the 1820s, a professor of anatomy named Johann Purkinje had pointed out that everyone's fingerprints are different, and suggested a crude method of classification. But in 1858, an Indian Civil Servant named William Herschel had asked a contractor with whom he was concluding a friendly agreement to sign the back of the contract with a print of his hand.

Two years later, when he was a magistrate near Calcutta, Herschel found himself confronted with the problem of how to prevent illiterate pensioners from coming back twice for their government pensions. His solution was to make them sign by pressing a finger dipped in ink on the receipt. The cheating immediately ceased. And in 1877, Herschel wrote a letter to the Inspector-General of Bengal prisons outlining his ideas on fingerprinting.

At this time, a Scottish doctor named Henry Faulds who was living in Tokyo, and teaching physiology to medical students at the Tsukiji Hospital, noted the fingermarks on Japanese pottery, and began studying the 'whorls' known as papillary lines. Two years later, Faulds used his knowledge of fingerprints to clear a suspected burglar. The police, who knew of his interest in fingerprints, told him that a thief had left sooty fingerprints on a whitewashed wall near Faulds's home. They arrested a man soon after, and the conscientious Faulds decided to test his theory that fingerprints could be used to identify criminals; he asked permission to take the accused man's fingerprints. To his surprise, they were quite different from those on the wall, and Faulds pointed out that they must have the wrong man. A few days later they arrested the man whose fingerprints were found on the wall, and who proved to be the burglar. In October 1880, Faulds wrote a letter to the scientific journal *Nature* about his theory of the use of fingerprints to identify criminals. Herschel, who was now in retirement in England, read the letter, and wrote to *Nature* describing how he had first used fingerprints for identification in 1858. Faulds was enraged. He was a highly aggressive man, and it seemed to him that Herschel was simply trying to steal the credit for his discovery. He dashed off dozens of letters to various public figures and scientists, including Charles Darwin, and even to the Parisian Prefect of Police, the same Louis Andrieux who had snubbed Bertillon in the previous year. (Andrieux; of course, ignored the letter.) After all this activity, Faulds embarked for England, determined to assert his priority in the face of this impostor.

Fortune was not with him – as indeed it seldom is with paranoid individuals whose driving force is a sense of their own importance. Back in England he became a police surgeon, and did his best to interest Scotland Yard in fingerprinting; but he allowed initial failures to embitter him. This in turn made him unpopular, and may explain why, when a distinguished scientist asked the editor of *Nature* to help him track down the founders of fingerprinting, they sent him only the address of William Herschel.

The scientist was 66-year-old Sir Francis Galton, a cousin of Charles Darwin, who had been in his time a sportsman, explorer, meteorologist and psychologist. Galton might be regarded as another disciple of

Quételet, for he was also obsessed with collecting statistics on the human faculties and attributes – for example, he once went to the trouble of collecting data on the distribution of beauty in the British Isles. In 1884 he had set up an 'anthropometric laboratory' to study such statistics as the strength, height, size, and acuteness of the senses of large numbers of people. And among the things he studied were fingerprints. In 1888, the year Bertillon was appointed chief of the Department of Judicial Identity in Paris, Galton was asked to deliver a lecture at the Royal Institution about *bertillonage,* and with his usual thoroughness, he went to Paris to study it at first hand. Bertillon obligingly demonstrated. Galton was impressed; but it also struck him as too complicated. Fingerprints, he saw, would constitute a far more straightforward method of identifying a criminal. He recalled the correspondence in *Nature* of eight years earlier – one of Galton's most amazing characteristics was his cross-indexing memory. The editor sent him Herschel's address, and Galton hurried to Littlemore, near Oxford, to see him. Herschel was only too delighted at this sign of interest. His original letter to the Inspector of Prisons in Bengal had met with a cautiously polite response that revealed unmistakably that the inspector thought the Indian climate had affected Herschel's mind. Now an eminent man of science was showing interest, Herschel unhesitatingly handed over all his material.

Galton's first task was to make quite sure that fingerprints are unique – or at least, that duplication is rare. It took three years of careful study to assure himself that, in fact, no fingerprint is identical with that of another person. That was a marvellously promising beginning. But it would obviously be quite useless unless he could find some convenient method of classifying them. Professor Purkinje had devised such a method in 1823, but it was complicated, with its spirals, ellipses, double whorls and so on. But Galton eventually perceived a less complicated possibility. Most fingerprints are centred around a triangular shape, which Galton called the delta (whose Greek sign is a triangle). In 1891, Galton published a paper on fingerprints in *Nature,* in which he acknowledged his debt to Herschel. The immediate result was a letter from Faulds claiming that *he* was the true inventor of fingerprint identification – which happened to be untrue; Faulds was only the first to apply it to police work. Galton ignored this, since he felt that questions of priority are of no importance in science. And he went on to write the first book on fingerprinting in the following year.

The Home Secretary, Herbert Asquith, was at this time giving urgent consideration to the question of introducing *bertillonage* into England, since Scotland Yard's criminal identification system was as appallingly inefficient as that of the Sûreté had been before Bertillon. He was on the point of giving the notion his support when someone handed him Galton's book on fingerprints. This led him to decide to postpone the decision until both systems could be studied. In the typical English manner, a committee was appointed. It was headed by a Home Office official named Charles Edward Troup. Its other two members were Major Arthur Griffiths – whose *Mysteries of Police and Crime* is still the finest textbook on crime in nineteenth-century Europe – and Sir Melville Macnaghten, who had become Assistant Commissioner of Police a few months after the notorious Jack the Ripper murders of 1888. The Troup Committee was deeply impressed by the simplicity of fingerprinting, and dismayed that Galton had not yet devised a workable system of classification. They went to Paris, where Bertillon received them with hospitable enthusiasm, took them on a tour of the Paris underworld, and demonstrated his latest devices for scientific crime fighting. The Committee was impressed, yet was still unable to make up its mind. Other countries had no such misgivings. In Austria, the 'father of criminology', Hans Gross, urged the introduction of *bertillonage* in his great textbook *Criminal Investigation,* and ten years later, in 1898, this came about. It had already been introduced into Germany in the previous year. And it had actually reached Argentina as early as 1891, when the La Plata Chief of Police, Guillermo Nuñez, read about it and ordered a subordinate to introduce the system.

The subordinate was a Dalmatian named Juan Vucetich, who had been in Argentina a mere seven years; in 1891 he was the head of the Statistical Bureau of the La Plata police. In no time at all, he and his assistants were measuring criminals with the same efficiency as Bertillon's team. And at this point he saw an article on Galton's work in the *Revue Scientifique;* it was by H. de Varigny, and admitted that Galton had not solved the basic problem of classification. This was an irresistible challenge to Vucetich, who hurled himself at the problem with all the enthusiasm of a brilliant novice. As a practical police officer, he was not too concerned with devising the perfect system; all he wanted was something he could put to immediate use. Like Galton, he realized that the triangle, or delta, was the essential feature of a fingerprint. Like Galton, he also recognized that there were four basic types: those with no triangle, those with a triangle on the right, those with a triangle on the left, and those with two triangles. He labelled these 1, 2, 3, and 4 (using the letters A, B, C, and D for thumbs). So if he fingerprinted a criminal, the classification on the card might read: B, 3, 2, 2, 4. These were easy to arrange in filing drawers, beginning with the letter denoting the thumb.

Vucetich also set up Bertillon systems in other cities, but he lacked enthusiasm, for, like Galton, he felt that fingerprinting would suffice. His chiefs were less certain. But in July 1892, Vucetich's faith in fingerprinting was triumphantly vindicated. In June, a double murder had occurred in the small coastal town of Necochea, in the province of Buenos Aires. The victims were two young children whose mother, 26-year-old Francisca Rojas, was unmarried. They were lying in bed, their skulls smashed, and Francisca denounced a farm-worker named Velasquez, who had been importuning her to marry him. She claimed that she had found the door open when she came home from work, and that Velasquez had rushed past her; she had found the two children, a boy of six and a girl of four, dead in their bloodstained bed.

Velasquez was arrested, and interrogated by Police Chief Alvarez. He agreed that he had threatened violence when she had told him she loved someone else, but insisted that these were merely empty words. In his frustration, Alvarez turned to the well-tried method of the Middle Ages, and had Velasquez subjected to a 'third degree'. And when that failed to work, he reverted to another ancient practice, and had Velasquez tied up and laid on the bed next to the dead children. The next morning, Velasquez still denied it, and Alvarez began to experience a suspicion that he might be telling the truth. Nevertheless, for good measure, he had him tortured for another week. And when the battered and bruised farm-worker still insisted on his innocence, Alvarez began to give careful consideration to the alternative theory that Francisca had killed her own children. He had learned that she had a younger lover, who had been heard to remark that he would marry her if it were not for her illegitimate brats. Still operating according to some medieval police manual, he tried terrifying Francisca by spending a night outside her miserable hut, moaning and muttering threats in an attempt to convince her that he was an avenging spirit. Francisca was made of stronger stuff, and the next morning looked as if she had enjoyed a good night's sleep.

Now Alvarez did what he should have done in the first place – he spent some time in the hut, when Francisca was at work, searching for clues. The quest was unsuccessful until a beam of sunlight came in through the window, and illuminated a dark smudge on the thin, cheap wood of the door. Alvarez peered at it through a magnifying glass; it was undoubtedly a fingerprint, and an unusually good one. He hurried out to borrow a saw, removed the square of wood containing the print, and took it back to the station. Then he had Francisca brought in, and her prints taken with an ink pad. The magnifying glass left him in no doubt: the bloody print was of her right thumb.

'You say you didn't touch the bodies of the children?'

'No.' She had no idea what was coming, or would doubtless have changed her story.

'Then how did this thumbprint get onto your door?'

When he showed her the print under the magnifying glass, and placed the inked thumbprint beside it, even Francisca could see they were identical. She broke down and confessed: she had killed the children with a rock, then taken it and thrown it into the well. After that she had washed her hands. But she had failed to notice the bloodstain on the door. Even if she *had* noticed it, she would have thought it unimportant; after all, it could have been left by the man she accused ... Francisca Rojas was tried and found guilty, although no record exists of her sentence.

Vucetich, of course, could hardly claim any credit for this success, since his classification system had had nothing to do with it. But then, Alvarez would not have known about fingerprints except for a conversation with Vucetich. So in the history books, Vucetich receives the credit for the solution of the first fingerprint murder.

6

The case brought Vucetich the same kind of celebrity in Argentina that the Ravachol case had brought Bertillon in France. But in the long run, this newspaper publicity was not to his advantage. Bertillon's fame brought him a certain independence from official interference, but in a Latin American country, with its tradition of authority, Vucetich was still regarded as a minor official whose job was to obey his superiors. His fingerprint system soon proved its value – within a short time he had identified a suicide and a murderer – but his superiors objected to his insistence that fingerprinting was a better system than *bertillonage*, and in the year after the Rojas case, they actually ordered him to abandon his own preferred method. He retaliated by writing two books on identification in which he argued the superior merits of fingerprinting, and was threatened with dismissal.

Moreover, he incurred the hostility of Bertillon. Bertillon was never, as the legend has it, hostile to fingerprinting; on the contrary, he quickly added it to *bertillonage,* leading to an equally inaccurate legend that he was the founder of fingerprinting. But he resented the suggestion that fingerprinting made his original system redundant – resented it the more, no doubt, because his own intellectual acuity must have made him aware it was true. When Vucetich went to Paris in 1913, and hastened to call on Bertillon – looking forward to a profound discussion of criminal identification – Bertillon glared at him and said coldly: *vous avez essayé de me faire beaucoup de mal* ('You have tried to do me a great deal of harm') and slammed the door in his face. Poor Vucetich was not a lucky man. Three years later, in 1916, it looked as if he had achieved the major triumph of his lifetime when the Argentine government decided to set up a General Register of Identification that would involve fingerprinting everybody in the country. But there were riots, and the law was repealed. All records made so far were destroyed. Vucetich retired to the country in disgust, and died at the age of 67 in 1925. Bertillon had predeceased him in 1914. Yet by that time, 'dactyloscopy' (as he called fingerprinting) had triumphed; as early as 1896 it had replaced *bertillonage* in Argentina, and in the first decade of the twentieth century, spread to every major country in South America.

But why did Vucetich's system establish itself so triumphantly in Argentina when, at the same time, Sir Francis Galton was confessing his inability to devise a satisfactory system in London? The answer is simple. Vucetich was a practical policeman whose only aim was to arrest criminals; it did not matter to him if his system was crude and imperfect. But Galton was a scientist who knew that fingerprinting would eventually have to be applied to millions of criminals. His problem was to devise a system that would enable a policeman to locate a particular fingerprint in a few minutes, even in a file containing a million. And anyone who looks at an impression of a fingerprint will see why it was so difficult. All fingerprints have the same basic 'whirlpool' or eddy information. Unfortunately, apart from that they seem to be as different from one another as clouds in the sky. It is easy enough to look at two fingerprints and see they are identical, as Alvarez did with Francisca Rojas'. But how would you *describe* the difference between two prints – if, for example, you had to do it over the telephone? One obvious method would be by identifying various features – describing different types of 'whirlpool' (circles, ellipses, etc.), counting the lines in them, mentioning small lines due to creases in the skin, and so on. But it would be easy to end up with 50 such features. In that case, how would they be filed and made easy of access? No wonder Bertillon thought that his system would never be replaced by the fingerprint – his 11 basic measurements were easy to file in numerical order. Of course, it was true that, as the files swelled, it might take an hour to locate a particular card; but that simply couldn't be helped.

At the time Vucetich was setting up the first *bertillonage* system in South America, a British Civil Servant had decided to do the same thing in India. Edward Richard Henry looked every inch the English gentleman, with his classic features and military moustache. He had been in India since the age of 23, and by the time he was 41, in 1891, he was the Inspector-General of Police in Nepal. He introduced a simplified version of anthropometry into Nepal – using 6 measurements instead of 11 – and it soon proved its value in picking out men with previous convictions. But, like Vucetich, he soon came to feel that it was too complicated, and too liable to be misused by lazy and incompetent measuring clerks who didn't care whether a man's arm was 789 centimetres or 790. At this point he read Galton's book on fingerprints, published in the previous year, and saw that if he could solve the classification problem, he would be able to virtually eliminate human error – a fingerprint is quicker and easier to take than a series of measurements.

On leave in England he called on Galton, who unhesitatingly placed all his material at Henry's disposal. And, back in Calcutta, Henry pored over Galton's photographs of different patterns, and realized why he had admitted defeat. (The Troup Committee had settled for a typical British compromise – a mixture of *bertillonage* and fingerprints.) Like Galton and Vucetich, he could easily distinguish four basic types of 'whirlpool' (in fact, Henry decided there were five – two types of arches, two types of loops, and whorls). But how could these be classified and easily identified?

It was on a railway journey in December 1896 that Henry had his sudden insight into the solution. If you look at the top of your fingers or thumbs, you will see parallel lines; further down, towards the centre of the top joint, these lines turn into various types of eddies and whirlpools. These eddies are in the form of long loops, which 'trail off' to the right or left. So inevitably, between the loop and the arch of parallel lines above and around it, there is bound to be a 'leftover' space which is triangular in shape. These are what Galton called the deltas. The only fingerprint that does not have a delta is the simple 'arch', whose lines trail off equally to the right and left, leaving no 'leftover' space.

What Henry saw on that railway journey was that the solution of his problem lay in the deltas, with their convenient triangular shape, which lends itself to geometrical measurement. These deltas, wrote Henry, 'may be formed by either (a) the bifurcation of a single ridge, or (b) by the abrupt divergence of two ridges that had hitherto run side by side'. All Henry had to do was to establish the limits of the triangle – what he called the 'inner terminus' and the 'outer terminus'. A line could be drawn between these two termini, and the number of papillary lines that it intersects counted with a needle. And this number was the core of Henry's classification system.

So, confronted by an unknown fingerprint, the detective had only to decide which of the five basic types it belonged to – loops, arches, whorls – and then count the number of lines, and he had the basic 'formula' for any fingerprint. Of course, there were many unusual cases to be taken into account – so-called 'accidentals', for example, that defy all the rules – but a little ingenuity could absorb them into the system. And the vast majority of fingerprints belong to the simple loop-and-delta system.

Why had Galton and Vucetich not grasped this obvious solution? The answer, presumably, is that it was not obvious until Henry pointed it out. At all events, the Governor-General of India quickly saw its merits, and in July 1897, decided that there was no point in wasting more time on Bertillon's system; fingerprinting became the sole means of criminal identification.

In the following year, Henry's new system demonstrated its value in a murder case. In August 1897, the manager of a tea plantation in the remote Jalpaiguri district of Bengal was found in bed with his throat cut; the safe had been robbed and the servants had all fled – no doubt worried in case the police decided to revert to the medieval method of obtaining a confession. The manager's wallet had also been rifled, and on a calendar in it, the police noted a smudged fingerprint in blood. Henry asked the police to take the fingerprints of everyone on the estate, including the murdered man, and to send them to him, together with the wallet. The print turned out to be that of a right thumb, and no such print could be found among those that had been taken. Henry enquired if the manager had any enemies, and someone recollected that, two years before, a servant named Charan had sworn revenge against him. Charan had been arrested for theft and sentenced to prison in Calcutta. 'Had his fingerprints been taken at the time of his arrest?' asked Henry. They checked the 'Bertillon card', and discovered that it contained Charan's right thumbprint. It matched the one found on the calendar, and an order was sent out for Charan's arrest. It took some weeks, but eventually, he appeared in court, charged with murder and theft. But the jury (known as 'assessors') were thoroughly unhappy with the fingerprint evidence. It was not that they did not believe that Charan had committed the murder – only that they would have preferred some 'stronger' piece of evidence, such as a confession. They reached an absurd compromise: Charan was found guilty of robbery, but not of murder.

But one thing was clear: Henry had tracked down a murderer who had otherwise left no clue. England's equivalent of Bertillon could not be left in an outpost of the empire. On 31 May 1901, Henry took up a new position as Assistant Commissioner at Scotland Yard, and in the following July, he created the Central Fingerprint Branch.

The statistics quickly proved the soundness of his judgement. In 1901, 503 suspects had been identified as previous offenders through the use of *bertillonage*. In the following year, when the fingerprint method came into full operation, 1,722 suspects had been identified. Fingerprinting was more than three times as efficient as *bertillonage*.

7

In Paris, the Sûreté heard the news of the new fingerprint bureau with scepticism. They simply failed to see how a fingerprint could be as reliably classified as Bertillon's measurements. Only one man did not share their doubts: Bertillon himself. Since 1900 he had been adding fingerprints to the other information on his file cards.

On the morning of 17 October 1902, Bertillon was summoned by an examining magistrate named Joliot to the scene of a crime. It had taken place in a luxurious flat in the rue Faubourg Saint-Honoré; the victim was the valet of a wealthy surgeon-dentist named Alaux. The body was sitting in a chair in the office, the legs outstretched, the shirt tails pulled out of the trousers. The valet, Joseph Reibel, had been manually strangled. The confusion in the room – overturned furniture – suggested a struggle, and the open cabinet and desk drawers indicated that robbery had been the motive. But closer examination threw doubt on this notion. The keys of the desk and cabinet were on the shelf, and very little had been taken.

Bertillon set up his camera on a tripod; the legs of the tripod could be extended for nine or ten feet, so that the camera could take an overhead picture of a crime. An assistant burnt magnesium ribbon to illuminate the scene as Bertillon photographed it.

In the drawing-room next door, the same procedure was repeated. Here there was less disorder, but the glass panel of a cabinet had been broken. The burglar had apparently cut himself – the shards were smeared with blood. As a police inspector was about to pick one of them up, Bertillon stopped him sharply: 'Don't touch that.' He used a pocket handkerchief to pick up one of the shards. 'You see? Fingerprints.' The thief had left an almost perfect set of fingerprints in the blood. Bertillon packed the glass with extreme care, in case he smudged them, and took them back to his laboratory. There he photographed them by a process he had developed himself – against a black background, with a powerful arc lamp within a few inches of the fingerprint. The result was an excellent photograph of a thumb and three fingers.

Now, for Bertillon, came the difficult part of his task. He had a few thousand fingerprints on file, but they were not classified under the Henry system; they were merely included on the usual Bertillon file cards. So there was nothing for it but to go right through all his file cards with a magnifying glass. It must have been a discouraging task, since there was no guarantee that the 'burglar' had ever been 'bertillonized'. In fact, by now Bertillon was fairly sure it was not a burglar. Only 1,600 francs had disappeared, hardly enough to justify a murder. That meant that the 'burglar' had deliberately rifled the place to mislead the police. In fact, the dead man's employer, M. Alaux, was fairly certain that his valet was homosexual, and that the murder had been committed by his lover, who was known only as Georges. And if Georges had no previous police record . . .

He had. At the end of three days, Bertillon experienced once more the elation he had felt when he found the file card of Dupont, alias Martin, 20 years earlier. The card belonged to a swindler called Henri-Léon Scheffer, 25 years old. In fact, the police had already been observing his movements, and they tracked him down with the aid of correspondence addressed to him in Marseilles. And while the Marseilles police were searching for him, Scheffer walked into a gendarmerie and gave himself up; he was at the end of his resources, financially and emotionally. He confessed to murdering his lover, and to attempting to make the crime look like a burglary that had gone wrong.

Nevertheless, as Bertillon's biographer points out, the inventor of anthropometry deserves the credit for being the first person in Europe to solve a murder by means of a fingerprint. Yet the Scheffer case should also have convinced Bertillon that his system was greatly inferior to fingerprinting, for *bertillonage* was only of use once the criminal was in the hands of the police; the fingerprint could identify a criminal who was still at large. Why was he not convinced? The answer is obvious. Bertillon's three-day search should have shown him that it would be sensible to adopt the Henry system of classification. But there would be no point in *adding* this to his own system, for that would be mere duplication. The sensible course would have been to scrap *bertillonage* and rely on fingerprints. And for Bertillon, that would have amounted to a confession of failure. The animosity he showed towards Vucetich revealed a determined refusal to recognize this failure. Yet the persistent ill health of his later years may amount to a subconscious acknowledgement of the truth.

The first murder to be solved by a fingerprint in Great Britain occurred in Deptford, south-east London, in 1905. But fingerprints had already proved their worth on Derby Day, 1902. Ever since the first Derby on Epsom Downs in 1780, the race course had also been the haunt of every pickpocket from Birmingham to Brighton. In his auto-biography *Days of My Years,* Sir Melville Macnaghten describes how Scotland Yard's fingerprint experts were on the course all day, taking the fingerprints of arrested men; that evening, they went through the files, and discovered that 29 out of 54 pickpockets were previous offenders. And when the men appeared before the magistrates the next morning, the records and photographs of the 29 were handed to the magistrates, who imposed sentences that were twice as long as on first offenders.

The first prisoner on this occasion gave his name as Green of Gloucester, and assured the interrogating magistrate that he had never been in trouble before . . . But up jumped the Chief Inspector, in answer to a question as to whether 'anything was known', and begged their worships to look at the papers and photograph, which proved the innocent to be Benjamin Brown of

Birmingham, with some ten convictions to his discredit. 'Bless the finger-prints,' said Benjamin, with an oath; 'I knew they'd do me in!'

In the same year, the fingerprint record led to the arrest of a burglar named Harry Jackson, who had made the mistake of touching some freshly painted wood when he burgled a house in Denmark Hill and stole some billiard balls. Detective Sergeant Collins, of the fingerprint bureau, appeared in court on 2 September 1902, to present the evidence. He had already coached the barrister, Richard Muir. And it was Muir who succeeded in convincing a British jury that a fingerprint was sufficient evidence on which to convict a man; Jackson received a seven-year sentence.

At 7.15 on the morning of 27 March 1905, a small girl playing on the pavement outside a shop in Deptford saw the door open slowly, and a man with a bloody face looking out. Then he closed the door again. The small girl, accustomed to the sight of blood (Deptford had several slaughter houses) paid no attention. At half past eight, the shop assistant arrived, and was surprised to find the door still locked; he went off to fetch the landlord, a Mr Chapman, who lived nearby. The boy clambered through a back window. The shopkeeper, whose name was Farrow, was found lying dead in the back parlour. Mrs Farrow, was lying in a bloodstained bed, still alive but unconscious. By half past nine, Scotland Yard men were at the scene. As the news of the murder spread, a milkman came forward to say that he had seen two men leaving the shop at about 7.15.

It was not difficult to reconstruct the crime. Medical evidence showed that the Farrows had been violently attacked around seven o'clock that morning; the two intruders had been wearing black stocking masks, which they left behind. The door had not been forced, and Farrow was partly dressed, suggesting that he had come downstairs in answer to a knock, expecting an early customer – perhaps a painter on his way to work, since he sold paint and oil. The men had attacked him with a jemmy or some other heavy instrument, then gone upstairs and attacked his wife. After that they had forced the cashbox, which was found under the bed. Local rumour had it that the Farrows kept a large sum of money in the house. They were mistaken; the shop takings – less than £10 a week – were banked regularly.

One of the killers had left a vital clue – his bloody thumbprint in the lid of the cashbox. It was found by Sir Melville Macnaghten himself.

Macnaghten had the box sent straight to the Yard's fingerprint department. Then he took the fingerprints of the shop-boy and Mr and Mrs Farrow. (It was the first time the prints of a corpse had been taken in England.) A check in the fingerprint record – now amounting to 80,000 or so – failed to identify the bloody thumbprint.

Straightforward detective work was making more progress. Two brothers, Alfred and Edward Stratton, were known to the local police as unsavoury characters, but had not yet acquired criminal records. They were no longer to be found in their usual haunts. The younger brother Alfred had a mistress, and when the police located her, she showed signs of a recent beating. And she was sufficiently resentful about Alfred to tell the police that he had left via the window in the early hours of Monday morning – the day of the murder – and returned by the same route after dawn, warning her to say that he had spent the whole night with her. The landlady of the elder Stratton was able to tell the police that she had once come upon black stocking masks hidden under his mattress. Macnaghten gave orders for the arrest of both brothers. When they were taken into custody a week later, Mrs Farrow had died in hospital, turning it into a double murder inquiry.

At the Tower Bridge police court, both brothers were noisy and abusive, and the magistrate was inclined to feel that there was almost no case against them. But he remanded them in custody for a week. Then the brothers were fingerprinted. That afternoon, the fingerprint expert came into Macnaghten's office saying: 'Good God, sir, I've found that the print on the cashbox corresponds exactly with the right thumb of Alfred Stratton.'

On 5 May 1905, the brothers appeared at the Old Bailey charged with murder. The prosecuting attorney was Richard Muir, the man who had succeeded in convicting the Denmark Hill burglar, Jackson. Detective Sergeant (now Inspector) Collins was the fingerprint expert for the prosecution. And Muir was startled to see that the chief expert for the defence was none other than Henry Faulds, the Scot who had discovered fingerprinting in Tokyo. In the intervening two and a half decades, Faulds had become increasingly embittered as his contribution was ignored, and his noisy insistence on his priority had alienated most of the other experts. And sitting beside Faulds, Muir was greatly intrigued to recognize Dr J. G. Garson, a man who had developed his own system for classifying fingerprints, but also failed to achieve recognition when Henry's greatly superior system was adopted. These were the men who had briefed the defence.

And in the cross-examination of Inspedor Collins by the defence, it soon became clear what advice they had given. The defence argument was that Alfred Stratton's thumbprint and the bloody thumbprint on the cashbox were *not* identical; there were various points of difference. That, replied Collins, was natural, because different pressures cause various discrepancies. And he proved his point beyond doubt by taking the prints of the juryrnen several times over, and showing that the same differences occurred.

The defence case was shattered. But they had one slight hope. Dr Garson might still succeed in throwing some doubt into the minds of the jury. Dr Garson was called to the stand. Muir was ready for him. He held out a letter. Had Dr Garson written him this letter, offering to testify on behalf of the prosecution? Dr Garson reddened, and admitted that he had. 'But I am an independent witness . . .' The icy voice of the judge interrupted him. 'I would say a completely untrustworthy one. Kindly leave the witness box.'

Both brothers were condemned to death. And the evidence of the bloodstained fingerprint became front page news throughout the British Isles.

8

By the end of the first decade of the twentieth century, most countries in Europe had adopted fingerprinting, including Russia. The main exception, of course, was France, where Bertillon still reigned as the giant of criminology. It seems sad that his obsessive nature found it impossible to accept the replacement of anthropometry with a good grace – after all, it had been the very foundation of scientific criminology, and the fact it was being superseded was in no way to Bertillon's discredit. But Bertillon was irritable and thin-skinned, and he declined to accept relegation to the ranks of 'interesting pioneers'.

Two cases helped to undermine Bertillon's standing with his countrymen. The first became so notorious that it was enough to refer to it simply as 'l'Affaire'. This was the accusation of spying that led to the imprisonment of Captain Alfred Dreyfus in 1895 – a time when Bertillon's reputation was at its height. It began in September 1894, when a French intelligence officer named Henry managed to get possession of a letter offering to send various secret army documents to the German embassy – a cleaner had retrieved it from the waste-paper basket of the German military attaché. On the strength of the handwriting, the author of the letter was identified as a Jewish captain, Alfred Dreyfus. And a chemist and handwriting expert named Gobert called on Bertillon soon after Dreyfus's arrest, and asked him to photograph the notorious letter, known as the *bordereau* (list). Bertillon was not a handwriting expert, but as a scientist, he felt he was qualified to pronounce upon it. His first Holmesian deduction was that since the *bordereau* was written on thin onion paper, the writing on it had probably been traced. But why trace it? In order to disguise the handwriting. Close examination of the *bordereau* confirmed his opinion; certain words and syllables were written *identically,* while real handwriting had many minor variations. Moreover, the spacing between the words was also identical, which was equally unusual. But a similar method of exact spacing is used on military maps. That, to Bertillon, suggested that the writer was a staff officer – as Dreyfus was.

It was a pity that Bertillon's ingenuity should have led him to formulate this complex and unlikely theory, for his first opinion was that the *bordereau* was not in Dreyfus' handwriting. His tracing-paper theory led him to change his mind; if the handwriting differed from that of Dreyfus, it was because Dreyfus had traced someone else's handwriting – probably that of his brother Mathieu. But he had still been unable to suppress certain basic characteristics of his own handwriting . . . This was the theory that Bertillon argued at Dreyfus's trial, at the same time producing a convincing forgery of the *bordereau* by the very method he believed Dreyfus had used. And the evidence of the celebrated Bertillon undoubtedly played a major role in the condemnation of Alfred Dreyfus, and his sentence of deportation to Devil's Island.

But the Dreyfus case refused to die; France divided into Dreyfusards and anti-Dreyfusards, that is to say into Liberals and Conservatives. A Major Picquart, who had taken over the job of the man responsible for Dreyfus' arrest, became convinced that the real author of the *bordereau* was a ne'er-do-well called Major Esterhazy. Picquart was 'removed' and sent to Tunisia. The case erupted again when Picquart's new evidence was leaked to the Press. Esterhazy was court-martialled but acquitted. Letters incriminating Dreyfus were forged by French Intelligence; Major Henry, the original discoverer of the *bordereau,* virtually admitted his guilt by committing suicide. The scandal was tremendous. Dreyfus was retried, and this time no one had any doubt that he would be acquitted. And when he was found guilty yet again, public outrage exploded. The forces of reaction were obviously using every dirty trick to suppress the truth. Much of the mud that was flung stuck to Bertillon. Cowed by the uproar, the government granted Dreyfus a 'pardon'. Still his supporters fought on for his total acquittal, and this finally came in 1906. But it was regarded not merely as an exoneration of Dreyfus, but as a condemnation of his 'enemies', including Bertillon. And although Bertillon continued to receive many official distinctions, his reputation was badly tarnished in the eyes of the general public.

Bertillon's second failure was on an altogether smaller scale, yet in the personal sense, was even more disastrous. On 21 August 1911, someone stole Leonardo's *Mona Lisa* from the Louvre. It should, of course, have been a total impossiblity, with so many guards; but it happened on a Monday, when the Louvre was closed to the public. The painting, which is on a panel, was housed in a case with a glass cover. This case was found, empty, on the service stairs.

Bertillon was immediately summoned, and careful examination revealed fingerprints. A fingerprint is made by sweat – that is to say, the skin's secretions which include fatty substances; this comes from sweat pores along the papillary ridges, and also from contact of the fingertips with parts of the body where there are sebaceous glands, such as the face. Latent or invisible prints on smooth surfaces can be made visible by dusting the surface with fine powder, such as talc, aluminium or lead powder. (On white surfaces, such as china, a black powder is used.) And when Bertillon dusted the glass with powder, he realized with delight that the thief had left behind a good set of finger-prints. And now if the thief happened to have a criminal record, it should be a matter of the utmost simplicity to identify him . . .

And if the theft had taken place in London or Berlin or Madrid, it would have been. But Bertillon's fingerprints were still unclassified. And since 1902, when he had solved the Scheffer case, he had accumulated more than 100,000 additional cards. So, in fact, it was an impossible task. Bertillon and his assistants searched for weeks and months – Bertillon was such an obsessive that he probably went through every card individually. But after a few hundred prints, the eyes grow tired, and the attention flags. Bertillon must have ended day after day in a state of exhausted defeat. Nothing could have brought home to him more clearly that his system was a waste of time, and that he should have adopted Henry's fingerprint classification, as improved by Inspector Collins.

Two years later, the thief was arrested in Florence. The police had been tipped off by an art dealer named Alfredo Geri, who had been offered the painting in a letter signed 'Leonard'. Leonard proved to be an Italian house painter named Vicenzo Perrugia, and he was carrying the *Mona Lisa* with him. His story of the theft caused astonishment, and some amusement at the expense of the Louvre authorities. The crime had not been planned. Perrugia had been a friend of a painter working in the Louvre, and the guards were familiar with him; they let him past without question. Finding himself quite alone in the Salon Carré with the famous painting, the temptation had been too much. He had simply lifted the case off the wall, walked down the service staircase, and extracted the painting, leaving his fingerprints on the glass. Then he had hidden the painting – which is small – beneath his smock and walked out unchallenged. For the next two years the *Mona Lisa* lay hidden under his bed.

But for Bertillon, the final bitterness must have been that he had Perrugia's card in his file, for Perrugia was a petty thief who had been arrested several times.

Significantly, it was in this year 1913 that Bertillon was found to be suffering from pernicious anaemia. It is hardly surprising that he was so rude to Vucetich when the Argentinian arrived at his door in that same year. He began suffering from permanent lassitude, and his room needed to be at a temperature that made his family perspire. A blood transfusion from his brother Georges caused a temporary improvement, but further transfusions became less and less effectual. When it was realized that he was dying, the government decided it was time to offer him the ultimate accolade, the Rosette of the Legion d'Honneur. But the old problem remained: his involvement in the Dreyfus case meant that such an award would still arouse controversy. The official who was assigned the task of approaching Bertillon had to explain, as tactfully as he could, that as much as the Republic would like to offer Bertillon the Rosette, there was still the delicate problem of the *bordereau*. Did Bertillon still believe that Dreyfus had written it? Although he was lying exhausted on a couch, all Bertillon's old pride and irritability surged up in him. He forced himself upright, glared at the official, and informed him in a cold voice that his views remained unchanged. The official hastened to take his leave . . . It is typical of Bertillon that in spite of all the evidence proving Dreyfus' innocence, he refused to change his views. It is interesting to speculate on what he might have said if he been alive in 1930, when publication of the papers of von Schwartzkoppen, the German military attaché to whom the *bordereau* was addressed, conclusively proved Dreyfus's innocence. But our knowledge of his character leaves little doubt that he would have refused to change his mind.

On 13 February 1914, Bertillon sank into a light coma, and died at 11 o'clock that evening. He was buried with national honours, and a vast crowd attended his funeral in Père-Lachaise. But everyone who was concerned with the advance of criminology in France must have heaved a sigh of relief. History could at last start moving forward again.

9

Perhaps the most eminent of these criminologists was Professor Alexandre Lacassagne, who had achieved sudden fame in 1889 through his remarkable work in identifying an unknown corpse as that of a man called Gouffé (see p. 180). Lacassagne, Professor of Forensic Medicine at Lyon, became in France what Sir Bernard Spilsbury later became in England, the supreme authority. But it was his assistant, Edmond Locard, who was to become France's greatest criminologist. Twenty years Bertillon's junior, Locard was an ardent admirer of that remarkable man of genius. But he quickly realized that the future of crirninal identification lay in fingerprinting, not anthropometry. And even while Bertillon was still alive, the young Locard (born 1877) was developing his own interesting extension of fingerprinting: poroscopy. Locard was the first to realize that the pores that lie along the ridges, between 9 and 18 per millimetre, are as individual as the fingerprint patterns themselves – that they are, in effect, a fingerprint within a fingerprint. Moreover, if a fingerprint is fragmentary, so that there are doubts about matching it, a few millimetres containing pores can still prove its identity beyond doubt. An enlarged photograph of a papillary ridge shows dozens of pores so close together that at a casual glance it looks like a piece of string. Locard's discovery was used for the first time in 1912 in Lyon. On 10 June, an apartment at 6 rue Centrale was burgled; about 400 francs (in those days, £20) and numerous jewels were taken. There were no clues, but a rosewood box that contained jewels revealed latent fingerprints. These were 'developed' with powder and their photographs enlarged. Now fortunately, Lacassagne and Locard had no objection whatever to fingerprinting, and the

Vucetich method was in use in the Laboratory of Police Techniques in Lyon, founded in 1910. So it took no time at all to match one of the fingerprints with those of a man called Boudet, who was a known burglar, and who usually operated with a companion called Simonin. Both were arrested, and some of the prints on the box were revealed to be those of Simonin. These included a palmprint. But the two burglars were far from stupid. They knew that fingerprint evidence was relatively new, and that a jury would be unwilling to convict on this evidence alone. And they knew that there *was* no other evidence – no witnesses, no clues that might support the fingerprint evidence. So they flatly refused to confess.

But Locard was determined to convince the jury. And when Boudet and Simonin appeared at the local assizes, he had made photographic enlargements of the prints that clearly showed all the pores. He explained to the jury that the arrangement of the pores was as individual as the print itself; they were patriotic enough to feel proud that this was a French discovery. Then he counted the pores on a fingerprint found on the rosewood box, and counted the pores on a fingerprint taken from Boudet – 955 on the same area of each. The jury was overwhelmed by the demonstration, and found the pair guilty; they were each 'sentenced to five years' hard labour.

1912 was a good year for Locard and poroscopy. In his great classic work *Traité de criminalistique* he mentions no fewer than seven cases solved by this means in 1912 and the following year. One is of particular interest in that the malefactor wore gloves when he broke into a bar and drank several bottles of wine, taking others with him. But the gloves had a hole in one fingertip – enough to provide a single print, and enough to identify the guilty merrymaker as one Sabot. The fingerprint was fragmentary, but the number of pores on the papillaries left no doubt that it was Sabot's.

One of Locard's oddest cases concerned a female pedlar named Léa Camelin, who boarded a train at Perrache, near Lyon, on 12 October 1929. This 39-year-old woman was taking a basket of feminine underwear, worth 3,000 francs, to a nearby market. A quarter of an hour after she had boarded the train, it stopped at a place called Brotteaux, and a passenger who went into her compartment found her lying with her head wrapped in a gag; the compartment smelt strongly of ether. He gave the alarm, and Mme Camelin was carried into a room on the station, where she was revived. Her story was that two men had burst into the compartment, and one had grabbed her arms while the other held a pad smelling of ether against her face. She had then lost consciousness. The men, she said, had taken her merchandise and about 200 francs.

The bottle that had contained the ether was lying in the compartment, and the police picked it up carefully and placed it in a box, which they sent to the Lyon Police Laboratory. Locard's assistant, Grangeversanne, examined it for fingerprints, and found there were a great many. But what baffled him was that they were all of the victim herself. And it was obvious that, if the bottle belonged to the robbers, she could not have touched it, since she was unconsious. Only one conclusion was possible; Mme Camelin had anaesthetized herself. Under interrogation, she broke down and confessed. She had planned to commit suicide, but was worried about the disgrace to her family. So she had decided to make it look like murder. She had planned the suicide carefully. The fact that she was known to be on her way to the market in Pont-d'Ain, and that she would be found without merchandise or money, would make it look as if she had been etherized and then robbed. Unfortunately for this ingenious scheme, she had forgotten that the train would stop at the next station . . .

As to *bertillonage,* it vanished almost instantaneously with the death of its founder. Within weeks of his death, at a police conference in Monaco – one of the few places that still clung to *bertillonage* – Bertillon's successor, David, proposed that fingerprinting should be adopted as the standard method of criminal identification throughout Europe.

10

There is a case for arguing that Mark Twain deserves to be remembered, together with Herschel and Faulds, as the discoverer of fingerprints. His book *Life on the Mississippi* came out in 1883, the year after Bertillon's first success in Paris, and long before any police force had even heard of fingerprint identification. But the book's thirty-first chapter contains an anecdote in which a dying man tells how he tracked down the murderers of his wife and child by means of a bloodstained thumbprint. 'When I was a youth, I knew an old Frenchman who had been a prison-keeper for 30 years, and he told me that there was one thing about a person which never changed from the cradle to the grave – the lines in the ball of the thumb; and he said these lines were never exactly alike in the thumbs of any two human beings.' Posing as a fortune-teller who uses thumbprints for divination, Karl Ritter takes the prints of the whole company of a US cavalry regiment, and identifies the two assassins. One of them he stabs through the heart on guard duty; the other he refuses to help when he finds him dying of suffocation in a Munich mortuary. It is an absurd and nasty little story, but a remarkable anticipation of a scientific discovery that was then known to less than half a dozen men. Eleven years later, in *Pudd'nhead Wilson,* Twain used fingerprints again in a tale of a Mississippi lawyer who solves the murder of a judge through bloodstained fingerprints on the handle of a knife. By that time, Police Chief Alvarez had solved the Rojas murder in Argentina by means of a fingerprint, but the news had still not percolated north to America.

In the United States the problems faced by the police were far more acute than in England or Argentina – not simply because it was a less law-abiding country – with its post-Civil War crime wave, its 'Wild West', its Mafia, and 'Black Hand' – but because its sheer size made it easy for a wanted man to move to parts where he was unknown. In the early 1890s, the only hope seemed to lie in Bertillon's anthropometry, and 150 police forces and prisons adopted it as the best method of bringing some order into the chaos. At a meeting of police chiefs in Chicago in 1896, considerable dissatisfaction was expressed with *bertillonage,* the problem being simply that unless the men who took the measurements were as dedicated to accuracy as Bertillon himself, it was too unreliable. But it was a case at Leavenworth penitentiary in 1903 that suddenly made everyone aware of the superiority of fingerprinting. A Negro named Will West was brought into the *bertillonage* office to be measured and photographed. 'I've seen you before', said the measuring clerk, 'Don't we already have your measurements?' 'No, sir.' The clerk looked in the file under West's measurements and found, as he had expected, that he already had Will West. He asked angrily: 'What game are you playing?' But the man insisted that he had never been in Leavenworth before. 'Look, isn't this your photograph?' The man said that it couldn't be. Finally, the exasperated clerk sent out a query about Will West, and was stunned to learn that he was safe under lock and key in another part of the prison. The two Will Wests were brought together into the warden's office. They looked like identical twins. In fact, closer study of all 11 Bertillon measurements revealed that some were different. But no one could have divined this by looking at them.

Now it so happened that Warden McCloughty possessed a copy of Henry's book on fingerprinting and a simple apparatus for taking prints – they had been sent to him by a friend in England earlier that year. A comparison of the fingerprints of the two Will Wests soon revealed that their papillary lines bore no resemblance. The lesson was not lost on McCloughty, who is quoted as remarking: 'That's the end of *bertillonage.*' And as the story of the two Will Wests became known to the police chiefs throughout America, he proved to be correct.

This problem of identification had been bothering the police for many years, and would continue to do so for a few years more. As early as 1805, a man Thomas Hoag was brought to trial in New York for abandoning his wife and child two years earlier. He had vanished suddenly from his home in Haverstraw, New York. His sister-in-law had recognized him in a New York street and was responsible for his being brought to trial. But the accused declared that his name was Joseph Parker, and called eight witnesses, including his wife, who claimed they had been together since 1799. On the other hand, the Justice of the Peace who had married Hoag in 1800 had no hesitation in identifying him. Moreover, Parker had a scar on his forehead, a wen on his back, and a lisping voice, just like Hoag. The dilemma was resolved by a young athlete who used to run with Hoag until Hoag stepped on a knife and seriously injured his foot. The accident had left a scar. The judge ordered the prisoner to take off his shoes. When no scar was found, it was finally agreed that Parker was not Hoag and he was acquitted.

The classic English case of mistaken identity was that of Adolf Beck, a Norwegian mining engineer, who was accused of being a confidence swindler named 'John Smith' – real name, Wilhelm Meyer. Beck was 54 years old in December 1895, when a young woman named Ottilie Meissonier stopped him in Victoria Street, London, and accused him of stealing some of her jewellery. Beck went of his own accord to the police station, where the lady told her story – how a well-spoken man had introduced himself to her a month earlier, and invited her to go with him on a cruise of the Mediterranean on his yacht. He had identified himself as a cousin of the Prime Minister, Lord Salisbury, given her a cheque for £40, and taken some of her jewellery with him on the pretext of having it measured so he could buy her more expensive items. A few hours later she realized she had been 'conned'.

The *modus operandi* sounded like that of a swindler who had defrauded a number of women over the past two years. When they identified Beck as the man responsible, and it was revealed that he had run up an unpaid bill of £600 at the Covent Garden Hotel, the police had no doubt that he was the wanted confidence man. They decided that Beck was a man named John Smith who had been sentenced to prison in 1877 for defrauding women. A sample of John Smith's handwriting was found, and declared by an expert to be identical with Beck's. And in March 1896, Beck was sentenced to seven years' hard labour.

His tribulations were not over. Again and again he protested his innocence, but at that time there was no Court of Appeal. In 1898, Beck's lawyer unearthed a piece of evidence that should have freed his client; it was shown that 'John Smith' had been Jewish and was circumcised; Beck was not. Still the judge refused to believe that Beck was not the man who had taken Ottilie Meissonier's jewellery. Beck was released on parole in 1901. And three years later, the same incredible situation repeated itself. A girl accosted him in the street and accused him of swindling her out of jewellery. This time Beck ran away, and bumped into a policeman. He was still under arrest three months later when the real John Smith was arrested – he now called himself William Thomas. He had swindled two actresses out of some rings and been arrested as he was trying to sell them. Sir Melville Macnaghten personally intervened and took along one of 'Beck's' former victims to see Thomas; she unhesitatingly identified him as the swindler. So did all the other women who had borne witness against Beck. Beck was freed and granted £5,000 compensation, and Meyer took his place in the dock. No case could have revealed more clearly the need for a foolproof system of identification. Fortunately, that had existed since 1901 – the year of Beck's release – in the form of the new fingerprint department at Scotland Yard. It was largely through the repercussions of the Beck case – and partly through Conan Doyle's intercession in another flagrant miscarriage of justice, the George Edalji case – that the Court of Criminal Appeal was established in England in 1907.

In Scotland in 1908, the lack of a fingerprint system led to another tragic case of mistaken identity in which the creator of Sherlock Holmes became passionately involved. And old maid named Marion Gilchrist was battered to death in her flat in Glasgow. The murderer had been interrupted by the maid, Helen Lambie, and the tenant of the flat below, and had walked calmly past them and out of the building before they discovered the body. The murder weapon had been a chair, and there was a bloody handprint on it. But the Scottish police knew nothing of fingerprinting.

The motive for the crime was supposed to have been Miss Gilchrist's jewellery, but only one small item appeared to have vanished – a crescent brooch. A few days later, a cycle dealer told police that he had seen a man offering for sale a pawn ticket for a crescent brooch at his club. This man had now sailed for New York, and his name was Oscar Slater.

Slater was arrested in New York, and was so certain that he had nothing to fear that he waived extradition proceedings and accompanied detectives back to England. The pawn ticket had now proved to be a false lead – the brooch had been pawned well before Miss Gilchrist's murder – but still Slater was tried for the crime. The maid Helen Lambie identified him as the man she had seen in Miss Gilchrist's flat, and other witnesses who had glimpsed the murderer running down the street declared Slater was the man. Slater was found guilty and sentenced to death; this was later commuted to life imprisonment.

Conan Doyle heard of the case when Slater had been in prison for five years, and his efforts secured a retrial. And again Slater was found guilty. He had been in prison for 18 years when Helen Lambie, now in America, admitted that she had recognized the murderer when she saw him in Miss Gilchrist's flat, and that the man had not been Slater. The police had put pressure on her to indentify Slater. When another leading witness told a similar story, Slater was released pending investigation. After a new inquiry Slater's sentence was quashed. The man who actually killed Miss Gilchrist was almost certainly a scape-grace nephew whose motive was to steal certain papers – a box of private papers had been smashed open. But the police preferred to believe, in the face of all the evidence, that the criminal was Oscar Slater. The handprint on the chair could have proved his innocence and convicted the real killer.

Cases like these made every police official in Europe aware of the crucial role of fingerprinting in identification. Argentina, as he have seen, even debated a law ordering that every citizen should be finger-printed. But in America, it was less simple. Every state had its own laws, and co-operation between the police forces was minimal. When criminals protested that fingerprinting was a violation of their civil rights, many judges agreed with them – it was not until 1928 that New York ruled that fingerprinting of all offenders was legal. To add to the confusion, there was widespread corruption, with politicians in the pay of wealthy criminals, and the police in the pockets of the politicians. America's most famous policeman, Inspector Thomas Byrnes of New York – who can be seen in the photograph of four policemen holding down a crook who is being photographed – was the first American to establish a criminal identification system in the 1880s; he resigned hastily in 1896 after being forced to admit to a committee that the police tolerated brothels and gambling dens so long as they received part of the profits – Byrnes himself was very nearly a millionaire.

One result of this chaos is that there is no early American fingerprint case to compare with the Rojas case in Argentina, the Scheffer case in Paris, or the Stratton case in London. But some of the successes of Detective Sergeant Joseph A. Faurot, a colleague of Thomas Byrnes, deserve to be mentioned. In the spring of 1904, Faurot went to London to study fingerprinting under Inspector Collins of the Yard. But by the time he returned to New York, the police commissioner had been changed, and the new one believed that fingerprinting was an impracticable fad. Faurot proved him wrong in 1906 when he was patrolling the Waldorf-Astoria Hotel, and caught a man creeping out of someone else's suite in his stockinged feet. In a crisp upper-class British accent, the man assured him that he had been visiting a lady who was not his wife, and told him to mind his own business. Faurot declined to be cowed, and sent a copy of the man's fingerprints to the Yard Fingerprint Bureau. Two weeks later, the reply revealed that his suspicion was correct; the Englishman was a hotel thief named Daniel Nolan, alias Henry Johnson, who was wanted for burglary. Nolan alias Johnson received a seven-year sentence.

As a result of this case, Faurot became something of a celebrity with the New York reporters. In 1908, he followed up his success with a remarkable piece of sleuthing that combined the 'needle-in-the-haystack' method with fingerprint technology. The body of a pretty nurse was found in a rooming-house; the only clue was a whisky bottle found under the bed. Reporters had covered every clue in the room with their fingerprints, but Faurot assumed, correctly, that those on the bottle were those of the murderer, and tracked down every man with whom she had been acquainted. The prints proved to belong to a plumber named George Cramer, and confronted with the evidence, he confessed to beating the girl to death after a drunken quarrel.

But the first case in which a fingerprint tipped the balance between conviction and acquittal concerned a burglar named Caesar Cella, whose friends had raised $3,000 for his defence. Faurot testified that he had found Cella's fingerprints on a window of the burgled shop, and identified them from his file. The judge invited him to demonstrate in court, sending him outside, then asking various spectators to make index prints on a window. Finally, he asked one of them to make another index print on a glass table top. Back in court, Faurot studied the prints with his magnifying glass, and took only four minutes to identify the one that was on both the window and the desk top; Cella was convicted, and the story was told in every newspaper in the country, so that the year 1911 became the year every American learned about fingerprints.

In fact, America had a bigger crime problem than any European country. In the late 1870s, the Mafia (the initials standing for *Morte alla Francia Italia Anela*, or Death to France is Italy's Cry) moved from Sicily to America, first to New Orleans, then to other major cities with a large Italian community that could be terrorized and blackmailed. New York fought back successfully largely due to the efforts of one fearless detective, Joseph Petrosino; but Petrosino was murdered by the Mafia in 1909, on a visit to Sicily. The gangs soon realized that labour racketeering was safer than burglary or extortion, and every profitable enterprise from gambling and prostitution to rag-picking and dock labour was soon infiltrated by the gangsters. Obviously, what was badly needed was some central crime-fighting agency with its own national fingerprint file, but all the efforts in this direction by the IACP (International Association of Chiefs of Police) came to nothing until 1921, when Attorney-General Harry Daugherty agreed to create a Bureau of Investigation. The Leavenworth files were transferred to Washington (about 800,000 fingerprint records) and by 1923 the United States at last had a central criminal records bureau of the kind that had existed in Paris and London for decades. But it was crippled by lack of funds.

Since 1920, American law enforcement officers had had a new problem; the country's teetotallers had persuaded Congress to pass the Volstead Act, declaring all alcoholic beverages illegal. It turned the gangsters and bootleggers into the citizen's friend, and destroyed any hope of stamping out the Mafia. But in 1924, Attorney-General Harlan Fiske Stone decided to appoint a young lawyer named J. Edgar Hoover to do a 'house cleaning' job of the Federal Bureau of Investigation, an agency that had been created in 1908 by Theodore Roosevelt, and which speedily became as corrupt as most other government agencies.

In July 1924, two months after his appointment, Hoover succeeded in persuading Congress to donate $56,000 to get the fingerprint bureau into operation. By 1932, nearly 5,000 law enforcement agencies around the country were co-operating with the FBI. The number of its records would eventually exceed 200 million.

Yet even as late as the 1920s, American juries remained dubious about fingerprint evidence. In the first week of November 1926, the celebrated Faurot himself gave evidence that should have led to a guilty verdict against the defendants, and which was virtually ignored by the jury. The case was the great American *cause célèbre* of the 1920s, the Hall-Mills murder case. Four years earlier, on 16 September 1922, a courting couple taking a stroll near Brunswick, New Jersey, came upon two corpses in a country lane. They proved to be those of the local minister Edward Wheeler Hall, who was 41, and of one of his choir singers, Mrs Eleanor Mills, 34. Scattered around the bodies were various torn letters, and the minister's calling card was propped against one of his feet. Both had been shot dead; the woman's throat had been cut from ear to ear, and her tongue and vocal cords removed. The letters proved to be love letters from Mrs Mills to the Revd Hall, and proved conclusively that she had been his mistress for some time.

Clearly, this was a *crime passionnel,* and all the evidence pointed towards the minister's wife Frances, seven years his senior, and her two brothers Willie and Henry – the latter was an expert shot. But quarrels between two lots of country police about their jurisdiction, and incredible official bungling, finally led a Grand Jury to decide that there was insufficient evidence to charge anyone with the murders.

Four years later, the case was reopened when the husband of a parlour-maid in the minister's household tried to get his marriage annulled, and made some amazing accusations. Arthur Riehl stated that the parlourmaid, Louise Geist, had learned that the minister and his mistress had planned to elope, and had passed on this information to Mrs Hall. On the night of the murder, Mrs Hall, her brother Willie, and Louise Geist drove out to the lovers' lane where the couple planned to meet, and killed the two of them. Louise received $5,000 for her part in the crime and for her silence. The newspapers made the accusation into front-page headlines, and Mrs Hall and her brothers were arrested.

Some of the most telling evidence against them came from a bizarre lady who became known as the Pig Woman; she was Mrs Jane Gibson, who ran a pig farm near De Russey's Lane, the scene of the murder, and who claimed that at 10.30 on the night of 14 September 1922 she had passed close to the crab apple tree under which the bodies were later found, and heard a quarrel, followed by shots. But the Pig Woman's mother, who was also in court, insisted that her daughter was a pathological liar. During the trial, the Pig Woman collapsed – she proved to be suffering from cancer – and had to give her evidence from a hospital bed in the courtroom.

But the most impressive evidence concerned the visiting card propped by the dead man's foot. It had been in a safe in the State Prosecutor's office since the day after the murder. And when examined in the Middlesex County fingerprint laboratory, it had been found to contain a fingerprint. Lieutenant Fred Drewen mounted the stand and testified that he had taken the fingerprints of Willie Stevens, and that the print on the visiting card was that of Stevens's left index finger. Next, the head of the Bureau of Records of the Newark Police Department, Edward H. Schwartz, testified that he had examined the card and found that the fingerprint on it was that of Willie Stevens. Finally, Joseph Faurot, who had ended as New York's Deputy Police Commissioner, mounted the stand. He not only testified that the fingerprint was that of Willie Stevens, but produced transparencies of the accused man's fingerprints, which he projected on a screen, explaining to the jury his reasons for having no doubt. In an English or French court of law, that would have settled the case; unless Willie Stevens could explain how his fingerprints came to be on the minister's calling card, the jury would have concluded that it was he who had placed the card against the dead man's foot.

Fortunately for the defendants, there was a dramatic interruption; Alexander Simpson, the prosecutor, announced that the Pig Woman was at death's door, and about to sink into a coma. So Faurot stood down to make room for the Pig Woman's doctor, and the judge announced that the trial would be adjourned for the time being.

Back on the stand a few days later, Schwartz and Faurot again insisted that the fingerprint on the card was that of Willie Stevens, although they agreed that being exposed to the weather for 36 hours might have impaired the print.

When the maid, Louise Geist, appeared on the stand, she testified that, on the morning after the murder, Willie had told her that 'something terrible happened last night'. And another witness, Marie Demarest, told how a private detective hired by Mrs Hall had tried to bribe her to suppress part of her testimony.

Things looked black for the defendants. Yet, incredibly, the defence made no real attempt to discredit the most serious piece of evidence: the calling card. Robert J. McCarter told the jury: 'I charge with all the solemnity that is involved in it that the card is a fraud.' But he made no attempt to explain how a fraudulent fingerprint could be fabricated, or how, if the card itself was a fraud, Willie Stevens had been induced to put his fingerprint on it. The jury was apparently incurious about this vital point. On 3 December 1926, after deliberating for five hours, they returned a verdict of not guilty. James Mills, the sexton and husband of the murdered woman, remarked that he was not surprised, since money could buy anything . . .

At this distance in time, the solution to this 'unsolved' murder case seems obvious. The defence was correct about one thing: Frances Hall had no idea that Eleanor Mills was her husband's mistress. When she found out – probably from overhearing a telephone conversation about an elopement – she summoned her brothers, and they hurried off to administer summary justice. Mrs Hall may have been doubly enraged because she genuinely liked Eleanor Mills and had always treated her with kindness. If the Pig Woman's testimony is correct, Hall was shot first, above the ear, while Eleanor ran away; they found her with the aid of a torch, dragged her back and shot her beside her lover. Then the infuriated wife slit her throat and removed the vocal cords that had been responsible for the sweet voice that had seduced her husband.

Then why was she acquitted, when all the evidence pointed to her guilt? The answer may lie in the flamboyant manner of the prosecuting counsel, a native of Jersey City, who had referred to the residents of Somerset County, where the trial took place, as country bumpkins. During the trial, his extrovert city manners evidently grated on the jury. It seems probable that the verdict was a gesture of defiance and contempt towards State Senator Alexander Simpson rather than an affirmation of belief in the innocence of Mrs Hall and her brothers.

But if fingerprint evidence failed to convict the killers of the minister and the choir singer, it scored a triumph in another remarkable case of the 1920s. On 23 May 1928, four men walked into the First National Bank in Lamar, Colorado, and waved guns at the customers and tellers. As they seized almost a quarter of a million dollars, the bank president, A. N. Parrish, grabbed a revolver from a drawer and fired at one of the bandits; he was shot dead. So was his son, who ran to his father's side. The killers rushed away, taking two hostages, E. A. Lundgren and Everett Kessenger. As the local sheriff started in pursuit of the getaway car, Lundgren was pushed out. Finally, in the face of heavy fire, the sheriff lost the trail.

A few hours later, a man called at the home of Dr W. W. Weininger and asked him to come and attend a man who had been injured in a tractor accident. They drove off in the doctor's car. Later, the doctor's bullet-riddled body was found in a ravine; the other hostage, Kessenger, was found dead in an abandoned shack. It was clear that the killers had summoned the doctor to attend the wounded bandit, then killed him to prevent him from testifying against them – a completely pointless murder.

R. S. Terwilliger, a fingerprint expert from the Kansas Police Department, inspected the doctor's car, and found that it had been wiped carefully with a damp cloth – evidence that America's criminals were becoming aware of the value of fingerprint clues. But after an inch-by-inch examination, he found one fragmentary fingerprint on the glass of the right rear door.

When the FBI's Identification Division received the enlarged photograph of the print two months later, they had to admit defeat; their system depended on a classification of all ten prints, although even then, single print classification was being considered. Hoover became personally interested in the problem – the ruthlessness of the crime had shocked the nation. He ordered his subordinates to study the fingerprint until they had memorized it. Then, if they came upon it by chance, it could be used to identify the killers.

In the pocket of the murdered doctor had been found a note denouncing the medical profession; this led the police to arrest a crook named Charles Clinton, who had developed an insane hatred of doctors since his wife died during an operation. With three criminal associates, he was charged with the bank robbery; various witnesses identified them, but their trial was delayed.

A year after the murders, an FBI fingerprint expert received a request from the sheriff's office in Stockton, California, asking him to verify that the fingerprints of a train robber known as William Holden were those of a crook named Jake Fleagle. Something about one of the prints intrigued the expert, and after a long and fruitless attempt to match it, he recalled that it was the Lamar hold-up fingerprint. He checked it against the print found on the doctor's car; it was undoubtedly that of Jake Fleagle.

Fleagle's brother Ralph was run down on a farm in Kansas, and implicated his brother and a man called Howard Royston; Royston was arrested and led the police to a third robber, George Abshier. Ralph Fleagle also admitted that he 'framed' Charles Clinton – with whom he had quarrelled – by writing the note denouncing doctors. The arrests occurred two days before Charles Clinton and his three associates were due to go on trial. They were cleared but re-arrested on other charges and sentenced to jail. Ralph Fleagle, Howard Royston and George Abshier were tried for the Lamar murders, and hanged. Jake Fleagle, whose fingerprint led to their arrest, was still at large; but he was cornered by police when about to board a train in Branson, Missouri, and killed in a gun battle.

11

The Fleagle case makes it obvious that what the FBI urgently needed was a *single* fingerprint collection. If only a single fingerprint is found at the scene of a crime, then it is no use trying to find it in a collection of all ten prints which is classified according to the right thumb. This problem had been obvious to Scotland Yard ever since Henry began the first fingerprint collection in 1901. But a single fingerprint collection would obviously be a tremendous task, since it would involve multiplying the original collection by ten, as well as finding new and subtler ways of classifying each fingerprint. But it obviously had to be done sooner or later. The US Navy was the first to attempt it, under the guidance of its Chief of Identification, J. H. Taylor, who devised his own system as early as 1921. At Scotland Yard, it was Inspector Collins's successor, Superintendent Harry Batley, who finally created the Single Fingerprint System in 1930. His assistant was Detective Inspector Fred Cherrill, later famous as 'Cherrill of the Yard', one of its most successful manhunters. In the following year, Batley and Cherrill decided that palmprints were just as useful as fingerprints, and began to include them in their collection. But these were included with the fingerprints, so that unless a burglar left a fingerprint as well as a palmprint, they were virtually useless.

The first crook to be convicted in England on palmprint and single fingerprint evidence was a burglar named John Egan, who had been breaking into suburban houses at Hendon, Watford and Staines. He had left a palmprint on a glass table top at one house, and enough fragmentary fingerprints at the others for him to be identified through the Single Fingerprint System, at that time only a year old. Cherrill had his palmprints taken, and had no difficulty in convincing Egan that it would be futile to challenge the evidence. Egan pleaded guilty, and received 14 months.

The first murder case that turned upon palmprint evidence took place in 1942. The victim was a 71-year-old pawnbroker named Leonard Moules. He was putting up the shutters of his shop when two passing men paused, and followed him back into the shop. One of the men struck him on the head with the butt of a revolver; the old man collapsed, but struggled to his feet and grappled with the men. He was again beaten to the ground. Then the men took his keys, opened the safe, and removed money and jewellery. The old man was found unconscious, and although detectives waited by his bedside, he died four days later without opening his eyes.

Cherrill was able to find one single palmprint, inside the door of the safe. This, of course, was of no use, for palmprints were not separately classified. But fortunately, the men were caught by police work. Hundreds of men in the area of the shop – Hackney Road, Shoreditch – were questioned, and a soldier finally mentioned that he had seen two men in a café examining a revolver on the day of the murder; he only knew them as 'George and Sam', but more lengthy enquiries revealed that 'George' was a 23-year-old machinist named George Silverosa, who lived in Pitsea. Silverosa soon confessed, declaring that it was his companion, Sam Dashwood, who had battered the old man to the ground. When their prints were taken, the palmprint in the safe was found to be Silverosa's. This may have sealed his fate; the judge rejected the plea that only Dashwood was the killer, since it was obvious that the men had had a common purpose, and that the pawnbroker had been killed in the pursuit if this common purpose; both men were hanged at Pentonville.

England's murder rate was low; throughout the 1920s and 1930s, it seldom exceeded 150 a year – less than most large American cities. And very few of these murders were solved by a fingerprint – one rare exception being the case of Stanley Hobday, a burglar who stabbed a householder to death in a struggle in August 1933, then left an excellent set of fingerprints on a milk bottle during the course of another burglary the same night.

But in America during the bootleg era, the operation of the finger-print bureau brought a new hazard into the lives of gangsters. The bureau in Washington had to deal with thousands of enquiries every day, for every time a man was arrested in any part of the country, the police wanted to know if he had a past record. The number of enquiries eventually reached a fairly stable total of 30,000 a day. Under the old state system, a criminal from the east coast could feel fairly secure in San Francisco or Los Angeles until he began to acquire himself a new police record there. After 1930, when Congress approved a permanent Division of Identification and Information within the FBI, a travelling crook was no longer safe in any part of the country.

This applied particularly to bank robbers like Machine Gun Kelly, Baby Face Nelson, Pretty Boy Floyd and John Dillinger. The latter's brief but spectacular career as Public Enemy Number One lasted from May 1933, the year Prohibition was repealed, until July of the following year, when he was shot down outside the Biograph Cinema in Chicago by Hoover agents. During that time the 'Dillinger mob' committed a series of robberies that occasionally netted as much as $75,000. But he soon realized that the life of a hold-up man was rather less peaceful and secure than that of a hunted fox, and began to brood on ways of being able to mix freely with his fellow citizens without constant anxiety about being recognized. One solution seemed to be a plastic surgical operation to change his face; he decided that he might as well have his fingerprints changed at the same time. If Dillinger had maintained a closer liaison with others of the bank-robbing fraternity he would have known that this was virtually impossible; early in 1934, two members of the Ma Barker gang – Freddy Barker and 'Creepy' Karpis – had allowed a doctor called Joseph P. Moran to slice off their fingerpads, only to discover that, as they healed, the original fingerprints reappeared. Dillinger's operation at the hands of Dr William Loeser and Dr Harold Cassedy was even more traumatic; under the anaesthetic he swallowed his tongue, and it was only when the doctor thrust his fingers down his throat and retrieved it that he was able to breathe again. Dillinger's general dissatisfaction with the doctors – reinforced by threats with a sub-machine-gun – made them decide to remove his fingerprints by a less drastic method, using acid. Yet when Dillinger was shot down outside the cinema (betrayed by a girlfriend) a few months later, the papillary lines were already beginning to show again.

Another gangster who became increasingly indignant as his fingerprints betrayed his previous record was a hold-up man named Robert Philipps. Philipps had first been arrested for automobile theft in 1932, at the age of 23, and spent much of the following ten years in prison. In March 1941, having narrowly escaped another jail sentence for lack of evidence, Philipps decided to try a new method of escaping detection by his fingerprints: he paid a Dr Leopold Brandenburg of Union City, New Jersey, to graft skin from his ribs on to his fingertips. The operation was fully as painful as the one performed by Dr Joe Moran in 1934 on the members of the Ma Barker gang (and which had resulted in the doctor's corpse being consigned to a lake). Having removed the skin from the fingertips, Brandenburg made Philipps sit for three weeks with his fingers strapped to the transplantation sites on his chest, until the skin grew over them. The effort was in vain – not because the operation was unsuccessful, but because when Philipps was again arrested – five months later in Austin, Texas – the police were baffled by the lack of fingerprints, and threw him into jail until they could establish his identity by other means. By checking the files of all escaped convicts and wanted robbers, the FBI eventually arrived at the conclusion that the unknown Roscoe Pitts in a Texas jail was Robert James Philipps. The question now was what crimes Philipps had committed since his fingerprints had been obliterated. And that question was not too difficult to answer, for the fingerprints had only been obliterated down to the first joint, and the prints on Philipp's file happened to show the left ring-finger below the joint. A print at a robbery showed the lines below the joint, and Philipps received a 20-year jail sentence. And Dr Brandenburg, who had formerly escaped justice on charges of abortion and planning a robbery, also went to prison for knowingly aiding a criminal to evade justice. The Philipps case caused criminals to reflect that fingers without fingerprints involved as great a risk of conviction as the normal alternative, and it was the last recorded case of an attempt to change fingerprints through surgery.

12

In England, where crime was on an altogether smaller scale, the history of fingerprinting proceeded more sedately during the war years and immediately after. With the exception of Gordon Cummins, the 'Blackout Ripper' (of whom we shall speak later), Fred Cherrill mentions no major investigation that was solved by fingerprint identification during this period.

Then, in 1948, came one of the most remarkable cases in the history of crime detection. It began shortly before midnight on 14 May, when a nurse entered the children's ward of the Queen's Park Hospital, and realized that one of the cots was empty. Three quarters of an hour earlier, 4-year-old June Devaney had been asleep in it. The nurse gave the alarm, but it was not until after three o'clock in the morning that the child's body was found lying beside the hospital wall. She had been raped, her left buttock had been bitten, and she had been killed by being swung against the stone wall by her ankles.

Footmarks on the polished floor revealed that the intruder had entered by a porch door, and looked into various cots before he had chosen that of June Devaney, who was the largest child in the ward; June had just recovered from a mild case of pneumonia and was due to go home the next day. A large Winchester bottle, which had been on a trolley, was lying beside the bed. On this bottle, Detective Inspector Colin Campbell, chief of the Lancashire Fingerprint Bureau, found an excellent set of 'dabs' (as the British called fingerprints). The fingerprint records revealed that they were not the prints of any known criminal. And a careful check against all fingerprints of hospital staff and visitors to the ward also eliminated this possibility. Detective Inspector John Capstick of Scotland Yard decided on a desperate expedient: to fingerprint every male in the town of Blackburn. There were 35,000 houses, and probably 50,000 males over the age of 16. And of course, there could be no compulsion for anyone to have his print taken. But the horror caused by the crime was so great that, in practice, there were no objections.

The immense operation began on 23 May, nine days after the murder. Five hundred cards a day were sent to the sorting office of the fingerprint bureau. At the same time, copies of the prints on the bottle were sent to every fingerprint bureau in the world. Yet two months after the murder, the fingerprint had still not been found. Forty thousand males in Blackburn had been fingerprinted, and no more could be found on the electoral register. Then an issue of ration books, which had continued after the war, made the police aware that there were at least 800 males still unaccounted for. On 11 July 1948, the police called at 31 Birley Street, Blackburn, and asked if they could take the fingerprints of 22-year-old Peter Griffiths, the half-brother of the householder, James Brennan. Brennan's little daughter Pauline had been in the hospital at the same time as June Devaney. Peter Griffiths allowed his prints to be taken, and the card went to the fingerprint bureau later that day. And it was on the following afternoon that one of the searchers yelled: 'I've got him! It's here!'

Peter Griffiths denied the crime, but then made a confession. He claimed he had got drunk, then accepted a lift from a man who offered to 'give him a spin', and who dropped him off near the hospital, a place Griffiths knew well, having spent weeks of his childhood there. In the children's ward, he claimed that a child woke up when he stumbled against her cot, and that he carried her outside to keep her silent. He said nothing of the rape, but claimed that he lost his temper 'because she wouldn't stop crying', and banged her head against the wall.

The defence pleaded diminished responsibility arguing that Griffiths was the son of a mentally ill father, and that he himself was generally regarded as 'queer' and childish. But the jury found him guilty of first degree murder, and on 19 November, seven months after the murder, he was executed.

It would be another seven years before the science of dactyloscopy again played such a crucial role in a British murder case. On the evening of 29 April 1955, Mrs Elizabeth Currell took her corgi dog for a walk on the golf course at Potter's Bar; she was 46 years old, but looked many years younger. The path ran along a railway embankment, and passed an old Second World War pillbox. A man watched from inside the pillbox as she walked along the path, then followed her on to the golf course. She turned round as he approached, and it seems probably that she recognized him. As he grappled with her, and she began to struggle, she told him not to be silly, and that he would get into trouble. Her mistake was in not screaming and trying to escape. The man struck her on the jaw, and she collapsed; then he tried to strangle her. She began to fight again, and he reached out and grabbed the nearest weapon – a tee-iron which marked the 17th tee – and began to hit her with it. She began to bleed heavily, yet was still sufficiently concerned for her dog to talk to it soothingly. Finally, when she stopped struggling, he raised her dress around her waist, tugged off her knickers, and knelt between her legs. At this point she began to vomit blood, and he put her coat over her face to stanch it. Then he heard voices nearby; wiping his bloody hands on her clothing, he hurried away.

Back at home, her husband, a lorry driver, became increasingly worried. Yet it was not until 11 o'clock that evening that he telephoned the police. He had been out to look for her and found the dog, but no sign of his wife.

It was at dawn the next day that a constable found the body, lying in a position of sexual assault. One of her stockings had been tied round her neck, but the pathologist, Dr Francis Camps, soon verified that she had been battered to death by the tee-marker. The rape had not been completed. And the Scotland Yard men who took charge of the case discovered a fragment of a palmprint on the murder weapon. Apparently the killer had pressed his hand on it as he pushed himself to his feet.

The police were faced with the same dilemma as in the Blackburn case. It was possible that the killer knew the golf course, and lived in the area; in that case, he would probably be caught in a mass finger-printing exercise. On the other hand, he might be simply a visitor to the area from some adjacent suburb of north London. The task was not quite so daunting as in the Blackburn case – there were only about 7,000 houses in the Potter's Bar area, compared with five times that number in Blackburn. Nevertheless, every other possibility had first to be explored. By now, Scotland Yard had a small palmprint collection – about 6,000. And when the bloodstained print was not found among these, the detectives began checking on the record of every known sex offender in six counties, and asking each one where he had been on the evening of 29 April 1955. And finally, they embarked on the task of taking palmprints at every house in Potter's Bar, as well as those of 2,000 employees who worked in the area but lived elsewhere. Fifty-seven detectives were engaged in this task, while 12 officers of the fingerprint branch compared the results with the fragmentary palmprint. Meanwhile, dozens of copies of the palmprint were sent to the police of six continents, with requests to check them against the prints of various residents of Potter's Bar who had travelled abroad since the murder.

Week after week went by without result. It was even possible that they had taken the palmprint of the killer, and failed to identify it; a small fragment of palmprint is not easy to identify, particularly if you have no idea of which part of the palm it came from. By mid-August 9,000 palmprints had been taken, and about half of them had been examined. On 19 August, one of the experts was studying the 4,605th print when he suddenly realized that he had a match. It belonged to a 17-year-old youth named Michael Queripel, who lived with his parents and brother close to the golf course.

In fact, the police had interviewed Michael Queripel five days after the murder. His mother had told them that Michael had spent the evening of the murder at a local garage with a friend. It was after this interview that Scotland Yard Commissioner Richard Jackson had approved the mass palmprinting operation. The police had called at the Queripel's house again on 3 July, and Michael had declined to have his palmprint taken, saying that it was against his principles. His brother Robert had commented: 'That's bloody silly Mick – it can't hurt anything.' So Queripel submitted. In the weeks that followed, he must have endured a great deal of mental agony, mitigated by the hope that the police had failed to match his print. But on 19 August, Chief Inspector Crawford and Detective Inspector Denis Hawkins walked into the town hall at Potter's Bar, where Queripel worked as a clerk, and asked him to go outside with them. One of them asked: 'You know what this is about?', and after hesitating, Queripel replied: 'Yes I know . . . But she was already dead when I found her.' He had already planned his story of how the palmprint came to be on the tee-marker.

'Why didn't you tell the police?', they asked.

After a long pause, during which they looked at him, Queripel said: 'I hit her. Then I tried to strangle her . . .'

Queripel's trial lasted only five minutes, and he was sentenced to be 'detained during Her Majesty's pleasure', a phrase that meant life imprisonment. In 1955, Queripel could have been hanged, but the fact that he was under 18 saved his life. He was only the second murderer to be convicted by a palmprint in Britain, the first being George Silverosa, the murderer of the pawnbroker Leonard Moules (see p. 158).

13

Perhaps the strangest story in the history of fingerprinting is recounted by Detective Chief Inspector Tony Fletcher, of the Fingerprint Bureau of the Greater Manchester Police. In the spring of 1961, Fletcher was approached by David Cohen, secretary of the Manchester branch of the Society for Psychical Research, who wanted to know if Fletcher would co-operate in trying to fingerprint a ghost. Fletcher himself was unwilling, but recommended Cohen to ask Sergeant Rowland Mason of the fingerprint bureau, a policeman who often seemed to his colleagues to possess second sight where criminals were concerned. Mason agreed to attempt the experiment.

It seemed that the ghost was that of a musician who called himself Nicholas. In 1959, Cohen had been approached by a widow who lived in a small terraced house in south Manchester with her son and daughter. Her son was taking violin lessons, and one night, the lady woke to hear the sounds of a violin coming from his room. It was playing Ravel's Bolero, and she was intrigued to observe that the performance revealed a technical command of the instrument that was beyond her son's normal powers. She crept to his bedroom and peeped in; he was fast asleep, and the violin had stopped.

The same thing had happened several times, until she was afraid that she was suffering from auditory hallucinations. Finally, she asked her son if he had been playing the violin in the night; he answered: 'No, it wasn't me, it was Nicholas.' Nicholas, apparently, was an old man who obligingly played the violin for the young learner.

The widow approached the Society of Psychical Research, and a number of seances were held at the house, under the direction of Mr Cohen. After a while, a pair of 'spirit hands' had begun to manifest themselves at the seances. And the reason for Mr Cohen's visit to the Manchester police headquarters was that he wanted to take the ghost's fingerprints, and compare them with those of everyone in the room, to eliminate trickery – one of the chief objects of the Society for Psychical Research, which was formed at a time when dozens of fake 'mediums' were deceiving their sitters.

Sergeant Mason agreed to attend a seance and see what happened. And Mason was impressed. The 'spirit' manifested itself with a series of knocks, after which the large round table at which they were sitting rose in the air until Mason had to stand on tiptoe to keep his fingers on it. A luminous tambourine flew round the room at a great speed, changing direction with an abruptness that made it clear that it was not simply being thrown or propelled on strings or wires.

Mason was intrigued enough to pay a second visit. And after the same manifestations as before, a pair of hands touched Mason on the shoulders and arms. Later, Mason held the hands. He described them as being slim, dry and scaly, and having lace cuffs at the wrists. This convinced his that it should be easy enough to fingerprint them. So before the next seance, he slipped into the empty room and carefully polished the tambourine to provide a clean surface for fingerprints. As soon as the room was in darkness and they were all sitting round the table, something struck him in the face – it was the duster he had used to polish the tambourine; the spirit was apparently telling him it knew exactly what he was up to. After this the tambourine flew wildly around the room. But when Mason dusted it with mercury powder, it proved to be devoid of fingerprints.

On the next occasion, the tambourine was powdered with mercury dust before the seance began. And in the darkness, they all watched the luminous tambourine rise from the sideboard and circle the room. Yet there were still no fingerprints on it.

They decided to ask 'Nicholas' whether they could take his fingerprints; the answer was a single knock, indicating agreement. In due course, Mason reached out in the darkness and took one of the hands in his own, then guided it to a chemically sensitized pad in front of him. After that, he pressed the fingers against sensitized paper. That procedure should, undoubtedly, have guaranteed a set of fingerprints. But when the sensitized paper was examined in the light, it was found to have only three scratches on it, such as might have been made by nails or by the claw of a bird.

Fingerprinting had obviously failed; the next step was to try infra-red photography – infra-red light is invisible in the dark but can still affect a photographic plate. An expert photographer, Constable John Cheetham, was chosen, and he and his wife attended a preliminary seance. There were loud knockings, the tambourine flew around the room, and the flowers from a vase were scattered around the room – the constable's wife was so terrified that she swore she would never re-enter the room. At this seance, Nicholas was asked if he would consent to sit in an armchair and be photographed, and agreed that he would. And in due course, John Cheetham pressed the button that should have photographed a ghost. When the photograph was developed, it showed an empty armchair and a creased cushion where a head would normally be resting. But on closer examination, everyone who looked at it saw the same faint image: 'a very old man, bearded and turned to the right, rather like the head of an old king on a coin . . . It was a remarkable coincidence that all present could see the same thing.'

At this point, the story leaked out to the Press, and the chief superintendant demanded explanations. After that, the investigation was discontinued. In his autobiography *Memories of Murder,* Tony Fletcher concludes with characteristic caution: 'If you were now to ask me if I believe in ghosts, I would reply that I do not readily disbelieve in the supernatural and that there are probably two reports still on file in police archives which bear witness to the events I have just related.'

The conclusion would seem to be that, whether genuine or fraudulent, 'Nicholas' possessed a capacity to eradicate his own fingerprints that would be the envy of the most innovative burglar.

14

In 1961, at the time Rowland Mason was trying to fingerprint the violin-playing ghost, it must have seemed to fingerprint experts that their science had reached a stage close to ultimate perfection – they could hardly foresee the remarkable advances to be made through the development of 'blood fingerprinting' in the mid-1960s and 'genetic fingerprinting' in the mid-1980s (developments that will be reserved for a later chapter). Even so, the advances made since Henry had solved the classification problem were as impressive as anything in more orthodox sciences. It had become possible, for example, to transmit fingerprints by wireless telegraphy. The principle is similar to television, and depends on a curious property of the element selenium, which becomes a better conductor of electricity according to the intensity of light shone on it; so a photograph only has to be scanned by a beam of light which is then reflected on to a bank of selenium (photoelectric) cells, and the resulting 'message' can be transmitted like any other. By the 1920s, the telegraphic transmission of fingerprints and wanted photographs was a commonplace. The French had also learned to make use of the light-sensitive qualities of silver nitrate – used in photography – for developing latent fingerprints on wood and other rough surfaces. Fingerprints contain a quantity of salt (from perspiration), and when sprayed with a fine spray of silver nitrate, would then 'develop' like a photograph when exposed to light. In the early 1930s, this was further developed in America by Dr Erastus Mead Hudson, and in the Lindbergh kidnapping case in 1932 (see Chapter 9), Hudson offered to use his technique to examine the ladder by which the kidnapper had gained access to the child's bedroom. It worked, revealing 125 marks and dozens of palmprints. Unfortunately, the ladder had been handled by so many people since the kidnapping that it was virtually impossible to identify most of them – the only eight that could be identified were those of policemen. If the ladder had been submitted to this test immediately after it was found, it would probably have identified the kidnapper – and later, murderer – of Charles Lindbergh jun.

Other methods of raising latent fingerprints on a porous surface – including cloth and wood-involved 'developing' with iodine fumes and spraying with ninhydrin. Even fingerprints on flesh could be 'visualized' with special X-ray techniques. The advance of computerization had made it possible to check the fingerprints of a suspect as easily and quickly as checking the licence number of a car. When this method was introduced into the San Francisco Bay area in 1984 – so that finger-prints can be checked within seconds – the result was an astonishing increase in the number of crimes solved.

Yet even with such advances, a number of crimes have remained obstinately insoluble. In the late 1960s, an unknown psychopath in the San Francisco area committed five murders and left two victims on the point of death; he preyed on courting couples. In letters to the Press, the killer called himself 'Zodiac'; he threatened more atrocities – for example, machine-gunning a busload of schoolchildren. On 20 September, a pudgy man with a hood held up two students who were picnicking near Lake Berryessa, tied them up, and stabbed them both repeatedly. Shortly after, a man with a gruff voice made a typical 'Zodiac' telephone call to the Napa police department, reporting a double murder. The call was traced to a telephone only a block away, and technicians were able to lift a good palmprint from the telephone. On 11 October, the killer shot a San Francisco taxi-driver in the back of the head, and came close to being caught as he escaped. Three bloodstained fingerprints were found on the passenger seat; since they were not those of the victim, Paul Stine, they had to be those of the killer. But the prints were not on record. They later enabled the police to eliminate several suspects, but have so far (2003) failed to lead to the killer.

In retrospect it seems obvious that a mass fingerprint operation might have trapped Zodiac. A great deal was known about him: that he was young (probably in his early 20s), that he was overweight, that he wore horn-rimmed glasses, and that he was so familiar with Napa and Vallejo that he probably lived in one of the two. It should have been within the bounds of possibility to fingerprint every male who answered that description in Napa and Vallejo – the operation would have been far less ambitious than the Blackburn or Potter's Bar mass fingerprinting – but it was not attempted. Fortunately; the murders ceased after the killing of the taxi-driver.

15

Another important application of fingerprint identification deserves at least a brief mention: identification of the dead. Every year, thousands of unidentified corpses find their way into city morgues, and are finally buried in unmarked graves – except in cases where the fingerprints of the deceased happen to be on file. On 30 March 1968, two children playing in an abandoned tenement on New York's Lower East Side found the body of a man. The arms of the corpse were covered with needle marks, but cause of death was recorded as hardening of the arteries and a heart attack. The unidentified body was consigned to a pauper's grave.

Eighteen months later, a dying man in Cedar Rapids, Iowa, expressed a wish to see his son, who had vanished some years earlier. The son had, in fact, been a famous film star. Bobby Driscoll was picked out of a mass audition of children at the MGM studios in 1943 – when he was six years old-and soon became a child star in a number of Walt Disney productions, including *Lost Angel, Song of the South,* and *Treasure Island;* in 1949 he won an Academy Award. Married at the age of 19, Driscoll had already been a drug abuser for two years, and by the age of 19, his Hollywood career was virtually over. He remarked bitterly, 'I was carried on a satin cushion and then dropped into the garbage can', but a court appearance on charges of assault, robbery, forgery, and possession of drugs made it clear that this was largely his own fault. At this point, he slipped into oblivion.

But because of his arrest, his prints were on record. And a check with fingerprint records at the FBI revealed that Driscoll was the unknown corpse found in the empty house.

Such cases are a powerful argument for a universal fingerprint register. Prints could be taken at birth, since they remain unchanged throughout life (except for a slight decrease in the number of papillaries). All unknown corpses could be immediately identified; so could criminals like Peter Griffiths and the Zodiac killer. The argument that universal fingerprinting would threaten the rights of ordinary citizens is emotive rather than logical. Sooner or later, it must be recognized that the rising crime rate constitutes the greatest of all threats to the community; when that happens, the result should be a reappraisal in favour of common sense.

4

Whose Body?

1

'To write the history of identification is to write the history of criminology', says Edmond Locard in his classic *Traité de criminalistique*. And the reader of the two volumes entitled *Proofs of Identity* can sense the author's almost obsessive involvement in the subject. For Locard, the question of identification is indeed the essence of criminology.

Locard's account of the famous case of Lesurques and Dubosq offers a key to his attitude. It began on the evening of 27 April 1796, when the Lyon mail-coach failed to arrive at the village of Melun, just south of Paris. Early the next morning, a search party found the abandoned coach near the Pouilly bridge. The driver and post boy had been brutally hacked to death, and more than five million francs was missing. One of the horses had also been taken, and it became clear that the wine merchant who had been the sole passenger had actually been a member of a gang of highwaymen. He had carried a large cavalry sword, and this had probably been the murder weapon. The other members of the gang, it soon became clear, were four heavily armed horsemen who had dined in the nearby village of Montgeron a few hours before the mail-coach went through.

The police picked up the trail remarkably quickly. The missing horse was found in Paris the next day. Then a stable-keeper reported that four sweating horses had been returned to his stable in the early hours of the morning by a man named Couriol. With luck and patience, the police traced Couriol to a village north of Paris and arrested him; he was found to be in possession of over a million francs, obviously his share of the booty.

On the morning Couriol was due to appear in court at the Palais de

Justice, a man called Charles Guénot went to the Palais to collect some papers the police had taken from him – they had found him in the same house as Couriol, but he was not suspected of being one of the gang. With Guénot was a friend called Joseph Lesurques, a well-to-do businessman from Douai, who had bumped into Guénot by accident that morning. Also in the Palais were two barmaids from Montgeron, who had served dinner to the highway robbers. When they saw Guénot and Lesurques, they became excited and told an usher that they recognized them as two of the robbers. Guénot and Lesurques were arrested. In due course, they were tried, together with Couriol and three other men who were accused of being accomplices. Guénot was acquitted; Lesurques. and Couriol were among those condemned to death.

Couriol immediately declared that Lesurques was completely innocent. And the judge who had ordered Lesurques's arrest – a man named Daubanton – was so disturbed by this that he went to see Couriol in prison. Couriol repeated that Lesurques was innocent. The barmaids, he said, had mistaken Lesurques for the real culprit, a man named Dubosq. It was true that Dubosq, unlike Lesurques, had dark hair, but he had worn a blond wig to take part in the robbery.

Daubanton had the case reopened. A commission was set up to re-examine the evidence against Lesurques. It was pointed out to them that Lesurques had no possible motive to get involved in highway robbery; he was already well off. Unfortunately, this piece of information backfired. The commission decided that perhaps Lesurques's relatives had offered to bribe Dubosq's relatives if he would declare Lesurques innocent. The Minister of Justice agreed with them. And the unfortunate Lesurques took a tearful farewell of his wife and children and went to the guillotine with Couriol.

But the police evidently believed Couriol. They went to considerable trouble to arrest four men named by Couriol, including the fake wine merchant, and these men were also condemned and executed. Judge Daubanton's campaign to have Lesurques declared innocent only damaged his own career.

Obviously, this is a classic case of mistaken identity, like that of Adolf Beck and Oscar Slater (described in the previous chapter). Yet we can see why Edmond Locard thought it so important. The brutality of the crime aroused a determination to punish it at all costs. When the barmaids indentified Guénot and Lesurques as two of the highway-men, everyone was understandably delighted. But when Guénot was found innocent, it should have been obvious that Lesurques was also innocent. Unfortunately, the authorities were so anxious to see justice done at any cost that Lesurques was executed. Identification, which Locard defined as the centre of any criminal inquiry, had failed utterly.

For Locard, this represented the greatest challege for the science of criminology. This is why his two volumes on the proofs of identity are the very heart of his great *Traité de criminalistique*. Dozens of pages are devoted to case after case of mistaken or doubtful identity, and again and again he points out the unreliability of eye witnesses. He is obviously fascinated by the controversial case of Anastasia, the woman who claimed to be the last survivor of the Russian Royal Family. On 16 July 1918, the Grand Duchess Anastasia, together with her parents – the Tsar and Tsarina – and her three sisters and brother, was taken down to a cellar in Ekaterinburg and shot. The bodies were destroyed by acid and thrown down a mineshaft. In February 1920 a girl tried to commit suicide in Berlin. A fellow patient in hospital declared that she recognized her as the Grand Duchess Anastasia. The girl herself later declared that this was true, and that she had escaped the massacre with the aid of a soldier named Tchaikovsky, whom she later married. After his death, she attempted to kill herself . . .

Various people who had known Anastasia went to see Mme Tchaikovsky. Her tutor, Pierre Gilliard, was at first convinced, but later changed his mind; Anastasia's uncle, the Grand Duke Andrei, was totally convinced; so was an officer who knew her well, when she addressed him by his old nickname. Soon, 'Anastasia' had hosts of people who thought her genuine, and hosts who were convinced she was a fraud. In 1938, she allowed a German lawyer to try to obtain for her a share of the Tsar's fortune lodged in foreign banks. The case dragged on for 20 years, but Mme Tchaikovsky never established her legal right to call herself the Grand Duchess Anastasia.

Locard's *Proofs of Identity* appeared in 1932, long before the law case; but the 20 pages he devotes to the identity of Mme Tchaikovsky leave very little doubt that 'Anastasia' was a fraud. Two photographs alone – one superimposing Anastasia's profile on Mme Tchaikovsky, the other superimposing Mme Tchaikovsky's profile on Anastasia-make it obvious that they are not the same person. The Grand Duchess has a smaller mouth, a smaller nose, a smaller ear; moreover, her nose is straight, while Mme Tchaikovsky's is 'tipped'. Even the fact that the photograph of the Grand Duchess Anastasia was taken at the age of 17, while that of Mme Tchaikovsky is taken two years later, cannot account for the difference; faces do not change so much in two years. Moreover, Locard shows that two photographs published in the *New York Evening Post,* purporting to be those of Mme Tchaikovsky and of the Grand Duchess Anastasia, and showing an astonishing resemblance are, in fact, both of Anastasia, one of them slightly retouched. Locard's analysis makes it clear beyond all doubt that Anna Anderson (as Mme Tchaikovsky later called herself) and Anastasia were two different people.

The riddle remains: how could a number of people who knew Anastasia intimately, like her uncle, have made such an extraordinary mistake? The answer is obviously that Anna Anderson *did* bear a close resemblance to Anastasia, and that people who had not seen Anastasia for several years were taken in by the resemblance. Locard also cites the extraordinary Tichborne case of the 1860s, in which a grotesque impostor was accepted by an English lady as her dead son. Roger Charles Tichborne was lost at sea off Brazil in 1854. Twelve years later, his mother, Lady Félicité Tichborne, received a badly spelled letter purporting to come from her long-lost son in Wagga-Wagga, Australia, asking her to send the money so he could come home. When Lady Tichborne finally went to see her son in his hotel in Paris, she was startled to see a vast whale of a man, weighing 26 stone, lying in a darkened room with his face to the wall – the son she remembered had been thin. Yet, incredibly, she accepted him as the missing Sir Roger (the son would have inherited his father's title) and allowed him a £1,000 a year until he could legally establish his claim. In due course, 'Sir Roger' became chief mourner at his mother's funeral. Like 'Anastasia', he aroused widespread support, and large sums were donated to prosecute his claim on the understanding that these supporters would be richly repaid when he won his case. This ended by costing £200,000 and dragged on for nearly a year. A commission that visited Australia had little trouble in showing that the claimant to the Tichborne millions was actually a butcher called Arthur Orton, also known as Castro. A pocket-book was found, which the claimant admitted to be his property, in which he had written: 'Some men has plenty money and no brains, and some men has plenty brains and no money. Surely men with plenty money and no brains were made for men with plenty brains and no money.' The jury had no difficulty in deciding that Arthur Orton and Sir Roger Tichborne were not the same person, and Orton was later sentenced to 14 years' imprisonment for perjury, of which he served 10. Here is a case in which there can be no possible doubt that the fraud was made possible only through the obsession of a half-blind old lady who refused to accept that her son was dead.

Far more baffling in every way is the case of the 'second Joan of Arc'. In May 1436, five years after Joan of Arc had been burnt at the stake by the English, her two brothers heard that she had returned and was taking part in a jousting tournament at Vaucouleurs, near Metz. They hurried along to denounce the impostor, but when a woman dressed in armour raised her visor, both of them greeted her as their sister Joan. In Metz, many people who had known her well in her days as a soldier accepted her as 'the Maid'. She returned to her home village of Domrémy, where her relatives, and apparently her mother, accepted her as Joan. Her brothers went to tell the king – whom Joan had crowned – that their sister was still alive, and in 1440, she went to the court. The king tried to deceive her by asking one of his men to impersonate him, but Joan was not deceived, and went and knelt at his feet, whereupon Charles VII said: 'Pucelle, my dear, you are welcome in the name of God.' Yet after this meeting, the king denounced her as an impostor. In spite of this, Joan returned to Metz and continued to be accepted as La Pucelle, the Maid. She married a knight and, as the Dame des Armoires, lived to an advanced age.

The greatest mystery that remains is: if Joan was not executed at Rouen in 1431, then who *was*? The crowd that witnessed her death was kept at a distance by 800 English soldiers. It is just conceivable that the English connived at her escape; she was a person who could command astonishing affection and loyalty, and when she complained to the Earl of Warwick that her two guards treated her disrespectfully, he was furious and immediately changed them. But if she was allowed to escape, we can only assume that some unfortunate woman – perhaps some derelict from the Rouen jail – was burned in her place. At this distance in time the mystery is clearly insoluble, but Locard's criteria of identification seem to suggest that the Dame des Armoires was Joan of Arc.*

Locard proceeds from problems of the identification of the living to the – criminologically speaking – more interesting problem of identifying the dead. Here he was able to draw upon the work of the greatest pioneers in this field, his friend and mentor Professor Alexandre Lacassagne, who, in a celebrated case of 1889, had demonstrated the techniques of identifying an unknown corpse.

*For a more detailed account of the case see *The Encyclopedia of Unsolved Mysteries*, by Colin and Damon Wilson, Harrap, London 1987.

2

In earlier centuries, the methods had been crude, and often ineffectual. A rare exception was the case of Catherine Hayes, which took place during the 'crime wave' in early eighteenth-century London. At daybreak on 2 March 1725, a watchman named Robinson saw a head lying on the muddy foreshore of the Thames at Westminster. Fortunately, the features were still intact, and the local magistrates ordered that it should be washed and have its hair combed, after which it should be placed on a pole in the local St Margaret's churchyard. Parish officers were ordered to place themselves around the churchyard, and be prepared to take into custody anyone 'who might discover signs of guilt on the sight of it'. (A footnote to the case in *The Newgate Calendar* of 1774 describes how the wounds of a corpse will bleed profusely if it is touched by the murderer.) But the head soon began to decay, whereupon the parish officers ordered that it should be preserved in a jar of spirits (probably gin).

Meanwhile, an organ-builder's apprentice named Bennet called on a woman named Catherine Hayes, who lived in Tyburn Road (now Oxford Street) and told her that he thought the head was that of her husband John. Catherine Hayes, a dominant, rather attractive woman in her mid-30s, assured him that her husband was perfectly well, and warned him against spreading false rumours. The same day, a Mr Patrick went into a pub called the Dog and Dial and remarked that the head looked like John Hayes. A youth named Billings was drinking in the pub; he told Mr Patrick that he was lodging with John Hayes, and that Hayes had been lying in bed when he left that morning. But some of Hayes's close friends were more persistent. When a man called Ashby asked her outright what had happened to her husband, Catherine Hayes told him in confidence that he had been forced to flee to Portugal, having killed a man in a quarrel. Ashby was unconvinced; he went to another friend of Hayes called Longmore, and asked him to go and put the same question. Mrs Hayes told him the same story – except that this time she claimed that the husband had fled to Hertfordshire. When the two men compared notes, they decided to go and tell their story to a magistrate. And the magistrate, a Mr Lambert, agreed that it all looked highly suspicious, and issued a warrant for the arrest of Catherine Hayes. Catherine Hayes had recently changed her lodgings, but was easily located. The officers found her in bed with the lodger, Thomas Billings. She and Billings were both arrested. So were two more lodgers called Thomas Wood – who was even younger than Billing – and a Mrs Springate.

Catherine Hayes now demanded to see the head, and was taken to the house where it was kept. On beings shown the jar, she cried dramatically: 'Oh, it is my dear husband's head!', and proceeded to kiss the jar. The man in charge of the head lifted it out of the jar by the hair, whereupon Catherine, declining to be unnerved, kissed it passionately and asked if she could have a lock of the hair. The custodian replied drily that it was bloody, and she had already had enough blood, at which the widow fainted away.

The young man Wood proved to be a weaker spirit. On being confronted with the evidence, he made a full confession. He and Billings were both Catherine's lovers. Catherine Hayes was a dominant, quarrelsome woman, and she was tired of her husband's meanness. So she persuaded her lovers to murder him. They had made John Hayes drunk on six pints of wine, and when he fell asleep, Billings had hit him on the head with a coal-hatchet; Wood completed the job with two more blows. Then they placed the neck above a bucket, and sawed off the head with a carving knife. Catherine wanted to boil it to make it unrecognizable, but the killers were too unnerved. They took the head away in a pail, and threw it on the foreshore of the river. Then they returned to the house and dismembered the body; the following night they tossed the pieces into a pond at Marylebone, where they were found just after Catherine's arrest. Mrs Springate, it seemed, had been unaware of the murder, and she was duly discharged.

Catherine Hayes was shocked when she learned that the charge against her would not be murder, but 'petty treason' – her husband was supposed to be her lord and master and she had rebelled against him. The penalty for this was to be burned alive. This finally led her to 'confess' that the other two had committed the murder. But it did no good. After she was condemned to be burned, she screamed all the way back to Newgate prison. Billings, with whom she was undoubtedly in love, was hanged. Wood died in jail of fever. And Catherine was duly burned alive – the executioner was trying to strangle her when the flames licked his hands and he was forced to jump back. The chronicle comments that she survived for a considerable time, trying to kick the burning faggots away, and that it was three hours before her body was reduced to ashes.

More than a century later, the science of identification was still in a primitive state when a tailor of Norwich called William Sheward had a furious quarrel with his wife about money matters, and slashed her throat with a razor. Sheward was not a violent man – he was, in fact, a rather inadequate alcoholic – and the realization of what he had done overwhelmed him with horror. But the thought of the hangman made him bold. He and his wife Martha had never got on together – she was a shrew, and many years his senior – and he was determined not to swing for her. Unlike Billings and Wood, he did not make the mistake of losing his nerve, but spent several days carefully dismembering the body, boiling the head to reduce the stench of decay. Then he proceeded to distribute the pieces in ditches around the area. He burned all the bloodstained nightclothes – he killed her in bed – as well as the mattress. Six days after the murder, a man who was out for a country walk wondered what his dog was chewing in a ditch; he called it, and the dog ran towards him with a human hand in its mouth. And for the next few weeks, other parts of the body were found in different places around Norwich.

The chief problem of murderers who kill their wives is to account for her sudden disappearance. Sheward told his neighbours that his wife had left him and gone to London. It was an unimaginative invention and hardly deserved to succeed. But luck was on Sheward's side. Doctors who examined the remains agreed that they were those of a woman in her 20s – Martha Sheward had been 56. She had taken good care of her hands, and Sheward had unintentionally created further confusion by boiling most of the members to reduce the smell. He also avoided another mistake made by Catherine Hayes, and cut up the head into small pieces. A magistrate ordered that the unidentified remains should be pickled in spirit, and kept in the Guildhall, and there they remained undisturbed for the next 18 years.

Sheward was a haunted man; he even gave up alcohol in case he betrayed his secret in his cups. But in 1862, 11 years after the murder, he felt sufficiently relaxed to marry again – this time to a lady of a less quarrelsome disposition, by whom he had two children. Oddly enough, he frequently tried his wife's patience by extravagantly praising the virtues of the deceased Martha; now she was gone, he allowed himself to indulge in sentimental reminiscences.

By 1869, his conscience was troubling him so much that he decided to commit suicide. For some reason, he chose to do it in London, where he had met his wife when he was a young man. On New Year's Day, he took a steamboat to Chelsea, and tried to nerve himself to cut his throat. 'But the Almighty would not let him do it.' Instead, he went and stood in front of the house in Walworth, where he had first seen his wife, then went up to a policeman standing on the corner, and declared that he wanted to confess to the murder of his wife. He was taken to the police station, and told the story in detail.

The remains in the Guildhall were now re-examined, and the doctor who had originally identified them as those of a young girl agreed that the hands could have been those of a older woman who had done little housework. By now, Sheward had regretted his confession and retracted it, realizing that there was no evidence against him but his own admissions. But the jury preferred to believe the original confession, and he was sentenced to death. And Britain's best-known pathologist, Alfred Swain Taylor (who had been asked to look at the pickled remains) remarked: 'The case shows the necessity of using extreme caution in giving an opinion respecting the age of bones, and of allowing sufficient latitude in years for the bones of adults.' But Taylor's own record as a forensic pathologist leaves some doubt as to whether he would have been any more successful in assessing the age of the dismembered corpse.

3

It was in 1889, 20 years after Sheward had been hanged, that a great pathologist transformed the identification of corpses into an exact science. His name was Jean Alexandre Eugène Lacassagne, and he was the Professor of Forensic Medicine at the University of Lyon. Lacassagne was an obsessive collector of facts. In 1885, an old man had been found dead in a locked bedroom in Savoy; he had been shot through the head, and a revolver in his hand seemed to indicate suicide. But there was one odd circumstance. The arms were under the bedclothes, which had been pulled up under the chin. Could a man blow out his brains, and then pull up the bedclothes under his chin? Called to examine the body, Lacassagne found other suspicious circumstances. There were no powder burns on the dead man's forehead, no powder grains embedded in the skin. Most people who shoot themselves in the head place the muzzle of the revolver against the skin; it is exceedingly rare for the suicide to hold the revolver at a distance. Nevertheless, the two doctors who had first examined the corpse had diagnosed suicide.

The eyes of the corpse were closed. Lacassagne now spoke to a number of nurses, and asked them for their observation of the eyes of corpses. He was told that when people die naturally, their eyes are usually closed. But people who die suddenly – of suicide, or of a heart attack – have their eyes open. In the case of violence, they may be staring. Lacassagne reasoned that, whether the old man committed suicide or was murdered, his eyes should have remained open. Therefore someone had closed them after death.

But what of the revolver clutched in the hand? Current medical wisdom insisted that this was a sure indication of sudden violent death. A French soldier killed at Sedan continued to hold his rifle with one hand while the other pulled back the ejector. Another whose head had been blown off by a shell sat with a cup half raised to his lips. So if the old man was holding the revolver, he must have shot himself. A gun placed in the hand after death will not be gripped.

Again Lacassagne decided that the only way to find out was by experiment. When he was in hospital in Lyon or Paris, he asked to be instantly notified when anyone died, and then tried closing the hands of the corpse around any convenient object. He discovered that the hand *could* be made to grasp a revolver after death – at least enough not to drop it. And if the corpse was found after rigor mortis had set in, usually around two or three hours, then the gun would be difficult to remove from the hand, producing the impression that it was tightly gripped.

These facts, taken in association with the pulled-up bedclothes and the lack of powder burns, led Lacassagne to assert that the old man had been murdered. The old man's son, who was under suspicion, was arrested and convicted of the crime. He had shot his father, placed the revolver in the hand, locked the door and then escaped through the window. He had made the obvious mistake of closing the eyes and pulling the bedclothes up under the chin; but these facts had escaped the attention of the local doctors, who had supported the suicide verdict. Only Lacassagne's obsession with experimental evidence revealed that a murder had taken place.

In 1889, Lacassagne was 45 years old. He had been an army doctor in North Africa in his youth, and had written a treatise on tattoos as a method of identifying corpses. It was in the November of that year that he was asked to undertake the most unpleasant task of his career.

Three months earlier, a roadmender had discovered a canvas sack hidden in some bushes by the riverbank at Millery, 10 miles from Lyon; it proved to contain the decomposing naked body of a dark-haired man. Dr Paul Bernard, one of Lacassagne's pupils, directed the police to take the corpse to the morgue in Lyon. There he examined the body, which had been wrapped in oilcloth and tied round with string. Bernard concluded that the man had been strangled. Meanwhile, another important piece of evidence had been found – the remains of a wooden trunk, which stank of rotting flesh. Fragments of labels indicated that it had been sent from Paris to Perrache, in Lyon, on 27 July.

Now on that date, a man had gone to the Paris police to report the disappearance of his brother-in-law, a bailiff called Toussaint-Augssent Gouffé. Gouffé was a 49-year-old widower who lived with his three daughters and had an office in the rue Montmartre. But he was a man of powerful sex drive, and spent most of his evenings pursuing the opposite sex in the cafés and night-clubs of Paris. He had last been seen on Friday 27 July. He was accustomed to spend Friday nights in beds other than his own, and as a result of this habit, he usually left the day's takings in his office overnight. The porter had heard a man go upstairs to Gouffés office at nine o'clock on Friday evening, and assumed it was the bailiff. But when the man came downstairs, he realized it was a stranger. He had started to ask the stranger his business, but the man hurried away. The next morning, the porter looked in Gouffés office, half expecting to discover a robbery. But everything was in perfect order, and a sum of 14,000 francs was found lying behind some papers.

The disappearance of Gouffé became something of a sensation in Paris, particularly when police investigation uncovered his fascinating love life. The detective in charge of the case was Assistant Superintendent Marie-François Goron, the man who had followed Pranzini's trail all over Europe two years earlier. When, one morning, Goron found two provincial newspapers on his desk, with accounts of the Lyon discovery, he lost no time in telegraphing Lyon for a fuller version of the events. Then he despatched the brother-in-law, a man named Landry, to Lyon, to see if he could identify the corpse. Lacassagne has an amusing account of the Lyon morgue, which was housed on an obnoxious barge on the river, and which, in mid-August, smelt like an open grave. His eyes watering with retching, Landry cast a swift glance at the corpse and fled back to the riverbank. His brother-in-law had chestnut hair, he said, and that of the corpse was black.

Goron was a stubborn man; he made his own way down to Lyon. This was against the advice of the examining magistrate, who assured him that the Lyon case was solved. A cabman had told the police that three men had unloaded a heavy trunk off the Paris train and driven off with it to a spot near Millery; there they had unloaded the trunk and thrown it into the bushes. The cabman had identified three convicts by their photographs in the rogues' gallery, and both he and they were now under arrest. But the cabman claimed this had happened on 6 July, before Gouffé had vanished. When Goron saw the label on the remains of the trunk, proving it had been despatched from Paris the day after Gouffés disappearance, he sent for the cabman and asked him what he was playing at. The cabman admitted that his story had been an attempt to 'get in well' with the authorities, since he was in danger of losing his licence. It is not recorded whether he was charged with wasting the time of the police.

Goron interviewed Dr Bernard, who told him that the corpse could not possibly be that of Gouffé, since the hair was the wrong colour. He produced a test tube with some hair taken from the head of the unknown man. Goron asked for some distilled water, and immersed the hair in it. To Bernard's embarrassment, this had the effect of removing caked dust and blood, and revealing that the hair was, in fact, auburn in colour . . . Goron lost no time in ordering the exhumation of the corpse.

The body was in an advanced state of decomposition when it finally arrived in Lacassagne's laboratory at the University. The genital organs had entirely rotted away, most of the hair and beard had also vanished. Parts of the skull were missing. There was little to do but concentrate on the bones and the hair. Lacassagne had some irritable things to say to Bernard about the previous autopsy.

He spent days removing the maggoty flesh until he finally had a skeleton; formaldehyde lessened but could not drown the stench. And when the skeleton finally lay on the dissecting bench, and Lacassagne could study it in detail, he observed that there had been something wrong with the man's right leg. The knee was slightly deformed, and the parts of the bones to which the muscles are attached revealed that the muscles must have been undeveloped. Lacassagne was able to tell Goron that the man had a limp, and had probably suffered from a tubercular infection of the leg in his youth. Checks with Gouffés relatives in Paris, as well as with his doctor and shoemaker, revealed that he *had* limped. Breaks in the thyroid cartilage convinced Lacassagne that he had been correct in believing that the man had been strangled, but Lacassagne thought the signs were consistent with manual strangulation rather than strangulation with a cord. Close examination of the state of the teeth led Lacassagne to conclude that Bernard had also been mistaken about the age of the corpse; Bernard had guessed 35 or so; Lacassagne decided he was closer to 50. Gouffé had been 49. Some of Gouffés hair, found on his hairbrush, was compared under the microscope with the hair of the corpse; again, Lacassagne concluded that Gouffé and the unknown man were the same person. In fact, when Goron came to the laboratory, Lacassagne turned to him with a flourish. 'Messieurs, I present you with Monsieur Gouffé.'

But who had murdered him? A friend of Gouffés had been suspected and placed under arrest, but released for lack of evidence. But by now, Goron had another possible suspect. Another friend of Gouffé's had told him that Gouffé had been seen drinking in a bar with a man called Michel Eyraud two days before the murder; also present was Eyraud's attractive young mistress Gabrielle Bompard. The mention of a pretty girl had aroused Goron's interest; by now he knew that the missing bailiff was the sort of man whose mouth watered at the sight of any attractive, or for that matter unattractive, girl. He tried to find Eyraud, without success. Eyraud sounded as if he might be in need of money. He was a married man of 46, but was separated from his wife; he had been a distiller in Sèvres, then become a salesman for a firm that went bankrupt; he was ugly and pockmarked, but apparently attractive to women. His 20-year-old mistress Gabrielle had been a prostitute – she claimed she had been raped under hypnosis as a child. Eyraud, like Pranzini, had been something of an adventurer, and some of his business deals had been distinctly unsavoury.

Back in Paris, Goron decided on a rather desperate expedient, a thousand-to-one chance. There was enough of the trunk left to have a copy made; this Goron had exhibited in the morgue, and begged the public to go and look at it. They did, in their thousands, since the Gouffé case was still discussed avidly. A trunk-maker ventured the opinion that it looked as if it had been manufactured in England. And a few days later, Goron received a letter from a Frenchman living in London, who had read about the case in French newspapers sold there. The previous June, an ugly, balding man named Michel had taken lodgings with him; he was accompanied by his daughter. They had bought a trunk from Zwanziger's in Euston Road, and departed for Paris with it. When her landlord had remarked that it seemed a large trunk for her possessions, the girl had laughed and answered that they would have plenty to put in it in Paris.

The hunt was now on for Eyraud and Gabrielle Bompard. The newspapers publicized the search. And, at this point, Eyraud virtually gave himself up. He wrote Goron a long letter, from New York, asking why he was being slandered in this way. He had nothing to do with the disappearance of his friend Gouffé. Perhaps Gabrielle had persuaded one of her lovers to murder him . . . He would, he promised, return to Paris soon and hand himself over to Goron.

A few days later, Goron was startled when Gabrielle herself came to see him. She was small and pretty, with grey eyes, good teeth and a large head. 'Corruption literally oozed from her', said Goron later in his memoirs. She was accompanied by a middle-aged man who seemed to be infatuated with her. And her purpose, incredibly, was to denounce Michel Eyraud as the killer of Gouffé, and to admit that she had been his willing accomplice. The crime had been committed in a room at 3 rue Tronson-Decoudray, but she had not been present. She had travelled with Eyraud to America, where she had met the gentleman who now accompanied her. Eyraud had planned to murder and rob him too, she had informed the proposed victim, and together they had fled back to France. Now her lover had persuaded her to go to the police and tell them everything. They were both obviously upset when the prefect, M. Lozé, told them that he was compelled to place Gabrielle under arrest.

The hunting down of Eyraud is another classic example of the needle-in-the-haystack method. Two detectives travelled around America and Canada searching for him, followed by enthusiastic pressmen whose stories gave Eyraud prior warning whenever the hunters came within 500 miles. But people who had been swindled and robbed by the fugitive kept the trail alive. In New York he had persuaded a Turk to lend him a costly oriental robe, claiming he wanted to be photographed in it; that was the last the Turk saw of Eyraud or the robe. And an American actor who is called by Goron 'Sir Stout' had been touched by Eyraud's account of how his wife had deserted him, and lent the distracted husband $80. Sir Stout was of the opinion that Eyraud was a great actor. In March 1890, the disgruntled detectives returned to Paris without their quarry. But in Havana, Cuba, a French dressmaker was offered a rich oriental robe by a pockmarked Frenchman, and a few weeks later, she read a newspaper description of the Turkish robe 'borrowed' by Eyraud. That day she saw the Frenchman standing before her shop and asked him if he still had the robe. Eyraud said no. The dressmaker then engaged him in conversation, and brought up the name of the assassin Eyraud. 'You look rather like him, you know.' The next day, the Frenchman came back to her shop with a newspaper that contained a poor photograph of Eyraud. 'Look, he's nothing like me.' But when he left, the dressmaker contacted the French consul. Now by an extraordinary coincidence too preposterous for a detective novel, one of Eyraud's former employees from the distillery happened to be in Havana at the time. The consul sent for him and told him that he thought Eyraud was in town. And as the man left the consulate, he bumped into Eyraud, who had been keeping the dressmaker under observation. There was no point in trying to disguise his identity, so Eyraud invited his former employee for a drink, and begged him not to betray him. But late that evening, when Eyraud tried to lead him down a darkened alleyway, the man suspected that Fyraud was contemplating a more certain method of ensuring his silence, and leapt into a passing taxi. The next day, the search was on; in Eyraud's room in the Hotel Roma, the police found his baggage packed, but learned that Fyraud had preferred to sleep at a seedy hotel opposite. That night, Eyraud tried to get into a brothel, but the Madame was suspicious of his down-at-heel appearance, and sent him packing. By chance, he again ran into his former employee, and remarked: 'It's all up with me now.' He was right. Half an hour later, a policeman saw the solitary wanderer, who looked aimless and tired, and took him back to the station. In the night, the man made an unsuccessful attempt at suicide, confirming the opinion of the Spanish police that they had captured the assassin of Gouffé.

Goron had already obtained an account – or rather, several accounts – of the murder from Gabrielle Bompard, but she was such a pathological liar that it was impossible to be sure of how much was true. Now Fyraud was back in Paris, it was at least possible to construct an accurate account of the crime. When they had bought the trunk in London, they had intended to use it to conceal a corpse, but had not yet chosen the victim. Eyraud had learned of Gouffés existence only two days before the murder; a mutual friend had described the bailiff who was reputed to be rich, and who left a large sum of money in his office before he went off for a Friday night's debauchery. It was Gabrielle who accosted Gouffé, and made an appointment with him for Thursday evening. This was the evening when Gouffé, Eyraud and Bompard had been seen in the Brasserie Gutenberg. She had then succeeded in making a 'secret' appointment with him for the following evening. Gouffé needed no persuading to go to her room; as they went in he

The police decided on shock tactics, and took Mrs Nack to view the remains. Pointing to the legs, the detective asked: 'Are those Willie's?'

Mrs Nack looked at him haughtily. 'I would not know, as I never saw the gentleman naked.'

But the *Journal* reporters had heard another story from the inhabitants of the boarding-house and from neighbours. They asserted that Mrs Nack and Willie Guldensuppe had been lovers for years. But they had quarrelled recently, the cause apparently being a fellow lodger, a young barber named Martin Thorn.

The police managed to forestall the *Journal* reporters at the barber shop where Thorn worked. There another barber named John Gotha told them that Thorn had confessed the murder of Willie Guldensuppe to him. Thorn's story was that Mrs Nack had seduced him when her regular lover, Guldensuppe, was away. But when Guldensuppe had found them in bed together, the brawny masseur had beaten Thorn so badly that the barber had to go into hospital. And when he reported for work with two black eyes, he was dismissed. Thorn decided to change his lodgings. But Mrs Nack had continued to visit him there. And Thorn had purchased a stiletto and a pistol, determined to revenge himself . . .

Martin Thorn was arrested, and the *Journal* headline declared: MURDER MYSTERY SOLVED BY JOURNAL. By now, both the *Journal* and the police had located the spot where the murder took place. It was in a pleasantly rural area on Long Island called Woodside, not far from the store where the oilcloth had been purchased. A farm stood next to the cottage, and on the day Willie Guldensuppe's torso had been recovered from the river, the farmer had been puzzled to see that his ducks had turned a pink colour. The reason, he soon discovered, was that they had been bathing in a large pool of pink-coloured water, which had issued from the bathroom drainage pipe of the cottage next door. But it was not until the farmer read of the arrest of Martin Thorn and Augusta Nack that he connected this event with a couple who had rented the cottage two weeks earlier. They had called themselves Mr and Mrs Braun, and had paid $15 rent in advance. But they had only visited the cottage on two occasions, the second on the day of the disappearance of Willie Guldensuppe . . . Belatedly, the farmer decided to pass on his suspicions to the police.

A revolver, a carving knife and a saw were found in the cottage; but, advised by their respective lawyers, the two declined to confess. Thorn succeeded in escaping to Canada and was brought back; yet even when shown the 'confession' he had allegedly made to John Gotha, he continued to insist on his total innocence.

The difference between the Nack – Thorn trial and that of Eyraud and Bompard is a measure of the difference between Paris and New York in the *fin de siecle* period; the French would have been horrified by the carelessness and levity of the American courtroom. Thorn was represented by a brilliant but not over-scrupulous lawyer named Howe, whose line of defence was simply that the two defendants were unacquainted with one another, and that neither of them knew the victim anyway. What evidence was there, asked Howe, that the assorted arms and legs belonged to Willie Golden-soup? (On other occasions he pronounced it Gludensop, Gildersleeve, Goldylocks and Silverslipper.) They might belong to any corpse. What evidence was there that the victim had ever existed?

This audacious line of defence might well have succeeded – New York jurors liked to be amused, and Howe had talked innumerable clients out of the electric chair – except that Mrs Nack decided to confess. Hearst had sent a Presbyterian minister to see her in prison every day, and one day he had brought his son, a curly-haired child of four, who climbed on to her lap and begged her to clear her conscience; Hearst naturally printed the story a day ahead of his rivals. And on the second day of the trial, Mrs Nack declared that she had seen the light, and gave a gruesomely detailed account of the crime. On the day before the murder, she and Martin Thorn had rented the cottage on Long Island. She then told Willie Guldensuppe that she had decided to run it as a baby farm, and asked him to come and give his opinion. When Willie entered the building, Thorn was waiting behind a door, and shot him in the back of the head. Then they threw him into the empty bathtub and, while he still breathed stertorously, Thorn sawed off his head. While Mrs Nack went out to buy oilcloth, Thorn dismembered the body – he had once been a medical student, which explained the surgical skill noticed by the police surgeon. He left the taps running, under the impression that the water would run down a drain and into the sewers; in fact, there was no drain, and it formed a pool in the farmyard, where the ducks were delighted at the opportunity of a midsummer bathe. Thorn then encased the head in plaster of Paris, and threw it in the river . . .

The narrative so upset one of the jurors that he fainted and had to be carried out of court. This caused a mistrial, and when the case was resumed, Thorn had changed his story. He now declared that the cottage had been rented only as a love nest, and that on the day of the murder, he had arrived to find Mrs Nack already there. 'Willie's upstairs. I've just killed him.' Once again, Howe rested his defence upon the assertion that there was no proof that the corpse was that of Willie Guldensuppe, and for a while it looked as if the absence of an American Lacassagne might sway the issue in favour of the accused. But the jury chose to be convinced by the negative evidence of the missing tattoo, and found them both guilty. Martin Thorn went to the electric chair; Mrs Nack was sentenced to 20 years. The *Journal* was jubilant, but the *World* took the view that Thorn was the victim of a scheming woman.

Mrs Nack was apparently an exemplary prisoner, and was parolled after ten years; she returned to her old neighbourhood on Ninth Avenue and opened a delicatessen shop; but for some reason, the neighbours found her cooked meats unattractive, and she retired into obscurity.

5

In the same year, a Chicago businessman named Adolph Louis Luetgart decided to dispose of his wife's body by a method that showed startling originality.

Luetgart seems to have been what is clinically known as a satyr – a man whose sexual appetites are insatiable. When his first wife died, he decided to marry again – a curiously ill-judged decision in view of his obsessive need for new mistresses. Louise Bicknese had been a maid in their home, and had probably been his mistress. And after he married her, he lost no time in according Louise's maid, Mary Simering, the same status. He also slept regularly with Mrs Christine Feldt, and with a saloon-keeper's wife named Agathia Tosch. His love life, which included regular visits to prostitutes, impaired his business efficiency, and by 1897 he was on the verge of bankruptcy.

His domestic relations had been strained for many years. On one occasion, he told a mistress that his wife had been seriously ill and he had sent for a doctor. 'If I had waited a little longer, the dead, rotten beast would have croaked.' Neighbours who heard her screaming one day looked through the parlour window and saw that her husband had her by the throat; when he realized he was observed, he released her. A few days later he was seen chasing her down the street with a revolver.

On 11 March 1897, Luetgart ordered 325 lb of caustic potash from a wholesale drugs firm – he explained he needed it to make soap. It was delivered to his business address, a sausage factory on Hermitage and Diversey, the next day. More than a month later, on 24 April, he ordered an employee known as Smokehouse Frank to take the metal drums of potash to the basement and crush it up with an axe. Then he and Frank placed the crushed potash in the middle of three vats, used for boiling the sausage meat. Luetgart turned on the steam, and the vat was soon full of boiling caustic potash, a liquid strong enough to dissolve flesh on contact.

At about 10.30 on the night of Friday 1 May, a young German girl who was passing the factory saw Luetgart and his wife going down an alley near the building. The night-watchman, Frank Bialk, was sent out on an errand, and when he came back, found the factory door was now closed. Luetgart told him to go to the engine room, which was apart from the factory. Later, the watchman was sent on another errand. The next morning, the man found Luetgart fully dressed in his office at an early hour. When he asked if the fire should be allowed to go out, Luetgart told him to bank it up. In the basement, the watchman noticed a gluey substance on the floor, with some flakes of bone in it. But since the vats were used for boiling meat, he thought nothing of it. On the following Monday morning, Smokehouse Frank was told to scrape up the gluey substance and flush it down the drain; whatever would not go down the drain should be scattered on the railroad tracks.

On 4 May, Mrs Bicknese's brother Diedrich came from out of town to see his sister; on being told she was not at home, he went away and returned in the evening. Luetgart then explained that he had not seen her since the previous Saturday – she had walked out of the house with about $18 in her handbag. He was convinced that she had simply left him.

Diedrich spent the next two days calling on relatives and friends looking for his sister; then he went to the police. Summoned before Police Captain Schuettler, Luetgart explained that he had not notified the authorities of his wife's disappearance because he was a respectable businessman and wanted to avoid scandal. Schuettler decided that Louise Luetgart had probably committed suicide, and began dragging the river. A week after her disappearance, they interrogated Smokehouse Frank and the night-watchman, and heard about the slimy substance on the basement floor.

The middle vat was still two-thirds full of a brown liquid like soft soap. Schuettler, now reasonably certain that he was looking at all that remained of Louise Luetgart, decided to drain it, using gunny sacks as filters.

Adolph Luetgart had been correct in his assumption that boiling caustic potash would turn a body into soap. But he had forgotten to remove his wife's rings. Two of these were found in the filters, one with the initials 'L.L.' engraved on it.

Even with this evidence, the outcome of the trial was by no means a foregone conclusion. The defence argued that the evidence was entirely circumstantial, and that Mrs Luetgart was probably still alive. In fact, she had been seen in New York by a man who had known her well. She had also been seen in Kenosha, Wisconsin, by several witnesses two or three days after the murder. Luetgart's 12-year-old son Louis insisted that he had heard his mother in the house after his father had left for the factory. The young German girl, Emma Schmiemicke, who claimed to have seen Luetgart and his wife going towards the factory, proved to be weak minded, and her testimony was discredited. Perhaps the most convincing argument of the defence was to point out that if Luetgart had dissolved his wife in caustic potash, he would hardly be likely to leave the incriminating evidence in the vat when he could pour it down the drain – many people felt that this was self-evidently true. They were forgetting that Luetgart believed that nothing of his wife remained in the vat, and that if he had poured the 'soft soap' down the drain, it would have been practically an admission of guilt.

The prosecution evidence was, admittedly, mostly circumstantial, but as such it was very convincing. Fifty years later, the medical evidence alone would have convinced any jury. Many experts identified the fragments of bone taken from the vat as human. Professor George Dorsey, an archaeologist from the Field Columbian Museum, testified that one of the bones found in a pile of animal bones in the basement was the left thigh bone of a woman. Other experts testified that fragments of bone found in the drain pipes leading from the vat were human: part of the humerus (or great bone from an arm), a fourth toe of the right foot, ear bones, a palm bone, fragments of a temporal bone, and a sesamoid bone from the right foot. (This was discussed with some passion, with the result that the sesamoid bone, which no one had heard of before the Luetgart trial, became part of normal conversation.) Mrs Luetgart had had false teeth, and part of an artificial tooth had also been discovered. Dr Charles Gibson and Professor de la Fontaine testified that the soapy substance was human flesh that had been boiled in caustic potash. All this should have been quite conclusive, but in 1897, American juries were as suspicious of experts as a British jury had been in 1832, when it rejected James Marsh's evidence that Farmer Bodle had been poisoned with arsenic, and set the murderer free.

The prosecution had no difficulty in demonstrating that Luetgart had behaved like a man with something on his conscience. When Mrs Tosch, the saloon-keeper's wife, enquired as to the whereabouts of his wife, Luetgart blenched and replied: 'I am as innocent as the southern skies' – recalling Helene Jegado's protestation 'I am innocent' before anyone accused her. And a detective had hidden under the bed of the night-watchman Bialk when Luetgart came to visit him, and overheard Luetgart ask nervously whether the police had found anything incriminating in the factory; when Bialk replied in the negative, Luetgart sighed 'That's good.' The large quantities of hunyadi water that Bialk had been sent out to purchase on the night Mrs Luetgart disappeared had later been purchased by a druggist, who testified to the sale, demonstrating that Luetgart had no genuine need for the 'nerve medicine'.

Luetgart's defence was simple; he had decided to make a large quantity of soft soap to give his factory a thorough cleaning, his aim being to persuade investors to provide more capital. The potash was not the only thing he had bought; there was also a quantity of grease – and a defence witness swore that he had delivered the grease. But the prosecution pointed out that it was absurd to spend $40 on potash to make soft soap when he could have bought enough soft soap to clean the factory for $1. And if he was really inspired with a desire to make soft soap, why spend all night doing it instead of paying one of his workmen to do it by day?

The jury was divided; when they failed to agree at the end of three days and nights, the judge discharged them. But at his second trial, they were able to reach a unanimous verdict of guilty. Luetgart escaped the death sentence; instead, he was sent to prison for life (where he eventually died, still protesting his innocence). The verdict reflected the doubt felt by the judge and jury that Mrs Luetgart just *might* still be alive. The defence in the Guldensuppe case relied on the same shadow of a doubt. In retrospect, the notion strikes us as preposterous. Yet in a missing body case, no jury has the right to make an absolute assumption of guilt, in case 'circumstantial evidence' happens to point in the wrong direction.

The classic case of such a miscarriage of justice occurred in 1660, at Chipping Campden in Gloucestershire, and because the mystery is still unsolved, has become known as the 'Campden Wonder'. On 16 August 1660, a 70-year-old steward named William Harrison disappeared while collecting rents, and his wife sent a servant named John Perry out to look for him. Perry did not return that night, and when a bloodstained hat was found on the road, Perry was suspected of murdering his master. Under interrogation, Perry declared that Harrison had been murdered by his mother and brother, Joan and Richard Perry, and that Richard had strangled Harrison with a hair net. All three were indicted, but one judge declined to try them because no body had been found. When he was finally tried, John Perry withdrew his confession, declaring that he was 'mad and knew not what he said'. But it was too late, and all three were hanged, and their bodies hung in chains. But two years later, William Harrison had reappeared, and described how he had been 'shanghaied' and taken to Smyrna, where he was purchased as a slave by an old Turkish doctor. When the old man died, he succeeded in getting a ship back to London. This extraordinary story was widely believed at the time, but everyone who has examined the case since then has pointed out its various absurdities and inconsistencies. The mystery remains insoluble: why William Harrison chose to disappear, why John Perry chose to hang his mother and brother as well as himself. All that *is* perfectly clear is that if the judge, Sir Robert Hyde, had chosen to sentence them to life imprisonment, a great injustice would have been avoided. The Campden Wonder remains a warning against the dangers of circumstantial evidence.

6

In England at the turn of the century, the science of forensic medicine had not yet recovered from the conspicuous misjudgements of Alfred Swain Taylor, particularly the Smethurst case. Smethurst's conviction and subsequent pardon caused widespread concern about the accuracy of medical experts, for it was clear that he could have gone to the gallows. Where laboratories and institutes of forensic medicine were concerned, England continued to lag far behind the Continent. France had its Institute of Legal Science at Lyon; Scotland Yard made do with Home Office pathologists and toxicologists who could be called upon when needed. Among the best of these were Dr A. P. Luff,

Dr William (later Sir William) Willcox, and Dr Augustus Joseph Pepper, all three of St Mary's Hospital in Paddington.

Pepper's name came to the attention of the wider public in 1903, when he figured in one of the most sensational murder trials of the year, that of Samuel Herbert Dougal, the 'Moat Farm murderer'. Dougal had spent most of his life in the army, and attained the rank of sergeant; during that time, two of his wives died under curious circumstances-according to Dougal, both of oyster poisoning. Discharged after he had spent a year in jail for forgery, Dougal paid court to a cultured and romantic spinster, Camille Holland, and induced her to elope with him; it was Miss Holland who purchased Moat House Farm in Essex in 1899. But when Dougal made an attempt to climb into the maidservant's bed, Miss Holland ordered him to leave. A few days later, she vanished; Dougal simply announced that she had taken a holiday. And for four years he lived at the farm and seduced a succession of maidservants, meanwhile gaining access to Miss Holland's bank account and securities by means of forgery. In March 1904 the police came to call to enquire about Miss Holland, and Dougal decided to flee. He was caught in London and charged with forgery. Meanwhile the police had succeeded in locating a ditch which had existed in 1899, and eventually uncovered a greatly decomposed female corpse. But could it be proved to be that of Camille Holland? It was Pepper who examined the remains, and established that it was that of a middle-aged woman who had been shot below the ear. Unfortunately, Miss Holland had no distinguishing marks, and the utmost forensic skill could not prove the identity of the corpse. This was finally accomplished by Miss Holland's shoe-maker, who identified the boots he had made for her by his own initials, worked into the heel in brass tacks. Dougal confessed to the murder as he stood on the scaffold.

Later that year, 1903, Pepper figured in another case involving identification – the Druce affair. Thomas Charles Druce died in 1864 and was buried in a vault in Highgate cemetery. In 1898, the wife of one of his sons, Anna Maria Druce, created a sensation by asserting that Druce had not been the prosperous draper everyone assumed, but the highly eccentric Duke of Portland, John Bentinck, who had died in 1879. According to Anna Maria, the duke had lost his reason because he had killed his younger brother George Bentinck, after a quarrel about a woman – George Bentinck had been found dead in a field, apparently having succumbed to heart disease. Anna Maria's contention was that the coffin in Highgate contained lead taken from a roof. She wanted the coffin opened to prove her contention. Thomas Druce's son Herbert opposed the exhumation, inevitably producing the impression that he had something to hide. A court supported his decision. The dispute dragged on for nine years and, as in the Tichborne case, many 'shareholders' were persuaded to contribute to the legal costs, on a promise of receiving a share of the Portland fortune. Several apparently credible witnesses testified that Thomas Druce and the Duke of Portland were the same person, and eventually, on 30 December 1907, the Highgate vault was opened, with Dr Pepper in attendance. Pepper was assisted by Sir Thomas Stevenson, the toxicologist who had figured in the Lamson case, and whose position as Home Office toxicologist Pepper had taken over in 1900. They were able to prove, on the medical evidence given by the doctor who had attended Thomas Druce in 1864, that the bearded man in the coffin was undoubtedly Druce, and not the Duke of Portland or a quantity of lead. Two witnesses were imprisoned for perjury, and the most sensational 'identification' drama since Tichborne ended in anticlimax.

Pepper had also figured in the prosecution of Arthur Devereux, a chemist's assistant who, in 1905, had poisoned his wife and twin sons with morphine, then concealed their bodies in a trunk, which he placed in storage. His motive was poverty, and the desire to devote himself completely to his eldest son, whom he adored. His mother-in-law revealed unusual talents as a detective, and tracked down the trunk to a Kilburn warehouse, where it was opened by the police. In this case, Pepper could only confirm that the victims had been poisoned with morphine; he was unable to combat Devereux's assertion that his wife had committed suicide. But Devereux had made the mistake of describing himself as a widower when he applied for a new job – some weeks before the death of his wife. This convinced the jury of his guilt, and he was hanged in August 1905.

So by the year 1907, Pepper was England's best-known pathologist – at least in his own narrow world of hospitals and police courts – a kind of Anglo-Saxon equivalent of Lacassagne. And, like Lacassagne, Pepper's reputation would be eclipsed by that of his most brilliant pupil. By 1905, Pepper had acquired himself a protégé', an earnest young medical student named Bernard Spilsbury. In fact, Spilsbury was not so young; he had become a medical student at the relatively late age of 22, in 1899, after three years at Magdalen College, Oxford. Son of a wholesale chemist who had wanted to be a doctor, Spilsbury was a quiet, introverted young man who gave his contemporaries the impression of being a mere plodder. Pathology was not the most popular subject at St Mary's, being known as 'the beastly science'. But Spilsbury was soon fascinated by it. No one has ever said so, but it is impossible not to suspect that Spilsbury was a devotee of the Sherlock Holmes stories, which had made Conan Doyle so famous in the 1890s; one merely has to look at a picture of Spilsbury looking down a microscope, with his serious, intellectual face, to be reminded of Holmes. By 1904, as his biographers Douglas Browne and E. V. Tullet remark, Spilsbury had been a medical student far longer than modern standards allow, and he would be almost 28 before he became a qualified doctor. He became Pepper's assistant at St Mary's, and married on a salary of £200 a year. When Pepper retired in 1908, Spilsbury was appointed to succeed him as pathologist. He was often called to give evidence in criminal cases, many involving death during abortion. But it was in 1910, when he was 33, that Bernard Spilsbury became a household word.

The Crippen case has been written about so often that it is difficult to discern the underlying reality. In his novel *We the Accused*, Ernest Raymond presented the story in a way that is sympathetic to the little doctor; since then, the case has been dramatized, filmed, even turned into a musical. The basic outline of the drama has the simplicity of a folk tale. The kindly, mild-mannered doctor is married to an aggressive and hysterical female who bullies him. He falls in love with his quiet, womanly little secretary, and is finally driven to murdering his wife – or, in other versions, kills her accidentally in the course of administering a drug to lessen her sexual demands. His dismemberment of her body so horrifies public opinion that he goes to the gallows, possibly innocent, certainly deserving of mercy.

The truth is rather more complex. Crippen was an American whose medical degrees, if they existed, would not have allowed him to practise in England; his diploma came from a college of homoeopathy, still regarded by many members of the medical profession as a crank aberration. He was a 30-year-old widower when he met a 19-year-old Polish girl who had Anglicized her name to Cora Turner. She was the mistress of a stove manufacturer, who had set her up in a flat and was paying for her singing lesson – Cora was convinced she would become a great singer. The notion of being a doctor's wife appealed to her, and she induced Crippen to propose by telling him that her lover wanted her to run away with him. The great depression of 1893 made life difficult;

when they were forced to move in with Cora's parents, she told him it was time to forget general practice and become a quack. Crippen remained, basically, a quack and a confidence man for the rest of his life. He worked as a salesman for a patent medicine company, and in 1897, became manager of its London office. His employer called himself Professor Munyon, and his cure for piles, advertised by a picture of himself with an upraised finger, gave rise to many ribald jokes. But Munyon fired Crippen when he found he was the 'manager' of a music-hall singer – Cora was now calling herself Belle Elmore and was on the stage – and from then on, Crippen was forced to struggle on as a low-grade quack selling worthless nostrums. He became a consultant to a firm of dubious ear specialists, Drovet's, and a magazine editor who called on Crippen had his ears examined with a filthy speculum which he made no attempt to disinfect. He was also startled by Crippen's flamboyant dress – the loud shirt and yellow bow tie, the enormous diamond stick-pin. For a quiet, unassuming little man, Crippen had an odd taste in clothes. He also had a reputation for meanness – he made a habit of offering to buy a drink, then discovering he had left his money at home, and borrowing half a crown. The editor commented on Crippen's 'flabby gills and shifty eyes'.

The 'ear specialist' Drovet went bankrupt when the firm was convicted of gross negligence in the death of a locksmith and other examples of what amounted to medical homicide. But it was there that Crippen met a 17-year-old typist named Ethel LeNeve (whose real name was Neave). She was a moaning hypochondriac whose endless complaints of headache and catarrh had earned her the nickname 'Not very well thank you'. She had been a miserable child, painfully conscious of a deformed foot, and hating her father because he insisted that it would cure itself if she walked properly. (He proved to be right.) She was also jealous of her vivacious younger sister. Yet underneath these unpleasant traits, she had a highly dominant character, and this is undoubtedly what attracted Crippen to her. Crippen was something of a masochist in his relations with women. This is presumably why he did not divorce Cora when he found she had taken an ex-prize-fighter as a lover, and why he put up with a series of lodgers who shared his wife's bed. With bankrupt stock purchased from Drovet's, Crippen set up his own business, with Ethel as his bookkeeper.

As Belle Elmore, Mrs Crippen became a moderate success in the London music-halls. The British liked American acts, and Belle seems to have been the sort of person that everyone liked anyway –

immensely vital, good natured, embarrassingly frank. She earned the enduring friendship of Marie Lloyd and many other music-hall artists. But at home, she became inclined to bouts of screaming temper. And most of her friends detested her husband, regarding him as a sponger.

Ethel was in love with her employer, and in some ways they were well suited. Crippen was a crook, although as a result of weakness rather than moral delinquency, and Ethel was a pathological liar, whose biographer Tom Cullen writes that she 'lied from sheer perversity – in fact she seemed incapable of telling the truth'. But she was also determined not to yield her virginity until they were legally married. It was not until Crippen discovered his wife in bed with the German lodger and Ethel, presumably, had reason to feel that his marriage was at an end – that she consented to become his wife in the physical sense of the term; the date was 6 December 1906, seven years after their first meeting. It seems to have happened in a hired hotel room during the day, as did their subsequent intimacies – Crippen continued to return home at night.

Crippen became a dentist, and Ethel his assistant. At one point, Ethel became pregnant; she was determined to have the baby, and for a while it looked as if it might transform their lives, and bring about the inevitable break with Belle. Then she had a miscarriage. And to make things worse, Belle went around telling the Music Hall Ladies' Guild members that no one was sure which of Ethel's many lovers was responsible. This may well have been the last straw. Instead of leaving her, which would have been the obviously sensible course, Crippen decided to murder her. On 17 January 1910, he bought no fewer than 17 grains of hyoscine, a vegetable poison that he had seen administered to calm the violently insane at London's Royal Bethlehem Hospital. There is a strong probability that Ethel knew that her lover intended to kill his wife – she may even have planned it. On the evening of 31 January 1910, two of Belle's music-hall friends came to dinner at the Crippens' house at 39 Hilldrop Crescent, Camden Town. They said goodbye to Belle at 1.30 the next morning; it was the last time Belle was seen alive. The following day, Crippen pawned Belle's diamond ring and ear-rings, and Ethel slept at Hilldrop Crescent. The following day, letters were received by the Secretary of the Music Hall Guild, signed Belle Elmore and resigning her membership; they explained she was leaving for America to nurse a sick relative. Just before Easter, in the third week of March, Crippen told his friends that Belle was dangerously ill in Los Angeles; soon after, he announced her death.

Belle's friends were suspicious. Someone checked with the shipping lines, and discovered that no one of that name had sailed for America in February. A music-hall performer called Lil Hawthorne paid a visit to New York with her husband John Nash, and they also made enquiries, which achieved no positive result. Back in London, they talked to Crippen, who sobbed convincingly, but told contradictory stories about precisely where Belle had died. The Nashes decided to go to Scotland Yard. There they spoke to Chief Inspector Walter Dew of the CID, who agreed to go and talk to Crippen. And Crippen smoothly admitted that his wife was still alive. She had simply walked out on him and gone to join her former prize-fighter lover in Chicago. Dew was completely taken in. A thorough search of the house convinced him that there were no suspicious circumstances. When Dew left the house, he was more than half convinced that Belle was alive.

Then Crippen made his greatest mistake; he decided to flee. He and Ethel left for Antwerp, and took a ship for Canada. Ethel was dressed as a boy. When Dew returned two days later, and found the house deserted, he called in his team of diggers. Beneath the coal cellar floor, buried in quicklime, he found the remains of Mrs Crippen.

On board the SS *Montrose*, Crippen's secret had already been discovered by Captain Henry Kendal, who quickly realized that 'Mr Robinson's' son was a girl in disguise. In a copy of the *Daily Mail* which he had taken on board, the captain found a picture of the wanted 'cellar murderer' Crippen. He handed his radio operator a message that began: 'Have strong suspicion that Crippen London cellar murderer and accomplice are among saloon passengers.' So it came about that Crippen was the first murderer to be caught by means of wireless telegraphy, for which Marconi had received the Nobel prize in the previous year. On the morning of 31 July 1910, as the ship lay off the mouth of the St Lawrence river, Crippen went on deck, and was greeted by Dew, who greeted him with 'Good morning, Dr Crippen.'

On the morning Cora Crippen's remains were found, Bernard Spilsbury was preparing to leave for a holiday in Minehead with his wife and child. Then he received a summons from his eminent colleagues Drs Pepper, Willcox and Luff, to go and view the body. Richard Muir, who had prosecuted the Stratton brothers, was in charge of the prosecution. (When Crippen heard this, he remarked dolefully, 'I fear the worst.')

Crippen was defended by the brilliant but unscrupulous Arthur Newton, who would later go to prison for forging Crippen's 'Confession' and selling it to a newspaper. As a defendant, Crippen was certainly his own worst enemy. His only chance of escaping the rope was to admit everything except intent to kill. But if Crippen pleaded guilty, the whole sordid story about Belle and Ethel would emerge. Crippen chose to protect Ethel and enter a plea of innocence. His defence was that Belle had left him, just as he said, so the body in the cellar must be that of some other woman, buried by some previous tenant, or hidden there during his tenancy. It was obviously an absurd story, and it amounted to suicide. And, of course, it left to the prosecution the fairly light task of proving that the corpse *was* that of Cora Crippen. So the forensic evidence lay at the heart of the case. On one side was the formidable team of Pepper, Willcox, Luff and Spilsbury, on the other, Drs Turnbull, Wall and Blyth. Turnbull had been accosted by the defence at a bridge party, and had casually agreed to give his opinion as to whether a piece of skin was from the stomach, and contained an operation scar; he decided it was from a thigh, and that the scar was merely a fold. Since the operation scar was almost enough in itself to identify Mrs Crippen, the defence was delighted. When Arthur Newton broke his promise not to call Turnbull as a witness, the doctor was horrified and tried to change his mind. But unless he was willing to make a public confession of error, it was too late.

Willcox had found hyoscine in the remains, and Crippen was proved to have bought 17 grains of the drug not long before his wife's disappearance. Spilsbury, an expert on scar tissues, had no doubt whatsoever that the fragment of skin was from a stomach, not a thigh. And when they found part of a rectus muscle of the abdominal wall attached to the skin, the identification was proved beyond doubt. In court, Turnbull identified the skin as coming from the thigh, and the scar as a fold. Spilsbury, with the calm, grave manner that later led juries to think him infallible, pointed out the older man's errors with a pair of forceps, and the harassed Turnbull left the box with an embarrassed flush. He was followed by Dr Wall, who admitted that he had changed his mind about the piece of skin, and that it came from the abdomen. Dr Blyth disputed the presence of hyoscine in the body, but made a poor showing. It was Pepper's team that carried the day, and it was the junior member of that team who made the most powerful impression in court.

Crippen's downfall was not due entirely to this medical team. Part of the body had been wrapped in a piece of pyjama jacket, and it contained the maker's name. One pair of Crippen's pyjamas had a missing jacket, but Crippen insisted that these had been purchased years before, in 1905 or 1906 – the intervening years would explain why the jacket was now missing. But Muir was able to establish that the pyjamas to which the jacket belonged had been purchased in 1909. Crippen was caught out in a direct lie, and this did as much as anything to convince the jury of his guilt. It took them only 27 minutes to reach their verdict. Crippen was hanged on 23 November 1910. Ethel was tried separately, but acquitted.

Ethel LeNeve emigrated to Canada, but she returned to England in 1916, took a job in a furniture store in Trafalgar Square, and married an accountant there. Her husband is said to have borne a strong resemblance to Crippen. They lived in East Croydon, and in 1954, she revealed her identity to the novelist Ursula Bloom, who had written a novel called *The Girl Who Loved Crippen*. Miss Bloom became a close friend, and it was to her that Ethel LeNeve remarked one day that she had never ceased to love Crippen. She died in 1967, at the age of 84.

Many writers have pointed out that the great mystery remains: why did Crippen kill his wife when he could simply have walked out of her life? In his novel, *Dr Crippen's Diary,* Emlyn Williams settles for the explanation that Crippen gave her hyoscine tablets in mistake for aspirin. Dr Ingleby Oddie, who worked with Muir for the prosecution, had a more plausible theory. It was his belief that Crippen intended to kill his wife with hyoscine, convinced that her death would be ascribed to a heart attack – which is highly likely. What Crippen did not realize is that a large dose of hyoscine does not invariably act as a sedative, but can have the opposite effect. Witnesses claim to have heard screams coming from 39 Hilldrop Crescent on the morning of the murder, and another neighbour heard a loud bang. Crippen possessed a pistol and ammunition. Oddie speculates that the dose of hyoscine, given in a 'night cap', caused her to become hysterical and start screaming. If neighours rushed in, all Crippen's plans would collapse; there would be an inquest, and hyoscine would be discovered. Crippen salvaged what he could of the murder plan, and shot her through the head – the skull was never found. Then he had no alternative but to dismember the body and seek a place to hide it . . .

7

Pepper, Willcox, Luff and Spilsbury were mainly responsible for changing the attitude of British juries to 'expert evidence'. Yet two years after the Crippen trial, Spilsbury witnessed a courtroom scene that made him aware just how easy it could be for an intelligent counsel to discredit the expert. The case centred around Frederick Henry Seddon, a 50-year-old insurance agent, who was accused, together with his wife, of poisoning his lodger, Miss Eliza Barrow, by the administration of arsenic. Seddon was a miser in the classic sense of the word; he was obsessed by pounds, shillings and pence. The overweight lodger who came to live with the Seddons in 1910 was just as miserly, and her habits more insanitary. But Seddon could be charming and persuasive, and soon induced Miss Barrow to transfer £1,600-worth of India Stock to him in exchange for an annuity of about £2 a week; when she assigned some leasehold property to Seddon, he raised it to £3 a week. In August 11 she became ill; she was subject to asthma, and there was danger of heart failure. In September, she died of an illness that her doctor diagnosed as heart failure due to epidemic diarrhoea. Her cash, £700, simply vanished.

When her cousin, a Mr Vonderahe, heard (accidentally) about her death, he wanted to know what had happened to the money, and when Seddon assured him there had been no money, he flew into a state of furious resentment and went to the police. Two months after her burial, Miss Barrow was exhumed.

Scotland Yard asked Spilsbury to examine the body. His conclusion was that her inner organs seemed to be sound, and her death was not due to heart failure. Then Willcox took over, and soon discovered that her stomach and other vital organs contained a quantity of arsenic. But Willcox was not content with that discovery; he wanted to be able to state precisely how much arsenic had been administered. He was one of the most brilliant toxicologists since Orfila, and had demonstrated this in the Crippen case when he had identified the poison as an alkaloid by dropping it into the eye of the hospital cat – it caused a contraction – then gone on to demonstrate that it was hyoscine by a new method involving the type of crystal it formed. Now he decided to try and determine the amount of arsenic in Miss Barrow's body by weighing the 'mirrors' it formed in the Marsh test. It required immense precision, but was not in itself a complicated operation. He first had to experiment with hundreds of samples of arsenic, and construct a table telling him what weight of 'mirror' corresponded to what weight of pure arsenic. (The mirror could be weighed by weighing the glass tube before and after.) He then assumed that the arsenic had become evenly distributed in Miss Barrow's stomach, and tested a piece of the stomach whose weight was exactly one two-hundredth of its weight.

Having obtained his arsenic mirror from this piece, he multiplied its weight by 200. And the same procedure was applied to the rest of the body. His final figure was about 131 milligrams of arsenic, or more than two grains. The fatal dose (according to Taylor) is between two and three grains. This much had been absorbed by the vital organs; Willcox did not bother to try and establish how much arsenic had been absorbed by other parts of the body and by the bones. He had established the presence of the fatal dose.

But in court, a brilliant defence attorney, Edward Marshall Hall, came close to overturning his calculations. Eliza Barrow had originally weighed 10 stone (140 lb) but when she was exhumed, evaporation of water from the tissues (the human body is more than 50 per cent water) had reduced her weight to 60 lb, less than half. This loss weight meant that the remaining arsenic was far more concentrated than it had been at the time of death. And, with some embarrassment, Willcox admitted that he had left this out of account. And if his 131 milligrams of arsenic was halved, then it was less than the fatal dose . . . In fact, if Willcox had extended his examination to other parts of the body, the total might have been as much as six grains, three times the fatal dose. Of course, the precise dose was not really the issue; the major question was how arsenic had got into Miss Barrow's stomach in the first place. But Marshall Hall had scored a good point. And he went on to score another that almost destroyed the prosecution case. The questioning turned on the amount of arsenic found in Miss Barrow's hair; Willcox had found one-eightieth of a milligram next to the scalp, and about a quarter of that amount at the far end. But for arsenic to reach the end of the hair, it must have been administered about a year earlier. And Miss Barrow had certainly shown no signs of discomfort at that period – the prosecution case was that the Seddons had administered the poison within two weeks of her death. It was a good point, for it seemed to suggest that Miss Barrow had been absorbing arsenic from some other source. Miss Barrow's room had been full of flies, and Seddon himself had pointed out that an old-fashioned arsenic flypaper, soaked in water, was on the mantelpiece in her room.

Again, Willcox was taken off guard, and had to admit that Hall had a point. But then, as the cross-examination continued, he suddenly saw the answer. After the autopsy, Miss Barrow's body had lain in the coffin in a certain amount of bloodstained fluid, and this fluid had contained arsenic. The hair had absorbed the arsenic from the fluid. Willcox took the opportunity to introduce this explanation, and Hall –

predictably – looked sceptical and implied that it was just an excuse. But Willcox proved his point by taking some hair from one of his patients and soaking it in the same fluid; at the end of three days, it had absorbed enough arsenic to indicate that the patient had also been poisoned.

In the end, it was Seddon himself who caused his own downfall. One of the major arguments of the defence was that Seddon had no need of Miss Barrow's money; he was quite adequately well-off already. But Seddon's performance in the witness box made it clear that he was an obsessional miser, and that £700 in cash was a more than sufficient motive for murder. Seddon was found guilty and sentenced to death; his wife was acquitted. The obsession with money stayed with him to the end; when, after his appeal had been dismissed, he heard of the poor price his property had fetched, he snorted: 'Well, that finishes it!'

Spilsbury's next major case was that of George Joseph Smith, the 'Brides in the Bath' murderer. Smith was a confidence man who made a habit of marrying susceptible spinsters, then drowning them in a zinc bath. The verdict was always death by misadventure. Earlier victims were merely deserted, but when a lady named Bessie Munday declined to part with her money or property, Smith persuaded her to make a will in his favour and drowned her. This was in July 1912, and in 1913 he made £600 from the death of a nurse named Alice Burnham. The third and last victim, Margaret Lofty, was found dead in her bath on 18 December 1914, Smith (who was calling himself Lloyd) meanwhile playing the organ to establish an alibi. When the death was reported in the newspapers, a relative of his second victim read the report, and was struck by the similarity of the circumstances; she went to the police.

The Director of Public Prosecutions, Sir Charles Mathews, agreed that the circumstances looked incredibly suspicious, but pointed out that it would be extremely difficult to drown someone in a bath – they would fight and struggle.

Examining the corpse of Margaret Lofty, Spilsbury was inclined to agree; there was no sign of violence, except a small bruise on the elbow. That she had died of drowning was obvious – there was foam in the lungs. (As incredible as it sounds, it was not until the 1890s that it was finally established that drowning was due to water entering the lung – an observation that seems self-evident to anyone who has ever swallowed a mouthful of tea the wrong way.) But if force had been used, how had it been applied? Spilsbury and Detective Inspector Arthur Neil decided to conduct experiments to find out. Young women in bathing dress were persuaded to sit in a bath of water while Spilsbury and Neil tried to drown them. It seemed impossible; even if the victim's head could be forced, her hands could still grip the sides and prevent further immersion while she turned over on to all fours. Then Neil saw the answer; he grabbed the girl by the knees, and raised them in the air. Her head slipped under immediately, too quickly for her hands to grab the sides. And, to Neil's alarm, she immediately became unconscious – the rush of water into the mouth and nose had caused an instant blackout. It took some minutes to revive her. But Spilsbury and Neil now knew how Smith had killed his bride.

In fact, the medical evidence played little part in convicting Smith; it was obvious to the jury that when three wives die in bathtubs in three years, coincidence may be ruled out. Smith was executed in a state of collapse, still protesting his innocence.

Two years later, in November 1917, the discovery of the torso and arms of a woman in Regent Square, Bloomsbury, looked as if it might provide Spilsbury with an interesting problem in identification. The remains were in a meat sack, and some brown paper scrawled with the words 'Blodie Belgiam' were also found. In fact, the body was quickly traced through laundry marks on the sheet in which it was wrapped: it was a Frenchwoman named Émilienne Gérard, aged 32, who had been missing for three days. An IOU found in her flat led the police to her lover, Louis Voisin, who was sitting in a bloodstained kitchen in Charlotte Street, Soho, with his latest mistress. In his cellar, the police found the victim's head and hands. Asked to write 'Bloody Belgium', Voisin wrote 'Blodie Belgiam'. Voisin was a butcher by trade, and Spilsbury noted that the mutilations had been performed by a skilled hand.

Voisin's defence was that he had found the dismembered body in Émilienne Gérard's flat in Munster Square, and had only tried to get rid of them. His story was apparently supported by bloodstains in the flat. But Spilsbury's examination soon established what had really happened. The blows that had battered the victim unconscious had been struck by a woman's hand; if the powerful Voisin had struck them, the skull would have been shattered. Then Voisin had dismembered the body, and gone back to the Munster Square flat to spread blood around and support his story of finding her there. Apparently unaware that medical science had now learned to distinguish human from animal blood, he insisted that the bloodstains in his own basement were those of a calf; Spilsbury had no difficulty disproving this. It finally became clear that the murder had been due to a quarrel between the two women, and that the new mistress, Bertha Roche, had battered the old one unconscious, after which Voisin had completed the job by strangling her with his bare hands. Voisin was sentenced to death. At the later trial of Bertha Roche, Spilsbury had to accompany the jury to the Charlotte Street basement and demonstrate – in dumb show – how the murder had been done. (His comments might have prejudiced the jury and caused a mistrial.) Bertha Roche was sentenced to seven years, but went insane after two, confirming the impression of the investigators that she had been mentally unstable at the time of the murder.

Asked at a banquet which of his cases he regarded as his most difficult, Spilsbury mentioned the Crumbles murder of Emily Beilby Kaye by her lover Patrick Mahon. A Liverpool Irishman with an abundance of good looks and charm, Mahon had been to prison for embezzlement and for breaking into a bank and knocking the charlady unconscious. He was also a philanderer with an impressive string of successful seductions. In 1923 he had seduced a 34-year-old secretary named Emily Kaye, and in 1924 she became pregnant. On the weekend of 12 April 1924, Mahon invited her to a bungalow on a desolate stretch of shingle known as the Crumbles, Eastbourne, and at some time during the weekend, murdered her – probably with a blow on the head – and then dismembered the body. At this point he recollected that he had a date with a young lady called Ethel Duncan, whom he had picked up just before the murder by offering to share his umbrella in a rainstorm; he hastened back to London and persuaded her to come down for the weekend. Emily Kaye's dismembered body was at this time in a trunk in a locked bedroom. When Ethel Duncan showed curiosity about the locked bedroom, Mahon sent himself a telegram recalling himself to London on business. There he deposited a Gladstone bag at the Waterloo station left-luggage office, and went back to his wife. But before returning to Crumbles to continue the task of disposing of the body, he decided to spend a day at Plumpton races. A friend saw him there and mentioned it to his wife. Mrs Mahon was already worried about her husband's mysterious movements, and now went carefully through his pockets; in one of them she found the ticket from the left-luggage office. She asked a friend who had been a member of the railway police to investigate. She probably suspected that the bag contained love letters or other proofs of infidelity; what the friend discovered was some bloodstained ladies' underwear and a carving knife. He went to the police. The next day, Mahon was arrested as he went to recover the bag.

His story was that Emily Kaye had died as a result of an accident; she had attacked him with a hatchet during a quarrel, and they had wrestled. She had fallen backwards, and he lost consciousness. When he recovered, he found that she was dead – her head had struck against the coal bucket . . . In a panic, he decided to get rid of the body, and went out to purchase a saw and a knife.

Spilsbury was called down to the Eastbourne bungalow. He found a rusty tenon saw that was covered with grease and had a piece of flesh adhering to it. On the fire there was a 2-gallon saucepan half full of a reddish liquid, and covered with a coating of solid fat; this proved to contain a piece of boiled human flesh. The trunk contained four segments of a body, and a hatbox another 37 pieces of flesh. A biscuit tin contained various inner organs.

Spilsbury took the pieces back to St Bartholomew's Hospital, and set about reconstructing the body. There were hundreds of fragments and Spilsbury's task was to recognize each and assign it to its proper place. And when it was finally reassembled, he discovered that the head and right leg were missing. (Mahon later admitted that he had taken parts of the body in the Gladstone bag, and scattered them out of the window of the train *en route* to London.) Apart from a heavy bruise on the left shoulder, there was no evidence to indicate how Emily Kaye had died. But Spilsbury's discoveries were enough to wreck Mahon's defence. The breasts told him that Emily Kaye had been pregnant; but the uterus, which would have shown the same thing, was missing. The inference was that Mahon had destroyed it for that reason, unaware that the breasts would tell the same story. As to the coal bucket, it was obvious to Spilsbury that if a head had struck it with sufficient force to cause death, it would have been badly dented; but it showed no sign of a blow.

The missing head was a problem. Mahon claimed that he had burnt it on the fire; but was that possible? The question was worth answering, for if it had not been destroyed, then it might be buried somewhere. And it would almost certainly reveal the manner by which Emily Kaye met her death. With his usual thoroughness, Spilsbury procured a sheep's head, and tried burning it on an open kitchen fire. In four hours, it was a charred remnant that could be smashed to pieces with a poker.

Mahon himself gave evidence in court, and turned on all his Irish charm. He had bought himself a new suit, and used some artificial sun tan to darken his skin. His story of the 'accident' was told with the skill of an actor. One part of his story caused a stir in the courtroom; he described how, when he had placed Emily Kaye's head on the fire, the heat had caused the dead eyes to open. This, and a crash of thunder from outside, so unnerved him that he rushed out into the storm. By an odd coincidence, a thunderstorm was taking place as Mahon recounted this incident in court, and he was clearly not acting when he went pale and stammered.

It was not entirely Spilsbury's evidence that convinced the jury of Mahon's guilt. Even if, as Spilsbury stated, it would be virtually impossible for Emily Kaye to have died by falling against the coal scuttle, it was still possible that she died accidentally, in the course of a quarrel. Here the crucial evidence was uncovered by the police. Mahon claimed that he went out and bought the chef's knife and saw four days after her death, on 17 April 1924. But the carbon of the receipt in the hardware store showed that he had bought them on 12 April, before her death. The inference was clear: the murder was premeditated. Mahon realized the seriousness of this piece of evidence, and summoned all his open-faced plausibility. He had, he admitted, made a mistake about the date. But the purchase had still been unpremeditated. He had gone into the shop to buy a lock for the bungalow, but found the saw and the carving knife so attractive that he bought them on the spot. However, he had not used the chef's knife to slice up Miss Kaye's body; she had handled the knife, and for sentimental reasons, he did not feel he could use it for such a purpose. So he had used the ordinary carving knife from the bungalow . . . But, as Spilsbury had pointed out, the ordinary carving knife would not have done the job; the chef's knife was specially designed to cut raw flesh.

It took the jury only 40 minutes to reach a guilty verdict; Mahon was hanged on 9 September 1924.

8

Later that same year, another pregnant mistress met her end in a lonely cottage, and once again, it was Spilsbury who conclusively disproved the murderer's story of how it came about.

Norman Thorne was a Sunday school teacher and an unsuccessful chicken farmer; his fiancee, a bespectacled 23-year-old typist named Elsie Cameron, was tired of waiting for marriage, and by the autumn of 1924, was ruefully aware that, in yielding her virginity, she had thrown away her trump card. On the late afternoon of 5 December, she made her way from Kensal Green down to Thorne's smallholding near Crowborough, Sussex, and was seen, attaché case in hand, by two farm-workers. She had told Thorne, untruthfully, that she was pregnant, and Thorne had countered with the equally untrue assertion that he was having a love affair with a girl called Elizabeth Coldicott. This is why Elsie was rushing down to see him on that dark December afternoon.

Five days later, Elsie Cameron's father sent Thorne a telegram asking for news of his daughter; Thorne replied by letter that he had been expecting Elsie, but she had failed to arrive. Mr Cameron went to the police, who called on Thorne and asked if they could look over the farm. He agreed willingly, and when they left, they were apparently satisfied. The Press heard of Elsie's disappearance, and descended in multitudes on the farm; Thorne allowed one photographer to take his picture feeding the chickens in the poultry run.

In the second week of January, a woman came forward to say that she had seen Elsie Cameron walking towards the farm on the afternoon of 5 December 1924. She only confirmed what the two previous witnesses had said, but this time the local police decided to take the sighting seriously, and Scotland Yard was called in. They arrived with picks and shovels, and soon found Elsie Cameron's dressing-case in a potato plot. Thorne was told that he would be charged with her murder, and replied with a line that has been used by many other murderers: 'I want to tell you the truth about what happened.' The truth, he claimed, was that he had stormed out of the hut that constituted the farmhouse after a quarrel about the 'other woman', and had returned to find that Elsie had committed suicide by hanging herself from a beam. He had panicked, and spent the night dismembering the body with a hacksaw. Then, in the dim light of dawn, he had buried it in the poultry run – in the exact spot where he had been photographed by the Press. That afternoon, he had taken Elizabeth Coldicott out to the local cinema. And for the next six weeks, he had behaved with a beaming self-confidence that hardly suggested a man who had panicked on discovering that his mistress had committed suicide.

The dismembered body was recovered from the poultry run, and taken to the Crowborough mortuary, where Spilsbury examined it. The head had been forced into a biscuit tin, so that it was difficult to remove. Spilsbury found several bruises on the body, but none of the marks on the neck that would have pointed to hanging – the extravasation (breaking of blood vessels) – due to the pressure of a rope.

Elsie Cameron's remains were buried at Willesden; but four weeks later they were exhumed for another examination. This was by the pathologist Patrick Bronte, an Irishman who had left for England after the establishment of the Irish Free State in 1922. By now the remains were badly decomposed; nevertheless, Bronte concluded that Elsie Cameron's throat *did* show signs of a rope mark.

But, like Mahon, Thorne had chosen the wrong defence. Police discovered that the dust on the upper half of the beam was undisturbed, but a rope would have made a mark in the dust. He had claimed that he left the hut after a quarrel, but denied striking the girl; but the heavy bruising on her body showed this to be untrue.

At Lewes Assizes, on 4 March 1925, it soon became apparent that the case would turn upon the medical evidence. Spilsbury's opinion was that the bruising – on the back of the head and on both temples, as well as on the leg – indicated that Elsie Cameron had been attacked with considerable violence, probably with some heavy instrument with a smooth surface. (Thorne possessed a pair of Indian clubs.) All this suggested that she had been thrown to the ground and beaten with a club. Dr Bronte produced slides which, he insisted, showed the extravasation characteristic of hanging, and mentioned creases or grooves on Elsie Cameron's throat. Spilsbury replied that these were the creases that could be found on anyone's throat. Bronte argued that some of the bruises could have been caused after death; Spilsbury replied that it is impossible to bruise a corpse. And although five other doctors supported Bronte's view that the signs were consistent with suicide by hanging, the jury remained unconvinced, and sentenced Norman Thorne to death.

The case nevertheless marked the beginning of a certain revolt against the tendency to regard Sir Bernard Spilsbury – he had been knighted in 1923 – as a kind of infallible Sherlock Holmes. One letter to a newspaper began: 'For some reason or other, Sir Bernard Spilsbury had now arrived at a position where his utterances in the witness box commonly receive unquestioning acceptance . . . But a reputation for infallibility . . . is quite out of place in medical and surgical matters.'

In fact, Spilsbury's evidence in the Thorne case raises a number of unsettling questions. He believed that the blows would have been sufficient to cause death from shock. But most young women can probably sustain a beating without dying from shock. Spilsbury might have been expected to point to some particular blow – perhaps to the back of the head – as cause of death, and support it with the evidence of injury to the skull or brain; but he did not do so. Therefore, in an important sense, the case against Thorne was incomplete. Now in fact, we know that Elsie Cameron was a highly neurotic woman, who had been out of work for six months before her death through 'neurasthenia'. On a visit to Thorne's parents she had become hysterical and difficult. All this suggests that when she went to Thorne's cottage with a false story about pregnancy to blackmail him into marriage, there was a violent quarrel with a great deal of screaming, and that Elsie Cameron's death took place as a result of this quarrel. The bruises of the legs support this view; a man who intends to murder an unwanted mistress does not cover her in bruises; he strikes a single blow. Thorne's fatal mistake was to choose a defence of suicide. But Spilsbury's disproving of the suicide defence should have made it obvious to the jury that Thorne had killed her during a quarrel, and allowed him a certain benefit of the doubt. Unfortunately, Spilsbury's quietly confident manner of giving evidence tended to leave the jury feeling slightly cowed. So in a sense, Thorne was not hanged by the medical evidence, but by Spilsbury's reputation. It was for this reason, rather than professional jealousy, that a certain resistance to Spilsbury began to build up during his later years.

There was another drawback to Spilsbury's world-wide fame; it made the criminal aware of the skills of the forensic scientist, and led him to take redoubled precautions – one result being that few burglaries were now solved by fingerprint evidence. And those who contemplated solving their problems by murder also became aware that a single hair or fibre could lead to their downfall, and planned with increased subtlety. At least one murderer of the 1930s demonstrated that he had learned his lesson.

On 17 June 1934, the Brighton cloakroom attendants noticed an unpleasant smell in the office. The police traced it to a cheap-looking trunk, and it was opened in the police station. It was found to contain the torso of a woman, wrapped in brown paper and tied with window cord. A word written on the paper had been half obliterated by a blood-stain, but its second half read: 'ford'.

Where was the rest of the body? Cloakroom attendants all over the country were asked to report suspicious packages, and the result was that a pair of legs was found in a suitcase at King's Cross.

The trunk and the suitcase had both been deposited on Derby Day, 6 June, between six and seven in the evening; the person responsible had estimated correctly that the cloakroom attendants would be too busy to remember who left any particular item. The Brighton attendant could only recollect that the trunk had been left by a man.

Spilsbury verified that the legs and the trunk belonged to the same body. She had been a woman in her mid-20s, and had been five months' pregnant. Various clues suggested that she had belonged to a reasonable income group: the hairs on the legs were bleached with sunbathing, and some light brown head-hairs found on the body suggested a permanent wave. The hands and feet were well kept, and the armpits were shaved; lack of callouses on the feet indicated well-fitting shoes. The brown paper in which the torso was wrapped had been soaked in olive oil – sometimes used by surgeons to stop heavy bleeding, and this might have suggested a restaurateur or some fairly well-to-do household. On the whole, it seemed likely that the victim's identity should be fairly easy to establish. Newspaper and wireless reports made certain that every adult in the British Isles knew about the crime. Yet although 700 women were traced, none proved to be the victim. The maker of the trunk was found, in Leyton, but he had no record of where it had been sold, or to whom; one of his employees had written the word 'ford' on the paper. Five thousand prenatal cases were traced and eliminated. At one point it seemed to the people of Brighton that the whole of Scotland Yard had moved into their hotels; the Royal Pavilion was used as a search headquarters. When eventually the trunk was traced to a big shop in Brighton, it looked as if all this effort was at last yielding some result; but once again, the trail petered out. The 'Brighton trunk murderer' had proved that it *was* possible to commit a perfect crime.

9

Oddly enough, one of the men who was questioned and then released was a certain Captain Ivan Poderjay, whose name also survives in the annals of crime for having committed a 'perfect murder'. In 1933, Captain Poderjay – a small, dapper, bald-headed man – was on a cross-channel steamer when he oberved a tall, attractive blonde lady suffering from incipient sea-sickness; he ushered her onto the deck, where she soon made a recovery. He introduced himself as an ex-army intelligence officer from Yugoslavia; he also mentioned that he was a millionaire inventor. If the lady, Miss Agnes Tufverson, a New York attorney, had happened to see the magazine *John Bull* for 12 March

1933, she would have discovered an article pointing out that Poderjay was a confidence swindler who preyed on rich women. As it was, the 40-year-old Miss Tufverson became the latest of Poderjay's dupes, and by the time he saw her off to New York, she was hopelessly in love. She had given him $5,000 to invest for her, although he had certainly spent half that sum entertaining her in London.

A few days after her return to New York, she received a love letter enclosing a draft of $500, a first return on her investment, and suggesting that she should send him another $5,000 to invest. Miss Tufverson was tempted – she entertained no suspicions about her new business adviser – but she urgently wanted to see him again. And, as she explained to her closest friend Julia Tilinghast, if she played hard to get, Poderjay would come to New York all the sooner. She was right. In November 1933, Poderjay arrived accompanied by an incredible quantity of flowers. On 4 December they were married, Poderjay wearing a full dress uniform. The fact that the top of his head scarcely came up to her breasts seems to have worried neither of them. On 20 December, they sailed off to England for their honeymoon on the SS *Hamburg*. Mrs Poderjay had sold off $38,000 worth of stocks and shares, since her husband had told her he could invest the money at a far higher rate of interest in Europe.

But the *Hamburg* left without them. Two hours after they had set out for the dock, they were back at her apartment, with Agnes in tears. No one saw her again. The next day, Poderjay went out and purchased a large trunk, as well as 800 razor blades and an immense quantity of vanishing cream. He told Agnes' friends that she had left on the *Hamburg,* and that he would follow on the *Olympic* after transacting some urgent business. The trunk, now a great deal heavier, was transported to the ship, with Poderjay sitting on top of it, and was placed in his cabin.

In January, Agnes' family received a cable stating that she loathed the British climate and was on her way to India. When they heard nothing more of her for another five months, her sister Sally came from Montreal to the Missing Persons Bureau in New York to ask for help. The bureau went to work, and traced Mr and Mrs Poderjay to the Hinterstrasse in Vienna. But Mrs Poderjay was not Agnes Tufverson, but a Frenchwoman whose unmarried name had been Marguerite Suzanne Ferrand. She and Poderjay had been married since 1931. A check with the *Hamburg* revealed that Mr and Mrs Poderjay had never been booked on board; but Captain Ivan Poderjay had booked his own passage a week earlier on the *Olympic*. Furthermore, the shipping company was able to tell them that Poderjay had insisted on a cabin just above the waterline. His cabin steward added that Poderjay had allowed no one to touch the heavy trunk, and that when the ship arrived at Southampton, he had caught a glimpse inside it and been surprised to discover that it was only half full.

All this information made very clear what had happened to Agnes Tufverson. She had been heavily drugged with sleeping pills when she had been carried on board in the trunk – Poderjay would not have risked killing her in case the trunk was opened before the ship set sail. He had then murdered her, probably by suffocation, and spent the voyage slicing the flesh from her bones with razor blades and feeding it to the fish. Finally, the skeleton, greased with cold cream, had also been pushed through the porthole. And when it vanished below the waves, Poderjay must have sighed with relief, and made sure that there was not the slightest sign of blood in the cabin or in the trunk – he had probably dissected the body on a sheet of rubber, after draining it of blood.

When the Vienna police arrested Poderjay, they discovered that his home contained a room full of every conceivable instrument of torture and sexual perversion. The most eminent Viennese psychiatrist, Sigmund Freud, was called in to report on the case. He diagnosed Mr and Mrs Poderjay as polymorphous perverts whose sex life together was one continuous fantasy. Poderjay was basically a female personality; his wife was male. As 'Count John' she treated her mistress 'Ita' with appalling savagery; Poderjay was Ita, who was having a lesbian affair with two of his wife's female personalities, Sonja and Jeanitason, as well as being Vanchette, who was flogged by Count John. Freud found it one of the most complex cases of sexual perversion he had ever studied. Now, at least, it was clear why Ivan Poderjay had chosen such an original method of disposing of the body; it had not been a gruesome chore, but a continuous delight.

Poderjay's arrest corresponded with the finding of the torso in the Brighton left-luggage office; it can be seen why the British police wished to question him on his way back to New York. But it was fairly clear that a man who has just acquired a fortune in dollars and is hastening back to the delights of the torture chamber would have no time or inclination to dissect a pregnant mistress in Brighton; besides, the girl in the trunk must have become pregnant in early January, at which time Ivan Poderjay was still on his way across the Atlantic.

Back in New York, Poderjay seemed to enjoy his days of intensive questioning by the police, and remained irritatingly bland – he was probably trying to provoke them to complete his happiness by administering third degree. His story was that Agnes had walked out on him, probably with another man; beyond that he refused to make any admissions. Poderjay's case history, forwarded by the Vienna police, revealed only that he had been born in Serbia in a poor family, had started life as a fortune-teller, joined and deserted the French foreign legion, then taken up his true calling as a confidence man. He had swindled at least two women out of their fortunes before he met his wife, Marguerite Ferrand, in 1931, and his interest in her fortune had swiftly deepened into warmer feeling when he learned of her desire to flog him. None of this brought the New York police any closer to provoking a confession of murder, and they relieved their frustration by charging him with bigamy. He emerged after a five-year prison sentence with only one eye and half his teeth, having infuriated a fellow convict with some unmentionable proposition. He remained cheerfully uncommunicative under further police questioning, and was deported back to Serbia. Some time after, he wrote to a New York newspaper from Belgrade insisting that Agnes Tufverson was still alive, and would probably reappear one day

10

It was another Derby Day killing, that of Agnes Kesson, that inspired one of the most ruthless and ingenious murder schemes of the early 1930s. The body of Agnes Kesson was found in a ditch near Epsom, where the Derby is held, on 7 June 1930. She had been strangled with a cord, and her murderer was never found. A 36-year-old commercial traveller named Alfred Arthur Rouse, whose personal life had reached crisis point, found himself reflecting on how easy it seemed to be to get away with murder.

Ever since a head injury, caused by a shell splinter during the First World War, Rouse had been a changed man. He had been a sober and conscientious character; now he became an obsessive seducer of women. As a commerical traveller, working for a garter manufacturer, he was earning £500 a year – a comfortable income in days when farm labourers earned £2 a week. But part of this had to be paid in maintenance to a French girl who had borne his child during the war, and part went to supporting other illegitimate children all over the south of England. It was later calculated that he had seduced about 80 women by posing as a carefree bachelor; in fact, he was married, and his wife was taking care of an illegitimate child of a servant girl named Helen Campbell, who was one of many that Rouse had married bigamously. By Derby Day 1930, his wife was threatening to leave him, one mistress was having her second baby in a London hospital, and another in Wales had announced that she was pregnant. She was a nurse from a middle-class family, and Rouse had persuaded her to pretend they were married when he visited her home; he had also told her family that they were about to move into a luxury home at Kingston upon Thames, and had invited her sister to come and stay.

Rouse decided that the solution to these problems was to vanish – in fact, to die. And as he meditated on the Agnes Kesson murder, he began to see how this might be done. She was a waitress who had probably been lured into a car by a customer, then strangled. And during the depression years, England was full of down-and-outs who could be lured into a car.

He put his plan into effect on Bonfire Night, 1930. On the Great North Road, near St Albans, he picked up a hitch-hiker, a man who, he noted, was of roughly the same build as himself. Towards two o'clock the following morning, Rouse stopped the car near Hardingstone, Northampton, and told his passenger he wanted to relieve himself. What happened next is not certain; but a mallet with hairs on it, found near the car, suggests that he knocked his passenger unconscious. Then he poured petrol over the body – which was stretched across the front seats, with the legs sticking out of the open door – and lit a trail of petrol leading to the car. As it exploded into flame, Rouse ran and hid in the nearest ditch. Then, when he felt the coast was clear, he climbed out and began to walk down the road. But within a few yards, he encountered two young men who were returning from a dance in Northampton. He hurried on past them, and when they asked what had happened, called back 'It looks as if somebody's got a bonfire up there.'

Rouse's perfect murder plan had failed, and he knew it. There was now no point in 'vanishing'. Instead, he went on to the home of the pregnant nurse, Ivy Jenkins, at Gelligaer in Wales. As soon as he arrived, he was shown a photograph of the burnt-out car in the evening newspaper, and it stunned him. The next day, the newspapers mentioned his name – and, worse still, his wife. But by now Rouse was on his way back to London, where the police met him off the bus at Hammersmith Bridge.

His story was that the death of his passenger had been an accident. He had asked the man to fill the petrol tank while he climbed over a hedge to relieve himself; the man must have lit a cigarette, for the car burst into flames . . .

What was obviously more difficult to explain was why he had walked away from the blaze without seeking help. His explanation was feeble; the shock had caused him to 'lose his head'.

Spilsbury was called to examine the charred remains. The first thing he discovered was a scrap of rag between the legs, still smelling of petrol – the tremendous heat had caused one of the legs to bend, trapping the rag. It had also caused the skull to explode, and destroyed all indications of the victim's sex, with the exception of part of the flies trapped between the thigh and the stomach. To Spilsbury, the position of the body indicated that the victim had been alive when the fire started. And the rag, and the smell of petrol on the trapped fly, showed beyond all doubt that the man had been soaked in petrol before his death. It was Spilsbury's evidence that destroyed Rouse's defence that the fire had started by accident. To the suggestion that the victim had kicked his way through the badly burnt door, Spilsbury replied: 'He would have been dead long before that.'

The jury took over an hour to find Rouse guilty of murder. His counsel appealed, on the grounds that newspaper publicity about Rouse's 'harem' could have influenced the jury. (All evidence about Rouse's sexual life was excluded from the courtroom.) The appeal failed. Just before his execution, Rouse confessed to the murder. But the identity of his victim was never established.

11

A week after Rouse was hanged at Bedford jail, another commercial traveller stood in the dock at Ratisbon charged with an almost identical murder. His name was Kurt Erich Tetzner, and he was accused of burning to death an unknown tramp in his car.

For Professor Richard Kockel of the University of Leipzig, a man who had established his right to be regarded as the German Spilsbury, the case began when he was asked to inspect a charred body that was about to be buried. The man, identified as Tetzner, had been found burnt to death in his car, which had apparently struck a milestone. What bothered the insurance agent who approached Kockel was that Tetzner had insured his life with three different companies, for the vast sum of 145,000 marks. His death seemed a little too convenient. Kockel performed an autopsy on the body, and quickly concluded it was that of a youth – he found a particular piece of cartilage that usually vanishes by the age of 20. But Tetzner was 26 years old. Moreover, the corpse had no soot in the mouth or windpipe, which argued that he was not breathing when he was burnt. Finally, miscroscopic examination of a section of the lung showed fatty embolisms blocking the blood vessels. This was a sign of death by sudden violence; a violent blow or injury drives fat from the tissues into the blood vessels, and they may be carried to the heart, causing a blockage. (This is what Spilsbury meant when he diagnosed Elsie Cameron's death as being due to shock.)

Kockel's conclusion was that the body was that of someone who had been murdered by Tetzner to perpetrate an insurance fraud. In which case, Tetzner must still be alive, and would probably be in contact with his wife. Accordingly, the police tapped Emma Tetzner's telephone, or rather, her neighbour's, for she had no telephone of her own. On 4 December 1929, a week after 'Tetzner's' death, a man who called himself Sranelli rang Frau Tetzner from Strasbourg; the policeman, posing as the neighbour, replied that Frau Tetzner was not at home, and asked Herr Sranelli to ring back that evening at six. Chief Superintendent Kriegern, who was in charge of the case, flew off to Strasbourg, and was there in time to arrest the suspect himself. Sranelli was obviously shocked. He was a fat, unhealthy-looking man with beady eyes, and he soon admitted that he was Erich Tetzner. And, still demoralized by the collapse of his foolproof plan, he made a confession to the murder. He had, he said, planned the insurance fraud some time ago, and advertised for a companion to travel with him. One young man had agreed to go, but become suspicious at the last minute. Then, on 21 November 1929, Tetzner had picked up a hitch-hiker named Alois Ortner, who was in search of work. Tetzner persuaded him to crawl under the car to look for some imaginary fault, then attacked him as he emerged with a heavy spanner and an ether pad. But Ortner had fought back, and escaped into the woods. He had, in fact, collapsed unconscious almost immediately, but fortunately, Tetzner had given up the chase and driven off. The Ingolstadt police, to whom this had been reported, dismissed the story as fantastic – they suspected Ortner of an unsuccessful attempt to rob a motorist.

On 27 November 1929, Tetzner had picked up another hitch-hiker, a young man of slight build. When the man was asleep, said Tetzner, he had poured petrol in the car, then tossed in a match and run away, burning the man alive.

The German legal system is more ponderous that the British one; by the following April, Tetzner's trial had still not begun, and he had decided to change his story. The victim, he said, was a man whom he had accidentally knocked down and killed. He had then decided that it was a heaven-sent opportunity to go ahead with his insurance fraud plan . . .

This story struck Kockel as altogether more plausible than the previous version, for no soot had been found in the victim's lungs. And at the trial of Erich and Emma Tetzner, which began on 17 March 1931, Kockel gave it as his opinion that the second of the two stories was more likely to be true, although it probably fell short of the horror of what actually happened. But if Tetzner thought that this support for his second story would influence the jury towards mercy, he was mistaken. What emerged in court was a nightmarish tale of greed and brutality that almost defied belief. Tetzner admitted that when he had learned that his mother-in-law was about to have an operation for cancer, he had dissuaded her for just long enough to insure her life for 10,000 marks, then suggested that she should go ahead after all; she died a few days after the operation, and the insurance company paid up. This easy profit led Tetzner to meditate on how he might make an immense fortune from the insurance companies. When he told his wife of his plan of killing a hitch-hiker, she suggested that it would be easier to dig up a newly buried corpse. Tetzner shook his head. 'No, there has to be blood around.' But after the fiasco with Alois Ortner, he changed his mind; now he thought that it would be easier to blind the victim with pepper, then set him on fire. But then, said Tetzner, the accidental killing of the hiker had enabled him to carry out his scheme without the need for murder . . .

It was clear that his brutal frankness was an attempt to convince the jury that he had decided to tell the whole truth. They declined to believe him, and he was sentenced to death. Shortly before his execution, he confessed to what had really happened. The thinly clad youth had complained of feeling cold, and Tetzner had wrapped a rug around him, immobilizing his arms. Then he had strangled him with a piece of rope. Even this version was probably less than the truth. Kockel was convinced that Tetzner had hacked off the top of the man's skull, to conceal heavy blows (which would still be visible even on a charred skull), and perhaps even his legs, which might have provided some clue – possibly the hiker was crippled. Tetzner was executed on 2 June 1931.

Yet his example had already inspired another 'insurance murder'. Some time during the summer of 1930, when the Tetzner case was being discussed in German newspapers, a young furniture store manager named Fritz Saffran walked into the store brandishing a newspaper, and exclaimed to his mistress, the bookkeeper Ella Augustin, 'Have you read about this man Tetzner? That's how we'll do it . . .'

The Platz Store, in the little town of Rastenburg, was apparently doing excellent business, and its friendly young manager, a former schoolteacher, was universally liked and admired. He had married the store-owner's daughter and taken over his father-in-law's business. The books showed large profits – but only because the plain but determined Ella was willing to falsify them on a massive scale. In fact, Saffran had sold far too much furniture on hire-purchase, and the recession was preventing his customers from keeping their side of the deal. It was then that he read about the Tetzner case, and saw a way out. His first step was to insure his life for 140,000 marks. His next was to take Ella Augustin and the store's chief clerk, Erich Kipnis, into his confidence, and explain that they had to find a body that could be destroyed in a fire. Like Tetzner, they decided that a corpse from a graveyard would not serve their purpose – to begin with, it would be too hard to obtain. Instead, they set up a 'murder camp' in the Nicolai forest. Every evening, Saffran and Kipnis drove off in the car, looking for a victim. They proved unexpectedly hard to find. One evening, near the village of Sorquitten, a man accepted a lift. But when Kipnis began hitting him with a life-preserver, Ella became hysterical and held him back; the man escaped, and apparently failed to report the incident. On another occasion, according to Kipnis' later confession, a hitch-hiker told them that he had six children, and they decided to let him go. But finally, on 12 September 1930, they passed a pedestrian near Luisenhof, and Kipnis got out of the car with his life-preserver and a revolver. When the car returned a few minutes later, Kipnis was waiting for them. 'He's there in the ditch – give me a hand.'

Saffran's original plan was to burn the body in the car, but he then had a better idea: burn it in the store, and also collect insurance for the building. So now they took the body back to the store, dressed it in

Saffran's clothes, placed his rings on the man's fingers and his watch in the waistcoat pocket, and doused the place in petrol. Then, leaving a trail, they hurried out of the store, and lit the end of the trail. Minutes later, there was a tremedous explosion. There were 30 people working in other parts of the building, and all managed to escape. And Erich Kipnis rushed to the home of Herr Platz, the store's owner, and babbled that Fritz Saffran had died in the fire. They had been passing the store after an evening in a café when they saw smoke, and Saffran had rushed into the building seconds before the explosion . . .

During the next 48 hours, it looked as if the plan had succeeded. Ella collapsed in a faint in the street, and everyone sympathized with her state of shock, for it was generally known that she cherished a hopeless passion for her employer. But a few days after the fire, the police began to hear curious rumours, to the effect that Fritz Saffran was still alive. A local doctor was asked to take a closer look at the charred corpse found in the store. He found traces of earth on the body, and concluded that it had been buried for some time before being burnt. The police began to make enquiries to find if any local graveyard had been robbed. (This is an aspect of the case that remained obscure – three days elapsed between the murder of the pedestrian and the explosion in the store, and it seems probable that the corpse was meanwhile buried in the forest.) Pictures of the teeth were also published in a dental journal, and they eventually led to the identification of the corpse. He was a 25-year-old dairyman named Friedrich Dahl, and he had been cycling home on the night he disappeared.

But by that time, the police were on Saffran's trial. Ella Augustin was arrrested on a charge of falsifying the accounts. She tried to smuggle a note to Saffran; it was intercepted, and told the police that he was staying with a relative of Ella's, a carpenter who lived in Berlin; Saffran had been there for seven weeks. But by the time the police arrived, Saffran had left. He had decided to escape abroad, via Hamburg. Stealing his host's identity papers, he boarded a train at Spandau, then a suburb of Berlin. By the kind of incredible bad luck that seems to dog so many killers, he was recognized by a guard who had once served with him in the local rifle brigade at Rastenburg. The guard telephoned the police, and the police telegraphed Wittenberg, the next station down the line, where Saffran was drinking coffee in the waiting-room as the police entered.

At the trial, Saffran and Kipnis tried to throw the blame on one another. When Frau Dahl, the wife of the murdered dairyman, appeared in court, both of them fell on their knees and tearfully begged her forgiveness until the public prosecutor snapped: 'Enough of this play acting.'

The police had also considered charging a chauffeur named Reck with complicity. It had been Reck who had unintentionally alerted the police by talking about a curious event that had occurred two days after Saffran's 'death'. Ella Augustin had asked him to drive her ailing mother to Königsberg, but when the chauffeur arrived at her house, it had been Fritz Saffran who had climbed into the car. Reck had taken him as far as the village of Gerdauen, then refused to go further, afraid of being implicated in the fraud. But he had agreed not to notify the police. He had, in fact, mentioned to friends that Saffran was still alive, and this is how the police had eventually heard about it. The chauffeur was charged with aiding and abetting, but the conspiracy charge was eventually dropped.

Saffran and Kipnis were condemned to death, Ella to five years' imprisonment. But an appeal was successful, and the two 'manhunters' spent the rest of their lives in prison.

12

The most remarkable feat of forensic reconstruction of the 1930s was not performed by Sir Bernard Spilsbury, but by Professor John Glaister of the University of Glasgow.

September 29, 1935, was a cool autumn day; a young lady had paused in her afternoon walk to lean on the parapet of a bridge across a pretty stream called the Gardenholme Linn. As she stared at the narrow, rocky stream, she noticed some kind of bundle that had jammed against a boulder. Something that looked unpleasantly like a human arm was sticking out of it.

The police were on the scene by mid-afternoon, and had soon discovered two human heads on the bank of the Linn, as well as four bundles, each containing human remains – thigh bones, legs, pieces of flesh, and an armless torso. One piece of newspaper wrapped round two upper arms proved to be the *Sunday Graphic* for 15 September 1935.

When, the following day, Professor John Glaister – author of a classic *Medical Jurisprudence and Toxicology* – arrived with his colleague Dr Gilbert Millar, he quickly realized that this killing was not the work of some terrified amateur; he had taken care to cover his tracks. He had not only dismembered the bodies, but removed the skin from the heads, to make the faces unrecognizable, and cut off the fingertips to make fingerprint identification impossible. He had made only one mistake: instead of tossing the remains into the River Annan, a few hundred yards downstream, he had tossed them into its tributary, the Linn, which had been swollen with heavy rains at the time. If the rain had continued, the parcels would have ended up in the Solway Firth. But there were a few days of fine weather; the stream dwindled to its usual trickle, and the parcels caught in the rocks.

The remains were sent to the Anatomy Department of the University of Edinburgh, and there treated with ether to prevent further decomposition and destroy maggots; then they were 'pickled' in a formalin solution. Glaister and Millar found themselves confronted with a human jigsaw puzzle of 70 pieces.

The first task was to sort the pieces into two separate bodies, and this was made easier by the fact that one was six inches shorter than the other. And when it was finally done, Glaister and his team found that they had one almost complete body, the taller one, and one body minus a trunk. There was also an item that caused much bafflement – an enormous single eye, which certainly did not belong to either of the bodies; by some odd chance, this eye, probably from an animal, had also found its way into the Linn.

What could be deduced about the murderer? First, that he was almost certainly a medical man. He had used a knife, not a saw, to dismember the body, and a human body is almost impossible to dismember with a knife without detailed knowledge of the joints. He had also removed the teeth, recognizing that they could lead to identification by a dentist.

Fortunately, the murderer had either lost his nerve or been interrupted, for he had left some of the hair on the smaller body – which, at first, Glaister thought to be that of a man. And when more parcels were found in the river, Glaister found that he had a pair of hands that still had fingertips. After soaking them in hot water, he was able to get an excellent set of fingerprints. And the discovery that the assorted pieces of flesh included three breasts also made it clear that both bodies were of women.

The next problem was the age of the bodies. Glaister determined this by means of the skull sutures. Sutures are 'joining lines' in the skull, and they seal themselves over the years; they are usually closed completely by the age of 40. In one of the two skulls, the smaller of the two, the sutures were unclosed; in the other, they were almost closed. This indicated that one body was that of a woman of about 40; the other was certainly under 30. X-rays of the jaw-bone of the younger woman showed that the wisdom teeth had still not pushed through, which meant she was probably in her early 20s. The cartilage, the soft material of which bones are originally made, gradually changes into 'caps', called 'epiphyses', and the age can also be estimated from how far this change has taken place. The epiphyses of the smaller body confirmed that this was a girl of 20 or so; the other was of a woman approaching middle age.

As to the cause of death, this was fairly clear. The taller woman had five stab wounds in the chest, several broken bones, and many bruises. The hyoid bone in the neck was broken, indicating strangulation before the other injuries had been inflicted. The swollen and bruised tongue confirmed this inference. Glaister reasoned that a murderer who strangled and beat his victim before stabbing her would probably be in the grip of jealous rage. As to the other body, the signs were that she had been battered with some blunt instrument. It hardly needed a Sherlock Holmes to infer that she had been killed as an afterthought, probably to keep her silent. The fact that the murderer had taken less trouble to conceal her identity pointed to the same conclusion.

Meanwhile, the police were working on their own clues. The *Sunday Graphic* was a special local edition, printed for the Morecambe and Lancaster area. And the clothes in which some of the remains had been wrapped were also distinctive: the head of the younger woman had been wrapped in a pair of child's rompers, and another bundle had been wrapped in a blouse with a patch under the arm . . .

And in Lancaster, a Persian doctor named Buck Ruxton had already attracted the suspicions of the local police. Five days before the remains were found in the Linn, Ruxton – a small, rather good-looking man with a wildly excitable manner – had called on the police and mentioned that his wife had deserted him. The police were investigating the murder of a lady called Mrs Smalley, whose body had been found a year earlier, and in the course of routine investigations, had questioned a domestic in Ruxton's household; he wanted to protest about this harassment. And when he spoke of his wife's disappearance, they were not in the least surprised; they knew that the relations between the two were stormy. Two years before, Mrs Isabella Ruxton had come to the police station to protest that her husband was beating her, and Ruxton had made wild accusations of infidelity against her;

however, he had calmed down, and 24 hours later the two were apparently again on the best of terms.

The parents of Mrs Ruxton's maid, Mary Rogerson, were not only surprised but incredulous when Ruxton came and told them that their daughter had got herself pregnant by the laundry boy, and that his wife had taken her away for an abortion. Nothing was less likely; Mary was a plain girl, with a cast in one eye, who loved her home and her parents, and spent all her spare time with them; she was as unlikely to get herself pregnant as to rob a bank. In spite of Ruxton's feverish protests, they reported it to the police. On the evening of 9 October 1935, ten days after the remains had been found in the Linn, Ruxton came to the police and burst into tears. People were saying that he had murdered his wife and thrown her into the Linn; they must help him find her. They soothed him and sent him away. But, in fact, Ruxton had been the chief suspect since earlier that day. The Scottish police had been to see the Rogersons, and had shown them the patched blouse. As soon as they saw it, they knew their daughter was dead; Mary had bought it at a jumble sale and patched it under the arm. They were unable to identify the rompers, but suggested that the police should try a Mrs Holme, with whom Mary and the three Ruxton children had spent a holiday earlier that year. And Mrs Holme recognized the rompers as a pair she had given to Mary for the children.

The police spoke to the Ruxton's charlady, Mrs Oxley. She told them that on the day Mrs Ruxton and Mary Rogerson had disappeared, Sunday 15 September 1935, Ruxton had arrived early at her house and explained that it was unnecessary for her to come to work that day – he was taking the children to Morecambe, and his wife had gone to Edinburgh. The following morning, she found the Ruxton's house – at 2 Dalton Square – in a state of chaos, with carpets removed, the bath full of yellow stains, and a pile of burnt material in the yard. A neighbour told the police that Ruxton had persuaded her to come and clean up his house to prepare it for the decorators, claiming that he had cut his hand badly on a tin of peaches. She and her husband had obligingly scrubbed out the house. And Ruxton had given them some blood-stained carpets and a blue suit that was also stained with blood.

On 12 October, the police questioned Ruxton all night, and at 7.20 the next morning he was charged with the murder of Mary Rogerson.

In spite of Ruxton's attempts to cover his tracks, and to persuade various witnesses to offer him false alibis, the truth about the murders soon became plain. Ruxton was pathologically jealous, although there was no evidence that his 'wife' – they were in fact unmarried – had ever been unfaithful. A week before the murder, Mrs Ruxton had gone to Edinburgh, where she had a sister, with a family named Edmondson, who were close friends of the Ruxtons. The Edmondsons and Mrs Ruxton had all booked into separate rooms; nevertheless, Ruxton was convinced that she had spent the night in the bed of Robert Edmondson, an assistant solicitor in the Town Hall. Ruxton had driven to Edinburgh to spy on them. The following Saturday, Isabella Ruxton had gone to spend the afternoon and evening with two of her sisters in Blackpool. Convinced that she was in a hotel room with a man, Ruxton had worked himself into a jealous frenzy, and when she came back far later than expected, he began to beat her – probably in an attempt to make her confess her infidelities – then throttled her unconscious and stabbed her. Mary Rogerson had probably heard the screams and come in to see what was happening; Ruxton believed she was his wife's confidant in her infidelities, and killed her too. He had spent the next day dismembering the bodies and packing them in straw; that night, he made his first trip north to dispose of the bodies . . .

Ruxton's counsel, Norman Birkett, must have known that his client did not stand a ghost of a chance. His line of defence was that the bodies found in the Linn were not those of Isabella Ruxton and Mary Rogerson, but of some other persons. But when the medical experts – Glaister, Millar and Professor Sydney Smith – gave their evidence, it was obvious that the identity of the bodies had been establlshed beyond all possible doubt. One photograph, which has subsequently been used in every account of the case, superimposed the larger of the two skulls on a photograph of Mrs Ruxton. She had a rather long, horsy face, and it was obvious that the two fitted together with gruesome exactitude. Ruxton seemed determined to trap himself in a web of lies and evasions. The result was a unanimous verdict of guilty, arrived at in only one hour. He was hanged at Strangeways jail, Manchester, on 12 May 1936.

Yet examination of the evidence – and of Glaister's famous book *Medico – Legal Aspects of the Ruxton Case* (1937) – makes it clear that Ruxton came very close indeed to getting away with murder. If he had taken the trouble to remove Mary Rogerson's fingertips, and destroyed the telltale breast tissue as well as the trunk (which was never found), the evidence against him would have remained purely circumstantial; and since British juries are unwilling to convict on circumstantial evidence, he might well have been given the benefit of the doubt.

Glaister's forensic skill and Ruxton's failure of nerve played an equal part in bringing him to the gallows.

13

In 1940, Sir Bernard Spilsbury suffered a stroke – partly as a result of shock at the death of his son Peter, a house surgeon who was killed in the blitz. He lived on for another seven years, and continued to perform 1,000 post-mortems a year; but it was obvious that the Sherlock Holmes of forensic medicine was slowing down. He had often talked of retirement during the 1930s, but was always dissuaded on the grounds that there was no one to take his place. But in the early 1940s, the British public began to hear about another rising star, Professor Cedric Keith Simpson, of Guy's Medical School. No two personalities could have been less alike. Simpson, like many pathologists, derived a certain macabre amusement from his gruesome trade, and when lecturing on murder enjoyed trying to make his students feel sick. But apart from Spilsbury, there was no pathologist in London of comparable brilliance during the 1940s.

Spilsbury had been 33 at the time of the Crippen trial; Simpson was 35 when he suddenly stepped into the limelight with the curious case of the body in the church basement, which he later described as 'the case of a lifetime'.

On 17 January 1942, workmen had started to demolish a bombed Baptist church in Vauxhall Road, south London, and one of them prised up a heavy stone slab in the cellar. Underneath, he found a skeleton with a few shreds of flesh clinging to it, and when he lifted the skeleton with his spade, the skull remained where it was. It looked as if this was another victim of German air raids; yet the fact that the body was lying under a slab raised some doubts. When Simpson inspected the remains in Southwark mortuary the next day, he noted the remains of a womb. It told him not only that this was a woman, but that she had been buried in the past year or so; flesh would not survive much longer.

With the skeleton back in his laboratory at Guy's, Simpson could see plainly that this was a case of murder. The head had been severed, and both legs were severed at the knee. A yellowish powder clinging to parts of the skeleton proved to be slaked lime – calcium hydroxide. More was found in the hole in which she had been buried.

Simpson was able to determine the age of the dead woman from the skull sutures; the brow plates were completely fused and fusion was in progress between the top plates; that placed her age between 40 and 50. The uterus proved to be enlarged, but not due to pregnancy; an X-ray showed a fibroid growth. The lower jaw was missing, but the upper jaw was complete, and fillings and the marks of a dental plate told Simpson that it should not be difficult to identify her if her dentist could be found.

This proved to be unexpectedly easy. Detective Inspector Keeling studied a list of missing persons, and noted that Rachel Dobkin, wife of a fire-watcher at the Baptist church, had been reported missing since Good Friday 1941. Her sister told the police that she had gone to collect arrears of maintenance from her husband, Harry Dobkin, and had not been seen since. Over the years, Dobkin had been in prison several times for failing to pay her maintenance. Mrs Dobkin's sister was also able to tell them that Rachel's dentist was Mr Barnett Kopkin of Stoke Newington. And Mr Kopkin was able to confirm that the photograph of the upper jaw was that of his patient. The doctor who had diagnosed a fibroid growth of the uterus was also found. There could be no reasonable doubt that the body was that of Rachel Dobkin. And a tiny blood clot on the voice box revealed that she had died by strangulation. Simpson completed the identification by imposing a photograph of Rachel Dobkin on the skull, the technique Glaister had used in the Ruxton case; the fit was perfect.

The defence did its best, trying hard to throw doubt on Simpson's findings, and then suggesting that, if the victim was Mrs Dobkin, she could have died naturally through a bomb blast. The jury declined to consider either possibility, and Dobkin was condemned to death.

Even before the trial of Harry Dobkin in November 1942, Simpson was deeply absorbed in an equally strange murder case. On 7 October 1942, marines exercising on Hankley Common, near Godalming, saw a mummified hand sticking out of the earth. The following day, Simpson was there, carefully digging the body out of the earth to ensure that it remained undamaged. It was a woman, lying face downwards, the legs apart, one arm outstretched. She was fully clothed, and the back of the skull was shattered.

The body was moved back to Guy's, and placed in a carbolic tank; Simpson devoted all his spare time to it. 'Spare time' was usually tea time, when he and his secretary Molly Lefebure would sit beside the tank with their tea and sandwiches, and she would take notes at his dictation. Simpson's associate Dr Eric Gardner often came to help.

Their conclusion was that the dead girl had received stab wounds to the left top side of the head. And some of the smaller indentations revealed that a knife with a hook-like point had been used – neither Simpson nor Gardner had ever seen anything of the sort. The girl had apparently fallen heavily on her face, knocking out some of her front teeth. Then there had been a tremendous blow to the back of the head with some blunt instrument, shattering the skull. When Simpson and Miss Lefebure had finished wiring together the skull fragments, they could see a depressed fracture across the back of the head – it could have been made with a stake or a bough. This is what had killed the girl. Her teeth and bones put her age in her late teens.

The task of discovering the girl's identity was less complicated. Detective Inspector Ted Greeno of Scotland Yard made enquiries at Godalming about a blonde teenager who wore a green and white summer dress with a lace collar, and learned that a girl called Joan Pearl Wolfe was known to the local police – she lived like a tramp, and was often seen with soldiers from a nearby camp. She was not a prostitute, but had apparently run away from home. A search of the area where the body was found revealed Joan Wolfe's identity card, her rosary (she was a Roman Catholic) and a letter to a Canadian private called August Sangret, telling him she was pregnant. A few more enquiries revealed that Sangret had been spending his weekend leaves with her in home-made 'wigwams' made of branches, which he built for her – Sangret was half Cree-Indian, half French Canadian.

Interviewed at the Canadian army camp, Sangret told Greeno that he had not seen Joan for more than three weeks, and had reported her disappearance to his provost sergeant. But a little further enquiry revealed that Sangret had told contradictory stories about her disappearance to various friends. And the police search revealed new evidence that made it clear that Sangret was the man they were looking for – a bloodstained army blanket and battle dress, both of which had been ineffectually washed, a birch stake with bloodstains and blonde hairs on it, and, finally, a clasp knife with a 'hooked' point, which was found obstructing a washhouse pipe – someone recollected that Sangret had excused himself to go to the washhouse while he was waiting for his first interview with Greeno. What had happened was clear. Joan Wolfe and August Sangret had met on Hankley Common on the afternoon of 14 August 1942, and she had pressed him about marriage. They had quarrelled, and Sangret had attacked her with the knife – the point of the clasp knife fitted the indentations in the skull. She had fled and tripped over a military trip-wire, knocking out her teeth, and Sangret had smashed in her skull with a blow of the birch stake as she lay there. Then he had wrapped her body in a blanket, hidden it under bushes for 24 hours or so, then dragged it to the top of the ridge to bury it – possibly following some burial ritual of his Native American ancestors.

In court, Simpson produced the skull and the knife, and the jury took them with them when they retired. It took them two hours to find Sangret guilty, with a strong recommendation to mercy, but he was hanged in Wandsworth jail.

While he was still working on the 'wigwam case' (as it came to be known), Simpson was called to view the body of an unknown woman found in some reeds by the River Lea, near Luton. The body was trussed up in four potato sacks, the knees against the chest. In the mortuary, Simpson quickly diagnosed the cause of death as strangulation, followed by a blow to the side of the face from a heavy blunt instrument. Bruises caused by the ropes indicated that she had still been alive when trussed up. The woman was in her mid-30s, had had at least one child, and was again pregnant.

Since she had been dead only about 24 hours, the face still looked virtually as it had when she was alive; it was photographed, and the result exhibited in local shops and cinemas. Yet no one seemed to recognize her. There was nothing for it but to apply the 'needle-in-the-haystack' method. The police traced 404 missing women, went to all dry cleaners to check on women's clothing that had been left uncollected, and searched rubbish dumps for discarded female clothes. A cast of the dead woman's remaining teeth was taken – she had also worn dentures, which had been removed by her killer – and the photograph published in the British Dental Journal. And when, after three months, all this activity had brought no result, Chief Inspector Chapman, who was in charge of the case, decided once more to study all the evidence collected so far. This included a piece of black coat found on a rubbish dump; a piece of attached tape indicated that it had at some time been sent to the local Sketchley dry cleaners. From the tag, the dry cleaner was able to tell Chapman that the coat had been brought in by Mrs Rene Manton of Regent Street, Luton. The 8-year-old girl who opened the door bore a strong resemblance to the unidentified corpse; she explained that her mother had left home. A photograph of Rene Manton supplied by the child left no doubt in Chapman's mind that the victim was Rene Manton, who had been missing since 18 November 1942.

Chapman's next call was on Mrs Manton's mother. When she told him that she had received several letters from her daughter, who was living in Hampstead, Chapman wondered for a moment if he was pursuing a false lead. But the old lady was half blind, and hardly able to read the handwriting. He noted that 'Hampstead' was spelt without the 'p'.

His next call was on Rene Manton's husband, Bertie, who was in the National Fire Service, at the Luton station. Manton told him that his wife had left him on 25 November, a week after the discovery of the body, after a quarrel about her association with soldiers. Shown letters to his mother-in-law, Manton identified the handwriting as that of his wife. Asked to write a sentence containing the word 'Hampstead', he spelt it 'Hamstead'.

Manton told the detective the name of his wife's dentist, and the dentist provided the final piece of evidence – the teeth left no doubt that the victim was his patient Rene Manton.

Confronted with this evidence, Manton confessed. He and his wife had quarrelled about soldiers, and she had thrown a cup of tea in his face. He had then struck her to the ground with a footstool. Convinced she was dead, he had stripped the body and hidden it in the cellar, then cleared up the blood before his children returned from school for their tea. Later, he tied it in the sacks, and wheeled it to the river on the handlebars of his bicycle.

Mrs Manton's 17-year-old daughter had seen the photograph of her mother flashed on to the screen at the local cinema, but the swelling due to bruises had prevented her from recognizing it. The two sons, aged 14 and 15, had also seen the photograph in a local tobacconist's window and told their father they thought it looked like their mother; he said their mother had gone away to Grantham and they believed him.

The final piece of identification evidence was collected by Fred Cherrill, of Scotland Yard's fingerprint department. Going over the Manton house, Cherrill found a thumbprint on a pickle jar which matched that of the dead woman.

Manton's defence was that he had killed his wife in a fit of fury with a single blow, and that it was therefore manslaughter. But Simpson pointed out that marks on her throat showed that he had throttled her – not once, but twice. Moreover, Manton had struck her twice with the stool. All this seemed to indicate a deliberate intention of killing her rather than a single blow struck in a rage. Manton was found guilty and sentenced to death.

Simpson's most famous murder case was still to come. By the late 1940s, he was known to the general public largely as the pathologist who had figured in the most widely publicized murder trial since the war, that of the sadist Neville George Clevely Heath. The 29-year-old ex-Borstal boy was an incorrigible fantasist who loved to pose as a colonel or group captain. On the evening of 20 June 1946, Heath booked into the Pembridge Court Hotel, Notting Hill, with an amateur artist named Margery Gardner, who also happened to be a masochist. Her naked body was found the next day, apparently suffocated accidentally by a gag, the flesh covered with distinctive whiplash marks; her nipples had been bitten off, and her vagina was torn from the insertion of some blunt instrument. When Simpson examined the body he remarked to Detective Chief Inspector Barratt: 'If you find that whip you've found your man.' The hotel register had been signed 'Col. and Mrs G. C. Heath'. Heath meanwhile had gone to the Tollard Royal Hotel in Bournemouth, and booked in under the name 'Group Captain Rupert Brooke'. There he met a pretty ex-WRNS named Doreen Marshall, and persuaded her to have dinner with him, then to allow him to walk her back to her own hotel. Heath returned alone. Five days later, a swarm of flies alerted a passer-by to her naked body lying in some bushes; like Margery Gardner, she had been sexually mutilated – this time with a knife. The manager of the Tollard Royal told the police she had dined with 'Group Captain Brooke'. The detective constable who questioned 'Brooke' recognized him as the man wanted by Scotland Yard for the murder of Margery Gardner. In Heath's pocket they found a cloakroom ticket, which led them to an attaché case containing the riding whip of distinctive pattern. Heath was found guilty of the murder of Margery Gardner – a curious verdict since her death was obviously accidental – and he was executed at Pentonville on 16 October 1946.

The sensation caused by the Heath murders was eclipsed three years later by the case of the 'vampire murderer' John George Haigh. On Sunday 20 February 1949, a man and a woman arrived at the Chelsea police station and explained that they wanted to report the disappearance of an elderly lady, Mrs Durand-Deacon, who was a fellow guest at the Onslow Court Hotel in South Kensington. The man – dapper and well-dressed, with a neat moustache – explained that he had arranged to meet Mrs Olivier Durand-Deacon two days earlier, to take her to his place of business in Sussex, but she failed to keep the appointment; now, with her friend Mrs Constance Lane, he had come to alert the police. When the police checked on him at the Criminal Records Office, they discovered that John Haigh had been in prison for swindling.

Crime reporters flocked to the Onslow Court Hotel, and Haigh gave a kind of impromptu press conference, emphasizing his own concern for the missing woman. But the West Sussex Constabulary was already looking at Haigh's 'place of business', Hurstlea Products, at Crawley. He rented a two-storey brick-built storehouse from the firm, using it for 'experimental work'. The police broke in, and found a revolver, and a receipt for a Persian lamb coat from a firm of cleaners. The coat proved to belong to Mrs Durand-Deacon, and further enquiries revealed that her jewellery had been sold by Haigh to a jewellers in Horsham. Haigh was arrested and taken to the police station. At first he told obviously concocted lies about his relationship with Mrs Durand-Deacon, hinting at blackmail. Then he suddenly asked the police inspector what the chances were of anyone being released from Broadmoor, the criminal lunatic asylum. Inspector Webb was non-committal. 'Well', said Haigh, 'if I told you the truth you wouldn't believe me . . . Mrs Durand-Deacon no longer exists . . . I have destroyed her with acid!' He gazed at the incredulous policeman with a bland smile. 'How can you prove murder if there is no body?' Like many murderers, Haigh made the mistake of believing that the phrase *corpus delicti* means the corpse, without which murder cannot be proved; in fact, it means the body of the offence or crime. Fellow convicts who knew Haigh in his earlier days in Dartmoor had nicknamed him 'old *corpus delicti*' because he liked to expound his view that a killer could not be convicted so long as there was no body.

Haigh added: 'You'll find the sludge that remains at Leopold Road [Crawley]. I did the same with the Hendersons and the McSwanns.'

Haigh had decided that his best means of escaping justice was a defence of insanity; he continued to pursue this objective by telling the police that the motive for the killings had been a desire to drink the blood of his victims; he had an insatiable lust for blood, and after each murder, filled a glass with his victim's blood and drained it. (In fact, blood is an emetic, and a glassful would undoubtedly have made him vomit.)

Haigh had embarked on his career of mass murder with the deliberation of a businessman. After a number of spells in jail for petty fraud, he decided that the best way to avoid being caught was to kill his victims and dispose of their bodies. In 1936 he had been employed by an amusement arcade owner named McSwann; after coming out of prison in 1943, he had met their son Donald again, and proposed a business partnership. Donald was lured to Haigh's basement 'workshop' at Gloucester Road in September 1944 and bludgeoned to death; then Haigh dissolved his body in a vat of concentrated sulphuric acid – he had already experimented on mice in the prison workshop and decided that this was the perfect method of destroying his corpses. He emptied the 'sludge' down the drain. McSwann's parents were told he had gone off to Scotland on business. Ten months later, the elder McSwanns were lured separately to the basement and disposed of in the same way. Haigh then disposed of their considerable property, forging the necessary documents, for about £4,000.

By September 1947, Haigh had spent the £4,000, and looked around for more victims. He saw an advertisement for a house, and introduced himself to its owners, Archie and Rose Henderson, and offered them £10,500 for it. The deal 'fell through', but Haigh continued to see the Hendersons, posing as a rich businessman. On 12 February 1948, Archie Henderson accompanied Haigh to his 'workshop' at Leopold Road, Crawley, and was shot in the back of the head. Haigh then went and collected Rose Henderson, telling her that her husband was ill, and killed her in the same way. Various letters were despatched to relatives of the dead couple, explaining that they had been close to a 'bust-up', and were travelling while their relationship was repaired. Haigh forged these letters so expertly that all suspicion was finally allayed. Then he disposed of their property, collecting some £7,700.

Other possible victims – including the widow of a Wakefield businessman – slipped through the net. By February 1949, Haigh was again in debt, and realized that he had to find a victim within the next week or so. To Mrs Durand-Deacon, who always dined at the next table at the Onslow Court Hotel, Haigh suggested a business deal involving the manufacture of plastic fingernails. And on 18 February 1949, Mrs Durand-Deacon made her fatal visit to the Crawley workshop. Twelve days later, on 2 March, Haigh was charged with her murder.

When Professor Keith Simpson travelled down to the Crawley workshop on 1 March, he had little hope of finding evidence of murder; Haigh had already told the police that he had poured the 'sludge' over the ground several days earlier. The sludge was lying on an area of ground about six feet by four, and was about three inches deep. Simpson was staring intently at this sludge when he exclaimed: 'Aha, gall-stones.' He had seen an object about the size of a cherry, lying among some pebbles that were, to the inexpert eye, indistinguishable from it. After this find, the police carefully shovelled the sludge into boxes, to be removed to the Scotland Yard laboratory. There it was searched by spreading it thinly in steel trays; because the acid was so strong, the searchers had to wear rubber gloves. But the effort was worthwhile: the sludge proved to contain a partially dissolved left foot, and intact upper plastic denture, a lower denture, three gall-stones (easy to distinguish at close quarters by their facets), 28 lb of greasy substance, 18 fragments of human bone, the handle of a red plastic handbag and a lipstick container. Haigh had left more than enough of Mrs Durand-Deacon to hang him.

Simpson took the bones to his laboratory at Guy's. He discovered the presence of osteo-arthritis in some of the joints – Mrs Durand-Deacon suffered from osteo-arthritis – and was able to identify most of the bone fragments as human. Meanwhile, the police had made a plaster cast of the left foot, and checked it against Mrs Durand-Deacon's left shoe; the fit was perfect. The plastic dentures were identified by Mrs Durand-Deacon's dental surgeon as having been supplied to her two years earlier. Haigh had no way of knowing that the false teeth were of plastic, and therefore would not dissolve in acid, nor of knowing the gall-stones cannot be dissolved in acid.

Bloodstains found on the whitewash of the storeroom were tested and found to be human. Bloodstains were also found on the Persian lamb coat, and on the cuff of one of Haigh's shirts. The handbag strap was identified as belonging to the handbag Mrs Durand-Deacon had carried when she drove with Haigh down to Crawley.

Haigh's major mistake had been in confessing to the murders, and trusting to a defence of insanity. If he had said nothing about the 'acid bath', the sludge might not have been examined for many weeks, and Simpson later admitted that by that time, the acid might have consumed everything but the gall-stones and the human fat. And in themselves, these would not have constituted sufficient evidence of identity.

In prison, Haigh continued to build up the notion that he was insane, claiming that there had been three more victims – all penniless – whom he had killed for their blood alone. He explained that the urge to drink blood developed after an accident with a lorry in 1944, when his car overturned. After this, he said, he began to have a recurrent dream of a forest of crucifixes which turned into trees that dripped blood . . . He also claimed that the murders were divinely inspired. When aware of being observed, he drank his own urine.

All this was useless. A number of doctors and psychiatrists examined Haigh, and all but one concluded that he was perfectly sane. A woman friend who visited him in prison observed that he was playing the role of mass murderer with tremendous gusto, delighting in his belated 'fame'. The newspapers were full of accounts of the 'vampire murderer' – probably no case of the century has received so much publicity – and one of them, the *Daily Mirror,* went too far and was fined £10,000, while its editor was sentenced to three months in prison. But at the trial, which began on 18 July 1949 at Lewes Assizes, all the evidence revealed Haigh as a calculating killer who had murdered for gain, and who was shamming insanity. Dr Henry Yellowlees, for the defence, argued that Haigh was genuinely paranoid, but the jury was so unimpressed that they took only 15 minutes to bring in a guilty verdict. Haigh was executed at Wandsworth on 6 August 1949.

Simpson, who was responsible for the medical evidence that convicted Haigh, later commented on the absurdly small profits that Haigh had made from five years of murder – a mere £12,000. The last murder, of Mrs Durand-Deacon, would have brought him only about £150 for the coat and the jewellery. He could have made more money in almost any honest occupation.

Keith Simpson died in 1985, at the age of 78. Like Spilsbury, he was inclined to overwork, and his publisher J. H. H. Gaute remarked in an obituary that this was the cause of his death. But his enthusiasm for his gruesome occupation was so great that he was unable to stay away from the morgue and the 'path lab'. Gaute recalls how, after lunching with Simpson at Guy's, Simpson asked him if he would like to come down to the mortuary, and seemed surprised when the publisher declined. 'Not the keen type, eh?' he remarked drily.

The present writer (Colin Wilson) did not decline a similar invitation, and was taken into the mortuary to view the body of a male child of about seven, who had – according to a teenage baby-sitter – died after a fall downstairs. Simpson expertly opened the body in a few minutes, then, as if he knew exactly what he was looking for, plunged in his hand and drew out the liver, which was broken in half. 'That wasn't caused by a fall downstairs. It's an impossibility. He must have been kicked in the stomach.' Since the baby-sitter had been alone with the child at the time of the 'accident', the evidence suggested that he was the culprit. I never found out the sequel to the story. But I retained the impression that Simpson had known intuitively that he was looking at a case of murder.

14

Since Lacassagne and Locard initiated the science of identification in the late nineteeth century, forensic pathology had again and again demonstrated its ability to identify human remains from even the smallest clue. But a case in Chicago in 1945 demonstrated that a prosecution for murder can be successful even without the slightest trace of the *'corpus delicti'*, as Haigh would have said.

On 28 February 1945, a man who identified himself as Milton Michaelis, of Clyde Avenue, Chicago, rang the Woodlawn police station to report that his wife had been missing for several hours. It was the first time in their 36 years of married life that she had gone off without telling him. When the police made a routine call, the anxious husband showed them some house keys and the heel of a shoe that he had found in a nearby alleyway since making the call. The police looked in the alleyway, which was beside the apartment building, but could find nothing more. The door to the basement proved to be unlocked, and the janitor, Joe Nischt, told them that he had seen nothing. He had been to collect his pay, stopped for a few beers, and now – towards midnight – was completing various tasks he should have finished earlier. When the police asked him if they could search his furnace room, he agreed immediately. One of the officers even glanced into the furnace, but the glowing coals made it impossible to see anything.

Working on the assumption that Rose Michaelis might have been the victim of a hit-and-run driver, the police again searched the alleyway at first daylight. This time they found some ominous clues: hairpins, fragments of broken glass, and some bloodstains on a telephone pole. Milton Michaelis thought that his wife might have gone out to get water from a nearby filtration plant; she disliked the Chicago tap-water. The broken fragments looked very like those of the type of bottle she used to collect the water. If Mrs Michaelis had been struck by a hit-and-run driver, then he must have dragged her into his car.

Investigations of the janitor's alibi revealed that he was telling the truth; he had collected his pay, then stopped at a few bars on the way back to the apartment building. A check of the criminal record files revealed that he had been arrested twice for assualting women in barroom brawls. On both occasions he had been released with a caution; but it was clear that he was likely to become aggressive towards women when drunk. The police asked him to come in for questioning.

And when he seemed sullen and uncooperative, they decided to book him on suspicion of murder. But his union promptly filed a writ of *habeus corpus*, and he was released the next day.

That same evening, a woman called at the police station; she was carrying a copy of the evening paper, which contained a photograph of the janitor. 'This man knocked on my door three nights ago and asked if he could see my husband. I told him my husband wasn't at home, and asked if I could help. And he put his hands over his face and said: "No one can help me. I just killed a woman." Then he went away. I thought he was drunk . . .'

Once again the police called in Joe Nischt for questioning. And when they told him of the woman's story, he covered his face with his hands and began sobbing. He described how he had approached the attractive, middle-aged housewife and tried to pick her up. When he became too suggestive, she lost her temper. He struck her so hard that he knocked her head against the telephone pole. Then he dragged her into the basement . . . He was not specific about what happened next, but he confessed that he had pushed her body into the furnace, and that she was probably still alive. He signed a statement to this effect.

He was held in a cell while the police doused the furnace, then sent the ashes to the laboratory for examination. The results were disappointing. There was not the slightest trace of a human body – not even the tiniest bone fragment. The police were in the position that Keith Simpson might have found himself in if Haigh had not told the police about the acid 'sludge' – in fact, worse, since they could not even offer a single gall-stone in evidence. And, like Simpson, they were aware that juries are highly suspicious of murder cases in which there is no trace of the body. The Assistant State Attorney Blair Varnes realized that, in spite of the confession, his case was almost non-existent. Nischt only had to repudiate his confession, claiming that it had been obtained under duress, and the state would have no case. And this is, in fact, precisely what happened. Moreover, Nischt's lawyers declared that it was impossible to destroy a body totally, and that this would be the line of their defence.

This, at least, offered the prosecutor a possible line of attack. He decided to consult Professor Wilton Krogman, and anthropologist at the University of Chicago, who was often consulted by the FBI as an expert witness on bodies. Varnes and Krogman visited various crematoria to find out just how long it took a human body to turn to ashes, and at what temperature. They learned that, at a temperature of around 3000° Fahrenheit, it took an hour or so to reduce a body to ashes. The temperature in an ordinary furnace would be far lower than that, but the one in the Clyde Avenue basement had had three days to do its work. If the prosecution could prove beyond all doubt that the furnace could destroy a body in that time, then they had a reply to the main defence argument.

From the Chicago morgue, Krogman obtained the unclaimed body of a woman of about the same age and weight as Rose Michaelis. Then he staged a gruesome reconstruction – placing it in the furnace of an apartment building, and raising the temperature to its maximum. The furnace achieved very nearly the same temperature as a crematorium, and the unknown body was reduced to ashes in three and a half hours. At the end of that time, not a single identifiable fragment remained. When this evidence was presented to the grand jury – whose business was to decide whether there was a case to prosecute – the janitor was indicted on a murder charge.

In court the case attracted nation-wide attention – since it was the general belief that it was impossible to prove a murder without a body. Many newspapers recalled the parallel case of the other Chicago killer, Adolf Luetgart, and pointed out that the few bone fragments and the initialled ring had proved his undoing. Nischt's attorneys argued that it was impossible to destroy a body so completely that no fragment remained. And when Professor Krogman produced his triumphant refutation, they were obviously shaken. Suddenly, Nischt announced that he wanted to change his plea to guilty. The defence offered to do a deal – life imprisonment in exchange for a guilty plea. And although Varnes felt that he had won his case, he realized that a jury of laymen might still be swayed by the 'no body' argument. He accepted, and Joe Nischt was sentenced to life imprisonment in the State Penitentiary at Joliet.

The science of forensic identification has made further leaps forward in recent decades – often through cooperation with specialists in apparently non-forensic fields of knowledge. A prime example was Dr Zakaria Erzinclioglu – a Turkish born entomologist (insect expert) who spent most of his career at Cambridge and Durham universities in the UK. Over the last three decades of the twentieth century, Doctor Zak – as he was invariably called for practical as well as affectionate reasons – was often asked to help with homicide investigations, especially where the time of death was considered to be of key importance.

It is a common misconception that forensic experts can determine the exact time of a murder by examining the corpse. In fact, even today, the best that can be done is to make an educated guess; in the Raymond Chandler novel, *The Big Sleep,* a pathologist is asked when a murder victim died, to which he replies laconically: 'I might be able to tell you that if he ate supper last night; and then only if you can tell me what time he ate it.' In real life, pathologists are rarely even that certain. And, of course, in cases where a body has lain days, weeks, months or even years before discovery, the matter becomes even harder to judge with any degree of accuracy.

Dr Erzinclioglu was an expert on many forms of British insect life, but his academic speciality was the life and habits of the blowfly, the common pest whose eggs and maggots are often found on corpses, even just a few hours after death. Given access to the blowfly young found on a corpse, Erzinclioglu could give investigators a reasonably accurate *minimum* estimate of the time that had passed since death occurred, based on the maggots' level of growth. Obviously blowflies do not lay eggs on living hosts, thus giving a minimum period of death, but unless there was proof that the body had been exposed to such wildlife immediately after death (and had not, for example, been hidden in a car boot or a similar sealed area) a maximum time dead could not be determined with certainty by this method.

Disgusting as all this is to the layman, Dr Erzinclioglu soon realized that combining a Sherlock Holmesian methodology with general entomology could prove an invaluable tool to homicide investigations. He began to study all the insects that take advantage of decaying human bodies, with an eye to aiding murder investigations. His research eventually led him to become the director of the Forensic Science Research Centre at Durham University, and his evidence helped convict dozens of British murderers. In the early 1980s (shortly before Alec Jeffreys announced his DNA fingerprinting technique) Dr Erzinclioglu was contacted when West Yorkshire police found what they believed were the dismembered skeletal remains of a teenage girl in a house in Wakefield. Neighbours of the Perera family had noticed that their thirteen-year-old adopted daughter, Nilanthi, had not been seen in some time. Initial suspicions had been allayed by the Perera parents' assurances that Nilanthi was fine, but as the year wore on into a hot summer and the usually gregarious girl did not appear outside, the neighbours decided to contact the authorities.

The police were told by Dr Anthony Samson Perera – Nilanthi's fosterfather – that she was 'a jungle girl' who was unable to adapt to life in England and had been sent back to her native Sri Lanka.

Checking with Sri Lankan police failed to find any evidence of Nilanthi's return, but it was not until a colleague of Dr Perera at Leeds University – Perera was a lecturer in Oral Biology – reported that he had brought some dirt-encrusted human bones into the university laboratory that police decided to search the Perera home.

They found what looked like human vertebrae and some rotting meat under the plants in several indoor pots. Fleshless leg and arm bones were also found under the floorboards in the living room and a recently disturbed patch of ground in the garden gave up more human bones as well as long strands of black hair that resembled that of Nilanthi. The body (if all the bones and flesh belonged to the same corpse) had been very thoroughly dismembered and a significant proportion of it remained missing.

Despite the apparent weight of evidence, Dr Perera refused to confess to any wrongdoing. He claimed that the human body parts were the remains of a dead body he had obtained legally (under Sri Lankan law) from Peredeniya University for the purpose of anatomical study. He had concealed it after he had dissected it to avoid unnecessary red-tape with the British authorities. When charged with Nilanthi's murder he replied confidently: 'You prepare your case inspector. I'll prepare mine.'

In fact both cases were on rather shaky ground. The police had human remains, and an affidavit from Peredeniya University that they had not sold Dr Perera a cadaver, but extensive forensic study of the partial skeleton and the small fragments of rotting flesh could not conclusively show the age, sex or racial decent of their owner. With such gaps in the evidence, a good defence council might sow a shadow-of-a-doubt in the minds of the jury and get a not guilty verdict. On the other hand, Dr Perera's main hope lay in convincing the jury that he was being totally truthful and that the whole matter was just a horrible misunderstanding. It was here that Dr Erzinclioglu's evidence proved vital. He showed that the species of mite found on the leg bones under the floorboards were of an outdoor-only variety. This indicated that the bones had been buried in the garden, then later dug-up and placed beneath the living room floor. As Dr Perera had flatly denied that he had exhumed any of the 'medical cadaver' after burying it, this showed him to be dishonest. His credibility dashed, Perera was found guilty and sentenced to life imprisonment.

Dr Erzinclioglu was also involved in one of the most remarkable cases of victim identification in British legal history – one that combined several new forensic disciplines to crack a case that might otherwise have been impossible to solve. On 7 December, 1989, workmen doing rebuilding work on number 29 Fitzhamon Embankment in Cardiff dug a trench in the garden of the terraced house to install a new sewer pipe. A few feet down they found a buried human skeleton wrapped in a carpet. The police were initially stumped – the rundown house had been rented to numerous people in the past few years, any one of whom might have buried the body – their list of potential suspects was enormous. Without more information, they would be very unlikely to catch the murderer (if it was murder).

Dr Erzinclioglu was called in and, after studying the effects left by the various creatures that had reduced the body to a skeleton, was able to confirm the body was at least five years dead – and probably had been for several years before that. He also noted that the corpse must have lain exposed to the elements for at least a day before it was buried.

This information reduced the size of the police investigation considerably: any missing person reports that were less than five years old could be ignored, as could all residents of the property within the last five years. But investigators were no closer to identifying the corpse.

The skull still sported a quantity of long blonde hair, indicating that the victim had been a woman. This was confirmed after examination by Professor Bernard Knight, who reported that the skeleton was that of a teenaged girl, five feet four inches tall. Unfortunately, thorough questioning of the neighbours and anyone else involved with 29 Fitzhamon Embankment failed to find anyone who remembered a girl of this description seen staying at or visiting the property.

The remains were then sent to doctors Theya Molleson and Christopher Stringer – anthropologists at the Natural History Museum in London. They reported that the features of the skull indicated a Caucasian extraction, but that she had probably not been totally Anglo-Saxon. Unfortunately, this did no more than confirm that she was white – a fact the police had already assumed because of the naturally blonde hair. After hundreds of interviews and thousands of man-hours, the case could go nowhere without an identification of the victim.

It was then that an officer on the investigation picked up a magazine. Inside was an article about Dr Richard Neave of Manchester University, the 'medical artist' who had reconstructed the face of Philip of Macedon from just the dead king's bare skull.

Combining an expertise in sculpture with an in-depth knowledge of the musculature of the human face and head, Dr Neave could 're-build' the features of a face onto its original skull. During the process, called facial reconstruction, strips of clay are built-up on the skull, reproducing the sections of muscle, cartilage and tendon that make up the face. When a final 'skin' layer is added, a reasonable reproduction of the original face is produced. Even the shape of the nose and the lips can be accurately deduced by examination of the contours of the skull.

Dr Neave was recruited to help the investigation and, using a plaster copy moulded from the original, facially reconstructed the Cardiff head. The result was shown at a press conference along with a request to the public to help identify the victim. Two different social workers rang the investigation to identify the girl as Karen Price, who had run away from a state children's home eight years before. One of them even had a photograph of Karen, and the similarity to Dr Neave's reconstruction was striking. (As doctors Molleson and Stringer had guessed, Karen was white, but was a mix of British, Greek, Spanish and American forebears).

Karen Price's dental records were obtained and an exact match to the teeth of the skull was made, but the investigating officers still felt that something more might be needed to convince a jury of the identification of the skeleton. One of the officers mentioned to Dr Erzinclioglu that they had hoped to use the new technique of DNA fingerprinting to identify the victim definitely as Karen Price, but they had been advised that the age of the bones might be too great to get a sample of DNA. Erzinclioglu, who had worked on DNA recovered from insects trapped for millions of years in amber, replied that a decade was nothing in such cases. On his recommendation Dr Erika Hagelberg in the John Radcliff Hospital in Oxford was asked to compare the skeleton's DNA with that of Karen's parents. The result was a success: the victim was certainly Karen Price.

The main question remaining, of course, was who had buried Karen (presumably after murdering her)? The answer came when the BBC's Crimewatch program broadcast an update on the case. A small-time crook called Idris Ali recognized the reconstruction of Karen and was persuaded by his friends to contact the police. He confessed that he had been Karen's pimp over the years 1981 to 1982. At sometime in that period (he could not remember exactly when) he had witnessed a client of Karen's beat her and strangle her to death when she refused to pose for pornographic photographs. Ali insisted that he had not been directly involved in the murder at 29 Fitzhamon Embankment, but he had helped the killer, Alan Charlton, to bury the body.

Found guilty, Charlton was sentenced to life imprisonment, while Ali, who was under age at the time of the murder, was detained at Her Majesty's Pleasure. On appeal Ali had the sentence changed to one of manslaughter and was immediately released (having already served the sentenced period in jail).

The Karen Price case combined forensic entomology, anthropology, facial reconstruction, dental identification, DNA fingerprinting and, arguably most telling of all, the clever use of the national media to solve a case that, five years earlier, might have been considered virtually unsolvable.

5

If Blood Could Speak . . .

1

The science of bloodstains is probably the most important single advance in the history of crime detection. 'For at least as long as recorded history, man has been interested in and mystified by blood', remarks Addine G. Erskine in his standard textbook *The Principles and Practice of Blood Grouping*. Yet until the early twentieth century, there was no reliable way of distinguishing a human bloodstain from an animal bloodstain. This is the reason that bloodstains seldom played a central role in early criminal investigation. And a Scottish case of 1721 served as a warning against placing too much reliance on this type of evidence. William Shaw, a native of Edinburgh, was known to be on bad terms with his daughter Catherine because of her association with a man he disliked. One day, neighbours in the same tenement heard a violent quarrel, followed by groans, and the slamming of the door. When this was succeeded by silence, someone went to the door and knocked. It was locked, and there was no reply. The neighbours sent for the police, who broke in, and found Catherine lying in a pool of blood, with a knife beside her. She was still alive, but unable to speak. Asked about the quarrel with her father, she nodded her head; asked if he was responsible for her present condition, she nodded again. Soon after, she died. William Shaw was taken into custody as soon as he returned, and he was obviously badly shaken when taken into the presence of his daughter's body. The police noted the bloodstains on his clothing, and he was arrested and charged with her murder.

The defence was that she had committed suicide. The accused man insisted that he had not even struck his daughter, but left the room in a rage. He claimed that the blood on his clothing was his own – he had been bled a few days earlier, and the bandage had worked loose. But the jury was particularly impressed by the evidence of a neighbour who had heard the girl scream, that her father was the cause of her death. Shaw was condemned to death, and executed in November 1721, continuing to protest his innocence.

The next tenant of the room discovered a letter in an opening near the chimney; it was a suicide note from Catherine Shaw, stating that she intended to kill herself because her father would not allow her to marry the man she loved. The letter ended by stating that her father was the cause of death.

When the handwriting was proved to be that of the dead girl, the authorities realized they had hanged an innocent man. Orders were given for Shaw's body to be taken down from the chains in which it had been hung, and given a decent burial, with semi-military honours – no doubt as a kind of belated apology.

There is one impressive exception to the statement about the role of bloodstains in early criminal investigations. Gustave Macé, one of the most remarkable of Vidocq's successors, solved his first murder case through the discovery of a bloodstain. We have already encountered Macé in an earlier chapter – he was one of the senior policemen who opposed Bertillon's early experiments with anthropometry. But this, perhaps, should not be held against him, for Macé was one of the greatest exponents of the old-fashioned school of 'needle-in-the-haystack' detection.

In late January 1869, a restaurateur of the rue Princesse, off the boulevard St-Germaine in Paris, received protests from customers about the quality of his water, and decided to investigate the well in the basement. It was 60 feet deep, and covered with a kind of grill within a few feet of the surface of the water. Floating on the surface was a parcel wrapped in cloth, and its stench left no doubt that it was the cause of the trouble. With some difficulty, the man fished it out, and was horrified to discover that it contained the lower half of a human leg. He reported it to the Sûreté, and a new recruit named Gustave Macé was sent to investigate. Macé was not simply a policeman, but a lawyer whose duties included crime investigation and prosecution – an 'investigating magistrate'. He soon realized that there was another parcel floating just below the surface. It proved to contain another leg, encased in part of a stocking.

The doctors who examined the legs concluded that they were those of a woman. Macé noted that both legs had originally been tied in a piece of black glazed calico, about a yard square, tied at either end; this, he remarked in his first report, was a method in use among tailors and seamstresses. With marvellous thoroughness, he checked on the way seamstresses tied parcels, and observed that it was slightly different – they folded the corners inward in the shape of a cross. And so, concluded this remarkable forebear of Sherlock Holmes, it seemed to him probable that the parcel had been tied by a journeyman tailor. The 'journeyman' inference arose from the fact that the material was cheaper than the kind that would be used in a first-class establishment. There was an odd mark on the stocking: '+B+', which Macé soon discovered was not a laundry mark. He began checking the file of missing women, 122 in all, a number he was able to reduce to 84. But at this point, the great doctor Ambroise Tardieu, author of the earliest treatise on hanging, examined the legs, and declared that they belonged to a man. All Macé's labours so far had been wasted. With a sigh, he prepared to start all over again.

The state of decay of the legs suggested that their owner had been dead a fairly long time – perhaps six weeks. A few days before Christmas, a human thigh wrapped in a blue jersey had been taken from the river and deposited in the morgue. A human thigh bone had been found in the rue Jacob at about the same time. Two days later, a laundry propietor had seen a man scattering pieces of meat from a basket into the river; he explained that he 'was baiting the fish'. But since then, some fairly large chunks of flesh had been pulled out of the river and the St-Martin canal. On 22 December two policemen had seen a man wandering in the early hours of the morning with a parcel in one hand and a hamper in the other; they had questioned him in case he was a robber, and the man had explained that he had just arrived in the capital by train, and been unable to find a cab. The parcels, he explained, contained hams. He looked so honest that they let him go. They described him to Macé as short, plump, round-faced, with a black moustache and confident manner. The laundry proprietor gave the same description of the 'fisherman'.

Macé felt he was now on the right track. Why had the murderer deposited the lower limbs in the well? Almost certainly because being stopped by the policemen had given him a nasty shock, and he was unwilling to take further risks. He had been stopped close to the rue Princesse, not far from the restaurant. That argued that he lived close by, or at least knew the place well.

Macé had a conversation with the old and inefficient concierge of the restaurant building. No, she said, there was no tailor living there.

But there had been a tailoress – a waistcoat-maker known as Mathilde Dard (her real name was Gaupe) – who worked for a little tailor. He used to annoy the concierge by fetching water from the well and making splashes on the stairs . . . Mathilde had had many male friends (said the old lady with disapproval) but she had now left – the concierge had no idea where she had gone. But she was able to tell Macé that one of the girl's male callers was a chemist's assistant who worked nearby, and the assistant was able to tell Macé that the girl was now a cafe *chanteuse*. The police made enquiries around the cafés, and soon traced a singer named Mille Gaupe, who came willingly to the police station. She told Macé that half a dozen tailors had given her work. But the one who had annoyed the concierge by spilling water was called Voirbo. Yes, she cheerfully acknowledged, she had been his mistress. But now he was married. He used to live in the rue Mazarin, but she had no idea where he lived now. She went on to say that he was a strange man who seemed to do very little work, yet he always seemed to have money.

'Did he have any special friends?' asked Macé. The girl recalled a little old man Voirbo often drank with. He introduced him as Père Desiré. And on another occasion, Voirbo had introduced her to Père Desiré's aunt, 'Mother Bandage', who lived in the rue de Nesle.

Mother Bandage proved easy to trace. Père Desiré, she said, was her nephew Desiré Bodasse, an upholsterer of mean habits, whose investments brought him an income of 1,800 francs a year – not a fortune, but ample for a man with such a niggardly temperament.

Macé recalled the '+B+' mark of the stocking – 'B' might stand for 'Bodasse' – and took Mother Bandage to the morgue to see the remnants in which the limbs had been wrapped. She immediately identified the '+B+' mark – she had sewn it on herself. She was also able to identify the jersey and a part of her nephew's trousers.

Why had no one missed the old man? Because, said Mother Bandage, he was an eccentric recluse who liked to be alone. On one occasion he had vanished for six weeks; it turned out that he had spent that time in hospital, masquerading under another name, so the hospital authorities could not trace him and make him pay for his treatment.

They went to call at Bodasse's apartment in the rue Dauphin. Here Macé met with a surprise. The concierge was certain Bodasse was still alive. She had seen him in the street that morning, and on the previous evening, they had seen his shadow on the blind of his room.

It looked as if the whole investigation had collapsed again. Macé left a note for Bodasse, and decided to go and interview Voirbo, who certainly sounded like the man with the hamper.

But, as Mathilde Gaupe had said, Voirbo was no longer at his old apartment in the rue Mazarin. From the landlady, Macé learned that Pierre Voirbo was a man of dissipated habits who was also a police spy. He pretended to be an anarchist, and made rabid anti-authoritarian speeches, when all the time he was reporting the activities of the comrades to the police. He had recently married for the second time, but his old friend Bodasse had not attended the wedding. Voirbo said they had quarrelled because the old miser had refused to lend him 10,000 francs to begin housekeeping.

When Mother Bandage insisted that the articles of clothing *were* the property of her nephew, Macé decided to break into Bodasse's apartment. The place proved to be in perfect order. The clock was ticking. And on the mantelpiece, there were two candle holders, each holding eight candles. These contained 15 stumps and one complete candle, while in the grate were 17 used matches. Macé inferred that someone had been visiting the apartment for the past 15 days, lighting one candle per evening to give the impression that Bodasse was still there.

Mother Bandage was able to show Macé the secret drawer where Bodasse had kept his wallet and his securities. It was, as Macé expected, empty. But when Macé opened the case of a watch hanging over the bed, a slip of red paper fell out. It contained a list of numbers of Italian Government stock. The stock were pay-to-bearer securities, which could be negotiated like banknotes.

Back at Voirbo's lodgings, Macé confirmed that the landlady had heard nothing more from him. He asked about rent, and learned that Voirbo had paid up his arrears when he left. He had paid with an Italian Government security, and the landlady directed Macé to the money changer she had used to cash it. This man had kept a record of its number. It was one of the securities listed in the back of the watch. Voirbo had, at last, connected himself to the disappearance of Desiré Bodasse.

The charlady of Voirbo's flat also had an interesting story. He was usually the laziest and most untidy of men. But one morning in mid-December – she thought it was the 17th – she had found Voirbo already up when she arrived, and the whole place scrubbed. He had explained that he had dropped a bottle of cleaning fluid, which had made such a smell that he had to clean out the whole place. The charlady thought this was an unlikely story – why should he clean the place up himself when she was coming the next day?

Macé was hoping to catch Voirbo red-handed in Bodasse's lodgings, and placed two plain-clothed policemen on guard. But after a week, Voirbo had still not appeared. Then Macé learned that Voirbo had approached the building, seen the detective, who was an old acquaintance, and asked him what he was doing there. And the detective, without dreaming that he was talking to the man they wanted to trap, told him the whole story . . . So Voirbo now knew the police were after him. And Macé knew he still had no case. Even the evidence of the Italian security could be discounted, for Voirbo would undoubtedly say that it was a loan.

It was time for Macé to confront his quarry. Voirbo was asked to call at the police station. Face to face with him at last, Macé summed him up as a highly dominant and energetic individual, although he described his slightly hangdog manner as that of a broken-down stockbroker or a commercial traveller who adulterated his wines. Thirty years of age, round faced, with dark eyes and a dark complexion, he was obviously a man of considerable physical strength. He talked to Macé as if they were colleagues – which was, in a sense, true – and remarked blandly that he had thought of offering his services to Macé, but had been told that, due to Macés youth and inexperience, this would be pointless. Macé declined to take offence. Instead, he told Voirbo that he heard his name mentioned favourably and thought of asking for his help in trying to find Bodasse. Voirbo, no doubt wondering what kind of fool Macé took him for, said he would be glad to offer his assistance. His own theory, he said, was that Bodasse had been killed out of jealousy, and that the killer was a butcher named Rifer, a heavy drinker. He also mentioned that he thought Rifer had three accomplices. Then he took his leave, accepting 100 francs for expenses. Macé immediately set out to learn what he could about Rifer and his 'accomplices'. Two of them had perfect alibis – they were in jail throughout most of December.

Macé now saw that Voirbo was spending his expenses on drinking with the chief suspect, Rifer, and plying him with so much drink that Rifer could hardly walk. There was nothing Macé could do about it. One morning, Rifer had DTs and was dragged off to an asylum, where he died that night. The next morning, Macé found Voirbo seated in his office when he arrived, asking whether Macé meant to drop the case now Rifer was dead.

Macé was determined that the time had come to arrest Voirbo and put an end to the farce. But he was a small man, and no match for

Voirbo. So he excused himself, explaining that he had to write a letter, and offering Voirbo the morning papers. Then he wrote instructions to his subordinates to surround Voirbo and arrest him. He also ordered all exits to be closed, and instructed a messenger to remove the fire irons on the pretext of replenishing the coal bucket. As Voirbo was expounding his latest theory about a girl who had helped Rifer to kill Bodasse, he fumbled in his pocket for an address, and a card fell out. Macé handed it to him politely – noting as he did so that it contained the address of a shipping agent. His bird was intending to fly.

The precautions proved unnecessary. As the policemen came in to arrest him, Voirbo went pale, but made no resistance. He insisted that he knew nothing whatever about Bodasse's death, and skilfully parried all the questions. His demeanour showed that he felt that Macé had no evidence. And he was right. As an examining magistrate, Macé knew he lacked proof that Voirbo was a murderer. Voirbo was searched, and in his pocket, Macé found a ticket from Le Havre to New York in a false name – Saba.

In front of an instructing judge, Voirbo sullenly refused to answer questions. Meanwhile, Macé went to Voirbo's present apartment at 26 rue Lamartine. Voirbo's wife was there, a fragile little creature, who obviously had no idea of the true character of her husband. She told Macé that she had brought Voirbo a dowry of 15,000 francs, and that he had brought 10,000 francs to the marriage – the precise amount of Bodasse's securities. But when they forced the box that should have held the securities, it was empty.

A side table contained a pile of newspapers. Macé found these intriguing. Several were about the mystery of the legs found in the well in the rue Princesse. Others were about the murder of a man called Bernard at Aubervilliers. Voirbo also seemed extremely interested in the murder of a servant girl called Marie Carton in the rue Placide. Finally, there were a number of newspapers about a recently executed killer called Charles Avinain, who had intercepted farmers on their way to market with loads of hay, and offered them a better price than they could normally expect. The farmer was invited back to Avinain's hut near the river at Clichy and murdered with a hammer blow; the dismembered body was then thrown into the river, and the hay sold. But finally one of the victims escaped, and the police called at the riverside hut, and caught Avinain as he tried to escape through a trapdoor into the cellar. Avinain's last words from the steps of the guillotine had been: 'Never confess.' Obviously, Voirbo felt he had something to learn from Avinain.

The search for the missing bonds continued. In the cellar there were two barrels of wine. Macé's keen eye noted that the bung of one of them was slightly higher than the other, suggesting that it fitted less tightly. Closer examination showed that it held a piece of string. When Macé pulled on the string, a soldered tin cylinder came out. It proved to contain the missing securities.

Back at the commissary, Macé told Voirbo he wanted to have him photographed.

'Why this additional outrage?' asked Voirbo angrily

Macé replied: 'So I can show it in Aubervilliers and in the rue Placide.' Voirbo indicated, with some strong language, that nothing would induce him to hold still long enough for a photograph to be taken – evidently he had good reason to avoid being recognized.

The next day, Macé decided to make one more attempt to extort a confession. He took Voirbo back to his former lodgings in the rue Mazarin, now occupied by a young couple. His first task was to discover precisely where the furniture had been during Voirbo's tenancy. This convinced Macé that there was only one spot in the room where Voirbo could have dismembered the body – on a round table in the centre. Macé had also noted that the tiled floor sloped down towards a bed in a recess. If Macés own account is to be believed, he then proceeded to make the kind of speech that ficitional detectives make in the final scene when all the suspects have been gathered together in the same room. 'You are now going to see how very important an accessory may be in a criminal case and how the most trifling detail may enable us to complete an enquiry . . .' And after five minutes or so of this sort of thing, he concluded: 'In short, in this very room which was once Voirbo's, an accessory is going to reveal to us the name of the murderer . . .'

He then took in his hand a carafe of water, and raised it in the air. 'You observe a perceptible slope down towards the bed. If a body was dismembered in this room, the blood must have run down like this . . .' and Macé poured the water. Voirbo watched with horror as it flowed across the floor, to form a pool under the bed. Then a workman was brought in, and ordered to remove the tiles. As each tile came up, dried bloodstains could be clearly seen on the sides and underneath. Voirbo was now trembling, and when Macé asked him to hold a candle while a cupboard was searched, he burst out: 'Don't continue. I am guilty. I will tell you everything. But take me away from this accursed place.'

Voirbo's confession, cited at length in Macé's *My First Crime*, is one of the most fascinating documents in criminological history. He admits that his real name is not Voirbo, but says he prefers to be regarded as an orphan, since he hated his father, who often screamed at him: 'You shall perish by my hand.' 'Perhaps he is the cause of all my misfortunes', says Voirbo, and for once this sounds like something more than the usual self-pitying rationalization so typical of criminals. Voirbo was determined to achieve success and security, by fair means or foul. Marriage to Mlle Rémondé seemed the answer; but he had told her parents that he possessed 10,000 francs in securities, and he had to produce it. The miserly Bodasse refused to lend him the money, so Voirbo decided that he had to die. Bodasse often went to Voirbo's room, in the hope of meeting some of his workgirls. (In those days – the 1860s – most workgirls would accompany a gentleman for 10 francs, which was a day's wages.) Voirbo lured him there on 14 December 1868, telling him that his fiancée would be spending the evening there. Then he struck him a tremendous blow from behind with a flat iron. And when Bodasse still moved, Voirbo slit his throat with a razor. After that, he undressed down to his underwear and chopped up the body – not hacking at it with a cleaver, which would have made too much noise, but placing the sharp edge against the flesh, then striking it with a metal bobbin.

And, just as Macé had supposed, it had been the encounter with two gendarmes when he was carrying parts of the body to the river that decided Voirbo to dispose of the remaining limbs down the well in the rue Princesse – a decision that eventually cost him his life. Voirbo did not die on the guillotine, but cut his throat with a razor smuggled in a loaf of bread.

2

But Voirbo had made an even more serious mistake: failing to pay heed to the advice of the murderer Charles Avinain: never confess. In 1869, and for many decades afterwards, there was no method of discovering whether a bloodstain was animal or human. Microscopic examination could distinguish a bloodstain from an iron stain or fruit juice, by showing the corpuscles, but only if the blood was fresh, or clotted; once blood dries, the corpuscles become indistinguishable. As early as 1841, a French doctor named Barruel believed he had found a method of determining whether blood was animal or human, by heating it with sulphuric acid; he claimed that human blood gave off a sweat-like odour. But, as far as is known, this absurd claim was never tested in court. Around 1850, Ludwig Teichmann had developed a test based upon the shape of blood crystals; the suspected blood was mixed with acetic acid on a microscope slide, and a grain of salt added; then if heated delicately over a bunsen burner, haematin (or haemin) crystals would form. But it needed a highly skilled analyst to distinguish between, say, human blood and bullock's blood; moreover, if he was not careful, he burnt his fingers, and the slide shattered. Voirbo *could* possibly have been convicted by this test, but it is doubtful – even if the blood had been proved to be human, he could have protested that it might be due to some previous tenant giving himself a bad cut . . .

After 1859, the invention of the spectroscope (by Bunsen and Kirchhoff) provided an infallible test for haemoglobin (the red colouring matter in blood) by its characteristic spectral lines; but this could still not distinguish between animal and human blood. But science was taking some slow and cautious steps in the right direction. It had started in the 1650s when young Dr Christopher Wren – later the architect of St Paul's – invented what was basically the first hypodermic syringe – a slender quill with a pointed tip, attached to a bladder. By 1667, Jean Denys, a professor of mathematics at Montpellier, was curing some of his patients with injections of lamb's blood. But in the following year, a patient died, and he was ordered to stop. Why had the patient died? Herein lay the secret forensic scientists were still seeking two centuries later. Around 1814, Dr James Blundell, whose speciality was midwifery, began experiments in blood transfusion, and discovered that a dog could be virtually drained of blood, and then revived by the blood from another dog. But if he used sheep's blood, the dog died. By 1818, Blundell was ready to try human blood transfusions. And, like Jean Denys, he was baffled by the fact that they were sometimes triumphantly successful, and sometimes the patient died. When this happened, the first symptom was a pain in the arm and rapid heart rate, then back pains, vomiting, diarrhoea, and black urine. The answer was not discovered until 1875, when the German physiologist Leonard Landois noticed that if red blood cells from one animal were mixed with the serum – the blood's basic liquid – of an animal of a different species, the red cells 'clumped' together like lumps in porridge; sometimes they even burst, which seemed to account for the black urine. But how could this explain why human blood sometimes caused human blood to react in the same way? There could be only one answer: there must be several types of human blood.

By the end of the nineteenth century, blood transfusions were still being attempted by many enterprising doctors, but the patient's chances were only 50:50. It was obviously of immense importance to discover why. The Viennese surgeon Theodore Billroth had theorized that there must be different types of blood that were incompatible; but how did one go about identifying them? In 1900 a young doctor named Karl Landsteiner, Assistant Professor at the Institute of Pathology and Anatomy in Vienna, asked five of his colleagues to give him samples of their blood, and also took a sample of his own. In each of these, he separated the colourless serum from the red blood cells (he did it with a centrifuge machine, but it works just as well if the blood is simply left exposed in a test tube), then put serum from one of the participants, Dr Stork, into six test tubes. Then he mixed red blood cells from the six participants into each test tube. In four out of six cases, it 'clumped' (or agglutinated, to use the correct scientific term). He took six test tubes of another lot of serum, and repeated the experiment – this time only two lots clumped. And when this had been repeated six times over, Landsteiner had an interesting table that told him something quite new: that there were not just two different human blood types, but three. It was a matter of simple mathematical reasoning. Landsteiner could see that there must be something in the serum which 'opposed' certain blood cells, and he called this something agglutinin, while the factors they seemed to dislike he called agglutinogens. If there were only two types of blood, it should have been quickly possible to predict each reaction in advance, as he dropped one lot of blood cells into another lot of serum. But it proved to be more complicated than that, and he had to assume that blood came in three types, A, B, and C (C was later called O). Two years later, one of Landsteiner's donors, Dr Adriano Sturli, discovered a type of blood serum that did not clump A or B – which meant that it must have characteristics of both. This 'typeless' blood group became known as AB.

In the year after Landsteiner's experiment, a young doctor named Paul Uhlenhuth, another assistant professor – this time at the Institute of Hygiene in Greifswald – announced an equally important discovery: he had learned how to distinguish between animal and human blood. His insight derived from Pasteur's tremendous discovery of the principles of vaccination in the late 1870s. Pasteur had been studying a new treatment, invented by a doctor named Louvrier, for the deadly

disease anthrax. The treatment did not work; but two of the cows
Pasteur had injected with anthrax recovered on their own. And when he
tried injecting them with an even more virulent dose of anthrax, it had
no effect at all; the cows had developed 'resistance' to anthrax. Pasteur
discovered that he could 'weaken' germs by subjecting them to heat,
and that these 'attenuated' germs could be injected into animals, or
humans, without endangering life. Moreover, the result was a
'resistance' that brought immunity from more powerful forms of the
same germ. Pasteur demonstrated his method triumphantly by injecting
a small boy who had been bitten by a mad dog with a weakened version
of the rabies virus; it took 14 injections, which set up an immune
reaction before the original virus could do its deadly work, and the boy
recovered.

What was actually happening was discovered in 1890 by Emil von
Behring, the assistant of Pasteur's great rival Koch, the man who
isolated the germs of tuberculosis and cholera. Von Behring realized
that when the blood is invaded by a toxin – a protein poison – the
serum develops an anti-toxin to resist it. Five years later, the Belgian
Jules Bordet, working at the Pasteur Institute in Paris, tried to understand the basic principles of 'immunity', and founded the science of
serology – the study of body fluids, such as blood. (*Sera* is a Sanskrit
word meaning 'to flow'.) He first identified the factors in blood serum
that destroy bacteria by causing the cell wall to rupture, then went on
to discover that these same factors will also destroy foreign blood
cells. Moreover, if milk or egg-white was injected into guinea pigs,
their blood developed the same defensive reaction against it. And if a
few drops of milk or egg-white was then mixed with the guinea pig's
blood serum, their protein came under attack, and was deposited as a
white precipitate. The defensive substances became known as
precipitins.

It was the Viennese doctor Paul Uhlenhuth who saw the consequences of this discovery. If proteins produce these defensive reactions
in blood serum, then presumably one type of blood – say, a goat's will
produce an immune reaction in another type – say, a rabbit's. In fact,
Bordet had already shown this by his experiment in which 'foreign'
blood cells were ruptured in serum. Uhlenhuth tried injecting chicken
blood into a rabbit. It worked like Bordet's egg-white in guinea pigs
and produced a defensive reaction. Then he took a test tube of the
immunized rabbit's serum and introduced a drop of chicken blood; it
instantly turned cloudy. And when a rabbit was injected with human

blood, its serum would react just as readily to a drop of human blood. And not only to blood; it would react just as well to a bloodstain dissolved in salt water.

To us, it is obvious that these two discoveries – of human blood groups and of the precipitin test – were among the most important advances ever made in forensic science. Yet the contemporaries of Landsteiner and Uhlenhuth showed themselves curiously unapprecia- tive of their achievement – Landsteiner had to wait until 1930 before his discovery was rewarded with the Nobel prize. The French were quicker to grasp the importance of Bordet's discovery, and in 1902, a French murderer was sent to the guillotine by the precipitin test, when it proved that the blood on his clothes was human, and not, as he claimed, the result of skinning a rabbit. As a consequence, the precipitin test generally became known in Europe as the Bordet test – and this in spite of the fact that Uhlenhuth had already used his test to establish the guilt of a murderer in 1901.

3

Around 1 p.m., on 9 September 1898, the mothers of two small girls in the village of Lechtingen, near Osnabrück, became worried when they failed to return home. And when Jadwiga Heidemann and her neigh- bour Irmgard Langmeier called at the school, they learned that their children had not been to classes that day. The whole village joined in the search, and at dusk, the dismembered body of 7-year-old Hannelore Heidemann was found in nearby woods – some parts had been scattered among the trees. An hour or so later, the remains of 8-year- old Else Langmeier were found hidden in bushes; she had also been mutilated and dismembered.

The police learned that a journeyman carpenter named Ludwig Tessnow had been seen entering Lechtingen from the direction of the woods, and that his clothes seemed to be bloodstained. Tessnow was soon arrested, but insisted that the stains on his clothes were of brown woodstain. A powerful microscope would have revealed that this was a lie, but the Osnabrück police knew nothing of forensic science, and let him go for lack of evidence. But a policeman visited Tessnow in his workshop, and contrived to knock over a tin of woodstain so that it ran down Tessnow's trousers. In fact, it dried exactly like the other stains. And since Tessnow continued to work in the village, his neighbours concluded that he must be innocent. He remained until January 1899, when he went to work elsewhere.

Two and a half years later, a frighteningly similar crime occurred near the village of Göhren, on the Baltic island of Rügen. On Sunday 1 July 1901, two brothers named Peter and Hermann Stubbe, aged 6 and 8, failed to return home for supper, and parties went into the nearby woods, carrying burning torches and shouting. Shortly after sunrise, the bodies of both children were found in some bushes, their skulls crushed in with a rock and their limbs amputated. Hermann's heart had been removed, and was never found.

The police interviewed a fruit seller who had seen the two boys in the late afternoon; they were talking to a carpenter named Tessnow. Tessnow had recently returned to Rügen, after travelling around Germany, and was regarded as an eccentric recluse. Another neighbour recollected seeing Tessnow returning home in the evening, with dark spots on his Sunday clothes.

Tessnow was arrested and his home searched. Some garments had been thoroughly washed, and were still wet. And a stained pair of boots lay under the stone kitchen sink. Tessnow remained calm under questioning, and seemed to be able to account satisfactorily for his movements on the previous Sunday. Again, he insisted that stains on his clothing were of woodstain.

Three weeks before the murders, seven sheep had been mutilated and disembowelled in a field near Göhren, and their owner had arrived in time to see a man running away; he swore he could recognize him if he saw him again. Brought to the prison yard at Greifswald, the man immediately picked out Tessnow as the butcher of his sheep. Tessnow steadfastly denied it – he was not the sort of man, he said, to kill either sheep or children . . .

The examining magistrate, Johann-Klaus Schmidt, now recalled a case in Osnabrück three years before, and contacted the police there. When they told him that the name of their suspect was Ludwig Tessnow, Schmidt had no doubt that Tessnow was the killer. But how to prove it? At this point, his friend Prosecutor Ernst Hubschmann of Greifswald recollected reading about a new test for human bloodstains. And at the end of July, Uhlenhuth received two parcels containing Tessnow's Sunday clothes, brown-stained working overalls, and various other items, including a bloodstained rock, probably the murder weapon. It took Uhlenhuth and his assistant four days to examine over a hundred spots and stains, dissolving them in distilled water or salt solution. The overalls were, as Tessnow had claimed, stained with wood dye. But they also found 17 stains of human blood and nine of sheep's blood. It took the Rugen prosecutor a long time to bring Tessnow to trial – German justice was extremely slow-moving- but when he eventually appeared in court, Uhlenhuth was there to give evidence and explain his methods. Ludwig Tessnow was found guilty of murder and sentenced to death.

4

England, as usual, was far behind the Continent in making use of the new discoveries. Spilsbury's mentor Dr William Willcox – who gave evidence at the Crippen trial – was the expert the Home Office called upon when the evidence concerned identification of bloodstains. Around the turn of the century, the chief methods in use depended on the power of haemoglobin to attract oxygen. When hydrogen peroxide was poured on a bloodstain, it foamed. A West Indian shrub called guiaiac produced an extract that turned blue in the presence of oxygen; when mixed with turpentine and blood, it turned blue because the haemoglobin extracted oxygen from the turpentine. The same thing happened with a substance called benzidine, developed at the turn of the century; this also turned blue in the presence of blood. These were the tests known to Dr Willcox, although he became aware of the 'Bordet test' (which, as we know, is basically identical to the Uhlenhuth test) at about the time it became known to French criminologists.

The first British murder case in which the identification of blood played a crucial role occurred in 1910 in Slough. A 70-year-old widow, Isabella Wilson, was discovered in the back room of her second-hand clothes shop in the High Street with a cushion tied over her face with a scarf; she had died of suffocation. Marks on the side of her head indicated that someone had given her two or three violent blows, perhaps with a blunt instrument. Mrs Wilson was known to carry a purse in the pocket underneath her apron, sometimes with as much as 20 gold sovereigns in it. The purse was now empty, so it was obvious that the motive for the attack had been robbery. On the table there was a piece of brown paper with circular marks on it, and Mrs Wilson had been known to keep her sovereigns wrapped in brown paper inside her purse; the murderer had left it behind.

Police investigations soon pointed towards a man called William Broome, a 25-year-old unemployed motor mechanic. Until recently his family had lived next door to the dead woman's shop, but they had now moved. But on the day of the murder, several local people had recognized Broome walking around Slough. Two days after the murder, patient sleuthing tracked down Broome in Harlesden, and he was asked to go to the police station and make a statement. As soon as Broome insisted that he had been in London all day on Friday 15 July – the day of the murder – the police must have known they had their man; they had a dozen witnesses to say he had been in Slough. Asked if he had any money, Broome produced a few shillings, and said that he had 20 sovereigns back in his room in Albany Street, Regent's Park – the exact amount the dead woman usually carried on her.

The dead woman's fingernails were long, and one of them was broken – it looked as if she had scratched her assailant. Broome had two scratch marks on his face, and several people had asked him about them. Broome had told each of them a different story; now he told the police that the scratches had occurred during his fight with a bookmaker about money he had won on a race – an obvious attempt to account for the 20 guineas.

In court in Aylesbury on 22 October 1910, it soon became obvious that Broome's major mistake was in claiming that he had not been in Slough on the day of the murder – the prosecution was able to produce witness after witness who had seen him.

But the part of the trial that excited most interest was what the local newspaper, the *Bucks Herald,* called 'the sensational evidence of Dr Willcox', 'fresh from his part in the sensational Crippen trial'. Scotland Yard had asked Dr Willcox to examine various items, including a pair of the prisoner's boots – worn on the day of the murder – and fingernails snipped from the dead woman, as well as some of Broome's clothing. Broome had carefully cleaned and polished the boots after the murder, but had failed to notice a bloodstain on the instep. Willcox had tested this bloodstain and found it to be 'mammalian'. Asked if this meant it could be human, Willcox replied yes. He was also able to say that there was human skin on one of the victim's nails, and that it had blood on it. A German or French pathologist would have taken pride in determining whether the blood was human, and whether it was of the same blood group as the murderer or victim. Willcox had evidently decided that it was not worth so much trouble. To do the doctor justice, he may have felt that the evidence against Broome was so conclusive that his work would have been wasted. He himself made it more conclusive by describing how he had examined the brown paper under a microscope, and found minute specks of gold, proof that it had wrapped gold sovereigns. Other pieces of brown paper made it clear that the number of sovereigns had been exactly 20 – the number found in Broome's lodgings.

The outline of the crime was now clear. Broome had obviously gone to Slough that day with the specific intention of robbing Isabella Wilson; and since she knew him well, he must also have intended to kill her. The blood on his instep indicated that, after knocking her to the ground, he must have stamped on her head – if he had merely stepped in her blood, the bloodstain would have been on the sole or the heel. Then he went into a nearby pub for a pint of beer, and caught the next train back to London. After the judge had summarized this evidence, the jury took only 13 minutes to find him guilty and he was sentenced to death.

A few days after Broome had been found guilty, Willcox gave evidence at another murder trial. The name of the accused was Mark Wilde, and he was charged with the murder of a rich industrialist named George Henry Storrs. The 'Gorse Hall murder' has become known as one of the strangest mysteries of the century. On the evening of 1 November 1909, a slightly built man with a blond moustache broke into Gorse Hall – situated on a lonely moor in Cheshire – and threatened the cook with a revolver. Storrs grappled with him while his niece and some servants ran for help; but when they returned to the house, Storrs was dying from 15 stab wounds, and the intruder had escaped. But he had left the revolver behind. It proved to have no firing pin, but was of a peculiar type known as a 'Bulldog'.

A man named Cornelius Howard, a cousin of Storrs, was arrested and charged with the murder. The evidence against him looked black, but it was entirely circumstantial, and when he produced a strong alibi, the jury acquitted him.

Five months later, the police made another arrest, this time a man named Mark Wilde. They had found several witnesses who swore that the Bulldog revolver belonged to Wilde. On the night of the murder, Wilde had returned home with bloodstains on his clothes, and told his mother that he had been in a fight. Police also discovered that he had owned two more revolvers, but that he had dismantled them and disposed of the pieces – he admitted that this was in case he was suspected of the Gorse Hall murder. Wilde was charged with killing

Storrs, and his bloodstained jacket and trousers were sent to Willcox for examination.

What Willcox did was to apply the Uhlenhuth test to the bloodstains; he discovered that they were human blood. But since Wilde had already admitted this, it made no real difference to the outcome. Once again the jury decided that the evidence was inconclusive. Mark Wilde was acquitted, and the Gorse Hall mystery remains unsolved.

In fact, it seems fairly certain that Storrs knew the identity of the man who stabbed him, although he denied it as he lay dying. Seven weeks earlier, in September 1909, Storrs had asked the local police for protection. He claimed that, on the previous evening, as they were sitting at dinner behind drawn blinds, a man's voice had shouted: 'Hold up your hands or I'll shoot', and that a shot had then broken the window. Storrs claimed that he raised the blind, and saw a revolver pointing at him. He wanted to run outside to tackle the man, but his wife prevented him . . .

This story sounds highly unlikely. Would the man shout 'Hold up your hands' when he could not see the family behind the drawn blind? Would Storrs have raised the blind after a shot had been fired through the window? If the man intended to kill Storrs, why did he not then fire a second shot? It sounds as if Storrs made up the story – and fired a shot through his own window – to provide a plausible reason for asking for police protection. Why did he not tell them the true reason? Presumably because he preferred to keep it to himself. Did his wife and niece know the true reason? That also seems unlikely; but they probably believed whatever Storrs chose to tell them.

During the next seven weeks there was a police guard at Gorse Hall, and an alarm bell was installed which could be heard in the neighbouring town of Stalybridge. On the night of the murder the guard was withdrawn because there was a local election, and all police were required for keeping order. Whoever killed Storrs knew this, and chose his opportunity. As he burst into the dining-room, he shouted: 'Now I've got you.' He was a man with a grudge, and most writers on the case seem to agree that the likeliest reason for the grudge was that Storrs had seduced some mill-girl – perhaps the man's wife or sister. Whatever the reason, Storrs chose to die without naming his assailant.

Could Willcox have done more to solve the mystery? There was one possibility that he overlooked: to test the stains for their blood group. In 1902, Uhlenhuth's colleague Max Richter had tried testing dried bloodstains to ascertain their blood group, and discovered that the reaction was weak if the stains were more than a few weeks old. Yet there were abundant bloodstains on Wilde's jacket and trousers, and there must have been bloodstains at Gorse Hall – made when Storrs was dying – to compare them with. The reason that he did not do so is almost certainly, as incredible as this sounds, that he had never heard of Landsteiner's discovery of blood groups.

5

For, in fact, Landsteiner's achievement remained virtually unknown for many years. The man who first grasped the significance of his discoveries for criminology was not an Austrian or a German, but an Italian lecturer on forensic medicine in Turin, Dr Leone Lattes. During his postgraduate studies, Lattes had met Max Richter, and learned of his experiments with bloodstains. He also learned of Richter's conclusion that it is not easy to determine the group of a bloodstain once it is more than a few weeks old.

In 1915, Lattes proved him wrong. An absurd domestic drama was brought to his attention by a local doctor. A construction worker named Renzo Girardi was being tormented to death by his wife's insane jealousy. And three months earlier, he had provided her with reasons for a particularly violent outbreak; he had returned home unusually late one Saturday night, and the next morning his wife had discovered bloodstains on his front shirt-tail. She was quite convinced that Girardi had been consorting with a woman, and had made his life a misery ever since. He asked Dr Lattes to help him prove his innocence.

If Richter was correct, the case was hopeless, for the bloodstain was now three months old. But Lattes was willing to try. First, he took a blood sample from Girardi, and ascertained that it was group A. Girardi's wife Andrea was persuaded to give a blood sample: she was group O. And a friend of Andrea Girardi's who had been in the house at the time was also persuaded to give a sample – she had been menstruating, and it was just conceivable – although she indignantly denied it – that she might have wiped herself on the shirt-tail after Girardi had removed the shirt. She also proved to be blood group A, like Girardi.

Lattes became fascinated by this ridiculous little problem, and went to immense pains to solve it. First he soaked the bloodstains out of the cloth with distilled water, going to extraordinary lengths to determine their exact weight. (All this care was to avoid 'pseudo-agglutination', an apparent 'clumping' which appears when the serum is too strong or there are too many red blood cells in the test solution.) And in spite of the age of the stains, he succeeded in manufacturing several drops of liquid blood. And when the blood was placed in tiny 'wells' on dimpled microscope slides, and drops of fresh blood – both A and B – were added, he observed that the unknown blood 'clumped' with group B. That meant it had to be group A. So it could have been Girardi's own, or that of the family friend. But examination under a microscope revealed none of the epithelial (skin or mucus) cells that would be present in menstrual blood. (If Lattes had merely wished to disprove that Girardi had picked up the bloodstains from a menstruating mistress, he could have confined his efforts to this test alone.) A medical examination of Girardi revealed that he suffered from prostate trouble which caused occasional bleeding. Mme Girardi was convinced, and her husband's domestic life became, for the time being, more peaceful.

Lattes had shown that even three-month-old bloodstains can reveal the group to which they belong (which suggests that the Gorse Hall case could probably have been solved by the same method). And he was so delighted with his triumph that he went on to a systematic study of serology – all bodily fluids – and its application to crime detection. His enthusiasm increased when, soon after the Girardi case, he was able to prove the innocence of a man accused of murder by demonstrating that the bloodstains on the man's coat were of his own group, and not that of the victim. Of course, it would have been unfortunate for the suspected murderer if he and the victim had shared the same blood group – by now, it had been established that 40 per cent of people are group A, 40 per cent group 0, 15 per cent group B, and 5 per cent AB. But it was clear that, while blood grouping could not finally establish the guilt of a suspected killer, it could sometimes establish his innocence. Lattes went on to invent a greatly simplified method of testing, placing tiny flakes of blood on the microscope slide, adding fresh blood, and placing another slide on top. The serum in the fresh blood would do all the work of dissolving the suspect blood cells and, where the blood was of another group, produce clumping.

In 1922, Lattes gained some of the recognition he deserved when he published a treatise on *The Individuality of Blood,* which soon became a criminological classic. (One of its incidental effects was to bring Landsteiner, who had now emigrated to America, some of the recognition that had long been his due.) And in 1926, his intervention in a preposterous *cause célèbre* of mistaken identity momentarily made the Italian public aware of the importance of the new science of blood grouping.

The Bruneri–Canella Affair is virtually an Italian version of the Anastasia controversy, but with distinctly comic overtones. In March 1926, the caretaker of the cemetery in Turin saw a man apparently praying, but when he looked more closely, noticed that he was stealing a bronze vase from a grave, and trying to conceal it under his coat. The man was chased into the church, and attempted suicide. When he was caught, he insisted that he had lost his memory, and was confined in the asylum at Collegno. Whether the doctors believed his story of amnesia is unclear, but some Italian newspapers printed the man's photograph, asking if anyone knew his identity. In Verona, a certain Professor Canella thought he recognized the photograph as that of his brother, who had been a headmaster until he vanished during the Macedonian campaign in the First World War. The professor hastened to the asylum, and was convinced that he had found his long-lost brother. His parents and friends had mixed opinions about the man's identity, but when the man's wife came, she instantly declared that the amnesiac was her missing husband. The ex-headmaster was released and he and his 'wife' went off for a second honeymoon.

Soon after, the Préfecture in Turin received an anonymous letter declaring that Canella was an impostor named Mario Bruneri, a printer of Turin who was wanted for fraud. Bruneri had a criminal record, and when the police finally checked his fingerprints with those of the amnesiac (taken in the asylum) they were found to be identical. That obviously settled it – except that Italian public opinion remained unconvinced. An inquiry instituted by Professor Mario Carrara, using the identification techniques described by Locard, also concluded that 'Canella' was a fraud. But 'Canella's' family insisted that he was the missing headmaster, and his wife seemed contented to accept him as her long-lost husband.

Now the highly respected Professor Lattes intervened. We can almost certainly establish the truth, he declared, by simply examining the blood of 'Canella', and of his parents and children. Blood groups are hereditary, and if both parents turned out to be group A, and 'Canella' was B, then he would certainly not be their son. If Canella was 0, and his children were A or B, the same would apply. I need, said Lattes, merely one tiny drop of the blood of each individual concerned, and I can almost certainly establish beyond all doubt whether 'Canella' is really the thief Bruneri.

It would be highly satisfactory to record that Lattes carried out his test, and settled the question once and for all. Unfortunately, he was flying in the face of human nature. 'Canella' did not want the test; neither did his wife or family. Like the Tichborne claimant, Canella continued to play his game of evasion, frequently infuriating the magistrates with barefaced effrontery. When one of Bruneri's own children ran towards him crying 'Papa, papa!' 'Canella' replied: 'Go, little one, and find your family as I have found mine.' Someone asked him: 'Why deny that your son recognizes you?', and 'Canella' replied with a wink: 'It's not for the son to recognize the father, but for the father to recognize his son.' And since Mme Canella remained convinced that she had regained her husband, the science of blood grouping was as helpless as the science of fingerprinting to dislodge the impostor.

In the autumn of 1928, the problem of human blood grouping became the central issue in a German murder case, and suddenly made forensic experts aware of the importance of the 'Lattes test'. (The case may also have been instrumental in securing Landsteiner the Nobel prize in 1930.) On the morning of 23 March 1928, a 19-year-old student, Helmuth Daube, was found dead in the street outside the family home in Gladbeck, in the Ruhr – his father was a school principal. The student's throat had been cut from ear to ear, and at first, suicide was suspected. But when a doctor began to undress the corpse, he realized that the genitals had been mutilated with a knife. This was murder, probably with sexual overtones. On the previous evening, Daube had been to a neighbouring town to a students' fraternity meeting, and he had walked back home with another student called Karl Hussmann. Hussmann was fetched from his home nearby, and asked to account for his movements; he claimed that Daube had walked him home to his front door, then left him. But the police inspector investigating the death noticed that Hussmann's shoes were heavily bloodstained. And when it emerged that Hussmann was a homosexual with sadistic tendencies, and that he and Daube had at one time been sexually involved, the inspector became fairly certain Hussmann was the killer. Enquiries among their fellow students indicated that Hussmann liked to dominate Daube, even to the point of causing him physical pain, and that Daube had recently worked up the determination to make a break.

Hussmann's first excuse was that the blood on his shoes came from a cat that he had killed when he caught it 'poaching'. Then he remembered that he had found a frog and torn it to pieces on his way home the night before. The Uhlenhuth test soon disproved both these stories, revealing that the blood was human. Even faced with this evidence, Hussmann maintained his innocence. Now, finally, the shoes and other bloodstained items of wearing apparel were sent to the Institute of Forensic Medicine in Bonn, and tested by its director, Dr Viktor Müller-Hess. He discovered that there were two sets of bloodstains on the clothing, group A and group O. Hussmann was type O, while Daube was A. This evidence should have convicted Hussmann of murder. But, as in so many other cases involving 'expert evidence', the jury was sceptical, and returned an acquittal verdict. From the point of view of justice, the case was a failure. But it had the effect of making forensic scientists aware of the importance of Landsteiner's discoveries, and the methods that Leone Lattes had developed to apply them to criminal investigation.

The next important step forward was taken by Fritz Schiff, the Berlin serologist who had arranged the translation of Lattes's book *The Individuality of Blood* in German. Like many fellow serologists, he was troubled by certain shortcomings in the Lattes method. This, as we have seen, depended on Landsteiner's discovery of 'agglutinins' in the serum and 'agglutinogens' in the red blood cells. In the red blood cells, the agglutinogens can be of two types, antigen A and antigen B. The corresponding bodies in the serum are called antibody α and antibody β. In the various blood groups, these are distributed as follows:

Group A: Antigen A in the cells, antibody β in the serum.

Group B: Antigen B in the cells, antibody α in the serum.

Group O: No antigens in the cells, antibodies α and β in the serum.

Group AB: Antigens A and B in the cells, no antibody α or β in the serum.

So cells of type A showed clumping when mixed with B serum, because B serum contained antibody α. They also clumped in O serum, which also contains antibody α. But type O blood cells could be mixed with all three other sera without clumping – as can be seen from the table above. So in theory, it was easy for a serologist to determine the group of an unknown sample by a simple process of elimination.

Unfortunately, experience showed that the β antibody in type O lost its strength much quicker than the a antibody, so type O could easily be mistaken for type B. The β antibody might vanish from a group A bloodstain, so it appeared to be type AB. Such a complication might seem to make the blood test virtually useless. But Fritz Schiff saw that there was a solution. Fortunately, the antigens in the red blood cells retain their strength. So if the cells from an old dried bloodstain were added to a fresh serum they ought to produce *some* effect, even if they have lost their ability to 'clump'. They ought, in fact, to attract and absorb some of the serum's antibodies. And if a method could be discovered of measuring *exactly how much* of the antibody was absorbed, then the group of the old bloodstain could still be determined. It was a matter of measuring the effectiveness of the serum before and after the cells had been added to it. But although Schiff worked hard at this problem, he was unable to solve it. The method was discovered by a young forensic scientist named Franz Josef Hoizer. He used a 'dimpled' microscope slide – a glass slide into which a number of tiny wells have been drilled. Into each of eight 'wells' he dropped group O serum, diluted with salt solution. Each well contained a solution twice as dilute as that in the previous one. Now he dropped fresh blood cells into each – exactly the same quantity – and examined each well to find out how much each serum had agglutinated the red blood cells. This allowed him to determine how much each serum would 'clump' the red cells. He then repeated the same test with his unknown bloodstain, and then re-checked each serum to see how far it had lost strength. It was then again a simple matter of elimination. (A type O bloodstain would produce no clumping at all; AB would produce twice as much as A or B, since it contained both antigens, and so on.)

In 1931, Holzer demonstrated the effectiveness of his method in a rural murder case. A farmer named Franz Mair was found dying in his own barn, his skull split open with several blows of a sharp weapon like an axe; he was inclined to carry his money and his bank-book in his pocket, and these were now missing. The dead man's stepbrother Karl summoned the police. Karl's story was that he had been asleep when awakened by the screams of Franz Mair's mistress-housekeeper. Blood on the toe of Karl's slipper made him a leading suspect. Holzer, who was an assistant at the Forensic Institute at Innsbruck, not far from the murder site, was summoned to examine the scene of the crime. He took the slippers, and a pair of Karl's trousers with a small bloodstain, back to his laboratory. To his disappointment, he obtained no result with the ordinary Lattes test for blood groups. The slipper stains had been absorbed into the leather, and for some reason, the dried blood on the trousers proved equally difficult. He then turned to his own more delicate method, using his dimpled slides, and was delighted when this yielded unmistakable results; the blood was group O, the dead man's blood group. Karl Mair had allowed his own blood to be tested; this proved to be group A. Faced with this evidence, Karl Mair finally broke down, and confessed to attacking his stepbrother with a hoe, which he afterwards cleaned thoroughly. He had taken Franz's money and bank-book and hidden them in the hay, where they were subsequently found. Hoizer's evidence led to a guilty verdict against Karl Mair.

One obvious problem was that if Karl Mair and his stepbrother had both been group O, then Karl would probably have got away with the murder. And since A and O are the major bloodgroups, the possibility that murderer and victim happen to share it is obviously great. So considerable relief was felt in forensic circles as researchers began to discover other substances that made one lot of blood different from another. Group A was made up of two different strengths labelled A1 and A2. Then, in the mid-1920s, Landsteiner and his assistant Philip Levine discovered another blood group system by injecting rabbits with human blood. The consonants of the words 'immune' suggested calling these new groups M and N. A person could be either M, N or a combination of the two, MN. The M group was found to have various other properties (or 'specificities'), given such labels as M^v and M^A, all of which are found in all humans, but only some of which are found in apes (whose blood is otherwise very similar to that of human beings). Experiments with rhesus monkeys in 1940 by Landsteiner and Alexander S. Weiner led to the discovery of another M factor which was labelled rhesus, or Rh. In 1927, Landsteiner and Weiner had identified yet another factor labelled P. And so the discoveries continued: the 'Lutheran' factor in 1945, the Kell factor the following year, then the Lewis, Kidd, Duffy and Diego factors, named after their discoverers in 1946, 1950, 1951 and 1955, and Yt, I, Xg and Dombrock in 1956, 1956, 1962 and 1965.

Obviously, all these additional discoveries made it increasingly simple to identify the blood of a certain individual, just as Bertillon's 11 measurements each helped to pin down a particular individual. What was emerging was, in effect, a kind of 'blood fingerprinting'.

Yet even more exciting was Landsteiner's realization that 'serology' literally applies to all the secretions of the human body, such as saliva, mucus, tears, semen and sweat. All this culminated in the discovery in 1984 of 'genetic fingerprinting', the ability to identify an individual by his sperm – or by a hair follicle – as precisely as by his fingerprint – a subject we shall discuss at the end of this chapter.

6

In Great Britain, the first major case solved by forensic serology occurred in 1934. The pathologist involved was one of Spilsbury's most active contemporaries, Dr (later Sir) Sydney Smith. Born in Roxburgh, New Zealand, in 1883, Smith studied medicine at Edinburgh, and was greatly intrigued by stories of the late Dr Joseph Bell, the man on whom Conan Doyle based Sherlock Holmes; Bell often astonished his students by deducing the occupation of his patients from their appearances. When serving in Egypt as the principal medico-legal expert of the Egyptian government, Smith was asked to report on the body of a British official who had been found shot through the head. It could have been suicide, but there was no suicide note. Smith observed a small nick on one of the fingers of the right hand, and noticed that the man's shirt and waistcoat were unbuttoned. He deduced that the nick had been made when pulling back the bolt of the pistol, and that the only reason for unbuttoning the waistcoat and the shirt must have been that he had originally intended to shoot himself in the heart, then changed his mind. The result of these observations was a verdict of suicide.

The case of the murder of 8-year-old Helen Priestly in Aberdeen called upon Smith's powers of deduction. The child lived with her parents in a tenement in Urquhart Road, and on the afternoon of Friday 20 April 1934, her mother sent her to the local Co-operative store to buy a loaf of bread. When Helen failed to return after a quarter of an hour or so, her mother went out to look for her. A search was instituted, which became more frantic when a local boy said he had seen Helen being dragged up the street by a man. Late in the afternoon, a man noticed a sack sticking out from a recess under the stairs. It contained Helen's body, and her bloomers were missing. Blood trickling between her thighs suggested that this was a sex crime. The child had been strangled.

Everyone in the tenement building was questioned. But when the police doctor discovered that there was no sperm on the child's combinations or in her vagina (semen stains show up blue under ultra-violet light, and sperm can be clearly seen under the microscope), and that the injuries seemed to have been inflicted with some instrument like a poker or a pudding spoon handle, they realized that the killer could have been a woman.

Next to the stairwell where the body had been found lived a family named Donald: the husband, John, was a hairdresser. He had been at work at the time Helen had disappeared. The wife, Jeannie, had a reputation as a woman of violent temper. Her daughter, also called Jeannie, had once been a friend of Helen Priestly, but they had quarrelled, and the two families were not on speaking terms. Jeannie Donald was known to dislike Helen, because the child used to run past her door shouting the nickname 'Coconut'. The Donalds were the only family in the tenement who had not taken part in the search for Helen.

Questioned routinely by the police, Jeannie Donald seemed to have an excellent alibi; she had been out shopping for food, and also called at a shop to buy some fabric. On her way back, she said, she had seen a crowd of women standing at the street corner, and Mrs Priestly crying. But when examined more closely, the alibi began to seem less convincing. She had named the prices she had paid for various items, such as eggs, but had given the prices charged the *previous* Friday. The shop where she claimed she had searched for fabric had been closed that afternoon. The group of women had not seen her pass them, but she could have seen them from a tenement window. Now the police searched the Donalds' flat, and found some stains in a cupboard that might be blood. A police doctor said they *were* bloodstains, and the Donalds were both arrested. In fact, laboratory examination showed that the stains were not of blood. But by now, the police were reasonably certain that Jeannie Donald had killed Helen Priestly.

Sydney Smith was then Professor of Forensic Medicine at Edinburgh, inheritor of Britain's first chair in legal medicine. Regarded by many as one of Spilsbury's chief rivals, he was now asked to see what he could make of the Helen Priestly case. If Jeannie Donald had murdered Helen in a fit of temper, then the evidence had to be sought in the Donalds' flat. Like Sherlock Holmes, Smith studied the clues. First, there was the sack; it was made of jute, had contained cereals, and had a hole in the corner. In the sack there was a double handful of washed cinders, some human and animal hairs, and a little household fluff. Most working-class families reused their cinders on the fire, but Jeannie Donald was the only housewife in the tenement who got rid of the ash by washing them. In the 'trap' in Jeannie Donald's sink wastepipe, the police found cinders similar to those in the sack. The sack had come from Canada filled with cereals, and had arrived in Aberdeen via London and Glasgow. Jeannie Donald's brother worked near a farm, and often brought her potatoes in a sack. Sacks such as this one were found on the farm. The hole in the corner had apparently been made when the sack had been hung on a hook; in the Donalds' flat there were other sacks with similar holes.

The human hairs in the sack were not from Helen Priestly's head, and they showed signs of having been 'permed'. Smith managed to obtain samples of Jeannie Donald's hair from a hairbrush; it had the same signs of artificial waving. Under a comparison microscope, the fluff – made up of around 200 types of fibre – proved to be similar to that found in the Donalds' flat, and not in any other flat in the tenement.

But most significant were a number of small bloodstains found on such items as newspapers (dating from the day before the crime), linoleum, washing cloths and a scrubbing brush. Smith's laboratory tests found them to be type O, the same as that of Helen Priestly; but could it also be that of Jeannie Donald? Mrs Donald refused to have a blood sample taken (which was her legal right), but Smith managed to obtain one of her used sanitary towels; it revealed that she was of a different blood group. (In his account in his autobiography *Mostly Murder*, Smith does not specify which.)

But the clinching evidence came from blood on the dead child's combinations. The article that had been used to simulate rape had ruptured her intestinal canal, releasing bacteria. Smith sent samples of the child's bloodstains, and those on articles from the Donalds' flat, to the bacteriology laboratory at the university. The Professor of Bacteriology, Thomas Mackie, discovered that Helen's intestines had contained a rare bacterium that he had never seen before. And the same bacteria were found in the bloodstains on the kitchen floorcloths. It was irrefutable evidence that the cloth had been used to mop up Helen's blood.

Smith was not inclined to believe that Jeannie Donald intended to kill Helen Priestly. He had learned that Helen had an enlarged thymus, and that this gave her a low resistance to various infections; it also meant that Helen would be more prone to fainting than a normal child. Smith theorized that Helen had run past the Donalds' flat chanting 'Coconut', and that on her way back, Jeannie Donald had been waiting for her, prepared to chastise her. She was a vengeful woman – the police learned that she had once wrung the necks of all the chickens in a hotel because the chef had reprimanded her – and probably grabbed

Helen by the throat or shoulders. Helen fainted. Believing her dead, Jeannie Donald decided to simulate a rape murder, and rammed some hard object into her vagina. The child woke and began to scream (a slater working next door said he had heard a scream at about the correct time) and Jeannie Donald tried to silence her by throttling. In fact, the pressure caused the child to vomit, and it was probably the vomit in her windpipe that caused her to suffocate.

If Smith was correct, Jeannie Donald was not guilty of murder but of manslaughter. He suggested this to the defence. But they under-estimated the strength of the scientific evidence, and decided to plead not guilty. It took the jury only 18 minutes to find Jeannie Donald guilty of murder, and she collapsed in the dock – the first sign of emotion she had shown during the trial. Her death sentence was later commuted to life imprisonment, of which she served ten years.

7

It must be admitted that the latest discovery in serology – that bodily fluids like saliva and semen also contain the 'blood fingerprint' – proved to be less successful in practice than the scientists had hoped. It is true that the Japanese solved a rape murder by this method in 1928, but this was largely because the murderer confessed. The victim was a 16-year-old itinerant fortune-teller named Yoshiki Hirai; she had been killed not far from the town of Nugata, and two suspects were arrested. One of them, a mentally defective beggar, confessed to the crime; but Dr K. Fujiwara, director of the Forensic Medicine Institute in Nugata, soon ascertained, from the rapist's sperm, that his blood group was A, and that the beggar's was O. But that of the other suspect, Iba Hoshi, was A, and when confronted with this evidence, he confessed. Without this confession, there would have been no case against him, for Yoshiki Hirai might have been raped by any number of men with A-type blood. In a sense, it was a new version of the old medieval problem: that the only evidence that would finally convince a jury was a confession.

And this, as Jürgen Thorwald points out in *Crime and Science,* was the major problem confronting the forensic serologist in the mid-twentieth century. One of Spilsbury's best-known cases of 1939 concerned the murder of a 9-year-old schoolgirl named Pamela Coventry, who disappeared on her way back to school on the afternoon of 18 January. Her naked body was found in a ditch near the

Hornchurch aerodrome the following morning, her knees bound against her chest with insulated wire. A bruise on her chin suggested that she had been knocked to the ground with a blow, then she had been strangled manually. But either the rape had not been completed, or there was not enough sperm for a determination of blood group. However, as the limbs were straightened out, the butt of a home-rolled cigarette fell out – the murderer had evidently been smoking as he bound her.

The police inferred that the girl had been dragged into some house or out-building after being knocked unconscious; there was snow on the ground, and the killer would not have risked a sexual assault outdoors in the early afternoon.

Spilsbury's colleague Dr Roche Lynch, director of the Department of Pathological Chemistry at St Mary's, decided to try to determine the killer's blood group from his saliva on the cigarette butt. This depended on whether the man was a 'secretor' – that is, whether his bodily fluids contained blood antigens. Fortunately, only 14 per cent of the human race are non-secretors. But unfortunately, the killer of Pamela Coventry proved to be one of these non-secretors.

Police suspicions now centred on a factory worker named Leonard Richardson, who had been away from work on the afternoon of Pamela's murder; his wife was in hospital having a baby, so he was alone in the house. Richardson was a non-stop smoker who rolled his own cigarettes. Tiny blood spots were found on his raincoat, and the precipitin test showed them to be of human blood; but determination of blood group then required a fairly large stain, and there was simply not enough. By examining some dirty handkerchiefs belonging to Richardson, Lynch was able to determine that, like the killer, he was a non-secretor. But although laboratory tests showed that the tobacco and cigarette paper were of the same type used by Richardson, the jury found the evidence unconvincing; the trial was stopped on its fifth day, and Richardson allowed to go free.

A second case of the same year proved to be equally frustrating for the police and the forensic experts. On the evening of 21 May 1939, a well-to-do businessman named Walter Dinivan was battered unconscious at his villa in Bournemouth, and died later the same night. On the table in his sitting-room there were two glasses, suggesting that Dinivan had been offering a drink to someone he knew during the course of the evening. The safe had been opened with his own keys, and emptied. Police enquiries showed that Dinivan sometimes

Scenes during the kidnapping and death of Colonel Lindbergh's
young son at Hopewell, New Jersey, USA.

The remains of Charles A. Lindbergh Jr were found on 12 May 1932,
in a shallow grave in the woods near the Lindbergh home.

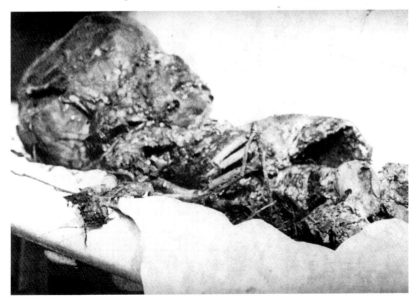

A sketch from the *Illustrated Police News* showing Dr George Bagster Phillips, Whitechapel Divisional Police Surgeon, examining the body of Annie Chapman. Dr Phillips felt the murderer had some anatomical knowledge.

Police crime scene photographs of Mary Jane Kelly's body as found in her bed.

The second police crime scene photograph of Mary Jane Kelly's body, taken from the opposite side of the bed and showing a table piled with flesh in the background.

François Lacenaire

The tracking down of François Lacenaire, one of the most ruthless and intelligent of French criminals, was an example of the needle-in-the-haystack method; employed in the days before the arrival of scientific crime detection.

Finding the body of Patrick O'Connor. He was murdered by Frederick and Maria Manning. Maria Manning served as a model for the attractive but murderous Hortense in Charles Dickens's *Bleak House*.

Jonathan Wild became a kind of eighteenth-century Al Capone. Eventually the law caught up with him, and he was hanged in 1725.

Marie Lafarge was accused of poisoning her husband with arsenic, and arrested. As soon as the arrest was reported in the Paris newspapers, Marie's case became a *cause célèbre* because of her aristocratic connections.

Madeline Smith

Madeline Smith was accused of murdering her French lover with arsenic. The case aroused the same excitement as the Lafarge poisoning; the notion of a young girl becoming the mistress of a Frenchman horrified Scottish public opinion. The jury eventually brought in a verdict of 'not proven', which implied that they regarded her as guilty, but found the proof insufficient.

Close up of bone fragments found on the property where Leonard Lake lived. Authorities believed that as many as 25 people may have been slaughtered at the site in sex-torture killings.

Interior view of the room considered to be the sex-torture chamber where Leonard Lake could spy on his captives through a one-way mirror installed in his sleeping quarters in the adjoining room of the concrete bunker at his Sierra foothill cabin.

John George Haigh, handcuffed to a police officer, as he arrived at Horsham Magistrates Court for his fifth appearance on the charge of murdering Mrs Olivia Durrand-Deacon.

The notices of Haigh's execution, posted on the gates of Wandsworth Prison. On the left is the surgeon's confirmation of death and on the right the Sherrif's notice, signed by the Prisoner Governor and Chaplin – certifying carrying out the death penalty.

CERTIFICATE OF SURGEON

31 Vict. Cap. 24

I, the Surgeon of His Majesty's Prison of WANDSWORTH hereby certify that I this day examined the Body of JOHN GEORGE HAIGH, on whom Judgment of Death was this day executed in the said Prison; and that on that Examination I found that the said JOHN GEORGE HAIGH was dead.

Dated this 10th day of August 1949

(Signature)

DECLARATION OF SHERIFF
AND OTHERS

(31 Vict. Cap. 24)

We, the undersigned, hereby declare that Judgement of Death was this Day executed on JOHN GEORGE HAIGH in His Majesty's Prison of WANDSWORTH in our presence.

Dated this 10th day of August 1949

Sheriff of London

Justice of the Peace

for

Governor of the said Prison.

Chaplain of the said Prison.

entertained prostitutes in his home, and it was one of these who led them to a man called Joseph Williams, a cantankerous old man who knew Dinivan.

The police had two promising clues: a thumbprint on a glass that had contained beer, and a number of cigarette butts. Chief Inspector Leonard Burt of Scotland Yard was able to identify the thumbprint as that of Williams. By stealthily abstracting a cigarette butt that Williams had smoked while being interrogated, Burt was able to provide Roche Lynch with material for a blood group test. Williams proved to be a secretor whose group was AB – the smallest of the blood groups – which proved to be the same as that on cigarette butts found in Dinivan's sitting-room. Circumstantial evidence was also strong: Williams had been broke up to the time of the murder, and had since apparently had plenty of money – he claimed he had won it on a racehorse.

The case against him seemed watertight. Yet the jury ignored the fingerprint evidence, ignored the blood group evidence, and returned a verdict of not guilty. The same night, in a fit of alcoholic remorse, Williams admitted to *News of the World* reporter Norman Rae that he had murdered Walter Dinivan. But it was too late. The reporter revealed his secret only after Williams's death in March 1951.

Yet it could be argued that the scepticism of the jury in these two cases was not entirely unjustified, for the techniques of blood testing have never been as straightforward – and therefore as reliable – as fingerprint evidence. In 1948, in a brilliant piece of investigation, the fingerprint expert Superintendent Fred Cherrill, was able to identify a killer who had left no other clue than two partial fingerprints. The victim was an old lady called Mrs Freeman Lee, who lived alone in a house in Maidenhead. When she failed to take in her milk for two days, police broke in and found her body in a chest in the hall; she had died of suffocation. The killer was evidently an intruder who had taken care to leave no fingerprints. But Cherrill found the lid of a tiny cardboard box under the bed, with two faint partial fingerprints on its sides which were only five-sixteenths of an inch in width. They were nevertheless enough to identify a housebreaker named George Russell, who lived in the area and who was duly hanged for the murder.

Yet eight years later, in 1956, German forensic science came close to convicting the wrong man on bloodstain evidence. In the first six months of 1956, there occurred a horrific series of apparently motive-less murders around Düsseldorf – the city that, in the late 1920s, had been terrorized by the sadistic murders committed by the sexual pervert Peter Kürten. On 31 October 1955, two lovers, Friedhelm Behre and Thea Kürmann, had vanished after an evening out. A month later, a car was found submerged in a pond near Düsseldorf, and the bodies of the lovers were found in the back seat. They had apparently been battered into unconsciousness while lovemaking, and the killer had then driven the car into the pond, jumping clear when it reached the edge.

On 7 January 1956, two men were seated in a car in a secluded spot on the bank of the Rhine when a man wearing a stocking mask wrenched open the door and shot one of them, a homosexual lawyer named Servé, through the head. Another man climbed into the car and struck the other man – a young workman with whom Servé was having an affair – on the head, at the same time whispering to him to sham dead. This saved the workman's life. After an unsuccessful attempt to start the car, the man in the mask took Servé's wallet and vanished.

On 7 February 1956, another car vanished, and its owner reported that his chaffeur, a young man named Peter Falkenberg, had vanished with it. At the same time, a Frau Wassing reported that her daughter Hildegard had not returned from a date with a chaffeur named Peter. It was found parked with its headlights on, and pools of blood inside indicated that some violence had taken place. Later, two bodies were found in a burnt-out haystack; both had been battered unconscious, and the man had also been shot.

It looked as if a sexual pervert who preyed on courting couples was responsible for all five murders. In the town of Büderich, detectives heard of a young man called Erich von der Leyen, who lived close to the burnt-out haystack, and who had a reputation for oddity – he was said to have attacked children with a hayfork. Von der Leyen proved to be a travelling salesman for an agriculture firm, and his alibi for the night of the murder – that he had been at home – was uncorroborated. The entry in his log-book for the night of the murder also seemed implausible. Finally, spots like bloodstains were found in his Volkswagen. When these were examined by the Forensic Institute, they were reported to be human bloodstains. The Institute also said that stains on von der Leyen's trousers were human blood. Some of the spots were blood group A, others AB. Von der Leyen's bloodgroup was A_2. But the victims Friedhelm Behre and Thea Kürmann had both been group B; so had the chauffeur Falkenberg. The police asked a forensic expert to see if he could determine the age of the bloodstains on the trousers. In the course of examining them, he came upon more stains which were undoubtedly blood – but blood which showed epithelial cells under the microscope, indicating that it was menstrual blood. Further tests showed that it was the blood of a dog. In fact, von der Leyen had insisted that the only way he might account for the blood in his car was that a girlfriend's dachshund had leapt into the car when it was on heat. Following this discovery, the police asked the Forensic Institute to re-check the bloodstains on the seat covers. With embarrassment, the Institute admitted that a mistake had been made. Their Uhlenhuth test had indicated that the blood was human, but when tested again, it proved to be dog's blood. The Institute blamed the company that had supplied the serum. Erich von der Leyen was immediately released – he had been intensively interrogated for many days, on the assumption that he was the killer, and would eventually confess.

On 6 June 1956, a forester named Spath was patrolling woods near Büderich. When he saw a courting couple embracing in a parked car, he stood still; at the same time, he realized that a man was creeping towards the car holding a revolver. Spath ran towards him, and the man fled, throwing away the gun. He caught up with him in a hollow, and told the man he was under arrest. At the police station in Büderich, the man identified himself as Werner Boost, a 28-year-old mechanic from Düsseldorf; he protested that he was married and the father of two children, and hardly the type of man to attack courting couples. But his police record showed that he had started life as a juvenile deliquent, had been in prison for robbing cemeteries, and fined for possessing firearms without a permit. Confronted with the evidence of the revolver, Boost explained that he was a moralist who detested sexual licence, and that he intended to frighten the couple. 'These sex horrors are the curse of Germany.'

As he interrogated Boost, Kriminal Hauptkommissar Mattias Eynck recalled that in 1945, about 50 people had been killed near the town of Helmstedt, trying to cross from the Russian to the British zone. At that time, Boost had been in Helmstedt, acting as a guide to refugees who wanted to cross the border. When he had left Helmstedt, the killings had ceased.

While Eynck was interrogating Boost, a man named Franz Lorbach asked to see him. He was a nervous man with watery eyes, and Eynck recalled an entry he had found in Boost's diary: 'Lorbach seems in need of another shot.' Lorbach, he thought, looked like a drug-taker.

Lorbach was there to denounce Boost as the unknown sex killer. In

1952, he explained, he and Boost had teamed up to poach in the woods around Büderich. Boost was obsessed by courting couples, whom he seemed to hate. When they came upon a couple engaged in love-making, Boost and Lorbach would spy on them, then Boost would threaten them with a gun and rob them. These couples never reported the attacks. Then Boost graduated to rape. In a home laboratory he concocted narcotic substances and gases that could cause unconsciousness, and used these on courting couples. He and Lorbach would then rape the unconscious women.

Dr Servé, it seemed, had been murdered by accident. Boost assumed the lovers in the car were male and female, and wrenched open the door, killing the man. Lorbach opened the other door and struck the young workman, ordering him in a whisper to pretend to be dead.

Lorbach went on to write a full-length confession, telling also how Boost had planned robberies; Lorbach had been in agony for months, trying to avoid taking any further part in Boost's crimes. This is why, as soon as he heard of Boost's arrest, he had hastened to the police; he was afraid that Boost might talk himself out of jail.

The revolver found in the woods proved to be the one that had killed Dr Servé. In a laboratory in Boost's cellar, the police found materials for the manufacture of cyanide gas, and toy balloons, which Boost used to fill with the gas and release in the cars of his victims. At his trial, Boost was found guilty of the murder of Dr Servé, and sentenced to life imprisonment; Lorbach received six years. If a perceptive forensic scientist had not noticed the menstrual bloodstains on the trousers, Erich von der Leyen might have been sentenced instead of Boost.

8

So, by the end of the 1950s, the record of serology in the solution of violent crime was rather less impressive than that of fingerprinting or the microscopic examinaton of fibres. Even in cases where a bloodstain might have played a crucial part, it was often unidentifiable, either because it was too small, or was on material that confused the issue.

On 29 July 1950, the body of a woman was found lying in the road in south Glasgow; her injuries suggested that she had been struck by a heavy lorry. But when the police studied the scene of the accident, they began to have doubts. There were *two* sets of intersecting skid marks on the road, and it seemed unlikely that the victim had been struck by two vehicles. There were also signs of blood and skin tissue ground into the road for some distance from the body, as if she had been dragged under a vehicle. But there was no broken glass, or other evidence of an accident, near the body.

The woman was identified as Catherine McCluskey, a 43-year-old blonde who was the mother of two illegitimate children. She lived not far from the place where her body was found, and the police discovered that she had many male friends.

In the pathology laboratory at St Mungo's College, the body was examined by Professor Andrew Alison. The first thing that struck him was the absence of the expected injuries on the woman's legs. Those who are knocked down by a car usually have some injury at bumper-level; lack of such injuries suggested that although the woman had been killed by a car, she had not been knocked down by one. And that combination of circumstances sounded like murder.

Interviews with Catherine McCluskey's friends suggested that one of her boyfriends included a policeman; she had told a woman friend that the policeman was the father of one of her children. Inspector Donald MacDougall of the CID made discreet enquiries, and learned that, on the night Catherine McCluskey had died, a policeman named James Ronald Robertson had told a colleague that he intended to take some time off from his beat to see a blonde. In fact, gossip indicated that Robertson was an enthusiastic pursuer of the opposite sex. And on the night of the murder, he had told the constable who shared his beat that he intended to take a short time off to run someone home in his car. In fact, he had been away two hours, and when he returned, seemed tense and agitated; his trousers were dirty and he told his fellow constable that his car exhaust had fallen off.

Robertson was arrested and his house was searched. There the detectives found a quantity of stolen property, including car registration books and a radio. Robertson's car, a large black Austin, was also discovered to be stolen. The number plates were found to be those of a tractor. Robertson admitted that the car was not his own – he claimed that it had been abandoned in a road near his home, and he had finally decided to 'claim' it.

Robertson also admitted what the police experts soon confirmed: that his car had been the vehicle that caused Catherine McCluskey's death. His story was that they had quarrelled, and she had got out of the car to walk home. He relented, and reversed the car to pick her up; instead, he knocked her down and ran over her. He tried to drag her out from under the car, but her clothing was entangled in the propellor shaft. So he moved the car backwards and forwards until the body was free, then drove away . . .

There were two major objections to this story: first, that the lack of leg injuries indicated that she had not been knocked down accidentally, second, that the propellor shaft was boxed in, so it could not possibly catch her clothing.

Professor John Glaister – the man who had reconstructed the bodies in the Ruxton case – felt there was a more plausible explanation. When Robertson was arrested he had been carrying a cosh, and there was a bloodstain on it. Glaister believed that Robertson had used the cosh to knock Catherine McCluskey unconscious, then had deliberately driven the car over her, and reversed it over the body. Her injuries were consistent with this theory. Unfortunately, the bloodstain on the cosh was too small to test by the Lattes method – obviously, the evidence against Robertson would have been very strong indeed if the blood had proved to be of the murdered woman's group. In spite of which, it was bloodstain evidence that finally convinced the jury of Robertson's guilt – or rather, the completely inexplicable lack of it. If, as he claimed, Robertson had tried to drag the body free of the car, his trousers and cuffs would have become heavily bloodstained. There were no such bloodstains. It followed that Robertson had simply driven the car over the unconscious girl after he had struck her to the ground. Then he had driven away without touching the body. On this evidence, Robertson was convicted of murder – his motive, apparently, was to cease paying maintenance for his illegitimate child – and he was sentenced to hang.

The case is an example of the best kind of crime detection – the combination of forensic skill with logic and common sense. If Glaister had been a slightly less old-fashioned pathologist, he might well have applied the latest serological methods to the bloodstained cosh, and perhaps succeeded in demonstrating that the blood was of the victim's group. Yet in the event, the forensic evidence about her injuries combined with the lack of bloodstains on Robertson's trousers built an overwhelming case for calculated murder.

Unfortunately, the combination was not always so satisfactory. Four years after the Robertson case, slipshod forensic work and a certain carelessness on the part of the police led to one of the most controversial murder trials of modern times. The defendant was a brilliant young neurosurgeon, Dr Sam Sheppard, of Cleveland, Ohio. On the night of 3 July 1954, Sheppard's wife Marilyn was murdered in her own home, and her husband apparently knocked unconscious by an intruder. What actually happened is still – long after Sheppard's acquittal and death – a matter of controversy.

Sheppard's story – as told to the police – was that he had fallen asleep while watching television, although two dinner guests were still in the room. He was awakened, he claimed, by his wife's screams, coming from her bedroom. He rushed upstairs, only to be struck on the head from behind and knocked unconscious. When he woke up, he realized that his wife had been violently attacked. He ran to his son's bedroom, and was relieved to see that the boy was peacefully asleep. Then he heard a noise downstairs, and ran down to see a shadowy figure running from the back door towards Lake Erie. He gave chase, but was again knocked unconscious. When he woke up again he found himself half-in and half-out of the lake. For some reason, his assailant had pulled off his T-shirt. When he got back into the house he realized that his wife was dead, and rang the local mayor, who soon brought the police. Sheppard's brother Richard also arrived, together with the coroner, Samuel Gerber. They discovered that Marilyn Sheppard was dead, struck on the head repeatedly with a blunt instrument; she was clad only in a pyjama top. The place was in chaos, with drawers pulled out and their contents scattered. Sheppard said that the 'burglar' had been a big, bushy-haired man. But if he *was* a burglar, why had he apparently taken nothing, and even ignored money? Coroner Gerber quickly reached the conclusion that there had been no bushy-haired intruder; Sheppard had killed his wife during a quarrel, then tried to make it look like a burglary. His wife had died – according to medical evidence – at a round 4 a.m., yet it had been another two hours before Sheppard had telephoned the mayor. His own account was that he had been dazed and unconscious much of the time; Gerber suspected that he had used the time to get rid of the murder weapon (if it was a blunt metal instrument, he only had to scrub it, dry it and replace it in the tool shed) and to set the scene of the 'burglary'.

In later accounts of the case, Gerber has come in for a great deal of harsh criticism; it is alleged that he was jealous of Sheppard's success and went out to 'get' him. Yet anyone who studies the above account of the murder can see why he was suspicious. According to Sheppard, Marilyn had left him asleep in an armchair (wearing a corduroy jacket, according to the dinner guests) and gone off to bed. He sleeps on for between three and four hours – an unlikely contigency; most people who doze off in the armchair – particularly with the light on – wake up after half an hour or so and realize where they are. He is awakened by his wife's screams – an intruder has broken into the house, possibly walking past the sleeping man, and gone upstairs, where he proceeds to rifle drawers. When the woman wakes up, he attacks her to keep her silent – but does not content himself with knocking her unconscious, but goes on battering her with about 35 blows. Downstairs, the husband pauses to remove his corduroy coat and place it on the settee before he rushes upstairs to see why his wife is screaming. He is knocked unconscious by the intruder; but the intruder, instead of making off, goes downstairs and waits around until the husband again rushes down to pursue him out of the house. Yet again, the man somehow succeeds in knocking him unconscious, and he lies in the lake for a considerable period – perhaps an hour – before waking up, going indoors, and discovering that his wife has been murdered . . .

The whole story was highly suspicious. Why did the dog not bark when the intruder broke in? If Sheppard had been lying with his head on the beach, why was there no sand in his hair? Why was Sheppard's bloodstained watch – which he had been wearing presumably when he fell asleep – found in the garden, in a canvas bag he used on his boat? Sheppard explained later that the watch had become bloodstained when he felt for his wife's pulse; in which case, why remove it and put it in the garden? Gerber felt, understandably, that Sheppard had noticed the bloodstains while he was frantically trying to 'stage' the burglary, and hid it outside.

By the time the inquest was convened on 26 July 1954, the investigation had discovered that Sheppard had been having an affair with a pretty technician at the hospital; she had moved to California, and Sheppard had been to stay with her a few months before. At the inquest, Sheppard declared indignantly that he had never had any sexual relation with the girl, Susan Hayes. Since the police knew this to be untrue, they must have found themselves wondering how many other things Sheppard was lying about. Four days later, Sheppard was arrested and charged with his wife's murder. The local newspapers were all convinced of his guilt, and announced it without regard to the laws of libel.

There were, of course, certain points in Sheppard's favour. If he had killed Marilyn with a bludgeon, he would have been sprayed with blood; but he had only one bloodstain on the knee of his trousers, and he claimed this must have happened when he was taking his wife's pulse. His brother had seen a cigarette stub floating in the lavatory; but

Sheppard was a non-smoker, and Marilyn smoked filter tips; this was not a filter stub. Sheppard's medical bag had been up-ended, and an ampoule of morphine capsules was missing, which suggested that the intruder could have been a drug addict, crazed with the desire for a 'fix'. But then, Sheppard had time to get rid of bloodstained clothes – perhaps rowing out into the lake, and weighting them with a stone. (This seemed a more likely explanation of the loss of his T-shirt than that the 'burglar' had taken if off him because his own was blood-stained.) The cigarette butt could have been thrown there by one of the policemen, or by one of the two dinner guests. (It vanished when a policeman flushed the toilet.) And he could have got rid of the morphine as easily as the clothes and the murder weapon. (A lake is a convenient item for a murderer to have at his back door.) Finally, the strange absence of fingerprints in the house could be interpreted in two ways – as an attempt by the intruder to destroy all evidence of his presence, or as another attempt by Sheppard to substantiate his burglar fabrication . . .

The prosecution rested its case after Susan Hayes had appeared in court and admitted to having an affair with Sheppard that started 18 months before the murder; she confessed that they had made love in cars and in a flat above the clinic. She also admitted that Sheppard had spoken to her about getting a divorce. After all this, the defence had an uphill task to depict Sheppard as a wronged innocent. On 21 December 1954, Sheppard was found guilty of second degree murder (because there was no evidence of premeditation) and sentenced to life imprisonment.

In June 1957, the Sheppard case became headline news again when a convict named Donald Wedler, serving a 10-year sentence for a hold-up in Florida, confessed to the murder. He claimed that he had been in Cleveland that day, and had taken a shot of heroin. Late at night he had stolen a car, then looked for somewhere to burgle. He had entered a big white house on the lakefront, seen a man asleep on the settee, and gone upstairs. A woman had awakened as he had been rifling her dresser, and he had beaten her with an iron pipe. Then, as he fled downstairs, he had encountered a man, whom he had also struck down with the pipe. Then he had flung the pipe in the lake and driven away. The story was obviously inconsistent with the one Sheppard had told – first, about being struck down from behind in the bedroom, and second, in failing to mention the struggle in the garden. Although a lie detector test seemed to indicate that Wedler was telling the truth, no further action was taken.

But in 1966, when Sheppard had been in prison for 12 years, an appeal finally succeeded – on the grounds that the newspaper stories had made a fair trial impossible. The conviction was quashed, and a new trial ordered. A young Boston lawyer, F. Lee Bailey, appeared for the defence. He embarrassed the police by revealing that their search for clues had been very casual indeed – they had not even tried to get fingerprints from the watch found in the duffle bag, as well as a key-ring and chain. Bailey accused Gerber of being out to 'get' Sheppard through jealousy, and Gerber's angry reply made a bad impresssion on the court. But the turning point of the case was a photograph of Sheppard's bloodstained watch. The face contained specks of blood, such as would have been made if Sheppard had been wearing it when he battered his wife to death. Bailey noticed that there were also 'flying' bloodspots *inside* the wristband, which indicated clearly that it had not been on Sheppard's wrist at the time his wife was battered to death, and that therefore the bloodspots had got inside the wristband after Marilyn was killed. This was the kind of Agatha Christie reasoning that impresses juries, and this time, they decided that Sam Sheppard was innocent.

Yet in retrospect, it is difficult to follow their reasoning. If there were spots of blood inside the wrist band, we have to suppose that the watch was lying beside the bed when Marilyn Sheppard was murdered. But it should have been on the wrist of her husband, who was just awakening downstairs. The only other logical explanation is that Sheppard went up to bed after the guests had left, leaving his corduroy jacket downstairs (whether it was on the settee or lying on the floor was a point of controversy at the trial), and removing his watch before getting into bed. We then have to suppose a violent quarrel, perhaps brought on by some talk of divorce, or perhaps by Sheppard's jealousy of his wife (who also seems to have had her admirers) and Sheppard's murder of his wife with a blunt instrument . . .

The fact that Marilyn Sheppard had admirers led one writer on the case, the Chicago journalist Paul Holmes, to propound an extraordinary theory in his book *The Sheppard Murder Case*, written before Sheppard's final acquittal. Holmes suggested that one of these admirers had observed the light in the Sheppard's house, assumed the doctor was out on a call, and let himself in to enjoy a little hasty love-making. Unfortunately, he was followed by his wife, who battered Marilyn Sheppard to death . . . But this fails to explain why Sheppard failed to see the enraged wife when he rushed into the bedroom.

In his account of the case in *Cause of Death, The Story of Forensic Science,* Frank Smyth argues strongly in favour of Sheppard's innocence, as does Jürgen Thorwald in *Crime and Science.* Yet, as this re-examination demonstrates, the evidence of Sheppard's guilt remains highly convincing. All the same, the plausibility of Wedler's confession reminds us that the murder *could* have been committed by a burglar who was probably a drug addict. But if that is so, it only underlines the total failure of forensic science in a case where it might have been expected to reach important conclusions.

In 1963, while still in prison, Sheppard had announced his engagement to a wealthy – and beautiful – young divorcee from Düsseldorf, who had flown to America to see him. They married, but after his release she sued for divorce, alleging that he carried a heavy axe and a knife, and had threatened her. Sheppard subsequently became a professional wrestler, teaming up with a man named Strickland, and married Strickland's 19-year-old daughter. But it seemed clear that many people still believed he had killed his wife, and Sheppard's health began to fail; he died in 1970 at the age of 46.

9

What was becoming clear, in the 1950s and 1960s, was that in spite of the increasing skills of the forensic scientist, serology had not achieved the same pinpoint accuracy as other branches of scientific crime fighting. A criminal could be convicted by a single hair or a single cloth fibre, but seldom by a single bloodspot. In 1966, the newspapers announced the discovery of the 'blood fingerprint' by Drs Margaret Pereira and Brian Culliford; but they were not referring to some method of identifying the blood of a single individual, but only to new methods of increasing the likelihood that blood came from a certain individual by studying the rhesus factors. Such a method was invaluable in paternity disputes, but not necessarily to a 'disappearing body' case in which the only clue might be a single bloodstain. Even cases involving dozens of bloodstains might still constitute a baffling problem in crime detection. Such, for example, was the case of Stanislaw Sykut, a farmer who disappeared from the remote Welsh farmhouse he shared with his fellow Pole Michial Onufrejczyc (pronounced Ono-free-shic) in December 1953. The two ex-soldiers proved to be poor farmers, and their financial problems became increasingly serious; things were made worse by Onufrejczyc's complaint that his partner was lazy, and on one occasion, Sykut complained to the local police that he had been beaten up. Sykut gave his partner notice that he wanted to leave, and asked for the return of the £600 he had paid for a half share in the farm. The last time he was seen alive was on 14 December 1953; when his mail at the post office remained uncollected, the police went to the farm to check up. Onufrejczyc's explanantions left them more unsatisfied than ever, and they searched the farmhouse (which was at Cwm Du, near Llandilo, Carmarthenshire) and found the kitchen full of bloodstains – thousands of flying bloodspots which suggested that someone had been beaten to death. One of them even contained a small fragment of bone. Onufrejczyc claimed that Sykut had simply gone back to Poland, and that the blood came from rabbits. Forensic tests showed that it was human blood; whereupon Onufrejczyc changed his story and claimed that his partner had cut his hand in the hay machine.

For months the police searched for the body, with total lack of success. In September 1954, almost a year after Sykut's disappearance, they finally decided to charge Onufrejczyc with his partner's murder. At the trial in Swansea, the defence poured scorn on the circumstantial evidence and argued that there was no case to answer. There was no body, which meant that Sykut might still be alive. The jury disagreed, and found Onufrejczyc guilty of his partner's murder. But in view of the doubts that still lingered, he was sentenced to life imprisonment rather than to death. And in spite of more than 1,000 bloodspots, all the skill of Britain's forensic scientists was unable to resolve those doubts.

In 1981, the Hampshire police found themselves investigating a case in which there was even less evidence. Twenty-seven-year old Danny Rosenthal was an intelligent but highly disturbed young man who lived alone in a bungalow at 7 Nordik Gardens, Hedge End – a suburb of Southampton. He had turned his bedroom into a laboratory, where he was trying to transplant chickens' brains into fertilized eggs. He had a history of mild mental disorder, and had been diagnosed schizophrenic. In a strange letter to the FBI, he had accused his parents, Milton and Leah Rosenthal, of committing serious crimes against him.

His parents had been separated since he was 12; his mother lived in Israel, while his father, a retired UNESCO official, had a flat in Meudon, a suburb of Paris. And in the early autumn of 1981, it became clear that both his father and mother had vanished. Leah Rosenthal had been staying at a health farm in August 1981 – she suffered from multiple sclerosis and could walk only with the aid of crutches. Then she had decided to go and see her son in Southampton; a family friend, Dr Hussein, had put her on the train. On 26 August, she had telephoned Dr Hussein to say she was worried about Danny – the implication being that she thought he was going insane – and wanted to go and discuss it with her husband in Paris. Dr Hussein agreed to go with her. But after that, he heard no more. A few days later, he rang Danny to enquire about his mother, and was told that she had returned to London. Dr Hussein reported his worries to the Hedge End police, who went to question Danny. He repeated his story that she had left for London in a taxi. He allowed the police to look over the house, and although the place was a shambles, with ivy growing down the wall in the living-room, there was no sign of anything suspicious. The police next tried to trace the taxi-driver. But neighbours had not noticed a taxi arriving, and no Southampton driver reported going to Hedge End to pick up a lady with crutches.

On 3 September 1981, Danny Rosenthal was taken to Bitterne police station, and detectives searched the bungalow. Again, they found nothing suspicious; but they asked the Home Office for a full scientific examination of the bungalow. Later that day, Dr Mike Sayce and Dr Sue Sims of the Aldermaston Central Research Establishment began their own search. They found the place looking like a rubbish dump, with books, papers and clothing on the floors.

The police had found bottles of acid, which led Sayce to suspect that Mrs Rosenthal had been disposed of in the same way as the victims of Haigh, the 'acid bath murderer'; but the bath revealed no sign of acid damage. And in the outside drain they found a live frog, which indicated that no noxious chemicals had been flushed down recently.

In the bedroom, Sayce found traces of blood on the floor and skirting board. These could have been from the chickens, which Danny claimed he had killed; but tests back at the laboratory showed that they were human blood, and that its group was B. Danny's was O. And when Sayce examined a hacksaw found in a second bedroom (used as a workshop), he found human skin and muscle tissue, as well as bone. This left him in no doubt that Mrs Rosenthal had been killed in the bungalow. They returned to search the bedroom, and this time found bloodspots on the legs of furniture, radiating away from the centre of the floor. It looked as if Leah Rosenthal had been killed there, probably by a blow, and dismembered after she was dead. Bloodspots were no higher than nine inches off the floor, and if she had been alive at the time, the blood would have spurted higher – perhaps even to the ceiling.

There were also traces of blood on the bathroom taps, on washed male clothing in the bath, and in a bucket beneath the kitchen sink. It looked as if Leah Rosenthal had been dismembered on a bedroom carpet, which had since been destroyed, then the house had been thoroughly mopped. Danny Rosenthal must have been certain that he had not left the slightest trace of blood; the Home Office team showed that this is far more difficult than it looks.

There was still no direct evidence of murder – Danny could have alleged that his mother had died of a heart attack, and that he had panicked and disposed of the body. But by now, the police had tried to contact Danny's father, Milton Rosenthal, in Paris, and learned from his housekeeper that he had also vanished. 'Milton is dead – Danny killed him' said Quibillah Shabbaz. She had reported her suspicions to the Meudon police on 17 August, but since she had a record as a drug addict, they had ignored her.

It seemed that Danny Rosenthal had gone to visit his father two weeks before the disappearance of Mrs Rosenthal, and that Milton Rosenthal had not been seen since. On 12 August 1981, the housekeeper had gone to Milton Rosenthal's flat – she lived in the basement – to do some typing. Danny had admitted her with obvious reluctance, and had retired to the bathroom, where he had run water continuously for two or three hours. That sounds like a cleaning-up operation. After Danny had returned to England, the housekeeper had found blood-stained paper and clothing, and plastic bags and string in the flat.

Now Dr Sayce went to Paris to search the flat. The French police had already found traces of blood around a light fitting on the bathroom ceiling, and a hacksaw. When Sayce arrived he found that the bathroom was lit by an extremely dim bulb. But he had brought his own lighting, and this soon showed traces of blood on the bathroom floor, which someone had tried to mop up – a bloodstained 'squeejee' mop was found in the kitchen. Cracks between the lino tiles in the living-room also contained traces of blood, and there were drag-marks in blood from the living-room to the bathroom. Careful examination revealed two fragments of bone. It looked, then, as if Milton Rosenthal had been killed with a heavy blow in the living-room – perhaps only minutes before the housekeeper had arrived – and had been dragged into the bathroom. Then he had been dismembered and put into plastic bags.

Study of the hacksaw again revealed fragments of human skin, bone and muscle. There was now clear evidence that Danny Rosenthal had killed both his mother and father – possibly killing his mother when she announced her intention of going to see the father. He was charged with the murder of his mother by the Southampton police, even though an exhaustive search had revealed no sign of the body. Two weeks before his trial, in June 1982, the French police announced that some human remains had been found at Troyes, 100 miles south-east of Paris – the trunk, pelvis and leg of a male of about Milton's Rosenthal's age; they had been dismembered with a hacksaw. Dr Sayce hurried over to view the remains. Since the head and hands were missing, identification was difficult. But from the long bones, Sayce was able to determine the man's height as just over five and a half feet, like Milton Rosenthal. The blood group was B, like Rosenthal's. As a final test, the hacksaw was used to cut wax, putting black powder on the blade to show the marks of the teeth. Comparing the wax with the bones revealed that the same hacksaw had cut both.

The plastic bin liners in which the remains had been found still bore the store label, and it was found to be close to the travel agent from which Danny Rosenthal had purchased his ticket to Paris. A final item of proof was a metal plate found in Danny Rosenthal's workshop; it bore the name 'Zimmer', the manufacturer of Leah Rosenthal's crutches.

At his trial, Danny Rosenthal stubbornly insisted that his parents were still alive, but he was found guilty of the murder of his mother. His mental condition was found to be such that he was confined in Broadmoor.

10

For the forensic scientist, the most satisfying type of case is that in which he is able to help the police establish the identity of an unknown killer. This is what happened in 1983, the year that might be regarded as the centenary of *bertillonage* – for it was in February 1883 that Bertillon had first established the identity of a criminal through his system of measurements.

The Laitners were a wealthy Jewish family who lived in a luxury home in the fashionable Sheffield suburb of Dore. Basil Laitner, a 59-year-old solicitor, lived there with his wife Avril, his son Richard, who was taking a medical degree, and his youngest daughter Nicola, who was 18. On 23 October 1983, Laitner's eldest daughter Suzanne married an optician, and the wedding reception was held in a marquee on the lawn of the Laitner home. Unfortunately, the guests were unaware that they were being closely observed by a man who was hiding in the shrubbery, and that he was fascinated by the beauty of one the bridesmaids – Nicola Laitner.

Late that night, Nicola was awakened by sounds of a struggle outside her door; as she lay there, wondering if this was a nightmare, she heard her mother's screams. Then, suddenly, her bedroom door opened; the beam of a torch fell on her, and a man with a 'Geordie' accent ordered her to keep quiet or he would kill her. He told her that he had killed her mother and father, then added: 'I don't want to kill you – I want to fuck you.' At knifepoint, he forced her to get out of bed and go downstairs. On the way, they passed a body lying face downward, the head pointing downstairs – her father. The man – who was wearing a blood-stained blue T-shirt – took her out to the marquee on the lawn, and there raped her. He was dirty, smelt of sweat, and had cropped curly grey hair and an incipient beard. Like many rapists, he seemed to believe that his victim should enjoy it. 'You've got to enjoy it or I'll kill you. That's where your mum went wrong – she made a fuss.' When the rape was over, he took her back into the house – perhaps because she was wearing only a thin nightie and was cold – and in her bedroom, raped her twice more. Then he tied her up, and left the house at dawn, ordering her to 'tell the police it was a black man'. After a long struggle she succeeded in freeing herself from her bonds. The workmen who arrived early to take down the marquee were startled to be met by a weeping girl dressed in a bloodstained nightgown, who told them that her family had been murdered.

When the police entered the house, they found three corpses. Nicola's brother Richard had been stabbed through the heart as he lay in bed – the killer later admitted that he had entered the bedroom, seen a bridesmaid's dress hanging behind the door, and assumed that the figure in the bed was a girl. Hearing noises from upstairs, Basil Laitner – who had only just returned from an evening out – had run up to see what was happening; the man was lying in wait and plunged the knife into the back of his neck. Laitner fought hard, but the man forced him face-downwards over the banisters, and drove the knife into his back so hard that the point came out of his chest. Avril Laitner heard the sounds and came out of her downstairs bedroom to investigate; she was met by a blood-covered man who was wielding a knife, and who chased her back into her bedroom. The man's intention was probably rape – as his comment 'That's where your mum went wrong' implied – but as Avril Laitner fought back, he stabbed her again and again and cut her throat. Then the killer made his way up to Nicola's bedroom.

The investigators called in a team from the Home Office Forensic Science Laboratory at Wetherby. It was clear from the beginning that the man who would be at the centre of the scientific investigation would be the man in charge of the serology laboratory, Mr Alfred Faragher.

His problem, of course, was that there was too much blood, most of it – perhaps all of it – from the victims. But on Nicola Laitner's bed, there was one bloodstain that appeared more promising. It looked as if it was at about the knee level of a person lying in bed. And since Nicola Laitner had no cuts on her legs, it was a fair assumption that it came from the killer during the course of his rape. At this point in the investigation, the police had a list of about 200 suspects – men who, because of their criminal records, might well be capable of the crime.

Even by the end of the 1960s, so many new blood group factors had been discovered that the popular press was talking about the 'blood fingerprint'. This was a gross exaggeration, for there was no way of testing a bloodstain to determine which individual it had come from. Yet each new discovery helped to narrow the field: the new M and N factors, the P factor, the Rh and Hr factors. Sometimes, protein analysis of the serum could reveal a factor that was found in only one in a million of the population; others might be found in one in ten. It should be obvious that if a serologist can find the one-in-a-million factor in a blood sample, it can identify a suspect almost as reliably as a fingerprint.

In the case of the bloodstain in Nicola Laitner's bed, Faragher's team discovered a combination of factors that would be found in only one in fifty thousand of the population. And this combination was already familiar to Alf Faragher, since he had already encountered it in the blood of a suspect that had been sent to him for analysis a month earlier. On 28 September, a man named Arthur Hutchinson, a 42-year-old petty-thief, had escaped from the Selby police station by jumping out of a second-storey toilet window and then climbing a 12-foot wall topped with barbed wire. The offence for which Hutchinson had been arrested was not theft but rape. After hiding in the undergrowth of a garden in Selby, he had broken into the house when it was empty, and hidden in the roof space. The house was owned by a 45-year-old saleswoman who had recently come into an inheritance; it had been a newspaper report of this inheritance that gave Hutchinson the idea of robbing and murdering her – he had dug a grave in the undergrowth. During his two days hidden in the house, he had spied on the woman having bondage-sex with a young lover. And when the woman was alone, Hutchinson had walked naked into her bedroom, and raped her repeatedly at knifepoint. As he left her, he warned her not to contact the police; in fact, she telephoned them immediately, and Hutchinson was soon arrested. He had spent a month in custody when he escaped by jumping through the glass of the toilet window. Fortunately, the police had taken a sample of Hutchinson's blood while he was under arrest.

Hutchinson was not known as a violent man, although he had served five and a half years in prison for carrying firearms and threatening his half-brother with a shotgun. Most of his prison sentences had been for minor offences.

Rape is a serious but fairly common crime, so the hunt for 'the Fox'- as Hutchinson was known – had caused little public stir. Nicola Laitner's description of the rapist-killer had led the police to suspect that it could be Hutchinson; but Hutchinson had no record of murderous violence. But Faragher's comparison of the bloodstain found in the bed with a bloodstain from the earlier crime left no doubt that Hutchinson was now a killer; the chances that the murders had been committed by another man with the same fifty-thousand-to-one blood combination were too remote. Televisions all over the country broadcast descriptions and Identikit pictures of Hutchinson, and his description was circulated to all hotels and boarding-houses. Hutchinson had a reputation for being able to live rough in 'foxholes' – hence his nickname; in fact, as reports from boarding-house proprietors showed, he had a preference for comfort. In the 12 days after the Laitner murders, he stayed in York, Scarborough and Manchester. Then he grew alarmed as he read reports that the barbed wire that had torn open his leg had been specially treated, and was likely to turn his leg gangrenous. In fact, the police knew that Hutchinson was inclined to call at hospital out-patients departments for treatment; he was captured in a turnip field on his way to a hospital in Hartlepool.

At the trial, which began on 4 September 1984, Hutchinson's defence consisted of the assertion that he had been invited to the house by Nicola Laitner, whom he had met in a pub with two girlfriends, and that the sex had been with her consent. The real murderer, he said, was Mike Barron, a crime reporter on a Sunday newspaper, who had entered the house after he, Hutchinson, had left. However, the jury also heard that Hutchinson had at first denied ever being in the Laitner's house. But a palmprint found on a champagne bottle found in the marquee left no doubt whatsoever that Hutchinson had been there. A piece of cheese in the refrigerator contained impressions of teeth, and a dental consultant, Geoffrey Craig, gave evidence that these matched impressions of Hutchinson's teeth, taken after his arrest.

It was at this point during the trial that Hutchinson changed his story, and alleged that he had returned to the house in the early hours of the morning – after having had sex with Nicola, with her consent – and found that Nicola had been raped and her family murdered. Nicola, he claimed, had named the killer as Mike Barron. The prosecution had no difficulty in convincing the jury that this version of events, like the previous ones, was a lie. The defence argument that, if Hutchinson had been the murderer, he would not have left Nicola Laitner alive, also failed to convince them. He was found guilty, and sentenced to three terms of life imprisonment, eight years for rape, and five years for aggravated burglary; the judge recommended that he should serve a minimum of 18 years in prison.

11

If the Hutchinson case is one of the most remarkable examples of serological detection, the Backhouse case of the following year is a textbook example of the collaboration of many forensic experts in the solution of a carefully planned murder.

Graham Backhouse had been a successful hairdresser before he made the mistake of turning to farming. By 1984, things were going badly at Widden

Hall Farm, near the village of Horton – about ten miles from Bristol. Two years of crop failures had left Backhouse £70,000 overdrawn at the bank. Moreover, some of his neighbours seemed to regard him with intense dislike. This became apparent on the morning of 30 March 1984, when Backhouse's herdsman discovered a sheep's head impaled on the fence, with a note that read: 'You next.' Backhouse told the local police that this was the latest incident in a campaign of harassment that had been going on for months, with threatening telephone calls and poison-pen letters, one of which accused him of seducing the anonymous writer's sister. This should have given Backhouse some clue to the identity of the writer; the problem was simply that, in the past 20 years or so, the 44-year-old farmer had seduced a great many people's sisters. Even after ten years of marriage, he still had a reputation as the local Don Juan.

On the morning of 9 April 1984, Backhouse asked his wife Margaret if she would drive into town and pick up some antibiotics for the livestock. She climbed into her husband's Volvo – her own car was having starting problems – as the farmer went to the cowshed with the herdsman John Russell. As she turned the key, there was a loud explosion that came from underneath her, and the car filled with smoke. In agony, feeling as if her legs had been blown off, Margaret Backhouse succeeded in pushing open the door and falling out onto the ground. Her husband failed to hear her screams – there was a radio playing in the cowshed – but she was seen from a passing school bus, and rushed to hospital.

Forensic examination of the car revealed how lucky she had been. The bomb had been made from a length of steel pipe, which had been packed with nitro-glycerine and shotgun pellets; the detonator was exploded when the ignition switch was turned. It was virtually a minia-ture sawn-off shotgun, which fired upward through the driver's seat. Fortunately, the bottom of the Volvo had been weak enough to release most of the blast downward; as it was, Margaret Backhouse had lost half a thigh, and had to have thousands of pellets and fragments of shrapnel removed. Soon after she had been removed to hospital, the postman brought another threatening letter. This was passed on to Mike Hall, the Document Examiner at the Birmingham Forensic Laboratory. Hall realized that the handwriting would be practically impossible to identify – the writer had disguised it by 'overwriting' – going backwards and forwards over each letter. But the original 'You next' note was more interesting; on the back of it there was the imprint of some kind of doodle, which had been made on the next sheet of the writing pad; it suggested that the writer had been idly doodling with a ball-point pen while listening on the telephone . . .

Backhouse at first insisted that he had no enemies – at least, no one hated him enough to plant a bomb in his car (for it seemed obvious that the bomb had been intended for him rather than for his wife). On second thoughts, he was able to supply the names of a number of people with whom he had had unsatisfactory business deals or personal relationships. There was, for example, his neighbour Colyn Bedale-Taylor, a carpenter who lived close by; he and Backhouse had quarrelled violently about a right of way. Bedale-Taylor had been severely depressed since the death of his son in a car crash two years before. Another possible suspect was a man who worked in a local quarry, and therefore had access to explosives; Backhouse admitted to having an affair with the man's wife recently. But when the police began to follow up rumours of sexual irregularities in the village, they realized that Backhouse was not the only adulterer; wife-swapping seemed to be the local sport . . .

For nine days after the bombing, Backhouse was given police protection. This was withdrawn after he made an angry telephone call to Detective Chief Inspector Peter Brock, asking him to get his men off Widden Hall Farm. Brock had no alternative than to comply, but he warned Backhouse against taking the law into his own hands – he was aware that Backhouse kept a shotgun in the house. The farm remained connected to an alarm at the local police station.

This alarm sounded on the evening of 30 April 1984. Police who rushed to the farm found Backhouse covered in blood, and a dead man lying in the hall at the bottom of the stairs. Backhouse had knife wounds to the left side of his face, and a deep gash that ran from his left shoulder down across his body.

The dead man was Colyn Bedale-Taylor. Backhouse's story was that Bedale-Taylor had called to enquire about his wife, and he had invited him into the kitchen for a cup of coffee. Then, according to Backhouse, his neighbour had announced that God had sent him. When Backhouse laughed derisively, Bedale-Taylor grew angry, and accused Backhouse of being responsible for the death of his son. Backhouse claimed that Bedale-Taylor admitted planting the bomb, and declared that he would be successful next time. At this point, he pulled out a Stanley knife and slashed Backhouse's face, then his chest. Backhouse fled down the hall, and grabbed a shotgun that was standing on the stairs. As Bedale-Taylor rushed him, he fired two shots into his chest, killing him instantly.

The story sounded convincing enough, and seemed to solve the mystery of the car bomb. And when the police searched Colyn Bedale-Taylor's land, and found the rest of the length of pipe from which the 'bomb' had been sawn, the conclusion seemed doubly certain. Then there was the fact that the Stanley knife found in the dead man's hand had the intials 'B.T.' scratched roughly on its handle. Yet this in itself planted the first seeds of doubt in the minds of the investigators. In Bedale-Taylor's workshop there were other tools with his intials; but these were all neatly engraved – for he was a man of meticulous habits .

Dr Geoff Robinson, the forensic biologist who studied the scene of the crime, had more serious doubts. There was a great deal of blood on the kitchen floor, but the spots were the wrong shape. They were all neat and round, as if they had dripped on to the floor – and furniture – by a man who was standing still. If Backhouse had been fighting for his life, many of the spots would have had 'tails', as if flying. Moreover, Backhouse had no defensive wounds on his hands, which seemed extraordinary in view of his account of the struggle. And when Geoff Robinson noticed that there was no trail of blood down the hallway, although Backhouse claimed that he ran along the hall to escape his assailant, he became almost certain that Backhouse was lying.

The evidence of the forensic pathologist, Dr William Kennard, confirmed that suspicion. Kennard was puzzled by the fact that the Stanley knife was still clutched in the dead man's hand, when it should have been lying on the floor. There was a great deal of blood on Bedale-Taylor's shirt-front – far more than might have been expected. When this blood was tested, Kennard was surprised to discover that by far the larger part of it came from Backhouse. How had it got there in the course of a knife attack in which Backhouse was on the retreat? It looked as if Backhouse had stood over the body and deliberately allowed his blood to drip onto Bedale-Taylor's shirt . . .

All this left the police in little doubt that Backhouse's story was false. He had invited Bedale-Taylor to the house with the intention of murdering him, and after killing him with the shotgun, had then deliberately slashed himself with the Stanley knife. But although the evidence pointed in this direction, it was purely circumstantial. There was not enough to justify Backhouse's arrest.

Geoff Robinson came up with the most interesting clue so far. The envelope that had contained the first threatening letter had been sent to him for a saliva test, to see whether the man who licked the envelope had the same blood group as Backhouse. The letter had been opened with a paper knife, and when Robinson unsealed the flap, he found a tiny clump of wool fibres stuck to the gum. Under a microscope, he could see that they were probably from a woollen sweater, of the type Backhouse usually wore. The police soon obtained samples of wool from sweaters and jerseys in Backhouse's farmhouse. The comparison microscope left no doubt whatsoever that one of these was the sweater that the letter-writer had been wearing as he sealed the envelope.

Now certain they were on the right trail, the police made another search of the farmhouse, with Backhouse watching gloomily. In a drawer of stationery, a detective found a spring-backed notepad. And as he went through it page by page, he suddenly came upon the doodle that had pressed through onto the back of the 'You next' note. Mike Hall, the document examiner, made blow-up photographs of the doodle and the impression; superimposed upon one another, it was obvious that they were identical. It was the final link in the chain of evidence that proved beyond all doubt that Graham Backhouse had written himself the threatening letters, and that this had all been part of a plot to murder his wife.

The motive became clear when it was discovered that, a month before the car bombing, Backhouse had increased the life insurance on his wife from £50,000 to £100,000. The murder plot had failed, and Backhouse had made the supreme mistake of trying to 'close the case' by murdering his neighbour. A century earlier, a detective like Gustave Macé would have been helpless to establish the killer's guilt. In 1984, it took the aid of four forensic scientists – a pathologist, a biologist, a document examiner, and a bomb expert – to establish beyond all doubt that Graham Backhouse had murdered Colyn Bedale-Taylor and had attempted to murder his wife.

On 18 February 1985, Graham Backhouse was found guilty as charged, and sentenced to two terms of life imprisonment.

12

The most important single discovery in the history of serology, DNA fingerprints, was made by Alec Jeffreys, of the University of Leicester, in September 1984; this at last enabled the forensic scientist to pin down the identity of an individual from whom a blood sample had been taken. But before we speak of DNA fingerprinting, it is necessary to summarize some of the more important serological discoveries of the past two or three decades.

During the late 1940s and early 1950s, blood testing not only ceased to advance, but actually seemed to be slipping backwards – we have already considered the sad cautionary tale of the Werner Boost case. This was not the fault of the scientists so much as of the police specialists, who failed to grasp the importance of extreme precision and exactitude; the Uhlenhuth test, for example, could very easily yield mistaken results if the sample was even slightly contaminated. Yet in 1949, the Swedish scientist A. Ouchterlony had discovered a new and far more accurate method of applying the Uhlenhuth test to distinguish human from animal blood. It was he who discovered that gelatine could greatly simplify the process, since it will allow the serum to spread out in a circle around a hole punched in it. He covered a microscope slide with a substance called agar gel, made from seaweed, in which tiny holes had been punched around a central hole. The blood to be tested is placed in the central hole, and the various antisera in the holes around it; the slide is then placed for 24 hours in a moist chamber at 980 Fahrenheit. As the circles start to overlap one another, a horizontal line develops between the central hole and the antiserum of the same type. This not only saves a great deal of work with test tubes and pipettes, but means that a minute trace of blood can be tested. The same discovery – that antigens and antibodies would diffuse through the gel – led to the method known as gel electrophoresis, developed by Culliford, in which protein molecules are separated on an 'electric racetrack'.

Another important discovery involved the 'rhesus factor' identified by Landsteiner and Weiner in 1940. This was discovered to be respon-sible for a percentage of stillborn babies. The rhesus factor is not present in all human beings; those who have it are called rhesus positive (Rh+) and those without it rhesus negative (Rh–). If the father was rhesus positive and the mother rhesus negative, the mother might develop a rhesus antibody, which could kill the baby by destroying its blood cells.

Anti-rhesus serum could reveal the presence of the rhesus factor in the father. But it proved far more difficult to find a way of revealing the presence of anti-rhesus factors in the mother, for it failed to cause 'clumping' in many cases.

The problem was eventually solved – in a typically roundabout way – by the Cambridge immunologist R. R. A. Coombs in 1945. The trouble, it seemed, was that instead of 'clumping' red blood cells, the anti-rhesus factors only coated them. The anti-rhesus factors consisted of proteins known as globulins (present, for example, in haemoglobin). The problem was to make the globulin visible. What Coombs and his colleagues did was to inject human globulin into rabbits, thus producing a serum that was anti-human globulin. Now let us suppose that the problem is to discover whether a wife who had produced a stillborn baby has anti-rhesus factors in her blood. The Coombs anti-globulin serum is added to a sample of the husband's rhesus positive blood, mixed with some of his wife's blood serum. If anti-rhesus factors had coated the husband's blood cells, the result is clumping as the anti-globulin serum attacks the globulin-coated cells.

But the process is not quite as straightforward as it sounds. It is not enough to add the Coombs serum to a mixture of the husband's blood and the wife's serum, for the mixture will contain other globulins which will clump, spoiling the whole experiment. It is necessary to separate out the 'coated' blood cells, and to add these alone to the Coombs serum; this is done by washing them in saline solution to remove all traces of the wife's serum. Like so many processes in modern serology, the Coombs test is a 'fiddly' job. Yet its sensitivity made it invaluable. Moreover, it could also be adapted to the same purpose as the Uhlenhuth test. If a very small quantity of Coombs serum is contaminated with human protein, it fails to clump when anti-rhesus serum is added because its antibodies have already absorbed the human protein. So if a suspect bloodstain is added to a tiny quantity of Coombs serum, then anti-rhesus serum is added, it will instantly identify the serum as animal – by clumping – or as human – by not clumping. But again, it is an extremely 'fiddly' process. Ouchterlony's gel method came as an immense relief to serologists, who could simplify the test by dropping tiny quantities of their sera into holes in the gel, and waiting for the 'lines' to appear.

But perhaps the most important single discovery of this post-war period was a simple and reliable way of testing old bloodstains; it was invented by Stuart S. Kind, of the Home Office Forensic Laboratory at Harrogate, and was christened the absorption elution test. This came to replace the complicated Holzer method, using 'dimpled slides', and which depended on finding out the exact amount of antibody that had been absorbed.

To simplify this explanation, let us think of the antigens in the blood cells as Yale locks, and the antibodies in the serum as Yale keys. Clumping occurs when keys combine with locks. The problem with old bloodstains is that some keys lose their strength sooner than others, so type O, with withered B keys and normal A keys would react like type A. But the 'locks' in the blood cells retain their strength. So if locks from an old bloodstain are added to fresh serum, they will absorb some of its keys. And if the serum can be tested to find how many keys it has lost, then we shall know what type of lock the old bloodstain had. But

Hoizer's method, using a microscope slide with eight 'dimples', was long and complicated.

In the 1920s, a colleague of Lattes named Syracusa saw another possible solution. If the antiserum, with its keys, is added to an old bloodstain, with its locks, some of the keys will combine with locks. Holzer's method was to try to *count* the number of keys combined with locks. Syracusa wondered whether it might not be possible to 'discombine' the keys from the locks by heating them gently. He would then have a solution containing the original locks from the bloodstain, and the discombined (or 'eluted') keys from his new lot of test serum. How could he go about testing these keys to find out whether they are A or B? Simple. Merely add fresh A and B cells to the liquid, and see if clumping takes place. If the A cells clump, then the keys were A, and the old bloodstain was A. If B cells clump, then it was B. It is obviously a highly ingenious method, which takes advantage of the fact that keys decay quicker than locks, and tests the stain by fitting it out with new keys.

Where Syracusa went wrong was in not being very clear about what to do with his solution full of newly discombined keys. He felt he ought to drain off the liquid containing the keys before he tried testing it with new cells. But during this complicated process the temperature inevitably dropped, and his keys recombined with the locks, aborting the whole process. So Syracusa finally decided his idea was unworkable.

Kind knew nothing about Syracusa's failure, and in what he calls a 'state of original ignorance', he decided not to bother with separating-off the liquid containing the keys. Instead, he divided the liquid – still containing the bloodstain – into two, and put A test cells in one lot and B test cells in the other. The result was that when the temperature was lowered, one of his samples would clump, revealing whether the original bloodstain was type A or B.

Why did this simple method work? Because although some of the keys recombined with locks from the original bloodstain as soon as the temperature was lowered, most of them would combine with locks from the new blood cells. To understand why this is so, we have to stop thinking about keys and locks for a moment, and recognize that what actually happens is that the antibody in the serum combines with the antigen on the surface of the blood cell. New blood cells have more surface than old ones, as a fresh pea has more surface than a dried one. So Kind's marvellously simple method worked, and saved the endless lengthy process of trying to count the keys on a dimpled slide. Kind's 'absorption-elution' test is now the standard way of testing old bloodstains in all forensic laboratories.

For a brief period, it had a rival in a process known as the 'mixed agglutination' method. This depended on a curious discovery first made by Wiener in the late 1930s, and rediscovered by Coombs in the mid-1950s: that even when a key is combined with a lock, it still had a certain capacity to form a link with another lock – as if the key had two identical ends, so to speak. Coombs discovered that skin cells have blood group characteristics – they are, in effect, small locks. And if serum is added – anti-A or anti-B – they unite with the keys in the serum. Yet if the correct blood cells are added, clumping still occurs – as if, so to speak, the serum had two hands, and could hang on to the skin cell *and* the blood cell. Now obviously, this ought to be the simplest method of all, since it cuts out the intermediate step of 'discombining' the locks and keys by heating them. Unfortunately the method proved to be unreliable. In his *Crime and Science,* Jürgen Thorwald remarks that 'by August 1962 the mixed agglutination test was well on its way to acceptance by all the serological laboratories of the world'. In fact, the test has now been dropped by most laboratories, and replaced by Kind's absorption elution test – so that, for example, it was the Kind test that Faragher used to determine the ABO characteristics of the bloodstains found in Nicola Laitner's bed.

Yet in spite of these remarkable advances, the ultimate goal, the 'blood fingerprint', continued to elude the scientists. And in 1984, Dr Alec Jeffreys, of the University of Leicester, made the discovery superfluous when he stumbled upon a completely new method of 'typing' an individual: the DNA fingerprint.

For readers whose knowledge of biology is minimal, an account of DNA fingerprinting should begin with the explanation that each individual is made up of about 100 million million cells, each of which consists of protein surrounding a nucleus; the latter is made of a substance called nucleic acid. In 1911, the biochemist P. A. T. Levene discovered that there are two types of nucleic acid, known as RNA and DNA, according to whether they contain a sugar called ribose or deoxyribose. Unfortunately, the cell nucleus was transparent, so it was hard to tell what was going on inside it, until someone discovered a method of staining it with dye. This showed that when cells divide into two – which is how they reproduce – the nucleus turns into a number of thread-like objects called chromosomes. There are 46 in all, 23 contributed by the father's sperm, 23 by the mother's egg. And the staining process revealed that the chromosomes appeared to be largely made up of DNA. In the 1940s, it became clear that DNA is the 'transforming principle' in living things – the material which carries genetic information, and which determines whether you are born with red or black hair, an aquiline or snub nose, brown or blue eyes.

But if the DNA gives all these orders, how does it transmit them? The answer was, obviously, by means of a code – which could be compared to those plastic biscuits with notches along their edges, which housewives sometimes used for 'programming' their washing machines. The DNA code, as everyone knows, was finally solved by Watson and Crick in the early 1950s; they showed that the DNA molecule has a thread-like structure, and looks like two interlocked spirals – the double helix – held together by pairings of chemical building blocks as a ladder is held together by its rungs. The building blocks are four bases called adenine, guanine, cytosine, and thymine, and these are strung together in apparently meaningless permutations, such as ATTGGGTTCCC, and so on. This order of the bases determines the characteristics of a human being as the order of the notes of the scale determines a symphony. When the cell splits into two, the two spirals come apart, and each one attracts to itself various molecules – of adenine, guanine, etc. – that make it a duplicate of the original helix. This is the basic mechanism of the genetic code, and it explains why a human female gives birth to a human baby and not, say, to a dog or cat.

Now, obviously, long sections of this DNA (which is about three feet long) remain the same from person to person – since we all have heads, limbs and so on. But in 1980, it was discovered that there are stretches where the code differs dramatically in each individual – except identical twins, whose genetic material is identical. They were labelled 'hypervariable regions', and were found to consist of short sequences of bases repeated over and over again like a stutter. The next question was to find out whether there was any molecular motif shared by these hyperactive regions. A simple analogy might help to make this clear. Imagine a Martian astronomer examining some newly built town on earth through a powerful telescope. He sees that it seems to consist of more-or-less identical straight roads with identical houses on either side. But every few streets he notices a church, which looks quite different from all the other buildings. The churches are of many different designs, and his problem is to study them through his telescope and see if he can find some basic building-block which is the same in all the churches . . .

Jeffreys made his discovery in 1984, when he was studying genes coding for myoglobin proteins, which carry oxygen in the muscles. He discovered a kind of basic building-block made of repeated sequences within the DNA, each 10 or 15 bases long.

Next he isolated two of these 'blocks', and cloned them – that is, mass-produced them. The blocks – or genetic markers – were then made radioactive. Jeffreys wanted to see if he could use them as 'probes' to detect hypervariable regions in other genetic material. (The blocks will tend to home-in on other blocks like themselves, like birds of a kind flocking together, and then wave a radioactive flag.) Jeffreys next obtained genetic material from members of a family, and set out to see whether his method could discover the relationships. The 'fingerprints' of the hypervariable regions appear as dark bands on an X-ray film, so they look like long columns with a couple of black stripes of lines spread out against a white background. By placing the columns from parents and children side by side, Jeffreys was able to see that all the bands of the children derive from the mother or father, and that the same applies to the parents and to their parents.

There was great excitement in Jeffreys's laboratory when this discovery was made. It was obvious, for example, that it could resolve the majority of paternity cases – to which all books on blood grouping devote a section. Blood factors can help to determine whether a certain man could or could not be the father of a certain child, but they cannot state beyond all doubt that it *has* to be a certain individual. Jeffreys's new method was almost as precise as a fingerprint. In one of his early cases, a Ghanaian boy who was born in Britain had returned to Ghana to rejoin his father. When he wanted to come back to Britain, the immigration authorities disputed whether he was the woman's son. The father was in Ghana, so he was not available for tests. But Jeffreys was able to get genetic material – from white blood cells – from the mother and three undisputed children. (Red blood cells have no nucleus, and so are not suitable for genetic fingerprinting.)

The process begins by separating the DNA from the proteins that surround the nucleus. Then the DNA is chopped up into a kind of genetic confetti with the use of an enzyme – a catalyst material (of which the digestive juices are an example) – and sorted into various sizes on the 'electric racetrack' of gel electrophoresis, which separates them into bands. The bands are then stuck to a nylon membrane, and the radioactive 'probes' added. All that remains is to place a radio-active-sensitive film over the membrane. The bands show where the probe has combined specifically with the 'highly variable' DNA.

When this method was applied to the Ghanaian family, the boy's 'autoradiograph' showed bands that were either present in the mother, or as paternal characteristics in the undisputed children: in short, it revealed unmistakably that the children all had the same mother and father. The Home Office was forced to admit that the boy had a right to enter Britain.

Soon after Jeffreys's discovery, his small daughter Sarah fell down in the playground at school and cut her face. Jeffreys was forced to cancel a lecture he had scheduled on his new technique to take her to hospital. The accident proved to be a remarkable piece of luck. If Jeffreys had given the lecture, the resulting public disclosure would have made it impossible to patent his process. As it was, it was licensed to ICI, and has proceeded to generate a considerable revenue, which Jeffreys has poured back into basic research. (ICI charge for each test performed, each one of which takes about three weeks and costs – at the time of writing – about £120.)

The new technique revealed its value as a tool of forensic science in a rape case that came to trial in November 1987. In January of that year a man broke into a house in Avonmouth, Bristol, where a 45-year-old disabled woman lived alone. After robbing her of jewellery, he raped her. Some time later, a labourer named Robert Melias was arrested for burglary; and was identified by the woman as the rapist. A year earlier, his defence might have argued mistaken identity. But when the semen stains from the woman's petticoat were sent to the Home Office Forensic Research Establishment at Aldermaston, Dr D. J. Werrett was able to compare them with Melias's own genetic material and show the DNA fingerprint to be identical. The chances of someone else having the same 'fingerprint' were about four million to one – rather shorter odds than in the case of real fingerprints, but still 80 times greater than in the case of the 'blood fingerprint' that convicted Arthur Hutchinson of the murder of the Laitners. On 13 November 1987, Melias was sentenced to eight years for rape and five years for burglary.

The case that excited nation-wide attention was heard in the following January. It had begun more than four years earlier, in November 1983, when a 15-year-old schoolgirl named Lynda Mann set out from her home in Narborough, near Leicester, to visit a friend in nearby Enderby. She took a short cut through a footpath known as the

Black Pad. The next morning her body was found lying near the footpath; she had been strangled with her own scarf and raped. A lengthy police investigation led nowhere but – as usual in such cases – the rapist's semen stains were preserved.

Three years later, in July 1986, another 15-year-old schoolgirl, Dawn Ashworth, who lived in Enderby, failed to return from the house of a friend. It was three days before her body was found near another footpath, less than a mile from where Lynda Mann's body had been discovered. She had been battered to death and brutally raped; multiple injuries to her head, face and genitals showed how violently she had resisted her attacker. A 17-year-old youth named Richard Buckland had been seen close to the murder site, and he was arrested and charged with the killing of Dawn Ashworth. But the police decided to check Buckland's DNA fingerprint at the University of Leicester, and Jeffreys was asked to undertake the task. His tests showed conclusively that Buckland could not be the rapist, and this was confirmed by the Aldermaston laboratory. So four months into their investigation, the police had to begin all over again.

It seemed probable that the rapist came from the small area surrounding Enderby and Narborough, and including the village of Littlethorpe. The police decided to invite all the young males in this area to give blood samples. It was an immense task for the Aldermaston forensic team, involving 5,000 analyses. It was only possible to process such a large number by eliminating a large proportion of blood samples through conventional genetic markers, and then processing many others in parallel. (Most of the three weeks is spent waiting for the reaction to reach completion and X-ray films to develop.) The result was disappointing; although every young male in the area had volunteered a blood sample, the screening still failed to turn up the rapist's 'fingerprint'.

The testing was still going on when the police heard of a promising lead. A man having a lunchtime drink in a Leicester pub had boasted to a companion that he had 'helped out' a friend by offering the police his own blood sample in place of that of his friend, who lived in Littlethorpe. The drinking companion reported the conversation to the police. A 23-year-old bakery assistant, Ian Kelly, was questioned, and admitted that he had acted as a 'stand-in' for his friend and fellow worker Colin Pitchfork. A check with police records revealed that Pitchfork, of Haybarn Close, Littlethorpe, had a number of convictions for indecent exposure. According to Ian Kelly, when the police had asked for blood samples, Pitchfork had begged several workmates to impersonate him, explaining that, with his record for 'flashing', he was afraid the police might 'fix him up'. He offered one man £50, and another £200. Kelly was finally persuaded to forge Pitchfork's passport and his signature, and to learn details of his family background by heart. The deception was successful; Kelly – who lived in Leicester – identified himself as Colin Pitchfork, and gave a blood sample.

Pitchfork was arrested, and a blood sample was sent to the Home Office laboratory; his 'bar code' proved to be identical with that of the rapist. But by the time this was confirmed, Pitchfork had already admitted both murders. On both occasions he had been out looking for a girl to whom he could expose himself. On both occasions, the realization that the girl was alone and that there were no witnesses led to murder and rape. In the case of Lynda Mann he had taken his wife to night school, and committed the murder before picking her up again.

On 22 January 1987, Pitchfork pleaded guilty to both murders at Leicester Crown Court, and was sentenced to life imprisonment. His 'stand-in' was given an 18-month suspended sentence.

13

On 9 May 1986 – two months before the murder of Dawn Ashworth – Nancy Hodge, a 27-year-old computer operator from Disney World, returned home late to her apartment in Orlando, Florida. She was removing her contact lenses in the bathroom when she heard a noise, and found a man standing behind her in the bathroom doorway. She was able to see his face before she was pushed to the floor, beaten, and threatened with a knife. The man covered her face and raped her three times. Then he took her handbag and left.

It was the first of a series of break-ins and rapes – or attempted rapes; there were another 23 during the remainder of 1986. But now the rapist took care not to allow the victims to see his face, covering the woman's head with a sheet or blanket beforehand. One of his odder habits was to turn on the light several times during the attacks, presumably for visual stimulation. Another was to study the victim's driver's licence, occasionally taking it away with him. On 22 February 1987, he broke into the home of a 27-year-old woman during the early hours of the morning, and raped her repeatedly, beating her and cutting her with a knife. Because her two children were asleep in the next room, she was afraid to make a noise. The man wrapped a sleeping-bag around her head to prevent her from seeing his face; but he was careless enough to leave behind two fingerprints on the window screen.

A police team studied the patterns of the rapes, and staked out the neighbourhoods where he was most likely to strike. In the early hours of 1 March 1987, a woman rang the police to report a prowler on Candlewick Street. A patrol car containing members of the surveillance team was there within minutes, and saw a blue car speeding away. They gave chase, and after two miles, the car – a 1979 Ford Granada – turned a corner too fast and crashed into a telegraph pole. The driver proved to be a 24-year-old named Tommie Lee Andrews, who worked at a local pharmaceutical warehouse, and lived three miles from the scene of the original rape.

The next morning, at a photo line-up, Nancy Hodge immediately identified him as the man who had raped her. Andrews was charged with the attack, and with the rape of the young mother a week earlier.

Yet in spite of the victim's identification, the case was far from watertight. Nancy Hodges had only glimpsed him for a few seconds, and she could have been mistaken. None of the other victims had seen his face. The fingerprints left on the window screen proved that Andrews was the burglar who had raped the young mother, but this case would be tried separately. A sample of the accused man's blood was compared with semen taken from the victims, but the result was inconclusive; the result fitted Andrews, but it also fitted 30 per cent of American males.

In August 1987, the Prosecutor and Assistant State Attorney, Tim Berry, heard about the Pitchfork case in England, and about the new technique of DNA fingerprinting. The attorney who described the case also mentioned that he had seen an advertisement for a DNA testing service called Lifecodes, with a laboratory at Valhalla, New York. Berry rang Lifecodes, spoke to its forensic director Michael Baird, and agreed to send him the samples of the rapist's semen and blood samples from the accused man. The tests were carried out by Dr Alan Giusti. And when the X-ray film was finally ready, in early October, it showed beyond all doubt that the blood and the semen came from the same man; their 'bar codes' were identical.

Now the only problem was to convince the jury that a technique as new as DNA fingerprinting was trustworthy. At a pre-trial hearing, the judge agreed that the DNA evidence was admissible. And on 27 October 1987, Tommie Andrews stood trial on a charge of raping

Nancy Hodge. She went into the box and identified Andrews as the man who had attacked her. Andrews's defence was that he had spent that whole evening at home, and this was supported by his girlfriend and his sister. But when the prosecutor was challenged to justify his assertion that the DNA evidence revealed that there was only one chance in 10 billion that Andrews was wrongly accused, he was caught unprepared; rather than venture into a specialized field beyond his competence, he withdrew the figure. This may have been one reason why the jury was split, and declared themselves unable to reach a verdict. The judge was obliged to declare a mistrial.

Two weeks later, Andrews stood trial on the second rape charge. This time, the prosecution made sure that the statistics were correct, and were ready for any challenge. Moreover, the case was bolstered by the two fingerprints found on the window screen, which were undoubtedly made by the accused. This time the verdict was guilty, and Andrews received a sentence of 22 years, the first man in the United States to be convicted by a DNA fingerprint.

At the retrial of the Nancy Hodge case in February 1988, the DNA fingerprint evidence again played a central role. Once again, Andrews insisted that he had been at home that night, and his evidence was backed by his sister and girlfriend. This time, there was no supporting prosecution evidence, except the victim's insistence that she recognized her assailant. Everything turned on the DNA evidence. The defence attempted to challenge it by arguing that not all the DNA molecule had been analysed, only its hypervariable regions. Baird explained at some length that there would be no point whatever in analysing the rest of the molecule, which contains human characteristics to be found in all of us – only the regions that differ. This time, the jury was convinced; after a 90-minute absence, they announced a verdict of guilty. Tommie Lee Andrews received a further 78-year sentence for rape, 22 years for burglary and 15 for battery, bringing his total sentence to over 100 years.

In the spring of 1989, two more British cases demonstrated the value of genetic fingerprinting as a 'last resort' when all other resources of scientific crime detection had failed.

Between 1982 and 1988, a series of rapes occurred in London's Notting Hill area. All the victims were single women, living alone in basement or ground floor flats around a communal garden. In most cases the rapist broke in through French windows, and was waiting for the girl when she returned from work. She would be seized from behind as she entered the flat, and the intruder would assure her that he was a burglar and had no intention of harming her. Then, just before leaving, he would rape her.

On two occasions the police came close to catching the rapist, but he tore himself free and escaped. And when a 32-year-old ex-paratrooper named Tony Maclean was caught in the communal garden with anti-crime paint from the fences on his hands, he was released because of an error in the police records; the blood group of the rapist (determined from his semen) had been wrongly entered on the computer. Finally, a semen sample taken from a rape victim was sent to Alec Jeffreys in Leicester, and its genetic fingerprint determined. Meanwhile, a Notting Hill policeman, PC Graham Hamilton, had become increasingly convinced that Maclean was the rapist, and Maclean was asked for a second blood sample. Aware that the previous sample had eliminated him, Maclean agreed. But the genetic fingerprint of the new sample proved to be identical with that of the rapist's sperm – the chance of error was 2,750,000 to 1 – with the result that, on 13 April 1989, Maclean received three life sentences for rape.

Even more remarkable was a case in which a man was convicted of murder although the police were unable to produce the body of the victim. On 9 February 1988, Helen McCourt, a 22-year-old computer operator, vanished during the 300-yard walk from the bus stop to her home in Billinge, Merseyside. Ian Simms, the landlord of the local pub, the George and Dragon, came under suspicion when his name was found in Helen's diary. Three weeks later, her clothes were found in a plastic bin liner. And on a slag heap three miles away, police found bloodstained male clothing that proved to belong to Simms. But without Helen's body, the blood could not be proved to be hers. Then a forensic scientist, Dr John Moore, saw the solution: that even though Helen was missing, blood samples from her parents could establish whether the blood on Simms's clothing was hers. Their genetic fingerprints established this beyond all doubt, and it was largely on this evidence that, on 14 March 1989, Simms was sentenced to life imprisonment. It was a historic legal precedent: the first murder conviction to be achieved with genetic fingerprints 'by proxy'.

6

Every Bullet Has a Fingerprint

1

On 1 December 1882, the cobbled, gaslit streets of east London were wrapped in choking fog as a young constable set out from Dalston police station on a beat that took him down a narrow thoroughfare called Ashwin Street. As he turned the corner, he came to a sudden halt as he saw a man placing a lantern on top of the wall outside the Baptist chapel, and beginning to scramble over. PC Cole took a swift step forward, laid his hand on the man's shoulder, and asked: 'What do you think you're doing?' For a moment, the man – who seemed little more than a youth – looked as if he was going to resist; then he changed his mind and agreed to 'go quietly'. But PC Cole and his captive had only gone as far as the pub on the corner when the man broke loose and ran. Cole ran after him and grabbed him by the left arm; as he did so, the man reached into his pocket, pulled out a revolver, and fired three shots. A woman who was walking towards them screamed and fled; as she ran, she heard another shot. Moments later, she encountered two policeman in Dalston Lane, and led them back to the scene of the shooting. PC Cole was lying on the pavement outside the Baptist chapel, his head in the gutter; a trickle of blood ran from the bullet hole behind his left ear. He died five minutes after being admitted to the local German Hospital.

Inspector Glass, who took charge of the case, ordered a search of the area where the policeman had been found; on the wall of the Baptist chapel, the burglar had left his dark lantern; behind the railings, a chisel, a jemmy and a wooden wedge had been left on the ground. The only other clue was a black billycock hat, which the burglar had lost in the course of the struggle. The woman who had seen him running away described him as short and slightly built; another witness gave the same description.

There was one man in the Dalston police station who believed he knew the identity of the murderer. Only minutes before Cole had arrested the burglar, Police Sergeant Cobb had been walking along Ashwin Street with another sergeant, Branwell, when they had noticed a man standing under a streetlamp. Cobb recognized him as a young cabinetmaker named Tom Orrock, and when he saw the policeman, he looked furtive and uncomfortable. Orrock had no criminal record, but he kept bad company – thugs and professional criminals – and it seemed a reasonable assumption that he would one day try his hand at crime. As they passed Orrock that night, Cobb had been tempted to arrest him for loitering. But standing under a streetlamp was no crime, and Cobb had decided against it. Now he regretted it, and was inclined to blame himself for the death of PC Cole, who was a young married man with children.

Informed of Sergeant Cobb's suspicions, Inspector Glass was inclined to be dismissive – to begin with, he disliked Cobb, regarding him as too unimaginative and too conscientious. But he ordered Tom Orrock – who was 19 – to be brought in for an identity parade. When the witnesses who had glimpsed Cole's captive failed to identify him, Orrock was released. Soon after that, he disappeared from his usual haunts.

Months after the murder, the investigation was at a standstill. The clues seemed to lead nowhere. The hat bore no marks of identification, and the chisels and the large wooden wedge might have belonged to anybody. But the bullets looked more promising. All four had been recovered – two from the policeman's skull, one from his truncheon, another from the truncheon case. They were unusual in that they had been fired from a revolver that was little more than a toy – the kind of thing ladies sometimes carried in their handbags. The science of ballistics was unknown in 1882, but the rarity of a gun suggested that it might one day provide a valuable piece of evidence.

When studied through a magnifying glass, one of the chisels also yielded an interesting clue. A series of scratches near the handle looked like an attempt at writing, probably with a sharp nail. And when the chisel was photographed for the case file, the letters could be seen more clearly, and they resolved themselves into a capital R, followed by what looked like an o, a c, and a k. Rock. Could it be short for Orrock? Cobb began calling in every tool shop in the Hackney and Daiston area, asking if they recognized the chisels, but met with no success.

Cobb refused to give up. A year after the murder, he was talking with an acquaintance of the missing cabinetmaker named Henry Mortimer, who occasionally acted as a police informer. And Mortimer's rambling discourse suddenly arrested the sergeant's attention when he mentioned that Tom Orrock had possessed a revolver – a nickel-plated, pin-fire miniature affair. Orrock had seen it advertised in the *Exchange and Mart,* and he and Mortimer had gone to Tottenham to purchase it from the owner for the sum of half a guinea. They had also been accompanied by two men named Miles and Evans, both professional – if unsuccessful – criminals. On the way home, the four men had stopped on Tottenham Marshes and used a tree for target practice. At Cobb's request, Mortimer accompanied him to Tottenham and showed him the tree. The following day, Cobb returned alone, and dug some bullets out of the tree with his penknife. One of them was relatively undamaged, and was obviously of the same calibre as the bullets that had been fired at PC Cole.

Now Cobb was sure he had his man, and that view was confirmed when Mortimer admitted that Orrock had virtually confessed to killing PC Cole. When Mortimer had expressed disbelief, Orrock had replied: 'If they can prove it against me, I'm willing to take the consequences.' This is precisely what Cobb now set out to do.

The first step was to lay the new evidence before his immediate superior. Inspector Glass was still inclined to be indifferent, but he agreed to ask for help from New Scotland Yard in trying to trace the shop that had sold the chisel. And it was the Scotland Yard team that finally located a woman named Preston, a widow who carried on her husband's tool-sharpening business. She recognized the chisel because she always made a practice of scratching the name of the owner near the handle; she remembered the young man who brought in the chisel for grinding had given the name Orrock, which she had shortened to 'Rock'.

Now at last, they had the kind of evidence that might impress a jury. All that remained was to locate Tom Orrock. Scotland Yard was asked to circulate his description to every police station in the country. This would normally have brought prompt results, for in those days before the population explosion, most police stations were aware of any strangers who had moved into their district. So when another year failed to bring news of the wanted man, Glass was inclined to assume either that he was dead or that he had gone abroad. Cobb refused to believe it. And one day he had an inspiration. One place where a man could 'lie low' with reasonable chance of escaping recognition was prison. Once again, Cobb began painstaking enquiries – enquiries that entitle him to be ranked with Canler and Macé as a distinguished practitioner of the needle-in-the-haystack method. And he soon learned that a man answering Orrock's description had been serving a term for burglary in Coldbath Fields for the past two years. Coldbath Fields, in Farringdon Road, was one of London's newer prisons, and had a reputation for severity. The name under which the prisoner was serving his sentence was not Tom Orrock, and when he was summoned to the governor's office, the man denied that he was called Orrock or had ever been in Dalston. Sergeant Cobb attended an identity parade, and had to admit reluctantly that he was unable to recognize Orrock among the seven uniformed convicts who now faced him. But as the men filed out again, they passed under a light, and Cobb suddenly recognized the profile of the man he had last seen standing under a gaslamp in Dalston more that two years earlier. He stepped forward and laid his hand on the shoulder of Thomas Henry Orrock.

Now it was a question of building up the web of circumstantial evidence. Orrock's sister, Mrs Bere, was questioned, and admitted that on the night of the murder her brother had returned home with a torn trouser leg, and without his hat, claiming that he had been involved in a street brawl. Orrock's two friends Miles and Evans were questioned separately. They admitted that they had spent the day of the murder drinking with Tom Orrock in various pubs, and that soon after 10 o'clock in the evening, the three had been in the Railway Tavern in Ashwin Street when Orrock boasted that he intended to embark on a criminal career by 'cracking a crib' – stealing the silver plate of the Baptist church, which he attended regularly, and taking it to his brother-in-law to be melted down. Orrock had then left the pub. Not long after, Miles and Evans heard the sound of revolver shots, but claimed they had taken them for fog signals. All the same, they had left the pub and been among the crowd that gathered around the wounded policeman. Three weeks later, when a reward of £200 had been offered for information leading to the capture of the murderer, Orrock went to Evans and begged him not to inform on him; Evans swore that he would not 'ruck' on a comrade even for a thousand pounds.

But all this was merely hearsay evidence. The vital link between Tom Orrock and the murder of PC Cole was the revolver. This had disappeared – one witness said that Orrock admitted throwing it into the River Lea. But the police were able to track down the man who had sold Orrock the revolver – his name was McLellan – and he unhesitatingly identified bullets and cartridge cases as being the calibre of those he had sold to a young man in the last week of November 1882, one week before the murder. McLellan's description of the purchaser fitted Thomas Henry Orrock.

A few decades later, all this corroborative evidence would have been unnecessary. Examination of the bullets under a comparison microscope would have proved that the bullet found in the tree at Tottenham was identical with the bullet that killed PC Cole.

But in the year 1884, no one had yet thought of studying the pattern of rifle marks on the side of a bullet; it would be another five years before Edmond Locard's mentor, Professor Alexandre Lacassagne, would provide the evidence to convict a murderer by studying bullet grooves under a microscope. Nevertheless, when Tom Orrock came to trial in September 1884, it was the bullet evidence that carried most weight with the jury. The bullet found in the tree at Tottenham was 'precisely similar to the one found in the brain of the dead constable', said the prosecution. 'If the prisoner purchased the revolver, where was it? A man did not throw away a revolver that cost him 10 shillings without good cause.' The jury was convinced. On Saturday 20 September 1884, Thomas Orrock was convicted of the murder of PC Cole and sentenced to be hanged. The jury added a special recommendation to Sergeant Cobb for his persistence in tracking down the killer. But the chronicler relates that, in after years, Inspector Glass liked to claim credit for capturing Orrock, and 'has often remarked that the man who in reality put the police in possession of their information to this day is ignorant that he disclosed to them this knowledge' – from which it would appear that Glass continued to resent the success of his subordinate and to deny him any of the credit.

2

The discovery of gunpowder – in China, around AD 1000 – changed the history of the world, and some two centuries later, the Chinese firecracker was converted by some Arab inventor into the first hand-gun. At the time when Sir Thomas Malory was immortalizing King Arthur and his knights, the knight in armour had become obsolete, for a well-aimed bullet could penetrate his armour as if it were cardboard. But compared with poison, hand-guns were such an expensive and noisy way of despatching an enemy that it was many centuries before they began to represent a problem for law-enforcement officers.

In Shakespeare's England, the use of guns was confined largely to wealthy sportsman. But the wars of the seventeenth century taught the working classes how to fire a pistol, and the result was a sudden rise of the 'highwayman' around the middle of the century.

These early pistols were loaded by pouring gunpowder down the barrel, followed by the lead ball, then a paper wad to keep the charge in place; finally, a ramrod was pushed down the barrel to tamp it down. The pistol was 'primed' by pouring powder into a pan at the rear of the barrel; in the centre of this was the 'touch hole'. The powder was then ignited by touching it with a match (in fact, a piece of string soaked in saltpetre), or by sparks from a fragment of flint or pyrites. Such pistols were, of course, capable of firing only one bullet. An eighteenth-century chronicler tells the story of a tailor who was crossing Hounslow Heath – notorious resort of highwaymen – when he was ordered to stand and deliver. After handing over his purse, the tailor asked the highwayman a favour. 'Would you mind firing your pistols through my hat, to make it look as if I put up some sort of resistance?' The highwayman obliged, whereupon the tailor drew a small pistol from his own pocket and took back his purse.

Muzzle-loading was inefficient and inconvenient; without a paper wad, the bullet could easily fall out. In the mid-eighteenth century, a manufacturer of sporting guns realized that it would be simpler to place a hinge between the barrel and the stock, so the gun could be 'broken' in the middle. The bullet and the powder could then be inserted in the end of the barrel thus exposed – the breech – saving both time and labour. And since the bullet no longer had to be rammed down the whole length of the barrel, it was possible to design bullets that were a more exact fit – the older models were often so loose that the exploding gases could pass around them and so lose half their force.

The earliest known case of forensic ballistics occurred in 1794. A man called Edward Culshaw was shot through the head at Prescot, in Lancashire, and the surgeon who examined the body found a wad of paper in the wound; this proved to contain an extract from a street ballad. Suspicion fell on an 18-year-old youth named John Toms, and when the rest of the ballad was found in his coat pocket, he was charged with murder, and sentenced to death at Lancaster Assizes on 23 March 1794.

In 1860, a paper wad led to the conviction of a murderer named

Richardson, who killed a policeman with a double-barrelled pistol. As a wad he had used a piece torn from a six-year-old copy of *The Times*. The wad was found beside the body. Richardson was taken into custody, and in the unfired barrel of the pistol, the police found another paper wad. The problem was to prove both pieces of newspaper came from the same issue, and it was solved only by appealing to the editor of *The Times,* who was able to show that they both came from the same issue of 27 March 1854. Richardson was convicted of the murder and hanged.

As late as 1891, a French *crime passionnel* was solved in the same way. Charles Guesner had been married for only a few months when, on 29 July 1891, a man broke into the bedroom where he and his wife lay asleep, and shot Guesner in the face. Mme Guesner fainted when she found her husband was dead, and the killer made his escape. The motive was puzzling, for Guesner seemed to have no enemies. The only clue was the pistol wad, a page from the *Lorraine Almanach*. Before her marriage, Mme Guesner had been courted by a man named Bivert. His room was searched, and the police found the almanac with the missing page. Bivert was found guilty and sentenced to 20 years' hard labour.

We have already noted that Bow Street Runner Henry Goddard probably deserves the credit for being the first man to employ forensic ballistics when, in 1835, he exposed a butler who had faked a burglary (see p. 30). In America, the first case to be solved by ballistics occurred three years later; William Stewart of Baltimore murdered his father in order to inherit his fortune, and tried to disguise the dead man's identity by smashing his face with a hatchet. But the pistol balls were identified by their manufacturer as being specially made for William Stewart's pistol, and Stewart was sentenced to life imprisonment. In 1869, a French expert, M. Roussin, solved a murder by the chemical analysis of the bullet. The victim was the *curé* of Bretigny, who was shot through the head by an unknown assassin. Suspicion fell on a watch-maker named Cadet, who was a man of bad character who had reason to detest the *curé*. But the bullets in the *curé* 's head had shattered into fragments by the impact, so could not be compared with the bullets found in Cadet's room, nor could their calibre be compared with those of two pistols found there. M. Roussin established the melting point of the fragments, their precise weight, and their exact chemical composition in terms of tin and lead, and showed that they were identical to the balls found in Cadet's room; as a result, Cadet was found guilty.

But by that time, the old-fashioned one-shot pistol had been long superseded by a new type of gun called the revolver, because it had a revolving chamber of bullets. Revolvers had been invented in the eighteenth century, but they were expensive and unreliable, for they still depended upon the old method of powder and flint; consequently they remained a rarity. Around 1820, someone invented the percussion cap – a metal cap that exploded when struck with a hammer – and it ceased to be necessary to rely on loose powder. Ten years later, a 16-year-old youth named Samuel Colt ran away from his home in Hartford, Connecticut to become a cabin boy, and in the following year, he carved the parts of a hand-gun with a revolving chamber out of wood. The revolving cylinder was rotated by cocking the hammer. He was only 21 when he patented the idea, and in his factory in Paterson, New Jersey, was soon turning out the first Colt revolvers. But they were expensive – $5 – and complicated, with 24 springs, cogs, ratchets and so on. In 1842, the New Jersey factory went bankrupt. Yet the Colt had already proved its value as a weapon of self-defence. In 1841, a Texas Ranger named Jack Hayes had been trapped by a small band of Comanches at Enchanted Rock. The Indians knew that when a white man fired his rifle, it took some time to reload, and that he could be overcome during that time. After Hayes had been lying in his place of concealment for an hour, the Comanches advanced, and Hayes fired his rifle. Then, as they ran forward, Hayes drew his revolver and shot them all down.

So the Texas Rangers needed the Colt revolver, and in 1846, Captain Hamilton Walker offered to finance a new factory. He and Colt redesigned the revolver until it had only five simple parts. And the new six-shooter made Colt a millionaire.

Now the Colt revolver was not designed as a hunting gun; it was intended for shooting people. It was known as 'the equalizer', because a contemporary rhyme stated:

> Be not afraid of any man
> No matter what his size
> Just rely on me and I will equalize.

It was the ideal weapon for the new brand of American highwayman who came into existence after the Civil War – the hold-up man and train robber. It was reliable and cheap – Colt's machines could turn out thousands of guns a day. (The revolver was the first mass-produced article offered to the American public.) And when it reached Europe, it was the ideal weapon for the burglar and footpad. The gun Richardson used to murder the policeman in 1860 was an old-fashioned two-barrelled pistol; 22 years later, Tom Orrock was able to buy the revolver that killed PC Cole for a mere half guinea.

The new cheap hand-gun was to present police with their greatest challenge since the poison epidemic of the seventeenth century. Orrock had been hanged by a bullet, but if the defence had chosen to argue that the bullet in the tree and the bullet in PC Cole's skull had not been fired from the same revolver, he might well have escaped the gallows. A bullet looked anonymous; to the naked eye, there was no difference between a bullet that had been fired and its companion still resting in the chamber of the revolver. There was such a general ignorance about guns that in the Moat Farm murder trial of 1903 a gun expert told the court that if the bullet had been fired at a greater distance from Miss Holland's skull, it would have attained a greater speed and made a cleaner hole. (A bullet, of course, can only lose speed after it leaves the barrel.)

But Edmond Locard's master, the great Alexandre Lacassagne, realized that bullets have their own fingerprints. In the eighteenth century, gunmakers had realized that the accuracy of a bullet could be improved if the barrel contained grooves. In some early models, the grooves ran straight down the barrel, but it was soon noticed that if they were cut into a spiral, the bullet would rotate, and that this spin would give it additional accuracy. In the *Traité de Criminalistique,* Locard describes the Echallier affair of 1889, in which a revolver was found under the floorboards of a suspected murderer. It was of the same calibre as the bullet found in the head of the victim, but that proved nothing. Lacassagne studied the bullet under a microscope and saw that it had seven grooves, and that the revolver belonging to the suspect also had seven grooves in its barrel – the number might have been five or six. Locard does not say so, but we may assume that Lacassagne fired a test bullet from the same gun, and showed that its grooves were identical. His evidence led to the conviction of the suspect.

Yet, as with so many of the great discoveries in crime detection, Lacassagne's brilliant piece of investigation went unnoticed, and the firearms experts who were sometimes called at murder trials failed to realize that their greatest ally was the microscope. Nevertheless, there were still some creditable attempts at scientific precision. The expert who made the absurd mistake about the speed of a bullet in the Moat

Farm trial – a certain Edward J. Churchill – demonstrated his own originality in his approach to the problem of the bullet hole in Miss Holland's skull. It was his contention that Camille Holland had been shot at close range, and if the body had been found soon after death – instead of four years later – this would have been fairly easy to establish, for a gun fired close to the flesh produces powder burns, and the 'bow wave' of air that precedes the bullet can cause the flesh to explode outward. Churchill obtained the skull of a sheep, then fired bullets taken from Moat Farm at various distances – two yards, one yard, two feet, and six inches. The first three drilled small holes in the bone; the fourth smashed a large hole of the same type as the one found in Miss Holland's skull. Churchill's testimony convinced the jury that Camille Holland was shot at close range, which was consistent with the prosecution argument that Dougal had driven off with her in the horse and trap and then produced the revolver and shot her as they drove.

Edward J. Churchill was also to play a central role in a case that is still regarded as one of the oddest unsolved mysteries of the century. On the afternoon of 24 August 1908, Major-General Charles Luard, who was 69 years old, returned home from the golf club at Ightham, near Sevenoaks, and was surprised to find that his wife was not there to receive a neighbour who had been invited to tea. Luard dispensed the tea, then went to look for his wife. He found her lying dead in a neighbour's summer house in the woods, shot through the head. Valuable rings were missing from her fingers. Her dress was torn, indicating a struggle, and the autopsy disclosed that she had been shot twice with a .32 revolver.

Luard himself owned several revolvers of this calibre, and these were sent to Churchill – who ran a gun business in the Strand – for examination. Churchill employed the same procedure as Lacassagne in the Echallier case: he fired test bullets from each of the revolvers, then examined them under a microscope. The difference in the rifle marks established that none of them had fired the murder bullet. The Major-General also had an unshakable alibi – he had been at his golf club at the time various people had heard shots coming from the direction of the summer house. Even so, Luard began to receive poison-pen letters accusing him of the murder, and on 18 September 1908, he committed suicide by throwing himself under a train. A year later, an old tramp was accused of the murder, but released for lack of evidence.

Sixty years later, in 1959, when I was compiling *An Encyclopedia of Murder,* a correspondent sent me a copy of a paper on capital punishment by C. H. Norman, who had been at one time an official shorthand writer to the Court of Criminal Appeal. In this paper – which I include as an appendix in the *Encyclopedia* – Norman stated his conviction that the killer of Mrs Luard was the 'railway murderer' John Dickman, who was convicted in 1910 of murdering a wages clerk named Nisbet on a Newcastle train, and stealing £370. Nisbet was shot in the head five times. Sir S. Rowan-Hamilton, who edited the trial of Dickman for the *Notable British Trials* series, told Norman in a letter: 'All the same Dickman was justly convicted, and it may interest you to know that he was with little doubt the murderer of Mrs Luard, for he had forged a cheque she had sent him in response to an advertisement in *The Times* (I believe) asking for help; she discovered it and wrote to him and met him outside the General's and her house and her body was found there. He was absent from Newcastle those exact days . . . I have seen replicas of the cheques.'

Whether this is the true solution of the Luard mystery will never be known. The only conclusive piece of evidence would have been the gun with which Caroline Luard was shot. But the two guns used to kill Nisbet were never found; and if Dickman shot Caroline Luard, he undoubtedly took the same care to dispose of the .32 revolver that he used. Even as early as 1910, murderers who used guns were becoming aware of the danger posed by firearms experts.

But it was at a Congress of Legal Medicine held in Paris in May 1912 that the new science finally took its rightful place beside finger-printing and *bertillonage* as a powerful technique of crime detection. The eminent medico-legal expert Professor Victor Balthazard gave a lecture about a case on which he had recently been consulted. A man named Guillotin had been killed by several bullets; the chief suspect was a man named Houssard, who owned a revolver of the correct calibre. Firearms experts in Tours were asked to study the bullets taken from the corpse, and the bullets fired by Houssard's revolver, but were unable to state definitely that the murder bullets had been fired from the revolver. Professor Balthazard was dissatisfied with this conclusion; he made enlarged photographs of the bullets, then pointed out no fewer than 85 similarities between those fired from the gun and those taken from the corpse; on this evidence, Houssard was convicted of killing Guillotin. At the Congress of Legal Medicine, Balthazard described the case, and explained his method of studying various markings on the bullet. Not only are the grooves – or striations – quite distinctive, but the marks on the cartridge case are also stamped with the peculiarities of the gun. The firing-pin leaves characteristic markings; so does the breechlock, and the extractor and ejector. All this, Balthazard argued, means that every bullet that has been fired has its own individuality – in fact, its own fingerprint. In the following year, Balthazard published these findings in the *Archives of Criminal Anthropology and Legal Medicine,* and established his own claim to be regarded as the founder of scientific ballistics.

3

When Edward J. Churchill died in 1910, the business passed into the hands of his 23-year-old nephew Robert. Churchill was unhappily married, and his biographer Macdonald Hastings suggests that this explains why he was a 'workaholic' who devoted his whole life to ballistics. He had been fascinated by guns – and by murder – since his childhood, and when he inherited his uncle's position as an expert firearms witness, he began systematically cataloguing the rifling of various kinds of guns. The inside of a gun barrel has a series of flat-bottomed grooves, which are separated by raised 'plateaux' known as lands, and these, as already noticed, are cut into a spiral, so that the bullet is spinning as it leaves the barrel. It was Churchill's ambition to be able to tell at a glance what type of weapon any bullet had been fired from. This involved noting the width, depth and pitch of grooves (the pitch being the length of one complete turn of the screw and whether they spiralled to the right or the left). But although Churchill was soon able to determine the make of gun from which a bullet had been fired, he was still a long way from Balthazard's objective of being able to distinguish the individual gun.

The problem was illustrated in the 'hooded man' case of 1912. On the evening of 9 October, the telephone rang at the Eastbourne police station, and a woman with a Hungarian accent told Inspector Albert Walls that a man was lying concealed on the wooden porch above her front door. Her coachman had noticed him just as she was setting out for a dinner engagement. Walls hurried round to the house in South Cliff Avenue, and was able to see the burglar lying above the front door. He called 'Now then, my man, just you come down.' There were two shots, and the inspector fell dead. The burglar scrambled down and fled.

The police took moulds of footprints found in the garden, and tried to trace a hat that had been found in the gutter; neither clue looked promising. But routine interviews with local residents disclosed that, on the afternoon of the murder, a man and a heavily pregnant young woman had been seen sitting on a bench at the end of South Cliff Avenue, and that the young woman had also been seen there alone, while the man wandered along South Cliff Avenue. It sounded as if he might have been spying out the lie of the land.

The following afternoon, a swarthy man asked to see Chief Inspector Bower, who was in charge of the case. He identified himself as Edgar Power, and said he knew the identity of the murderer of Inspector Walls. It was, he said, a man named John Williams, who was staying in Eastbourne with his pregnant girlfriend Florence Seymour. Power was a friend of Williams' brother, who bore the family name of McKay; Williams' name was George McKay, but his career as a burglar and petty crook made him prefer a *nom de guerre*. That morning, Williams's brother had received a desperate plea for money, and had travelled from London to Eastbourne with his friend Power, who had offered to act as emissary. The brother gave Power two sovereigns, and allowed him to keep the letter. Power pocketed one of the sovereigns and handed over the other to John Williams. Then he hurried off to the police to betray Williams. His motive, it seemed, was that he was in love with Florence Seymour, who was a remarkably beautiful girl. In the hope of seducing Florence, he was willing to betray his best friend's brother.

The following day, with Power's connivance, Williams was arrested at Moorgate Street station. Taken back to Eastbourne, he was 'hooded' with an apron as he left the train, in case press photographers should influence some future witness in identifying Williams – this was why the Press labelled Williams 'the Hooded Man'. But as it happened, the precaution was unnecessary; neither the Hungarian countess whose house he was about to burgle, nor her coachman, had glimpsed the face of the murderer, and were unable to pick out Williams in any identity parade. The case was virtually at a standstill. Now Power once again volunteered his help. He had been busy 'consoling' Florence Seymour, who was unaware that he had betrayed her lover (the police had arrested Power as well as Williams at the railway station). Florence admitted that Williams had buried his revolver on the beach at Eastbourne. Somehow, Power convinced her that the police were likely to find the revolver, and that it must be hidden in a safer place. He and Florence travelled down to Eastbourne, and she took him to the place on the beach where she had seen her lover bury the gun. Police pounced on them, and Florence became hysterical. The revolver was quickly uncovered and Florence was subjected to several hours of questioning at the police station, which led her to make a number of statements that incriminated her lover.

The gun was brought to Robert Churchill. Its hammer and spring were missing, but Churchill put new ones on it, and fired test bullets. They proved conclusively that the bullet that had killed Inspector Walls had been fired from a revolver of the same make and calibre. But that, of course, was not the same thing as proving that it had been fired from Williams' revolver. Chief Inspector Bower decided that more science would be needed to impress the jury; he placed a photographic expert at Churchill's disposal, and set them the task of photographing the inside of the barrel of the revolver, and of various other revolvers for comparison. In the days before the invention of the micro-camera this was a virtually impossible task; Churchill solved it by coating the inside of the barrels with melted dental wax, then easing it out with a knife, and photographing the result. The method was obviously far from satisfactory, but it served its purpose in impressing the jury, and Williams was sentenced to death.

Yet although it seems reasonably certain that Williams was guilty, the case still leaves an unpleasant aftertaste. Williams admitted that he had been a burglar, but that he was now a reformed character. He also pointed out that a professional burglar would not climb up on to a porch while the tenant was still in the house, but would wait for the lights to go out and then force his way in. This sounds a reasonable comment. He insisted that he had fled from Eastbourne only because he possessed a revolver and had a criminal record. A modern jury would probably have acquitted him for lack of evidence. But the case received an unprecedented amount of publicity, and established Churchill's reputation as the Spilsbury of ballistics.

4

The case that was to change the history of forensic ballistics occurred on the other side of the Atlantic. Early in the morning on 22 March 1915, a farmhand named Charles Stielow – a massive German who spoke English imperfectly – discovered that his employer Charles Phelps and his housekeeper Margaret Walcott had been murdered.

Both had been shot dead and the motive was obviously robbery. Autopsies revealed that they had been shot with a .22 revolver. (The number – known as the calibre of the gun – refers to the diameter in inches of the inside of the barrel.) At the inquest a few days later, Stielow declared that he had never possessed a revolver. So when a private detective discovered that Stielow possessed a .22, and uncovered the weapon, Stielow was an obvious suspect. Eventually, under 'third degree' questioning, Stielow – whose IQ was that of a child – 'confessed' to the murders. But later, in court, he insisted that it had been obtained by force, and withdrew it.

A firearms expert known as Dr Albert Hamilton – the degree was almost certainly bogus – declared that the test bullets fired from Stielow's revolver were identical with the murder bullets, and pointed especially to marks on the murder bullets that indicated that the gun had scratches inside the muzzle. The defence objected that no such marks were visible on the test bullets, or in the muzzle of Stielow's revolver. Hamilton replied that he had accidentally photographed the wrong side of the test bullets, and that the marks *were* there on the other side. He explained that the lack of marks in the muzzle of Stielow's revolver was due to the fact that they had been filled in by the lead from the bullet. And the jury was so convinced of Stielow's guilt that they accepted these extraordinary explanations, and declared him guilty. He was sentenced to die in the electric chair.

But the deputy warden of the prison became convinced that his child-like prisoner was innocent, and persuaded some New York ladies with humanitarian views to finance an investigation. They learned that two tramps named King and O'Connell had been seen in the area of Phelps's farm in Orleans County, New York and that both were now serving long sentences for theft. A female lawyer, hired by the ladies, saw one of the tramps in jail, and induced him to confess that he and his companion had murdered Phelps and Mrs Walcott. But, oddly enough, news of his confession only caused consternation in Orleans County, for it meant the cost of another trial. Various law officials from Orleans County interviewed King and persuaded him to withdraw his confession. When the Governor of New York heard of this suspicious change of heart, he asked a lawyer named George H. Bond to look into the case. Bond's assistant was an employee of the New York State Prosecutor, Charles E. Waite.

Waite and Bond talked to Stielow, and were soon convinced of his innocence. Next, Waite called on his own firearms experts to examine

Stielow's revolver: Inspector Joseph Faurot, who had brought finger-printing techniques to America from Scotland Yard, and Captain Jones. They examined the revolver, and declared that the amount of dirt and grease in the barrel proved that it had not been fired for years. They then fired test bullets, and compared them with the murder bullets; the difference was visible even to the naked eye. Moreover, no scratches were found, either on the test bullets or on the murder bullets – Hamilton had imagined them. Quite clearly, he was a charlatan. Moreover, the lands in the murder revolver must have been twice as wide as those in Stielow's.

The photographic evidence was conclusive, and it led Governor Whitman to grant Stielow a pardon – he had by now served three years in prison. King once again confessed to the murders, but the legal authorities in Orleans County were unwilling to face the costs of a new trial, and declined to indict him.

It was the Stielow case that made Charles Waite determined to devote the rest of his life to creating a science of firearms identification that would make all such miscarriages of justice impossible in the future. He was already past middle age, yet the task of cataloguing all the guns in use in America failed to daunt him. In 1912, Robert Churchill had listed 119 automatic pistols with a calibre of .25, 50 it seemed within the bounds of possibility to list the specifications of all guns manufactured in America since the first Colt revolver. It was simply a question of approaching firms like Colt, and Smith and Wesson, and asking for their help.

In 1922, after three years' work, Waite felt he was in sight of his goal. Then he was shattered to realize that thousands of European weapons flooded into America every year – more than half a million in 1922. With a sigh, Waite left for Europe, and set out to visit all the major arms manufacturers. Now, with some 1,500 guns in his collection, he was ready to begin his catalogue of world firearms. There were still many small firms in remote parts of the world that he had been unable to trace, but the chances of one of their weapons being used in a murder case were almost infinitesimal.

And now Waite rediscovered the insight that Professor Victor Balthazard had announced to the medico-legal society in 1912: that every gun has so many imperfections and peculiarities that it virtually leaves its own fingerprint on the bullet. He approached an expert in optics, Max Poser, of the Bausch and Lomb Optical Company in Rochester, and asked him to construct a microscope for studying bullets. Then, together with a physicist named John H. Fischer and a chemist named Philip O. Gravelle, he set up the Bureau of Forensic Ballistics in New York. Fischer solved the problem of looking down gun barrels with an instrument called a helixometer, a hollow probe fitted with a lamp and a magnifying glass, while Gravelle invented the comparison microscope, in which two halves of separate bullet images could be joined together under the same lens, to compare the marks on each. In 1923, 34 years after Lacassagne had solved a murder by studying the bullet under a microscope, the science of ballistics was finally born in the laboratory.

In 1925, Waite acquired his third – and in some respects most important – collaborator, an ex-colonel and army medical officer named Calvin Goddard. Like Robert Churchill in England, Goddard had been fascinated by guns and crime since childhood; now, after a brief association with the charlatan Albert Hamilton, whose inefficiency soon disgusted him, Goddard became Waite's assistant in the Bureau of Forensic Ballistics. And when Waite died of a heart attack in November 1926, it was Goddard who stepped into his shoes, and became the world's foremost ballistics expert. His *History of Firearms Identification* (1936) is still the classic work on the subject. And it was no accident that it was published in Chicago; during the 1920s, Chicago had become the home of some of America's most notorious bootleg gangs, notably that run by Johnny Torrio and his young assistant Alphonse Capone. On 8 November 1924, the Torrio–Capone gang had eliminated one major rival, Dion O'Banion, by riddling him with bullets as a member of the gang shook his hand. O'Banion's chief lieutenant, Hymie Weiss, swore vengeance, but was eventually machine-gunned down in 1926. Three years later, on 14 February 1929, Capone's last major rival, Bugs Moran, became the target. On the morning of St Valentine's Day, five men – two in police uniforms – went into the garage owned by Moran, lined up everyone they found against a wall – seven in all – and shot them down with machine-guns. Moran was not among them, but he ceased to represent a threat to Capone.

At the coroner's inquest on the victims of the massacre, some jurors asked why the police were keeping the murder bullets, and were told that ballistics experts might be able to identify the guns from which they had been fired. Now it so happened that Calvin Goddard had been called from New York to give his opinion on the firearms used in the massacre. When two wealthy members of the jury offered to finance a crime laboratory at Chicago's Northwestern University, Goddard was asked to become its director, and consented. This is why his textbook was published from Chicago. Moreover, Goddard went on to 'solve' the St Valentine's Day Massacre. When a Michigan policeman was shot, the killer was traced through his car licence number; in his apartment the police found a cupboard full of weapons, including two 'tommy guns'. Goddard's laboratory was able to establish they had been the weapons used in the massacre. The apartment was owned by a Capone henchman named Fred Burke, who was duly sentenced to life imprisonment. Capone himself was by then in prison for carrying concealed weapons; on his release, he was re-arrested and sentenced to 11 years for tax evasion.

5

By the time of the establishment of the Northwestern Crime Laboratory, most Americans had been made aware of the importance of ballistics in one of the most sensational trials of the decade: that of the anarchist 'martyrs' Sacco and Vanzetti. On 15 April 1920, two payroll guards were shot down with ferocious brutality during a robbery in the small town of South Braintree, Massachusetts. The men, Frederick Parmenter and Alessandro Berardelli, were carrying two boxes containing $16,000 into the Slater and Morrill shoe factory, when they passed two loiterers, one of whom drew a gun and shot down Berardelli; Parmenter ran away, and was also shot down – although he had already dropped his box. The second robber, who had a dark handlebar moustache, bent over Berardelli and fired more shots into him. Then the gunmen carried the payroll boxes into a waiting car, which already contained three men, and drove off.

The brutality of the crime caused widespread shock, and there was intense police activity. One of the few leads was the discovery of the car that had been used in the hold-up, a stolen Buick, found abandoned in nearby woods two days after the shootings. This was also thought to be the car used in an attempted payroll robbery in a shoe factory in nearby Bridgewater the previous December. Police heard that an Italian named Boda had been seen in the car, and when they received a tip that Boda had gone to a garage in Bridgewater to collect another car, they rushed to arrest him. But Boda and a companion had already escaped on a motorcycle. Two other men who had accompanied him were arrested on a streetcar; they were Nicola Sacco, 29, and his heavily moustached companion, Bartolomeo Vanzetti, 32. Both insisted that they did not know Boda, and that neither of them owned weapons. In fact, both were carrying revolvers, and Sacco's was a .32, the same calibre as the gun that had killed the guards. Both were members of the anarchist movement, whose advocacy of violence still aroused immense public indignation – there had recently been a spate of 'bomb outrages'. Vanzetti was a fish pedlar, Sacco – significantly – worked in a shoe factory. And when witnesses of the attempted Bridgewater robbery identified Vanzetti as one of the men, he was tried at Plymouth and sentenced to 10–15 years in jail. Sacco was able to establish that he had been at work at the time of the attempted robbery.

Eleven months later, on 31 May 1921, the trial of Sacco and Vanzetti for the double murder opened at Dedham, Massachusetts, under Judge Webster Thayer, who had presided over the trial of Vanzetti at Plymouth. There was little doubt that Thayer was deeply prejudiced against the accused – he had referred to them in his club as 'those anarchist bastards'. The prosecutor, District Attorney Frederick Katzmann, also made no secret of his detestation of anarchist politics. Yet the records of the trial show that both did their best to make it a fair one. It was the defence counsel, Fred Moore, who set out to drag politics into the trial, and to imply that his clients were the victims of a witch hunt.

This was patently untrue. The evidence of the Buick undoubtedly connected Boda with the robberies (Boda had fled to Italy) and a firearms expert would testify that Sacco's .32 was the murder weapon. So Moore's tactics did a great deal more to ensure the conviction of his clients than the obvious prejudice of the judge and prosecution.

The trial began with dozens of identification witnesses – 59 for the prosecution and 99 for the defence. All this conflict only produced confusion. And the ballistics evidence that followed was almost as bad. One prosecution expert testified that the bullet that had killed Berardelli had been fired from Sacco's revolver, while another expert would only say that it could have been. (This was three years before the invention of the comparison microscope.) Two defence experts testified that the fatal bullet had not been fired by Sacco's revolver. The defence also tried hard to prove alibis for both prisoners. But when the jury finally returned, on 14 July 1921, they decided that both were guilty. Judge Thayer sentenced them to death.

Within days there was an international outcry. Left-wing political parties in every country – including England – declared that this was an example of capitalist justice, and that Sacco and Vanzetti were obviously innocent. A Red Aid committee raised money for a retrial. And the irrepressible 'expert' Albert Hamilton took the opportunity to step once more into the limelight. Asked by Fred Moore to examine the bullet, he announced with his customary conviction that his examination proved Sacco and Vanzetti to be innocent. When Moore heard that Captain Proctor, one of the prosecufion experts, had also changed his mind about the bullets, he hastened to obtain Proctor's testimony. Proctor only restated what had said in court: that the fatal bullet *could* have been fired from Sacco's pistol; but he, he now added, personally thought it unlikely. Asked why he hadn't said so at the time, he replied that the prosecution had taken care not to ask him.

When a retrial was requested, the prosecution asked the other firearms expert, Charles Van Amburgh, to take another look at the bullets. By this time, in the autumn of 1923, some of the advances in ballistics for which Waite was responsible were available to the experts. Van Amburgh 'blew-up' the fatal bullet with micro-photography, and did the same with test bullets fired from Sacco's revolver. His conclusion was that Sacco was guilty. And when Judge Thayer considered the motion for a retrial, the egregious Albert Hamilton confirmed the conclusion by a barefaced attempt to switch revolvers. He took two new Colts into court, and then disassembled them – as well as Sacco's revolver – to demonstrate some point. Then he put one of the new barrels back on Sacco's revolver, and tried to leave court with the two Colts. Thayer caught him at it and recovered the switched barrel. As a result, the motion for a new trial was rejected.

The international furore continued and, in June 1927, a committee was appointed to re-examine the whole case. And this time, America's leading firearms expert, Calvin Goddard, was called in. He brought his comparison microscope, and one of the defence firearms experts, Augustus Gill, agreed to witness the experiment. A bullet was fired from Sacco's revolver into cotton wool, and placed beside the murder bullet on the slides of the comparison microscope. The result, Goddard announced, was that the murder bullet had undoubtedly been fired from Sacco's revolver. And Gill, peering through the microscope, whistled and had to agree. The other defence expert, James Burns, also looked through the microscope and changed his opinion. There could be no possible doubt about it. Whether or not Vanzetti was innocent, Sacco was beyond all doubt guilty. The committee reported accordingly. And on 23 August 1927, Sacco and Vanzetti died in the electric chair in Bridgewater jail.

What is the truth? The truth is undoubtedly that Nicola Sacco fired the shot that killed Alessandro Berardelli. This particular anarchist cell was murderous and ruthless; in the earlier Bridgewater robbery they had opened fire from a car, but the payroll guards had fired back, and driven them off. Now they were determined to kill without giving the guards a chance to hand over the money. But was Vanzetti on that earlier robbery, and did he later take part in the two murders? In a modern court of law, he would probably be acquitted for lack of evidence. Yet he was one of four men who went with Sacco that evening to collect Boda's car, and there are strong reasons for believing that Boda was one of the robbers. Vanzetti insisted that he was not acquainted with Boda, and that he owned no weapons; later he had to admit that he was lying on both counts. So whether or not he was the moustached gunman who also shot Berardelli, it seems likely that he was one of the gang. It is impossible to believe that Sacco and Vanzetti were innocent martyrs who died solely for their belief in human freedom.

The controversy raged on for years, and Judge Thayer's house was bombed. Goddard himself was accused of being a corrupt tool of capitalist oppression. But when, in 1961, another forensic team re-examined Sacco's revolver and the murder bullet, they concluded that there was no doubt whatsoever that the bullet had been fired by Sacco's revolver.

It was undoubtedly a mistake to execute them; if their sentences had been commuted to life imprisonment, the Left would have been robbed of a propaganda triumph. As it is, there can be little doubt that the myth of Sacco and Vanzetti's innocence will never be dispelled.

6

In 1926, the year before the execution of Sacco and Vanzetti, the 33-year-old Sydney Smith – whose acquaintance we have made in an earlier chapter – read an article by Calvin Goddard in the *Military Surgeon,* and learned about Philip Gravelle's comparison microscope. Smith had decided to accept a post under the Egyptian Ministry of Justice in 1917, and had developed a forensic laboratory as fine as Spilsbury's. Cairo was a good place to learn about crime detection from experience; compared with England, the murder rate was enormous. And two years after Smith's arrival, Egyptian nationalists, fretting under British rule, began a series of revolutionary demonstrations and political murders. As his morgue filled up with bullet-riddled bodies, Smith began to study the bullets under a microscope, and soon grasped the essential difficulty – that he had to remember what one bullet looked like while he studied another; even two microscopes side by side were no real solution to the problem. And so at about the same time that Philip Gravelle was building the first comparison microscope in New York, Smith was tinkering together a similar device in Cairo.

As an increasing number of Smith's friends died in the attacks, he studied the bullets, and recognized at least two that were distinctive: automatic bullets that had been fired from a Webley .45 revolver, and bullets fired from a .32 Colt with a fault that produced a characteristic scratched groove. A well-known nationalist and Member of Parliament named Shafik Mansour was suspected of being involved, but there was no positive evidence to incriminate him.

Then, on 19 November 1924, the terrorists succeeded in killing the British Commander-in-Chief of the Egyptian army, Sir Lee Stack, who was officially called the Sirdar. As his chauffeur slowed down at a tram line in the heart of Cairo, several men ran forward and emptied their guns into the car, then escaped in a waiting taxi. Stack died of loss of blood the following day.

Smith examined the bullets, which were .32 automatic ammunition, but fired from a Colt – Smith deduced this from characteristic ejection marks on the cartridge cases. They had been filed across the end to turn them into expanding – or dum-dum – bullets. And the bullets that had killed the Sirdar had been fired from the Colt with the characteristic groove.

The police now made use of a spy to infiltrate the group – a man who had served a jail sentence for an attempt on the Prime Minister in 1914. He was accepted by the terrorists, and was able to tell the police their identities. He also added that two young student brothers named Enayat – aged 19 and 22 – were most likely to crack under pressure. The traitor was instructed to tell the brothers that they were about to be arrested, and advise them to flee. They took a train to Tripoli, and the police swooped in the middle of the desert, capturing both. At first they could find no weapons, until a policeman knocked over a basket of fruit, and four automatics fell out. There were also bullets that had been filed to convert them into dum-dums.

Two of the pistols were .25s, so Smith ignored these. But the two .32s looked more promising. A test bullet fired from one of them – a Sûreté – gave no definite result, although it looked like one of the murder bullets; but the cartridge case had a series of scratches and nicks that were identical with those on a case found near the spot where the Sirdar was assassinated. And the comparison microscope left no doubt whatsoever that the Colt had been used in the same crime. It had the scratched groove Smith had been looking for.

The brothers finally broke down, both of them hoping that confession might save their lives. Their confessions led to the arrest of six other gang members, including Shafik Mansour. In the house of one of them the police found a vice and cutting files that could have been used to file the bullets.

At first, Mansour was confident, since all the members had sworn not to betray one another; then, when he learned that the brothers had confessed, he became desperate. Thinking the others were in nearby cells, he shouted: 'Deny, all of you, your safety lies in denial' – then, realizing he had incriminated himself, pretended to be mad, talking to himself and tearing his clothes. Smith examined him and concluded that he was shamming. In due course, his nerve broke and he confessed. At the trial, Smith's ballistic evidence was of central importance in convincing the jury of the guilt of the eight accused; all were sentenced to death.

In another case of the same period, Smith was able to demonstrate his skill as a forensic Sherlock Holmes. On the morning of 15 January 1923, a housemaid received no reply when she knocked on the bedroom door of a rich merchant named Max Karam. She went in, and found her employer sitting on the floor by the bed, entangled in the mosquito netting; he proved to be dead. In the mortuary, a doctor discovered that Karam had been beaten about the head, and also shot behind the ear. Keys to the safe, which Karam usually kept under his pillow, were found in the middle of the room, but the safe itself had not been opened. All the evidence indicated that Karam had been killed by a burglar, who had become alarmed at the report of his revolver, and fled without his booty. The iron bar which had caused the lacerations of the scalp was found by the side of the bed.

It became clear that the burglar had entered by drilling a series of holes in a door, and knocking out the panel. He had then put his hand inside and withdrawn the bolt. After that, he had cut the wires of the bell-pull which might have summoned the servants, and also the telephone wires.

The police observed that there seemed to be more sawdust outside the door than inside, and reached the conclusion that the holes had been drilled from the inside, in an attempt to make it look like burglary. They also felt that the cutting of the bell wires and telephone wires indicated an intimate knowledge of the household. All this led them to suspect that the merchant's widow had plotted the death of her husband, probably in association with a lover – Mme Karam was said to be having an affair with a man who had been a guest at a dinner party the evening before.

In the hot climate of Alexandria, it was necessary to bury the dead man fairly quickly. But Sydney Smith was approached for his opinion of the evidence. He was intrigued by the description of the dead man's injuries. He had been shot in the side of the head, while the injuries from the iron bar were to the front. But surely a burglar who beat him with an iron bar would shoot him from in front? Smith began to suspect that he was dealing with two burglars.

Examination of the scene of the crime confirmed this opinion. Powder burns on the mosquito netting showed that the merchant must have been out of bed, and behind the net, when he was shot. But there was also a powder burn on the elbow of his nightgown, which indicated that he had raised his hand to his head at the moment he was shot. This must have been to defend his head against blows from the iron bar. So he was facing one assailant when the other shot him from the side.

Examining the door with a hole drilled in it, Smith soon concluded that the police were simply mistaken in believing that the holes had been drilled from inside; to his experienced eye, they had undoubtedly been drilled from outside.

But the police officer who accompanied him had another reason for suspecting Mme Karam of complicity. She claimed that in the early hours of the morning, she had heard a sound like a window-shutter banging, and had toured the ground floor of the house with her maid to make sure that all was well. Finding nothing amiss, she claimed to have gone back to bed. But, said the police officer, no one could mistake the sound of a shot for a banging shutter. Smith was doubtful about this. So they retired to Mme Karam's bedroom, while a policeman stayed in the bedroom of the murdered man, and fired a shot. Smith had to agree that no one could mistake it for a banging shutter. They went back to the merchant's bedroom – and found the policeman struggling with a jammed pistol. 'I'm sorry, I haven't been able to fire it yet.' 'But we just heard a shot', said the police officer. At that moment they heard another 'shot' – and realized that it was, in fact, a window-shutter banging in the wind.

So now Mme Karam was absolved of all complicity, and the police set about tracking down the killers. In was, in fact, Mme Karam who solved their problem by offering a £2,000 reward for information leading to the solution of the crime. This brought information from a prostitute called Henriette. She knew a German called Ferid Merkel who had boasted of being involved in a burglary that had ended in a shooting. Merkel occupied a room in Alexandria with another man. But when the police arrived, both had gone. However, they found burgling equipment, and a brace and bit that fitted the holes drilled in the door.

Now it was simply a matter of patient police work, and the two men were eventually identified as two professional thieves named Herman Klauss and Fritz Doelitzsch, who had now left Egypt by sea. Klauss was tracked down to India, and a man named Magnus Klausen arrested and sent back to Egypt. It proved to be a case of mistaken identity. But at this point, a remarkable coincidence came to the aid of the police. The Indian police sergeant who had accompanied Klausen was shown a photograph of Herman Klauss, and recognized him as a man who was now in jail in Calcutta. Klauss was brought back to Egypt, while Doelitzsch was tracked down to Trieste and arrested on a ship there.

In court, the men admitted the burglary. But each tried to throw the blame on the other, aware that under Egyptian law only one could be found guilty of murder. According to Doelitzsch, Karam had awakened while he was searching for keys under his pillow, and had attacked Doelitzsch, who had struck him with a jemmy in self-defence. Then Klauss had shot the merchant. Klauss's version was that Doelitzsch had battered the merchant with the jemmy *and* shot him. But Sydney Smith had already shown that whoever had used the pistol had not inflicted the blows, and vice versa. So it became clear that Doelitzsch's version must be the true one, and Klauss was the actual killer.

The defence contended that there was so much doubt about who had fired the shot that both should be acquitted of murder. The court disagreed, and decided to break with precedent and find both men guilty of murder. Klauss and Doelitzsch were both sentenced to life imprisonment.

7

It was taking a surprisingly long time for the forensic experts to recognize the importance of ballistic evidence. A case that took place in South Africa in 1926 provides an example of the old, haphazard approach that could still be found throughout Europe.

On a farm named 'Waterval' (Water Falls) in the Potgietersrust district of the Transvaal, two middle-aged men lived a pleasant and leisurely existence, hunting during the day, and smoking on the verandah in the evening. William Nelson, who had retired from gold mining when he contracted tuberculosis, was 60, and his companion Thomas Denton was 55. Since life was quiet, they were not entirely displeased to see two strangers, who arrived on 1 December 1925, explaining that they had not eaten for days. The kindly Nelson offered them work plastering the house, and told them to rest for the remainder of the day. The following day, the guests were invited out on a shooting trip. After a large evening meal, all retired to bed.

At two in the morning, native labourers were awakened by the crackling of flames and a series of explosions that sounded like bullets. The farmhouse was on fire. By the light of the flames, the farmhands saw two men hurrying away from the burning building. The police were not summoned until the following morning. They smelt burning flesh as they entered the ruins of the farmhouse. Nelson and Denton were lying in their charred beds, their faces covered with burnt sacking. But fragments of skull and brains on the pillows indicated that both had been shot. There were many cartridge cases lying around the room, all exploded by the heat.

Dr George Melle, the District Surgeon, noticed the hole in the left side of Nelson's head; removing the top of the skull, he found a gunshot wound that had gone upward and backwards. Denton's skull was smashed, but at the base there was a hole about an inch in diameter. Below this Melle found a few buckshot pellets and a flattened slug.

The men had vanished, and the police had no clue to their identity. Detective Sergeant Daniel J. Malan had a vast area to search; he drove hundreds of miles a day in search of information. The first break in the case came when a taxi-driver reported driving two strangers to a remote farm, and driving them back to Potgietersrust the following day; they had succeeded in escaping without paying their £15 fare. Detective Malan visited the farm, and learned that the men had stayed there the night. The owner of the farm was unable to help; but where one of the men had shaved, Malan found a piece of paper that had been used to wipe a razor – it was a receipt for clothes made out to 'A. Van Niekerk'. And the criminal records file revealed that Andries Petrus Van Niekerk was a habitual criminal who had recently been released on probation from Pretoria's Central Prison. Also released at the same time was Edward William Markus. And the description of the two wanted men corresponded closely to that of Niekerk and Markus. Photographs of the ex-convicts were circulated to police all over the country.

Eight hundred miles from Pretoria, on the railway station at Cathcart, a policeman was watching incoming trains. He had heard about two suspicious characters who had sneaked out of a boarding-house in nearby Queenstown without paying their rent, and hurried to the station. Their landlord had caught up with them on the platform, but one had escaped on foot, while the other had jumped onto the moving train. When the policeman glanced into the guard's van, he saw a man who resembled the photograph of Van Niekerk, and challenged him. The man insisted that his name was De Wet, then made a bolt for it. The policeman caught him and took him to the local police station. The following day, travelling back to Queenstown in handcuffs, Van Niekerk threw himself out of the open window of the moving train. The detective pulled the communication cord, and ran in pursuit, shooting as he ran. He caught up with the man and hit him on the head, then dropped his gun; the man pounced on it, pointed it and pulled the trigger. Fortunately, it was now empty. Van Niekerk was escorted back to Queenstown.

Markus was found hiding in a native hut near Queenstown, and surrendered without resistance.

Two days later, Markus offered to 'confess'. His story was that the murders had been committed by Van Niekerk, who had forced him to co-operate by threatening to blow out his brains. Markus was 25, Van Niekerk ten years older. Van Niekerk had been in and out of prison since he was a teenager. Markus claimed that he had been entirely under the domination of his companion, and that he was terrified of Van Niekerk because the man was insane. On the night of the murder, he claimed that Van Niekerk had forced him into the bedroom of the two old farmers at gunpoint, then had shot both men through the head. Then Van Niekerk had taken money out of a trunk under the bed, and set the place on fire with paraffin. Ever since then, said Markus, Van Niekerk had threatened to kill him if he tried to escape . . .

When Van Niekerk heard of his companion's confession, he went beserk with rage. Then he made his own confession, insisting that he had killed Nelson with a revolver, while Markus had killed Denton with a shotgun.

If Markus's version was true, then he might well be acquitted. Everything depended on whether the ballistics evidence proved his story. And since both bodies had been badly damaged by fire, this was not easy to determine. The New York or London police would have sent for ballistics experts, and carefully photographed the skulls and the wounds. Dr George Melle, who had examined the scene of the crime, was not a ballistics expert, or even a forensic scientist. He had found a flattened bullet under Denton's skull, as well as shotgun pellets. Which had killed him? Melle was inclined to believe it was a shotgun, and that the flattened bullet had been from the exploding ammunition.

It was an issue of some importance. For if a microscope had revealed that the flattened bullet had been fired by the same revolver that killed Nelson, then Markus could be telling the truth about his own reluctance to have any part in the killings; this in turn would support a plea of insanity by Van Niekerk's defence. But such evidence was not introduced. At their trial – which began on 11 February 1926 – Dr Melle argued that Denton had been killed by a shotgun or a rifle, which argued that both defendants were killers. Markus' defence attorney called a firearms expert named Captain George Cross, whose contribution was to argue that, even though the two wounds were of a different nature, they *could* both have been caused by Van Niekerk's revolver, 'for the same weapon . . . can produce totally different wounds'. Next, Markus gave evidence of Van Niekerk's insanity – how he lay naked in the blazing sun of the veld, how he was subject to violent changes of mood – and how he himself had been forced at gunpoint to take part in the robbery. But the prosecution made a telling point when they reminded Markus that he had intended to take Van Niekerk to visit his own family, and that this was hardly consistent with his belief that Van Niekerk was a homicidal maniac.

Van Niekerk's defence told at length the appalling story of his life – how his father had been a lunatic, who drove the child away from home when he was 12, threatening to thrash him to death, and how many subsequent prison sentences had embittered him. Then a psychiatrist argued that Van Niekerk was a 'moral imbecile' who could not be held responsible for his actions. Van Niekerk himself informed the court that he was now a Christian convert and was washed in the blood of the lamb. But the jury declined to be moved or convinced; they sentenced both men to death. They went to the scaffold 'uncomplaining and unrepentent', on 13 April 1926.

8

The case that made all Europe aware of the importance of ballistic evidence began on the evening of 26 September 1927, when two petty crooks named Frederick Browne and William Kennedy set out to steal a car. Browne was a powerfully built man with a heavy moustache and a reputation for violence; Kennedy, an altogether weaker character, was a Scot of Irish parentage, who had met Browne in prison and was dominated by him. That night they went by train to Billericay in Essex, hoping to steal a Riley that Browne had noted earlier; but a barking dog scared them off. Since it was now too late to return by train, they decided to find another car to steal; Browne forced open the garage doors of a Dr Edward Lovell and let the car – a Morris Cowley – run down the slope to the road before starting it. But in a back lane a few miles on, they were waved to a halt by a policeman with a lantern. When Browne ignored him and drove on, he blew his whistle, whereupon Browne stopped. Police Constable George William Gutteridge approached the car, shone his torch on Browne, and asked where he was going. As Gutteridge was writing in his notebook, Brown drew a gun and shot him. Gutteridge fell down, and Browne got out of the car and stood over him. The policeman's eyes were open. 'What are you looking at me like that for?' asked Browne, and shot him through both eyes. Then they drove off. Browne was so nervous that at one point he drove the car off the road and damaged its bumper on a tree. A few hours later, they abandoned it in Brixton and returned home – to Browne's garage in Northcote Road, Battersea – by tram.

Dr Lovell reported his car stolen the next morning, at about the time it was discovered in Brixton. The body of PC Gutteridge had already been found soon after dawn, huddled beside the road.

In the stolen car the police photographer found a cartridge case, which the head of the CID, Major-General Sir Wyndham Childs, recognized as a Mark IV, manufactured at the beginning of the war at Woolwich Arsenal. And the base showed a tiny raised blister that had been imprinted by a fault on the breech shield of the gun that fired it.

Chief Inspector James Berrett, in charge of the case, studied a list of thieves and hold-up men inclined to violence, and came upon the name of Frederick Guy Browne, 46, who had often attacked prison officers when he was in Parkhurst. But there was no evidence to connect Browne with the murder, and the car yielded no other clues. So Browne, concluding that he had got away with murder, resumed his career of car theft and hold-ups. In Sheffield the following January, driving a stolen Vauxhall, he forced a van driver into the wall, and the man took his number. A policeman later saw the Vauxhall, stopped it, and asked the driver for his name and address. He also noted a man in the passenger seat. When a summons for dangerous driving was delivered to the address, it proved to be false, like the name the man had given. But the policeman had recognized the passenger – a man with a criminal record – and when he was run to earth by the Sheffield police, he told them the driver's real name: Frederick Browne. Then the old lag went to the Sheffield police and told them that Browne and an associate called Kennedy were responsible for a spate of recent robberies, and that he suspected they were the men who had killed PC Gutteridge. On 20 January 1928, the police waited outside Browne's garage in Battersea until a car driven by a man in chauffeur's uniform came in. Then ten officers moved in, and seized him as he got out of the car. It was just as well they waited until he was clear of the car; in its side pocket they found a revolver, and Browne confessed that he would have shot as many as possible before killing himself. On Browne's premises they found several more revolvers, and £2,000 in notes in a lavatory cistern.

Charged with the theft of the Vauxhall, Browne was obviously relieved. Relief turned to anxiety when he heard that William Kennedy had been arrested in Liverpool, and had tried to shoot the detective who arrested him – only the jamming of the gun saved the policeman's life. Kennedy had thrown away his only chance of escaping the gallows. In fact, Kennedy then went on to make a full confession to the murder of Gutteridge – insisting, of course, that he himself had played no part in it.

Browne, in turn, wrote a letter to his wife with a message written between the lines in urine – the most primitive kind of invisible ink – begging her to find witnesses to swear that he had exchanged guns with Kennedy before they set out on the night of the murder.

Among the guns found in Browne's possession was a Webley revolver. An enlarged photograph showed a small flaw in the breech block. The gun was sent to Robert Churchill, who fired a test bullet –

the obsolete Mark IV, with its equally obsolete black powder – and verified that this was the gun that had killed Gutteridge.

At the trial of Browne and Kennedy in April 1928, Churchill's evidence played a conclusive part in their conviction; both were sentenced to death. This was the first British case in which ballistic evidence played a central role.

One month after the Gutteridge murder, in October 1927, there occurred another shooting tragedy in whose solution Churchill's expertise played a central role. Towards midnight on 10 October, a poacher named Enoch Dix hid his bicycle in a hedge near the village of Twerton, near Bath, before making his way to a little wood known as Whistling Copse. Within minutes he had killed a pheasant with a shotgun. But gamekeepers overheard the blast, and hurried into the wood. Suddenly, they came face to face with Dix, who raised his gun and fired. The head keeper, William Walker, fell dead, shot in the throat. The under-keeper, 18-year-old George Rawlings, fired both barrels after the poacher as he ran away.

Dix, an obvious suspect, was arrested at home the following day and taken to the police station. Asked to strip, he made excuses; when his clothes were finally removed, the police saw why. From his neck to his thighs, his back was peppered with buckshot, much of its still under the skin.

It was obviously pointless to deny his part in the affair. But Dix's story was that he had only fired accidentally after being hit by the gamekeeper's buckshot. The case hinged upon the question: who was telling the truth – the under-keeper, who said Dix had fired first, or the poacher? Churchill was asked for his opinion, and measured the distances in the wood. The tree by which Dix had been standing when he received the charge was also peppered with buckshot – in fact, the tree had taken most of the pellets, and Dix had been lucky that he was only hit by the fringe of the shot. Churchill conducted a series of experiments with the shotguns, to see how far the shot spread. These left him in no doubt that Dix had been 15 yards from the under-keeper's gun when he had been hit. On the other hand, the gamekeeper had been hit at close quarters – Churchill judged the distance to be five yards. Therefore, it was impossible that the under-keeper had fired first, unless Dix had been running towards him – an impossibility, since Dix had been shot in the rear.

A sympathetic jury found Dix guilty only of manslaughter, but an unsympathetic judge gave him a maximum sentence of 15 years.

9

The Browne and Kennedy case caused an extraordinary sensation throughout Europe – perhaps through the gruesome detail of the shooting-out of the policeman's eyes. (One widely held theory was that Browne believed the old story that a dead man's eyes 'photograph' the image of the last thing he saw.) The result was that within two years, all the major forensic laboratories in Europe had comparison microscopes, helixometers and other delicate measuring devices. Yet even this impressive battery of new technology could not guarantee freedom from the kind of errors that arise when experts become too confident of their own opinions. In this respect, the case of John Donald Merrett remains one of the saddest cautionary tales in British criminal history.

At the age of 18, John Donald Merrett was a rather unprepossessing young man with big ears, a thick nose, and a heavy, sensual mouth. He was born in New Zealand in 1908, but his parents had separated, and he had accompanied his mother to England. He was clever, but spoilt and badly behaved, particularly where the opposite sex was concerned. A scandal involving a girl had forced his mother to withdraw him from Malvern College after only a year. This led her to abandon her plan to send him to Oxford; instead, she decided to go and live in Edinburgh, and to send him to the university there, where she could keep an eye on him in the evenings. They moved into the ground floor of a house at 31 Buckingham Terrace. But young Merrett soon found maternal supervision tiresome, and began to deceive her. He would set out for the university in the mornings, and play truant all day. In the evening, he would apparently retire to bed early and lock his door; then he would climb out of the window and make his way to the local dance-hall.

On the morning of 17 March 1926, the daily help, a married woman named Rita Sutherland, was in the kitchen when she heard a shot. Then Donald Merrett ran into the kitchen shouting: 'Rita, my mother's shot herself.' Bertha Merrett was lying on the floor, blood oozing from a wound in her head. According to Merrett, he had been reading in a recess at the far end of the room when he heard the report – he had bought a pistol, a Spanish .25 automatic, a few days before.

Mrs Merrett was rushed to hospital, the case being treated as attempted suicide. Donald took his girlfriend – a dance hostess – out in the afternoon, and to the cinema in the evening. He called at the hospital to ask: 'Is my mother still alive?', and, on being told she was, went away.

Mrs Merrett was unconscious when she arrived at hospital, but later recovered consciousness enough to speak and even sign cheques. Her story was that her son had been standing over her while she was writing, and that she had said: 'Go away Donald, and don't annoy me.' Then she had heard a loud bang and lost consciousness. She asked a nurse: 'Did Donald do it? He's such a naughty boy.' Yet in spite of this, no one seems to have suspected her son of murder. Two weeks later, on 1 April 1926, she died.

Her estate, which brought in about £700 a year, was left in trust to her son; meanwhile, relatives moved into the flat to look after Donald. But his behaviour continued to be appalling; at one point he went off to London with an under-age girl and had to hitch-hike back. His uncle and aunt were so worried that they had him examined by a psychiatrist, who pronounced him perfectly sane and normal. And, some months after his mother's death, it became clear that he had been forging cheques on his mother's account for some time. His pocket-money had been 10 shillings a week, yet he had been spending large sums on the dance hostess, and bought himself a motor-cycle. The forged cheques amounted to about £450. Clearly, he had had a strong motive for killing his mother. In November 1926, he was charged with her murder.

William Horn, the Procurator Fiscal of Edinburgh, who was responsible for the indictment, soon realized that he had a poor case. Nine months had gone past since the shooting, and no one had attempted to gather evidence that might indicate Merrett's guilt or innocence. No one had even taken down Mrs Merrett's statements in hospital. The letter she was writing at the time of her death had disappeared – it might have indicated her state of mind.

The autopsy on Mrs Merrett had been conducted by Professor Harvey Littlejohn, of the University of Edinburgh, and he had recorded that he found a wound behind her right ear, with the bullet hole slanting upward. He had decided that this was 'consistent with suicide'. But since hearing about Merrett's exploits since his mother's death, Littlejohn had begun to have serious doubts about his own verdict. He spoke to the two doctors who had treated Mrs Merrett in hospital, and they also suspected murder; there had been no powder burns around the wound, which would normally be expected in a case of suicide.

By now, Sydney Smith was back in Edinburgh, and had published a textbook of forensic medicine with a chapter on ballistics. Since he had been a pupil of Littlejohn's, it was natural that the professor should consult him about the death of Bertha Merrett. Smith's conclusion was that it sounded like murder. On Smith's advice, Littlejohn tried experimenting with the Spanish pistol that had killed Mrs Merrett, and found that it caused powder burns at any distance less than eight inches. All this led Littlejohn to tell the Procurator Fiscal that he now believed Bertha Merrett's death to be a case of murder.

The Procurator suggested that they should get another opinion – Professor John Glaister, whose work on the Ruxton case would bring him widespread recognition ten years later. Glaister came to Edinburgh, conducted his own tests with the gun, and concluded that Mrs Merrett had been murdered.

But the defence had made a brilliant move: they had engaged Sir Bernard Spilsbury, and Spilsbury had gone to Robert Churchill for his opinion. Spilsbury and Churchill had not asked for the Spanish pistol that had killed Mrs Merrett; instead, they had selected one of similar calibre. And they had concluded that such a pistol did not necessarily leave powder burns – or that, if it did, they could easily be washed off.

Merrett's trial began in Edinburgh on 1 February 1927, and at first, things went badly for the defence. A parade of witnesses testified about Mrs Merrett, and about her bullet wound, and Littlejohn insisted that if the gun had been fired close to her head, there would be powder burns. But when Churchill appeared in the witness box, the tide began to turn. Asked by Craigie Aitchison, the defence counsel, if he had ever seen a similar case of suicide – with wounding *behind* the ear – he said yes. Would this not force her to hold the revolver in an awkward position? No, said Churchill; women tend to flinch and turn away the head when pulling the trigger. And he demonstrated how, in his view, Mrs Merrett had held the pistol.

After Churchill came Spilsbury, who explained his view that Littlejohn was wrong in believing that the pistol would inevitably produce powder marks. No one thought to challenge him on the fact that he and Churchill had not used the Spanish pistol, and that therefore their conclusions were bound to be suspect.

The judge was impressed, as his summing-up revealed. The jury was only slightly less so; they brought in a Scottish verdict of not proven on the murder charge, although Merrett was found guilty of forgery. He was sentenced to 12 months in prison. And soon after his release, he married a 16-year-old girl named Veronica Bonnar. Within a short time, they were in trouble for obtaining £300-worth of jewellery with a worthless cheque; Merrett received another nine months in prison. When he came out, he decided to change his name to Chesney. And he settled down to the relatively easy task of spending the £50,000 he had inherited from his mother. When that was gone, he turned back to swindling and petty crime.

During the Second World War, Chesney served honourably in motor torpedo boats. Captured by the Italians, he escaped to Gibraltar. After the war he became a smuggler, working out of Tangier. Sentenced to prison in France, he escaped to Belgium in 1949. In 1951 he was convicted at Lewes Assizes of smuggling currency, and sentenced to a year in prison. When he came out, he changed his name to Milner, and lived in a houseboat on the Thames. One of his biographers writes: 'He was a man born four hundred years too late, a swashbuckler . . .' And he began to think about the £8,400 he had given his wife so many years ago, when he had inherited his mother's wealth.

Veronica Merrett and her mother were running an old people's home in Ealing. Veronica had refused to divorce her husband, since she was a Catholic. She had also refused an invitation to visit him on the Continent, suspecting that he intended to arrange a convenient 'accident' for her. She was right. And since she declined to leave home, 'Chesney' decided to take the accident to Ealing.

It was an ingenious plan, worthy of Agatha Christie. He visited his wife and mother-in-law – known as Lady Mary Menzies – in February 1954, and returned to Germany, but not before stealing a passport from a man in a pub. On 11 February, he returned to England on the false passport, entered the old people's home unseen, plied his wife with large quantites of gin, then carried her to the bathroom and drowned her in the bath. It was the perfect murder. But as he left the house, things went wrong; he encountered his mother-in-law. There was only one thing to do, and he did it – kill her. Having beaten her unconscious with a coffee pot, he strangled her and made his escape. And when the double murder was discovered the next morning, the police announced that they were anxious to interview Ronald Chesney, formerly John Donald Merrett. There was an international manhunt. Four days after the murders, on 16 February 1954, Chesney shot himself through the head in a park in Cologne.

When Sydney Smith had heard of Merrett's acquittal – he was back in Cairo at the time – he had remarked: 'That's not the last we shall hear of young Merrett.' When he came to write his autobiography in 1959, he quoted that comment with justifiable pride. But Spilsbury had no chance to learn of his mistake; he had already died – by his own hand – in 1947. Robert Churchill's biographer, Macdonald Hastings, does not record what Churchill thought when he heard of the Chesney murders. But he acknowledges that it is unlikely that either Churchill or Spilsbury believed Merrett innocent.

10

The Spilsbury–Churchill team was not invariably successful. In the next sensational murder trial in which they shared the limelight, they were brillantly out-manoeuvred by one of the most intelligent advocates of his day, Sir Patrick Hastings.

At 27, Elvira Barney was a spoilt, self-willed nymphomaniac who lived in a mews maisonette not far from her wealthy parents. During the 1920s she had been one of the 'bright young things', but by 1932 her good looks had vanished and she was running to fat. The house in Williams Mews had a cocktail bar, a library of pornographic books, and a collection of instruments of sexual perversion. Mrs Barney, long separated from her husband, had a preference for young lovers from the homosexual underworld. The latest of these was a young man named Michael Scott Stephen who described himself as a dress designer, and who was three years her junior. His father was a wealthy banker, but by the spring of 1932 he had cut off his son's allowance. This may explain why Michael Scott Stephen chose to live with a woman with whom he often had screaming quarrels.

On the evening of 30 May 1932, Mrs Barney and her lover gave a cocktail party at the maisonette, then went to a Soho night-club. Arriving home drunk at four o'clock in the morning, they began to quarrel. Long-suffering neighbours, who could hear all too clearly, heard Mrs Barney whining: 'Chicken, chicken, come back to me.' Then there was a woman's scream, followed by the sound of a revolver shot. Mrs Barney's doctor, Thomas Durrant, was awakened by a frantic telephone call. 'Come at once – there's been a terrible accident.'

Michael Scott Stephen was lying dead on the stairs, a gunshot wound in his chest. When a policeman asked Mrs Barney to go to the police station to make a statement, she slapped his face, and insisted that he should wait until her parents, Sir John and Lady Mullin, arrived. Then she went to the station and made a statement in which she swore that she had threatened to kill herself, and that her lover was trying to take the revolver away from her when it went off and shot him. After signing it, she was allowed to go home with her parents.

Churchill and Spilsbury were both at the mews flat within hours. Churchill examined the revolver, a Smith and Wesson .32, and concluded that it could not be fired accidentally – it required too strong a pull on the trigger. This view supported Spilsbury's own conclusion that the gun could not have been discharged during a struggle such as Mrs Barney had described. There was no powder blackening or scorching on Stephen's clothing, which argued that the gun had been fired from some distance away. In short, the evidence indicated that Mrs Barney had pointed the gun at her lover and deliberately shot him.

The evidence of neighbours further undermined Mrs Barney's story of an accident. One neighbour had heard her shout 'I'll shoot you', while another was certain she had heard more than one shot. They described how, a few days earlier, Mrs Barney had leaned out of the window with nothing on, and fired at her lover in the mews below; he had spent the night sleeping in a van. Mrs Barney was obviously a woman with a strong temper and a determination to have her own way at all costs. Nothing was more probable than that she had killed her lover when he threatened to walk out on her. Three days after the shooting, Elvira Barney was arrested.

On the opening day of her trial, on 4 July 1932, the waiting crowds were so large that a police cordon failed to hold them back. And the crowds of fashionably dressed people in court chattered so loudly that the judge, Travers Humphreys, had to threaten to clear the court to obtain silence.

It was appropriate that the defence should be conducted by Sir Patrick Hastings, whose demeanour in court sometimes suggested a Noel Coward play; he was cool, sophisticated, rather offhand, and had never been known to raise his voice or make an emotional appeal. Hastings knew that his chief opponent was not the prosecuting counsel, Percival Clarke, but Sir Bernard Spilsbury. He therefore decided upon an unusual step – to request that Spilsbury should not be allowed in court except to give his own evidence. Hastings knew that if Spilsbury listened to the defence – of accidental shooting – and was then asked by the prosecution: 'Do you think that is possible?', he only had to reply 'No' to undermine the whole defence. If he was not in court, that question could not be asked. So when the judge sent Spilsbury out of court, Hastings had gained his first victory.

The prosecution case opened with testimony from various neighbours. One of them described the episode in which Mrs Barney had fired at her lover from the upstairs window, and Hastings elicited the apparently unimportant piece of information that she had fired it with her left hand. When the woman described seeing a puff of smoke, Hastings asked her casually if she knew that cordite cartridges made no smoke. It was undoubtedly an unfair comment, for all guns make some kind of flash when they are fired, and this was certainly what the woman meant. But the jury was impressed by Sir Patrick's apparently exhaustive knowledge of firearms.

Hastings was aware that Churchill was quite as dangerous an opponent as Spilsbury. And when Churchill testified that the Smith and Wesson was one of the safest revolvers ever made, and that it required a pull of 14 lb on the trigger, it looked as if Mrs Barney's defence was hopelessly undermined. But Hastings seemed unperturbed. After getting Churchill to confirm that it was virtually impossible to fire such a revolver accidentally, Hastings pointed it at the ceiling and proceeded to fire it again and again; the clicks followed one another at considerable speed. Churchill said that it would require a stronger pull if held loosely. 'Would it?' said Hastings, who changed his grip, and proceeded to pull the trigger at the same speed. It was, as Hastings later admitted, a trick – he confessed that the force required had made his finger sore.

After this, Hastings turned to the vital matter of how many shots had been fired. Two bullets were missing from the chambers of the revolver; but oddly enough, they were not adjoining bullets – there was an unfired cartridge between them. Hastings asked Churchill: 'Have you noticed something peculiar about this revolver – that if you only half pull the trigger, it makes the cylinder rotate?' Churchill admitted that he had noticed this, and Hastings dropped the matter. He had made his point: that a struggle for possession of the revolver could have rotated the cylinder to leave a bullet unfired. It made no difference whether one or two bullets had been fired if they had been fired accidentally during the course of a struggle. (In fact, Churchill had discovered another bullet hole in the wall, but without a bullet inside it, suggesting that someone had dug it out.)

So, in fact, Churchill had been manoeuvred into being a witness for the defence. But there was still Spilsbury to come. In response to the questions of the prosecution, he stated his opinion that an accident seems improbable; if Mrs Barney's account was correct, there should have been scorch marks on the dead man's clothes. And if Stephen had grabbed the barrel, there should have been powder burns on his hand. Therefore, it seemed, there was no struggle, and Mrs Barney must have fired the shot when they were standing apart . . .

All this was bad enough, but at least Hastings had prevented Spilsbury from tearing the defence to pieces. Now Hastings rose to his feet, and the audience prepared itself for a struggle of the giants. But Hastings knew that such a battle would be fatal; Spilsbury's cool precision would sway the jury. Therefore he concentrated on the bare essentials. Spilsbury's contention was that the bullet had been fired horizontally, with the pistol pointing straight at Stephen, not upwards, as it would be in the course of a struggle. So his first question was how Spilsbury had decided that the bullet must have travelled horizontally. Spilsbury replied that he had made tests on a skeleton. But, asked Hastings smoothly, do not human bones vary in their position? Spilsbury agreed that they did. In that case, said Hastings, would not the best way of testing the line of flight be a post-mortem examination? Spilsbury agreed that this was also true. And at this point, Hastings sat down. The 'battle' was over, and the audience was slightly bewildered. Hastings had deliberately avoided the kind of confrontation they expected. For, as he later explained, Spilsbury had said nothing that actually contradicted the defence theory of the shooting. (This was quite untrue; but when Hastings made a statement with an air of total conviction, he could make the jury believe that black was white.)

There was still one more hurdle – the statement of the female witness that Mrs Barney had fired the revolver with her left hand. Hastings was asking them to believe that Mrs Barney had not fired at her lover, but had simply discharged the revolver in the room, as a dramatic gesture. Somehow, doubt had to be thrown on this witness's testimony. Hastings did it with a magnificent piece of theatre. He asked the usher to place the revolver in front of Mrs Barney. Hastings turned to face the judge, and then, as if he had changed his mind, whirled round to face Mrs Barney and snapped: 'Pick up that revolver.' Mrs Barney looked startled. Automatically, she reached out and picked up the gun – with her right hand.

The trial was virtually over. The final speech for the defence made no effort to stir the emotions of the jury; it would have been unnecessary. Hastings had performed a feat of hypnosis – convincing everyone in court, against their better judgement and against the judgement of the forensic experts, that Elvira Barney was a pathetic little rich girl who had accidentally killed the man she loved, and who was now broken and contrite. Even if she had been guilty, the jury would probably have forgiven her. But the verdict delivered by the foreman of the jury was not guilty, and Mrs Barney cried 'Oh', and stuffed her handkerchief in her mouth.

In a work of fiction, the shadow of the gallows would have converted her into a changed character; in reality, she lost no time making up for the sex and alcohol she had been missing during the trial, and died a few years later in Paris.

11

With the invention of the comparison microscope, ballistics became a science in its own right; during the 1930s, most forensic laboratories set up a separate ballistics department. (In Great Britain, the first Police Forensic Science Laboratory was established at Hendon in 1934.) New techniques were developed, such as the use of the 'periphery camera', which could photograph the whole curved surface of a bullet, so that photographs could be laid out side by side for comparison. A closely related technique involved making a gelatine cast of the bullet, which could be slit open and spread out flat. A test was also developed to establish whether a suspect had recently fired a gun; known as the dermal nitrate test, it depended on the fact that residue from an exploding cartridge is driven backwards on to the hand that pulls the trigger. The suspect's hand was coated in paraffin wax, which was then tested for nitrates. But this test eventually became obsolete because so many common substances – such as fertilizers – contain nitrates, and could lead to misleading positive results. In 1974, six Irishmen were accused of being responsible for bomb explosions in two Birmingham pubs, which had killed 21 people; an appeal against their conviction was based upon the fact that some of them had been playing cards shortly before they were subjected to the nitrate test for explosives, and the backs of the playing cards contained nitrates. Although these appeals were rejected in 1988, the unreliability of the dermal nitrate test was accepted in court.

Compared with fingerprinting or blood serology, forensic ballistics has obvious limitations. A bullet distorted by impact is almost impossible to match. And although every gun has its 'fingerprint', there is obviously no equivalent of the fingerprint classification system that could allow the expert to track down a particular gun; unless he happens to have the weapon that fired the bullet, his experience is virtually useless.

But in the United States, at least one forensic expert brought a new precision to the science of ballistics. His name was Herbert Leon MacDonell, and the originality of his approach led one journalist to dub him the Isaac Newton of ballistics. MacDonell was an expert in porous glass technology, and during the 1960s he worked for the Corning Glass Works in New York State. He was also a Fellow of the American Academy of Forensic Sciences, and often lectured on forensic medicine; in America he was known as a 'criminalist'. It was in 1969 that MacDonell achieved a degree of national celebrity through his investigation of the Black Panther gun battle in Chicago; but in earlier cases he had already demonstrated an approach that would have appealed to Alphonse Bertillon.

In April 1966, MacDonell was asked to apply his skills to a case of accidental shooting during a deer-hunt. Robert Ferry, a fellow employee of MacDonell's at the Corning Glass Works, had joined the hunting party on the last day of the deer-hunting season, 7 December 1965. In the dusk, he had raised his rifle to fire at a doe in a gully, and been shocked to hear the cry of a wounded man. Another member of the party, Roy Roxbury, had been shot in the throat, and died shortly after. Ferry was arrested and charged with manslaughter; if found guilty of negligence, he faced a prison sentence. The local sheriff announced that too much negligent shooting was going on in the area, and he proposed to make an example in this case.

MacDonell was called into the case – by Ferry's lawyer – four months after the shooting. Ferry's problem was that he had been in a state of shock when he made his statement, and had failed to mention that he had seen a deer – he only mentioned firing in the direction of a noise. The dead man had, admittedly, been in the wrong place; he had obviously crawled forward from his assigned position to get an advantage over the rest of the party. But it looked as if Ferry had heard the sound of his movement and fired straight at it, assuming it to be a deer. If true, this constituted criminal negligence.

When MacDonell examined the shotgun pellet that had killed Roxbury, he was intrigued by the fact that a piece of wadding was still attached to it. In a shotgun cartridge, the wadding is packed between the explosives and the pellets or slug, its purpose being to drive the mass of pellets *en bloc;* but it usually falls away after a few yards. Something had caused this wadding to stick to the slug. On closer examination, MacDonell detected a particle of wood fibre clinging to the slug. Moreover, weighed on a fine balance, the slug was considerably lighter than it should have been.

At the trial, MacDonell unveiled his own theory of the shooting. The wood particle indicated that the slug had ricocheted off a tree, losing 14 per cent of its weight in the process; some of the metal had formed a hook, bonding the wadding to the slug. He produced a magnified photograph of the piece of wood fibre to support his case, and pointed out that the fact that no other lead was found in the victim's body suggested that the slug had lost 14 per cent of its weight in flight. The jury agreed, and found Ferry not guilty. When MacDonell later visited the scene of the tragedy with Ferry, he was able to find the tree from which the ricochet had occurred, and establish the presence of lead at the point of impact.

The outcome of a 1968 case was altogether less satisfactory, yet it again revealed MacDonell's talent for the kind of precision associated with Sherlock Holmes. The accused man was a vet named Gary Greene, and the case seemed to have the hallmarks of a *crime passionnel*. Greene had been having a love affair, but the woman had taken up with a younger man named William Hodiak, who was a convicted drug-pusher. Late at night on 12 May 1967, Greene and his ex-mistress had quarrelled bitterly over the telephone, and Hodiak had snatched the receiver to tell Greene he was coming over to 'beat the shit out of him'. When the Volkswagen arrived, Greene went out with a shotgun 'to scare him off'. As Hodiak hurled open the door of the Volkswagen, it struck the gun, which exploded and killed him. Greene was being accused of premeditated murder.

MacDonell studied the Volkswagen microbus. The shot had broken the middle panel of the window, torn away part of Hodiak's skull, and struck the roof of the bus. If the defence could prove that the door was opening at the moment the shotgun exploded, they could sustain their defence of accidental shooting.

MacDonell ran a tape measure from the point of impact on the roof, through the window, and in a straight line down to the ground. This, according to the prosecution, was the trajectory of the shot. But if it was, then the blood splashes would have remained inside the microbus. In fact, some of them were on the bumper that curved round the door, proving that the door must have been opening as the blood splashed. And further tape measurements established that other blood splashes could only have been made if the victim had been leaning into an open door. Moreover, some of the splashes on the bumper could only have been made if the door had been open more than two feet. Yet the position of other splashes indicated that the door had been open about nine and a half inches when the shotgun went off. The inference was that it was being flung open so violently that it had continued to open after the gun had fired. This verified Greene's story that Hodiak had flung open the door with considerable force.

Unfortunately, these technical calculations failed to impress the jury – even in MacDonell's own account* they are somewhat obscure – and Greene received a sentence in excess of three and a half years for manslaughter. This was better than being found guilty of murder; but if MacDonell was correct, Greene was innocent.

The case that made MacDonell known throughout America began in the dawn hours of 4 December 1969 when a raiding party of 16 Chicago police officers burst into a house on West Monroe Street and shot dead two Black Panther leaders, and wounded four other members of the organization. The Black Panther Party was a militant political organization that had been formed in 1965 by young blacks who were disillusioned with the slow progress of the Civil Rights movement. They admitted openly that they had no objection to violence – one of them said it was 'American as apple pie'. So few Americans were sympathetic when the news reports of 4 December stated that the two Panthers had been killed in a wild-western style shoot-out with the police. The story put out by the Cook County Attorney Edward V. Hanrahan was that the police had entered the building and knocked on the door of a room in which the Panther leader Fred Hampton was sleeping. A shotgun slug had torn through the door from inside as they pushed it open. A young woman lying on a bed in a corner opened fire on them with a shotgun. The Panthers began to shoot, ignoring the demand of Police Sergeant Daniel Groth that they surrender peaceably. The shooting continued for several minutes, during which time Groth called out several times to suggest

*The Evidence Never Lies, by Alfred Allan Lewis, with Herbert Leon MacDonell, New York, 1984.

a truce. When it was over, two Panthers lay dead. Seven others were arrested and charged with attempted murder.

The police admitted that the raid was the result of a tip-off from an informer, who had told them that the house at 2337 West Monroe Street was a Black Panther arsenal. The informer had advised them to time their raid for eight in the evening, when most of the Panthers would be away at a political education class, but the police decided that a dawn raid would give them the element of surprise. They had found, they said, 13 firearms.

Three days later, MacDonell was contacted by the man who acted as attorney for the Panthers, Francis 'Skip' Andrews, who asked him if he was willing to look over the house where the shooting took place. Andrews's view was that the police had fired first, and that their aim in raiding the house was to 'get' 21-year-old Fred Hampton, who looked as if he might shape into another Malcolm X, the formidable leader of the Black Muslims. MacDonell explained that he was not interested in the political aspects of the case. He told Andrews: 'My examination is going to be impartial. It would make no difference to me if I'd been hired by Hanrahan instead of you. My conclusions would be the same. Mr Andrews, if you don't want the whole truth, don't hire me.' Andrews's reply was to tell him to be on a plane for Chicago the following day.

The building in West Monroe Street had once been a brothel, and it now looked derelict. It was dirty, and full of stained mattresses and old junk. The room that interested MacDonell was the bedroom in which the shooting had taken place. The walls were full of bullet holes. There were two holes in the door – one made by a shotgun slug that had been fired from inside the room, another by a revolver fired from outside and into the room. MacDonell had two major tasks: to determine which side fired which shots, and – most important – to decided who fired first. Andrews was confident that the police had fired the first shot, but MacDonell was uninterested in his convictions; he was simply there to study the evidence.

This was not easy. The Panthers had already turned the house into a kind of martyrs' museum, and were escorting parties of sympathizers through the rooms, lectured by a guide. But in the course of a 12-hour day, MacDonell succeeded in reconstructing most of what had happened.

The first and most obvious thing was that most of the shots had poured *into* the room. In fact, apart from the shotgun slug that had penetrated the door from inside, there was no evidence that the Panthers had fired. Mark Clark, who had discharged the shotgun, had been killed almost instantly.

MacDonell began by tracing the trajectory of the shotgun slug. It had gone through the door and hit the opposite wall 18 inches below the ceiling. The slug had then gone through the wall, and into an upstairs apartment. Climbing the stairs in this apartment, MacDonell found the dent in the plaster where the slug had finally impacted; the slug itself lay below on the stairway. MacDonell ran a piece of string from the impact crater, through the hole in the opposite wall, down through the door in the bedroom where the shoot-out had taken place – he had to open the door to make the string continue in a straight line – and finally, to the point from which Clark had fired the shotgun.

Next he traced the course of the revolver bullet that had been fired through the door from outside. This had gone across the room and into the wall opposite. MacDonell was able to dig it out of the wall. It was impossible that this shot had been fired by the policeman who was opening the door, for obviously, his shot would have gone *straight* into the room, not obliquely. The evidence indicated that it had been fired by a policeman who had been standing behind the door as it opened, using the door as a cover. But which of the two had fired first – the Panther or the policeman?

The chief evidence for the police story of a gun battle was the wall of the living-room, which contained no fewer than 45 bullet holes, and the door of a second bedroom, riddled with two dozen bullet holes, all of which had entered from the bedroom side. (It is obviously easy to tell which way a bullet has passed through a door panel by the direction of the splintering.) It looked as if the police had been greeted by a hail of shots from the bedroom. But if the shots had been fired from inside the bedroom, they would have gone across the living-room beyond, and into a bathroom door on the other side. There was no sign of any such shots in the bathroom door. But when MacDonell opened the door towards the bullet-riddled wall separating the living-room and bedroom, it was obvious that the bullets had come *from* the living-room, and passed through the wall and the open door. In other words, the bullets had been going in the opposite direction from that claimed by the police. They must have been fired by the police themselves.

MacDonell proved his point by passing straws through the bullet holes, so they showed the exact direction of the bullet, then pushing thin metal rods through the straws. With these rods, he was able to show that the bullet holes in the door were in an exact line with those that had come through the wall.

Another question that intrigued MacDonell was why the hail of police gunfire had not killed *all* the Panthers in the bedroom where Hampton and Clark died. The answer seemed to be that the police had concentrated their fire on the bottom end of the bed, where Hampton's head was lying. It looked as if Andrews could be right in saying that they intended to 'get' Hampton – their informer had told them which way Hampton lay in bed.

Back in Corning, with an exact scale plan of the rooms where the shootings had taken place, MacDonell finally assessed the evidence. It showed conclusively that the door had been only partially open when the police bullet had gone through it, and almost completely open when the shotgun slug was fired. There could be no doubt that the police had fired first. Clark's shot had been the only one fired at the police; all the other bullets had been fired by the police. Their story of a 'shoot-out' was totally untrue.

In spite of this evidence, MacDonell had a hard time in court; the prosecution suggested that his testimony was biased and 'defence-oriented'. MacDonell protested that he was simply truth-oriented. But his evidence produced some effect; the Grand Jury reprimanded police inefficiency and cast doubts on their credibility. But they also attacked the Panthers for being uninterested in justice. 'Revolutionary groups simply do not want the system to work.' But in this case, the system eventually worked in favour of the Panthers. The FBI was ordered to turn over its own forensic evidence to the Cook County state attorney, and it was found to agree with MacDonell's conclusion that the Panthers had fired only one bullet. The case against the seven Panthers was dismissed, and in 1982, the Panthers obtained $1.85 million damages from Cook County on the grounds that the raid had violated their civil rights.

In 1972, MacDonell finally left the glass works to become a full-time investigator of crime; in the meantime, his book *Flight Characteristics and Stain Patterns of Human Blood* (1971) had already become a classic of forensic medicine.

12

In England, one of the longest and most disputatious murder trials involving ballistic evidence was resolved by the use of the latest electronic technology.

Colin Chisam was a garage proprietor of Berwick upon Tweed, who lived with his wife and a young man who was virtually an adopted son. He was a rigid, intolerant man with a distinctly paranoid streak, and one of his obsessive aversions was to 'Teddy Boys' or young hooligans. The forensic expert in the case, Dr H. J. Walls, described him as 'a man who found it hard to distinguish between himself and God'. Chisam was also, unfortunately, a gun collector.

Around midnight on 5 August 1962, three young men called Tait, Henderson and Johnson, who had been out drinking with their girlfriends, were walking back to their holiday lodgings and playing a transistor radio at a fairly high volume. As they walked past Chisam's house, he rushed out and asked them to switch the radio off. Apparently they did so but, according to Chisam, they were abusive about it. Chisam went indoors, grabbed a .22 repeater rifle, and fired two shots after them. No one seems to have been hit, but the young men realized someone was shooting at them, and ran back in a fury. Chisam beat a hasty retreat, and the youths proceeded to force the front door. Chisam's 'adopted son', Ninian Sanderson, got up to investigate the noise, and Chisam told him to ring the police. The angry men burst into the front hall, and a fight commenced, during which Sanderson was knocked to the ground. Then the young men retreated out of the front garden. As they did so, Tait collapsed, while Henderson began to groan with pain. Johnson telephoned for an ambulance; by the time it arrived at the hospital, Tait was dead. Both he and Henderson were found to have puncture wounds in the chest and back. Chisam at first denied any shooting, then admitted that he had fired two shots after them as they went up the street. Two empty cartridge cases were found near his front gate.

If Tait had died of a bullet wound, then Chisam was likely to end on the gallows, for murder with a firearm still remained a capital offence. But Chisam's contention – and that of his defence – was that he had seized a swordstick, and that as the young men had attacked him on the ground, one of them had become impaled on it. If Tait *had* been killed with the swordstick, then Chisam could not be hanged.

No bullet was found in Tait's body; if he had been killed by a bullet, then it had gone straight through him. One of the puncture wounds was a hole in the breast, while another in his back could have been the exit wound of a bullet. The Home Office pathologist, Dr Colin Corby, was quite certain these were bullet wounds. Two medical experts called for the defence disagreed, and said they had been caused by a swordstick.

Dr H. J. Walls, who was the director of the police laboratory at New Scotland Yard, and was the author of a textbook on forensic medicine, also appeared for the prosecution. It so happened that Walls possessed an ancient swordstick, and he hurried back to his laboratory and tried it out on a corpse. The experiment was unsatisfactory, for Walls felt a certain revulsion at trying to impale a corpse with a thrust of the swordstick, and probably failed to apply the necessary enthusiasm; at all events, the result was inconclusive.

On the other hand, experiments with the dead man's clothing yielded an interesting piece of information. The exit hole of a bullet tended to have a 'collar' of fibres around it, while the entrance hole of a sword-stick also had a collar of fibres, produced when the sword blade was withdrawn. The hole in the back of the dead man's coat had a 'collar' of fibres, which seemed to prove that Tait had been shot. But having explained the distinction in the witness box, Walls was discomfited when the defence handed him two pieces of cloth with holes in them, and asked him to say which was a bullet hole and which had been made by a swordstick. Walls could see that no forensic test could answer the question, and decided to guess. In fact, he guessed wrong, so that part of his evidence was discredited in the eyes of the jury.

The defence experts contended that Tait had been killed by the swordstick. They argued that the only bullets that had been fired had been the two fired after the retreating youths. But the autopsy on Tait had revealed that his heart had been pierced, in which case, he should have dropped dead rather than running back to start a fight.

The wrangle of the medical experts continued for five days, leaving the jury bewildered. It finally struck Walls that if the deadlock was to be broken, he had to produce some more convincing scientific evidence that Tait had been shot by a .22 bullet made of lead. But by now it was too late for further scientific tests. The prosecution had been taken off balance by the defence argument that Tait had been killed by a swordstick. At the end of a nine-day trial, the jury retired for three hours, and announced that they found Chisam guilty of murder, but with diminished responsibility. The judge told them that such a verdict was unacceptable, and that they would have to change it to manslaughter. They did this, and Chisam was sentenced to life imprisonment.

For his own satisfaction, Walls conducted sensitive chemical tests on the bullet hole in the front of the dead man's jacket, and found traces of lead. Then, recalling that leaden bullets are hardened with antimony, he asked the Forensic Laboratory at Aldermaston to test the hole in the jacket. The laboratory used a sophisticated instrument called an electron-beam probe, which was able to detect tiny amounts of metals; it showed conclusively that the hole was surrounded by quantities of antimony as well as lead. Walls had proved his point, that Tait had died from a gunshot wound, but too late to influence the verdict. Moreover, in view of the psychiatric report on Chisam – that he was suffering from 'a paranoid disorder that made him feel that he was always right and everyone else always wrong' – it seems likely that the jury would still have arrived at their verdict of manslaughter. Nevertheless, Walls had the satisfaction of knowing that he had discovered a new method of detecting the entrance wound of a leaden bullet.

13

The Chisam case was unusual in that it depended on the simple issue of whether a man had been killed by a bullet. Few cases involving ballistic evidence are as straightforward as this; to begin with, most of them involve robbery, and the criminal takes the main piece of evidence – the gun – away with him. When the weapon happens to be a shotgun, the problem becomes twice as difficult.

At a few minutes before half past midday, on 10 November 1966, a man walked into Barclays Bank, Upper Ham Road, in Richmond, Surrey. He pointed a sawn-off shotgun at the 20-year-old clerk Angela Wooliscroft, and demanded money. The girl took £2,500 from the drawer, and pushed it across the counter. Then the man raised the shotgun and fired, smashing the glass and hitting her in the chest and hands. The gunman turned and walked casually out of the bank; without hurrying, he crossed the road into a crowd of workers who were streaming out of a factory for their lunch break. Angela Wooliscroft died on her way to hospital.

Detective Chief Superintendent James Sewell, of Scotland Yard's Murder Squad, was placed in charge of the investigation. A few bank employees had noticed the gunman, and from their descriptions Sewell was able to piece together a portrait of the killer: a man of about 25, with hollow cheeks and a dark or tanned complexion, wearing dark sunglasses, blue jeans and a blue raincoat. Two witnesses outside the bank had noticed the man: one had noticed him because he was walking slowly when everybody else was in a hurry, the other because he was carrying a shotgun. Other witnesses observed that he arrived and left in a dark-coloured car, which he parked opposite the bank; it may have had a 'C' on its number plate. There were two other clues that had been dropped by the killer: a woman's yellow raincoat, and an empty plastic fertilizer bag. And in the raincoat pocket there were two pieces of paper: one, a photocopied entry from a wine-making competition run by the Weybridge Wine Club, the other a shopping list. The wine entry was signed 'Grahame'.

Both items were publicized on the radio. As a result, a man named Grahame Marsh came forward to say that he had signed the paper. And the shopping list was written by his sister. Miss Marsh was able to tell the police how she had lost the raincoat. On the morning of the robbery she had parked her car, an Austin A40, at a car park in Kingston. When she came back after lunch, she noticed that the car was in a slightly different place. She had left a door unlocked, and assumed that an attendant had moved it to a more convenient place. She also noticed that her yellow raincoat and sunglasses were missing. The robber had taken the car, driven it to Richmond and committed the murder, then returned it to the same car park.

Every motorist who had used the Kingston car park on the day of the robbery was traced and interviewed; several of them recalled the Austin A40 returning to the car park after lunch – there had been a queue, and the driver had attracted their attention by hooting impatiently.

There was mud on the back of the car, which led Sewell to theorize that the man had driven it to some open ground at some point; he used a helicopter to fly between Richmond and Kingston, looking for every open space, in the hope of finding tyre tracks; but a great deal of work produced no result. But the murder hunt was not entirely barren; the widespread police investigation led to the uncovering of many other crimes, and to 65 arrests.

Meanwhile, the forensic investigation produced interesting results. Ballistics expert Brian Arnold was able to say that Angela Wooliscroft had been killed by a 12-bore shotgun, and the fact that the pellets weighed 1.3 grains meant that the shot was No.7 size. There are two basic types of shotgun pellet: game shot and trap shot. Game shot is softer than trap shot – the latter is used for clay pigeon shooting, and needs to be hard enough to shatter the target. The extra hardness is obtained by adding more antimony. Chemical analysis of the shot by the Special Services branch revealed that it must have been game shot. Next, Brian Arnold simulated the shooting in the laboratory, firing No.7 game shot from a 12-bore shotgun at a glass screen exactly like the one in the bank; a high speed camera was triggered by the sound of the gun. It revealed that when the gun was placed close enough to the glass to make a hole of exactly the right size – which meant within a few inches – a shower of glass blew back on the clothing of the man firing the gun.

In Miss Marsh's car, police found fragments of glass. A forensic chemist, Roger Davis, tested these to determine their refractive index. (This is done by covering them with oil, and gently heating; the refractive index of the oil changes as it warms up, and when the glass 'disappears', it means that the index of the oil is now the same as that of the glass; since the refractive index of the oil at that temperature is known, that of the glass must be the same.) The glass proved to be identical with that in the cashier's screen.

In the course of this investigation, more that a hundred suspects were interviewed, including every 'villain' who had served time for armed robbery. A member of the public notified Sewell that he had seen a petty crook named Hart transferring an object that looked like a shotgun from one car to another, and Hart was one of those interviewed. Michael George Hart was at present on bail, awaiting extradition to France; in a shoot-out at a French airport, he had shot a policeman. The magistrate had allowed him bail in the face of strong opposition from the Hampshire police – Hart lived in Basingstoke, 25 miles from the scene of the robbery. He was obliged to report to a police station twice a day, and had done so at 9.30 on the morning of the robbery and again at mid-afternoon. There was nothing to connect Hart with the murder of Angela Wooliscroft, and a search of his house revealed nothing incriminating, so he was allowed to go.

On 22 November 1976, Hampshire police were alerted about an attempted robbery at a Basingstoke garage, and the description and number of the getaway car were given. Not long after this, two police constables in a patrol car saw the car, a Ford Consul, driving past them at high speed. They gave chase, and the car pulled on to some open ground near the road; the man inside ran away. But they had recognized him as Michael Hart. In the boot of the car, they found a Hendal .22 automatic pistol and 72 rounds of ammunition. They went to Hart's home in St Peter's Road, Basingstoke, and there found a box of shotgun cartridges, Eley No. 7s. But they were trap-shooting cartridges, not game-shooting. Yet another piece of information indicated that Michael Hart was the wanted killer. A gun shop in Reading had reported that a burglar had broken in six days before the murder, and taken a Hendal .22 automatic, as well as a Reilly 12-bore shotgun and a Webley revolver. This seemed too great a coincidence, and Sewell ordered the 'trap shot' to be analysed chemically; it proved, as he suspected, to be game shot. The factory that had made it, Eley Kynoch of Birmingham, acknowledged that a mistake had been made, and that, due to a computer error, the cartridges had been wrongly labelled. But the error was helpful in building up the case against Hart, for it was possible to trace the wrongly labelled cartridges to the Reading dealer, from whom they had been stolen.

Hart had disappeared; unknown to the police, he was living with a girlfriend in a caravan. But on 20 January 1977, he went to collect some wages owed to him for building work at a petrol station in Hounslow; the garage had already been asked to notify the police if he appeared, and they arrested him while the manager kept him talking. He was driving a stolen car.

At the police station he denied all knowledge of the Richmond bank robbery, but when the police asked him about the automatic pistol found in his car, he was obviously shaken. Later that day, Hart was found hanging in his cell. He was rushed to the West Middlesex Hospital, where he recovered. And finally, he was ready to admit to the murder of Angela Wooliscroft.

But, he insisted, it was an accident. He had become impatient because she was bending down, her hands below the counter, and begun to suspect she might be signalling for help. He had knocked the muzzle of the gun impatiently against the glass, and it had exploded. Sewell knew this to be untrue; the girl's hands and arms had been peppered with shot, so she must have had her hands in view.

In the course of a detailed confession to the robbery, Hart described how he had thrown the sawn-off shotgun into the Thames, and took police to the spot at Hampton. Police frogmen recovered it, and Brian Arnold cleaned it, and allowed the wood to shrink back to its normal size. Then he tested it to see if it could be made to fire accidentally by knocking it against glass. It proved to be impossible. The trigger required a pull of 6.5 lb compared with a normal pull of 4 lb. Arnold tried knocking it against plate glass like that in the bank; even light blows distorted the muzzle. He finally hit the glass violently enough to break it, and still the gun would not discharge. In fact, nothing could make the gun discharge accidentally. This was the evidence that finally convinced a jury that Hart was guilty of murder, not of manslaughter. He was sentenced to life imprisonment, with a recommendation that he should serve at least 25 years. The girlfriend who had sheltered him, Sharon Stacey, was sentenced to three years' imprisonment for cheque fraud.

But why did Hart kill Angela Wooliscroft when she had already handed him the money? The answer seems to be that, ever since he was charged with the French airport shoot-out, he had known that he would be spending a long time in prison; he told his girlfriend that he was determined to enjoy himself while he could. Ever since his return from France he had been on a crime spree – owing to a magistrate's ill-advised decision to grant him bail – and his behaviour had become increasingly disturbed. The death of Angela Wooliscroft was due to a legal error of judgement that never should have occurred.

14

The Hart case is an interesting demonstration of the resources of a modern forensic science laboratory, and of the collaboration between different kinds of expert which finally brought about the murder conviction. But it should be clear that luck also played a major part in the case; Hart would never have been arrested if he had not bungled his second attempt at armed robbery. In fact, few major crimes are solved without this element of luck. The following case may serve both as an illustration and as a cautionary tale.

On the evening of 6 August 1985, armed police surrounded a farmhouse near Tolleshunt D'Arcy, in Essex; after waiting for four hours, they broke in, and discovered that the five people inside were dead. Sixty-one-year-old Neville Bamber, his wife June, their adopted daughter Sheila, and Sheila's twin sons, Daniel and Nicholas, had all been shot with a rifle.

The police had been summoned by a telephone call from Jeremy Bamber, the adopted son of the murdered couple; he said that he had just received a telephone call from his father saying that his sister Sheila had gone berserk with a rifle; then the line had gone dead. This is why the police had waited four hours before bursting in; they suspected Sheila Bamber might be waiting to fire on them. But the five bodies had been dead for many hours. June Bamber and Sheila were in one bedroom, the twins in another, and Neville Bamber, an ex-fighter pilot and a local magistrate, lay in the front hall. He had two black eyes and had obviously fought for his life. Sheila Bamber – a pretty 27-year-old model known as Bambi – was holding the murder weapon, a .22 automatic rifle; she was holding a Bible in her other hand.

The case presented certain puzzling aspects. Neville Bamber was a strong man who stood six feet four inches tall; it seemed strange that he had had to fight for his life against a slim girl. Moreover, 'Bambi' herself had been shot twice, in the head and neck; that made suicide seem highly unlikely. Could her death be murder? It was rumoured that she had taken refuge with her parents because she was more than £20,000 in debt to drug dealers, and it seemed just possible that the underworld had caught up with her. On the other hand, the beautiful Bambi was known to be mentally unstable; she had had a mental breakdown not long before the murders, and had told a psychiatrist that she thought her two 6-year-old sons wanted to seduce her. On the evening before the murders, according to her brother Jeremy, her parents had talked to her about having the children fostered. She disliked her mother, June Bamber, who was a religious fanatic with strong puritanical tendencies; as a child, her mother had caught her in a compromising position with a boyfriend, and told her 'You are the Devil's daughter.' Episodes like this had made her neurotic and unstable, and her broken marriage had convinced her that she was destined for unhappiness. Under the circumstances, murder followed by suicide seemed a possible explanation of what had happened that evening. The two bullets in her body could be explained if the rifle had been fired by a reflex action after the first shot.

But could she have shot herself in the throat with a rifle? A local constable conducted an experiment: his arms were roughly the same length as Bambi's, so he cut a length of broom handle to exactly the same length as the rifle barrel, and tried placing it against his throat at arm's length. Spilsbury had encountered a similar problem in January 1918, when a corporal named Dunkin was found shot through the head with a .303 Lee Enfield rifle, which was lying beside his body.

But Spilsbury had demonstrated that the bullet must have been fired five inches from Dunkin's head, and that his short arms would have made it impossible to reach the trigger – another soldier named Asser was convicted of the murder. But the Essex police decided, on the evidence of the broom handle experiment, that Sheila Bamber could have committed suicide with the rifle. It if was not Sheila, who else could it have been? There were only two sets of fingerprints on the rifle, that of Sheila Bamber and her brother Jeremy. But Jeremy had been in his own cottage three miles away at the time of the shooting – he had telephoned the police from there – and he admitted that he had used the gun for shooting rabbits that afternoon. Besides, the farmhouse had been locked from the inside – the police had to break in. All this led the police to conclude that Sheila Bamber had killed her family, then herself.

Local villagers found this hard to accept, and the pub landlord told reporters: 'No one round here believes Sheila did it.' A cousin of the family, David Boutflour, also had his doubts. As soon as he could gain access to the farmhouse, he conducted his own search. In the gun cupboard, he found a six-inch long silencer, with blood and grey hair on the end. This seemed to explain one of the more puzzling aspects of the case – that the villagers had not heard the shots. But if the silencer had been on the rifle, it would have made it far too long for Bambi to have shot herself. Boutflour called the police and notified them of his find. Two days later, the rifle was collected. But by the time it arrived at the forensic science laboratory, the grey hair had vanished . . .

Five weeks after the murders, the police were compelled to reopen the case. Twenty-one-year-old Julie Mugford, Jeremy Bamber's girlfriend, went to the police and told them that Jeremy had been responsible for the murders; he had – he confessed to her – hired a 'hit man' to do it. Bamber – who, like Bambi, was 27 – was arrested in London and taken to the police station at Chelmsford, where he was questioned for 18 hours. He denied having any connection with the murders, but finally admitted that he *had* been responsible for a burglary in a caravan that served his father for an office, and that he had taken money. He was charged with burglary and released on bail. The Assistant Chief Constable of Essex admitted, with visible embarrassment, that the assumption that no outside person was involved 'may have been a mistake'. And eventually, Jeremy Bamber was charged with the murders.

When the evidence was examined more closely, it seemed self-evident that Sheila Bamber could not have committed the murders. The gun had been reloaded twice, yet her nightgown showed no trace of oil residue from bullets, and her fingernails were immaculate, not chipped, as might have been expected from someone handling a bolt-action rifle. Sheila would not have been strong enough to have fought with her father and inflicted facial cuts and two black eyes; and if she *had* done so, she would also have had bruises. Someone had removed the silencer after the murders . . . But all this only underlines the basic problem of crime detection: that nothing is 'self-evident' unless the detective happens to be looking for it. Detective Inspector Ronald Cook admitted that the farmhouse had not been carefully searched 'because we did not consider at that particular moment it was relevant . . .' The police had been called to a locked farmhouse (Bamber later admitted that he was able to enter and leave the house through a bathroom window), expecting to find a woman who had gone berserk with a rifle, and that is exactly what they appeared to find. Bamber himself was clever enough to recognize this principle of 'obviousness'; that is why he placed the silencer in full view in the gun cupboard. To condemn the police for inefficiency is to overlook an important point: that detection only comes into its own when the investigator is aware that he has something to detect.

Once Julie Mugford had told her story, everything was suddenly clear. She told how Jeremy Bamber had talked about his plan to murder his family – for the half million pounds inheritance – for weeks before he carried it out; she had thought this was fantasy, since he was inclined to self-dramatization. She described how he had drugged rats with marijuana, then strangled them manually 'to see if he had the nerve to kill'. His original plan had been to poison his family, then set fire to the farmhouse, but had discovered that the insurance was not high enough. He made meticulous preparations for the murders, calculating how long it would take him to cycle from his home to the farmhouse. His basic motive seems to have been resentment – he worked for his father, and felt he was underpaid. (His salary was £20,000 a year, and he supplemented it with drug dealing.) He was on bad terms with his mother, who objected to his girlfriend and called her a harlot. His sister Bambi seemed to be a mental wreck; she believed she was evil, and even her children were disturbed. She had a violent temper, and on occasions raved and beat the walls with her fists. Bamber had told his girlfriend that he felt he would be doing his family a favour by putting them out of their misery.

The trial began at Chelmsford Assizes on 2 October 1986. The defence case was that Julie Mugford had invented the whole story out of resentment, because her lover had jilted her for another woman. She admitted that she had been jilted, but insisted that it was the 'terrible burden of her secret' that had finally driven her to go to the police.

The crucial piece of medical evidence concerned the murder weapon; a pathologist pointed out that it would have been physically impossible for Sheila Bamber to have placed it against her throat, with or without the silencer, and then pulled the trigger. A policewoman demonstrated to the jury that, no matter what position she adopted, it was impossible to place the muzzle against her neck and pull the trigger. Another small but crucial point made it clear that Bamber was lying. He had claimed that his father rang him to say that his sister had gone berserk; then the line had gone dead. In fact, the telephone in the farmhouse was off the hook. But in that case, Bamber's telephone would also have been dead, since he was still connected to the farmhouse, and he would not have been able to telephone the police.

On 28 October 1986, the jury returned from a 24-hour retirement to announce a verdict of guilty. Describing Bamber as 'evil beyond belief', the judge sentenced him to life imprisonment, with a recommendation that he should serve at least 25 years.

15

All the advances in ballistics have only underscored the central problem: that in large areas of the world, firearms are too easily available. In England around the turn of the century, one type of small revolver was known as the 'suicide special' because so many suicides used it. But it was not until the 1930s – when cases like Browne and Kennedy, Elvira Barney, and John Donald Merrett made the problem obvious – that the British introduced a law – the 1937 Firearms Act – forbidding the ownership of guns by private citizens except by special permit; this had the effect of dramatically reducing deaths from shooting in Great Britain. Most other European countries went on to introduce their own restrictions.

In America, where the Constitution permits every citizen to carry arms, and where there are 60 million hand-guns, a powerful 'gun lobby' (supported by arms manufacturers) has opposed any attempt to change the law, and the number of gun-related deaths has continued to rise steadily. The American murder rate has always been far higher than that of Great Britain; in 1960, the United States had 10,000 murders a year compared with Great Britain's 150, although the population was only three times as large. By 1975, the murder rate had risen to 500 a year in Great Britain and 21,000 in the United States – of which 16,000 (more than two-thirds) were shootings. Milton Helpern, the Chief Medical Examiner of New York, records that on the hot weekend of 22 July 1975, there were 57 murders in New York, including 26 shootings – he comments that this is an unusually low proportion. In his autobiography, *Autopsy,* Helpern remarks: 'I feel very strongly about this crazy notion that all Americans must have the sacred freedom to carry guns. We are not pioneering across the West now. . .' But the opinions of America's pathologists, and most of America's police force, have failed to break the stranglehold of the 'gun lobby'.

America's gun problem is not so much social as psychological, stemming from Samuel Colt's notion of the pistol as an 'equalizer'. In a society with a high rate of competitiveness, it is inevitable that there will also be a high rate of feelings of personal inadequacy, and that many of these people will regard the 'equalizer' as the solution. The years since the mid-century have seen an alarming increase in the number of mass murders committed with guns, and most of these, inevitably, have been in America. On 6 September 1949, a 28-year-old ex-GI named Howard Unruh walked out of his house in Camden, New Jersey, carrying a German Luger pistol, and in the next 12 minutes he killed 13 people. His motive, it seemed, was increasing resentment about the neighbours, particularly a Mrs Cohen who had once addressed him 'Hey you'. He planned the murders for two years, and carried them out with grim efficiency, walking from door to door, pausing to lean in the window of a car at a traffic light to shoot the driver, her son and her mother, then casually killing a small boy who had rushed to the window to see what was happening. When he ran out of bullets he returned calmly home, and gave himself up when the police used tear gas. He later told a psychiatrist: 'I'd have killed a thousand if I'd had the ammunition.' He was interned in New Jersey State Mental Hospital.

On 30 December 1950, a young psychopath named William Cook stopped a car driven by Carl Mosser, and also containing Mosser's wife, three children, and family dog. Brandishing a gun, he made Mosser drive around Texas for 72 hours, then, when the wife and children became hysterical, killed them all – including the dog – and threw their bodies down a well. He killed another car driver, and drove into Mexico, where a police officer finally disarmed him. He was executed in the San Quentin gas chamber in December 1952.

In January 1958, 28-year-old Charles Starkweather lost his temper with the parents of his 14-year-old girlfriend Caril Ann Fugate, and shot them both with a rifle; he choked her 2-year-old sister to death by pushing the rifle down her throat. Then the two went on a murder rampage across Nebraska and Wyoming, during which Starkweather shot seven people, including a 16-year-old girl, whom he raped first. In court, he implicated his girlfriend so that she received life imprisonment; he was executed in the electric chair.

On 31 July 1966, Charles Whitman stabbed his mother and his wife to death, then went up to the observation deck of the campus tower at the University of Texas, killing the receptionist with a blow of the rifle butt on the way. He shot three people who walked into the room, then went to the top of the tower and began sniping, killing 16 and wounding 28. An hour and a half later he was shot dead by police who burst into the tower; a post-mortem revealed that he was suffering from a brain tumour.

On 19 October 1970, a disaffected 'Beatnik', John Linley Frazier, walked into the home of an eye specialist, Dr Victor Ohta, near Santa Cruz, California, and killed the doctor, his wife and two children, and his secretary, 'executing' each with a shot in the back of the head, then dumping the bodies in the swimming-pool. Identified through fingerprints found on the door of the doctor's Rolls-Royce, Frazier was sentenced to death – although the suspension of the death sentence in California in 1971 meant that he joined a queue of convicted killers in San Quentin.

In the autumn of 1972, a paranoid schizophrenic named Herb Mullin began a murder rampage in California, killing an old tramp with a baseball bat, stabbing and disembowelling a girl to whom he had given a lift, and stabbing a priest to death. When his 'voices' ordered him to kill more, he bought a pistol. On 25 January 1973, he killed a man and his wife, then a mother and her two children. On 6 February, in the State Park near Santa Cruz, he walked up to a tent with four teenagers and shot them all dead. On 13 February, he approached an old man in his front garden and shot him. A neighbour witnessed the shooting, and within minutes, Mullin was under arrest. He was sentenced to life imprisonment for the 13 murders.

These cases constitute only a small proportion of mass murders by the use of firearms in the United States. England has so far (1989) had only one case. On 19 August 1987, a gun fanatic named Michael Ryan went berserk and killed 16 people, wounding 14 more, before he committed suicide. Ryan, 27, who was a member of a pistol club, lived with his widowed mother and had no record of violence. But that morning, he approached Mrs Susan Godfrey as she was picnicking with her two children aged four and two, in Savernake Forest, and ordered her to go with him into the forest, taking the groundsheet she had brought. His intention was probably rape; but Mrs Godfrey seems to have tried to run away. Ryan shot her with a burst from a Kalashnikov AK-47 rifle, and she fell dead. Ignoring the children, who were strapped in the car, Ryan drove to a nearby service station, and fired at the attendant with a shotgun; she dropped to the ground in time and, as Ryan drove off, rang the police. Assuming it was an attempted hold-up, they radioed two police cars to investigate. Meanwhile, Ryan had returned to Hungerford, the small Berkshire market town where he lived, and began a massacre. A man of 84 was shot dead as he sunbathed on the lawn. Then Ryan returned to his home in a cul-de-sac called South View, killed the two next-door neighbours, and shot and wounded the woman who lived opposite. He then set the house on fire, shot dead another passing male neighbour (who had ignored warnings that there was a gunman on the loose), riddled a police car with bullets, killing the policemen, and shot two more neighbours, killing one and seriously wounding the other. When Ryan's 60-year-old mother ran out of house to plead with her son, he shot her dead with four bullets. As he strode on, a deaf old lady shouted at him: 'Is that you making all that noise? . . . You stupid bugger', but he ignored her.

Ryan was now making for the John O'Gaunt School, which he had once attended. *En route* he shot at a couple in a car, killing the husband and wounding the wife, then killed a taxi-driver, a man walking his dog, and a woman driving past in her car. After this he burst into a house and killed an old couple, an invalid and her husband. Back in the street he shot a van driver who had been accidentally diverted into the killer's path by police who were now trying to isolate Ryan. A magistrate's clerk was also shot as he drove past with his wife and children; he died later. Finally, he took refuge in the school, which was quickly surrounded by police. For 90 minutes he held a reasonable and lucid conversation with them, telling them that 'It's like a bad dream.' He said that killing his mother had been a mistake, and added: 'It's funny. I've killed all those people, and I haven't the guts to blow my own brains out.' Tying a white handkerchief to the barrel of the Kalashnikov, he threw it out, together with the magazine of a Beretta pistol. Then he shot himself in the head with the Beretta with the one last round he had kept in the chamber. The fire at his home gutted three other houses; there police found the remains of his Labrador dog, which had also been shot.

Britain's newspapers wanted to know how a private citizen had been allowed to amass much an armoury in a country whose gun laws are the tightest in the world. The answer, apparently, was that as a member of a gun club, Ryan had been allowed to own rifles, pistols and shotguns. Within days, the Home Secretary, Douglas Hurd, announced that he intended to introduce legislation to ban semi-automatic weapons like Kalashnikovs, to restrict pump-action and semi-automatic shotguns, and introduce tighter controls on all shotguns. An indignant outcry from the 'gun lobby' – pointing out that hardly any weapons used in crimes are licensed anyway – was ignored, and the new restrictions duly introduced.

In the United States, all attempts to introduce similar laws have been passionately opposed by the gun lobby, supported by private citizens who invoke their constitutional right to carry guns. When Jim Brady, a White House secretary, was permanently disabled in 1981 by John Hinckley jun. (the man who wounded President Reagan), his wife Sarah sponsored the amendment to the law demanding registration of all hand-guns. The National Rifle Association immediately mobilized its 2.8 million members to fight a bill 'that would deny you your constitutional rights'. In fact, the amendment was merely designed to impose a seven-day waiting period on hand-gun sales to enable checks to be carried out on the background of the purchaser; it would do nothing whatever to restrict Kalashnikovs or Uzi sub-machine-guns, both of which are popular with the drugs underworld.

One of the major arguments of the gun lobby, that there is no proof that gun control would lower the incidence of murders, was conclusively disproved in 1988 by research conducted by Dr John Henry Sloan and a team of colleagues at the University of Washington in Seattle. They studied the crime statistics in Seattle, and in Vancouver, just across the Canadian border, between 1980 and 1983. The cities are 140 miles apart, and had approximately the same populations (about half a million); but Vancouver has the same gun control laws as Great Britain. The frequencies of robberies and burglaries were almost identical as was the frequency of assaults with weapons other than guns. But the Seattle murder rate was 63 per cent higher, most of this being accounted for by murder with firearms.

7

The Microscope As Detective

1

Perhaps the most important event in the history of crime detection occurred more than two centuries before the birth of forensic science. The day and the month have not been recorded, but the year was fairly certainly 1607. In the town of Middelburg, in Holland, two brothers named Johann and Zacharias Janssen practised the trade of spectacle-makers. One day, Zacharias heard a cry of excitement, and discovered that his two children were playing with lenses. They had found that if they held two lenses at a certain distance from one another, whatever they looked at became larger. They could clearly see the cock on the spire of the local church – although it appeared upside-down. Zacharias Janssen was inspired to put the lenses at either end of a tube, and so invented the telescope. But he was inclined to regard his invention as little more than a toy because it turned things upside-down – which is what happens if both lenses are convex. Another local optician named Johan Lippershey realized that if he placed a concave lens in the end of the tube nearest the eye, it turned the image the right way up again, although it diminished the magnification.

Now the principle of the lens had been known since about 1290, when a Florentine nobleman named Salvano degli Amati began to make concave lenses, and went on to invent spectacles.* And within half a century, other glass manufacturers had discovered that very tiny lenses will produce enormous magnification, so that a wasp's sting looks like a rapier. But a very tiny lens – a fraction of an inch wide – is hard to make, and almost equally hard to look through, so the 'micro-scope' (which is what such tiny lenses are called) failed to catch on.

*In fact, the earliest lenses, of quartz, were discovered in the treasury of Nineveh and in ancient Carthage

But around 1670, a Dutchman named Antonie Van Leeuwenhoek, who ran a hardware store in Delft, began grinding small lenses – purely as a hobby – and using them to study all kind of tiny objects, from grains of pollen and legs of flies to muscle fibres and hairs. He was the first man to realize that a hair, far from being a smooth tube, is covered with overlapping scales like a coconut palm or tiled roof, and that underneath this is a layer consisting of many colours.

Even before Leeuwenhoek, Janssen and Lippershey had realized that the principle of the telescope could be applied to the microscope: that the tiny image seen through the lens could be magnified by an eyepiece at the other end of a tube, and save a great deal of eye strain. Robert Hooke, secretary of the Royal Society, built one of the first of these tubular microscopes – called compound microscopes – in 1665, although it was far less powerful than Leeuwenhoek's simple lenses. And so it came about that, by the time forensic science came to birth in the mid-nineteenth century, its most powerful and useful tool was already in existence.

The first known use of the microscope in a murder case occurred in France, and it was used to throw light on the most sensational crime of the year 1847, the notorious Praslin Affair.

Charles-Louis Theobald, the Duc de Choiseul-Praslin, married his wife Fanny – a daughter of one of Napoleon's general – in 1824, when she was 16 and he 19. She was a woman of fiery temperament, with lesbian inclinations, and by the time she was 34, and had borne nine children, she was corpulent and wrinkled. The duke, an introverted, withdrawn man, found her dominant ways intolerable, and ceased to frequent her bed. Yet there can be no doubt that the duchess continued to love her husband. Matters became increasingly strained when an attractive girl named Henriette Deluzy was engaged as the children's governess, and it soon became clear that the duke was strongly attracted to her. Whether she became his mistress is not known, but it seems certain that the duchess thought the worst. She told her husband to dismiss the girl; he replied that if Henriette left, he would go too. The duchess wrote him a number of pathetic letters, which make it clear that this was not the first time the duke had shown interest in other women, and that in spite of this, she still loved him.

Finally, the duchess got her way; Henriette Deluzy was dismissed – without even a reference. The duke continued to call on her, and the affair became the talk of Paris society. In June 1847, the duchess announced that she intended to seek a divorce, on the grounds of her husband's adultery with the governess. The duke was mad with fury; he would lose his children and his position at one blow. On the evening of 17 August, he went to see Henriette Deluzy, and returned home in the early hours of the morning. As dawn was breaking, the servants were electrified by a piercing scream. Then the bell connected to the duchess's bedroom began to ring. There was another scream. It looked as if burglars had broken in. The duke's valet and the duchess's maid crept to her door, and heard the crash of something falling over. They knocked and called, but there was no reply. They tried another door, but it had been wedged. A number of servants rushed to the garden, and looked up at the bedroom window; as they did so, the shutter opened, and several of them saw a man they recognized as the duke. It seemed that he had also heard the burglars and had entered his wife's bedroom. The servants rushed back indoors to help him fight the intruders. To their surprise, the bedroom door was now open. The room was in chaos, with overturned furniture, and splashes of blood on the walls. The duchess was sitting on the floor, half-propped against her bed; she was obviously dead. Her throat had been slashed, and her face bruised and battered.

As they were examining her, the duke walked into the room, and gave a scream as he saw his dead wife. 'Some monster has murdered my beloved Fanny! Fetch a doctor.' He claimed that he had only just been awakened by the noise.

Two passing gendarmes noticed that the front door was open, and came in to investigate. Soon the house in the rue Faubourg-St-Honoré was full of policemen, including M. Allard, Vidocq's successor as head of the Sûreté. It took him very little time to dismiss the theory about burglars – to begin with, the duchess's jewels were untouched. Under the sofa, he found a Corsican pistol, covered with blood.

'Does anyone know whom this belongs to?', asked Allard.

To his surprise, the duke answered: 'Yes, to me.'

To this Allard asked: 'But how did it get here?'

The duke's story was that he had heard cries for help, and rushed into his wife's bedroom, brandishing his pistol. Seeing that she was covered in blood, he had dropped the pistol to raise her up. As a result, he had become covered in blood. Seeing that his wife was dead, he went back to his bedroom to wash off the blood . . .

It was just plausible – except, of course, that he had told the servants that he had only just awakened. Allard went to the duke's bedroom, and pointed out that bloodstains led to his door. The duke replied that he had been dripping with his wife's blood as he had returned. But the state of the duke's bedroom left little doubt of his guilt; there was a bloodstained handkerchief, the bloodstained hilt of a dagger, and a piece of bloodstained cord. And when the severed end of the bell-pull from the duchess's bedroom was found under her husband's shirt, Allard told the duke he was under arrest.

But suppose his story were true? Or suppose, at any rate, that he continued to insist that it was true? Was there any point at which his account could be positively disproved? He could claim that the servants had misunderstood him when they thought he said he had only just been awakened by the noise. He could claim that the shock of discovering his wife's dead body had led him to act in a strange and confused manner, carrying off the bloodstained cord and the bell-pull. A court might disbelieve him, yet still have difficulty proving that he murdered his wife.

The bloodstained pistol was turned over to the eminent pathologist Ambroise Tardieu, he who had written the first treatise on hanging, proved the guilt of Dr de la Pomerais, and discovered 'Tardieu spots', the spots of blood that form under the heart of people who have been suffocated. What the police wanted to know was whether the pistol had been dropped in the duchess's blood, or used as a weapon to batter her to death. With characteristic thoroughness, Tardieu studied the pistol, first under a magnifying glass, then a microscope. The first thing he discovered was a chestnut hair close to the butt. Near the trigger guard, he found fragments of skin tissue. Further microscopic examination revealed a bulb, or root, of human hair, and more fragments of flesh. One of the fragments melted when heated, and formed a grease spot on a piece of paper. Moreover, some of the contused wounds on the dead woman's forehead had been made with a blunt instrument like the butt of the pistol. In short, there could be no possible doubt. The microscope revealed that the duchess had been battered to death with the pistol.

Tardieu's medical investigations revealed exactly what had happened that night. The Duc de Praslin had slipped into his wife's bedroom, probably through the bathroom, intending to kill her with one sweep of a sharp knife. But his nerve failed him, or perhaps she woke up as he bent over her. The blade made a deep cut in her throat, but failed to sever the windpipe; she screamed, and began to fight. He stabbed her again and again with a dagger, then began to beat her with the butt of the pistol; as she writhed on the floor, she bit his leg (a medical examination revealed her teeth marks). By this time the whole house was aroused; the servants were knocking on the door. His original plan – of killing her, then opening the front door and making it look like a burglary – had to be abandoned; instead, he decided to leave an open window. But as he threw back the shutters, he saw the servants in the garden. At least this allowed him to escape back to his own room. And now he made yet another mistake. He rushed into his wife's bedroom, pretending that the noise had awakened him, and screamed at the sight of his wife's body. And when the police arrived, and he was forced to change his story, he knew that his last chance of getting away with murder had vanished . . .

Before being taken off to the Luxembourg prison, the duke succeeded in swallowing a dose of arsenic. He died three days later, still refusing to admit to the murder. But Tardieu's microscope had made such a confession superfluous.

2

The basic principle of the magnifying glass is extremely simple. When you 'look at' an object, rays of light enter the retina of your eye. You therefore see the object in the position *from which the light seems to be travelling*. An obvious example is a mirror. You know that your own face is not really two feet in front of you; it only appears to be so because the mirror has reflected the light backwards, so it appears to be coming from the opposite direction. A similar thing happens if you stick a pencil in a glass of water; it appears to be bent because the water makes the light come from a different direction, owing to refraction. When two parallel beams of light enter either side of a magnifying glass, glass bends them inward. If you put your eye at the point where the two beams meet, your eye continues the line of both beams, so to speak, and sees the object as far wider than it is. A fairground distorting mirror works on the same principle, which is why a telescope can use mirrors as well as lenses.

Leeuwenhoek's microscope was simply a very small lens, and in order to see the magnified object clearly, he had to put his eye fairly close to the lens. It soon dawned on his successors that a second lens would magnify the already magnified image, and that if the original lens magnified it 20 times, and the second one another 20 times, the result would be a magnification of 400 times. In theory, a third lens ought to be able to magnify the object 8,000 times. But this proved to be impractical, because an object cannot be magnified beyond the wavelength of the light that is magnifying it; this limit proved to be about 2,000. (But an electron microscope, using electron beams of far shorter wavelength, can achieve as much as half a million.)

Now hair could be magnified until it looked like a tree trunk, the experts realized that there was a basic difference between human and animal hair, and that even within human hair there were many varieties. In animals, the cells of the cuticle (outer layer) were larger and less regular in shape, and the medulla, or core, more continuous and obvious, whereas in humans it is often invisible. There was an obvious difference between Negroid hair and that of other races. Morever, it was possible to distinguish armpit hair, pubic hair, scrotum hair, moustache hair, and facial hair from beards. The first treatise on hair appeared in 1857, and by the early years of the twentieth century – when scientists like Edmond Locard and Victor Balthazard took up the subject – the study of hair was virtually a branch of forensic medicine. The Paris Medical Examiner, Victor Balthazard – the man whose solution of the Guillotin case laid the foundations of ballistics – produced his own treatise on human and animal hair in 1910. In the previous year, his knowledge of human hair had enabled the police to solve a baffling murder mystery.

On Sunday 18 July 1909, a waiter in the Café Bardin, at 1 boulevard Voltaire, noticed blood oozing through the ceiling. It was coming from the kitchen of the flat above, which was occupied by a bachelor named Albert Oursel. The concierge tried to gain access to the flat, but it was difficult, since it had its own separate entrance, and the stairs that led up to it were closed off by an iron gate. The only other possible means of access was a transom window at the rear of the flat, but this also proved to be locked. A ladder placed against a bedroom window revealed that the room was in chaos. The concierge hastened to fetch the police. They broke a rear window and climbed inside. On the floor of the kitchen lay a dead woman, her naked legs spread apart, her face beaten beyond recognition. The concierge had no doubt about her identity; she was Germaine Bichon, the 16-year-old mistress of Albert Oursel. A half-eaten meal in the dining-room indicated that she had been surprised there by her assailant. There had been a struggle between the dining-room and the kitchen, where Germaine had finally been battered to death with a hatchet. Then the murderer had ransacked the bedroom, apparently looking for money, and escaped by means of the transom, which was now open.

But the mystery remained. If the iron gate had been locked, and the transom had been closed, how had the murderer got into the apartment in the first place?

The crime caused such a sensation – a large crowd had gathered in front of the building within minutes – that Octave Hamard, the chief of the Sûreté, himself decided to take over the investigation. His first question concerned the whereabouts of the girl's lover, Albert Oursel. It seemed that he ran an agency for domestic servants from the flat, and that he spent most weekends at his family home at Flint-sur-Seine, leaving his mistress alone in Paris. The absence of any sign of a break-in led Hamard to suspect that Oursel had returned to Paris, let himself in and killed Germaine. He had, it seemed, a motive; he was tired of the girl, who was pregnant, and who wanted him to marry her. But when Oursel returned to Paris the next day, Hamard had to admit that his alibi was unshakable; he had only just left church at the time Germaine was being hatcheted to death, and had then had lunch with his family.

Was it possible, then, that the killer was a jealous lover? That also seemed unlikely. Germaine was hardly the type to drive a man into a fever of jealousy; she was singularly free with her favours, having been raped by her father and brothers when she was a child. According to Oursel, it was probably some casual pick-up who was responsible for her condition; he himself took care to use contraceptives.

Could it, perhaps, be some woman who was in love with Oursel? The only likely candidate seemed to be Oursel's secretary, Suzanne Dessignol. She proved to be an unattractive woman of about 30, who admitted that she was probably the last person to see Germaine alive, apart from her killer. They had left the flat together on Saturday afternoon, after Oursel had departed for the country, and had separated soon after to go in opposite directions. Germaine might have picked up one of her lovers – or some total stranger – and taken him back to the flat. This seemed the likeliest explanation of how the killer had entered the apartment, for Germaine was far too nervous to admit any stranger who knocked on the door; she disliked being left on her own all weekend.

Suzanne Dessignol was also a possible suspect, for she had a key to the apartment. But there was no evidence to link her with the murder. And she had no injuries that she would probably have sustained in the struggle with a healthy country girl.

Mme Dessignol was at least able to provide one useful piece of information. Seven francs had vanished from a cash drawer and a further 30 from the bureau. Oursel himself was able to add that a gold watch chain, and a gold Russian rouble worth 40 francs, had also vanished. But it hardly seemed worth committing a murder for so little . . .

Other clues seemed relatively unimportant. The concierge's wife remarked that an unknown woman had passed her lodge soon after the discovery of the murder, and had said that she was looking for a maid named Adèle. Apparently Adèle was not at home, and the woman had asked the concierge to pass on a message saying that Angèle had called. The apartments above Oursel's flat were mainly occupied by domestic servants, so it was not improbable that the woman had been up there in search of Adèle. On the other hand, the transom through which the killer may have escaped was also on the staircase leading up to the servants' apartments. Hamard gave orders to try to track down a woman called Angèle, and his interest in her increased when he learned no one in the building seemed to know anyone of that name – including a servant girl called Adèle.

Victor Balthazard, the Medical Examiner, was out of Paris for most of the day of the murder, but as soon as he returned he hurried to boulevard Voltaire. His examination of the corpse told the police little that they did not already know: that she had been dead about six hours, that she had died in the course of a struggle, and that she was five months' pregnant. But at the conclusion of his examination he opened the dead girl's hands, and observed that she was clutching a number of hairs. The colour was light – as far as he could judge, a mousy blonde. And their length suggested that they were from the head of a woman. Since Suzanne Dessignol was a blonde, she was requested to provide a few of her own hairs for comparison. She agreed without hesitation.

Baithazard began by washing the hair in a weak solution of bicarbonate of soda to remove blood – probably the victim's own – then in distilled water with a little alcohol; after drying, it was coiled on a glass slide and held in place with colourless gelatine. Under a microscope, it could be seen that it was not blonde, but a light chestnut colour, quite different from that of Suzanne Dessignol. This eliminated Suzanne from the inquiry. But it meant that Germaine Bichon had been killed by an unknown woman, to whose identity the police had no clue whatsoever.

Meanwhile, the police continued to interview everyone who had known Germaine Bichon. The cleaning woman was able to confirm that Oursel and Germaine had not been on the best of terms for some months, and that he was anxious to get rid of her. She, on the other hand, seemed to be genuinely in love with Oursel, and wrote him love letters. Again, the finger of suspicion seemed to be pointing towards Oursel. Yet he hardly seemed the type to kill his mistress with a hatchet, or even hire someone to do so: he was a weak, nervous little man with an obsessive attachment to his mother. The cleaning woman had also recommended the police to speak to her predecessor, a woman called Rosella Rousseau. She was soon located – she was living with a workman named Martin – but was unable to help; she had not seen Germaine since she left the job several months ago.

Among the mass of interviews collected by his officers, Hamard discovered one curious piece of information. On the Saturday afternoon, the day before the murder, three servant girls had been separately accosted by a woman near Oursel's flat. She had explained that Oursel owed her money, and she wanted someone to go with her as a witness when she demanded it. All three girls had refused to get involved. The unknown woman had told one of the girls that her name was Mme Bosch. And as Hamard idly flipped through the various depositions, his eye was suddenly caught by another mention of a Mme Bosch. It was the married name of the previous cleaning woman, Rosella Rousseau. This could, of course, be coincidence. But when a criminal gives a false name, it is often connected with someone he knows, or with his own past. Hamard ordered Mme Bosch to be brought to his office for questioning.

She proved to be a slatternly, nondescript female of 38, a woman who had obviously 'been about'. She burst into tears when talking about Germaine Bichon, and professed deep sympathy for the girl and her plight. Her theory about Germaine's murder was that it must have been committed by someone with a key to the flat – which meant that it could only have been Oursel or his secretary Suzanne. Since both had been eliminated, Hamard had no hesitation in dismissing this notion.

Hamard brought the three servant girls to see whether they could identify her as the 'Madame Bosch' who had accosted them; disappointingly, none of them recognized her. One thought she looked like the woman, but could not be certain. The wife of the concierge also failed to recognize her as 'Angèle', the woman who had been looking for Adèle. There was obviously nothing to connect 'Madame Bosch' (or Martin) with the murder, nor could Hamard conceive of any reason why the cleaning woman should kill a girl she professed to love. Yet there was something shifty about her that made him order further investigations.

His officers soon unearthed a fact that made Mme Bosch a leading suspect. She and her present 'husband' were deeply in debt, and on the day before the murder, their landlord had given them an ultimatum: pay up or get out. The following afternoon, they had paid enough of their rent to lift the threat of eviction. Then they had gone looking for a dealer who would buy something. This 'something' could, of course, be the missing watch chain and gold rouble. Detectives found the dealer and questioned him; they were excited when he told them that she had wanted to sell a gold coin. But he insisted that he had not bought it. And all the efforts of Hamard's team failed to track down the rouble or gold chain.

At this point, Balthazard's report on the hairs reminded Hamard that he had forgotten this important clue. He had Mme Bosch brought in for further questioning, and obtained a sample of her hair. Back in his laboratory, Balthazard soon determined that this was of exactly the same colour and width, 0.07 millimetres, as the hair taken from the dead woman's fingers. There was, of course, no way of stating positively that they were from the same person; but it seemed highly likely. And now Balthazard recalled something else: the hair in one of the victim's hands was in a clump, with blood on the end, as if torn from the head of her assailant in one violent pull. The next day, Baithazard hastened to interview the suspect again. She was obviously depressed after her night in prison, and sat apathetically as Balthazard examined her forehead and temples. And on the left temple Balthazard found what he was looking for: a spot where a tuft of hair had been pulled out with a single tug.

Later that afternoon, confronted by this new evidence, Rosella Rousseau finally broke down and admitted that she had murdered Germaine Bichon. Driven to desperation by the eviction threat, she had decided to try to rob her former employer, Albert Oursel. She knew that he left for the country every Saturday afternoon, and that Suzanne Dessignol left soon after. If she could slip into the flat unseen, she might get a chance to steal money, and slip out when Germaine had gone to sleep – she remembered the transom that led out on to the rear staircase. But how could she get in unnoticed? The idea that occurred to her was to persuade some other woman to go with her, and while Suzanne Dessignol's attention was distracted, slip quietly into the flat. But the three girls she accosted all turned her down. Nevertheless, she went up to the apartment, and when Suzanne Dessignol's attention was distracted, succeeded in slipping inside. Some time later, she heard Suzanne and Germaine leave the flat; now was her opportuntiy. But she was afraid of being caught, and delayed too long. Germaine returned, and she was forced to hide in a closet overnight. Since the money she wanted was in the bedroom, she had to wait until Germaine got out of bed at midday the next day and went to get herself a meal. But as she stole out of her hiding-place and into the dining-room, she found Germaine already sitting at the table. She flew at her and they fought their way to the kitchen, where Germaine grabbed the hatchet to defend herself. She had wrenched it out of her hand and killed her with blow after blow. (In the restaurant kitchen down below, the waiter had heard Germaine's gasps and groans, and concluded that she was engaged in sexual intercourse.) Then she had forced open the cashbox and ransacked the wardrobe. Interrupted by noises from below, she began to wonder if anyone had heard the struggle, and went and peered out through the transom, standing on a chair – this is why the police later found the transom open. Then she took the key and let herself out through the iron gate at the bottom of the stairs, unaware that the police were already on their way. In case anyone saw her, she stopped by the concierge's lodge and enquired for 'Adèle'.

At her trial in February 1910, Rosella Rousseau withdrew her confession, alleging that it had been forced from her; then she tried pleading self-defence, insisting that Germaine had compelled her to snatch the hatchet from her to save her own life. But – as Locard puts it at the conclusion of his account of the case – 'the jury of the Seine would not accept that excuse, and the woman Bosch was condemned to death'.

3

A less-publicized murder case of 1909 reveals the new science of forensic analysis at its most impressive. It occurred in the port of Le Havre, and concerned a woman of dubious reputation called Marie Pallot. Mme Pallot, who was in her early 30s, lived in a house in the Passage des Mathurins, and was suspected by the police of being involved in receiving stolen goods. In the early hours of an October morning, a gendarme passing her front door gave it a routine push, and was surprised to find it open. Marie Pallot usually went to some trouble to lock her doors and bolt her window-shutters. He walked along the passageway beyond, and pushed open another door; the light of his lamp showed him a woman seated at a table, the back of her head matted with blood; she had been killed with one tremendous blow. A ransacked cupboard indicated that the motive was probably robbery.

In 1909 French criminology was still dominated by *bertillonage,* and it so happened that one of Bertillon's leading disciples, Professor R. A. Riess – the man who had founded the Institute of Police Science in Lausanne – was on a visit to Le Havre. On the morning after the crime, the Prefect of Police invited Riess to come and demonstrate his skills as an investigator. Like his British colleague Sherlock Holmes, Riess's mainstay was a powerful magnifying glass. With this he spent five minutes closely examining the front door in the Passage des Mathurins. The prefect pointed out that his had already been dusted for finger-prints, and that the result was negative.

'Nevertheless', said Riess, pointing to the spot where the door had been forced, 'the killer has left us a drop of his blood. In jemmying the door, he drove this large splinter into his finger. I would be surprised if he has not left a trail of blood inside.'

He crawled along the passageway on all fours. 'I can tell you one thing already. The murderer was left-handed, and it was his left hand that he injured.'

The prefect asked him to elucidate.

'There are blood spots on the left side of the passage. This indicates that his left hand was hurt. But there are also a number of grease spots on the right side of the passage. That shows that he carried a candle in his right hand. He would also be carrying a weapon – probably the instrument that forced the door and shattered her skull. Most of us would carry the weapon in the right hand, and the candle in the left. He must be left-handed.'

In the room where the dead woman was still sitting, Riess pointed to the injury on the left side of her skull. 'That confirms my observation – he wielded the blunt instrument with his left hand.'

In life, Marie Pallot had been a coarse but not unattractive woman; she was known to have come from Marseilles. In front of her on the table there was a glass and an empty spirit bottle. This, as the prefect pointed out, suggested that her killer knew her fairly well. He knew that she was inclined to drink strong liquor late at night, and he knew which cupboard to search. Now Riess studied this cupboard, and the carpet in front of it. This was stained with several spots of candle grease. That could mean only one thing: that the killer had still been holding the candle when he searched the cupboard, and that the apartment must therefore have been in darkness when he entered. This suggested that

Marie Pallot had already been asleep – probably drunk. The fact that the grease spots were on the left of the cupboard again indicated that he was holding the candle in his left hand.

Once again Riess crawled on all fours, this time examining every inch of the carpet. He muttered with satisfaction as he used a pair of tweezers to transfer two short hairs into an envelope. These were not long enough to be from the head of the victim. They might, of course, be animal hairs, but this would become clear under the microscope. Finally, Riess took scrapings of the candle grease, and placed these in another envelope.

When he next called on the Prefect of Police, Riess was able to tell him: 'The man you seek is a left-handed sailor who has recently been in Sicily. He has a cut on his left hand and a red moustache.' Under the microscope, the hairs had proved to be red, and their length and width indicated that they were from a moustache – Riess thought that the murderer had nervously tugged at his moustache as he stood over the corpse. Chemical analysis of the candle grease had led to the deduction about Sicily. Candles have a stearine basis, mixed with other substances, and Riess had made a study of their composition. After a chemical analysis of the grease, he had telegraphed the Sûreté to ask if they could suggest where it had been made; they had replied that this type of candle was made only in Sicily. Since few men could carry a candle for any length of time, it could probably be assumed that the owner of this one had recently been in Sicily. Since he was now in the port of Le Havre, it seemed a fair inference that he was a sailor.

The prefect made immediate enquiries from the harbour board, and learned that a ship called the *Donna Maria* had arrived from Sicily two days before. Detectives went on board to make enquiries. Almost immediately, they noticed a short, powerfully built man with red hair and red moustache, who was busy on deck. He was seized unceremoniously, and handcuffed, while he protested volubly in Italian. On the prefect's orders, he was taken to the scene of the crime, where Riess was waiting. Asked his name, the man identified himself as a native of Sicily called Forfarazzo. Riess ordered the police to remove the handcuffs, then extended a piece of paper. 'Please look at this.'

The man took it, and looking up in bewilderment said: 'It is blank.' But Riess and the prefect had observed that he took it with his left hand.

Accused of the murder of Marie Pallot, Forfarazzo denied knowing her. When told they were certain of his guilt he replied angrily: 'Prove it.' Riess asked him to turn out his pockets. Among the usual odds and ends there was the stump of a candle. Riess snatched it up, saying: 'I think we have our proof.'

As he suspected, analysis of the candle showed that it was of the same composition as the grease on the carpet. Under a microscope, hairs from the suspect's moustache were identical with those found behind the murdered woman. Upon this circumstantial evidence Forfarazzo was found guilty and sentenced to death. He strenuously maintained his innocence until shortly before his execution, then made a full confession. He had been doing business with Marie Pallot for a long time – she often purchased smuggled brandy from him. He had stayed in her house, and set out to try and learn where she kept her money. One day, when drunk, she took money from a cupboard. Next time he was in Le Havre, Forfarazzo determined to rob her. He had sold her a quantity of brandy, and knew her well enough to be fairly certain that she would be drunk when she retired to bed. He was carrying a quantity of heavy sling shot in a bag, to serve as a blackjack in an emergency. When he entered the room, he found her asleep at the table, her head in her arms. He was searching the cupboard when she suddenly stirred; he struck her on the head with all his strength, then went on searching until he found the money. Then he quickly left the house with his loot, not long before the passing gendarme had tried the door . . .

Riess was in Le Havre for only a few days, but he had demonstrated to the police that scientific crime detection was not an invention of Conan Doyle and Emile Gaboriau.

4

The French police were in need of such a demonstration. Bertillon's domination of criminology meant that France was at least 10 years behind the rest of Europe. In London and New York, criminalistics had been revolutionized by fingerprinting. In Germany and Austria, a new era had dawned in 1893 with the publication of Hans Gross's *Handbook for Magistrates,* published in English as *Criminal Investigation,* with its long sections on footprints, fibres, wood fragments, dust and hairs. Gross cites a typical case of the use of microscopic examination in a case of indecent assault. Three small girls were taking a rough-haired terrier for a walk by the sea when they were approached by a stranger, who gave them sweets and took them on the sand hills, where he persuaded them to allow him to commit sexual assault. The children told their parents, who in turn reported the incident to the police. The clothing worn by the children was immediately collected. The knickers of all three showed semen stains inside the crotch. The following day, one of the girls was out walking with her mother when she saw the man on the seafront. The mother called a policeman and the man was taken into custody. Examination of his trousers showed seminal stains on the outside of the flies, confirming the children's story that he had exposed his penis and placed it inside their knickers. There were also dog hairs identical to those of the terrier, and a number of coloured wool fibres which matched those of a knitted woollen dress worn by one of the girls. As usual in his accounts of such cases, Gross does not bother to give further details, but it seems clear that the man was convicted on this evidence.

Gross's book came to the attention of a brilliant chemist named Georg Popp, who ran his own company in Frankfurt. Popp loved chemistry for its own sake. But when asked to examine the spots on a suspect's trousers in 1900, he became fascinated by criminal investigation. Like Riess, who in 1903 wrote a book on forensic photography, Popp was convinced of the importance of fingerprints, and of the use of the camera to record them. On one occasion, he used his skills to track down a thief in his own laboratory. The thief had handled a piece of platinum, and also some copper salts. Many other laboratory employees had also touched the platinum. But Popp exposed it to vapours of ammonium sulphohydrate, which caused the thief's fingerprints to show up in black; the man was identified as someone who had frequent access to the laboratory.

In 1904, Popp photographed fingerprints found in the shop of a murdered piano dealer, as a result of which three men were arrested for the crime. Impressed by his feat, the police began to consult him regularly. And in October 1904, Popp achieved celebrity in his native Frankfurt when he solved a sex crime by means of the microscope. The victim, a 52-year-old dressmaker named Eva Disch, was found dead in a beanfield; lying in a typical rape position and strangled with her own silk scarf; there were also knife wounds on her neck. The corpse lay beside a footpath, and on this the police found a handkerchief. Popp was asked if he would go to Wildthal, near Freiberg, to study the evidence.

Under the microscope, Popp was able to see traces of blood that had been partly washed away by rain; the crime had been committed towards evening, and there had been a heavy rainstorm later. There were also tiny scraps of red and blue silk on the handkerchief – the same colour as the victim's scarf. There was nasal mucus stained with snuff, and quantities of coal and coke dust, as well as sand and fragments of the mineral homblende.

Popp told the police that the blood on the handkerchief and the fragments of silk indicated that it belonged to the killer. The man they should be looking for took snuff, and worked in a place where he was likely to breathe in coal (or coke) dust and sand. Since this sounded an unlikely combination, he probably worked at two jobs. In a place as small as Wildthal, it was not difficult for the police to trace such a person. He was an ex-legionnaire named Karl Laubach, who worked in a sand quarry, and who took snuff. When the police questioned him, he flatly denied having anything to do with the crime, but admitted that he had recently worked in a gas works, where he was in contact with coke. All this made him a prime suspect.

Fortunately for Popp, Laubach was not a man who attached much importance to cleanliness. There were faint traces of blood on his fingers and on his clothes. And in the plentiful dirt under his fingernails, there was sand mixed with homblende and mica, coke dust, and fragments of red and blue silk. Under a powerful microscope, all these 'traces' became enormous, so the coke dust looked like lumps of coal, and the sand grains like rocks. The most telling piece of evidence against him was a knife found in his room. It was not bloodstained (or if it had been, Laubach had washed it clean), but it contained minute traces of dried blood and cloth fibres. These fibres proved to be identical with those of Laubach's trousers; he had evidently used the knife to try to scrape off dried blood. Popp was even able to establish that the mud on Laubach's trousers came from the footpath between the scene of the crime and Laubach's home. Faced with all this evidence, Laubach broke down and confessed. When news of Popp's triumph percolated back to Frankfurt, one newspaper printed the story in an article aptly entitled 'The Microscope as Detective', and other newspapers hailed Popp as a real-life Sherlock Holmes. In his own account of the case, written in 1918 for the *Archives of Criminology* under the title 'The Microscope in the Service of Criminal Investigation', Popp studiously under-dramatizes the story, and does not even bother to mention whether Laubach was sentenced to death or life imprisonment.

In the same article, Popp describes one of his most remarkable successes, the affair of Andreas Schlicher. It took place four years later, and once again involved the murder of a woman out for a country walk. On 29 May 1908, an architect named Seeberger informed the police that his housekeeper, Margarethe Filbert, was missing; she had failed to return from her afternoon off the previous day. She had taken a train to a nearby village, then walked home through the attractive valley of Falkenstein, with its ruined castle. Two members of the Royal Bavarian Police picked up her trail in the village of Falkenstein, where people had noted a skinny woman with a parasol walking towards Rockenhausen; she had also been seen picking flowers. A search of the woods was organized, and on 30 May, two days after her disappearance, the headless corpse of Margarethe Filbert was found lying among the bushes. It looked like a sex crime; she lay on her back, her legs apart and her skirt and petticoat up over her head – or where the head should have been. But the autopsy was to establish that there had been no sexual assault. That evening, District Attorney Sohn of Kaiserslautern arrived at the scene with a district judge and a doctor. He noted immediately that Margarethe was exceptionally well dressed – like a 'lady' rather than a servant – and that this could have explained why her killer thought her worth attacking. Her purse was missing, and so were the hat, jacket and parasol. One glove was still on her hand, the other had been pulled off enough to expose the fingers, as if someone had been looking for rings. Leaves caught in the dress indicated that the body had been dragged from further up the slope where it was found. The pathologist who performed the autopsy concluded that she had been strangled, then beheaded with a sharp knife.

District Attorney Sohn had read Gross's *Handbook for Magistrates* with deep attention, and he prepared himself to apply its principles of minute observation. He took possession of some hairs clutched in the dead woman's hand, and also of some fragments of flesh found further up the slope. And at this point, he happened to see one of the Frankfurt newspaper articles about Georg Popp and his Holmesian powers of deduction. He telegraphed Frankfurt, received a reply from Popp, and sent off the various clues, including the woman's bloodstained clothing. Within 24 hours, Popp had established that the hair came from a woman's head, and that the pieces of flesh were from a mole.

Meanwhile, the local police were questioning the inhabitants of Falkenstein about possible suspects. The mayor had no doubt that only one man was capable of the crime, a factory-worker who owned the field next door to where the body had been discovered. The man's name was Andreas Schlicher, and he was disliked and feared by his neighbours, being known as a bully with violent inclinations. He was also known to the police, who had been trying for years to catch him in the act of poaching.

Schlicher owned a small farm, and he denied being anywhere near the field in question on the day of the murder, which happened to be Ascension Day, a public holiday. He had been out to inspect other fields at mid-afternoon, then stayed at home. The testimony of a woman who had heard cries for help coming from the woods that afternoon enabled them to place the time of death at five o'clock. But the local tavern-keeper told the police that Schlicher's alibi was false: he had been seen coming out of the wood later in the evening. Unfortunately, the man who had volunteered this information was terrified of Schlicher, and could not be induced to repeat it to the police.

The examining magistrate, Seeberger, took over the case. Schlicher had been arrested, and Seeberger interrogated him; but Schlicher stuck to his story of being at home at the time of the murder. A search of the farmhouse revealed nothing suspicious. But scrapings were taken from underneath Schlicher's fingernails, and the material was sent to Popp in Frankfurt. Popp applied the Uhlenhuth test, and found traces of human blood among the dirt. The net was beginning to close around Schlicher. But no jury would convict a man on the evidence of his fingernails. More was needed. Popp asked Seeberger to send him Schlicher's clothing, but the magistrate – who had not read Gross – thought it a waste of time and ignored the request.

The victim's head was still missing, and the search was extended throughout the woods around Falkenstein. But it was not until they examined the ruined castle that the searchers found more evidence. In a cellar they found a rusty rifle, a box of shells, and a pair of trousers wrapped in a woman's blouse. Police investigation established that the trousers belonged to Schlicher, and the blouse to his wife. But Popp himself was now in a state of intense frustration. Magistrate Seeberger insisted that Schlicher's clothes had been examined, and flatly refused to turn them over for microscopic investigation. But he at least agreed to Popp's suggestion that Schlicher's home should be searched again. The shotgun shells had been sealed with circles cut from a postcard. And a search of Schlicher's farm turned up the postcard with round holes cut in it.

District Attorney Sohn felt that the police were losing the initiative, and asked for the help of a skilled detective; the inspector who was sent from Darmstadt immediately sent all Schlicher's clothes off to Popp. Popp thought he saw traces of blood on the knees, and soaked them in salt water, then applied the Uhlenhuth test. The serum turned cloudy, indicating human blood. More spots of blood were found on the jacket, although someone had tried to wash them out.

This evidence made Seeberger recognize the error of his ways; he hastened to send Popp the shoes Schlicher had worn on the day of the murder. Popp went to Falkenstein, and visited the various fields that Schlicher claimed to have inspected, as well as the murder site, and Schlicher's own farmyard. Then he carefully removed the soil from Schlicher's shoes and sliced it into layers with a razor. The layer closest to the instep contained goose droppings, such as Popp had found in the farmyard. Next came a layer of mud containing grass fragments, as if Schlicher had crossed a meadow. Then there was a layer of red, sandy earth, such as that found at the scene of the crime and in the field next to it. This was of great importance because this type of soil was not found in any of the other fields Schlicher claimed to have visited. But there was something even more significant – tiny fragments of wool and cotton fibre, some purple, some reddish brown. Study of the victim's skirt and petticoat established that they were made of similar materials. In order to establish this beyond all doubt, Popp subjected them to spectroscopic tests. The spectroscope had been invented by Popp's master, Bunsen, in 1859, and by his friend Gustav Kirchhoff, and it depended upon the discovery that the spectrum of each element has its own individual fingerprint – the fingerprint being a series of bright lines called emission lines. The spectroscope had enabled Kirchhoff to announce confidently what elements were to be found in the stars. By comparison, it was relatively simple for Popp, using a related instrument called the spectrophotometer – for measuring intensities of light of different wavelengths – to discover what dyes had been used in the fragments of cloth found in the mud of Schlicher's shoes, and to ascertain that they were identical with the dyes of the skirt and petticoat.

All this left no doubt of Schlicher's guilt. Faced with the evidence of his own shoes, Schlicher hastily acknowledged that he *had* been at the scene of the murder, but only after the body had been discovered. Fortunately, his wife insisted on a different story – that she had cleaned his shoes on the evening of the murder, and that they had not been worn since. Popp's analysis disproved the first part of her story, and the second part contradicted her husband's line of defence. Although Schlicher continued to deny knowledge of the crime, a jury was so impressed by Popp's evidence that they found the accused man guilty. After sentencing, Schlicher finally decided to confess. He had seen Margarethe Filbert as he was on his way to his field, and had assumed from her clothing that she must be carrying money. He strangled her; then, when he discovered that she was almost penniless, he cut off her head in a rage – an indication of the vengeful temperament that made him a terror to his neighbours. Then he buried the head under a heap of stones – where it was finally recovered – and washed the bloodspots off his coat and trousers in a pond. Because the trousers were so badly stained, he had decided to hide them in the cellar of the castle, where he had also hidden the gun he used for poaching.

The sentence of execution was commuted to life imprisonment, and Schlicher paid tribute to the man who had been responsible for his conviction by admitting grudgingly: 'That chemist fellow was right.'

5

The great Lacassagne, who had solved the Gouffé case (see p. 180), was a friend of Bertillon – which was unusual, for that notoriously prickly man had few friends – yet he was too good a forensic scientist not to recognize that Bertillon was blinded by his own obsession with 'anthropometry'. So he lost no opportunity in impressing on his pupils at the Lyon Institute of Forensic Medicine the importance of the microscope. One of his best students, Émile Villebrun, wrote his thesis on fingernails and their importance in legal medicine (1883). This dealt with the characteristics of scratches made by fingernails, as well as with the microscopic examination of the dirt underneath them. In 1887, the postmistress of Beauval, in northern France, was murdered in the course of robbery; she was also raped. A man named Gillard was arrested; he had deep scratches on both cheeks. Gillard claimed that these were made when he fell down among some brushwood, but the doctors who examined him could easily see that this was impossible. When human nails enter flesh, they make a groove, then tear away the skin in a distinctive manner; this groove, and the shape of the nails, can easily be seen under a powerful magnifying glass. Nail marks on both cheeks left little doubt that the woman had scratched him as he was raping her, and this piece of evidence led the court to condemn him to death. Villebrun cites a similar case of a man suspected of a sex murder, who had two straight scratches on the right cheekbone, and claimed that these had been made in a fall against a wall. Villebrun thought this was just possible, but that it was far more likely that they were scratches made by the nails of a robust woman such as the victim. In fact, her nails proved to be short and square, exactly like the scratches on the man's face.

In due course, Villebrun's thesis was eagerly read by a young man called Edmond Locard, who had been born in Lyon. Locard was only 6 when Villebrun submitted his thesis, but he was already an avid reader. A French translation of *The Adventures of Sherlock Holmes* filled him with a vision of an ultimate science of crime detection. Locard was undoubtedly a romantic – but, fortunately, a romantic with the determination and the funds necessary to pursue his vision. He talked to Bertillon in Paris, to Riess in Lausanne, then extended his criminological tour to Rome, Berlin, Brussels, New York and Chicago. What he saw disappointed him; apart from fingerprinting – which he recognized immediately as far as more efficient than *bertillonage* – there was nothing that could be called a genuine advance in crime detection. Back in Lyon, he tried to persuade the police department of the need for a genuine crime laboratory, apart from Lacassagne's department at the university. Like Bertillon 30 years earlier, he met with total indifference. But he was persistent and, like Bertillon, he knew a few people of influence. Finally, one day in 1910, he established his own police laboratory – two attic rooms in the Palais de Justice – and began the task of transforming forensic medicine into an exact science.

His earliest success was in helping to convict a gang of comers. The Paris police had been trying to trace the source of false franc coins, and had succeeded in arresting some of the gang who were distributing them; but their suspects refused to reveal the identity of the coiners. Finally, an informer told the police the names of three men, and these were taken in for questioning. But it was impossible to connect them with the counterfeiting. Locard heard of the case, and asked the inspector in charge of the case to allow him to see the clothes of the men; it took several requests before the inspector reluctantly sent along the garments of one suspect. Locard carefully brushed the clothes – paying special attention to the sleeves – over a sheet of white paper, and studied the dust under a microscope. There were unmistakable fragments of metal. Chemical tests showed these to be made up of tin, antimony and lead. Moreover, precise analysis revealed that these were in exactly the same proportion as in the counterfeit coins. On receiving this information, it dawned on the inspector that this young man was not simply an upstart busybody, but a valuable ally; he lost no time in sending Locard the clothes of the other two suspects. They yielded the same information, and the coiners were convicted.

From now on, the Lyon police realized that Locard could detect evidence not visible to the naked eye, and began to call upon him whenever confronted by a baffling case. In 1922, Locard described many of these cases in his book *Policiers de roman et policiers de laboratoire (Detectives in Novels and Detectives in the Laboratory)*. One of them concerned a 13-year old girl who had been lured into a garage and violently raped; she accused a taxi-driver, but the man denied it. Locard was sent the girl's knickers for examination, and immediately noticed a number of dark-coloured spots. Under the microscope, they proved to be spots of thick oil containing grit and dust. Chemical analysis also revealed traces of iron. Comparison with oil on the wheels of a motor car in the garage showed that it was identical. On this evidence, the taxi-driver was convicted.

Another case may be told in Locard's own words:

In June 1922, the postal authorities received complaints about the disappearance of registered letters and packets. As usual, instead of consulting the police, they decided on an internal enquiry. The results were not particularly enlightening: they came to suspect only that the thefts were committed in a specific post office and that the opening of the letters happened in the same place.

The ingenious postmaster suspected that the delinquents locked themselves in the lavatories to perpetrate their misdeeds. He found some men of good will to lock themselves in the attic above the cubicles, and survey the goings-on through a hole in the ceiling. After having witnessed a great deal of toilet-flushing, the watchers had the pleasure of seeing a postman in uniform who had locked himself in the toilet for reasons that were not purely digestive; he opened letters, chose paper money and postal orders, and put them in his inside pocket.

But nothing resembles the head of one postman more that the head of another, so that the spies felt they would be incapable of pointing out the squatter when the time came. Not daring to hope that he would raise his face towards them, they decided to make some kind of mark on him; and striking with their feet and knees the thin ceiling partition, they succeeded in detaching some fine flakes of plaster, which fell on to the shoulder and left elbow of the violator of correspondence. The latter, finding his retreat less secure than he thought, fled immediately.

When it came to recognizing the culprit by this mark, they realised that it had only one small defect: that it was invisible. So they had recourse to the police laboratory. Although the coat had been carefully brushed, microscopic and chemical analysis of the shoulder and elbow of one of the suspects revealed an appreciable quantity of sulphate of lime.*

Cases like these greatly enhanced Locard's reputation with the Lyon police. But the case that made him a minor celebrity occurred about a year after the setting-up of the laboratory. (Locard is economical with dates, so it is impossible to be more precise.) It concerned a local bank clerk named Émile Gourbin, who had fallen violently in love with an attractive young lady named Marie Latelle, whose parents lived in a villa on the outskirts of Lyon. This is why, when Marie was found strangled one morning in the parlour, the local policeman was called in rather than someone from the Palais de Justice where Locard worked.

Émile Gourbin was the obvious suspect. He was accepted, more or less, as Marie's fiancé, but Marie was inclined to flirt with other men, and Gourbin – who professed to be shattered by her death – admitted that he was jealous. But he had a perfect alibi. The doctors placed Marie's death at around midnight, and Gourbin had spent the night at the house of friends who lived some miles away; they had eaten well, drunk a great deal of wine, and played cards until 1 a.m., when Gourbin had yawned and mentioned that it was time for bed. His friends agreed, and they had all retired. Unless they were lying, Gourbin had been playing cards when Marie was strangled.

The local police decided they were out of their depth, and asked for help from their colleagues in Lyon. This is why Locard went to examine the body, taking with him, according to one account, an eight-foot long microscope of his own invention, through which he could also take photographs. But he needed only a magnifying glass to see that what the police had taken for fingerprints on the girl's throat were

*Traité de Criminalistique, Vol. II, p. 895.

actually spots where the skin had been scraped off by the pressure of the murderer's fingers.

Next, Locard asked to see Émile Gourbin. He sat opposite the young man, and asked if he could see his fingernails. Gourbin held out his hands, and Locard was relieved to see that the nails had not been cleaned recently. Gourbin sat there listlessly while Locard took scrapings from under his nails, and carefully transferred these on to a sheet of paper.

In his laboratory, Locard studied the scrapings under a microscope. He reasoned that the balls of a man's fingers would not tear away the flesh, no matter how hard he squeezed. But when hands are clutched round a throat, the thumb nails will dig into the flesh, and as the thumbs press inward, they will also scrape off a layer of skin. At the same time, the fingernails will dig into the back of the neck with the same scraping movement.

Under the microscope, Locard discovered epithelial tissue – skin cells – and blood cells. Gourbin might have collected these in scratching himself. But there was also a granular dust whose particles appeared as regular crystals. This was powdered rice, the basic constituent (in 1911) of face powder. He also found other chemicals that were used in cosmetics: iron oxide (for colouring), bismuth, magnesium stearate and zinc oxide. The skin found under the nails had been covered with pink face powder.

Locard asked the police to search the dead girl's bedroom for pink face powder; they brought him a box full of it. It had been made specially by a local chemist's shop, and its constituents proved to be exactly the same as in the powder found under Gourbin's nails.

Confronted with this evidence, Gourbin confessed – although it is interesting to speculate whether, had he maintained his innocence, a jury would have convicted him on the evidence of Locard's microphotographs. The friends had been innocent dupes; Gourbin had advanced the wall clock from 11.30 p.m. to 1 a.m. Befuddled with wine, his friends made no attempt to check the time. Instead of going to bed, Gourbin had slipped out of the house and hurried to meet Marie. According to his own confession, she had refused to marry him, and he had strangled her in a rage. But the prosecution emphasized the advancement of the clock, and argued that this showed he had every intention of killing her; the jury agreed, and found him guilty of premeditated murder. In retrospect, this seems a miscarriage of justice. Gourbin had no motive for murdering Marie Latelle, even though she made him jealous. It seems far more probable that she had agreed to meet him after her parents had gone to bed, and that he expected to spend the night with her. For some reason, she rejected him – perhaps because he had obviously been drinking – and in a fury of disappointment, he strangled her. If this is so, then his alteration of the clock was not a sign of premeditation to murder, but of impatience to join his mistress and a desire to preserve her reputation.

6

On 15 September 1929, Locard came to visit his colleague Edmond Bayle in his Paris laboratory; Bayle had succeeded Bertillon as the head of the Paris forensic science department. While Locard was there, a man who was obviously deranged succeeded in gaining admittance, and proceeded to explain his grievance at such incomprehensible length that Bayle lost his temper, and told him to get out, saying: 'You belong in a loony bin.' The man looked stricken, and left quietly. Locard claims, in his Memoirs, that he was possessed of a sudden intuition, and remarked: 'Bayle, you are going to be murdered.' The following day, as Bayle was entering the Palais de Justice, he was shot dead by a madman with a grievance – he was angry because Bayle had taken his landlord's side in a dispute about a forged contract. Bayle was just 50 years old at the time of his death, and had shown the same kind of genius for crime detection as his friend Locard. His main achievement was to introduce a new degree of precision into spectroscopic analysis.

Bayle's most remarkable case, and the one that reveals the breadth of his knowledge and incredible persistence, began on 8 June 1924, when the body of a man, wrapped in a sheet, was found in the Bois de Boulogne by a man out for a Sunday morning cycle ride. The corpse proved to be that of a respectable-looking old gentleman who seemed to be dressed for a day at the office. On his striped shirt there were marks of coal dust. The corpse was identified as that of Louis Boulay, who was 70 years old, and worked in the office of a paper manufacturer. He had vanished nine days earlier, on 30 May, when he had left the office to buy stamps and post letters. These letters had all reached their destinations. The motive, it seemed, was robbery, since Boulay's wallet and his gold watch were missing.

Edmond Bayle was asked to see what clues he could find on the body. Boulay had died from blows on the head, which had stained his shirt and jacket with blood. His hair seemed to be unusually dirty, and on close examination, Bayle detected river sand and sawdust – he later identified it as a mixture of oak and pine. There was also coal dust, of the same type as that on his shirt. Bayle inferred that the man had been battered to the ground, and had fallen on earth covered with sawdust and coal dust, as well as sand.

Bayle spent hours removing all the particles of dust from the man's hair; he took this with him back to his laboratory. He also took the bundle containing the dead man's clothes.

The police found the case baffling. Boulay had apparently been a perfectly normal, respectable citizen, with no secret life. His colleagues in the office had known him for 17 years, and could shed no light on the mystery. His wife told the police that her husband was as regular as clockwork – he caught a train every morning from the George V Metro, and returned home at seven every evening. He had no enemies, hardly drank, and was scrupulously honest.

It was several days before Chief Inspector Riboulet, in charge of the investigation, uncovered his first clue. Under the cushion on Boulay's office chair, he discovered a newspaper which contained tips for horses, and in which two of the runners were underlined – Libre Pirate and Star Sapphire. This elicited the information that Boulay occasionally placed a small bet – but never more than a few francs. By no stretch of the imagination could he be described as a gambler.

Yet since this seemed to be the only lead, Riboulet had no alternative than to follow it. At every café and bar where gamblers might be found, his men showed a photograph of Boulay and asked if anyone recognized it. Eventually, in a small bar near the Gare St-Lazare, the proprietress recognized it as a customer she knew as Père Louis. It seemed that he was a racing enthusiast who loved to talk horses with other punters, and who acted as a bookie's runner. Here, at last, the police had a possible motive for the murder. A bookie's runner often carries large sums of money. Libre Pirate and Star Sapphire had both won their races – two days before Boulay had disappeared. Perhaps he had been to collect winnings – some of the customers had money to come. Now all Riboulet had to do was to find the bookmaker with whom Boulay had placed the bets, and from whom he had collected his winnings. But this, again, proved unexpectedly difficult. Riboulet's team interviewed dozens of bookies, legal and illegal, and none of them would admit to knowing Boulay. And, for the next five months, the investigation languished. All Bayle's interesting remarks about a cellar with river sand and sawdust were useless unless he knew where to look.

That November, one of Boulay's fellow clerks came to see Riboulet – he had remembered an incident which might just possibly be of some significance. On the floor above the office, there lived a man called Boulet, and in the previous May he had accidentally received a letter addressed to Boulay; tearing it open, he had found a message from a bookie offering a red-hot tip. Boulet took it down to Louis Boulay, apologizing for having opened it by mistake, and Boulay had remarked: 'Oh, it's only from Tessier . . .' The clerk was not quite sure that this was the name, but it was something like it. And when he had mentioned this incident to the chief clerk, the latter had also recalled that Boulay had mentioned a bookie named Tessier – and had then gone on to say that he was transferring his business elsewhere, because he didn't like the cellar in which Tessier conducted his betting operations. He even recalled Tessier's address – Boulay had mentioned the rue Mogador.

Now back on the trail at last, Riboulet checked on bookies who lived in the rue Mogador. He soon discovered that this 'Tessier' had already been interviewed. In fact, his name was Lazare Teissier, and he was a concierge at 30 rue Mogador. Teissier was an illegal operator, and he had insisted that he had not been taking bets since he had been arrested the previous year.

Teissier and his wife were brought in for questioning. Riboulet meanwhile set his team to find out what they could about the concierge. It soon became clear that the man was thoroughly dishonest, and that his customers were far from satisfied with him. On the other hand, there was no evidence that he had known the dead man.

Teissier had a cellar, and the next step was to search it, with Edmond Bayle present. Bayle's analysis of the dust found in the dead man's hair had been a work of art. He had identified the coal dust as anthracite by determining its precise density. He had discovered that some stone dust came from a grinding wheel. Under the microscope, the sawdust was seen to be of oak and pine. There was a tiny piece of yellow cardboard, and Bayle had even determined that its fibres were made of straw. There were two insects, both of which lacked eyes – an indication that they lived in total darkness. He had even centrifuged some parts of the clothing covered with a greenish fungus, and had found micro-organisms – those on the hat were of yeast, and characteristic of wine cellars.

Teissier led the investigators down to the cellar. In fact, there were two. The first had too much light to be the home of the eyeless beetles; but there was sawdust and coal dust on the floor, and a large coal-bin big enough to hide a body. This cellar was obviously Teissier's 'office'. The other contained the boiler. There was also a quantity of cardboard similar to the piece Bayle had analysed, and a partially sawed-up board painted red – Bayle had also found stripes of red paint on the victim's trousers containing a component called rhodamine. Bayle filled bags with the dust, and carried it off back to his laboratory. The results were almost all he had hoped. The coal dust, the sand, the paint, and the cardboard were all of the type found on the dead man's clothing. There was only one disappointment – no eyeless beetles. Nevertheless, the scientific evidence was now strong enough to justify an arrest, and Teissier was taken into custody. He simply denied all the charges.

One thing was clear: Teissier had been heavily in debt before the murder; his brother-in-law told how Teissier had asked him for a large loan. Another tenant had lent Teissier 2,000 francs in April, and Teissier had repaid it in early June. His money troubles had obviously eased by then.

Twice more Bayle returned to the cellar, the second time with powerful lamps. These revealed that a new patch of grey paint on the wall was surrounded by spots that looked like spatters of blood, and there was a bloodstain at the foot of the stairs – it even had a hair stuck in it.

Teissier declared that a cat had had kittens in the cellar; Bayle replied that the Uhlenhuth test proved that it was human blood. Teissier countered by replying that the tenants brought soiled clothing down to the cellar to wash it, and that the stain could be menstrual blood. Bayle asked why, in that case, was the stain surrounded by spattering, such as occurred when a violent blow was struck?

Finally, Bayle obtained his final piece of the jigsaw. The tenant who had lent Teissier the 2,000 francs mentioned that he allowed Teissier to use his own cellar under the stairs, and that in June he had to complain about an unpleasant odour, which Teissier had attributed to the drains. In this tiny cellar, Bayle found what he was looking for – total darkness, and tiny eyeless insects. He also found green cloth fibres, of the same type he had found on Boulay's clothes. Elsewhere in Teissier's flat they found the tattered green jersey they came from.

The detectives hurled themselves into a final search, and this produced the most conclusive evidence of all – in the dust of the cellar there were fragments of a torn Métro ticket from the George V station, and it was dated 30 May 1924, the day Boulay had vanished.

The story was now clear. On that morning, Boulay had left the office to post letters, and had taken the opportunity to call on Teissier to place bets and collect winnings due on the two horses. Teissier had taken him down to his 'office', and had struck him violently on the head from behind. Then he had concealed the body in the coal-bunker. But this place was too dangerous; someone might look inside. So he transferred the body to the cubby-hole under the stairs, which was kept locked. When the smell grew unbearable, he knew he had to move it. This he did on the night of 7 June, the day before the body was discovered. The police suspected that he was aided by another brother-in-law who was a cab-driver, but were unable to prove it.

Teissier refused to confess, so the case against him depended entirely upon Bayle's forensic evidence. But this convinced the jury, who found Teissier guilty of manslaughter – since the prosecution was unable to produce evidence of premeditated murder they decided to give him the benefit of the doubt. Teissier received a 10-year sentence, and had to pay 30,000 francs compensation to the dead man's widow.

When, three years later, Edmond Bayle was murdered by a madman, France undoubtedly lost a forensic scientist who would soon have ranked with the world's greatest.

7

By the end of the First World War, police forces all over the world had come to recognize the importance of the forensic scientist and his microscope. Admittedly, there were places where it was at first treated with suspicion, a fad that was unconnected with the realities of crime detection. In provincial Lyon, it was Edmond Locard who transformed this attitude with his work on the Gourbin case. On the other side of the world, in Melbourne, Australia, it was a scientist named Charles Anthony Taylor who first made the police aware of the importance of the microscope.

Taylor came into crime detection by a circuitous route. Born in Maryborough, in the central highlands, in 1885, he had been a mining engineer, a science master in high schools and an industrial chemist before, in 1921, he was appointed Government Food Analyst. He soon revealed an unusual talent for the unravelling of mysteries. Two floors of a concrete building had collapsed, and two men were killed. It was suspected that the concrete had been mixed in the wrong proportions, but no one knew how to go about testing such a theory. Taylor did it by pounding the concrete to powder, then demonstrating the exact amount of sand and cement in the mixture.

In the year Taylor became Government Analyst, a fellow Australian named Colin Ross took over the lease of the Australian Wine Shop in Melbourne's Eastern Arcade, a dubious area frequented by prostitutes and pickpockets. And it was in a narrow thoroughfare called Gun Alley that the naked body of a girl was found on the last day of 1921. The corpse was lying on its back, the legs tucked under it, and the girl's red-gold hair was spread out on the pavement like a halo. The derelict who discovered it fetched a policeman. It was only a few minutes after six in the morning, but a crowd of sightseers soon gathered in the entrance to the alleyway; the police decided to shift the body to the mortuary, and the pathologist of the Victoria State Government, Dr Crawford Mollison, was called in to examine it.

Mollison saw immediately that she was an adolescent; her breasts were still immature. The smear of blood on the inside of her thigh indicated that this was a sex crime, and a vaginal swab verified this. She had been strangled, and beaten about the face and head.

She was quickly identified as a schoolgirl who had been missing since the previous day. Her name was Alma Tirtschke, and she was 13 years old. The family were South African, and Alma lived with her grandmother in the suburb of Hawthorn. She was a quiet child, and was top of her class at the local high school.

Detectives Frederick Piggott and John Brophy were in charge of the investigation, and they had already made a number of basic deductions. The way that the hair was spread out on the pavement suggested that the girl had been lying on a blanket, which had been pulled from under her. She had been placed in the alleyway after 1 a.m. – a prostitute had been patrolling down Little Collins Street until that hour, and would have seen anyone carrying a body. An hour later, a constable on his beat passed the end of the alley; he was supposed to walk up it, but decided there was nothing worth his attention, and went on. How had the body been transported? It could have been brought by car, or in a horse and cart. But in that case, why bring it to a place like Gun Alley? It seemed more likely that the killer lived nearby, and had killed her on his own premises. That she had been murdered in the privacy of a house was made evident by one curious fact noted by the pathologist: the corpse had been carefully washed.

The detectives began door-to-door enquiries among the tradesmen of the area. A man who kept a doss house in Little Collins Street told them that he had been sitting on a chair on the pavement from 8 p.m. until 12.30 a.m. – it was a hot night and had noticed a young man walking up and down several times, as – if looking for something or waiting for someone. As the man passed under a streetlamp, he had recognized him as Colin Ross, who kept the Australian Wine Shop in Eastern Arcade.

The detectives called on Ross to ask him about his movements on the evening of the murder. Ross was a pleasant-looking man, slim and athletic, although his gold teeth did nothing to improve his smile. He had, it seemed, been the manager of a hotel at nearby Donnybrook before deciding to try his luck as a tavern-keeper. The lease of the wine shop had been an experiment – in fact, it had run out on the day of the murder. He was able to give good reasons for walking up and down Little Collins Street on the evening of the murder, and the police spoke to him for only a few minutes. But a day or two later, as the two policemen were walking down Little Collins Street, they saw Ross walking ahead, and Piggott decided, on impulse, to go and speak to him again. And this time, Ross suddenly volunteered the information that he had seen Alma Tirtschke on the afternoon of the murder. She was walking up and down, as if waiting for someone. And she was wearing a pleated skirt, a white blouse, a white hat with a red band, and boots.

Neither of the policemen showed any sign of their interest as they listened. But the same thought had struck them both: that this description was remarkably accurate for someone who had merely seen the child walking up and down the street. Of course, it was possible that Ross had looked closely at her, and that it had only struck him after the murder – when he had seen descriptions in the newspapers – that this might be the murdered girl. But the newspapers had not given such a precise description of her clothing. Piggott decided that Colin Ross was suspect number one.

Other witnesses also linked Ross with Alma Tirtschke. Two men had seen Alma standing near the wine shop, and Ross had been lounging in the doorway; they had glanced back from the end of the arcade, and both figures had vanished. A derelict known as 'Staring Eyes' insisted that he had seen Ross staggering across Little Collins Street carrying something wrapped in a blanket at 2 a.m., but unfortunately he vanished before the coroner's inquest. A prostitute named Olive

Former Utah law student Ted Bundy conducting his own defence at his murder trial.

Police recover nine bodies from the crawl space beneath the home of John Wayne Gacy on December 27 1978. Gacy was executed by lethal injection.

Cook County medical examiner Dr Robert Stein stands alongside bodies in the morgue as he discusses their possible identification with reporters. The bodies are some of the 22 uncovered by police in their search of the home of John Wayne Gacy.

Hawley Crippen

Ethel LeNeve in her disguise

Mrs H. H. Crippen (Miss Belle Elmore)

A remarkable picture taken of Landru in his cell, closely guarded,
waiting for the jury to decide his fate. His self-possession throughout
the trial was one of its outstanding features.

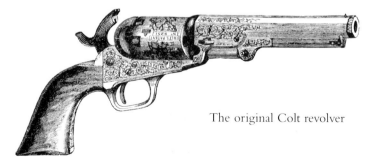

The original Colt revolver

Doctors Taylor and Rees performing their analysis for the trial of William Palmer.

ARCH.

LOOP.

WHORL.

COMPOSITE.

The four main forms of fingerprints.

Journalists looking at the spot where Elsie Cameron's body was found buried.

A general view of Norman Thorne's chicken farm and huts.

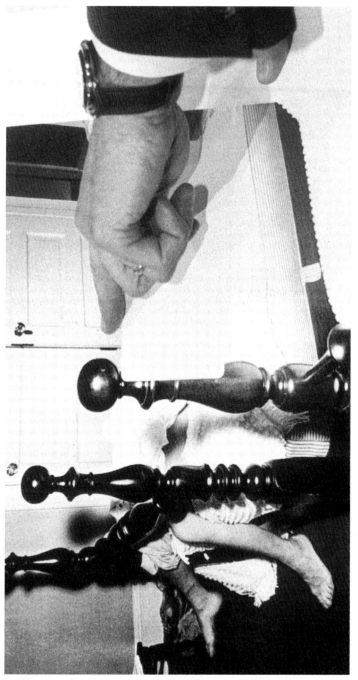

Terry Gilbert, lawyer representing Dr Sam Sheppard's son, points to the bedroom closet door, on a photo, where a blood spot was found to match the blood of the convicted killer Richard Eberling, just inches from the beaten body of Marilyn Sheppard (the photo shows her legs sprawled at the edge of the bed).

A policeman stands guard in the derelict back garden of 10 Rillington Place, Notting Hill, London, where the bodies of four murdered women were found in the ground floor flat once occupied by tenant John Christie.

Maddox claimed that she had been in the wine shop at mid-afternoon, and as Ross had walked out of his private room behind the bar, parting the bead curtain, she had glimpsed a schoolgirl sitting on the settee and drinking a glass of wine. A barmaid also claimed to have seen Alma in the wine shop that afternoon.

The detectives now felt they had enough evidence to arrest Ross. In addition to the wine shop, he had rented a house in nearby Footscray; it was in the Ballarat Road. On 12 January 1922, the detectives knocked on his door. Ross did not seem surprised to see them, and agreed to go back to police headquarters. When they asked him what had happened to the blankets that had covered the settee in the wine shop, he handed them over. These were sent immediately to Charles Anthony Taylor, at the Melbourne Police Laboratory.

There were two blankets. At first glance, neither had any significant marks. Taylor draped the first over a white plywood screen, then took a powerful magnifying glass, and spent the next hour examining every inch of the blanket, holding the lens six inches away. He found nothing whatsoever – no specks of powder, no bloodstains or seminal stains, nothing that might indicate who might have been in contact with it. But as soon as he began to study the second blanket, Taylor became excited. In the top left-hand corner, he found a hair – a red-gold hair. And in the course of the afternoon, he found another 21.

The hairs were all mounted on a strip of white cardboard. By now Taylor was convinced that these were from Alma Tirtschke's head, and that they had been tugged out as her killer had pulled the blanket from under her. Some hairs – the long ones – had been pulled out by the root. Shorter ones showed signs of having been broken off. The long ones were often more than 12 inches, a convincing proof – in 1922 – that they came from a girl's head.

The next step was to study the hair under a microscope and to establish that it was human. This was easily done – animal hair, as Villebrun had noted, has a continuous central core, while in human beings, parts appear to be missing. This hair was unusually coarse, but clearly human. Each hair was of a clear auburn colour – and this offered Taylor a clue to the age of the person from whom it came. Human hair takes on a distinct colouration at the age of 5 or 6, and it reaches its peak at about 13. After 30, it usually begins to decline. That, at least, placed the age of the hair at 13 or over.

For Taylor, all this was unknown territory; he had never heard of Villebrun or Locard – and neither had many other people in Australia.

Everything had to be learned from scratch. Taylor and his assistant Charles Price felt they needed to learn more about redheads in general. They both began to make a habit of falling closely in step with any redhead who passed, and peering at her hair; on a few occasions, the indignant lady threatened to call the police. But they soon learned what they wanted to know. The hairs on the blanket were from the nape of the neck. Again and again, they observed that, in red-headed women, the hairs become lighter in colour close to the the the bulb. So the hairs came from the nape of the neck. This confirmed their theory that the blanket had been pulled from under her as she lay on her back, pulling up the hair so it spread around the head in a halo.

At the trial, which opened in February 1922, the defence argued that most of the witnesses who claimed to have seen Ross with Alma were criminals or prostitutes, and that their evidence was therefore suspect. They also argued that the red hairs found on the blanket could have come from at least three redheads of Ross's acquaintance. Ross seemed to be a man of high sexual drive, and a number of women of dubious reputation had been in his back parlour. Ross insisted that the hairs were those of a woman called Gladys Wain. Taylor disproved that by taking samples of Mrs Wain's hair and studying it under the microscope; it was fine and golden, quite unlike Alma Tirtschke's.

The chief witness against Ross was the former manageress of his bar, Ivy Matthews. She refused to say much about her past – probably because the prosecution might have used it to discredit her – and so became known as 'the mystery woman'. It was she who had told Piggott she saw Alma drinking wine in Ross' back room. She claimed that she had later asked Ross: 'Why did you do it? It was that little girl I saw in the shop yesterday.' And Ross had burst into tears and admitted: 'The moment I'm in the presence of a child I seem to lose my head. She was dead before I knew where I was.' Later, Ross had written her two notes, urging her not to turn on him, and she had showed these to the police. Later, though, she had torn them up, so the most damning piece of evidence against Ross was no longer in existence. Ross' story was that the police were deliberately trying to 'frame' him.

There was other convincing evidence against Ross. On the evening of the murder he had left the wine bar early and taken a tram back to Footscray. His intention was clearly to establish an alibi, for he deliberately created a scene on the tram, refusing to pay his fare. But the conductor had noticed that, when he alighted, he walked back towards the city instead of towards Footscray. Alma's school tunic was found out at Footscray. But this kind of evidence could be dismissed as circumstantial. What could not be dismissed was the evidence of the forensic scientists. It was the first time such medico-legal evidence had been used in an Australian court, but it was so clear and unambiguous that the jury could have no doubt that the hairs found on the blanket were those of Alma Tirtschke.

The evidence that emerged at the trial enables us to reconstruct the story. Colin Ross was a man with powerful sexual urges, with a taste for schoolgirls – he admitted to a friend: 'I prefer them without feathers.' This is why he moved from the small community of Donnybrook – where everything he did was under constant observation – to the dubious Eastern Arcade area of Melbourne, where no one would notice what he did. This is why he rented a cheap wine bar whose licence had less than a year to run (and which he knew would not be renewed). And it is probably why, on the day before the licence was due to expire, he decided to seize his last opportunity when a pretty schoolgirl stood waiting outside his shop. He invited Alma in for a glass of wine, then told her she would have to drink it in the back room, where she would not be seen by the police. He was hoping to make her drunk and then seduce her. Alma objected to his advances; he had to strangle her to prevent her cries being heard. Then he undressed her and raped her, probably on the floor. (He could not use the sofa in case someone looked through the bead curtain.) From then until closing time he was in a fever of anxiety; he could hardly wait to get rid of his customers. At six sharp he locked the door, and settled down to cleaning up the room; there was dried blood on the floor, and probably excrement – strangulation produces loss of bowel control. Before he wrapped her in a blanket, he also had to wash the body, to make sure no traces were left on it. After that he took the tram in the direction of Footscray to create his alibi, making sure he was remembered by arguing with the conductor. Now came the most difficult part – getting rid of a body on the busiest night of the week. He had already settled on a place of concealment – the wide drain at the end of a cul-de-sac that ran off Gun Alley. Again and again he went out to see if the coast was clear, but there was always someone about. Finally, at 2 a.m. he decided to risk it, and hurried out of the shop with the body still wrapped in the blanket; an old derelict saw him crossing the road to Gun Alley. But as he was trying to pull up the grating of the drain, he heard the sound of a policeman on his beat. If the man walked into Gun

Alley, he was lost. For a moment, a torch played over the dustbins behind which he was crouching. Then the footsteps moved on. Almost sick with relief, he decided to take no further risk; the body could lie where it was. Then he made his fatal mistake. Instead of rolling the girl off the blanket, or tugging it from under her feet, he pulled from above her head. The jerk doubled the legs underneath the body, and tore out hairs from the nape of the neck. Ross tucked the blanket under his arm and hurried back to his shop. Forty years later, Detective Frederick Piggott, now a superintendent, admitted that it still made him angry when he thought of the policeman who was too lazy to walk a few yards into Gun Alley.

The body was disposed of, but he still had problems. Someone must have seen Alma outside his shop; a few customers had probably glimpsed her behind the bead curtain. When the police questioned him, he had to admit that he had noticed her, for if he denied it, then someone reported seeing her in the shop, it would be an admission of guilt. If he admitted seeing her, and someone talked to the police, he could quickly change his story: yes, he *had* given her a glass of wine, but then she had left to go home; someone else must have killed her. They might not believe him, but they couldn't disprove it. And at this point he made his second mistake: he described the girl's clothes with such exactitude that he suddenly became the chief suspect.

On 24 April 1922, Colin Ross was hanged in Melbourne jail – the first man in Australia to be convicted of murder purely on forensic evidence.

8

In 1931, a few red hairs led to the solution of one of the most baffling murders ever encountered by the Bucharest police department.

One summer morning in 1931, shortly after daylight, a schoolteacher named Mme Pocanza walked across the courtyard of 55 avenue Magureanu – an apartment building – and saw a body lying close to the locked gates. Even several yards away, the smell made her feel sick. She lost no time in telephoning the police, and they arrived within minutes. The body proved to be that of a young man with red hair, about 21 years old, and the smell revealed that he had been dead for some time.

Chief Inspector Franculescu was confronted by an extraordinary mystery. The tall wrought iron gates were locked, so it was obvious why the body had been abandoned. But how had the murderer got into the house? The obvious answer was that he must be one of the tenants. But the tenants would all know that the gates were locked at midnight. Mme Pocanza had been awakened shortly before dawn by the sound of someone dragging something heavy down the stairs. She had called out, but there had been no reply. As soon as daylight came, she went down to investigate and found the corpse.

When he saw the corpse in the morgue, Franculescu could understand why the murderer had made too much noise; the young man was large and powerfully built. The pathologist had established that he had died by strangulation – not manual strangulation, but with some sort of ligature like a scarf. He had been dead for about two weeks.

The most puzzling question was where he had been kept during that time. The police searched every cupboard and pantry in the house, and could find no evidence suggesting that a corpse had been stored there – for example, a lingering stench. Finally, Franculescu asked the superintendent of the building about the space under the roof. This sounded altogether more promising. There were attics, used for storing old junk, and they were not kept locked. When he investigated, Franculescu could see why; no one would want to go into these dark cubby-holes full of dust and cobwebs. Most of them were lit by small and grimy windows. And in one of them, he found what he had been looking for: a large packing case without a lid. The lid, in fact, lay on a pile of rubbish. The heads of its nails were rusty, but their points were bright; that suggested that it had, until recently, been nailed to the packing case, otherwise the points would have rusted too. The lid yielded further information. Some nails were in their original holes, while others had been hammered straight through the wood. Whoever had closed the packing case had been in a hurry.

Even in 1931, the Rumanian police understood the importance of dust clues. Franculescu wiped a clean rag over the inside of the packing case, to obtain a sample of its dust and debris; then he wiped another rag over the dusty floor; later, on his way downstairs, he wiped another rag over one of the steps.

Close examination of the inside of the case with a powerful torch revealed a few red hairs caught in the rough wood, as well as a torn piece of newspaper with stains that looked like blood. These were sent to the forensic science laboratory. Meanwhile, the scientists had examined the scrapings from under the dead man's nails. They had found fragments of skin and blood cells, and some fine hairs. Their colour was red, like the dead man's, and the scientist guessed that they were from the face of a man who had a growth of hair on his face – not a beard, but a stubble. So the murderer had been a man with red hair, like his victim, and his face had been scratched in the struggle. This was confirmed by an examination of the red hairs from the packing case. All but three were from the victim's own head. But the other three were from the killer; they had different characteristics.

There was a mark on the back of the dead man's neck, suggesting that he had been attacked from behind. And the murderer had then pulled down his trousers and made a cut on the buttock – a cut in the shape of a figure four. That seemed to point clearly to a revenge killing. But what could the four – if that is what it was – signify?

The newspaper had also yielded interesting clues. The dust on it was unlike that found in the attic or on the stairs. Nothing indicated that it came from a factory or workshop or warehouse; it was simply the kind of dust that would be found in someone's living-room – a badly dusted living-room. The bloodstains on the newspaper were those of the murderer – at least, they were of a different group from the blood of the victim.

The packing case proved to be the property of a family who had once lived in the building, and who had now moved to a distant part of the country. Since he had no other leads, Franculescu checked their alibis with immense thoroughness. It was obvious that they had no connection with the case. Three weeks into the investigation, he had run out of leads.

The Chief of Police was pressing him for results. For the hundreth time, Franculescu reviewed all the evidence. And it was as he was studying the photographs taken by the police photographer that he experienced a forlorn hope. There were photographs of the corpse, of the packing case, of the courtyard where the body had been found. This picture showed a group of morbid sightseers, most of whose faces were clearly distinguishable. Franculescu remembered tales about murderers who had been unable to resist revisiting the scene of the crime – the Bucharest newspapers had recently carried stories about the Dusseldorf sadist, Peter Kürten, who had made a habit of joining the horrified crowds around the bodies of his victims. Franculescu ordered enlarged copies of the photograph, and told his men to try and track down everyone in it. What he wanted to know was whether any of the sightseers had red hair. It seemed a remote possibility, but it was worth trying.

After several days, one of his squad reported success. A bar-owner recognized one of the men as having red hair. Moreover, he recalled that this man had been drinking with another young man with red hair at about the time of the murder. They looked like brothers. But he had no idea who they were.

Once again faced with a dead end, Franculescu's mind returned to the question of how the two men had gained access to the building. They might have walked up to the attic in broad daylight, but that seemed unlikely. Franculescu went up to the attic, and clambered out of the small window. He found himself standing among the chimney pots, looking out over various other buildings. These roofs were not steep and dangerous; a man with good balance would find it easy to walk among the chimneys. Yet after walking to every corner of the roof, he had convinced himself that there was only one other building from which this one was accessible. It stood slightly higher than 55 avenue Magureanu, and there was a window in its mansard roof. If a man climbed out of this window and slid down to the edge of the roof, he could easily jump across the narrow gap between the two houses.

The house with the mansard roof was, it seemed, occupied by a major in the Rumanian army, and he was at home when Franculescu called on him. When he was shown the photograph, he immediately pointed to the red-headed man. 'That's Bardica.'

'Who is he?'

'He was my batman – the worst I ever had.' It seemed that Alexander Bardica was not a good soldier, and when he had left the army a few weeks before, Major Mihail had been glad to see the last of him; the man was lazy and dishonest. And before his discharge, Bardica had lived in the major's house. The room, as Franculescu expected, was the one whose window looked out from the mansard roof. The major was unable to help Franculescu to establish the identity of the dead man, but this proved to be unnecessary. Alexander Bardica was easily traced, living in a working-class district of Bucharest under his own name. When confronted with the evidence against him, he made a full confession.

The motive, as Franculescu had suspected, was revenge. The dead man's name was Ladislas Jurca and, like Bardica, he had been a conscript in the Rumanian army. Together with two other red-headed conscripts, they had formed a group who called themselves the Four Musketeers, spending most of their leaves together in Bucharest. But Ladislas Jurca was a good soldier, and in due course he was promoted to corporal. And he declined to show favouritism to his former comrades; in fact, he proved to be a disciplinarian who seemed to enjoy giving them orders. Bardica's reaction was one of tremendous bitterness; he came to detest his former friend with a deep and vengeful loathing. He liked to indulge in day-dreams of horrible retribution.

As the major's batman, he spent many hours in his attic room. When he noticed that the attics a few yards away were obviously empty, he began to contemplate burglary; one evening he clambered out of his window and on to the next roof. On the whole, the expedition was a disappointment; even when he gained access to the attics, there was nothing worth stealing. But when he met his old comrade one day, and realized that he loathed him as much as ever, he worked out a plan of revenge. As they were drinking together, he told Jurca that he had gained access to the attic in the avenue Magureanu, and found a packing case full of things that would fetch a good price. If Jurca was not afraid of heights, they could start removing it now . . . It was the kind of challenge Jurca could not resist. They went straight back to Bardica's attic room, and clambered out of the window. A few minutes later they were in the room with the packing case. And as Jurca bent over it with a screwdriver, a leather belt was pulled around his throat. He managed to turn and fight, scratching Bardica's face, but his enemy's grip was too strong. Five minutes later, Ladislas Jurca lay dead inside the packing case. Before he left, Bardica scored a figure four in the flesh of his buttock, in memory of the Four Musketeers.

Two weeks later, Bardica was out of the army. But would it be wise to leave the corpse in the attic until its smell gave away its presence? The police would realize that the only access to the roof was from Bardica's own window. Therefore it had to be moved elsewhere – preferably to the nearby Dimboritza River, a tributary of the Danube. On his last night in Major Mihail's house, Bardica returned to the attic, and levered open the packing case. But the corpse proved to be heavier than he expected; he was forced to drag it most of the way. And on the last flight of stairs, the bumping of Jurca's feet awoke the schoolteacher, who called out to ask who it was. Hardica ignored her, praying that she would not come to investigate – otherwise he would be forced to commit a second murder. Then, in the courtyard, he realized that all this effort had been wasted – the gate was locked. There was nothing for it but to abandon the corpse and climb over the gate. Even if the police were intelligent enough to discover how he had entered the attic, there was no clue to connect him to the dead man. He had no suspicion that the clue lay under the dead man's nails, and in three hairs caught inside the packing case.

Alexander Bardica was found guilty of murder, and sentenced to life imprisonment in the convict mines of Kimpolung.

9

America, with its delight in technical innovation, was one of the first countries to recognize the potentialities of forensic science. As early as 1912, the microscopic study of fibres played a major part in solving a baffling murder.

The victim was a 78-year-old millionaire named George Marsh, and on the afternoon of 11 April, he was found shot dead on the highway beside some salt marshes near Lynn, Massachusetts. The question of motive baffled the police. His well-filled wallet and his gold watch were untouched. Then could he have been killed by some relative, anxious to inherit his fortune? An examination of his will refuted that theory; he had left all his money to charity, with the full knowledge and approval of his relatives, who were also wealthy. Marsh seemed to have no enemies, and there was not a scrap of evidence for the theory that he had been murdered by anarchists as a blow against capitalism.

There was only one clue: a pearl-grey overcoat button with a small piece of cloth attached; this had been found a few yards from the body, and might have belonged to the murderer. But unless they could find the overcoat, this clue was also useless.

Appeals to the public for information led to a number of reports about a young man who drove a light-blue open roadster, and who had been seen in the area of Marsh's home; it had been seen there on the day Marsh was murdered. The keeper of a boarding-house had let a room to a young man who drove such a car, and had been baffled by the strange way in which he spent most of his days: sitting at his window with a pair of binoculars, peering at the back view of George Marsh's house. The man had given his name as Willis A. Dow.

Another landlady reported that she had been letting a room to Willis A. Dow at the time of the murder, and that when he departed, he had left behind an overcoat from which all the buttons had been removed. Here at last was a clue that might connect the mystery man with Marsh's murder. But the police of Massachusetts had no forensic laboratory; it was impossible for them to state positively that the grey button came from this overcoat. And at this point, the police chief, Tom Burckes, recalled that nearby Lowell had many textile mills, and that it was the home of the Lowell Textile School. He telephoned them and explained his problem; they told him to send over the button and the overcoat immediately. These were examined microscopically by Professor Edward H. Baker and Louis A. Olney, who were able to report back immediately that the fragment of cloth on the button was identical with the cloth of the overcoat. It had the same weave and texture, and the same unusual colours: sea green, lavender, burnt orange, yellow, tan brown and dark brown. They could identify the place from which the button had been torn, with its broken threads. George Marsh had pulled it from the coat of his killer before he was shot; the killer, in turn, had cut off all the other buttons, and probably destroyed them, in an attempt to prevent such an identification being made.

The clue that led to his identification was the gun itself, a .32 Colt automatic, which he had been stupid enough to throw away only 50 yards from where Marsh had been killed. This was found by a fisherman, and a check on the serial number at the Colt factory in Hartford, Connecticut, enabled the police to trace it to a sporting store in Stockton, California, and in turn to a young man named William A. Dorr. The place itself was significant, for it was the home of George Marsh's adopted daughter Orpha. And enquiries by the Stockton police revealed that Orpha Marsh, a 38-year-old spinster, was having an affair with the owner of a motorcycle shop named William A. Dorr, and that she had made a will in his favour. Unfortunately, George Marsh was Orpha's trustee, and there was no way in which Dorr could get his hands on her fortune while Marsh was alive. This explained why Dorr had sold his motorcycle business and crossed the country to Lynn, Massachusetts, to remove the first major obstacle to inheriting Orpha Marsh's money. And now, quite obviously, he was on his way back to Stockton to remove the second obstacle . . .

A police guard was placed on Orpha Marsh's house, and her telephone was tapped. When William Dorr rang her from a nearby restaurant, the police were there within minutes, and Dorr was arrested before he could leave the telephone booth. He went to the electric chair in Charlestown, Massachusetts, on 24 March 1914.

The Marsh murder was probably the first case in the United States in which the microscope played a key role. In 1912, America had no equivalent of Locard or Balthazard. But within ten years this had ceased to be true: a chemist named Edward Oscar Heinrich had become known as 'the Edison of Crime Detection'. Before he became Professor of Criminology at the Berkeley campus of the University of California, Heinrich had been the city chemist at Tacoma, in Washington. By the mid-1920s, he was regarded as America's leading forensic scientist.

The case that brought him celebrity began on 11 October 1923, when a train bound from Oregon to San Francisco was held up by bandits in the Siskiyou Mountains. The train was crawling through a tunnel when two men dropped off the roof of the engine tender and pointed guns at the engineer and fireman; they were made to stop the train and then marched up a slope at gunpoint and made to stand with raised hands. A third man placed a large package beside the mail car – which was half-way out of the tunnel – and ran. A moment later, there was a violent explosion, which blasted open the car and set it on fire. Then the engineer and fireman were ordered to pull the rest of train out of the tunnel. This proved to be impossible. The bandits were becoming increasingly panicky, and when the brakeman ran out of the tunnel to see what was happening, one of them raised a shotgun and shot him dead. Then the engineer and fireman were deliberately executed. And the bandits, who realized that they were not going to get into the blazing mail car, disappeared. A mail clerk named Edwin Daugherty was burned to death.

Police from Ashland, Oregon, found a detonating device with batteries near the tunnel. Nearby there was a revolver, a pair of shoes, and a pair of greasy denim overalls.

Posses galloped off in all directions looking for the robbers. Meanwhile, the sheriff examining the detonator wondered whether its batteries might not have come from a nearby garage. He hurried there, and arrested the mechanic he found working in a pair of greasy overalls that looked very similar to those found near the detonator. But the mechanic maintained his innocence, and the police were unable to find the slightest shred of evidence to link him with the crime.

Edward O. Heinrich was obviously the man to approach, and the police sent him the overalls found at the scene of the crime. Within two days he told them over the telephone: 'You are holding the wrong man. The grime on these overalls is not car grease. It is fir pitch. In the pocket I found particles of Douglas fir needles. The man who wore these overalls is a left-handed lumberjack. He is between 21 and 25 years of age, about five feet ten inches tall, and he weighs about 165 lb. His hair is medium light brown, his hands and feet are small, and he is a man of fastidious habits.'

Later, Heinrich explained how he had made these deductions. The fir chips were in the right-hand pocket, which meant that the man stood with his right side towards the tree as he was chopping it down; a right-handed man stands with his left side to the tree. Besides, the left-handed pockets were more used than the right, and the overalls were buttoned on the left. The overall bottoms had been folded to fit into boots, and the position of the suspender buckles indicated the height and build of the wearer. A single hair adhering to a button told Heinrich that the man was white – African American hair or Native American hair is quite different. Nail clippings that had been caught in a front pocket had been cut with a precision that indicated a man of fastidious habits. The size of the shoes had indicated a man with small feet, and it followed that his hands were also small.

Heinrich had found another clue. In the pencil pocket of the overalls he had found a scrap of folded paper that the police had missed. It was a receipt for a registered letter bearing a code number. The Post Office was able to tell the police that it had been issued in Eugene, Oregon, as a receipt for $50 sent by a man called Roy D'Autremont to Ray D'Autremont in Lakewood, New Mexico.

It was easy to locate Paul D'Autremont, the elderly father of the brothers, in Eugene. He told them that his three sons – the twins Roy and Ray, and their brother Hugh – had been missing since the day of the hold-up. And Roy was a left-handed lumberjack.

Heinrich's examination of the gun found near the detonator left no doubt that the D'Autremont brothers were the bandits. A hidden number led the police to the store in Seattle where it had been purchased by a man calling himself William Elliott. Heinrich, who was also a handwriting expert, was able to state that Elliott's handwriting was that of Roy D'Autremont.

Even the reward of $15,000 offered by the railway company failed to produce information of the brothers' whereabouts. But in March 1927, an army sergeant saw a 'Wanted' poster, and thought that Hugh D'Autremont resembled a private he had known in the Philippines. Hugh D'Autremont was arrested in Manila. A month later, Roy and Ray were recognized at the steel mill in Steubenville, Ohio, where they were working. All three brothers were sentenced to life imprisonment.

But perhaps Heinrich's most remarkable piece of crime detection was his solution of the mystery of Charles Henry Schwartz, an inventor who lived in the small town of Walnut Creek, not far from Berkeley, where Heinrich had his laboratory. Schwartz ran a company called the

Pacific Cellulose Plant, and spent his days working in his laboratory. He was a swarthy, smallish man of 30 who seemed to be happily married and reasonably prosperous. To some of his friends in Walnut Creek, he confided his secret – that he had invented an artificial silk that was indistinguishable from the real thing. He showed them samples, and they agreed that it was of exceptionally fine quality. Schwartz said he was trying to sell his process, but that various dubious characters were hoping to obtain it for far less than it was worth.

On 25 July 1925, the laboratory was shaken by a tremendous explosion, then burst into flames. When firemen were able to enter the building, they found the charred body of a man, whom Mrs Schwartz tearfully identified as her husband. It was soon clear that this was a case of murder – incendiary devices had been found in the ruins. A child who had run towards the blazing building testified that Schwartz's car had hurtled past him, almost knocking him down. Police soon decided that the man they were searching for was a travelling missionary named Gilbert Warren Barbe, who looked extraordinarily like Schwartz, and who had often been seen walking with him. Barbe had now disappeared.

Since Heinrich was so close, he was obviously the man to examine the scene of the crime. His first move was to have the corpse sent to his laboratory and X-rayed. He immediately observed that a molar was missing from the right upper side of the dead man's jaw; Schwartz's dentist was able to tell the police that he had removed it not long before. His next discovery was that the man had already been dead when the explosion occurred; he had been battered to death with a blunt instrument. It looked as if Barbe had been hired to kill Schwartz by someone who wanted his process of silk-manufacture; he had battered him to death, and then set out to make it look as if Schwartz had died in an accident.

A few days later, the police had another puzzle on their hands. Mrs Schwartz telephoned to say that someone had broken into her house when she was out, and had taken every photograph of her husband. This seemed an extraordinary crime; who could want photographs of the murdered man? In fact, Heinrich had already asked the police to find him a photograph, and now it looked as if they would be unable to oblige. Fortunately, Mrs Schwartz recalled that her husband had recently had his photograph taken in a studio in Oakland; the photographer still had the negative. Heinrich asked if he could have it in an enlargement.

As he stood by the charred remains of the corpse, with the photograph in his hand, Heinrich suddenly knew that he was not looking at the body of Charles Schwartz. The face was burnt, but an ear was still intact. And the ear lobe was a different shape. Close study of the jaw revealed that the missing molar had been removed violently and that the socket was still raw; that indicated that it had been pulled out shortly before or after death. The eye sockets were also empty, and now Heinrich studied them through a magnifying glass, he found evidence that the eyes had been gouged out. A query to Mrs Schwartz revealed that her husband's eyes had been brown, and that those of his friend Barbe had been a watery blue. It began to look increasingly as if the body in the laboratory was that of Barbe, and that Schwartz had been the man who had escaped in the car.

One obvious way of finding out was to check fingerprints. The hands of the corpse had been badly burned, but when he studied the fingerprints that remained, Heinrich realized that there had been an attempt to burn away the fingerprints with concentrated acid. This was verified when his chemical tests found traces of acid on the skin.

What motive could Schwartz have in faking his own death? As the police probed into his background, they found the answer. Schwartz claimed that he had been a flier in the First World War, and had since studied chemistry. In fact, he was only nine when the war broke out. And his background was that of a minor confidence man, not a scientist. For the past year or so, he had been living on his wife's money. But this was nearly all spent. She was not worried – she believed that his silk-making process would make them rich. By tracing Schwartz's cancelled cheques, the police were able to discover that he had bought the 'Chinese silk' in a dry goods store in San Francisco for $8 a skein.

These cheques also revealed that he had advertised for a chemist's assistant, and had rather oddly specified that he must have small hands and feet. This was clearly an attempt to find a victim. It had been unsuccessful, as a check with the Missing Persons Bureau revealed – no chemist's assistant had vanished since the previous June. Then Schwartz had met the travelling missionary, Warren Barbe, and decided that they looked sufficiently alike to deceive the police. Barbe was three inches taller than Schwartz, but fire causes bodies to contract, and this would probably remain unnoticed.

In the laboratory, in a locked closet, Heinrich found traces of blood, and some fragments of printed paper that were badly burnt. But with the aid of a magnifying glass and a microscope, Heinrich was able to determine that they were the remains of religious pamphlets. And under the microscope, he could see the remains of handwriting on the charred paper of the cover. Eventually, he was able to read the name: 'G. W. Barbe', and a few words such as 'Amarillo, Texas'.

As he studied the remains of Schwartz's laboratory, Heinrich concluded that it had never been used as a laboratory; to begin with, there was no water and no gas, and the electricity bills showed that he had burned only enough electricity to keep a single light burning.

The problem of the motive proved simple enough. Schwartz had insured his life for $185,000. When the excitement had died down, he evidently meant to contact his wife and persuade her to flee with him. In fact, the police stopped the insurance company from paying as soon as Heinrich's enquiries revealed that the death was suspicious. But they now decided that the simplest way of luring Schwartz out of hiding was to allow the newspapers to drop hints that she had been paid. Meanwhile, hoteliers and boarding-house proprietors were warned to be on the lookout. And one of these reported a mysterious lodger named Harold Warren, who had rented a room in Oakland on the day after the explosion. He was an exceptionally taciturn man, who kept himself to himself. But one day, when someone mentioned the rumour that the body in the laboratory was not Charles Schwartz, he had suddenly declared positively that he had no doubt that it was. His landlord had stared at him in astonishment. How could he be so certain? The more he thought about it, the more suspicious he became.

The police quickly surrounded the rooming-house in Oakland; then one of them rapped on the door of the unknown man. There was no reply. When they threatened to break down the door, there was a single shot. They burst into the room, and found a man lying on the floor, a smoking revolver in his hand. He was identified as Charles Schwartz. The police had arrived only just in time. Schwartz had packed his bags to leave, and in his wallet there was a thick wad of bills. On a table there was a note addressed to his wife. In this, Schwartz insisted that he was not guilty of murder. The body in the laboratory, he claimed, was that of a stranger who called looking for work, and tried to rob him; they had scuffled, and Schwartz had accidentally killed him with a blow on the head . . . But the evidence uncovered by Edward Heinrich left no doubt that Schwartz was one of the most ruthless killers in California's criminal history.

In 1927, Heinrich made use of another invaluable laboratory technique to trap a murderer – ultraviolet radiation. On the night of 21 August 1927, an ex-stablehand named Jesse Watkins broke into the apartment of stable-master Henry Chambers in San Francisco's Presidio (an area of military parkland), intent on revenge – Chambers had dismissed him for laziness. Chambers woke up, seized a revolver, and fired three shots; only one struck Watkins, and lodged in his cheek. He snatched the revolver and beat the old man to death with it. Then he stole whatever cash he could find and hurried back through the foggy streets – the fog was so thick that no one noticed the blood on his clothes. He washed the bloodspots out of his shirt and the next day, as a double precaution, sent it to the laundry. He told his room-mate that he had been attacked by a hold-up man who had shot him in the cheek – the room-mate, a man named Cahill, removed the bullet with tweezers.

For weeks the San Francisco police were baffled. Then one of the stablemaster's subordinates mentioned Watkins as a man with a grudge against Chambers. When the police visited Watkins's apartment in Lombard Street, Cahill told them the story about the bullet. Now certain that Watkins was the killer, they arrested him. Watkins was certain that they had no evidence, but he had overlooked two important items. The room-mate had kept the bullet, and Edward Heinrich used the recently invented comparison microscope to show that it had been fired from Chambers's gun. And when the laundered shirt was exposed to ultraviolet light, the invisible bloodstains became visible. In 1927, the jury might have been doubtful about the value of the comparison microscope and bullet identification; but the bloodstain evidence convinced them, and Watkins was sentenced to life imprisonment.

10

It is inevitable that murder cases should play a major part in the story of forensic science; yet it should be borne in mind that by far the greater proportion of crimes solved in the laboratory are less serious offences, the most frequent being robbery and burglary. Most such cases lack the dramatic appeal of a murder mystery. But a series of safe robberies that took place in New York in 1944 is a remarkable exception.

The thieves were 'cracksmen' of unusual ability, highly skilled professionals who burned their way into bank safes with an oxy-acety-lene torch. But the real mystery was their apparent ability to walk through solid doors. In the majority of cases, the police were unable to discover how the men had broken into the bank. Moreover, the thieves were able to walk the streets with heavy oxygen tanks, apparently without attracting attention. These abilities led one reporter who worked on the case, Edward Radin, to christen the robbers 'the phantoms'.*

The first robbery took place on the night of 19 October 1944, at the Long Island City Savings and Loan Association. But the thieves had either been interrupted, or forced to abandon the job because of defects in their equipment. A hole had been burned neatly through the door of the safe, but the contents remained untouched. And the door of the building was locked, exactly as it had been when the manager had left the previous evening. There were no fingerprints – the police did not expect any, since all burglars wore gloves as a matter of course.

In the days of the D'Autremont brothers, safe-breakers had used explosives – usually nitro-glycerine – or 'can-openers', huge jemmies that can rip off a safe door. In 1944, oxy-acetylene was the most sophisticated method.

Twelve days later, the 'phantoms' broke into a safe in Brooklyn and removed sugar coupons and rationing stamps; again, there was no sign of forced entry. An almost identical robbery took place in Queens 13 days later. Twelve days after that, the thieves got away with $11,000 in cash and $5,000 in war stamps; this time they had entered by a rear window. A robbery at another Brooklyn Savings and Loan Association in January was less successful – the thieves got away with blank war bonds. But again, the detectives could find no obvious means of entry

The police interviewed every bank burglar in New York and eliminated most of them from their enquiries; the rest were kept under surveillance. This seemed to deter the 'phantoms'; there were no more robberies for two months, and the next one occurred in Newark, New Jersey; the thieves drove off with the safe containing $7,000, and it was found the next day, with the neat burn-hole that had become the trademark of the raiders. But in March 1945, after the retirement of Captain Richard A. Fennelly, the man who headed the 'Safe and Loft' Squad – specializing in safe-crackers – the 'phantoms' moved back to New York and committed a series of robberies. Fennelly's assistant, Lieutenant Maguire – now promoted to chief of the squad – decided to keep a watch on all savings and loan associations. It required a vast number of officers, but it seemed to be the only way to approach the baffling case.

*Twelve Against the Law, by Edward G. Radin, New York, 1950.

One day, two policemen sitting in a car in downtown Manhattan noticed two men standing outside a bank. Neither of the men was a known safe-breaker, but the policemen nevertheless felt they looked familiar. Then one of them remembered: they had seen them a week before near a savings and loan association. One was big and muscular, the other small and slim. Now the policemen watched them enter the building, pick up an advertising booklet, then stand by the door, apparently deep in conversation, while they glanced around the room. After this they strolled across to a restaurant opposite. Within a few minutes, two additional police cars had been summoned. When the men emerged from the restaurant and entered a grey Dodge sedan, a plain-clothed detective strolled past and noted its number.

A check with the Bureau of Identification revealed that it was registered in the name of Stanley Patrek, of Clay Street, Brooklyn. A check with the Motor Vehicle Bureau uncovered Patrek's driving licence, complete with a physical description. The Bureau of Criminal Identification was then able to tell Maguire that Patrek, who had been born in 1915, had a record as a hold-up man. He had been paroled in the previous year. His description indicated that he was the shorter of the two men.

Patrek and his companion were shadowed to a garage in Astoria, and later to their separate addresses. The following day, a plain-clothed detective in an unmarked car saw the heavily built suspect come out of his apartment building, looking as if he was on a shopping errand. The detective slipped into the building and waited on the stairs. When the man returned, he observed which apartment he entered. A name on the door identified him as Joseph Stepka. He, it seemed, had a criminal record as a burglar as well as a stick-up man.

Now the two men were carefully shadowed; it was the constant aim of the police to make sure they had no suspicion they were under surveillance. If they were suspicious, both had sufficient money from robberies to lie low indefinitely. Both men seemed to be happily married, and spent much time at home playing with their children. But they also spent a good part of most days patrolling the streets and surveying loan association offices. One night, the detectives observed them having dinner with two attractive blondes, and deduced that they were deceiving their wives – the women proved to be a dance-hall hostess and a cigarette girl.

On 28 May 1945, a night of torrential downpour, the men left home late at night and returned to their Astoria garage. Three police cars proceeded to trail them as they drove off in the Dodge sedan. But near the Triboro Bridge, the suspects began to weave in and out of side streets, and the police lost them. The following morning, Maguire learned that the 'phantoms' had struck again at the Whitestone Savings and Loan Association, and got away with a safe containing $9,000. Again, there was no sign of forced entry, and the door was locked normally when the manager came to open the bank.

The following day, detectives trailed the two men from bank to bank as they made small deposits totalling $9,000. And when Maguire checked with the banks, he discovered that similar deposits had always been made in the past on days following the 'phantom' robberies.

On the night of 1 June 1945, Patrek and Stepka again left home late in the evening and drove to the Astoria garage, lifting a bulky suitcase into the trunk. Once again they were shadowed as they followed a circuitous route to their destination, which proved to be Yonkers. The police lost them again, but eventually found the grey sedan parked not far from the Yonkers Savings and Loan Association on Broadway. For the next three hours they waited in darkness. Then the two men returned, both carrying heavy objects. The police ordered them to halt, and both men turned to run. Shots fired in the air made them change their minds. Stepka proved to be carrying the oxy-acetylene equipment, while Patrek held a briefcase containing more than $15,000.

The two men surrendered philosophically, and admitted that they had no idea they had been under surveillance for months. The Astoria garage proved to contain elaborate and expensive safe-breaking equipment – the most elaborate the police had ever seen.

But although they had been caught red-handed, there was no conclusive proof that Patrek and Stepka were the 'phantoms' who had committed the previous robberies; understandably, they preferred to leave this problem to the police. The Astoria garage was studied carefully, and the detective in charge noticed some metal filings on the floor. These were turned over to the Technical Research Laboratory. The safe from the Whitestone Savings and Loan Association, which had subsequently been found abandoned, was also handed over. Under the microscope, the floor sweepings were found to consist of asbestos as well as metal filings, a strong indication that they came from a safe – most safes at that time were fire-proofed with asbestos inside the door, and often in the rear wall. Then samples of the filings and asbestos were compared with samples from the safe by means of the spectroscope. In emission spectroscopy, the sample is placed between two carbon electrodes, and a spark struck between them; the light from the burning sample is then split into a spectrum, whose emission lines are as distinctive as a fingerprint. The spectroscope revealed beyond all doubt that the filings and asbestos came from the Whitestone safe.

The chief mystery remained: how had the phantoms succeeded in walking in and out of locked doors? They refused to say; but a small box in their garage workshop finally revealed the secret. The box contained a well-known make of lock, together with an extra cylinder – the part the key slips into – and a tiny screwdriver. If the lock could be approached from the inside – the side that became accessible when the door was open – the screwdriver could be used to loosen a screw in the cylinder. Once this screw had been loosened, the cylinder could be worked out of the lock by pushing in a key, and twisting it back and forth. Eventually, it could be slipped out of the lock, and another cylinder – to which the thieves had the key – substituted. When the robbery was over, the original cylinder was replaced, the screw tightened, and there was no sign of the substitution.

Another lock in the box, partly sawed away, revealed how the thieves had stumbled upon this interesting secret. One of them had obviously made a scientific study of every make of lock until he found one with this flaw. When the watching detectives had observed Patrek and Stepka engaged in earnest conversation as they stood in the doorway of the bank, they had assumed that the men were simply observing the layout of the place; in fact, Patrek was unobtrusively inserting the screwdriver, using the big man's body as cover, and loosening the screw. Here was a case in which the thieves applied to crime the same scientific techniques that forensic experts were applying to their solution. It was a relief for the New York police when both men received long prison sentences for grand larceny.

11

In the years following the Second World War, the spectroscope and the spectrophotometer began to assume as much importance in the crime laboratory as the microscope. A mere shred of fibre left behind as someone brushes against a door-jamb can be analysed in the spectrophotometer by passing a beam of light through it, and analysing its spectrum. The absorption bands reveal what chemicals have been used in its composition. But substances also absorb the light that lies just beyond visible light at either end of the spectrum – infra-red and ultraviolet – and these can often identify a substance even more precisely. Salt is invisible to infra-red rays – they pass straight through it – so in infra-red spectrophotometry, the sample is mixed with salt. When the light has been passed through the substance, it emerges *minus* the rays that have been absorbed by the chemicals, and the spectrum of this light will reveal what is 'missing' – the spectrum is turned into a series of waves and troughs on a graph.

This technique, together with emission spectroscopy – vaporizing a sample between two electrodes and analysing the spectrum of the light – have become increasingly valuable to police in the solution of hit-and-run accidents. The accident usually leaves minute traces of car paint on the victim, and the victim's clothes leave minute fibres behind on the car. The following case is typical.

A woman riding her bicycle in London's rush-hour traffic was swiped by the wing of a car that passed her too close and too fast, and was thrown on to her head on the pavement. The driver of the car was obviously aware of what he had done; a witness said that he slowed down, and then, as other cars came up behind him, drove on. The witness said it was a black car, possibly an Austin, and that he thought he saw the letters PN on the number plate. The woman's condition was critical, although she eventually recovered.

On the handlebar of her bicycle, near the rubber grip, there was a flake of black paint. And in the police laboratory, under a microscope, it was seen that it consisted of four layers, two of them green, two of them black. The car – if this is what the paint came from – had orginally been green. Next, a fragment of the paint was placed between the electrodes of a spectroscope and vaporized; its emission spectrum was then photographed. It proved to be cellulose paint of the type used on cars.

The Motor Car Registration Office had so far been unable to help, since there would probably be thousands of black Austins with PN in the number. But this new information – that the car had originally been green – gave them more to work on. A lengthy search – the accident occurred in the days before all such information was stored on computer – revealed nine such cars in the London area. The police set out to check them all. Eight drivers were able to prove that they were nowhere near the scene of the accident at the time it occurred. But the ninth, a man named Cameron who lived in Ealing, admitted that his route home from work took him past the spot. The investigating officer asked to see his car, and noticed that the right wing had been retouched recently. Cameron explained that he had caught it when reversing out of a narrow alleyway.

The wing mirrors of the car were, like many such mirrors, mounted on springs concealed beneath the mudguard, so that if struck, they would merely turn sideway. Examining the right wing mirror closely, the policeman noticed a few fine strands of wool caught in its base. As he carefully pushed the mirror sideways and removed these, he noticed Cameron looking pale and nervous. But he quietly agreed to allow the officer to take a small flake of paint from the wing.

The woman involved in the accident had been wearing a grey woollen cardigan, hand-knitted and of loose texture. In the police laboratory, the spectrophotometer revealed that the strands found trapped in the wing mirror were identical with strands from the cardigan. The spectroscope revealed that the black paint from the wing was identical in composition to the paint found on the handlebar. These two pieces of evidence together indicated clearly that it had been Cameron's car that was involved in the accident. Faced with this evidence he admitted his responsibility, and was charged with failing to report an accident and failing to stop after an accident; he received a three-month prison sentence.

In 1956, a similar technique led to the conviction of a murderer. On the morning of 7 February, an elderly spinster, Lily Lockwood, made tea, and then sat down to wait for her neighbour, Ida Hinchcliffe, to arrive. They had arranged to meet when they parted the previous evening, after watching television together in Lily Lockwood's house. Finally, wondering if her neighbour had overslept, Miss Lockwood knocked on the door and called through the letterbox. When there was no reply, she called the police, who forced their way in through a window.

Ida Hinchcliffe was lying dead on the settee in the living-room; she had been battered to death with a blunt instrument. Drawers had been searched, indicating that the motive had been robbery.

The forensic scientist Stuart Kind was called to the scene, together with a pathologist, whose verdict was that the weapon had probably been a hammer – although no hammer was found in the house. Stuart Kind made a search to try to establish how the killer had entered the house, since the front door was locked. He found that the cellar window had been smashed, and that the intruder had then climbed steps to a cream-coloured door, which he had attempted to open with a jemmy, then burst open with his shoulder. Kind took paint samples from this door, and from the back door, which also showed signs of an unsuccessful attempt to force it. He also took samples of the glass from the broken window.

There were no fingerprints to point to the identity of the intruder. But interviews with neighbours revealed that Miss Hinchcliffe was sometimes visited by the husband of her great niece, a young man called Harold Whitwam. Whitwam was at the moment separated from his wife and living with his parents. He insisted that he had not seen Ida Hinchcliffe for more than two months. But when the police examined his suit jacket, they found stains that looked like blood on the cuff buttons.

At the police station, Stuart Kind studied the jacket, and soon confirmed that the marks were blood; he also found more on the sleeve and collar. Kind also discovered a tiny fragment of maroon paint, similar to that on Miss Hinchcliffe's back door, caught on the fabric.

Whitwam's story was that the blood was his own – his wife had struck him with a coal shovel during a quarrel. Mrs Whitwam verified this. And in fact, the blood on Whitwam's collar proved to be of his own group, A. The blood of the victim was group O. It began to look as if there was no conclusive evidence against Whitwam.

At this point, Kind tested the blood on the cuff, and found that it was group O. Suddenly, Whitwam was again the prime suspect. Yet blood group O is so common that it seemed unlikely that a jury would convict him on this evidence alone.

At this point, Kind placed the flake of maroon paint under the microscope. Under powerful magnification, it was found to consist of several layers – exactly like a paint sample taken from the back door. And when a vacuum cleaner device was applied to the jacket, it sucked up two fragments of cream paint, and some slivers of glass. Microscopic examination of this paint was even more conclusive. It was found to consist of several layers of different colours – cream, white, fawn, dark brown, light brown and pale green. Again, this matched exactly a paint sample taken from the cellar door. There was even a fragment of wood from the cellar door – red deal – attached to the samples found on Whitwam's jacket.

For good measure, Kind tested the glass fragments for specific gravity and refractive index; these also proved to be identical with the cellar window. All this evidence convinced the jury of Whitwam's guilt, and he was sentenced to death.

A few fragments of green paint, identified by the spectroscope, also played a major part in solving one of the most widely publicized terrorist crimes of the 1970s. On 27 August 1979, holiday-makers on the beach at Mullaghmore, in County Sligo, watched the yacht of Earl Mountbatten of Burma sailing out towards Donegal Bay for a day's fishing suddenly, there was a tremendous explosion, and the yacht dissolved into matchwood. Seventy-nine-year-old Louis Mountbatten, the Queen's cousin, died instantly, as did his 14-year-old grandson Nicholas Knatchbull and his boat-boy Paul Maxwell. Four others on board, including Mountbatten's daughter, son-in-law, and another grandson, were injured. The bombing received world-wide publicity, which was undoubtedly one of the major aims of the Provisional IRA, who later acknowledged responsibility.

Mountbatten had been spending summers at Cassiebawn Castle, on the north-west coast of Ireland, for many years, and enjoyed fishing and dropping lobster pots from his yacht *Shadow V*. The IRA terror campaign, which had begun in 1969, had not made him alter his habits, and he had even asked for discreet police surveillance to be withdrawn, asking: 'What would they want with an old man like me?'

Later that same day, 18 British soldiers were killed in a land-mine explosion in County Down, but even this catastrophe was overshadowed by the news of Mountbatten's assassination.

A few hours after the explosion, an Irish policeman at Granard stopped a car for a routine check; noticing that the driver and passenger seemed nervous, he arrested them on suspicion of being members of the IRA. The car driver was a 24-year-old farmer named Francis McGirl, and his passenger was later identified as Thomas McMahon, who was a member of the IRA.

Forensic examination established that the yacht had been blown up by a bomb that had been planted in its engine room; it had been set overnight, and detonated at 11.45 the next morning by a radio signal transmitted from the cliff above Mullaghmore. The yacht had been painted green, and traces of green paint were found on McMahon's boots. Subjected to spectroscopic examination, these proved to be identical to the paint of the *Shadow V*. Moreover, sand on his boots was found to be identical to that of the slipway at Mullaghmore. But the finally conclusive evidence consisted in the traces of nitro-glycerine, detected by chemical analysis, on his clothes. In November 1979, this forensic evidence led to the conviction of Thomas McMahon, and he was sentenced to life imprisonment. The driver, McGirl, was acquitted for lack of evidence.

12

Recognition of the importance of car paint led the American Law Enforcement Assistance Administration to announce in 1976 its expansion of a pilot scheme to supply car paint samples to crime laboratories. In 1975, the Administration had collected hundreds of samples of paint sprayed on 1974 cars, and sent these to 171 crime laboratories, at a cost of $36,000. The samples led to the arrest of so many hit-and-run drivers, and of rapists who dragged their victims into cars, that it was decided to expand the scheme, and in 1976 the cost rose to $50,000.

In Great Britain, paint analysis proved its value in 1984 when it led to the arrest of a multiple rapist known as 'the Fox'.

On the night of 11 April 1984, a 74-year-old woman was awakened in her house in Linslade, Bedfordshire, by a man who had broken into her house. After shining a torch on her face, he felt under the bedclothes and tried to indecently assault her; she fought back and shouted so violently that he fled.

In the weeks that followed, there were many more break-ins over five counties, mostly in a triangle formed by three towns, Tring, Leighton Buzzard and Dunstable. The police became aware that these burglaries were the work of the same man because of one peculiarity: he took out photograph albums and laid out pictures of women on the table.

On 10 May 1984, the man broke into a house in Cheddington, Buckinghamshire, when the owner was out, and found two guns, one of them a shotgun with cartridges. He also found £300 in cash. When the owner, a man of 34, came home, he found himself confronted by a hooded man pointing his own shotgun at him. It may be that the burglar was hoping that he would encounter a female victim, but his sexual appetite seems to have been eclectic; he tied up the man and subjected him to a homosexual assault. He took the guns with him.

This acquisition of weapons was to be the turning point in the life of the criminal who soon became known as 'the Fox'. So far, he had been an unambitious burglar. The guns gave him a feeling of power, of invulnerability, and this combined with a highly developed sexual instinct to turn him into a dangerous rapist. The motive behind the burglaries was not, primarily, the desire to steal. The ordinary burglar takes what he can find and gets away as quickly as possible. The Fox enjoyed the process of entering someone else's house, cutting the telephone wires, and then treating it as his own. On 9 June, three days after a burglary in which he had stolen yet another shotgun, he broke into a house in Leighton Buzzard, helped himself to food, then settled down to watch television, with a blanket arranged as a kind of tent to prevent the owners from noticing the light from the screen as they arrived home. But for some reason he decided not to wait – possibly because his sexual excitement reached a premature imaginative release – and he left the house before their arrival. He took £113. Then, obviously frustrated at having rejected the opportunity, he broke into another house. There was a struggle with its male occupant; the shotgun exploded, and the man lost a finger. As usual, an extensive police search failed to find any trace of a burglar.

The police decided to co-ordinate their operations. By now it was clear that they were hunting a burglar who had turned rapist, and who moved freely over three counties. Those who had heard the burglar's voice said he had a northern accent. The Criminal Records Office provided the police of Bedfordshire, Hertfordshire and the Thames Valley with information on all burglars who had migrated from the north of England. This sounded a promising approach, but the computer produced no fewer than 3,011 names. The task of tracing that many burglars was tremendous.

In America, in similar cases, teams of police have concentrated on the areas where the rapist is likely to strike next, and have achieved remarkable success with this technique. But the Fox moved over such a wide area that this approach would have required the combined police forces of Great Britain. Whole villages were surrounded; policemen hid in certain houses in areas where the burglar had operated before. Even so, on 6 July, the Fox returned to Linslade and pointed his shotgun at a newly married couple. The wife screamed so loudly that he fled.

So far, his attempts at rape had been unsuccessful. But on 10 July, he broke into a house in Leighton Buzzard, and satisfied his peculiar power fantasy by tying up the husband, then raping the wife while the husband looked on. Children who were in the bedroom, through which he had forced an entry, slept on, unaware of what was happening.

Three days later, on Friday 13 July, he broke into a house in Edlesborough, Bedfordshire, where three teenagers – a brother and sister, and the sister's boyfriend – were spending an evening watching television and playing records. At 2 a.m., a man wearing a hood and leather gauntlets, and carrying a shotgun, walked into the room. The girl was ordered to tie up her 17-year-old brother and her 21-year-old boyfriend with electric flex. Then she was marched into her bedroom and left tied on the bed, with a pillowcase over her head. The burglar went to the kitchen and helped himself to a drink. Then he returned to the bedroom and raped her. The family dog was brought into the bedroom – the man apparently hoped to make it commit an act of bestiality – but it failed to become excited. The two boys were then brought upstairs and both ordered to have sex with the girl; both simulated the act. The burglar then raped her a second time, and committed indecent assault on the males. After this he went downstairs and sat watching videos before he left.

The reports of these rapes led to a public outcry and to feverish police activity. Every village in the 'triangle' seemed to be swarming with police. Burglar alarm companies had to go into top gear; thousands of households acquired big guard dogs. People who lived alone moved in with neighbours for the night. And the Fox, as the newspapers reported these activities, seemed indifferent to all this excitement. In fact, it gave him a sense of power and invulnerability.

A month later he made the mistake that was to lead to his arrest. On 17 August 1984, he set out to drive up to Newcastle to see his mother. Driving along the M18 motorway, he saw the lights of a small village, and again felt the familiar impulse to satisfy his sexual urge. He drove into a field, and uprooted a sapling to hide the reflection of the windscreen from passing traffic. He was not carrying his mask, but he made one out of a pair of dungarees. Then he walked into the village of Brampton, and broke into the home of an accountant – again through a bedroom where children were asleep – and tied up the man and his wife. After ransacking the house, he returned to the bedroom, and tied the legs of the 37-year-old housewife apart, one ankle shackled to the bedpost, the other to the leg of her 41-year-old husband. When she resisted, he rammed the shotgun into her face, and raped her. After this, he displayed the extent to which he was 'security conscious'. He washed the woman's body to remove saliva traces or hair samples, then cut out the square of sheet on which there were sperm traces. He took this with him. In 1984, the DNA fingerprint had not yet been discovered, but the rapist knew that his blood group could be detected from his semen and saliva traces. In fact, he had left such traces behind after earlier crimes; but his intention at the moment was to try to prevent police from recognizing that the Fox had left the south and was on his way back north. It could provide them with a valuable clue.

On the way back to the parked car he had another thought. As soon as the alarm went out, there would be road blocks. Therefore it would be dangerous to take the evidence – the shotgun and the square of sheet – with him. He left the shotgun concealed beneath a mound of leaves. His precaution proved unnecessary; no police patrols stopped him on his drive north.

The next day, the village of Brampton was full of police. And an alert officer noticed footprints going across a field towards the motorway. Tyre tracks showed them where the car had been parked. And a tiny flake of yellow paint on a tree revealed that the Fox had backed carelessly and scraped the wing. A careful search of the area also revealed the square of sheet, the dungaree-mask, a leather glove – obviously dropped by accident – and a carrier bag containing £38. The hooded rapist was becoming careless.

The police were fairly certain that the wanted man was the Fox, and that he was on his way north. There was a possibility that he might stop on his way back to recover the shotgun and the missing evidence. They ordered a blackout on Press and television coverage, and a fake motorway accident was staged to explain the police cars in the area. Then the police set up an elaborate trap. Infra-red cameras were installed in the copse where the car had been parked. Sensitive sound recording devices that could pick up the movements of a rabbit were hidden in the undergrowth. Police with special night binoculars lay in hiding around the copse. But it was all wasted effort; the Fox decided not to return. Police on the case were to say that he seemed to have a sixth sense for danger.

The night following the rape, he broke into a house in Peterlee, County Durham, and tried to rape a Chinese woman at knifepoint. When she fought back and bit his hand, he punched her in the face and fled.

Back in the south, he returned to his old area. On 9 September, he broke into a house in Milton Keynes and woke up a sleeping woman. Once again, a knife was not sufficient to cow her; she fought back, and he cut her stomach. When she screamed in pain, he fled.

But the paint had already provided the police with the clue they had been seeking. It was Harvest Yellow, and laboratory analysis revealed its exact composition. The British police had not established a scheme like that of the American Law Enforcement Assistance Administration, sending samples of all car paints to crime laboratories; but the British car industry was smaller and spread over a smaller area. The manufacturers of the Austin Allegro were able to identify the yellow paint as one that had been used only on Allegros. Now the problem was to identify a northern burglar who drove an Allegro.

The solution came almost by accident. The massive police operation – code-named Peanut because the burglar had stolen peanuts in one early break-in – was still directed to checking on the 3,011 crooks who had moved from the north to the south. On 11 September, two days after the rape attempt at Milton Keynes, two policemen were sent from Dunstable on a 'routine and eliminate enquiry' (known as an RTE) to a house in Kentish Town, north London, to check on yet another man with a police record who had moved south. They had only two pieces of information that might help identify the Fox: that he drove a yellow Allegro, and that he was left-handed – a fact noted by several of the victims.

The two constables had travelled on a railway warrant – the enquiry was not rated of sufficient importance to justify a police car. But as they turned into Oseney Crescent, NW5, they both stopped to stare. A thin-faced young man was washing a Harvest Yellow car outside the address they were looking for. Both had an instant 'hunch' that they had found the Fox. They introduced themselves to the man, whose name was Michael Fairley, and he invited them indoors, into the flat he occupied with his wife and two children. Asked about his recent movements, his alibis sounded weak. The police went out to examine the car – an Allegro. One wing showed signs of having been scuffed against bushes and had flakes of paint missing. The man's wristwatch was lying in the car; when he picked it up, he strapped it on to his right wrist – he was left-handed. A search of the car revealed a pair of dungarees identical to those used in the Brampton break-in. Michael Fairley was placed under arrest. Faced with the overwhelming body of evidence against him, he quickly admitted to being the hooded rapist.

In Fairley's flat, the police found pornographic videos. What surprised them was Fairley's admission that it was such videos that had turned him from a burglar into a rapist. Scenes of rape of schoolgirls, of group sex, of intercourse with animals, had made him feel a compulsion to try it for himself. During the period when he was committing the rapes, he had continued to have frequent intercourse with his wife.

Fairley, it seemed, had always been a 'loner'. The youngest of nine children, he had been educationally subnormal, and had spoken with a stammer; other children bullied him. He had preferred to spend much of his time in a tent above the housing estate where he lived rather than in his overcrowded home. In 1984, at the age of 31, he had drifted down to London and lived in a lodging-house until he was joined by his family. He made a living by burglary, until pornographic videos turned him into the hooded rapist. He showed no awareness of having done wrong. Asked by a policeman how he felt about a woman he had raped, he replied: 'She was good, just great.' Asked if he felt sorry he answered: 'I'm sorry I was caught.'

In court at the Old Bailey, Fairley admitted to 79 crimes between March and September 1984, and asked for 68 other offences to be taken into consideration – an average of a crime a day. He was sentenced to six periods of life imprisonment for rape, and several periods of 14 years for burglary. A single flake of yellow paint had ended the career of the hooded rapist.

8

The Sexual Criminal

1

As strange as it sounds, sex crime is a relatively modern phenomenon. Of course, invading armies have always committed rape; so have brigands and burglars. But these might be regarded as crimes of opportunity. A sex criminal like Michael Fairley is an obsessive, for whom sex is the most important thing in life. And as we look back over the history of crime, we find that such people were virtually non-existent before the nineteenth century.

The reason is obvious. In earlier centuries, most people lived in a state of continuous insecurity. If you are on the verge of starvation, or likely to freeze to death in winter, sexual satisfaction is bound to seem a secondary affair. One of the few true sex murderers of earlier times is the French Marshall Gilles de Rais, executed in 1440 for the sadistic murder of children, who also happened to be at one time the richest man in France; but Gilles began killing children in the course of 'magical' operations to make gold, which he believed required human sacrifice. The evidence at the trial makes it clear that, for this spoilt and bored aristocrat, paedophilia and sex murder simply developed into a habit. The case of Gilles makes it plain why 'obsessive' sex crime was a rarity in earlier centuries.

The same remains true down to the late eighteenth century, although by now there were a great many spoilt and bored aristocrats. It was the attitude of mind that was absent. The wealthy man who was so inclined could have an endless procession of mistresses and concubines; sex, like good dinners, was easily available. The first comprehensive survey of crime to be published in England, *The Newgate Calendar* (1774), reveals that murder committed in the course of robbery was the commonest offence, and that rape was a rarity. Of its 200 or so cases, only two or three involve 'rape', and even in these there is room for doubt. The Revd Benjamin Russen, executed at Tyburn for the rape of a child named Anne Mayne, was charged with committing the offence several times during a period when his wife was in bed having a baby, and a surgeon who examined the girl could find no sign of violence; it sounds like a case of seduction rather than rape. In 1817, a domestic servant was raped by three boatmen in Rickmansworth, Hertfordshire, and the local justice was so incensed that he financed a private investigation to track down the three men to Derbyshire; but when the victim and one of the rapists published their marriage banns, the charges were dropped.

Another case of 1817 poses an interesting riddle in crime detection; H. T. F. Rhodes devotes a chapter to its consideration in *Clues and Crime*. At 6.30 on the morning of 27 May 1817, a labourer on his way to work noticed a pair of shoes and a bundle of clothes lying close to the edge of a deep pool. He also observed, about 40 paces away, a patch of blood on the grass, and the impression of a human body lying full length; the blood was in the area of the lower part of the impression. There were also imprints of large-toed shoes, and some bloodspots leading towards the pond.

The labourer summoned help; the pond was dragged, and the body of a 20-year-old girl named Mary Ashford discovered in it. Medical examination later established that she had been a virgin, and that she had recently had sexual intercourse; the dress she was wearing was spotted with blood. The men made a careful study of the field, and showed that they had a real flair for detection. They noted several sets of footprints of a man and a woman, and that in one place, there was evidence that the man had run behind the woman to try to catch her up. Other footprints indicated that they had dodged one another. Finally, they had walked together. Then the girl had lost her virginity. No footprints led from this spot to the pond, from which the searchers deduced – rather oddly – that the man had carried her to the pond and thrown her in.

Mary Ashford lived at Erdington, near Birmingham, with her uncle, a small farmer, and was known as the village belle. On the night of the tragedy, Mary had arranged to go to a dance at a small village called Tyburn with a friend named Hannah Cox. She arrived at Hannah Cox's house with her dance frock tied in a parcel, and wearing a pink dress and a straw bonnet. At Hannah's she changed into her dance frock and shoes, and she and Hannah went to Tyburn. There she met the son of a neighbouring farmer named Abraham Thornton, and danced with him a great deal. Hannah and a friend left the dance around midnight; so did Mary and Abraham Thornton. At three o'clock, a man who knew Thornton passed him standing at a stile with Mary and said good morning. At 3.30 she was seen walking towards Hannah's house. There, at about 4 a.m., she changed back into her pink dress, and wrapped her dance clothes in a bundle. But, for some reason, she continued to wear her dancing shoes. Hannah watched her change, and said she seemed perfectly normal, and that her clothes were not blood-stained. At 4.15, Mary left Hannah's and began walking back towards her home – three people saw her on the road. (The unusual amount of activity in the area may have been due to the fact that the dance was a major annual event.) Two hours later, the labourer found her clothes in the field near the pond.

The obvious suspect was Abraham Thornton. He had walked back home to Castle Bromwich, arriving about 5.35. When told the next day of Mary's death, he certainly behaved like a man with nothing to hide: 'What! I was with her until four this morning.' And he also admitted that he had been responsible for the loss of her virginity – he had told a friend at the dance that he intended to try and seduce her later. He also seemed to have a sound alibi. At roughly the time Mary Ashford must have reached the field where she died, he was seen walking back home by three people, and was at a distance of three miles from the pond. Nevertheless, he was charged with Mary Ashford's murder, and tried at Birmingham. It took the jury only six minutes to find him not guilty.

In retrospect, we can see that the question of his guilt or innocence could have been easily established, even allowing for the condition of forensic science in 1817 (when Orfila was just making a name for himself in Paris). A microscope would have revealed whether the blood on her dress was menstrual blood, or due to her deflowerment. We know that there were spots of blood on her dance frock, which means that she had bled while still wearing it. If it was normal blood, then Mary had voluntarily given herself to Thornton in the field, and gone back to Hannah Cox's to change. In that case, she began to bleed more heavily on her way home, and lay down in the field, near the pond, in an effort to ease it – hence the blood on the grass. (She would naturally raise her dress to prevent it becoming more badly stained.) This scenario suggests that her death was accidental – she walked to the pond to wash off the blood, and slipped in, perhaps weak from loss of blood.

If the blood was menstrual, then Thornton was guilty. He admitted to possessing her, and it is highly unlikely that a girl who is starting to menstruate would feel like surrendering her virginity. In that case, Thornton must have waited for her to return across the field and run after her. She was raped and probably fainted; then Thornton threw her into the pond. But if, in fact, he was seen as early as 4.35 at a farm three miles away, then he cannot have been Mary's killer. Since no other footprints were found in the field – Mary's shoes and Thornton's shoes both fitted the footprints – it seems unlikely that she was attacked by some stranger. In that case, the jury was correct to find him innocent.

Local people were certainly outraged by the 'not guilty' verdict; they may have felt that this conceited Casanova – there is some evidence that Thornton regarded himself as a ladies' man – deserved some punishment. A fund was raised to enable Mary's brother William to bring an appeal. And at the appeal, in front of the Lord Chief Justice Lord Ellenborough, Thornton caused considerable surprise by offering to defend his innocence by engaging in single combat – a medieval law that had never been repealed. He threw down a glove on the floor, and William Ashford was on the point of picking it up when he changed his mind – he was apparently a much smaller man than Thornton. So Thornton walked out of the court a free man, and Parliament hastened to pass an act abolishing the 'wager of battel'.

Rhodes has pointed out that if Mary Ashford had changed into her walking shoes at Hannah Cox's, the case would be solved. If some of the footprints in the field had been those of her walking shoes – particularly those that showed her walking with Thornton – then it would prove that Thornton was present immediately before her death, and was probably guilty of it. Since Mary neglected to change her shoes, her death must remain an unsolved mystery. Yet even so, there is still one more piece of evidence to take into account – the running footprints. The field next to the one that contained the pond had recently been harrowed, and it was in this field that the amateur detectives found signs that the man had pursued the girl across the field and caught up with her; then they had, apparently, walked to the place where blood had been found on the grass. More of the man's footprints – again running – were found going back across the harrowed field in the opposite direction. Now it seems unlikely that this had all occurred earlier in the evening; Thornton was seen talking to Mary at a stile that led to the fields, so why should he then pursue her, unless they had decided to play hide-and-seek at half past three in the morning? It seems more likely that Thornton was unsuccessful in his attempts at seduction, waited for her on her way home, and made an attempt to take her by force. The rape completed, and the unconscious girl assigned to the pond, he then ran back across the field in an attempt to make up for lost time and establish an alibi. Simple logic makes it seem that the acquittal of Abraham Thornton was a miscarriage of justice.

2

1828 saw the trial of Burke and Hare, the Edinburgh 'body snatchers'. The case might be regarded as a typical example of the type of 'economic crime' which is so fully documented in *The Newgate Calendar;* because anatomists would pay a few pounds for corpses (the price between £5 and £10) Burke and Hare decided that it would be a simple matter to manufacture corpses by suffocating vagrants after getting them drunk. After a dozen or so murders they became careless and were caught. Hare turned King's evidence, so only Burke was hanged; Hare later died, a blind old beggar, in London.

But the period that saw the archetypal 'economic' murder case also saw the rise of a vigorous new industry: pornography. A kind of pornography had existed in France in the eighteenth century, but it was really a type of anticlerical satire, consisting mainly of tales of monks seducing their penitents and impregnating nuns. In 1740, Samuel Richardson's novel *Pamela, or Virtue Rewarded* caused a sensation, with its tale of a virtuous servant girl who resists all her master's attempts to rape and seduce her; it was the first novel, in our modern sense of the word. Nine years later, a penniless drifter named John Cleland produced the first pornographic novel, *Fanny Hill,* full of minutely detailed descriptions of seduction; but the government awarded him a pension on condition that he wrote no more pornography, and Cleland found few imitators; Henry Fielding's contemporaries were less interested in reading about sex than in doing it. After the French Revolution, the works of the Marquis de Sade caused considerable scandal; but Sade was so obviously a pathological case – writing about horrible tortures – that people read them to be shocked rather than sexually titillated.

But by 1820, a new generation was learning from Sade and Cleland, and England was importing large quantities of pornography from France. Books like *The Lustful Turk* (1828) and *The Ladies' Telltale* differed from their earlier models in one basic respect. Instead of Rabelaisian accounts of seductions, or nightmarish sadism, they concentrated on the forbidden – peeping through cracks in doors at women undressing, drilling holes in lavatory partitions, hiding under beds. Seduction of innocence was a favourite subject: little girls who see the butler in bed with the chambermaid, and persuade him to initiate them into the 'game', schoolmasters who deflower their female pupils after whipping their bare backsides . . . And as we observe the rise of pornography, we can see that the blame should be laid squarely at the door of the virtuous Samuel Richardson, the printer who claimed that his novels were intended as a warning against vice. V. S. Pritchett observed accurately:

> Prurient and obsessed by sex, the prim Richardson creeps on tiptoe nearer and nearer, inch by inch. . . he beckons us on, pausing to make every kind of pious protestation, and then nearer and nearer he creeps again, delaying, arguing with us in whispers, working us up until we catch the obsession too.

In *Pamela,* the virtuous housemaid holds out for marriage, but in its successor *Clarissa,* the heroine is kidnapped, taken to a brothel, and there drugged and raped.

But Richardson's real importance is that he taught Europe to day-dream. *Don Quixote* and *Robinson Crusoe* had been mere fairy stories; by comparison, *Pamela* and *Clarissa* were soap operas about the people who live next door; they had the compulsive quality of gossip. Within a decade, the novel had conquered Europe as the cinema would conquer the world 150 years later. The novel was a kind of magic carpet to a more interesting world.

Under the circumstances, it is surprising that it took so long for unscrupulous hacks to realize that the magic carpet could make highly profitable day-trips to the land of sexual fantasies. But when it happened, pornography ceased to be a vehicle of anticlerical satire, and became an independent literary form, like the historical novel or the Gothic fantasy.

Now the novel in itself might be regarded as a mixed blessing. Human beings learn to cope with life by knocking themselves against its hard corners; personal development is limited by reality. But the world of imagination offers another kind of development, just as authentic in its way, but uncontrolled by harsh realities. Cervantes had already treated this theme satirically – the dreamer who ventures out into the world prepared only by a diet of fantastic day-dreams. In the early nineteenth century, thousands of young people served their apprenticeship to life through the pages of romantic fiction, and then found themselves overwhelmed by the physical actuality – one result being an appallingly high rate of suicide.

Pornography offered an alluring alternative to real sex – day-dreams of seduction in which the innocent maiden never offered any real objection to the lustful male, and in which all the normal laws of social reality were suspended; daughters yielded to their fathers, mothers to their sons, and no one ever became inconveniently pregnant. In Victorian brothels, clients enacted their fantasies with women dressed as nursemaids or schoolgirls. The male ego was able to blossom like a hothouse plant – for male sexual fulfilment is based upon the assertion of the ego. Sooner or later, all this fantasy was bound to try to come to terms with reality, and the inevitable result would be sex crime.

What prevented an explosion of sex crime in the mid-Victorian era was not religious or social inhibition, but the fact that women were so easily available. The male who walks through a modern city knows that most of the women are unavailable – unless he happens to be a film star or pop idol. In the Victorian age, most of the working-class women *were* available, if he happened to have a few sovereigns in his pocket. The anonymous author of the Victorian autobiography *My Secret Life* describes endless encounters with teenage pick-ups who yielded their virginity for five shillings in some hired room. Only children were 'forbidden', and this explains why about three-quarters of Victorian rape cases involved children. But in the second half of the century, an increasing number of women began to earn their own living. We have seen that, in 1841, female shop assistants like Mary Rogers were such a rarity that they became minor celebrities and ensured the success of the business; by the 1890s, every large store employed hundreds of them, and although a few of them might be available to the predatory male, most were intent on marriage. And since Victorian morality preached the importance of virtue, the female sex was suddenly divided sharply into two classes: respectable women and whores. Now that most women were 'forbidden', children ceased to constitute the majority of the rape statistics. Yet social taboos were still so powerful that the rape of a shop assistant or typist was still a relatively rare crime.

This explosive situation was complicated by Victorian prudery. The

Victorian heroine, particularly as portrayed by female novelists, was a high-minded creature who would have regarded sex out of wedlock as horribly sinful. These same novelists made sure that the 'fallen' woman always ended in ruin and despair. As far as the normal Victorian male was concerned, this only made them ten times as desirable, so that the very idea of femininity became sexually stimulating. In 1886, the Victorian medical establishment was deeply shocked by Dr Richard von Krafft-Ebing's *Psychopathia Sexualis,* a book that revealed the extraordinary extent of sexual deviations on the Continent. Many of these deviations were variants of sadism and masochism; but the majority were forms of fetishism, in which sexual excitement is derived from some object connected with women – hair, shoes, night-caps, underwear, even crutches. 'Woman' had become so forbidden and so desirable that her magic could operate just as potently even, so to speak, at second hand.

Yet at the time of the publication of *Psychopathia Sexualis,* sex crime was still rare. In 1867, a clerk named Frederick Baker had lured an 8-year-old girl named Fanny Adams away from her companions and then dismembered her. The main piece of evidence was an entry in his diary reading: 'Killed a young girl today. It was fine and hot.' Baker tried to persuade a jury that it merely meant: 'Killed today – a young girl. The weather was fine and hot', but they disbelieved him and he was executed. But Baker came from a family with a history of mental illness, and the murder was regarded as an expression of 'moral insanity' rather than as an explosion of obsessive sexuality. Four years later, in 1871, a Frenchman named Eusebius Pieydagnelle became obsessed by the smell of blood in the butcher's shop where he worked, and committed six murders with a knife, mostly of young women; he admitted that the murders were always accompanied by orgasm. In Italy in the same year, a youth named Vincent Verzeni was charged with a number of sex crimes, including two murders – he experienced a compulsion to strangle women until he experienced orgasm. And in Boston, Massachusetts, in 1874, a 14-year-old boy named Jesse Pomeroy was charged with two sex murders of children, and sentenced to life imprisonment. In 1880, 20-year-old Louis Menesclou lured a 5-year-old girl into his room in Paris and killed her; he concealed the body under his mattress overnight. When neighbours complained about choking black smoke issuing from the chimney, police found a child's head and entrails burning in his stove. Menesclou denied raping the child, but became embarrassed when asked why the genitals were missing; a poem in his notebook began: 'I saw her, I took her.' But what all these cases had in common was that the murderer was mentally subnormal, so the sexual motivation could be subsumed under the heading 'hereditary degeneracy' and dismissed.

3

The Jack the Ripper murders, which occurred in 1888, created a world-wide sensation because they refused to be dismissed – they were, in fact, the first 'sex murders' in our modern sense of the term. All occurred in the Whitechapel area of east London and the known victims total five, although it is possible that a prostitute named Martha Turner, stabbed 39 times on the landing of a slum tenement on 7 August, brings the total to six.

Most of the murders displayed the same gruesome trademark; the disembowelling of the victim and the removal of certain inner organs, such as liver or kidneys. In the early hours of the morning of 31 August 1888, a prostitute named Mary Ann Nichols was found lying on the pavement in Bucks Row, Whitechapel; when removed to the mortuary, it was discovered that her stomach had been cut open. Death was due to the severing of the windpipe. Eight days later, on 8 September, a prostitute named Annie Chapman was killed in an almost identical manner in a backyard in Hanbury Street; the head was almost severed from the body, and her kidneys and ovaries had been removed and taken away. On 28 September, the Central News Agency received a letter signed 'Jack the Ripper', threatening more murders; two days later, the 'Whitechapel maniac' killed two women in a single night. Interrupted soon after he had cut the throat of a prostitute named Elizabeth Stride in the backyard of a working men's club, the Ripper immediately went in search of another victim. In Mitre Square, half a mile away, he met a prostitute named Catherine Eddows, who had just been released from police cells, and killed and disembowelled her in less than a quarter of an hour – a policeman passed the spot at half past one and a quarter to two, and found the body on his return.

The final murder was the only one that took place indoors. On the morning of 9 November 1888, a rent collector peered through the broken window of a room in Miller's Court, and saw a mutilated body lying on the bed. The victim was a 24-year-old prostitute named Mary Kelly, and the murderer had obviously spent several hours in the room, opening the body and removing most of the inner organs, and stripping the skin from the legs; he had apparently worked by the light of rags burning in the grate.

This was almost certainly the last of the crimes of 'Jack the Ripper', although three other murders with similar features occurred during the next three years. The general public was horrified at the sheer savagery of the mutilations, and the fact that the women were prostitutes touched some deep spring of morbidity in the Victorian mentality. Prostitution was unmentionable in decent society; the kind of men who made use of such women were supposed to be unspeakably degenerate, while the women themselves were – in modern phraseology – 'non-persons'. Yet the thought that such 'creatures' existed aroused mixed feelings in the Victorian middle classes, a mixture of revulsion and envy. (They were known euphemistically as 'daughters of joy', apparently in the belief that they did it for pleasure.) By drawing attention to these women in such a horrifying manner, Jack the Ripper had aroused, in an amplified form, these same morbid emotions of revulsion and envy. And, for the first time, the Victorians became aware of the immense reservoir of sexual frustration that lay just below the surface of their prim and orderly society.

The police were horrified for a more practical reason. For more than half a century – since the foundation of Scotland Yard in 1829 – crime detection had been improving steadily. And crime detection meant discovering a link between the crime and the criminal, and tracing the thread back to the criminal. Yet these casual sex murders by a maniac with a knife seemed virtually unsolvable. In theory, they should have offered no more difficulty than a series of burglaries – for, after all, the burglar also selects his target more or less at random. But the burglar may be identified by his *modus operandi,* by clues he leaves behind, and by his method of disposing of the stolen goods. By comparison, Jack the Ripper might have been the Invisible Man.

A mere nine years after the Ripper murders, fingerprinting solved its first murder in India (see p. 134), and within another four years, was in use at Scotland Yard. But would fingerprinting have enabled the police to catch the Ripper? On the available evidence, the answer is no. Mary Kelly's murderer undoubtedly left behind fingerprints in her room in Miller's Court, but unless they were the prints of a known criminal, or of someone the police arrested as a suspect, they would have been unhelpful. In fact, Jack the Ripper might have gone on killing for years, if he had chosen to do so, and remained uncaught – as Peter Sutcliffe, the 'Yorkshire Ripper' (whom we shall discuss later) demonstrated in the 1970s. After half a century of scientific crime fighting, the police found themselves virtually back to square one – to the sense of helplessness that had led the police of earlier centuries to rely on torture.

Why *did* the murders cease? The police were inclined to assume that it was because the Ripper committed suicide, or was confined in a mental home. This is why their favourite suspect was an unsuccessful barrister named Montague John Druitt, who committed suicide by throwing himself into the Thames on 3 December 1888. Druitt was named in the papers of Sir Melville Macnaghten as his chief suspect – together with two other men named Kosminki and Ostrog. But then Macnaghten came to the Yard in the year after the murders, and so had no direct experience of the case. And the information he gives about his suspect – in his private papers, and in his autobiography *Days of My Years* – is so inaccurate that it throws doubt on the whole theory. Macnaghten describes him as a doctor who lived with his family, and who committed suicide immediately after his last murder, when his mind collapsed as a result of 'his awful glut'. Druitt was a barrister (although he never practised) who lived alone in the Temple; he committed suicide four weeks after the murder of Mary Kelly, not 'immediately' after. And we know precisely why he committed suicide, since he left a suicide note: because his mother had become insane, and he was afraid that the same thing was happening to him. He was also undoubtedly depressed because he had been dismissed from the school in Blackheath where he worked as an usher – possibly for homosexual offences. And only six hours after the murder of Annie Chapman, Druitt was playing cricket at Rectory Field in Blackheath – he was an enthusiastic cricketer. On the whole, it seems likely that Macnaghten was merely repeating garbled rumours when he named Druitt as his chief suspect.

Other suspects* have included the Duke of Clarence (Queen Victoria's grandson), Clarence's tutor, J. K. Stephen (the cousin of Virginia Woolf) and the Queen's physician, Sir William Gull. The Duke of Clarence must be excluded, since he was celebrating his father's birthday at Sandringham at the time of the last murder. His tutor and close friend J. K. Stephen was a homosexual aesthete who seems an even less likely candidate than Clarence. The Sir William Gull

*For a comprehensive discussion of the murders and suspects, see *Jack the Ripper: Summing Up and Verdict*, by Colin Wilson and Robin Odell (1987).

theory, advanced by Stephen Knight in a book called *Jack the Ripper: the Final Solution,* was based on a story told by Joseph Sickert, the son of the painter Walter Sickert, according to which the Duke of Clarence had outraged his grandmother by marrying a Catholic artists' model named Annie Crook, who bore him a child. Mary Kelly, the final victim, was the nurse of this child. Annie Crook was kidnapped on the orders of the Royal Family, and Sir William Gull induced to perform a sinister brain operation to destroy her memory. Then, since Mary Kelly and some of her Whitechapel friends were trying to blackmail the Royal Family, Gull was given the task of hunting them down and murdering them one by one.

Soon after Knight's book appeared, Joseph Sickert admitted that his whole story had been a hoax. But since Gull had suffered a severe stroke in the year before the Ripper murders, he could have been excluded as a suspect even without this admission.

If the Ripper murders produced dismay at Scotland Yard, the police must have been encouraged by their success in arresting two more mentally disturbed killers, both of whom have been suspected of being Jack the Ripper. Dr Thomas Neill Cream, who obtained his medical degree in Canada, was a bald-headed, cross-eyed man, who arrived in London in 1891. He picked up young prostitutes in the Waterloo Road area, and persuaded them to take pills containing strychnine, apparently from motives of pure sadism; four of them died in agony. But Cream was undoubtedly insane: he wrote confused letters accusing well-known public men of the murders, and went to Scotland Yard to complain of being followed by the police. A young constable who had followed him from the house where two prostitutes had been poisoned explained why he suspected the cross-eyed doctor, and Cream's arrest followed swiftly. After his arrest, he wrote to a prostitute to tell her that his name would be cleared by a Member of Parliament, who had over 200 witnesses to prove his innocence. Cream should undoubtedly have been found guilty but insane; he told one prostitute that he lived only for sex, and was probably suffering from tertiary syphilis, with softening of the brain. After his execution in 1892, it was frequently suggested that Cream was Jack the Ripper. This seems unlikely for two reasons. No sex murderer has been known to change his *modus operandi* from stabbing to poisoning; and at the time of the Ripper murders, Cream was serving a term in Joliet penitentiary in Chicago for the murder by poison of his mistress's husband. So although Cream's last words on the scaffold were: 'I am Jack the . . .', there can be no doubt that he is the least likely suspect.

George Chapman, a Pole whose real name was Severin Kiossowski, *was* in Whitechapel at the time of the Ripper murders, and was suspected at the time by Detective Inspector Frederick Abberline, one of the officers in charge of the investigation. A doctor named Thomas Dutton suggested to Abberline that he should be looking for a Russian or Pole with a smattering of surgical knowledge – it was often asserted, inaccurately, that the mutilations showed medical skill. Chapman, who was 23 in 1888, practised the trade of 'barber-surgeon' – one writer asserts that he rented a shop in the basement of George Yard Buildings, the slum tenement where Martha Turner was stabbed 39 times. But in 1888, Klossowski had no known criminal record. In 1890, he married (bigamously) and went to America. In 1892 he returned to England, met Annie Chapman, a woman with a private income, and allowed her to set him up in a barber's shop in Hastings. But in 1897, she died after a great deal of vomiting; her death was attributed to consumption. In the following year, Klossowski – who was now a publican – married his barmaid Bessie Taylor; she died in 1901 after a long period of vomiting and diarrhoea. He married another barmaid, Maud Marsh, but his mother-in-law became suspicious when her daughter fell ill, and even more suspicious when she herself almost died after drinking a glass of brandy prepared by Chapman (as he now called himself) for his wife. When Maud Marsh died, an autopsy revealed arsenic poisoning, and Chapman was arrested. A second inquest revealed that the poison was antimony, not arsenic; and when the bodies of the previous two women were exhumed, it was discovered that they had also died from antimony poisoning. Although there was no obvious motive for the murders, the evidence against Chapman was overwhelming, and he was sentenced to death.

Abberline had continued to regard Chapman as a prime suspect in the Ripper murders; he had questioned the woman who was his mistress at the time – Lucy Baderski – and she said that Chapman was often out until four in the morning. When Chapman was arrested by Detective Inspector George Godley, Abberline remarked to Godley: 'You've got Jack the Ripper at last.' But although Chapman certainly had the opportunity to commit the Whitechapel murders, the same objection applies to him as to Neill Cream: a sadistic killer who has used a knife is not likely to switch to poison.

So although the police had reason to congratulate themselves on the arrest of two multiple murderers, they must also have recognized that detecting a poisoner is far easier than tracking down a sadistic 'slasher'. It was obvious that the Ripper-type killer was by far the most serious challenge so far to the science of crime detection.

This view was confirmed by a series of murders which began in France in 1894. In May of that year, a 21-year-old mill-girl named Eugénie Delhomme was found behind a hedge near Beaurepaire, south of Lyon; she had been strangled, raped and disembowelled. And during the next three years, the 'French Ripper' went on to commit another ten sex murders of the same type. The next two victims were teenage girls; then a 58-year-old widow was murdered and raped in her home. In September 1895, the killer began killing and sodomizing boys, also castrating them: the first victim was a 16-year-old shepherd, Victor Portalier. Later that month, back near the scene of his first crime, he killed a 16-year-old girl, Aline Alise, and a 14-year-old shepherd boy. Soon after this, he was almost caught when he tried to attack an 11-year-old servant girl, Alphonsine-Marie Derouet, and was driven off by a gamekeeper, who was walking not far behind her. A man was stopped by the police, but allowed to go after producing his papers. He was, in fact, the killer – a 26-year-old ex-soldier (and inmate of an asylum) named Joseph Vacher, whose face was paralysed from a suicide attempt with a revolver.

Imprisonment as a vagrant stopped the murders for six months, but almost as soon as he was released he raped and disembowelled Marie Moussier, the 19-year-old wife of a shepherd; three weeks later, he murdered a shepherdess, Rosine Rodier. In May 1897 he killed a 14-year-old tramp, Claudius Beaupied, in an empty house, and the body was not found for more than six months. The final victim was Pierre Laurent, another 14-year-old shepherd boy, who was sodomized and castrated. On 4 August 1897, he came upon an Amazonian peasant woman named Marie-Eugénie Plantier, who was gathering pine cones in a forest near Tournon, and threw himself on her from behind, clamping a hand over her mouth. She freed herself and screamed; her husband and children, who were nearby, came running, and her husband threw a stone at Vacher, who in turn attacked him with a pair of scissors. Another peasant appeared, Vacher was overcome and dragged off to a nearby inn. There he entertained his captors by playing the accordion while awaiting the police. The 'disemboweller of the south-east' (l'éventreur du sud-est) was finally trapped.

There had been a massive manhunt for the disemboweller, and

dozens of vagabonds had been arrested on suspicion. An extremely accurate description of Vacher had been circulated, which mentioned his twisted upper lip, the scar across the corner of his mouth, the blood-shot right eye, the black beard and unkempt hair. Yet he committed 11 murders over three years, and if he had not been caught by chance, might well have gone on for another three.

The great Alexandre Lacassagne, Locard's mentor, spent five months studying Vacher, and concluded that he was only pretending to be insane. Vacher insisted that he had been abnormal since being bitten by a mad dog as a child. Tried for the murder of Victor Portalier, he was sentenced to death in October 1898 and guillotined on 31 December. But there seems to be little doubt that Lacassagne was mistaken; Vacher was undoubtedly insane, and his random mode of operation had enabled him to play hide-and-seek with the combined police forces of south-eastern France.

It was a disturbing lesson for the police and the crime scientists; in the 1890s, the random sex killer constituted a virtually insoluble problem.

Fortunately, rippers and disembowellers remained a rarity. We have already seen how, in 1901, Paul Uhlenhuth was able to use his newly discovered precipitin test to help convict the sadistic child-killer Ludwig Tessnow (see p. 257). But it must be admitted that his contribution was not crucial; the jury hardly needed to be convinced that the man who had been questioned about the murder of two school-girls in 1898 was the same man who had murdered two schoolboys in 1901. All the same, it was plain that Uhlenhuth's method would one day spell the difference between a guilty and not guilty verdict for someone who had shed human blood.

4

On the morning of 11 June 1904, a boatmen on the River Spree in Berlin hooked a floating parcel; it proved to contain the torso of a young girl, whose developing breasts indicated that she had not yet reached adolescence. Two days earlier, a workman named Friedrich Berlin had reported the disappearance of his 9-year-old daughter Lucie; now, from the underwear on the body, the torso was identified as that of the missing child. The police surgeon established that Lucie Berlin had been raped.

She had last been seen shortly after lunch on 9 June, when she had asked for the key to the toilet on the next landing – the family lived in an overcrowded apartment building. A few doors away from the Berlins lived a prostitute named Johanna Liebtruth; but since she had been in jail on the day of Lucie's disappearance, the police decided she could tell them nothing. They also ignored her pimp, a man named Theodor Berger. They were seeking someone who had a penchant for young children. In due course, such a man was arrested, but proved to have a cast-iron alibi. And by this time the police had learned that the prostitute's male guest, Theodor Berger, was not a casual visitor, but actually lived with Johanna Liebtruth. And the occupants of the room above theirs reported that they had heard a child cry 'No!' at about 1.30 on the day of the murder.

Lucie Berlin's head was found floating in the ship canal, with two arms attached to it with string. The police took Berger to view the remains, hoping to shock him into confessing. Berger strenuously protested his innocence, claiming that his sister was in the room cooking his lunch at the time Lucie Berlin had disappeared. But a lengthy interrogation of Johanna revealed a new piece of information. She had quarrelled violently with Berger when she came out of prison because she discovered that a wicker suitcase was missing; Berger had finally confessed that he had had another woman up to the apartment – he was a highly sexed man who needed regular satisfaction – and that, having no money to pay her, he had given her the suitcase. And then, to Johanna's astonishment, he had taken her in his arms and declared that he had decided to marry her immediately, a promise that had the effect of dissolving all her resentment – they had been living together for 18 years and he had so far resisted all her attempts to drag him to the altar.

To the police, this was a highly significant admission. Why indeed should Berger decide to marry the woman who supported him, simply because she was angry about a missing suitcase? It argued that the suitcase was of considerable importance. The police let it be known through the newspapers that they were seeking a wicker suitcase in connection with the murder of Lucie Berlin. Berger and Johanna were taken into police custody. Meanwhile, a brilliant forensic investigator named Dr Paul Jeserich studied the Berger apartment at 130 Ackerstrasse through a magnifying glass, and left with a number of items that appeared to be bloodstained. By using Uhlenhuth's method, he could now tell whether it was human blood, animal blood, or only some fruit or wine stain. His results were disappointing. Most of the stains were not human blood. Some clothing contained a few light stains that could have been blood, but they had been carefully washed, making them too faint for forensic identification.

Two weeks after the discovery of the body, the break came: a bargeman reported finding a wicker suitcase soon after Lucie had vanished. He had simply not heard that the police were looking for one.

Johanna immediately identified the case as her own. And the police were delighted to notice a few brown spots on the inside of the case. It had been found floating close to the spot where Lucie's torso had been discovered.

Jeserich now repeated his Uhlenhuth test, and this time it gave a positive result: the spots were human blood. This forged the last link in the case, enabling the police to build up a picture of how Lucie Berlin became a murder victim. Johanna Liebtruth had known her well, and Lucie had often been in the apartment; she called Berger 'uncle'. In fact, on the day before Johanna had been taken to jail (for insulting a customer) Lucie had been playing with Berger's dog on the floor of the room, kicking her shapely legs in the air – she was exceptionally well-developed for her age. Berger was the kind of man who needed a woman every day; when drunk he became – in Johanna's words – 'like a bull'. When Lucie had gone up to the lavatory, on the day of her disappearance, neighbours had seen Berger standing in the doorway of his room. What had happened, almost certainly, was that Berger had invited her into the room to play with the dog, then made advances to her. Lucie had shouted 'No', and Berger, too sexually excited to stop, had throttled her, then raped her. Then, terrified of being found with the body, he had dismembered it, removed the limbs so it would fit into the suitcase – wrapping the limbs in newspaper to absorb blood – then taken them down to the river after dark.

The jury declined to believe Berger's insistence that he was 'as innocent as Christ', and he was sentenced to 15 years in prison.

5

On the other side of the Atlantic, the transition from the age of Victorian morality to the age of sex crime was less brutally obvious than in Europe; there were no American Jack the Rippers or Joseph Vachers. (The nearest American equivalent, H. H. Holmes, will be considered in the next chapter.) America's first recorded sex murder took place in 1852 – 15 years before England's Frederick Baker case; a man named Charles Steingraver raped and murdered a 10-year-old girl who was blind, deaf and dumb in Jackson, Ohio. Hundreds of spectators cheered as he fell through the trapdoor of the scaffold, and then seized his body and tore it to pieces.

The crimes of a Boston bell-ringer, Thomas W. Piper, challenge Jack the Ripper's claim to be the first sex killer in the modern sense of the term. Piper, a black-moustached young man in his mid-20s, was held in high esteem as the sexton of the Warren Avenue Baptist church in the early 1870s. In 1873, a curious change came over his character, and he began to cause scandal by leering at young ladies and whispering indecent suggestions in their ears. In December 1873, in nearby Dorchester, a servant girl named Bridget Landregan was attacked and battered to death with a club; then her killer stripped her, and was in the process of raping her when a passing stranger came to investigate the sounds issuing from a thicket. The killer ran away, leaving his club behind, and escaped over a railway embankment. Hours later, a girl named Sullivan was knocked unconscious and raped; she died later in hospital. The next victim was a prostitute named Mary Tynam, who was battered unconscious as she slept; she died later in hospital.

After church on 23 May 1875, Thomas Piper invited a 5-year-old girl named Mabel Young to come and see the pigeons in the belfry. Once there, he battered her unconscious with a cricket bat; but at that point, he heard the sounds of a search party ascending the stairs. He descended to a lower floor before they caught sight of him, and scrambled out of a window, dropping to the ground. Then he strolled back into the church. Meanwhile, his victim had recovered consciousness enough to scream in reply to the shouts of the search party. The door of the belfry was forced, and the child taken to hospital. But she died before being able to describe what had happened to her. However, the bloodstained bat was identified as Piper's, and he had been seen leaping from the window. Charged with the child's murder, he protested his innocence. But the evidence against him was overwhelming, and he was sentenced to death. A few days before his hanging, he sent for his lawyers, and confessed to killing Mabel Young, and to four earlier murders, as well as to several rapes of children. He was executed in May 1876. Piper seems to have been a heavy drinker – he admitted to being drunk when he attacked Mabel

Young – who experienced the urge to rape under the influence of whisky (He was also a drug addict who took laudanum.)

Twenty years later, a strangely similar case was to take place in San Francisco, and was duly recorded by Thomas S. Duke, a captain of that city's police force, in his *Celebrated Criminal Cases of America* (1910). Theodore Durrant was a medical student and a Sunday school teacher at the Emanuel Baptist church, a good-looking and highly regarded young man, who was much attracted by a pretty girl named Blanche Lamont. But Blanche was not entirely happy about her admirer. Some time before, he had taken her for a walk in the park, and made some bold advance that had outraged the virtuous young lady, who refused to speak to him for several weeks afterwards. Another girl named Anne Whelming had even more reason to avoid Durrant; he had invited her into the church library, made some excuse to leave her, then suddenly reappeared completely naked. The girl had screamed and fled, but decided to tell no one.

On 3 April 1895, Blanche Lamont left her cookery class in the early afternoon and met Theodore Durrant; they took a ride on a streetcar and he was seen toying with her glove. At 4.15, they were seen entering the Baptist church on Bartlett Street, to which Durrant had a key. What happened there is a matter of conjecture, but it seems likely that Durrant left her in the library, and reappeared naked. When she screamed, he strangled her, carried her up to the belfry, and stripped off her clothes. Three-quarters of an hour later, the church organist arrived, and found Durrant looking pale and shaken; Durrant explained that he had accidentally inhaled some gas . . .

Blanche vanished, and no one knew where to find her. A week after her disappearance, Durrant persuaded her friend Minnie Williams to accompany him into the church library. When he reappeared naked, Minnie screamed. Durrant pulled her skirt over her head and rammed it into her mouth to choke her screams. After this he raped her and stabbed her to death so violently that the walls were covered with blood; he then raped her a second time. Durrant then went off to attend a meeting of young church members. Towards midnight, he returned to the library, and probably raped her again.

The body was found the next morning by women who had come to decorate the church for Easter. They found the partially clothed body in the library, with the blade of a broken knife still in her breast. The police soon established that Theodore Durrant was the last person to be seen with Minnie Williams; he was arrested near Walnut Creek, where he was training with the state militia. Meanwhile, Blanche Lamont's body had been found in the belfry, looking 'white as marble', although it quickly began to decay and turn black when removed downstairs, so that the doctor who performed the post-mortem was unable to say whether she had been raped.

Durrant protested his innocence, but more than 50 witnesses had seen him with either Blanche or Minnie. (This seems to establish that neither crime was planned.) The jury found him guilty. For the next two years, Durrant made a series of appeals, and the case was widely publicized in European as well as American newspapers – an indication that sex murder was still a rarity. He was hanged on 7 Janaury 1898, but feeling against him was so strong that it took his parents six days to find a funeral parlour willing to cremate him.

In retrospect it seems clear that both Thomas Piper and Theodore Durrant were mentally abnormal, and that both were subject to violent urges that temporarily robbed them of all self-control. That is to say, both cases may be seen as a violent and irrational revolt against the rigid morality of the Victorians.

It is interesting to note that Duke's *Celebrated Criminal Cases of America* contains only two sex crimes – in more than 100 cases – and that the second of these would hardly rate a mention in a modern work on American crime.

On 8 January 1902, an advertisement appeared in the *San Francisco Chronicle and Examiner* asking for a nanny to take care of a young baby. A 15-year-old girl named Nora Fuller answered it, and was asked to go to a restaurant in Geary Street by a man who called himself John Bennett. She never returned home. A month later, an estate agent who had let a house to a man who called himself Hawkins sent someone to collect the rent. The house proved to be empty, but the naked body of Nora Fuller was found upstairs in bed. She had been raped and strangled, and the body mutilated. A letter addressed to 'Hawkins', and found in the dead girl's jacket, was postmarked ten days after her disappearance, indicating that her killer had returned to the house.

The room was probably full of the man's fingerprints – for example, on an empty whisky bottle on the shelf – but 1902 was too early for fingerprint identification in San Francisco. But a handwriting expert called Theodore Kytka decided to try and track down the killer by the old-fashioned 'needle-in-the-haystack' method. His examination verified that 'John Bennett' of the advertisement and 'C. B. Hawkins' of the house contract were the same person. Then he went through the only extensive collection of signatures in San Francisco – the Post Office's 'change of address' file. He had studied 32,000 signatures before he found what he thought he was looking for. A detective rushed off to Kansas City to question an ex-resident of San Francisco about the murder of Nora Fuller – only to find that the man had a watertight alibi.

At this point, a local newspaper told the police that a clerk named Charles B. Hadley had disappeared, taking some of the firm's cash with him. The mistress with whom he had lived produced a photograph of Hadley with his signature on the back. The initials were obviously the same as those of 'C. B. Hawkins', and the handwriting expert verified that they were written by the same hand. The mistress admitted that Hadley had shown an obsessive interest in the Nora Fuller case, reading every report about it. 'C. B. Hawkins' had a moustache, while Hadley was clean shaven; then it was discovered that Hadley had purchased a false moustache just before the crime.

Now the hunt was on for Hadley. His photograph – plus an added moustache – was published in all the newspapers. So was his signature. It should have been merely a matter of time before he was caught; the whole country was on the lookout for him. But Hadley was never found; Thomas Duke suggests that he committed suicide.

Eight years later, in 1910, handwriting analysis again played the central part in identifying a sex murderer. A 16-year-old stenographer named Ruth Wheeler received a postcard, forwarded from the Bankers' and Merchants' Business College of New York, asking her to call at an address in 71st Street, on the Manhattan waterfront, for a secretarial job. When the girl failed to return home, her sister found the postcard in her room, mentioning the address; the card was signed 'C. Walker'. The apartment proved to belong to a young German immigrant named Albert Wolter, who lived there with his common law wife. Wolter was obviously nervous, and he admitted that Ruth Wheeler had been to see him; but he insisted that she had left. And he denied knowing anything about the postcard signed 'C. Walker'.

The following day, neighbours noticed a sack on the fire escape outside Wolter's room. It proved to contain a charred body, so badly burned as to be unrecognizable, but a gold chain around the neck identified her as Ruth Wheeler. Still Wolter insisted that he knew nothing about her death. But the police noticed that the fireplace in Wolter's room had been repainted – obviously because a very large fire had caused its paint to peel. Wolter was asked to provide a sample of his handwriting; he did, but it looked different from the writing on the card. A handwriting expert suggested that Wolter had disguised his writing in the 'C. Walker' postcard, and suggested that he should be made to write page after page. And when Wolter did this, certain German characteristics – due to the fact that he had learned to write German script before English – began to emerge. The expert was able to point to the same characteristics in the handwriting on the postcard. Faced with this evidence, Wolter confessed. He had lured the girl to his apartment knowing that his 'wife' would be out all day, and had strangled and raped her. Then he proceeded to burn the body in the grate. But it was still unburnt when his wife returned; Wolter was forced to thrust the remains hastily into a sack and push it out onto the fire escape. It was a singularly inept crime, and Wolter died in the electric chair in Sing Sing.

These early sex crimes all have the same curious characteristics: an attitude of obsession on the part of the murderer that meant that his chances of escaping detection were minimal. Charles Hadley went to the length of renting a house and placing an advertisement in a newspaper; Wolter of writing to a business college; both left an obvious trail behind. A century earlier, such crimes would have been incomprehensible; no criminal would have felt it worthwhile to go to such lengths merely for sexual satisfaction. Such crimes spring out of a preoccupation with sex that was largely the result of Victorian prudery. And that preoccupation was shared by the rest of society. William Randolph Hearst was one of the first newspaper magnates to realize that sex will sell out edition after edition. That he understood his readers is demonstrated by the most widely publicized murder case of 1913.

On Saturday 26 April 1913, a 14-year-old girl named Mary Phagan went to the paper factory in Atlanta where she worked to collect her wages, then went to the toilet in the basement. She failed to return home, and the next day her body was found in the basement, her dress around her waist and a cord knotted tightly around her throat. An autopsy later revealed that she had not been raped, but the motivation was obviously sexual.

Two notes were found near the body, both written in an illiterate hand. The writer obviously hoped that police would assume Mary Phagan had written them; one of them stated that she had been attacked by a 'tall, sleam negro'. The night-watchman, who was tall, and slim and black, was arrested, but soon released. In his place, the factory manager, Leo Frank, was arrested; he was Jewish, and there was a great deal of anti-Semitism in Atlanta.

Another Negro named Jim Conley – who was short and fat – admitted that he had been sleeping-off a hangover in the basement that Saturday; he also insisted that he could not write, and was believed. When it was later discovered that he could write, he stated that he had written the notes on the orders of Leo Frank. It should now have been obvious to everyone that Conley, not Frank, had killed Mary Phagan; but the citizens of Atlanta preferred a Jewish scapegoat.

One obvious clue was ignored: there were teeth-marks on Mary Phagan's shoulder. A few years later, they would have led to the conviction of the murderer; yet even when it was shown that they did not correspond to Frank's teeth, this evidence was dismissed. The newspapers sold endless editions by headlining the Frank case, and they were largely responsible for his final conviction in August 1913. His attorneys published a letter of protest that contained the sentence: 'The temper of the public mind was such that it invaded the courtroom and invaded the streets and made itself manifest at every turn the jury made.' Appeals were rejected. But in June 1915, Frank's sentence was commuted to life imprisonment. On 16 August, a mob that called itself 'the Knights of Mary Phagan' broke into the Milledgeville prison, overpowered the guards, and dragged out Leo Frank; hours later, weak from beating and loss of blood, he was lynched in Marietta, 125 miles away. Although the identity of the 'executioners' was well known, no one was ever charged.

In 1982, Alonzo Mann, who had been a 14-year-old boy at the time of the Phagan murder, testified that he had seen Jim Conley dragging the body of Mary Phagan along the ground, and that Conley had threatened to kill him if he told anyone. Mann's evidence was validated by lie detector. In 1986, Leo Frank was granted a posthumous pardon by the State of Georgia.

6

Even after Frank's death, the case continued to exercise a morbid fascination; there were several books about it, and no fewer than three films. The newspaper accounts of the time make it obvious that, while everyone expressed horror, the underlying emotion aroused by the case was a kind of prurient interest. A journalist only had to invent some new absurdity – such as that the walls of Frank's office were covered with nude photographs – to sell out an edition of his newspaper.

What had happened was simply that half a century of Victorian morality and Victorian prudery – when even table legs were covered up in case they reminded people of the real thing – had generated a feverish sexual obsession. Now in a sense, there was nothing very new in this – we can observe the same thing in the novels of Samuel Richardson. But for all his gloating interest in seduction and rape, Richardson never for a moment presents Pamela and Clarissa as mere sex objects; they always remained individuals. It was not until the pornography of the 1820s that the 'heroine' ceased to be an individual, and became a completely unbelievable combination of modesty and nymphomania. It was the phenomenon that Karl Marx would call 'alienation', the breakdown of human relationships that causes human beings to treat one another as mere objects. But at this early stage, the social pruderies had not yet dammed-up the sex urge until it was ready to explode into violence; this happened only in the second half of the century. And even so, it remained a frightening rarity until the First World War. 1913, the year of the Mary Phagan murder, may be regarded as a kind of watershed: it was the beginning of the modern age of sex crime.

It seems to have been the anarchic violence of the First World War that released the age of sex crime on Europe. The dubious distinction of being its inaugurator probably goes to the Hungarian Bela Kiss, whose crimes presented an apparently insoluble problem to the Central Police Medical Laboratory in Budapest.

In 1916, the Hungarian tax authorities noted that it had been a long time since rates had been paid on a house at 17 Rákóczi Street in the village of Cinkota, ten miles north-west of Budapest. It had been empty for two years, and since it seemed impossible to trace the owner, or the man who rented it, the district court of Pest-Pilis decided to sell it. A blacksmith named Istvan Molnar purchased it for a modest sum, and moved in with his wife and family. When tidying-up the workshop, Molnar came upon a number of sealed oildrums behind a mess of rusty pipes and corrugated iron. They had been solidly welded, and for a few days the blacksmith left them alone. Then his wife asked him what was in the drums – it might, for example, be petrol – and he settled down to removing the top of one of them with various tools. And when Molnar finally raised the lid, he clutched his stomach and rushed to the garden privy. His wife came in to see what had upset him; when she peered into the drum she screamed and fainted. It contained the naked body of a woman, in a crouching position; the practically airless drum had preserved it like canned meat.

Six more drums also proved to contain female corpses. Most of the women were middle-aged; none had ever been beautiful. And the police soon realized they had no way of identifying them. They did not even know the name of the man who had placed them there. The previous tenant had gone off to the war in 1914; he had spent little time in the house, and had kept himself to himself, so nobody knew who he was. The police found it difficult even to get a description. They merely had seven unknown victims of an unknown murderer.

Professor Balazs Kenyeres, of the Police Medical Laboratory, was of the opinion that the women had been dead for more than two years. But at least he was able to take fingerprints; by 1916, fingerprinting had percolated even to the highly conservative Austro-Hungarian Empire. However, at this stage, fingerprinting was unhelpful, since it only told them that the women had no criminal records.

Some three weeks after the discovery, Detective Geza Bialokurszky was placed in charge of the investigation; he was one of the foremost investigators of the Budapest police. He was, in fact, Sir Geza *(lovag),* for he was a nobleman whose family had lost their estates. Now he settled down to the task of identifying the female corpses. If Professor Kenyeres was correct about time of death – and he might easily have been wrong, since few pathologists are asked to determine the age of a canned corpse – the women must have vanished in 1913 or thereabouts. The Missing Persons' Bureau provided him with a list of about 400 women who had vanished between 1912 and 1914. Eventually, Bialokurszky narrowed these down to 15. But these women seemed to have no traceable relatives. Eventually, Bialokurszky found the last employer of a 36-year-old cook named Anna Novak, who had left her job abruptly in 1911. Her employer was the widow of a Hussar colonel, and she still had Anna's 'servant's book', a kind of identity card that contained a photograph, personal details, and a list of previous employers, as well as their personal comments. The widow assumed that she had simply found a better job or had got married. She still had the woman's trunk in the attic.

This offered Bialokurszky the clue he needed so urgently: a sheet from a newspaper, *Pesti Hirlap,* with an advertisement marked in red pencil:

Widower urgently seeks acquaintance of mature, warm-hearted spinster or widow to help assuage loneliness mutually. Send photo and details, Poste Restante Central P.O.Box 717. Marriage possible and even desirable.

Now, at last, fingerprinting came into its own. Back at headquarters, the trunk was examined, and a number of prints were found; these matched those of one of the victims. The post office was able to tell Bialokurszky that Box 717 had been rented by a man who had signed for his key in the name of Elemer Nagy, of 14 Kossuth Street, Pestszenterzsebet, a suburb of Budapest. This proved to be an empty plot. Next, the detective and his team studied the agony column of *Pesti Hirlap* for 1912 and 1913. They found more than 20 requests for 'warm-hearted spinsters' which gave the address of Box 717. This was obviously how the unknown killer of Cinkota had contacted his victims. On one occasion he had paid for the advertisement by postal order, and the post office was able to trace it. (The Austro-Hungarian Empire at least had a super-efficient bureaucracy.) Elemer Nagy had given an address in Cinkota, where the bodies had been found, but it was not of the house in Rákóczi Street; in fact, it proved to be the address of the undertaker. The killer had a sense of humour.

Bialokurszky gave a press conference, and asked the newspapers to publish the signature of 'Elemer Nagy'. This quickly brought a letter from a domestic servant named Rosa Diosi, who was 27, and admitted that she had been the mistress of the man in question. His real name was Bela Kiss, and she had last heard from him in 1914, when he had written to her from a Serbian prisoner of war camp. Bialokurszky had not divulged that he was looking for the Cinkota mass murderer, and Rosa Diosi was shocked and incredulous when he told her. She had met Kiss in 1914; he had beautiful brown eyes, a silky moustache, and a deep, manly voice. Sexually, he had apparently been insatiable . . .

Other women contacted the police, and they had identical stories to tell: answering the advertisement, meeting the handsome Kiss, and being quickly invited to become his mistress, with promises of marriage. They were also expected to hand over their life savings, and all had been invited to Cinkota. Some had not gone, some had declined to offer their savings – or had none to offer – and a few had disliked being rushed into sex. Kiss had wasted no further time on them, and simply vanished from their lives.

In July 1914, two years before the discovery of the bodies, Kiss had been conscripted into the Second Regiment of the Third Hungarian Infantry Battalion, and had taken part in the long offensive that led to the fall of Valjevo; but before that city had fallen in November, Kiss had been captured by the Serbs. No one was certain what had become of him after that. But the regiment was able to provide a photograph that showed the soldiers being inspected by the Archduke Joseph; Kiss' face was enlarged, and the detectives at last knew what their quarry looked like. They had also heard that his sexual appetite was awe-inspiring, and this led them to show the photograph in the red-light district around Conti and Magyar Street. Many prostitutes recognized him as a regular customer; all spoke warmly of his generosity and mentioned his sexual prowess. But a waiter who had often served Kiss noticed that the lady with whom he was dining usually paid the bill . . .

Now, at last, Bialokurszky was beginning to piece the story together. Pawn tickets found in the Cinkota house revealed that the motive behind the murders was the cash of the victims. But the ultimate motive had been sex, for Kiss promptly spent the cash in the brothels of Budapest and Vienna. The evidence showed that he was, quite literally, a satyr – a man with a raging and boundless appetite for sex. His profession – of plumber and tinsmith – did not enable him to indulge this appetite, so he took to murder. He had received two legacies when he was 23 (about 1903) but soon spent them. After this, he had taken to seducing middle-aged women and 'borrowing' their savings. One of these, a cook named Maria Toth, had become a nuisance, and he killed her. After this – like his French contemporary Landru (whose career we shall consider in Chapter 9) – he had decided that killing women was the easiest way to make a living as well as indulge his sexual appetites. His favourite reading was true-crime books about con-men and adventurers.

Bialokurszky's investigations suggested that there had been more than seven victims, and just before Christmas 1916, the garden in the house at Cinkota was dug up; it revealed five more bodies, all of middle-aged women, all naked.

But where was Kiss? The War Office thought that he had died of fever in Serbia. He had been in a field hospital, but when Bialokurszky tracked down one of its nurses, she remembered the deceased as a 'nice boy' with fair hair and blue eyes, which seemed to suggest that Kiss had changed identity with another soldier, possibly someone called Mackavee; but the new 'Mackavee' proved untraceable. And although sightings of Kiss were reported from Budapest in 1919 – and even New York as late as 1932 – he was never found.

7

In the year 1913 another notorious sex killer committed his first murder. On a summer morning, a 10-year-old girl named Christine Klein was found murdered in her bed in a tavern in Köln-Mülheim, on the Rhine. The tavern was kept by her father, Peter Klein, and suspicion immediately fell on his brother Otto. On the previous evening, Otto Klein had asked his brother for a loan and been refused; in a violent rage, he had threatened to do something his brother 'would remember all his life'. In the room in which the child had been killed, the police found a handkerchief with the initials 'P.K.', and it seemed conceivable that Otto Klein had borrowed it from his brother Peter. Suspicion of Otto was deepened by the fact that the murder seemed otherwise motiveless; the child had been throttled unconscious, then her throat had been cut with a sharp knife. There were signs of some sexual molestation, but not of rape, and again, it seemed possible that Otto Klein had penetrated the child's genitals with his fingers in order to provide an apparent motive. He was charged with Christine Klein's murder, but the jury, although partly convinced of his guilt, felt that the evidence was not sufficiently strong, and he was acquitted.

Sixteen years later, in Dusseldorf, a series of murders and sexual atrocities made the police aware that an extremely dangerous sexual pervert was roaming the streets. These began on 9 February 1929, when the body of an 8-year-old girl, Rosa Ohliger was found under a hedge. She had been stabbed 13 times, and an attempt had been made to burn the body with petrol. The murderer had also stabbed her in the vagina – the weapon was later identified as a pair of scissors – and seminal stains on the knickers indicated that he had experienced emission.

Six days earlier, a woman named Kuhn had been overtaken by a man who grabbed her by the lapels and stabbed her repeatedly and rapidly. She fell down and screamed, and the man ran away. Frau Kuhn survived the attack with 24 stab wounds, but was in hospital for many months.

Five days after the murder of Rosa Ohliger, a 45-year-old mechanic named Scheer was found stabbed to death on a road in Flingern; he had 20 stab wounds, including several in the head.

Soon after this, two women were attacked by a man with a noose, and described the man as an idiot with a hare lip. An idiot named Stausberg was arrested, and confessed not only to the attacks but to the murders. He was confined in a mental home, and for the next six months, there were no more attacks. But in August, they began again. Two women and a man were stabbed as they walked home at night, none of them fatally. But on 24 August, two children were found dead on an allotment in Dusseldorf; both had been strangled, then had their throats cut. Gertrude Hamacher was 5, Louise Lenzen 14. That same afternoon, a servant girl named Gertrude Schulte was accosted by a man who tried to persuade her to have sexual intercourse; when she said 'I'd rather die', he answered: 'Die then', and stabbed her. But she survived, and was able to give a good description of her assailant, who proved to be a pleasant-looking, nondescript man of about 40.

The murders and attacks went on, throwing the whole area into a panic comparable to that caused by Jack the Ripper. A servant girl named Ida Reuter was battered to death with a hammer and raped in September; in October, another servant, Elizabeth Dorrier, was battered to death. A woman out for a walk was asked by a man whether she was not afraid to be out alone, and knocked unconscious with a hammer; later the same evening, a prostitute was attacked with a hammer. On 7 November, 5-year-old Gertrude Albermann disappeared; two days later, the Communist newspaper *Freedom* received a letter stating that the child's body would be found near a factory wall, and enclosing a map. It also described the whereabouts of another body in the Pappendelle meadows. Gertrude Albermann's body was found where the letter had described, amidst bricks and rubble; she had been strangled and stabbed 35 times. A large party of men digging on the Rhine meadows eventually discovered the naked body of a servant girl, Maria Hahn, who had disappeared in the previous August; she had also been stabbed.

By the end of 1929, the 'Dusseldorf murderer' was known all over the world, and the manhunt had reached enormous proportions. But the attacks had ceased.

The capture of the killer happened almost by chance. On 19 May 1930, a certain Frau Brugmann opened a letter that had been delivered to her accidentally; it was actually addressed to a Frau Bruckner, whose name had been misspelled. It was from a 20-year-old domestic servant named Maria Budlick (or Butlies), and she described an alarming adventure she had met with two days earlier. Maria had travelled from Cologne to Dusseldorf in search of work, and on the train had fallen into conversation with Frau Bruckner, who had given the girl her address and offered to help her find accommodation. That same evening, Maria Budlick had been waiting at the Dusseldorf railway station, hoping to meet Frau Bruckner, when she was accosted by a man who offered to help her find a bed for the night. He led her through the crowded streets and into a park. The girl was becoming alarmed, and was relieved when a kindly-looking man intervened and asked her companion where he was taking her. Within a few moments, her former companion had slunk off, and the kindly man offered to take the girl back to his room in the Mettmänner Strasse. There she decided his intentions were also dishonourable, and asked to be taken to a hostel. The man agreed; but when they reached a lonely spot, he kissed her roughly and asked for sex. The frightened girl agreed; the man tugged down her knickers, and they had sex standing up. After this, the man led her back to the tram stop, and left her. She eventually found a lodging for the night with some nuns, and the next day, wrote about her encounter to Frau Bruckner.

Frau Brugmann, who opened the letter, decided to take it to the police. And Chief Inspector Gennat, who was in charge of the murder case, sought out Maria Budlick, and asked her if she thought she could lead him to the address where the man had taken her. It seemed a remote chance that the man was the Dusseldorf murderer, but Gennat was desperate. Maria remembered that the street was called Mettmänner Strasse, but had no idea of the address. It took her a long time and considerable hesitation before she led Gennat into the hallway of No. 71, and said she thought this was the place. The landlady let her into the room, which was empty, and she recognized it as the one she had been in a week earlier. As they were going downstairs, she met the man who had raped her. He went pale when he saw her, and walked out of the house. But the landlady was able to tell her his name. It was Peter Kürten.

Kürten, it seemed, lived with his wife in a top room in the house. He was known to be frequently unfaithful to her. But neighbours seemed to feel that he was a pleasant, likeable man. Children took to him instinctively.

On 24 May 1930, a raw-boned middle-aged woman went to the police station and told them that her husband was the Düsseldorf murderer. Frau Kürten had been fetched home from work by detectives on the day Maria Budlick had been to the room in Mettmänner Strasse, but her husband was nowhere to be found. Frau Kürten knew that he had been in jail on many occasions, usually for burglary, sometimes for sexual offences. Now, she felt, he was likely to be imprisoned for a long time. The thought of a lonely and penniless old age made her desperate, and when her husband finally reappeared, she asked him frantically what he had been doing. When he told her that he was the Düsseldorf killer, she thought he was joking. But finally he convinced her. Her reaction was to suggest a suicide pact. But Kürten had a better idea. There was a large reward offered for the capture of the sadist; if his wife could claim that, she could have a comfortable old age. They argued for many hours; she still wanted to kill herself. But eventually, she was persuaded. And on the afternoon of the 24th, Kürten met his wife outside the St Rochus church, and four policemen rushed at him waving revolvers. Kürten smiled reassuringly and told them not to be afraid. Then he was taken into police custody.

In prison, Kürten spoke frankly about his career of murder with the police psychiatrist, Professor Karl Berg. He had been born in Köhn-Mulheim in 1883, son of a drunkard who often forced his wife to have sexual intercourse in the same bedroom as the children; after an attempt to rape one of his daughters, the father was imprisoned, and Frau Kürten obtained a separation and married again. Even as a child Kürten was oversexed, and tried to have intercourse with the sister his father had attacked. At the age of eight he became friendly with a local dog-catcher, who taught him how to masturbate the dogs; the dog-catcher also ill-treated them in the child's presence. At the age of nine, Kürten pushed a schoolfellow off a raft, and when another boy dived in, managed to push his head under, so that both were drowned. At the age of 13 he began to practise bestiality with sheep, pigs and goats, but discovered that he had his most powerful sensation when he stabbed a sheep as he had intercourse, and began to do it with increasing frequency. At 16 he stole money and ran away from home; soon after, he received the first of 17 prison sentences that occupied 24 years of his life. And during long periods of solitary confinement for insubordination, he indulged in endless sadistic day-dreams, which 'fixed' his tendency to associate sexual excitement with blood. In 1913, he had entered the tavern in Köln-Mülheim and murdered the 10-year-old girl as she lay in bed; he had experienced orgasm as he cut her throat. The handkerchief with intials P.K. belonged, of course, to Peter Kürten.

And so Kürten's career continued – periods in jail, and brief periods of freedom during which he committed sexual attacks on women, sometimes stabbing them, sometimes strangling them. If he experienced orgasm as he squeezed a girl's throat, he immediately became courteous and apologetic, explaining 'That's what love's about.' The psychiatrist Karl Berg was impressed by his intelligence and frankness, and later wrote a classic book on the case. Kürten told him candidly that he looked with longing at the white throat of the stenographer who took down his confession, and longed to strangle it. He also confided to Berg that his greatest wish was to hear his own blood gushing into the basket as his head was cut off. He ate an enormous last meal before he was guillotined on 2 July 1931.

Kürten was only one of many sex killers who gained notoriety after the First World War. Fritz Haarmann, a Hanover butcher who was also homosexual, picked up vagrant youths at the railway station – in the post-war period Germany was full of young unemployed workmen – and took them back to his lodging. There he murdered them, dismembered the bodies, and sold them for meat. He was also a police informer, so escaped suspicion of being the murderer who tossed bones and skulls into the river. It was only after his arrest for indecency in 1924 that his room was searched and various male garments discovered. Haarmann then confessed to a whole series of murders, all sexually motivated. He insisted to the end that he had killed his victims by biting them through the windpipe. He was guillotined in 1925.

Karl Denke, a church organist and landlord of a house in Munsterberg, Silesia, also made a habit of murdering strangers who were looking for lodgings. In December 1924, a coachman who lived above Denke heard cries and rushed down to investigate; he found Denke in the process of battering a young journeyman with an axe. When the police searched the house, they found the remains of 30 bodies pickled in tubs of brine, both men and women. Denke had been living off human flesh for at least three years, since 1921, and kept a ledger of his victims. Denke hanged himself with his own braces before he could be tried. In Germany in the mid-1920s, schoolchildren had a joke that went: 'Who is the world's worst murderer?', and the child being questioned was encouraged to answer: 'Haarmann, ich denke' – which may either be translated: 'Haarmann, I think' or: 'Haarmann, I, Denke.'

Georg Grossmann was a Berlin pedlar who had lived in a flat near the Silesian railway terminal since the beginning of the First World War; when he took it, he specified a separate entrance. In 1921, the tenant of the flat above heard sounds of a struggle and called the police; they found the trussed-up carcase of a girl lying on the bed, tied as if for butchering. For many years, Grossmann had been picking up girls in need of a bed and killing them, then selling the bodies for meat. The number of victims is unknown, but it was established that he had killed three women in the three weeks before his arrest. Like Denke, Grossmann committed suicide in jail before he could be brought to trial.

But the most extraordinary sexual criminal of the post-war years was undoubtedly the Hungarian sadist Sylvestre Matuska, the 'man who played with trains'.

On 8 August 1931, a bomb had exploded on the Basel-to-Berlin express near Jüterbog (not far from Potsdam) injuring 100 passengers, some of them seriously. On 30 January of that year, there had been an unsuccessful attempt to derail a train near Anspach, in Lower Austria, and it seemed likely that both crimes had been committed by the same man – perhaps for political motives. On a telegraph pole there was a notice with swastikas and 'Attack! Victory!'

Only a month after the Jüterbog attack, on 12 September 1931, a tremendous explosion shook the Budapest–Vienna express as it crossed a viaduct near the station of Torbagy, hurling five coaches into the depths below. Twenty-two people were killed, and many more injured. A 20-year-old reporter on the *Vienna Morning Post* named Hans Habe was asked to rush to the scene of the disaster. He found dozens of ambulances, stretchers taking away the injured, and wooden coffins beside the track. Some victims had been blown into pieces, and he saw two heads in one coffin and three legs in another. While Habe was talking to Superintendent Schweinitzer, who was in charge of the investigation, a short, well-built man with a military haircut came up to them. He introduced himself as Sylvestre Matuska, a Hungarian businessman who had been in one of the coaches. He seemed a lively, friendly man, and had apparently had a miraculous escape from one of the wrecked carriages that lay below the viaduct. Habe agreed to give him a lift back to Vienna. The next day, Habe met him by appointment in a café and found him describing the accident – complete with sketches – to a crowd of fascinated onlookers. 'I saw one woman with her arm torn off. . .' Habe quoted him at length in his story, which brought the young journalist much favourable notice from colleagues.

But Superintendent Schweinitzer was suspicious. Matuska looked healthy and unshaken – quite unlike a man who had just survived a train wreck. He questioned all the surviving passengers on the train; none could recall seeing Matuska. Forensic examination had established that the train had been blown up by an 'infernal machine' in a brown fibre suitcase – virtually a mine which had exploded by the weight of the train. A great deal of explosive must have been used, and explosive was not easy to come by. A few days after the explosion, a taxi-driver came to the Vienna police and told them that he had been hired by a short-haired man to take him on a long journey to two munitions factories, where he had bought sticks of dynamite. This raised the question of how the man had managed to obtain an explosives permit. The answer came a week later when a society woman name Anna Forgo-Hung went to the police with another piece of the jigsaw puzzle. Sylvestre Matuska had approached her about leasing some of her property, but had finally rented only a quarry, explaining that he wanted to do some blasting. This is how he had obtained his permit to buy explosives.

Matuska was arrested and charged with blowing up the Torbagy express. When Habe heard the news, he hastened to see Matuska's wife, a pretty blonde with an obviously gentle nature. Frau Matuska told him that her husband was undoubtedly innocent; he was travelling on the train himself, and she had seen his ticket. Yet her attitude convinced Habe that she herself had her suspicions; a wife who believes her husband incapable of a crime says so plainly, and does not talk about tickets and other 'proofs' of his innocence.

In fact, Matuska soon confessed. He *had* been on the train from Budapest; but he had got off at the next station, hired a car, and drove to Torbagy in time for the explosion. Forensic examination of the trousers he was wearing at the time showed semen stains, and psychiatrists who examined Matuska verified that he was a sadist. He was also, like Bela Kiss, a man of insatiable sexual appetite, who slept with a different prostitute each night when he was away from home on business trips. Yet his gestures in court – his trial began in Vienna on 15 June 1932 – were oddly effeminate. From the beginning, Matuska set out to give the impression that he was insane, declaring that he had been persuaded to wreck the train by a right-wing guru called Bergmann, who had tried to persuade Matuska to have intercourse with his incredibly beautiful wife – Matuska rolled the word 'intercourse' round his tongue – and then persuaded him to help him found a religious sect. Matuska spoke of spiritualist seances, and claimed that he had been under the telepathic influence of an occultist called Leo since he was 14. But perhaps the most interesting piece of evidence was that he had bought his son an electric train set, then spent all his time playing with it.

The jury was unconvinced by all this talk of mysticism and

occultism, and sentenced Matuska to life imprisonment – there was no capital punishment in Austria. He was retried in Budapest, and this time sentenced to death; but since the Viennese court had sentenced him to life imprisonment, the sentence was not carried out.

At the end of the Second World War, a reporter asked the Hungarian authorities what had become of Matuska, and learned – after many evasions – that the train-wrecker had been released.

In 1953, towards the end of the Korean War, an American patrol near Hong-Song captured some North Korean commandos who were about to blow up a bridge; they were led by a white man who seemed to be about 60. After long interrogation, during which he apparently failed to answer the questions, the man announced: 'I am Sylvestre Matuska'. His interrogator was obviously unimpressed, at which point the man explained with pride: 'I am Matuska, the train-wrecker of Bia-Torbagy. You have made the most valuable capture of the war.'

An American report of the incident stated that Matuska had been freed from his Hungarian prison by the Russians, and told them that he had wrecked the Jüterbog train on the orders of a Communist cell of which he was a member; this is how he came to be accepted as a volunteer on the side of the North Koreans. As a saboteur trained to blow up bridges, he must have felt as contented as a necrophile placed in charge of a morgue. Habe is of the opinion that Matuska betrayed Communist military secrets to the Americans, and was then released. What became of him after the Korean War is unknown.

8

In America, as in Europe, sex crime became increasingly frequent after the end of the First World War. And the American police, like their colleagues in Europe, found it equally difficult to deal with. Sex crime often appears to be strangely motiveless – as in the case of Matuska – and since most crimes are solved by tracing the motive back to the criminal, such crimes present the most baffling problem to the investigator.

On the morning of 22 May 1924, a Polish immigrant crossing a marshy area near Wolf Lake, not far from Chicago, saw two bare feet protruding from a culvert pipe above a pond. He summoned help, and the naked body of a boy was removed from the culvert. One of the workmen picked up a pair of glasses from the ground close to the body.

Later that day, the dead boy was identified as Bobby Franks, the 14-year-old son of wealthy Jewish parents. He had vanished after school on the previous day, and his parents had received a letter demanding a $10,000 ransom, assuring them that their son was safe and well. The boy had been killed by violent blows on the head, and the face had been disfigured with hydrochloric acid.

Clues seemed to be minimal. The spectacles might or might not not have been connected with the case – it seemed unlikely, since they were small, and probably belonged to a woman. The kidnap note had been written on a typewriter that had a worn 't' and 'd'; but unless this could be located, this clue was useless. Three of the dead boy's school-teachers were 'grilled' by the police for hours, but seemed to have no connection with the murder. One theory was that the boy had been killed by a sexual pervert, who had then lost his nerve and failed to complete the assault – there was no sign of sexual interference.

The area where the body had been found was a nature reserve. The game warden was asked for the names of frequent visitors, and mentioned that of a 19-year-old ornithologist named Nathan Leopold, the child of wealthy parents who lived in south Chicago. Three days after the finding of the body, Nathan Leopold was asked to go to the local police station; there he signed a statement declaring that he and another ornithologist had been bird-watching in the Wolf Lake area the Sunday before the murder. A few days earlier, Leopold had passed his exams in criminal law.

A week after the murder, a reporter named Alvin Goldstein, who was working on the case, attended a fraternity lunch for students of the University of Chicago, and discussed the case with Richard Loeb, another son of a wealthy Jewish family, and a close friend of Nathan Leopold. Loeb suggested that Goldstein should check with drug stores to ask about anyone making suspicious telephone calls soon after the murder; Goldstein, who respected Loeb's 'hunches', left early to pursue this line of enquiry.

Meanwhile, the police were following their only promising lead: the glasses. The lenses had been made by a huge optical firm called Almer Coe and Company, who were able to identify them as theirs. But both lenses and the frames were of a common prescription. However, the hinges were more distinctive, having been made by the Bobrow Optical Company of Brooklyn. The Almer Coe Company kept excellent records, and were able to state that, out of 54,000 pairs of spectacles sold by them in Chicago, only three pairs had the Bobrow hinges. And one of the three purchasers – who had each paid $11.50 for their glasses – was the young ornithologist Nathan Leopold.

This, of course, meant little; Leopold had already described his bird-watching trip of the Sunday before the murder. They had probably fallen out of his pocket. Nevertheless, he was brought in for questioning. He declared at first that his spectacles were at home. But when a long search failed to unearth them, he admitted that he had probably lost them on the bird-watching trip. How had he lost them?, asked the interrogators. Leopold said that he had stumbled at one point, close to the culvert where Bobby Franks was later found. They asked him to demonstrate; Leopold obligingly put the glasses in his top pocket, and then fell down flat on the floor. The glasses remained where they were. He tried again; the glasses still stayed in the pocket.

Now the questioners asked Leopold about his whereabouts on the day of the murder. His replies were irritatingly vague. But he insisted that, at about the time Bobby Franks must have been kidnapped, he and his friend Richard Loeb had picked up two young women. When the girls had failed to 'come across', they had dropped them off, then gone home . . .

Loeb was taken to another police station and questioned separately. At first he said nothing about the two women; then he described how he and Leopold had got drunk and picked up two 'cheap girls' in Leopold's roadster. The police became increasingly convinced that they were questioning two innocent men.

The reporter Goldstein was meanwhile doing a little sleuthing of his own. He had seen the ransom notes, and now decided to try and check against notes typed by Leopold. He learned that Leopold was a member of a group of law students who prepared information sheets for one another. He called on another member of the group, and succeeded in examining some of these sheets. He immediately noticed that two of those typed by Leopold were on different machines. And the law student remembered: in fact, Leopold had a second typewriter, a portable. Goldstein was excited; typewriter experts had declared that the ransom notes were written on a portable Underwood or Corona. Goldstein borrowed the information sheets, and took them back to his newspaper, the *Daily News*. The editor contacted an expert from the Royal Typewriter Company. And the expert pointed out similarities between the information sheets and the ransom notes: the 't' printed light, the 'i' was twisted, the 'm' was slanted . . .

Confronted with this new evidence Leopold admitted that he had used a portable typewriter, but insisted it did not belong to him, but to a friend who was now on holiday in Italy. However, it should still be in his house. . . A lengthy search failed to reveal the portable typewriter. But perhaps the friend had taken it away. Once again, the police decided that they were on the wrong track. Both boys had rich parents, and it would be impossible to hold them much longer.

The interrogator, Detective Bert Cronson, decided to try just one more possibility. The one person in the Leopold household he had not yet questioned was the chauffeur, Sven Englund; he asked a policeman to bring him in.

Englund remembered the day of the murder clearly because Nathan Leopold had asked him to repair the brakes on his sports car, a red Willys-Knight; they had been squeaking.

'Then they took the car and left?'

'No,' said Englund; 'the car stayed in the garage all day.'

Now Cronson was excited. 'Are you quite sure of the date?'

Englund said that his daughter had been to the doctor that day, and they had picked up a prescription from the doctor. The police hurried to see Mrs Englund, and she was able to find the prescription. It was dated 21 May, the day of the murder.

When Richard Loeb was asked about the car, he went pale and asked for a cigarette. Then he confessed. They had hired a car from the Rent-A-Car-Company for the murder, because Nathan's red sports car would be too conspicuous. Nathan had given his name as Morton D. Ballard, and his address as the Morrison Hotel. They had waited for Bobby Franks to come out of school, and offered him a ride. Then, according to Loeb, Nathan Leopold had struck the boy on the head with a heavy chisel. They had stripped the body, poured hydrochloric acid on it to render identification more difficult, and pushed it into the culvert near Wolf Lake. They had posted the kidnap letter, written by Leopold on a stolen portable typewriter, then gone to Richard Loeb's home, where they had burned Bobby Frank's clothes in the furnace. They had already thrown the chisel out of the car window – it was found by a night-watchman . . .

When Leopold was told Loeb had confessed, he laughed and said: 'Do you think I'm stupid?' But the details of the confession convinced him; he immediately decided to make his own confession, implicating Loeb as the killer.

Why had they chosen Bobby Franks as the victim? It had been pure chance. Leopold and Loeb had decided to commit a murder 'for kicks'.

They had driven around that afternoon looking for a child to lure into the car – male or female. (At one stage they had planned on kidnapping a girl and raping her.) The child had to be wealthy, so they could also demand a ransom; when Leopold wrote the ransom note, he had no idea to whom it would be addressed. They hid in an alleyway, watching a group of boys playing baseball through a pair of binoculars. But after two hours of looking for victims, they saw Bobby Franks walking towards them – he was a friend of Loeb's younger brother. And Bobby agreed to accept a lift home.

Leopold and Loeb, it emerged at their trial, had been lovers since Leopold was 13 and Loeb was 14. Loeb was daring, charismatic and handsome; Leopold was studious and shy. Leopold fell in love with Loeb, and Loeb agreed to submit to his desires if Leopold signed a contract agreeing to become a partner in crime. For years they committed petty crimes – such as breaking into the fraternity house where they stole the typewriter. It was all part of a fantasy game in which they were master criminals, Nietzschean supermen. Loeb was undoubtedly the leading spirit of the two; Leopold took a masochistic delight in describing himself as Loeb's slave. Eventually, master and slave decided to confront the ultimate challenge, murder. 'The plan was broached by Nathan Leopold', according to Loeb, 'who suggested it as a means of having a great deal of excitement, together with getting quite a sum of money.'

The state demanded the death penalty, but a brilliant defence by the lawyer Clarence Darrow led to life sentences. Nathan Leopold became the librarian in the Stateville penitentiary. Eleven years after his conviction, Richard Loeb was slashed to death with a razor by a fellow prisoner, who alleged that he had made homosexual advances.

After his release on parole in 1958, Leopold decided to sue the novelist Meyer Levin, whose novel *Compulsion* had fictionalized the murder; he demanded almost three million dollars for alleged invasion of privacy. The case was eventually dismissed, the judge pointing out that, since Leopold had 'encouraged public attention' by committing the murder, he could not complain at someone writing about it. Leopold's biographer Hal Higdon* speculates that what really upset Loeb was an episode towards the end of the novel in which a psychiatrist analyses the murder of Bobby Franks as a sex crime, with the chisel as a symbolic penis and the culvert into which the naked body had been thrust a symbolic vagina. The Freudian interpretation may

*The Crime of the Century, by Hal Higdon (1975).

lack subtlety; but there can be little doubt that the underlying compulsion of the murder was sexual.

9

The case illustrates the baffling and paradoxical nature of sex crime. Henry Fielding would have found it totally incomprehensible that two brilliant university students from wealthy backgrounds should have wanted to commit crimes as a kind of game. In Fielding's day, crime was motivated by quite straightforward 'deprivation needs', such as starvation. And even if someone had explained to him that Leopold and Loeb were *too* comfortable, and wanted to seek out challenges, like a mountain climber or explorer, he would still have found it quite absurd. Fielding would also have been baffled by the crime of Charles Hadley: to rent a house under a false name and lure a girl there, purely for the purpose of rape . . . He *would* have understood the compulsion that makes Lovelace, the villain of Richardson's *Clarissa,* lure the heroine to a brothel to drug and rape her. But to go to so much trouble for *any* girl – a girl Hadley had not even seen until she came to answer his advertisement: that would have struck him as a kind of insanity.

What Fielding would have found impossible to understand is that, in the course of two centuries, civilized man had learned to use his imagination, so that *he lives with only one foot in the real world*. We have become so accustomed to this condition, with books, films and television, that we accept it as normal; but in the evolutionary sense, it is thoroughly abnormal. Living in this strange, airless world inside our own heads, we experience a compulsion to 'get back to reality'. The sexual urge has this power to restore contact with reality; this is why the twentieth century has become 'the age of sex crime'. In that sense, Hal Higdon was right to describe the murder of Bobby Franks as 'the crime of the century'.

It is the fact that sex crime is the outcome of fantasy that makes the random sex criminal so difficult to detect. Two years after the murder of Bobby Franks, the American police found themselves confronting the same problem that had perplexed the London police force during the Ripper's 'autumn of terror'. On 24 February 1926, a man named Richard Newman went to call on his aunt, who advertised rooms to let in San Francisco; he found the naked body of the 60-year-old woman in an upstairs toilet. She had been strangled with her pearl necklace, then repeatedly raped. Clara Newman was the first of 22 victims of a man who became known as 'the Gorilla Murderer'. The killer made a habit of calling at houses with a 'Room to Let' notice in the window; if the landlady was alone, he strangled and raped her. His victims included a 14-year-old girl and an 8-month-old baby. And as he travelled around from San Francisco to San Jose, from Portland, Oregon to Council Bluffs, Iowa, from Philadelphia to Buffalo, from Detroit to Chicago, the police found him as elusive as the French police had found Joseph Vacher 30 years earlier. Their problem was simply that the women who could identify 'the Dark Strangler' (as the newspapers had christened him) were dead, and they had no idea of what he looked like. But when the Portland police had the idea of asking newspapers to publish descriptions of jewellery that had been stolen from some of the strangler's victims, three old ladies in a South Portland lodging-house recalled that they had bought a few items of jewellery from a pleasant young man who had stayed with them for a few days. They decided – purely as a precaution – to take it to the police. It proved to belong to a Seattle landlady, Mrs Florence Monks, who had been strangled and raped on 24 November 1926. And the old ladies were able to tell the police that the Dark Strangler was a short, blue-eyed young man with a round face and slightly simian mouth and jaw. He was quietly spoken, and claimed to be deeply religious.

On 8 June 1927, the strangler crossed the Canadian border, and rented a room in Winnipeg from a Mrs Catherine Hill. He stayed for three nights. But on 9 June, a couple named Cowan, who lived in the house, reported that their 14-year-old daughter Lola had vanished. That same evening, a man named William Patterson returned home to find his wife absent. After making supper and putting the children to bed, he rang the police. Then he dropped on his knees beside the bed to pray; as he did so, he saw his wife's hand sticking out. Her naked body lay under the bed.

The Winnipeg police recognized the *modus operandi* of the Gorilla Murderer. A check on boarding-house landladies brought them to Mrs Hill's establishment. She assured them that she had taken in no suspicious characters recently – her last lodger had been a Roger Wilson, who had been carrying a Bible and been highly religious. When she told them that Roger Wilson was short, with piercing blue eyes and a dark complexion, they asked to see the room he had stayed in. They were greeted by the stench of decay. The body of Lola Cowan lay under the bed, mutilated as if by Jack the Ripper. The murderer had slept with it in his room for three days.

From the Patterson household, the strangler had taken some of the husband's clothes, leaving his own behind. But he changed these at a second-hand shop, leaving behind a fountain pen belonging to Patterson, and paying in $10 bills stolen from his house. So the police now not only had a good description of the killer, but of the clothes he was wearing, including corduroy trousers and a plaid shirt.

The next sighting came from Regina, 200 miles west; a landlady heard the screams of a pretty girl who worked for the telephone company, and interrupted the man who had been trying to throttle her; he ran away. The police guessed that he might be heading back towards the American border, which would take him across prairie country with few towns; there was a good chance that a lone hitch-hiker would be noticed. Descriptions of the wanted man were sent out to all police stations and post offices. Five days later, two constables saw a man wearing corduroys and a plaid shirt walking down a road near Killarney, 12 miles from the border. He gave his name as Virgil Wilson and said he was a farm-worker; he seemed quite unperturbed when the police told him they were looking for a mass murderer, and would have to take him in on suspicion. His behaviour was so unalarmed they were convinced he was innocent. But when they telephoned the Winnipeg chief of police, and described Virgil Wilson, he told them that the man was undoubtedly 'Roger Wilson', the Dark Strangler. They hurried back to the jail – to find that their prisoner had picked the lock of his handcuffs and escaped.

Detectives were rushed to the town by aeroplane, and posses spread out over the area. 'Wilson' had slept in a barn close to the jail, and the next morning broke into a house and stole a change of clothing. The first man he spoke to that morning noticed his dishevelled appearance and asked if he had spent the night in the open; the man admitted that he had. When told that police were on their way to Killarney by train to look for the strangler, he ran away towards the railway. At that moment, a police car appeared; after a short chase, the fugitive was captured.

He was identified as Earle Leonard Nelson, born in Philadelphia in 1897; his mother had died of venereal disease contracted from his father. At the age of ten, Nelson was knocked down by a streetcar and was unconscious with concussion for six days. From then on, he experienced violent periodic headaches. He began to make a habit of peering through the keyhole of his cousin Rachel's bedroom when she was getting undressed. At 21, he was arrested after trying to rape a girl in a basement. Sent to a penal farm, he soon escaped, and was recaptured peering in through the window of his cousin as she undressed for bed. A marriage was unsuccessful; when his wife had a nervous breakdown, Nelson visited her in hospital and tried to rape her in bed. Nothing is known of Nelson's whereabouts for the next three years, until the evening in February 1926, when he knocked on the door of Mrs Clara Newman in San Francisco, and asked if he could see the room she had to let . . .

What disturbed the police about the Nelson case was that even after they had obtained a reliable description of the strangler from the three old ladies, it was still more than seven months before he was caught; it demonstrated that, where the unbalanced sex killer was concerned, crime detection had made no marked advance since the days of Jack the Ripper. The point was underlined by a widely publicized kidnapping that took place in the year of Nelson's execution.

10

On 28 May 1928, a mild-looking old man knocked on the door of a basement at 406 West 15th Street, in the Chelsea district of Manhattan; he introduced himself as Frank Howard, and said he was looking for the young man who had advertised for a job in the *New York World Telegram,* Edward Budd. The old man explained that he owned a farm at Farmingdale, Long Island, and would be willing to pay $15 a week for a good worker. The Budd family was delighted; Albert Budd, a doorman, found it hard to support his wife and four children. The old man agreed to return the following week for their decision. He failed to keep the appointment, but sent an explanatory telegram. The next day he arrived, full of apologies, and had lunch with the Budds, who were impressed by his expensive clothes and good manners. They were even more impressed when he took out a huge roll of dollar bills, and presented the eldest children with two of them to go to the cinema. And when the kindly old man offered to take their 10-year-old daughter Grace to a birthday party at the home of his married sister, they had no hestitation in giving permission. It was to be held in a house at 137th Street and Columbus. Grace went off in her white confirmation dress, holding the old man's hand.

When she had failed to return by the next morning, Albert Budd went to the police; they were able to tell him immediately that there was no such address as 137th and Columbus; Columbus only went as far as 109th.

There was also, of course, no Frank Howard in Farmingdale, Long Island. Nor was there any other clue to his identity. He had taken back the telegram he had sent, claiming that he intended to complain to the post office for getting Albert Budd's name wrong. The first thing that Detective Will King of the Missing Persons Bureau did when he was placed in charge of the investigation was to launch a search for the original telegraph form. It took three clerks 13 hours of sifting through tens of thousands of telegrams before they found it. It had been sent from the East Harlem office of Western Union. But the task of making a search of every house in East Harlem for the missing child would be immense. Instead, King set out to trace a pail of pot cheese that 'Frank Howard' had brought Mrs Budd as a present. The police had tried every hardware store in East Harlem before they found the street pedlar who had sold the pail. His description of Frank Howard was accurate, but he could give the police no further information.

Newspapers and radio stations publicized the kidnap; the police received hundreds of letters and tips from the public. All led nowhere. After several months, the police abandoned the case as hopeless. Only Detective Will King refused to give up. When he heard of a forger named Corthell, who had attempted to abduct a little girl from an adoption agency, he travelled 40,000 miles trying to track him down. Finally run to earth, Corthell proved to have a perfect alibi; he had been in jail in Seattle at the time of the kidnapping.

On 11 November 1934, six years after the disappearance of Grace Budd, her mother received an unsigned letter. It began by claiming that a friend of the writer named Captain John Davis had acquired a taste for human flesh in China, when children were eaten during a famine. On returning to New York, Davis had kidnapped two small boys, beaten them 'to make their meat good and tender', then killed and eaten them. When Davis told the letter-writer 'how good human flesh was', he decided to try it. As he was eating lunch with the Budds, and Grace was sitting on his knee, he had made up his mind to eat her. He had taken her to an empty house in Westchester, then left her picking flowers while he went in and stripped himself naked. Then he called her in. She began to cry and tried to run away. He stripped her, then choked her to death. After this, he cut her into small pieces, and took her back home, where he proceeded to eat her. 'How sweet her tender little ass was, roasted in the oven. It took me nine days to eat her entire body. I did not fuck her tho I could of had I wished. She died a virgin.'

Edward Budd brought the letter to Detective Will King almost as soon as it arrived. King had declined retirement two years before so he could fulfil a vow to track down the kidnapper of Grace Budd. Now, at last, he had his second clue – the first had been the telegram written by 'Howard'. When he compared letter and telegram, it was immediately obvious that they had been written by the same man.

The flap of the envelope contained a design that had been partly blacked out with ink. Under a spectroscope, this proved to be the letters of N.Y.P.C.B.A. From his Manhattan telephone directory, King deduced that this stood for the New York Private Chauffeurs Benevolent Association. Its address was at 627 Lexington Avenue. Later that day, King spent hours at the Association, comparing the handwriting of every employee – 400 of them – with the Grace Budd letter. In the early hours of the following morning he realized he had again reached a dead end; none of the signatures bore the least resemblance to the handwriting of 'Howard'.

Next, King addressed the assembled employees. Had any of them taken the Association's stationery for his personal use? If so, he need not be afraid to say so; no action would be taken. Then King sat alone in the president's office and waited. There was a knock on the door. A nondescript little man in chauffeur's uniform identified himself as Lee Siscoski, and admitted that he had used the Association's envelopes. King asked if he had given any of them away, or left them anywhere. Siscoski said that he had left some behind in a room at 622 Lexington. King rushed to the address, and borrowed a pass key to the room. There were no envelopes there. He telephoned Siscoski to ask him to think again. This time, the chauffeur recalled that he had also had a room at 200 East 52nd Street.

This proved to be a cheap boarding-house – what the Americans call a flophouse. When he described 'Frank Howard' to the landlady, she immediately nodded. 'That sounds like the man in number seven – Albert Fish.'

In the register, there was a signature 'A. H. Fish'. King saw at a glance that it had been written by the same man who had written the letter and telegram.

Where was Fish? He had moved away, said the landlady. But he would undoubtedly be back to collect his cheque – the monthly cheque sent to him by one of his sons. She expected him in a couple of days . . . King rented a room at the top of the stairs – where he could see down to the hallway – and settled down to wait.

He waited for more than three weeks. Then, on 12 December 1934, he found the landlady waiting for him. Mr Fish, she said, had been back half an hour; she was afraid he was going to leave. King checked his .38, then went and knocked on the door; a voice called 'Come in'. A little old man with a grey moustache and watery blue eyes smiled at him as he opened the door. He agreed unhesitatingly to go to headquarters for questioning. But as they neared the street door, the old man turned suddenly and lunged at King, an open razor in each hand. King grabbed his wrists, and pounded them against the banister until he dropped them. Then he handcuffed the old man, and searched his pockets. They were full of knives and razor blades.

Fish confessed to the murder of Grace Budd without any attempt at evasion. His original motive, he said, was to kill Edward Budd, the 18-year-old youth who had advertised for a job. Instead, he decided that he preferred Grace. They had caught the underground to Sedgwick Avenue, and Fish had left his bundle behind on the train. But Grace noticed it, and ran to fetch it before the train started. The bundle contained a saw, a cleaver and a butcher's knife.

They had walked out to a place in Worthington Woods, a cottage where Fish used to live. There – as he described in his letter – Fish had stripped naked, called Grace, then killed her. After this, he cut off her head, and drank some of her blood. It made him vomit, so he dissected the body at the waist with a knife . . .

The detectives took Fish back to the empty house, Wisteria Cottage. There they unearthed the bones of Grace Budd.

Back at headquarters, Fish at first denied that he had committed other murders. Then, under intensive questioning, he began to tell the story of his life. Fish ended by confessing to 400 child murders, committed between 1910, when he was 40 years old, and 1934. This figure was never verified, and is undoubtedly exaggerated, but there can be no doubt that Fish murdered dozens of children in 24 years.

The psychiatrist Frederick Wertham was asked to examine Fish in jail. Fish came to like and trust him, and the relationship between the two men was not unlike that between Peter Kürten and Professor Karl Berg; Wertham was later to include a chapter on Fish in his book *The Show of Violence*. In this he states that Fish looked 'a meek and innocuous little old man, gentle and benevolent, friendly and polite. If you wanted someone to entrust your children to, he would be the one you would choose.' He also described Fish as the most complex example of a 'polymorphous pervert' that he had ever encountered; Fish apparently practised every known form of sexual deviation, from sodomy and sadism to eating human excrement and driving needles into his scrotum. (X-rays revealed the remains of rusted needles still in his body.) He even enjoyed inserting cotton wool soaked in alcohol into his anus and setting it alight. Wertham's study convinced him that Fish was insane, and had been suffering from delusions and 'voices' for years. The jury disagreed, and Fish was sentenced to death. He told reporters: 'Going to the electric chair will be the supreme thrill of my life.' But his last words in the execution chamber were: 'I don't know why I'm here.'

11

By comparison with America and the rest of Europe, England remained relatively free of sex crime, and the few that occurred were usually solved by skilful detection.

Nellie Trew was the daughter of an employee of the Woolwich Arsenal in south-east London and, at the age of 16, she was also given employment there as a clerk.

On Saturday 9 February 1918, she went off to the Plumstead Public Library to change her book; when she had not returned home by ten o'clock that evening, her parents began to worry. At eight o'clock the next morning, her body was found on a corner of Eltham Common, not far from her home. She was lying on her back with her dress around her waist, and although her knickers seemed undisturbed, Spilsbury's medical examination established that she had been raped. Cause of death was strangulation.

It had been raining most of the night, and the grass close to the body was muddy and trampled. On this muddy patch a policeman found a military badge and a black overcoat button; the badge was of the Leicestershire regiment 'the Tigers'. The button had apparently been attached by a piece of wire, which was still on it.

Pictures of the badge and button were published in the newspapers. On the following Thursday morning, these were seen by a youth named Edward Farrell, who worked at the Hewson Manufacturing Company, off Oxford Street – a factory engaged in producing parts for aeroplanes.

The man who worked on the lathe next to Farrell was a recently discharged soldier named David Greenwood, who was 21; on the previous Saturday, he had been wearing a military badge displaying a tiger. Farrell asked him what he had done with it, and Greenwood explained that he had sold it to a man on a tram for two shillings. 'In that case', said Farrell, 'you ought to go to the police and tell them about it.' Greenwood agreed, and Farrell accompanied him to the Tottenham Court Road police station. There Greenwood made a statement to the sergeant in charge, describing how he had sold his badge to a man wearing a black overcoat and bowler hat, and speaking with a Belfast accent. He signed it and was allowed to go.

The detective in charge of the case, Chief Inspector Carlin of Scotland Yard, hurried to the factory and interviewed Greenwood in the office of the works manager. When he learned that David Greenwood lived close to Eltham Common, he must have been fairly certain that he was speaking to the murderer of Nellie Trew. But proving it was a different matter, even when Greenwood acknowledged that the tiger badge had belonged to him. A jury might not believe the story about the man with the Belfast accent, but might still feel obliged to give the young ex-soldier the benefit of the doubt. He asked Greenwood to accompany him to Scotland Yard. And when Greenwood returned wearing an overcoat without any buttons, Carlin asked what had happened to them. 'Oh, they've been off for a long time.'

Closer examination of the overcoat revealed that most of the buttons had been sewed on with thread, and that this was still sticking out of the overcoat. Only the bottom position but one had a ragged hole where the button should have been. Carlin picked up the overcoat button found near the body and placed it against the hole. It seemed an exact fit.

Greenwood was placed in custody, and Carlin once again interviewed the factory manager, whose name was Hewson. On his way through the factory, he picked up several pieces of wire from the floor – the factory manufactured its own wire. In Hewson's office he asked: 'Could you unfailingly identify your own wire?' Hewson said he could. 'In that case, would you mind going out of the room?' Carlin then placed several pieces of wire on the desk, including the length from the button. Hewson was called back in. Before he allowed him to see the wire, Carlin warned him of the gravity of what he was about to do. Hewson went pale; he understood that a man's life depended on what he said next. Carlin allowed him to see the pieces of wire.

'Which of these is yours?'

Hewson studied them for a moment and said: 'All of them.'

'Are you sure?'

'Quite sure.'

The experiment was repeated with the foreman, and the result was the same.

At the trial, Spilsbury gave evidence that the girl had been unconscious but alive when she was raped. (This would be indicated by the flow of blood; if the heart had stopped, it would be minimal.) The implication was that she had been killed during the course of the rape, or afterwards. Greenwood's alibi was that he was in the YMCA at the time the girl was attacked; but since this was close to the scene of the rape, it was hardly an effective alibi. Greenwood was sentenced to death. But there was a great deal of public sympathy for a soldier who had been discharged with shell-shock, and the sentence was commuted to 15 years.

Greenwood's crime was obviously committed on the spur of the moment. The curious case of Thomas Allaway belongs in the same premeditated category as those of Charles Hadley and Albert Wolter.

On 22 December 1922, the *Morning Post* carried an advertisement: 'Lady Cook (31) requires post in school.' The salary she demanded was a modest £65 a year. On the same day, Irene Wilkins received a misspelled telegram from Bournemouth: 'Come immediatly [*sic*] 4.30 train', and was signed 'Wood, Beech House.'

On the train she was noticed by an engineer called Frank Humphris, who later saw her in a green-grey touring car driven by a chauffeur in uniform. Since Humphris was waiting for a car to pick him up, he paid particular attention to this one, observing a luggage carrier of unusual design.

At half past seven the next morning, a farm-labourer on his way to work saw a woman's body lying in a field near Boscombe. He called the police, who discovered that the woman was lying on her back, with her dress pulled up. The face was covered with blood, and there was a trail of blood on the ground. Medical examination revealed that the woman – Irene Wilkins – had been struck in the face several times by a man's fist, then battered to death with a hammer. But her attacker had either been interrupted, or sickened by the injuries he had caused; the rape had not been completed.

On the other side of the hedge from the place where the body was found, the police discovered tyre tracks on the muddy road – it had been raining much of the night. The tracks had sunk more deeply into the mud at one point, indicating that the car had been parked there for some time. The road itself was so muddy that the police were able to follow the tracks for some distance in either direction. An expert identified them as those of a steel-studded Dunlop Magnum tyre. It had been on the nearside rear wheel.

Frank Humphris saw the newspaper account of the murder, and told the police about the grey-green touring car and the man in chauffeur's uniform. Every chauffeur in Bournemouth was interviewed. Among these was a man called Thomas Allaway, who worked for a Mr and Mrs Sutton. He drove a grey-green touring car, but the nearside rear wheel had a Michelin tyre; the other three were Dunlop Magnums. Asked if he changed the tyre recently, Allaway said no. He gave as his alibi a visit to the local pub. And since his employer said that the car had not been out of the garage after six that evening, the alibi was not even checked.

It seemed that Irene Wilkins was only one of several women that the unknown chauffeur had tried to lure to Bournemouth; in the week before the murder, two other telegrams had been sent from the local post office, requesting women to catch the next train to Bournemouth. The clerk recalled that these had been sent by a man in chauffeur's uniform; she had spoken to him, and thought she would recognize his voice.

Two weeks after the murder, Frank Humphris was on his way to Bournemouth station when he recognized the grey-green touring car with the distinctive luggage holder. He told his son to take down its number and later passed it on to the police. This should have been the turning point in the case. In fact, with incredible incompetence, the police failed to follow up the lead. They later explained that they were overworked.

The investigation was very obviously bogged down when, a month later, the female clerk who had spoken to the chauffeur was transferred to the Boscombe post office, and one day heard a voice which she recognized. She told a fellow clerk, but by the time she had reached the door, the chauffeur had gone. However, a few weeks later, the fellow clerk saw the same man standing by a grey-green car. She took its number and passed it on to the police. But the police had obviously given up interest in the case, and again failed to follow it up. A few days later, the clerk again saw the chauffeur, and told a fellow worker, who grabbed his hat and followed the man to an address in Portman

Mews, the home of Mr Sutton. And, incredibly, still the police did nothing.

In April, Thomas Allaway left Sutton's employment and took Sutton's cheque-book with him. As a result of several forged cheques, the chauffeur was arrested in Reading. And now, at last, the police began to review the evidence, and realized to their surprise that it all pointed towards Allaway as the murderer of Irene Wilkins. Betting slips were found in Allaway's pockets; they checked against the telegrams, and found the handwriting to be identical.

Allaway was an ex-soldier, 36 years of age and married; he also had a mistress. A week after the murder, he had driven his mistress to tea with her sister, and waited for her. Irene Wilkins's attaché case had later been found outside this house.

The police also looked more closely at the tyres on the car, and now observed that the Michelin tyre was badly worn, although the spare tyre – a Dunlop Magnum, was new. A witness was found who had seen Allaway changing the tyre – the Michelin had been the spare – on the day after the murder, when local newspapers had mentioned the Dunlop Magnum tyre tracks. The final piece of evidence was a garage key which Allaway's successor had found in Allaway's old room. Only Mr Sutton was supposed to have a garage key; Allaway had obviously had a spare key cut. This explained how he had been able to use the car without his employer's knowledge.

At the trial, Allaway insisted on his innocence; his defence rested on an alibi which, so many months after the murder, could not be positively disproved. His handwriting and the handwriting on the telegrams were not quite identical, but a handwriting expert testified that it had been disguised. And various misspellings in the telegrams convinced the jury that they had been sent by Allaway: asked to write 'immediately', 'Bournemouth', and 'advertisement', he spelt them all without the middle 'e'. Allaway was sentenced to death, and shortly before his execution, confessed to the murder of Irene Wilkins.

Yet here, even more than in the case of Hadley or Wolter, the most baffling question remains that of motive. If Allaway had been a single man, his attempts to lure women to Bournemouth might be just comprehensible – although he would certainly have found no lack of willing partners on the Bournemouth seafront. But he was a married man with a mistress. To describe him as a 'sex maniac' only begs the question. We are simply forced to recognize that, in the twentieth century, social tensions have produced a type of crime that would have been incomprehensible in the eighteenth, and accept that, under these conditions, the roots of crime are to be sought in the imagination as much as in social reality.

The Allaway case demonstrates that the Bournemouth police were rather less competent than their colleagues in America or on the Continent. The tyre tracks, which should have led to Allaway's arrest within 24 hours, were ignored, while the sightings of the car, which should have clinched the case, were simply overlooked. Altogether, the police displayed a vagueness that would have been endearing if it had not been so very nearly disastrous.

Fortunately, their colleagues at Scotland Yard had a more thorough training in scientific crime detection, as well as the support of an up-to-date laboratory. Both these advantages were brought to bear in the investigation of one of the most brutal sex crimes of the 1930s.

On the morning of 15 December 1931, a milkman entering a garden in Addison Road, Holland Park, saw the body of a child lying on the lawn. She was identified as ten-year-old Vera Page, who had been missing from her home at 22 Blenheim Crescent, in the Notting Hill area of London, since the previous evening. She had been raped and then manually strangled. When the body was moved, a finger-stall fell out from the crook of the arm.

A number of clues enabled the police to reconstruct roughly what had happened. Vera Page had last been seen alive at a quarter to seven on the previous evening; she had been on her way back from the house of an aunt, and had been seen looking in the windows of shops decorated for Christmas. Spilsbury's examination indicated that she had been raped and strangled not long after she was last seen, close to her home. Since she was a shy child, it seemed clear that she had been murdered by someone she knew and trusted. This man had probably taken her to a warm room – decomposition had already set in – and raped and killed her there. Then he had hidden the body in a coal cellar – this was indicated by coal dust on her clothes. The cellar had no electric light; this was suggested by spots of candle grease on the child's clothes. Some time around dawn, the murderer had retrieved the body and taken it to the garden in Addison Road, probably using a barrow. It had rained for much of the night, but the child's clothes were dry. As he removed his hands from under her arms, the bandage had slipped off his finger.

The murder caused intense public indignation, and the police mounted an enormous operation to track down the killer. Door-to-door enquiries were made over the whole area, and they quickly located a suspect. He was a 41-year-old labourer named Percy Orlando Rush, and he lived in a flat in Talbot Road, close to Vera Page. Moreover, his parents lived in the same house as Vera Page, so he often saw her. On the evening of the murder, his wife had been visiting her mother, and had not arrived home until later. So Rush could have murdered Vera Page, then taken her down to the coal cellar in the basement before his wife arrived home. Moreover, Rush had a wound on his left little finger, and had been wearing a finger-stall until recently.

The finger-stall was examined by Dr Roche Lynch, the Home Office analyst. He found that it had covered a suppurating wound, and that the bandage had been soaked in ammonia. Percy Orlando Rush worked in Whiteley's Laundry, near Earls Court, and his job involved placing his hands in ammonia.

There was another damning piece of evidence against Rush. At dawn on 15 December, a man of his description had been seen pushing a wheelbarrow covered with a red cloth near the garden where the body had been found. When the police searched Rush's home, they found a red table-cloth.

From the point of view of forensic science, the most interesting clue was provided by the candle grease. In the previous year, an Austrian engineer had invented a new method of testing candle wax. It was melted, with careful temperature control, on a microscope slide, and allowed to cool. Examined through a microscope under polarized light, the wax would reveal its 'fingerprinting', a characteristic crystalline structure. The wax on Vera Page's clothing was examined in this way, and compared with candles in her own home. They proved to be quite different. But it was identical with the wax of a candle found in Rush's home. So were certain spots of candle grease on Rush's overcoat.

But the crucial piece of evidence was the bandage. And here Superintendent George Cornish recognized that he may have made a mistake. He had let his suspect know about the finger-stall. And when he asked Rush for samples of bandage from his own house, Rush had handed them over with a faint smile that Cornish found disturbing. In fact, Roche Lynch's microscopic examination of the bandage established that it was not the same as that of the finger-stall.

Cornish's men scoured every chemist's shop in west London to try to find if anyone could recall selling bandages to Rush or his wife. If he could establish that Rush had bought some other type of bandage, and it proved identical with the finger-stall, then his case was complete.

Unfortunately, this attempt was a failure. The circumstantial evidence against Rush was overwhelming. But unless the bandage could be traced to him, the case had a fatal flaw. This became clear at the coroner's inquest, conducted by Dr Ingleby Oddie, on 10 February 1932. Rush proved to be a short, thick-set man who wore horn-rimmed glasses and a black moustache. His evidence was punctuated by angry cries of 'Liar!' from the spectators. But Rush stuck to his story that he had ceased to wear his finger-stall some days before the disappearance of Vera Page; he explained that he wanted to 'harden' the wound. All the coroner's questions – and those of jurymen – make it clear that they were convinced of Rush's guilt. But no one had actually seen Rush with Vera Page, and after only five minutes, the jury decided there was insufficient evidence to charge him with her murder.

12

Sex crimes invariably increase during wartime. This is partly because the anarchic social atmosphere produces a loss of inhibition, partly because so many soldiers have been deprived of their usual sexual outlet. Nevertheless, the rate of sex crime in England during the Second World War remained low, while the murder rate actually fell. One of the few cases to excite widespread attention occurred during the 'blackouts' of 1942. Between 9 and 15 February, four women were murdered in London. Evelyn Hamilton, a 40-year-old schoolteacher, was found strangled in an air raid shelter; Evelyn Oatley, an ex-revue actress, was found naked on her bed, her throat cut and her belly mutilated with a tin-opener; Margaret Lower was strangled with a silk stocking and mutilated with a razor blade, and Doris Jouannet was killed in an identical manner. The killer's bloody fingerprints were found on the tin-opener and on a mirror in Evelyn Oatley's flat. A few days later, a young airman dragged a woman into a doorway near Piccadilly and throttled her into unconsciousness, but a passer-by overheard the scuffle and went to investigate. The airman ran away, dropping his gasmask case with his service number stencilled on it. Immediately afterwards, he accompanied a prostitute to her flat in Paddington and began to throttle her; her screams and struggles again frightened him away. From the gas-mask case the man was identified as 28-year-old Gordon Cummins, from north London, and he was arrested as soon as he returned to his billet. The fingerprint evidence identified him as the 'blackout ripper', and he was hanged in June 1942. Sir Bernard Spilsbury, who had performed the post-mortem on Evelyn Oatley, also performed one on Cummins.

Of more interest, from the forensic point of view, is a murder that took place near an RAF camp in 1944. On the evening of 8 November, two WAAFs, Corporal Margaret Johns and Radio Operator Winifred Evans, attended a dance at an American army camp near Beccles in Suffolk, and returned to their own camp around midnight. Winifred Evans was due to go on duty, so the two women said good-night. At this point, Corporal Johns walked into the ablution hut, and discovered a man in RAF uniform leaning against a wall. He claimed that he had lost his way in the dark and asked how to get back to his own section of the camp. Corporal Johns did not believe his story, but she told him that he had better leave before he got into trouble. The man – a Leading Aircraftman – went off in the same direction that Winifred Evans had taken a few minutes earlier.

The following morning, a policeman cycling past the camp saw the body of a woman lying in a ditch. Medical evidence revealed that she had been raped after a violent struggle, and it was as a result of this struggle that she had died of asphyxia.

This had taken place very soon after Corporal Johns had sent the man on his way, so the search focused upon Leading Aircraftmen. An LAC named Arthur Heys had returned to his billet in the early hours of the morning, and had undressed in the dark, although some of his friends were awake and spoke to him. The next morning, he was seen cleaning mud from his shoes and trousers. And later that day, Corporal Margaret Johns picked him out of a line of men who were sitting waiting for their pay. Detective Chief Inspector Ted Greeno, who had been sent from Scotland Yard, was certain that Heys was the rapist; but he was also aware that the corporal's identification would not prove it to a jury. Heys' clothes were sent for examination to the Scotland Yard laboratory.

Microscopic examination revealed the remains of mud and brick dust on his trousers, in spite of a brushing that had apparently left them spotless. There were also some rabbit hairs. Examination of the dead girl's clothing also revealed the same brick dust, mud and rabbit hairs.

Meanwhile, the pathologist, Dr Eric Biddle, had found bloodspots on Heys' tunic. A blood test revealed that they were of the same group as the dead girl, but not of Heys himself. Heys was placed under arrest and charged with the murder of Winifred Mary Evans.

On the day before the hearing, 9 January 1945, the Commanding Officer of Heys's squadron received an anonymous letter, written in block capitals with a blue pencil. It read:

Will you please give this letter to the solicitors for the airman who is so wrongfully accused of murdering Winifred Evans. I want to state I am responsible for the above-mentioned girl's death. I had arranged to meet her at the bottom of the road where the body was found, at midnight. When I arrived she was not there. I waited some time, and decided to walk towards the WAAF quarters. Just before I reached this I heard a voice and stood close to the hedge. I heard footsteps. It proved to be an airman. I don't think he saw me. I then saw someone I recognized as Winnie. She said I should not have come down to meet her. A WAAF friend had offered to go along with her as the airman ahead was drunk and had lost his way. She had a bicycle with her. No one will ever find this.

The envelope bore a Norwich postmark, and Greeno's immediate suspicion was that Heys was the author. He discovered that prisoners in Norwich jail could borrow a blue pencil to write letters, and that its colour was identical with that of the anonymous letter. The next task was to find samples of Heys's block writing. In a watch taken from him at the time of his arrest, there was a slip of paper with the word's 'Hair spring straightening', evidently intended for the watch repairer. But this was not long enough for proper comparison; Greeno also went through all the leave application forms Heys had completed in the orderly-room files. These, together with the watch message, were all sent to the Yard's fingerprint expert Fred Cherrill, who explains in his autobiography: 'Fingerprints and handwriting have something in common. A fingerprint possesses a host of intricate and minute details. So does handwriting, if one has the ability to detect them.'

Cherrill was struck by the 'p' in 'watchspring', which was written in a distinctive manner – exactly like those in the anonymous letter. Other letters were also unusual, and Cherrill found many exact counterparts in the application forms.

When Cherrill appeared at Heys's trial at Bury St Edmunds, he found that the airman seemed confident and relaxed; when asked if he murdered Winifred Evans, he replied in a firm voice 'I did not.'

But Cherrill had noted something else about the anonymous letter: the phrase: 'as the airman ahead was drunk and had lost his way'. But if the letter-writer was *not* Heys, how did he know that the airman had lost his way? Heys had said this to Corporal Johns, and unless the 'stranger' had been lurking close enough to overhear this comment, then he could not possibly have known. When the prosecuting counsel, John Flowers, began to question Heys, the airman looked calm and self-confident; he denied writing the anonymous letter with an assurance that might have sprung from a clear conscience. But as Flowers read out the sentence about the airman being drunk, his gaze wavered. Flowers pointed out that Winifred Evans had parted from Corporal Johns before he – Heys – followed her into the darkness. So it was impossible that the 'WAAF' friend' (Corporal Johns) had offered to accompany her because Heys was 'drunk and had lost his way.'

'But *you* were the airman who had lost his way', said Flowers. 'How could anyone else in the world have the knowledge to put it in this letter but you?'

Heys was pale as he replied in a low voice: 'I did not write this letter.' At that moment, he must have realized that the letter was virtually a confession that he was the murderer.

Heys was sentenced to death, and his appeal was rejected. But, as the judge who rejected the appeal made clear, it was the anonymous letter rather than the handwriting or forensic evidence that established Heys' guilt beyond all doubt. Heys was hanged in Bury St Edmunds.

13

By 1950, it was obvious that sex crime had ceased to be a rarity, or an exceptional abnormality, as it had been in the days of Jack the Ripper, or even of Peter Kürten. Although crime figures in general began to fall in the early 1950s, sex crime continued to rise. A series of experiments performed by the American psychologist John B. Calhoun on rats suggested a possible reason for this.* Calhoun discovered that when rats are grossly overcrowded, a small proportion of them – 5 per cent to be precise – develop 'criminal' behaviour, such as cannibalism and rape. It had been known since early in the century that 5 per cent of any animal group possesses 'dominance' – certain leadership

*In 1954 at Palo Alto, and later at the National Institute of Mental Health at Bethesda, Maryland. See *Mysterious Senses,* by Vitus B. Dröscher, Hodder & Stoughton, London, 1962, Chapter 9: 'Degeneration of Community Life'.

qualities. Calhoun's experiment suggested that, under conditions of stress, this 5 per cent expresses its aggression in crime, including rape. In the early 1950s it was observed that the homicide rate in large American cities was three times higher than in small towns, and that the rate of sex crime was four times higher.

Calhoun's conclusions might seem to suggest that the criminal – particularly the rapist – is some kind of heroic rebel. But modern studies of the criminal personality make it clear that this is not so. In a study called *The Authoritarian Personality* (1940), sociologist Donald Clemmer presented the result of a survey of 110 inmates of San Quentin prison, and concludes that criminals are not genuine rebels with a feeling of sympathy for the underdog; on the contrary, they are inclined to be childishly self-centred and oblivious to the feelings – and the basic reality – of other people.

Similar conclusions were reached by two other sociologists, Samuel Yochelson and Stanton E. Samenow, in a remarkable study, *The Criminal Personality* (1976). Their studies of criminals in St Elizabeth's Hospital, New York – studies that will be further discussed in a later chapter – led them to conclude that the chief characteristic of the criminal is a self-centredness that often makes him almost oblivious of the existence of other people. But they also noted the close relation between sexuality and crime – a connection that had been noted as far back as 1864 by the 'father of criminology' Cesare Lombroso when he served in the army. Lombroso commented: 'From the very beginning I was struck by a characteristic that distinguished the honest soldier from his vicious comrade: the extent to which the latter was tattooed, and the indecency of the designs that covered his body.' And Yochelson and Samenow noted that a large percentage of the criminals they observed had started sexual activity very early – such as peeking through keyholes at sisters undressing or going to the lavatory – and had always indulged in a great deal of sexual fantasy. Sex was exciting because it was 'forbidden', and crime itself was an exercise in the forbidden, and therefore carried some of the excitement of a sexual act. This curious confusion between sex and criminality can be seen in the case of the teenage sex murderer William Heirens, a student at the University of Chicago, who began his career of crime as an underwear fetishist, breaking into apartments to steal women's panties; Heirens soon began to achieve orgasm as he entered the window – the window having become a kind of symbolic vagina. Like so many sex killers, Heirens was caught by accident, when someone heard him prowling around an empty apartment and contacted the police; fingerprints left at scenes of crime identified him as the murderer of ex-Wave Frances Brown – over whose body he had scrawled in lipstick 'For God's sake catch me before I kill more' – and of six-year-old Suzanne Degnan, whose body he had dismembered and thrown down manholes and sewers. In 1946 Heirens was sentenced to life imprisonment.

In November 1944, Los Angeles police had been confronted with a case that bore alarming resemblances to the Jack the Ripper murders. On 15 November, in a hotel at Fourth and Main Street, a chambermaid discovered the mutilated body of a woman lying on the floor. An enormous cut from the throat to the vagina had opened the body, and the intestines had been pulled out. One arm and one leg had been partly severed at the joint, and the breasts had been removed. These injuries had been inflicted by a carving knife that lay beside the body. The man who had accompanied the woman to the hotel on the previous day had been tall and slender, with a face resembling the film star Robert Taylor, and he had spoken to hotel staff quite openly – indicating that the crime had not been premeditated. The woman was identified as a prostitute named Virginia Lee Griffin, who had often been arrested for drunkenness.

Later the same day, a second 'mutilation murder' was reported from a hotel only three blocks away. This time the mutilations were less savage, but the woman's body had been opened from the throat to the left knee, and the face had been gashed. She was soon identified as a prostitute named Lillian Johnson, 38, and the man who had accompanied her to the room was evidently the same man who had killed Virginia Griffin.

It was obvious that the sex killer was choosing victims at random and would continue to do so until he was caught. The police decided to conduct a blanket search of the 20 blocks around the murder area, reasoning that since the killer had already chosen two victims there, he might now be looking for a third. One of the officers walked into a bar on Fourth Street and glanced around; in one of the booths he noticed a man answering the suspect's description, drinking wine and talking to a brunette in a tight red dress. The officer arrested the man on suspicion. The suspect identified himself as Otto Stephen Wilson – he preferred to be called Steve – and when he lit a cigarette, the policeman noticed that the match-book bore the address of the hotel where Virginia Griffin had died. Like Heirens, he was identified by fingerprints left at the scenes of crime, and confessed to both murders. He was examined by the psychiatrist Paul de River, who concluded that Wilson had strong sadistic tendencies that emerged when he was drunk. His first wife had left him because he liked to creep up on her when she was naked, and cut her buttocks with a razor; later he would apologize and kiss the wounds. He had experienced the compulsion to murder Virginia Griffin after they had gone to the room, and had gone out again to buy a large carving knife. Then he had strangled and mutilated her. After the murder he went to see a horror film, then picked up the second prostitute, took her to another hotel, and murdered her in the same way. Then he went out to a bar and picked up a third prostitute, who would undoubtedly have died later in the day.

From the point of view of crime detection, the most noteworthy feature of the case is that Wilson was so easy to catch. He knew the police had a good description of the killer; he knew he must have left fingerprints in the rooms. Yet he was sitting quietly in a bar close to the scene of both crimes, as if waiting to be arrested. Before his execution in the San Quentin gas chamber in September 1946, he declined any final requests. 'I've caused enough trouble for people already . . . I'll be better off out of the way.'

Compare this case with the 'phantom bank robbers' of the last chapter, who went to such immense trouble to cover their tracks, and we become aware that, in some basic sense, sex crime differs from most other types of crime. It seems to contain a powerful 'suicidal' element. The same element can be observed in the case of Neville Heath (see p. 232), who murdered Margery Gardner in a sadistic frenzy in June 1946, then killed a second girl in Bournemouth shortly after; he had then telephoned the police saying that he wanted to assist in their enquiries, virtually giving himself up. After the first murder, the second was a kind of gesture of abandonment, like throwing himself off a cliff. He had accepted that he had entered on a course of self-destruction. The same observation tends to support the view that Jack the Ripper committed suicide in 1888.

Another interesting psychological feature of sex crime lies in the number of false confessions received by the police. One of the most gruesome cases of post-war years was the murder of a 22-year-old waitress called Elizabeth Short, known as the Black Dahlia because of her preference for black underwear. In January 1947, her body was found on a vacant lot in Los Angeles, severed in half at the waist. Medical examination revealed that she had been suspended upside down and tortured to death. The horror of the case made it headline material for many months, and in a short time the police had received 28 confessions, all of which proved to be false. And as the years went by (the murder was never solved) they received many more. It was clear that the crime aroused a kind of *envy* in people suffering from psychological imbalance. Yet the morbid interest aroused by the Mary Phagan case three decades earlier makes it clear that this feeling is not restricted to the psychologically sick; we are speaking of an element of sexual obsession that permeates modern society.

Inevitably, then, such murders will give rise to imitative crimes; in the case of the Black Dahlia there were six in the Los Angeles area within a year – one victim had 'B.D.' scrawled in lipstick on her breast. This raises the frightening notion of a society in which sex crime continues to propagate itself like a nuclear reaction – a notion which, fortunately, disagrees with our observation of reality. The 'suicide factor', as illustrated in the case of Steve Wilson or Neville Heath, seems to operate in the same way as the heavy water that acts as the moderator in nuclear fission.

14

A case in point is the series of murders committed in the 1940s and 1950s by John Reginald Halliday Christie in London's Notting Hill area. Christie, a bald-headed, bespectacled hypochondriac, suffered from problems of sexual impotence that led him to prefer his victims to be unconscious or dead. He achieved this by an ingenious arrangement which enabled him to bubble coal gas through a mixture of Friar's Balsam, designed to clear the sinuses and cure catarrh. Women were lured to his shabby flat in Rillington Place, and persuaded to sit in a chair with their heads covered with a cloth, breathing in the steam of Friar's Balsam mixed with coal gas; when they were unconcious, they were raped and strangled. The first victim, an Austrian girl named Ruth Fuerst, was lured back to the flat in September 1943, when his wife was away visiting relatives; she was buried in the back garden. So was a woman from his place of work, Muriel Eady, three months later. For the next nine years there were no more victims; then, in December 1952, Christie strangled his wife Ethel and placed her body under the floorboards in the front room. After this, he seemed to lose all control, and murdered three more women in the course of a few weeks, placing their half-naked bodies in a large kitchen cupboard. Then he wallpapered the cupboard, abandoned the flat, and became a vagrant. The bodies were discovered almost immediately by the landlord; there was widespread public alarm, and Christie was frantically sought by all the police forces of Great Britain. The panic was unnecessary; Christie was wandering around harmlessly, sleeping in Salvation Army hostels and dozing over cups of tea in cheap cafés. Like Steve Wilson, he had simply given up; all the instinct of self-preservation had evaporated. When recognized by a policeman near Putney Bridge, he made no attempt to resist arrest or deny his identity.

The three corpses in the cupboard were all of women in their mid-20s: two prostitutes named Rita Nelson and Kathleen Maloney, and a woman named Hectorina MacLennan, who had stayed in Christie's flat with her boyfriend, then been murdered as soon as he left. The pathologist, Dr Francis Camps, found traces of sperm in the vaginas of all three. The bones of the two earlier victims were dug up from the back garden; one of them had been used to prop up a fence.

In the abandoned flat, police found a tobacco tin containing four lots of pubic hair, 'artistically arranged'. Three were taken from the three women in the cupboard; but whose was the fourth? It was not from Mrs Christie, whose body had been found under the floorboards, and it seemed unlikely that it dated back to the murders of ten years earlier. The likeliest assumption was that it came from another woman who had died in the house in 1949, Mrs Beryl Evans, for whose murder her husband Timothy had been executed. The Evanses, who lived above the Christies, had a one-year-old daughter named Geraldine, and in the summer of 1949, Beryl had become pregnant again. She and her husband – who was illiterate and mentally retarded – quarrelled a great deal. On 20 November 1949, Evans had walked into the police station at Merthyr Vale, in South Wales, and announced that he wanted to confess to 'disposing' of his wife, who had died in the course of an abortion operation – he later said it had been performed by Christie. He had pushed his wife's body down a drain, arranged to have the baby taken care of, and sold all the furniture.

The police had found no body down the drain, but they *did* find the bodies of Beryl and Geraldine Evans in the wash-house; both had been strangled. Soon after, Evans made a statement in which he described how he had struck his wife in the face during the course of a quarrel, then strangled her with a piece of rope. He had later strangled the baby with his tie. (The tie was still around the baby's throat when the body was found.) Thirteen days later, Evans retracted his confession. But it was too late. At his trial in January 1950, Evans accused Christie of strangling his wife and child, but no one believed him, and he was sentenced to death.

And now that Christie stood accused of six murders, it suddenly began to look as if there had been a terrible miscarriage of justice. And in fact, Christie soon added his confession of the murder of Beryl Evans to the others; his story was that she had wanted to commit suicide, and offered to let him have sexual intercourse if he would help her. He had rendered her unconscious by turning on the gas tap, then strangled her . . . That seemed to settle it. Evans was obviously innocent, and the apparently incredible coincidence of two stranglers living under the same roof shown to be an absurdity.

Christie was tried only for the murder of his wife. The defence was insanity, but it stood little chance of succeeding – Christie was so obviously a sane and thoroughly cunning individual. He had killed, quite simply, for the immense pleasure of sexual possession. (Francis Camps even found sperm on Christie's shoes, indicating that he had stood over the corpses and masturbated.) The jury took an hour and twenty minutes to decide that he was guilty, and he was sentenced to death. He was hanged on 15 July 1953.

Now only one question remained: was Timothy Evans innocent of the two murders for which he was hanged? In view of Christie's confession, the answer may seem self-evident. But we have to bear in mind that it was Christie's defence who suggested to him that he should confess to the murder of Beryl Evans, on the grounds that a man who had killed seven women might be regarded as slightly more insane than a man who had killed six. Christie replied cheerfully 'The more the merrier', and accordingly confessed. But clearly, this proves nothing, except that Christie wanted to be found insane.

In 1961, Ludovic Kennedy published a book called *Ten Rillington Place*, in which he argues strongly that Evans was innocent. Kennedy's belief is that Christie offered to perform an abortion, but that when Beryl Evans had undressed, he became so overwhelmed with excitement that he hit her in the face until he had subdued her, then strangled her with a rope. After this he raped her. When Evans came home, Christie told him that Beryl had died during the course of the abortion, and pointed out that they would both face criminal charges if her death was discovered. That night, he persuaded Evans to help him carry the body down to the wash-house. Later, Christie told Evans that he would arrange to have the baby looked after by some friends. That day,

Christie also strangled Geraldine, and placed her body in the wash-house. After this, he persuaded Evans to sell his furniture and flee to his aunt's house in Merthyr Vale . . .

There is an obvious objection to this scenario. If Evans was Christie's dupe from start to finish, why did he not denounce Christie as soon as he learned that Geraldine had been found dead in the wash-house? Why, in fact, did he then go on to confess – not once but three times – to murdering his wife and baby? Kennedy gets around this supreme difficulty by suggesting that Evans was in such a state of shock that he was virtually 'brainwashed', and would have confessed to anything. And he points out that Evans *did* later withdraw his confession and blame Christie, by which time no one believed him. But the difficulty remains. Surely no sane man is going to confess in detail to strangling his wife and baby when he knows he has been 'framed' by the real murderer? It is like asking us to believe that black is white.

In fact, after Christie's conviction – but before he was hanged – the question of whether Evans was innocent had become such a public issue that the body of Beryl Evans was once again exhumed. It took place at dawn on 18 May 1953, and the bodies of Beryl and Geraldine Evans were taken to Kensington mortuary, where they were examined by a team of London's three foremost pathologists – sometimes known to the Press as the Three Musketeers – Francis Camps, Keith Simpson and Donald Teare. Teare had, in fact, performed the original post-mortem on Beryl Evans in 1949. Christie's later confession alleged that he had gassed Beryl, then strangled her, but Teare had certainly noticed no sign of death from carbon monoxide poisoning – a distinctive pink coloration – at the first autopsy. What he *had* noticed was a black eye, bruising on the upper lip, and also on her thigh and lower leg. He had also noticed a bruise on the wall of the vagina, which could have been caused by an attempt at forced intercourse, or by a syringe she had used to try and abort herself.

How would it have been possible to decide whether Beryl Evans had been murdered by Christie or by her husband? Teare could, admittedly, have taken a vaginal swab at the first post-mortem – he was told by a policeman not to bother, since Evans had already confessed – and according to Kennedy, this would infallibly have revealed signs of Christie's sperm. Kennedy is probably correct; where he is incorrect is in believing that this would prove that Christie murdered Beryl Evans. According to Evans, he strangled Beryl before going to work, and left the corpse in the house all day. Christie was a necrophile. The conclusion is obvious: there would have been sperm present in the vagina whether Christie killed her or not.

But the pubic hairs could have been altogether more significant. Christie later took 'souvenirs' from his three final victims. If the fourth lot of hair in the tobacco tin was from Beryl Evans, then it would certainly be a strong additional piece of evidence that Christie killed Beryl too. Christie himself claimed that the fourth lot of hair was taken from his wife, but microscopic examination showed this was impossible. So *was* the fourth lot of hair from Beryl Evans? The answer was apparently no. Under the microscope, it was seen to be of the same type as Mrs Evans's hair. But the hair on Beryl Evans's pubis was uncut. If Christie had taken it from her, then it must have been months before her death, to allow it to regrow. Then whose hair was it? The answer may well lie in a comment in Kennedy's book (p. 675): '[Christie] had met Kathleen Maloney before. About three weeks before Christmas he, Maloney and a prostitute called Maureen had all gone to a room off Marylebone Lane where Christie had taken photographs of Maureen in the nude while Maloney looked on.' The fourth lot of hairs could have been taken from some prostitute in circumstances like these, if not on this actual occasion. This would also account for Christie's unwillingness to reveal their source; he always maintained a pose of being a highly moral man, who would never have confessed to taking 'dirty photographs' and persuading the woman to allow him to take snippings from her pubis.

The inquiry into whether Christie had murdered Beryl Evans was placed in the hands of Scott Henderson, QC. He interviewed Christie in prison, and concluded that his confession to the murder of Beryl Evans was false; his report, published on the day of Christie's execution, stated that Evans had undoubtedly murdered both his wife and child.

This was not the end of the matter. Books about Christie continued to insist on Evans's innocence, with the result that, in 1968, the case was reheard at the Royal Courts of Justice before Mr Justice Brabin. The hearing lasted for several months, and the case for Evans's innocence was powerfully presented by the psychiatrist Dr Jack Hobson. The final result was surprising. Brabin concluded that Christie's confession to the murder of Beryl Evans was false, and that it was probable that Beryl was murdered by her husband. But he added the startling rider that Christie probably killed Geraldine.

What evidence led him to this view? We have seen, to begin with, that Christie had good reason to confess to Beryl's murder; his defence was insanity, and 'The more the merrier'. In his book *Forty Years of Murder*, Keith Simpson points out the sheer unlikelihood of Christie's confession. Would Beryl Evans lie down passively and allow Christie to gas her? And if he had done so, there would certainly have been signs of carbon monoxide poisoning when Teare examined the body. Aware of this problem, Christie explained that 'the gas wasn't on very long, not much over a minute I think'. But, as Simpson points out, if it had been on long enough to cause Beryl Evans to lose consciousness, then it would have left the unmistakable pink coloration in the tissues. This pink coloration would certainly have vanished by the time of the second autopsy; four years later, as all the pathologists agreed. In fact, tests showed no carbon monoxide in the tissues. But Camps – who, unlike Simpson, was representing the prosecution – noted that the teeth showed pink coloration, and tested them for carbon monoxide. He found none, but in his book *Medical and Scientific Investigations in the Christie Case* (1953) nevertheless argues that the pink teeth *could* indicate carbon monoxide poisoning. That still fails to explain why a pathologist as experienced as Teare should have failed to notice it at the first autopsy. We may therefore take it as fairly certain that Beryl Evans was not gassed.

In that case, what of Ludovic Kennedy's suggestion that Christie was engaged in a pretended abortion when he became sexually excited and strangled her? It *is* possible – it would account for the black eye and the bruises. But, as Simpson points out, Christie hated violence – partly because he was convinced that he was a sick man. Moreover, if he battered Beryl Evans unconscious, surely she would have screamed and fought? And since there were workmen carrying out repairs in the yard below, she would certainly have been heard. On the other hand, we know that Beryl and Timothy Evans often had violent quarrels. According to Evans's confession, he and Beryl had been quarrelling about debts – particularly about some furniture, on which she had failed to keep up the payments. They had quarrelled several times on the Sunday before her death. The following morning she told him she intended to leave him and go home to her father; but she was still there when he came home from work. They quarrelled yet again. 'I told her that if she didn't pack it up I'd slap her face. With that she picked up a milk bottle to throw at me. I grabbed the bottle out of her hand . . .' The following day they were squabbling again. 'I came home at night about 6.30 p.m., my wife started to argue again, so I hit her across the face with my flat hand. She then hit me back with her hand. In a fit of temper I grabbed a piece of rope from a chair which I had brought home off my van and strangled her with it.' The following day, according to Evans, he fed the baby, left her in the cot, and strangled her when he came home from work that evening. This, as Ludovic Kennedy points out, is impossible. A one-year-old baby cannot be left alone all day without crying, and in a house the size of 10 Rillington Place, the Christies would have heard her. (Ethel Christie, of course, was still alive at this time.)

But at least the account of Beryl's murder has the ring of truth – the dreary squabbling that went on day after day, ending in a quarrel during which he strangled her. After signing this statement, Evans repeated it the following day – not once but twice, to a police inspector and to the prison medical officer. Yet two weeks later, he withdrew it and accused Christie of murdering his wife and child. Why?

The answer is suggested by Rupert Furneaux, in a book called *The Two Stranglers of Rillington Place* (1961). Furneaux reveals that while Evans was in Brixton prison, he met an accused murderer named Donald Hume, who had been charged with the killing of a dealer in stolen cars called Stanley Setty, and scattering parts of his body out of an aeroplane over the Essex marshes. Hume stuck to his story that he was merely an accomplice, and was sentenced to 12 years. In 1958, when Hume came out of prison, he confessed to the murder of Setty, and also admitted to the *Daily Express* that it was he who had caused Evans to change his plea. He had advised him: 'Don't put your head in a noose. Make up a new story and stick to it.' When Evans asked his advice on the 'new story', Hume asked him whether he murdered his wife, and Evans denied it. Hume then went on to make the following strange statement:

> He told me that when he and his wife went to live at Rillington Place, Christie came to an arrangement with his wife and that Christie had murdered her. Then he told me about the child. He said: 'It was because the kid was crying.' I said: 'So you did it?' He said: 'No, but I was there while it was done.' He told me that he and Christie had gone into the bedroom together, that Christie had strangled the kid with a bit of rag while he stood and watched.

Here, at last, we can begin to glimpse a plausible outline of what really happened. There seems to be no reason why Evans should tell

Hume that Christie murdered the baby – with Evans looking on – unless it really happened. Evans, then, was an accomplice in the murder, which would explain the sense of guilt that led him to confess. The confession to the murder of his own child is incomprehensible if Christie had committed the murder alone.

But if Evans stood by and consented to the murder of his own baby, the rest of the story immediately becomes suspect: that Christie killed Beryl, and later told Evans that she had died in the course of an abortion. Even if Christie had assured Evans that they would both go to jail if the truth should become known, this would still not explain why Evans was terrified enough to allow Christie to kill the baby. The very idea is an absurdity.

There is only one other explanation. Evans killed his wife, exactly as he confessed. *That* could be the only possible reason that he would allow Christie to kill the baby. His neck was already at risk because he had killed his wife. With a baby on his hands, he stood no chance of remaining undetected. But if both bodies could be concealed, he might escape. He went off to Merthyr Vale believing that Christie would put both bodies down the drain. In Merthyr, he was overcome by guilt and fear. The more he thought about it, the more obvious it became that the bodies must be found, and that he had admitted his own guilt by fleeing. His only chance lay in going to the police and telling a story in which he was only an accomplice. Such a story would, of course, put the blame squarely on Christie . . . But when he was taken back to London, and charged with the murder of his wife and child, he could no longer maintain the deception; he broke down and confessed. This time he admitted to killing the baby, for what point would there be in accusing Christie if he was already admitting to strangling his wife?

One other odd puzzle remains. What did Hume mean when he stated: '[Evans] told me that when he and his wife went to live at Rillington Place, Christie came to an arrangement with his wife . . .'? He appears to be saying that some kind of intimacy developed between Christie and Beryl Evans. This, admittedly, sounds unlikely. When Timothy and Beryl Evans moved into 10 Rillington Place, during the Easter of 1948, they were still a happily married couple. But they had been forced to move because Beryl was pregnant with Geraldine, and the single room in which they had been living would obviously be inadequate for a family. After the birth of the baby, tensions began to develop, and they often quarrelled. Both Beryl and her husband were immature; Christie became their friend and adviser. His only motive can have been that he was attracted by the 19-year-old Beryl. So it is not entirely inconceivable that some kind of intimacy developed between Christie and Beryl. If Hume was telling the truth, Evans seems to have thought that Christie and his wife became sexually intimate, or at least came close to it. The whole question could be regarded as irrelevant, except for one thing: the pubic hairs in the tin. These hairs bore a close resemblance to Beryl's. But Keith Simpson points out that they could not have been Beryl's, because the autopsy showed that Beryl's pubic hairs were intact; Simpson says that if the hairs in the tin were Beryl's, they must have been taken at least six months before, to allow Beryl's hair to regrow. Understandably, he dismisses this as an absurdity. Yet if there is any basis of truth in Hume's statement, then it becomes possible that the hairs in the tin *did* belong to Beryl, and not to some prostitute, or another unknown murder victim. The oddest thing – if Evans made such a statement – is that he failed to see that it also contradicted his assertion that Christie killed Beryl. Christie was a sex killer; if there was some 'arrangement' between her and Christie, then Christie would have had no reason to kill her.

From this tangled mass of assertion and counter-assertion, one thing seems to emerge clearly: that whoever killed Geraldine, it seems relatively certain that Timothy Evans murdered his wife.

15

To criminologists of the future, the year 1960 may seem a watershed in the history of crime. Until that time, most crime could be conveniently classified in terms of motives, as Locard does in the *Traité de criminalistique*. But in his seventh volume (1940), Locard has a section entitled 'Crime Without Cause'. And although he begins by admitting: 'this title is a decoy' *(leurre),* he nevertheless goes on to raise the problem of apparently motiveless crimes, and cites a curious case of 1886, in which a young chemist's assistant named Pastré-Beaussier poisoned several people without apparent motive. The first victim was his employer, M. Decamp, who kept a pharmacy in Havre. Decamp suspected his assistant of petty theft, and in April 1886, Mme Decamp died after drinking a cup of bouillon prepared by the assistant. The laboratory assistant, a youth named Perotte, was the next to fall ill; but as soon as he began eating his meals at home, the vomiting and nausea ceased. But his successor in the shop became equally ill. So did

M. Decamp's mother, although her symptoms disappeared when she returned home.

M. Decamps was the next to die. His successor, M. Delafontaine, also came to suspect his assistant of stealing; soon afterwards, M. Delafontaine and two his employers became ill with vomiting. One of these, the housekeeper Mme Morisse, died. At this point, M. Delafontaine took an action against his landlord, alleging that the drains were a health hazard. This finally led the town council of Havre to send three experts to investigate. They found nothing wrong with the drains, but a post-mortem on Mme Morisse revealed that she had died of arsenic poisoning. Further inquests revealed that M. Decamps and his wife had also died from arsenic.

The assistant, Pastré-Beaussier, was the only person who could have been responsible for the illnesses – this conclusion was reached by a simple process of elimination. Placed under arrest, he protested that he had no reason to poison anyone, and that the suspicion of petty theft was too trivial to be regarded as a motive. The jury believed him, and in spite of all the evidence of the experts, acquitted him.

Locard had no doubt whatsoever of his guilt; 13 poisonings could not be coincidence. But he adds: 'Pastré killed for pleasure, and perhaps, after his first murders, from habit.'

When Locard was writing in 1939, such cases were a rarity. (The only other one cited by Locard is that of the poisoner Jeanne Weber, which we shall consider in the next chapter.) By the late 1950s, their number was increasing. In 1958, a man named Norman Foose stopped his Land Rover in the town of Cuba, New Mexico, raised his rifle, and shot dead two children who were playing. He explained after his arrest that he was trying to do something about the population explosion. In 1959, a pretty blonde named Penny Bjorkland accepted a lift from a married man and shot him dead with a dozen shots; she explained that she wanted to see if she could kill someone 'and not worry about it afterwards'. In the same year, a man named Norman Smith left his caravan in Sarasota County, Florida, and went and shot dead a woman (who was watching television) through an open window. He had been watching a television progamme called 'The Sniper'.

By the mid-1960s, 'motiveless murder' had become commonplace. In November 1966, an 18-year-old student named Robert Smith walked into a beauty parlour in Mesa, Arizona, made five women and two children lie on the floor, and shot them all in the back of the head. He explained: 'I wanted to get known, to get myself a name.'

In England, the 'Moors murder case' of the mid-1960s, had this same strangely motiveless quality. Ian Brady and his mistress Myra Hindley – whose crimes will be considered more fully in the final chapter – abducted children in the Manchester area, killed them after sexual assault, and buried their bodies on the moors. They made a habit of going back to the moors to eat picnics on the graves of their victims, a kind of 'gloating response' often associated with sex murder. They were caught after they tried to involve Myra Hindley's brother-in-law in the murder of a youth named Edward Evans; the brother-in-law went straight to the police. But at the subsequent trial (1966), it became clear that these could not be classified simply as sex crimes. Brady wanted to be a master criminal, a kind of Public Enemy Number One, and the crimes were partly a defiance of society; in this sense they had something in common with the Leopold and Loeb murder. Brady and Hindley were sentenced to life imprisonment, still refusing to admit their guilt.

In the early 1970s, the trial of the Charles Manson 'family' caused much the same kind of sensation in America that the Moors trial had caused in Great Britain. The murder of film star Sharon Tate and three of her friends in a house in Hollywood had produced shock headlines all over the world. The murders of a supermarket owner and his wife the following night increased the sensation and led to panic over the whole Los Angeles area. In prison on another charge a few months later, one of the killers, Susan Aitkens, told a cell-mate about her part in the murders; the cell-mate passed it on to another prisoner, who talked to the police. The result was one of the most widely publicized – and most expensive – trials in American history. Yet, as with the Moors trial in England, there was something oddly frustrating about it for those who hoped to understand exactly what motives could lead to such crimes. The Manson family seemed to have no motive, except a vague resentment of 'society'. Killing had become a casual habit, rather like lighting a cigarette.

Locard had commented about 'motiveless murders':

Crime is a physical phenomenon conditioned by psychological fact. Neither in physics nor in psychology is there an effect without a cause. In vain do modern novelists do their utmost to depict such acts which, in the minds of their authors, are purely

gratuitous manifestations of 'play', expressions of a consciousness which wants to be free of the Kantian axiom, and moreover,
of all law. All punishable acts – in fact, all acts – have their cause.

There is obviously some truth in this; but Locard was leaving out of
account the acts committed by people who live in a vacuum, who feel
a sense of moral weightlessness, analogous to an astronaut floating in
space. Such acts may not be 'motiveless', but they are committed with
a degree of casualness that comes very close to it. The English
equivalent of the Pastré-Beaussier case occurred in 1971, at a photographic firm called John Hadlands, in Bovingdon, Hertfordshire. Two
storemen died after severe stomach pains, and two more employees
began to lose their hair and suffer pins and needles. A team of experts
sent to investigate the 'Bovingdon bug' became suspicious when a
recent employee named Graham Young asked whether the symptoms
were not consistent with thallium poisoning. They asked Scotland Yard
whether Young had a record, and were electrified to learn that Young
had spent some time in Broadmoor, the prison for the criminally
insane, for administering doses of poison to his family and killing his
mother – he had been 14 at the time. A fellow prisoner had died of
poison while Young was in Broadmoor. Young was arrested and found
to be in possession of thallium, and his diary contained his notes on the
progress of his poisonings. Young apparently felt superior to his
working-class family, and hated his boring environment. His habit of
referring to himself as 'your friendly neighbourhood Frankenstein'
makes it clear that murders were a kind of attempt at self-dramatization. Like Robert Smith, he wanted to 'make a name for himself'. His
sister also spoke of his 'craving for publicity and notice'. But this could
hardly be regarded as adequate motivation for murder. For his second
series of poisonings, Graham Young was sentenced to life imprisonment.

It is precisely this 'motiveless' element in sex crimes that makes
them such a baffling challenge to detectives and criminalists.

16

The increasing use of computers is in itself one of the most important
responses to this challenge, as well as being perhaps the greatest
advance in crime detection since the invention of fingerprinting. In one

of the most widely publicized cases of the 1970s, the use of a computer would undoubtedly have led to the arrest of the killer at a far earlier stage of the investigation.

On an evening in late August 1969, a prostitute walking down St Paul's Road, in the red-light area of Bradford, Yorkshire, was struck violently on the head by a brick in a sock. She followed her assailant, and noted the number of the van in which he drove away. The police soon traced the owner of the van, who told them that he had been in the red-light area with a friend, who had vanished down St Paul's Road late at night. The police went to see the friend, whose name was Peter Sutcliffe. He was a shy, rather inarticulate young man, who insisted that he had only struck the woman with the flat of his hand. Since he had no criminal record, he was let off with a caution. The attack was the first crime of the man who would become known as the Yorkshire Ripper.

This attack was not quite 'motiveless'. Two months earlier, Sutcliffe had become intensely jealous of his girlfriend, Sonia, who was seeing another man and – he believed – being unfaithful to him. To 'get even', he picked up a prostitute – the first time he had ever done such a thing – but the encounter was not a success. The woman took his £10, then got her pimp to chase him away. Three weeks later, he saw the woman in a pub, and demanded his money back; instead, she jeered at him and made him a laughing-stock. Sutcliffe was a shy, sensitive man, and the experience filled him with rage and embarrassment. It festered until he became a sadistic killer of women – innocent housewives and school-girls as well as prostitutes.

Five years later, on 4 July 1975, Sutcliffe walked up behind a pretty divorcee named Anna Rogulskyj, and struck her three times on the head with the ball end of a ball-pein hammer. Then, as she collapsed, he raised her blouse and made several slashes with a knife. He was about to plunge it into her stomach when a man's voice called out to ask what was happening. Sutcliffe fled. Anna Rogulskyj recovered after a brain operation. Six weeks later, on 15 August 1975, he crept behind a 46-year-old office cleaner named Olive Smelt, and struck her to the ground with the hammer. Then he raised her clothes and made some slashes on her buttocks with a hacksaw blade before going to rejoin a friend who was waiting for him in a car. When the friend asked him what he had been doing, he explained in a mumble that he had been 'talking to that woman'. Olive Smelt also recovered after an operation to remove bone splinters from her brain.

On 29 October 1975, Sutcliffe picked up a 28-year-old prostitute named Wilma McCann, and went with her to a playing field near her home. But he found it impossible to achieve an erection at short notice. When the woman told him he was 'fuckin' useless', he asked her to wait a moment, got the hammer from the toolbox of his car, and struck her on the head. Then he tugged down her white slacks and stabbed her nine times in the abdomen and five in the chest.

Wilma McCann was the first of 13 murder victims over the course of five years. Some of the victims were 'amateur prostitutes', mothers of single-parent families trying to earn money. Some, like 16-year-old Jayne MacDonald, were schoolgirls who happened to be returning home late at night. Some were working women, like 47-year-old Marguerite Walls, a Department of Health official who had been working overtime. Although Sutcliffe was later to insist that he was interested only in killing prostitutes, his craving to kill and mutilate extended to all women.

By the late 1970s, the murder hunt for the Yorkshire Ripper (as the Press christened him) was the biggest in British criminal history. Thousands of people were interviewed – including Peter Sutcliffe – but all this information was not computerized, and so overwhelmed the investigators. Sutcliffe was interviewed in connection with the murder of a prostitute named Jean Jordan, a 20-year-old Scot, whom he had killed in the Southern Cemetery in Manchester, stripping her naked and stabbing her in a frenzy. After the murder, Sutcliffe looked for her handbag, which contained the £5 note he had given her – a new one he had been paid in his wage packet. In due course, this was found by the police, and all the employees of 23 firms in Bradford were interviewed, including Sutcliffe. His wife confirmed his alibi, and the police filed a report saying they had found nothing to arouse their suspicions.

In 1978 and 1979 the police had received three letters signed 'Jack the Ripper', which had led them to mount an extensive investigation in the Wearside area, 100 miles to the north of Bradford. And on 26 June 1979, the police received a recorded tape beginning with the works 'I'm Jack', and taunting them for failing to catch him; the accent was 'Geordie' – again, from the Wearside area. After Sutcliffe's arrest, the letters and the tape were recognized as hoaxes, but at the time, most police officers on the case assumed that the Ripper was from somewhere around Durham.

In December 1980, after the thirteenth murder, the police decided to set up an advisory team consisting of four police officers and a forensic expert, Stuart Kind. There had been 17 attacks in all – including the ones of Anna Rogulskyj and Olive Smelt, and two more in the autumn of 1979 when the victims survived. The main clues were three sets of tyre tracks at three scenes of crime, three sets of footprints also found near three of the victims, and finally the new £5 note found in Jean Jordan's handbag. It will be recalled that this had been found far from the sites of the earlier Ripper murders, across the Pennines in Manchester, so it seemed highly likely that the 'Ripper' had taken it with him from Bradford – Sutcliffe had received it in his pay packet two days before the murder. But if the Ripper lived in the Bradford area, then the search of Wearside was a waste of time. In that case, the tape was probably also a hoax, for although the 'Geordie' Ripper might live in Bradford, the extensive police investigations had failed to pinpoint such a suspect. This is why, at the beginning of the investigation, the five-man team decided that the tape and letters should be dismissed as irrelevancies.

There was another reason. The team had gone to examine all the murder sites, including that of a Bradford University student, Barbara Leach, who was killed returning to her flat in the early hours of the morning. As they were looking at the site, one of the police officers, Commander Ronald Harvey, had one of these sudden hunches that come from years of experience, and he remarked: 'Chummy lives in Bradford and he did it going home.' What he was suggesting was that the Ripper lived in this area, and that he killed Barbara Leach on his way home, perhaps after an unsuccessful search for a victim.

The comment impressed Stuart Kind, for surely here was an important point: that a murder committed in the early hours of the morning indicated that the killer was not far from home, whereas a murder committed earlier in the evening suggested that he had driven far from home in search of a victim and had to get back. Anna Rogulskyj had been attacked in Keighley, close to Bradford, at 1.10 in the morning. But Olive Smelt, attacked at 11 p.m., had been in Halifax. Josephine Walker had been murdered in Halifax at 11.30 p.m. Helen Rytka had been attacked in Huddersfield – even further from Bradford – at nine in the evening. Vera Millward had been murdered in Manchester at nine in the evening. Admittedly, this pattern did not hold for all the 17 attacks – Emily Jackson had been murdered in nearby Leeds at seven in the evening – but it held for most of them.

So it looked as if the Ripper was probably a local man living in Bradford or Leeds, where 10 out of 17 attacks took place. Next, the team took a map of the area, and computed the 'centre of gravity' of the attacks. The basic principle was to stick a pin in the 17 sites, then to take an eighteenth pin, and join it to the other 17 by lengths of thread, minimizing the amount of thread required. The eighteenth pin proved to be squarely in Bradford. (In fact, the 'pin test' was carried out on the forensic laboratory computer.)

The team suggested that a special squad of detectives should concentrate their energies on Bradford. That would involve re-checking all the men in Bradford who had been interviewed. And since the £5 note was the most vital clue so far, the men who had been interviewed in this connection would have been top of the list. Since the police possessed samples of the tyre tracks of the Ripper's car, it would have been a simple matter to check the tyre tracks of each of these men.

It can be seen that this method should have led infallibly to Peter Sutcliffe, who was by then living with his wife Sonia at 6 Garden Lane, in the Heaton district of Bradford. That it did not do so was due to the simple circumstance that the Yorkshire Ripper was finally arrested within two weeks of the interim report being completed. On 2 January 1981, in the early evening, Peter Sutcliffe drove the 30 or 50 miles from Bradford to Sheffield, and in the red-light district there, picked up a black prostitute named Olive Reivers, and backed into a drive. She removed her knickers and handed him a condom; he unbuttoned his trousers and struggled uncomfortably across her in the passenger seat. But he was unable to obtain an erection. As he sat beside her again, telling her about his wife's frigidity, they were dazzled by the lights of a police car which pulled up with its nose to the bonnet of Sutcliffe's old Rover. Sutcliffe told Olive Reivers to back up his story that she was his girlfriend, and gave his name as Peter Williams. One of the policemen went to the nearest telephone and checked the car's number plates with the national police computer at Hendon; within two minutes, he had learned that the plates on the Rover actually belonged to a Skoda. Sutcliffe had stolen them from a car scrap-yard and fixed them on with Sellotape, because he knew the police were noting the number plates of cars in red-light areas.

As both policemen escorted Olive Reivers to the police car, Sutcliffe hurried behind a nearby oil storage tank, explaining that he was 'busting for a pee', and there managed to dispose of the ball-pein hammer and knife that had been concealed under his seat. The police then took him to Hammerton Road police station. There he revealed that his name was Sutcliffe, and explained that he was using false number plates because his insurance had lapsed and he was due to appear on a drunken driving charge. He was placed in a cell for the night. And at eight o'clock the next morning – Saturday – he was taken to the Ripper Incident Room at Leeds. Here it was immediately noted that the size of his shoe was the same as that of the footprint found at three of the murder sites. When he volunteered the information that he had been among those questioned about the new £5 note, and had also been questioned routinely as a regular visitor to red-light areas, the investigators suddenly became aware that this man could well be the Ripper. When they learned that his car had also been logged in Manchester, it began to look even more likely. Yet there was still no real evidence against Sutcliffe, and after a long day of questioning, during which he had been pleasantly co-operative, the police recognized this lack of evidence. But five and a half years of fruitless search for the Ripper had made them persistent; they decided to hold him for another night. And, back in Sheffield, the policeman who had arrested him heard that he was still being questioned by the Ripper squad. On an impulse, he went back to the oil storage tank where Sutcliffe had urinated. There he found the hammer and knife on a pile of leaves.

When Sutcliffe was told about the find, he admitted that he was the Yorkshire Ripper, then went on to dictate a statement describing his murders in detail.

Stuart Kind is inclined to take the view that the findings of the five-man team would inevitably have led to the arrest of the Yorkshire Ripper in the early part of 1981, and in the light of the team's deductions, it is hard to disagree with him. It should also be clear that the Ripper was caught by police work as much as by chance. He was one of hundreds of suspects who had been interviewed, and when he was taken into the Incident Room, the chance of his being the Ripper were hundreds to one. The size of his shoe shortened the odds; so did the fact that he had been involved in the £5 note inquiry, and that his name was on the computer as a 'punter' seen in red-light areas. The finding of the hammer and knife clinched the matter; but even if they had not been found, the Rover's tyre tracks would have narrowed the odds to a virtual certainty. So although, in terms of the history of crime detection, the Ripper inquiry must be labelled a police failure, closer analysis reveals that it deserves to be classified as a real – if belated – success.

17

Most crime writers who have discussed the Whitechapel murders of 1888 have posed the same question: would Jack the Ripper have been trapped by modern police methods? The answer has usually been a depressing negative. But the Yorkshire Ripper case demonstrates that the British police *were* finally mastering the art of trapping a serial sex killer through modern technology. Their chief problem was the sheer quantity of information accumulated over a five-year inquiry. If this had all been computerized, there can be no possible doubt that Sutcliffe would have emerged as the chief suspect at a far earlier stage. As far as the British police were concerned, this was the main lesson of the case. They lost no time in rectifying the omission, and the result was that the computer played a major role in the solution of Britain's next major case involving a serial sex killer.

In 1982, five women were raped by two men wearing balaclavas, one tall, one short. In the second half of 1984, the short rapist began to operate alone. In the following year, Detective Superintendent Ken Worker was placed in charge of an inquiry code-named Operation Hart to try to trap the rapist. Twenty-seven attacks had taken place in the London area, the majority around Camden Town and further north. It was observed that many of the attacks took place near railway lines, which led the team to formulate the theory that the rapist was a railway worker. He usually engaged the victims in conversation, then threatened them with a knife, tied their hands and raped them. He seemed to enjoy frightening them and committing the rapes with a great deal of violence.

On 29 December 1985, 19-year-old Alison Day set out to meet her boyfriend from his place of work in Hackney, east London. She never arrived. Seventeen days later, her body was found in the River Lea, which ran close to the printing factory where her boyfriend worked. She had been tied up, strangled and probably raped – the period in the river destroyed most forensic evidence. But her sheepskin coat was also found in the river, and when it was dried, revealed a number of fibres that might have come from her killer. The pathologist observed that she had been strangled with a tourniquet – a scarf knotted around her throat, then tightened with a stick. An additional knot in the scarf had obviously been tied to press on the victim's windpipe and cause unconsciousness.

Four months later, on 17 April 1986, 15-year-old Maartje

Tamboezer, whose father – an oil executive – had only recently moved to Britain, set out on her bicycle to buy sweets in nearby Horsley. Cycling along a short cut near the railway line, she was forced to dismount by a fishing line stretched across the path. A man dragged her into the woods, battered her unconscious with blows to the head, and raped her. He then strangled her, and made an attempt to burn the body. Particularly strange was the fact that he rammed burning handkerchief tissues into the genitals – obviously an attempt to eliminate his sperm traces. For the Surrey police, whose team was led by Detective Superintendent John Hurst, this suggested that he had some previous experience with blood group identification, and might have a previous record as a sex offender. As Surrey's largest ever manhunt developed, hundreds of possible witnesses were interviewed. The picture of the rapist that began to emerge was of a smallish man wearing a blue parka. He had been seen running frantically to catch the 6.07 train from East Horsley to London. Two million train tickets were examined, in the hope that the rapist had left his fingerprints behind; but although a number of possible tickets were located, none had fingerprints.

At least the police were able to determine the murderer's blood group from traces of sperm left on the dead girl's clothing. It was group A, and since the scientists had determined it from his sperm, he was a 'secretor' – one of those whose blood group can be determined from bodily fluids. One in three people are group A, so this was hardly a breakthrough. But an enzyme called PGM (phosphoglucomutase) enabled forensic scientists to make a closer determination that would eliminate four out of five suspects.

There was another important clue: Maartje Tamboezer's hands had been tied with a peculiar kind of brown string, which proved to be made of paper; it was called Somyarn, and the manager of the Preston factory which made it was able to say that the sample dated back to at least 1982, and that it had been made from an unusually wide 'edge' strip of the paper. If they could locate the rest of that ball of string, there would be a strong possibility that its owner would be the killer.

A month later, on Sunday 18 May 1986, a 29-year-old secretary named Ann Lock worked late at London Weekend Television, and set out for her home in Brookmans Park, in Hertfordshire; she had been married only four weeks, and had just returned from her honeymoon in the Seychelles. She never arrived home, and an extensive police search failed to find the body. In fact, it was discovered in some undergrowth near the Brookmans Park station some ten weeks later. She had been raped and allowed to suffocate, and there had again been an attempt to burn the body, apparently to eliminate traces of sperm. The blood group and the PGM reading pointed again to the 'railway rapist'.

By now it had struck Detective Chief Superintendent Vincent McFadden, who was in charge of the case, that the man he was looking for might also be the north London rapist, as well as the killer of Alison Day and Maartje Tamboezer. The various forces involved decided to link their computers to share information. Operation Hart – the team looking for the rapist – had started with a list of 4,900 sex offenders, which they had whittled down to 1,999. On this list, at number 1,594, was a man called John Duffy, an ex-British Rail carpenter, who was in trouble with the law for raping his ex-wife. This had happened in August 1985, two months after Margaret Duffy had left her husband because of his increasingly violent behaviour, and gone to live with Hungarian-born Imre Lovas. Duffy had attacked them with a knife and raped his wife. The following day he appeared before West Hendon magistrates on a charge of causing grievous bodily harm. He was remanded in custody until 19 September, when a judge granted him bail.

On 17 May, the day before Ann Lock vanished, Duffy had been arrested on suspicion for loitering near a railway station, and had been found to be in possession of a sharp knife. He explained that he was a student of Zen Budo, a form of Japanese martial arts which combines ju-jitsu and weapons training. He needed the knife, he said, for his classes in Kilburn, where he lived. This explanation was accepted, but the computer recorded the arrest.

With the sex charge and his arrest on suspicion, Duffy now figured on the suspect list for the railway rapist. The police were working their way slowly through the remaining 1,999, taking blood samples, and in due course, called in Duffy for questioning. This was on 17 July 1986. Duffy arrived with a solicitor, and declined to give a blood sample. The interviewers instantly realized that this ginger-haired, pockmarked little man – about five feet three inches tall – corresponded to the description of the railway rapist (although earlier descriptions had given him fair hair). They disliked his manner, which was glib and a little *too* helpful. The following day, the detectives reported to Ken Worker, the head of Operation Hart, that they thought Duffy was a likely suspect. But when they tried to follow up the interview, they discovered that Duffy was now in the Friern Barnet Hospital, apparently suffering from amnesia. A few hours after being interviewed, he had gone to the Hampstead police station, looking bruised and battered, and explained that he had been mugged and lost his memory. When the Operation Hart team tried to interview him at Friern Barnet, doctors declined to allow it. This should have placed Duffy at the head of the list of suspects. But they still had more than 1,000 to interview, and for the moment, Duffy was allowed to remain in the security of the hospital.

The police were also mounting a massive surveillance operation on British Rail stations that were unmanned at weekends, hoping to catch the railway rapist; but a Sunday newspaper revealed the secret, and it had to be dropped – an example of the Press actively hindering the search for a killer.

Meanwhile, Duffy – who was now a part-time patient at the Friern Barnet Hospital – raped another schoolgirl. She described the rapist as a short pockmarked man, with a dog named Bruce. For a while, police even suspected that the man might be a jockey, and sent detectives to every racing stable. All these enquiries led nowhere.

But the police were now willing to try another interesting experiment. Possibly inspired by stories of the new technique of 'psychological profiling' used in America (of which we shall speak in the last chapter), they asked a professor of psychology from the University of Surrey, Dr David Canter, to set up a team to review all the information, and see if he could reach any general conclusions about the rapist. Canter studied the reports of the rapist, and reached some interesting conclusions. The 'centre of gravity' method, used by the team in the Yorkshire Ripper case, enabled him to conclude that the killer lived in the north London area, within three miles of Finchley Road. He also concluded that he was, or had been, a semi-skilled worker, that his relationship with his wife had probably been a turbulent one, and that he had two very close male friends. Seventeen points were listed. And when Canter's analysis was matched against the 1,999 suspects, the computer instantly threw up the name of John Duffy . . .

Duffy, who lived in Barlow Road, Kilburn, was placed under close surveillance; detectives reported on his activities from the moment he left his home to the moment he returned. But at some point, Duffy realized he was being watched, and the detectives realized that he was enjoying trying to give them the slip – for example, jumping on a train just a moment before the doors closed. And when Duffy shaved off his moustache one day, Chief Superintendent John Hurst decided that he could no longer take the risk of a killer rapist committing a murder while under police surveillance; he ordered Duffy's arrest.

The 30-year-old Irish-born suspect proved a difficult man to question. He would neither admit nor deny that he was the railway rapist; his attitude was that if the police thought so, it was up to them to prove it. He had a disconcerting way of staring with wide open eyes at the questioner, his face blank, trying to force him to drop his eyes. The rapist's victims had described the same cold, dominant gaze. Hurst's position was a difficult one. Now he had arrested Duffy, he had 36 hours to find evidence sufficient to convince a magistrate that he ought to be held in custody. Duffy's home was searched, and many knives found. Duffy's ex-wife was interviewed, and was able to tell them that her husband had once told her that he had raped a girl and that it was her fault because she was frigid. Margaret Duffy also told the police that her husband liked to tie her hands and rape her; the more she struggled, the more he enjoyed it. On the other hand, if she submitted passively, he lost interest . . .

In the home of Duffy's parents, police found a vital piece of evidence – ball of brown string; it proved to be the unique Somyarn they were looking for. Yet even faced with this evidence, Duffy gazed back blankly, refusing to comment.

The clinching piece of evidence came from one of Duffy's closest friends, Ross Mockeridge, a fellow martial arts enthusiast. He went to the Romford Incident Room, and described how Duffy had persuaded him to punch him in the face and slash his chest with a razor – Duffy had explained that the police were trying to 'frame' him for rape. Mockeridge finally obliged. And Duffy hurried off to the Hampstead police station to report that he had just been mugged and lost his memory.

When five of Duffy's rape victims unhesitatingly picked him out in an identity parade, he must have realized that there was now enough evidence to ensure a guilty verdict. Yet he continued to fix his questioners with what one of them described as his 'laser beam stare' and to remain silent.

Detectives were confident that the string of evidence would link Duffy to the death of Maartje Tamboezer. But the Ann Lock case and the Alison Day case were more doubtful. Apart from similarity of method, there was nothing to link Duffy with either. Then, at the last minute, the forensic laboratory again came up with a vital piece of evidence. Seventy items of Duffy's clothing had been seized, and of these, 30 selected as the kind that might shed fibres when in contact with a rape victim. Under the microscope, 13 fibres taken from Alison Day's sheepskin coat – hurled into the river by her killer, with stones in the pockets – were matched with fibres from Duffy's garments, with such precision that one expert described the result as a 'fingerprint'.

Now, at last, the full story of the railway rapist had begun to emerge, largely with the help of his wife. The problem of the duo-rapes of 1982–1984 was not cleared up, although police were believed to know the identity of Duffy's fellow rapist. In 1983, Duffy and his wife were trying hard to have a child, but his sperm count proved to be too low; no rapes took place during that year. Duffy had lost his job as a British Rail carpenter, at Euston, in 1982, but had continued to use his free rail pass. His first attack as a solo rapist took place in November 1984, when a girl was raped at knifepoint at Barnes Common, in south-west London. By this time, Duffy and his wife were quarrelling all the time, and she left him in June 1985. Two months later he attacked her and raped her, also wounding her boyfriend. On 2 December 1985, Duffy appeared in Hendon magistrates court on the assault charge, and a member of the Operation Hart team took one of the rape victims to court to see if she recognized him. She did not; but Duffy undoubtedly recognized her, and realized suddenly the danger of leaving his victims alive. Three weeks later, he murdered Alison Day and carefully disposed of her body in the river, determined to leave no clues. Maartje Tamboezer and Ann Lock were murdered with the same ruthless efficiency. But after the death of Ann Lock, Duffy seems to have lost the stomach for murder – or perhaps decided that, after all, it was unnecessary.

In court, four rape victims gave evidence, all describing how Duffy had tied their hands behind them in a 'prayer' position – just as the hands of the murder victims had been tied. The last victim, a 14-year-old schoolgirl, described how Duffy had tied her with her own tights before raping her against a tree; she burst into tears as she gave her evidence. A 16-year-old rape victim was in court when the jury found Duffy guilty of four rapes and two murders – those of Alison Day and Maartje Tamboezer. (As the police had expected, Duffy was found not guilty of the murder of Ann Lock for lack of evidence.) Duffy stared impassively in front of him as the judge sentenced him to a minimum of 30 years in prison. He was the first sex killer in England to be caught by computer.

In January 2001 Duffy gave evidence against his former school friend, David Mulcahy, alleging that he had been his partner in many of the rapes and murders. Duffy's detailed evidence, together with conclusive DNA fingerprint evidence, convinced the jury and Mulcahy was found guilty of ten counts of rape and three of murder. The judge sentenced the 41-year-old father of four to life imprisonment.

Cynics who suggested at the time that Duffy was giving evidence against Mulcahy in order to improve his own chances of early parole got a surprise two months later. Duffy voluntarily admitted to a further seventeen rapes and was sentenced to a further twelve years in prison. Duffy himself admits he is unsure how many women he raped, on his own and with Mulcahy, and the police investigation into the Railway Rapists remains open-ended.

But it is also interesting to reflect that, by the time of his trial, the police had a choice: they *could* have proved his guilt by DNA fingerprinting, using the sperm from his rape victims. And this in itself was a watershed in the history of forensic science. Since the days of Jack the Ripper, the random sex killer had posed an apparently insoluble problem for scientific crime detection. With the introduction of the computer and genetic fingerprinting, those days were finally over.

9

The Craft of the Manhunter

1

The American equivalent of the great Vidocq was a Scottish-born detective named Allan Pinkerton. Like Vidocq, Pinkerton retired from the official police force to become a private detective, one of the first 'private eyes' in the business. (In fact, the term private eye is probably derived from the Pinkerton symbol – an open eye bearing the legend 'We never sleep'.) But in the second half of the nineteenth century, the Pinkerton detective agency developed an efficiency that surpassed that of Scotland Yard or the Sûreté.

Allan Pinkerton was a radical, who fled from Scotland at the age of 23 – in 1842 – to avoid arrest. Working as a cooper in Dundee, Kane County, Illinois, he became an ardent advocate of the abolition of slavery, and helped to smuggle runaway slaves over the border into Canada. And in 1846, chance introduced him to his true vocation: detection. Walking in the woods on an island, he found the remains of a camp fire and trails in the long grass. Many men would have minded their own business; but Pinkerton had a social conscience. The local sheriff accompanied him back to the island, and decided that the camp belonged to a gang of counterfeiters. With Pinkerton's enthusiastic help, he uncovered a cache of fake money and arrested the gang. Only one of them escaped, and Pinkerton, flushed with triumph, offered to help run him down. He tracked the man, pretended to be a fellow crook, and succeeded in getting him arrested. The result was an overnight reputation as a detective.

On Lake Michigan, not far from Dundee, there was a new city called Chicago – athough this little collection of wooden cottages and rooming-houses, with a population of 4,000, was hardly more than a town. Soon after his triumph with the counterfeiters, Pinkerton was asked to become a deputy in Kane County and Cook County, which included Chicago. Like Vidocq, he proved to be a born detective, with a phenomenal memory for faces and a sure instinct for the ways of criminals. But the Chicago police were poorly paid, and when the Post Office engaged Pinkerton as a special agent, he saw that there was more money in private work. This is why, in 1850, he founded the Pinkerton detective agency.

This new, fast-expanding America needed efficient detectives. A fastgrowing economy needs to transfer large amounts of money and valuables, and in the wide empty spaces, coaches and railway trains were a great temptation to bandits. The railway came to Chicago in 1852, and the new crime of rail theft was soon costing the express companies and their customers enormous sums of money. In this vast country, Pinkerton often had to behave more like an Indian tracker than a policeman. In 1858, he was summoned to New Haven, where robbers had forced open the Adams Express car and prised open the safes with crow-bars, taking $70,000 in cash and jewellery. Near Stamford, Connecticut, Pinkerton found a bag containing $5,000, and knew he was on the right track. At Norwalk he heard of three men who had tried to hire a buggy, and tracked them down to a house where they had stayed overnight. When he learned that their host had been seen the next day on a train, carrying a heavy package that evidently made him nervous, he guessed that it contained the rest of the loot. He tracked the man to New York, but found that he had already left for Canada – but without the package. And under his questioning, the man's niece led him to the money and jewellery, hidden in the cellar. The gang was arrested, and Pinkerton completed the job by arresting the leader in Canada.

One early case from the Pinkerton archives is so incredible that it sounds like fiction. In 1855, a young bank teller named George Gordon was murdered late at night when working in his office; he was the nephew of the bank president. The bank vault was open, and $130,000 was missing. Gordon had been killed by a hammer blow dealt from the left. In the fireplace there were remains of burnt papers and clothing-the murderer had stayed on to burn his bloodstained coat. The only clues were two pieces of paper – a bloodstained page containing some pencilled figures – found under the body – and a partly burnt fragment of paper that had been twisted into a 'spill' to light the fire. When Pinkerton unfolded this, he found that it was a note for $927.78, and that it was signed Alexander P. Drysdale, the county clerk, a man of unimpeachable reputation. The bloodstained page contained a subtraction sum – $1,252 minus $324.22 – the result being $927.78.

Pinkerton asked to see the bank balances of a number of prominent local businessmen whom Gordon might have admitted to the bank after hours. Drysdale's account showed a figure of $324.22. Now Pinkerton was able to reconstruct the crime. Drysdale had come to the bank in the evening to request a loan of $1,252. Gordon had agreed – but had subtracted from this sum the amount already in Drysdale's account. Then he had opened the vault. Overcome by sudden temptation, Drysdale had seized a hammer someone had left in the office and killed his friend.

Pinkerton was certain that Drysdale was the killer, but how to prove it? He began by finding an excuse to get Drysdale to write something, and noted that he was left-handed, like the killer. Next, he sent for three of his operatives from Chicago – an older man, a woman, and a young man called Green. They posed as visitors to the town, and began secretly investigating Drysdale's affairs. Green, a good carpenter, found himself a job in the local carpenter's shop, where all the old men gathered in the evening to gossip. The older detective, who was calling himself Andrews, learned by chance one day that young Green bore a close resemblance to the dead George Gordon. And when Pinkerton learned of this, he formulated an incredible plan. Not far from Drysdale's home was a spot known as Rocky Creek, reputed to be haunted. 'Andrews', pretending to be interested in a local plot of land, got Drysdale to take him through Rocky Creek at dusk, and as they rode among the trees, a ghostly figure walked across the path, its hair matted with blood. Drysdale shrieked; Andrews looked astonished and insisted that he could see nothing.

The woman operative had succeeded in getting herself invited into Drysdale's home as a guest of Mrs Drysdale, and she observed that her host was beginning to suffer nightmares and was prone to sleep-walking. Green, dressed as the ghost, kept up the pressure by occasionally flitting about outside the house when Drysdale was wandering around restlessly. Finally, Pinkerton appeared and arrested Drysdale, who protested his innocence. They took him to the bank, and when the 'ghost' appeared from behind the teller's counter, Drysdale fainted. When he recovered, he still continued to protest his innocence, and it began to look as if Pinkerton's bold strategy had failed. But when Drysdale was shown the two scraps of paper proving his involvement, he broke down and confessed. The stolen money was found hidden in a creek near his home.

But most of Pinkerton's early cases demanded persistence and courage rather than this kind of ingenuity. His most remarkable feat of the 1860s was undoubtedly his break-up of the Reno gang, America's first gang of organized outlaws. The five brothers – Frank, John, Simeon, Clinton and William – were the sons of an Indiana farmer who lived at Seymour, Indiana. John left home at 16 – in 1855 – and spent some time wandering around Mississippi, working on steamboats and learning to make a living by his wits. Back home, he propounded a scheme of amazing simplicity. The nearby small town of Rockford was prosperous and virtually unprotected. A series of arson attacks so terrified the inhabitants that they began moving elsewhere. Then the Renos bought most of Rockford at bargain prices.

During the Civil War, the Reno brothers served in the army; but most of them soon deserted. During the war, the bloodthirsty southerner William Clarke Quantrill led a band of guerrillas who were little more than robbers and murderers – it included Jesse James, 'Bloody Bill' Anderson, and Cole Younger – and although most of the gang was wiped out in 1865, James and Cole Younger went on to become wandering outlaws. Meanwhile, back in Seymour, the Reno brothers formed their own outlaw gang, specializing in robbing county treasury offices. And in 1866, they invented a new crime – holding up trains. They boarded the wood-burning Ohio and Mississippi railroad coach as ordinary passengers at Seymour, then strolled down to the Adams Express car, forced the door, and held up the messenger at gunpoint. They pulled the communication cord, stopping the train, and rolled the safe off it. But they were still trying to burst it open in the woods when a posse drove them to abandon it. Nevertheless, John Reno had succeeded in seizing $10,000 in notes.

Pinkerton was asked to take on the case. The bandits had worn masks, but he had no doubt they were the Renos. A few weeks later, a new saloon was opened in Seymour – the amiable, round-faced man who ran it was really a Pinkerton operative called Dick Winscott – and the Renos soon became customers. Winscott even succeeded in persuading the brothers to allow him to take a group photograph – possibly the first time photography was used in crime detection. (Pinkerton had copies made and circulated.)

Seymour was an armed camp run by outlaws, and there was no chance of arresting the Renos on the spot. Allan Pinkerton enlisted the aid of Dick Winscott. The Renos were being sought for a bank robbery in Gallatin, Missouri, and had been identified by witnesses through their photographs. One afternoon soon after, the train stopped in Seymour, and Allan Pinkerton looked cautiously out of the window. On the platform he recognized the jovial figure of Dick Winscott, talking to John Reno. Six muscular men, accompanied by a sheriff from Cincinnati – another city that held warrants for the Renos – strolled casually off the train, surrounded John Reno, and hustled him aboard. Reno bellowed for help, but although the other Reno brothers commandeered another train and pursued the kidnappers, John Reno was handed over to the Gallatin authorities and sentenced to 25 years in jail.

In February 1868, Frank Reno – now the gang leader – led a raid on the Harrison County treasury at Magnolia, Iowa, which netted $14,000. Using his skills as a tracker, Pinkerton found them hiding in the home of a pillar of the Methodist church in Council Bluffs, and arrested them in a sudden raid. But the jail in Council Bluffs was not strong enough to hold them, and when the sheriff arrived the next morning he found the cells empty and a chalked inscription: 'April Fool' – the date being 1 April 1868.

Local citizens were becoming enraged at the impunity the gang seemed to enjoy. The Reno brothers were not the kind of jolly outlaws who became folk heroes; they were bullies and killers. In desperation, some of the bolder Seymour residents formed a Vigilance Committee. The Renos heard the rumours, and made bloodthirsty threats.

After a train robbery at Marshfield, Indiana, which netted the gang $96,000, Pinkerton decided they had to be caught by cunning. He circulated rumours that $100,000 in gold was to be shipped via Seymour. The train's engineer pretended to agree to co-operate with the gang and tipped off Pinkerton exactly where the robbery would take place. And as the outlaws stopped the train and burst open the Express car, they were met by a volley of shots from Pinkerton's men. Most of the gang escaped, but the next day, three of them were captured in a thicket and arrested. But one dark night a few weeks later, the train on which they were being sent to their trial was stopped by men waving red lanterns; the three bandits were dragged off the train and lynched. A few weeks later, another three bandits who had been tracked down by Pinkerton were intercepted on their way to jail by a mob and lynched. The Reno gang left in Seymour began to fight back; members of the Vigilance Committee had rocks thrown through their windows; there were night raids, beatings and mutilations. When Simeon and William Reno were arrested by Pinkerton detectives in Indianapolis,

Vigilance Committee members received messages: 'If the Renos are lynched, you die.' The Vigilance Committee decided that if the Renos were not lynched, things would remain as bad as ever. The authorities decided to transfer the two Renos to the more secure New Albany jail. On 6 September 1868, there was a determined attempt by vigilantes to break into the Lexington jail, but the Renos had already been moved. They were joined in New Albany by their brother Frank, who had been arrested in Canada, together with a gang member named Charles Anderson. But on 11 December vigilantes surrounded the jail and burst their way in with a battering ram. The sheriff was beaten unconscious, and his keys taken. Then the Reno brothers and Anderson were dragged from their cells and lynched. As the vigilantes dispersed, prisoners watched from their cells and saw Simeon gasping for breath on the end of his rope; it took half an hour before he ceased to struggle.

The Vigilance Committee issued a notice, naming other members of the gang still in Seymour – including brother Clinton – and declaring that if they wished to remain as honest citizens, they would be welcome; otherwise they would meet the fate of the others. The gang accepted the ultimatum sullenly, and the outlaws ceased to be a power in Indiana.

Pinkerton was altogether less successful in his attempts to catch Jesse James. Like the Reno brothers, Jesse and his brother Frank came back from the Civil War, in which they fought for the South, wondering whether the methods of Quantrill's guerrillas could not be applied with equal success in peacetime. On 13 February 1866, ten men rode into Liberty, Missouri, and robbed the bank; on their way out of town, one of them shot down an unarmed student on his way to college, then, whooping and firing pistols, the gang rode out of town. It was the first of many pointless murders committed by the gang led by this modern 'Robin Hood'. In December 1869, the James gang robbed the same bank in Gallatin, Missouri, that the Reno brothers had robbed two years earlier, and James shot the manager in cold blood.

The Pinkertons began trailing the James gang at about this time, but had no success. In February 1874, a Pinkerton operative, John W. Whicher, succeeded in infiltrating the gang, but was recognized and murdered. On 6 January 1875, the Pinkertons received a tip-off that Jesse was visiting his mother, Mrs Zerelda Samuel; they surrounded the house and tossed in a 'smoke bomb'. It killed James' 8-year-old half-brother, and blew off his mother's arm. The incident brought much sympathy for the James brothers and indignant criticism of the brutality of Pinkerton. Jesse James was so angry that he spent four months in Chicago trying to get Pinkerton alone so he could kill him; he was unsuccessful.

On 7 August 1876, an attempt to rob the bank in Northfield, Minnesota, went disastrously wrong; the citizens all rushed outdoors with guns, and most of the bandits were either killed or wounded; James' cousin Cole Younger and his brother Bob were captured soon after and sentenced to life imprisonment. James formed a second gang, but it never met with the same success as the earlier one. On 7 August 1881, the gang committed its last train robbery, netting only $1,500. Harassment by the Pinkertons was breaking their nerve. On 3 April 1882, Jesse James was planning another robbery with two new gang members, Bob and Charlie Ford, when Bob Ford pulled out his gun and shot James in the back. He had agreed to deliver Jesse James to the state governor for reward money and amnesty. The murder of Jesse James – at the age of 34 – made him more of a folk hero than ever, and his brother Frank was acquitted several times of crimes he had obviously committed (he died of old age in 1915). Allan Pinkerton died two years after Jesse James, at the age of 65; but the agency continued with unabated success under sons and grandsons.

2

By the 1880s, the day of the American badman was drawing to a close – at least in the 'wild west'. But one of them was still to achieve – briefly – some of the same notoriety as Jesse James. Marion Hedgepeth was born in Missouri, and became a cowboy in Wyoming, then a hold-up man in Colorado. An exceptionally handsome man, he soon acquired the status of a folk hero when he began robbing trains in Missouri, on one occasion blasting his way in with dynamite. After netting $50,000 in Glendale, the 'Hedgepeth Four' (as they were known) moved to St Louis and perpetrated a number of audacious robberies by daylight. Allan Pinkerton's son William, now the head of the agency, rushed to St Louis to try and track down the gang. He failed, but a little girl playing in a shed found a hole in the corner, and discovered six-shooters and envelopes that had contained money stolen from Adams Express. The gang had left, but now Pinkerton had a lead, he tracked down the expressman who had agreed to ship their effects – including the loot – to Los Angeles. Hedgepeth's wife was arrested when she went to the Express office to claim the trunks. Hedgepeth escaped, but the Pinkertons knew he was associated with a crooked attorney who was fond of billiards. The attorney was watched, and one day when he had removed his tailcoat to play billiards, it was searched; in the pocket the detective found a letter to Hedgepeth which included the address of his latest hideout. Hedgepeth was quietly surrounded by detectives when out on a walk, and in St Louis was sentenced to 25 years' hard labour. In fact, he was released in 1908 with tuberculosis, and killed two years later in Chicago as he was trying to rob a barman of his takings.

But even in prison, Hedgepeth was to play an important role in criminal history; he was indirectly responsible for the capture of the worst mass murderer of the nineteenth century.

In June 1894, when Hedgepeth had been in prison for two years, a stranger with mild blue eyes and a gentlemanly manner was introduced into his cell. He introduced himself as Mr Holmes, a druggist, who had sold a drug store that did not belong to him in St Louis. Holmes was a man of 34, slightly built but with a winning smile and excellent manners. He asked Hedgepeth if he knew of a good – and not too honest – lawyer, and Hedgepeth recommended a man named Jephta D. Howe. Holmes, it seemed, needed a man who could be trusted, for he proposed to swindle an insurance company out of $10,000. Pressed by Hedgepeth, Holmes finally explained. He would insure the life of a friend called Benjamin Pitezel for $10,000, then arrange for Pitezel to be 'killed' in an accidental explosion. In fact, a corpse obtained from an undertaker would be substituted for Pitezel. In exchange for securing the co-operation of Jephta D. Howe, Hedgepeth would receive $500 of the loot.

With the help of Howe, the soft-spoken Mr Holmes was soon out on bail. And two months later, Hedgepeth learned that Pitezel had 'died' in an explosion. But Holmes failed to send the $500 he had promised, and Hedgepeth, having nothing else to do in jail, brooded on it until he was filled with resentment. Accordingly, he wrote a letter to the Fidelity Mutual Life Assurance Company, which had recently paid out $9,715.85 to Jephta D. Howe, denouncing Holmes as a swindler. And William E. Gary of the Mutual Life Agency promptly hired the Pinkertons to find out whether there was any truth in this story.

What had happened, it seemed, was this. On 22 August 1894, a carpenter looking for work had called at a house in Callowhill Street, Philadelphia, hoping to obtain a job with a 'patents dealer' named

Perry. Instead, he had found the decomposing corpse of Perry on the floor of his laboratory; he had apparently been killed in an explosion. An autopsy revealed chloroform in the stomach. Since no one claimed the corpse, it was buried in a public grave. However, before this happened, the St Louis branch of the Fidelity Mutual Life had received a letter from Jephta D. Howe, saying that he had reason to believe that Perry was really Benjamin Pitezel, whose wife Carrie had insured her husband for $10,000.

The agent who had insured Pitezel was asked if he knew anyone who could identify him, and he named a Mr Henry Howard Holmes of Wilmette, Illinois. Holmes was contacted, and he came to Philadelphia, together with Pitezel's 15-year-old daughter Alice. The corpse was exhumed, and proved to be badly decomposed; Holmes identified it as Pitezel, then the body was covered, all except for the teeth. Alice was now brought into the morgue and asked: 'Are those your father's teeth?' She said yes and burst into tears. So the company paid up the insurance. And now, a few weeks later, the letter from Marion Hedgepeth suggested that the whole thing was a swindle arranged by Holmes, and that Pitezel was still alive.

Oddly enough, the insurance company was disinclined to believe Hedgepeth; they suspected him of inventing the story for his own devious purposes. Nevertheless, they asked the Pinkerton agency to find Holmes. The agency tracked him from Canada to Detroit to New York to New Hampshire, and in the meantime discovered that he had a number of aliases, and that his real name was Herman Webster Mudgett. Finally, Holmes was arrested in Boston; he strenuously insisted on his innocence. The police were unhappy about the evidence against him in Philadelphia – after all, there was nothing to tie him to the death of 'Pitezel'. When they learned that he was also wanted in Texas, they telegraphed Fort Worth and asked what he had done. The answer was that Holmes was wanted for horse stealing, and also for questioning about the disappearance of two sisters called Williams. When told about the horse stealing charge, Holmes proved unexpectedly co-operative – he knew that Texans were inclined to lynch horse thieves without trial. So he admitted to being guilty of fraud in Philadelphia, and was promptly returned to that city. Here he explained that he procured a corpse in New York – he would not say where from – and passed it off as Pitezel. Pitezel was then given his share of the insurance money, and sailed for South America with three of his children . . .

Holmes asked the Pinkerton detective to deliver a note to a woman called Mrs Cook in Burlington, Vermont. The detective soon discovered that Mrs Cook was Carrie Pitezel, and she was placed under arrest. She had been living with her eldest daughter Dessie and her baby son; she explained that Mr Holmes had gone off with the other three – Alice, Nellie and Howard. And although she trusted Mr Holmes, she was worried about her husband and children . . .

Philadelphia detective Frank Geyer questioned Holmes, and soon decided that he was a born actor. He would talk with apparent candour, and his eyes would fill with tears; then, with a brave effort, he would master his apparently deep emotion and speak in a determined and forceful manner. And the more Geyer talked to Holmes, the more convinced he became that the children, like their father, were dead. But where were they? Geyer set out to track them down; he took with him photographs of Holmes and the missing children.

What followed was a masterpiece of dogged, old-fashioned 'needle-in-the-haystack' detection. First Geyer went to Cincinnati, where the Pinkerton detectives had traced Holmes. Enquiries at dozens of hotels finally revealed that a Mr Cook had stayed at one of them with three children; the clerk recognized the photographs of the children. Holmes had stayed only one night in the hotel, so it seemed probable that he had taken a house. A round of estate agents finally revealed that Holmes had rented a house in Poplar Street, paying $15 rent in advance and giving the name A. C. Hayes. Neighbours had seen a man and a small boy getting off a furniture wagon, and noticed that one piece of furniture he brought was a large stove. The next morning, Holmes had told his neighbour that he had changed his mind about occupying the house, and that she could have the stove. Apparently the curiosity of the neighbours had driven Holmes away . . .

The next stop was Indianapolis, where the Pinkerton detectives had found Holmes. There the usual search of hotel registers revealed that an 'Etta Pitsel' had stayed there for four days in the previous September. Geyer reasoned that Holmes had left 'Etta' (whom the clerk recognized from her photograph as Alice, the daughter who had identified her dead father) while he went to St Louis to cash the insurance cheque. Geyer next tracked Holmes to Detroit, where he had stayed in a hotel with the two girls – a discovery that convinced the detective that the small boy, Howard, had never left Indianapolis alive. Mrs Pitezel had also been in Detroit, apparently unaware that the children about whom she was so worried were staying in a hotel just around the corner, crying themselves to sleep with homesickness.

The Pinkertons had already established that Holmes had gone to Toronto. Geyer went to Toronto, and proceeded to make the round of estate agents, trying to find if Holmes had rented a house. When this brought no result, he called in the Press and told them the story. As a result, a man told him that he had leased a house to a gentleman called Holmes the previous October. This proved to be a false lead; after searching the property and digging in the cellar, they checked with the agent who rented the house; he looked at the photograph of Holmes and said it was not the same man. But by this time, another agent reported letting a house in St Vincent Street to a man who sounded like Holmes. The detective rushed to the house and persuaded its present occupant to let them dig in the cellar. Here, at last, they found what they were looking for – two naked bodies buried under three feet of earth. When Mrs Pitezel identified them as her two daughters, she had hysterics and fainted repeatedly.

More patient research – particularly into letters written by the children – revealed that the boy Howard had almost certainly been killed in Indianapolis in October. Finally, an estate agent recognized Holmes's photograph, and his office boy remembered that Holmes and a small boy had gone to a one-storey cottage at nearby Irvington. The place was searched, but Geyer could find nothing. Digging yielded no results. But after Geyer left, two children went on searching, and found a hole in the chimney; inside this they found pieces of bone and a set of teeth. Mrs Pitezel indentified them as the teeth of her son Howard.

Now, at last, the case against Holmes was complete. The corpse of the man found in Philadelphia had obviously been that of Pitezel, not some medical specimen purchased in New York. Holmes had persuaded Pitezel – a petty thief – to take part in the insurance swindle with a promise of half the proceeds. But he never had any intention of paying; instead, he intended to murder Pitezel, then kill his family one by one. Fortunately for Mrs Pitezel, Hedgepeth revealed the scheme before it claimed its final victims.

But now Holmes' face had appeared on newspapers all over America, those who had known him in the past began to tell their stories. He had lived in Chicago, and built himself a large house on 63rd Street – a place so big it had become known as his 'castle'. Dozens of people went to the police to complain of having been swindled by Holmes, whose favourite method of raising money was to buy something on credit and sell it for cash the next day. And when the police went to investigate the 'castle', they realized that it had been designed by a man whose life revolved around robbery and murder. There were secret rooms, trapdoors, rooms without windows which could be made airtight by closing the doors – one contained a huge safe with a gas-pipe running into it. But the most sinister discovery was a room lined with asbestos, with a gas-pipe that was designed as a giant blow-torch, in which a body could be incinerated. A large stove contained fragments of human bone, and in the chimney there was a bunch of human hair, a woman's. Chutes ran from the second floor down to the basement – chutes large enough to accommodate a human body.

Little by little, the full story of Holmes began to emerge, and even before it was complete, it was obvious that he was the most horrific mass murderer in American history. Born in Gilmanton, New Hampshire, on 16 May 1860, Herman Webster Mudgett had been a shy but brilliant child. He was also timid, and when mischievous school-fellows dragged him into an empty doctor's surgery to confront a skeleton, morbid terror began to turn into morbid fascination. So it was perhaps inevitable that he should decide on a medical career. He married at 18, but seems to have deserted his wife at an early stage. During his first year studying medicine at the University of Michigan, he went to Chicago, became an agent for a textbook publisher, and absconded with the funds He practised medicine in Mooers Fork, New York but soon devised a method of making a quick profit: insuring his life and then providing a substitute body. For various reasons, the scheme fell through, but he returned to it later in Minneapolis. Here, according to his later confession, he purchased a corpse from a medical college, insured himself for $20,000, then transported the corpse to a lumbering area of northern Michigan. Holmes disappeared into the forest, his 'corpse' was found pinioned under a tree a week or so later, and the insurance money was paid into Holmes's bank account.

This tale seems to bear some of the marks of Holmes's mythomania. What is undoubtedly true is that he moved to Chicago in 1886, and married a girl named Myrta Belknap – bigamously, of course – and that her family decided to break with Holmes when he forged the signature of Uncle John Belknap. Holmes invited Uncle John to go up to the roof of a new house to discuss the matter; some instinct warned Uncle John to decline.

Now he succeeded in obtaining a job as the assistant of a widow,

Mrs E. S. Holton, who ran a drug store at 63rd Street and Wallace in Englewood, Chicago. Business prospered. But after a few years, Mrs Holton and her young daughter vanished; Holmes declared that she had sold him the business. Now he purchased two vacant lots across the street, and began to build his three-storey 'castle', using borrowed money and money raised by petty swindles – one furniture company succeeded in recovering its furniture when a carpenter tipped them off about a secret room hidden behind a false wall. Holmes also bought a vast safe, but failed to pay; when the safe company sent men to recover it, they realized that there was not a door or window in the house that was large enough to take it through. So Holmes retained his safe. He also took the precaution of sacking gangs of workmen every few weeks, so that no one knew too much about the place.

According to Holmes' later confession, his first victim was a doctor friend, Robert Leacock of Baltimore, Michigan, whom he killed for $40,000 life insurance money in 1886, but he offers no further details. Once the castle was constructed, he settled down to the serious business of paying off his debts with murder and robbery. The drug store opposite brought in a good income, but it was not enough. A room in the castle was let to a Dr Russell, and one day Holmes killed him by striking him on the head with a heavy chair. He claimed that he sold the body to the Chicago Medical College for $45. He also killed a tenant called Rodgers, who had come to Michigan on a fishing trip, and a man named Charles Cole.

Holmes was an obsessive seducer, and he became involved with a woman called Julia Conner, whose husband Ned ran the jewellery section of the drug store. Ned Conner and his wife separated when it became clear that she was Holmes's mistress, and Mrs Conner and her eight-year-old daughter Pearl moved into the 'castle'. They also vanished, probably around Christmas 1891. Holmes later said that Julia Conner had died as a result of an illegal operation, and that he had been forced to poison Pearl. At the time, he told acquaintances that she had left him to marry a doctor.

The next victim, according to Holmes, was a domestic named Lizzie, who had begun to have an affair with the caretaker of the castle, Pat Quinlan. Afraid that Quinlan – who was married – was planning to elope with Lizzie, Holmes suffocated her in the basement, after forcing her to write letters saying she was going out west.

A woman named Sarah Cook began to work for Holmes, and her niece, a Miss Mary Haracamp, became Holmes's typist. Sarah Cook became pregnant. One evening, they came into the 'vault' (presumably the safe with its 'blow-torch') when Holmes was preparing his latest victim for shipment to the Medical School. According to Holmes, he slammed the door and gassed them both.

Some time in the spring of 1892, a beautiful girl named Emmeline Cigrand was lured to Chicago to work for Holmes; she had been employed at the Keeley Institute in Dwight, and Pitezel had been impressed by her when he went there to take a cure for alcoholism. It is typical of Holmes that Pitezel's descriptions of her led him to offer her a position as his bookkeeper and secretary. Her letters home to Dwight are full of descriptions of Holmes' kindness to her, and of how he often brought her flowers. She had one drawback; she was engaged to a young man in Dwight. Holmes claims that she became his mistress, but that was probably because he hated to admit failure. He became jealous enough to make plans to kill her fiancé, but these came to nothing. On the day in December when she came to say goodbye, Holmes pushed her into the vault, and offered to release her if she wrote a letter breaking off her engagement. He claims she did so, and that he then allowed her to suffocate. Since Holmes had no reason to want to get rid of her – unlike Julia Conner she had not become a nuisance – it seems probable that the motive was sexual: that this was his only way of possessing her.

The same probably applies to the next victim, another beautiful girl called Rosine Van Jassand, whom Holmes induced to work in his fruit and confectionery store. His story is that he 'compelled her to live with him', then poisoned her and buried her in the basement; it seems more probable that she clung to her virtue and that Holmes killed her for this reason.

Holmes had employed a caretaker named Robert Latimer, who had learned about his insurance schemes. When he tried to blackmail Holmes, he was also locked in the vault. Holmes claims that he allowed Latimer to starve to death, and in fact, police found that some of the bricks and mortar had been torn away by someone using his bare hands. All this makes it clear that Holmes was not merely trying to shock when he claimed that, 'like a tiger that has tasted human blood', he began killing out of a sadistic mania. This also seems to be confirmed by his next murder, that of a Miss Anna Betts, a customer at the drug store, in whose prescription Holmes inserted poison. Since she died at her home, the motive could only have been the strange delight in killing that also motivated Neill Cream and George Chapman. Holmes claimed that he also inserted poison into the prescription of a girl called Gertrude Conner – presumably a relative of Ned Conner – but that it was slow-acting, and she died only after returning home to Muscatine, Iowa.

But the motive of the next murder was purely financial; he convinced an unnamed woman in Omaha that the time had come to sell her real estate holdings in Chicago. She came to Chicago to collect the money, then died in the vault, Holmes taking back the money.

Since 1889, Holmes had been associated with a man named Warner in an enterprise called the Warner Glass Bending Company. Warner, it seems, had invented a new process, which involved a large zinc tank that could be filled with a fine oil spray, which was then ignited, producing a temperature hot enough to bend plate glass. When Warner had finished building his patent oven in Holmes' basement, he was pushed into it and incinerated 'In a short time, not even the bones of my victim remained.' The patent oven certainly existed. When police began investigating the 'castle' in July 1895, they sent for a plumber to knock down a wall that sounded hollow; a stench of decaying flesh came out. The plumber made the mistake of striking a match, where-upon there was an explosion that filled the cellar with flames and disabled several workmen. When the wall was demolished, police found a cylindrical tank which was ten feet long and six feet high, and made of wood; inside this was a zinc tank, with numerous pipes running into it. The gas fumes overpowered a fireman who ventured inside.

Holmes' confession claims that he next went into partnership with an Englishman who was an expert in financial swindles. A wealthy banker was lured into the vault and forced to sign cheques for $70,000, after which he was gassed; Holmes sold the body to the medical college. The motive of the next murder was also financial; he chloroformed a wealthy woman who lived above his restaurant, and presumably gained possession of her money.

The disappearance of the Williams sisters, for which Holmes was wanted for questioning in Texas, took place in 1893. Holmes had met Minnie Williams in New York in 1888, and in 1893, he offered her the job of secretary and bookkeeper. Minnie apparently had 'an innocent and childlike nature', and was soon induced to give Holmes $2,500 in cash and to transfer $50,000 in real estate in Texas. Minnie had a sister named Nannie, and she was persuaded to come to Chicago on a visit. Nannie was pushed into the vault and gassed, and in her violent struggles she left behind her footprint on the vault door, where it was later found by police. He then took Minnie on a trip to Momence, Illinois, and rented a house, where he poisoned her and buried her in the basement. In the spring of 1894, Holmes and Pitezel went to Fort Worth, Texas, and built a store on the land once owned by Minnie Williams.

Another 'business partner' was the next to die, Holmes having become disappointed with his business acumen. After that, Holmes found among Minnie Williams' papers an insurance policy on the life of her brother Baldwin, of Leadville, Colorado. This was too good an opportunity to miss, so Holmes hurried to Leadville, faked a quarrel with Baldwin Williams, and apparently shot him in self-defence. He was probably reckoning that in the wild west of the 1890s, no one was going to make too much fuss about a killing caused by a quarrel. Holmes' confession fails to explain how he induced the insurance company to pay him the money. The explanation of this discretion is probably that Holmes induced his latest 'wife', a pretty girl named Georgina Yoke, to pose as Minnie Williams and claim the money; Holmes seems to have been genuinely in love with Georgina, and burst into tears when she gave evidence at his trial.

It was after the murder kof Baldwin Williams that Holmes embarked on his plan to murder the whole Pitezel family for the $10,000 insurance money. In spite of his murders and swindles Holmes was apparently still urgently in need of money. But with his first encounter with the Pinkerton agency, his luck ran out and his arrest in Boston terminated three and a half years of murder.

At his trial in October 1895, Holmes was accused only of the murder of Pitezel. When Mrs Pitezel told her story, even the judge was so deeply moved that he had to grope for his handkerchief. So the defence argument that Pitezel's death was suicide was virtually irrelevant; Holmes was really on trial for the murder of the Pitezel children. It took the jury three hours to find him guilty of murder. Back in prison, Holmes wrote his confession to 27 murders, which was syndicated by the Hearst newspapers. It was so horrific that many believed that Holmes was simply writing it for the $10,000 that Hearst paid him (and which went to Georgina Yoke). But his jailer observed that, after the confession, Holmes behaved as if a great burden had been lifted from his mind; he announced his conversion to Catholicism. He was firmly convinced that his career of crime had caused physical changes – a shortening of one arm and one leg and the 'malevolent distortion' of one side of his face, which was so marked that he grew a beard to conceal it. That this was not entirely imagination is proved by photographs of Holmes reproduced in David Franke's book *The Torture Doctor*. In the November 1966 issue of *The Criminologist,* there is an article that discusses an old theory that the left and right sides of the human face reflect two different aspects of the character: that the left side is the 'natural' character and the right the 'acquired'. (If a mirror is placed down the centre of a photograph, so the face becomes two left sides or two right, an interesting difference often emerges.) The difference between the two halves of Holmes' face is marked enough to justify his assertion that 'I have commenced to assume the form and features of the Evil One himself.' The confession certainly reveals that, as in the case of the Yorkshire Ripper, killing became an addictive drug that literally turned Holmes into a monster.

Unpredictable to the very end, Holmes withdrew all his confessions on the scaffold on 7 May 1896, and declared that he had never killed anyone; Holmes always possessed a strong dramatic streak, and probably felt that he owed some last memorable gesture to the immense crowd that gathered to see him hanged. Even his death was dramatic. When the trap fell, it became obvious that the fall had not broken his neck; his body swayed and contorted for at least a minute, and two spectators fainted.

Holmes's celebrity had become so great that a number of people made offers for his body – a man who offered Holmes' lawyer $5,000 for it probably wanted to embalm it and show it at fairgrounds. Holmes thwarted this by ordering that his body should be encased in cement in its coffin; his lawyer went one better, and had the coffin buried ten feet deep, and covered with a two-foot layer of cement.

3

By comparison with the Holmes case, the murder of Henry Smith, which occurred in London in the year of Holmes' execution, has an old-fashioned, almost Dickensian air.

Henry Smith was a grey-bearded but vigorous gentleman of 80, who lived alone in the north London suburb of Muswell Hill. As a precaution against burglars, he had screwed down most of the windows in the house, and his gardener Webber had filled the garden with trip-wires connected to bells and detonating cartridges; these had already discouraged one burglar. But when Webber arrived for work on the morning of 14 February 1896, he found the kitchen door wide open, and the body of Mr Smith lying on the floor. He was wearing a blood-spattered nightshirt, and his hands and legs had been tied; there was also a gag in his mouth. Death was due to blows on the head from some blunt instrument. The old man had obviously disturbed two burglars – two sets of footprints were found in the flower bed outside the kitchen window, which had been forced with a jemmy. The bedroom safe had been opened, and the house thoroughly ransacked.

Chief Inspector Marshall of Scotland Yard was summoned to the scene by Inspector Nutkins of the local CID. They found only one clue, and that was a puzzling one: a child's toy lantern in the kitchen sink, together with a soaked box of matches. The neat way in which the trip-wires had been snipped, and the jemmy marks on various windows, indicated that the burglars were professionals; but the toy lantern seemed incongruous – surely professional burglars would carry the real thing?

The crime looked insoluble; scientific detection – in so far as it existed in 1896 – had no material on which to operate. The only possible approach to the mystery was the old-fashioned needle-in-the-haystack method, which had now become standard police procedure. For the next few weeks, Inspector Nutkins and his team went from door to door throughout the area, asking residents if they had noticed any suspicious characters around the time of the murder. Eventually, he found two witnesses whose stories sounded promising. A Mrs Good had been accosted by two rough-looking men a few days before the murder, and asked the way to Coldfall Woods. They had also asked her about late night trains from Muswell Hill. But their most significant query was about whether certain gardens had entrances leading into the woods. They mentioned various houses, and Mrs Good thought they had included Muswell Lodge, the home of Henry Smith.

Another neighbour, a Mrs Wheaton, had also seen two rough-looking strangers in a lane near Muswell Lodge two days before the murder; one of them turned and glared at her as though he thought she was spying on them. Their looks had terrified her.

Fingerprint classification did not exist in 1896 – or at least, had not reached Scotland Yard. But there was another type of classification that might be useful. That remarkable sleuth Adolphus ('Dolly') Williamson had already started a file in which criminals were classified by their methods – their *modus operandi*. Here were two professional burglars who worked in tandem. Marshall checked the file and noted a number of possible suspects. And he also sent out a directive to all metropolitan police stations to look out for rough-looking burglars who worked together. This was read by a detective named Ernest Burrell in Kentish Town, only a mile or so down the road from Muswell Hill. Burrell noted the suggestion that police should be on the lookout for 'ticket of leave' men – criminals on parole – who had failed to report to police stations; he knew that when such men return to crime, they usually stop reporting. One such ticket of leave convict was Henry Fowler, a huge, brutal man who looked like Dickens' Bill Sykes, and for some weeks now, Fowler had been drinking in the company of a crook named Albert Milsom. Burrell decided to check on Milsom, who lived in Southam Street; he was met by a pale, tired-looking woman, who said that her husband was away working, and she had no idea of his address. Further checks in the area revealed that neither Milsom nor Fowler had been seen in their usual haunts from two days before the murder until two days afterwards.

Later the same day, Burrell intercepted a letter written by Mrs Milsom to her husband; it told him that the police had been looking for him, and warned him that they were looking for Fowler because he had failed to report to the police station.

The police now had Milsom's address, but at this stage it would have been pointless taking him in for questioning. They had no evidence. Admittedly, Milsom and Fowler sounded like the two men described by Mrs Cook and Mrs Wheaton; but even if the two ladies identified them, that should still prove nothing. It was certainly tempting to arrest them and try and force a confession, for the murder had caused panic in north London. But while Marshall hesitated, Milsom changed his address.

Marshall was already following another line of enquiry: the stolen money. He talked to the old man's bank, and learned that he had drawn out a £10 note shortly before his death; and since £10 was a large sum in 1896 – more than twice the weekly wage of a detective – the clerk had recorded its serial number. This note had been among cash stolen from the safe, and its number was circulated to all banks. Six weeks after the murder, the Bank of England reported that it had been paid in. Marshall traced it to a firm of tea merchants, who thought that it had been paid to them by a grocer in the East End of London. The grocer was able to remember where it had come from: a local publican had used it to pay his grocery bill. And the publican clearly remembered changing the note. He had been unwilling to do so, but the man who had presented it was a big, powerful-looking individual with an unpleasant glint in his eye. That was a good description of Henry Fowler.

Meanwhile, in Muswell Hill, Inspector Nutkins had been following up the only real clue: the toy lantern. The Milsoms had two children, and Mrs Milsom's younger brother, a 16-year-old named Harry Miller, also lived with them. Nutkins knew that if he asked the children about the lantern, he would be told nothing – they had obviously been brought up to regard the police as natural enemies. So Nutkins secured the co-operation of a local boy, one of Harry Miller's friends, and entrusted him with the lantern, with instructions to produce it casually. It worked; Harry Miller demanded to look more closely, and promptly claimed it as his own. How could he be so sure? Because the original wick had not burned properly, and he had fashioned another wick from a strip of red flannel, which was still in the lantern. Besides, he recognized other distinctive features, such as the cracking of a green glass panel, and a place where he had scraped away some varnish . . . At that moment, Burrell happened to wander by, and listened without apparent interest. He asked how Harry Miller had come to lose his lantern; Harry said it had vanished from the kitchen dresser. When asked what Milsom had been doing that night, he recalled that his brother-in-law had not come home until seven in the morning. And when Harry had complained about the loss of his lantern, Milsom had told him to tell anyone who enquired that he had broken it and thrown it away.

Now Marshall knew he had found his killers; but where were they now? The police intercepted a letter from Milsom to his wife; it contained no address, but the postmark was Bow. It took some time to trace the pair in the Bow area of east London, and when they did, the wanted men had already left, saying they were going to Liverpool. This worried Marshall; they might already be on a ship to America. But in the dock area of Liverpool he picked up their traces again, and learned that they had been spending money freely – the old man's safe was said to have contained £700. From Liverpool, the pair were traced to Manchester, then to Cardiff – by now they were using the names Taylor and Scott. In Cardiff, they had gone to see a phrenologist who was travelling with a fair, and 'Professor Sinclair' had read their bumps. They told him they were seamen who were looking for work ashore, and were taken on as partners in Sinclair's waxworks business.

It was less difficult to trace the waxworks; it had moved to Swindon, then Chippenham, then Bath, and the police followed it to each of these places. They caught up with Milsom and Fowler – now calling themselves Stevenson and Walsh – in Monmouth Street, Bath. They had taken a room above a sweet shop, together with the 'professor'. That night – Sunday 12 April, eight weeks after the murder – the police burst into the room at 11 o'clock. Nutkins was carrying a loaded revolver. Marshall shouted 'Hands up, we are police officers', and Milsom groaned 'Oh my God!' But Fowler fought like a demon, and Marshall had to strike him on the head with his revolver before he fell to the floor and could be handcuffed. In the upholstery of the couch, the police found Fowler's loaded revolver.

At the local police station they were charged with murdering Henry Smith of Muswell Lodge; then they were separated. Fowler remained contemptuous and abusive; Milsom cowered and whined. Both denied the murder charge. Asked why, in that case, he had resisted arrest so violently, Fowler said he thought he was being arrested for failing to report at the police station. His alibi was that he was in a lodging-house in Kentish Town on the night of the murder.

The chief witness against them was the youth Harry Miller, who had been placed in a special home in case Milsom and Fowler learned of his betrayal. In court, it was soon obvious that the case against them was damning. At this point, it struck Milsom that he might save his own neck by turning Queen's evidence. Standing beside Fowler, he told the court that he had nothing to do with the murder. According to Milsom, Fowler had planned the 'job' with another crook, who had let him down at the last moment; on the evening of the burglary he had gone to Milsom's house, and finally persuaded him to join him. They had taken the toy lantern, and climbed into the old man's garden, carefully cutting the trip-wires. When it was dark, they broke in. The old man heard them and came downstairs with a light, shouting 'Police, murder!' Milsom alleged that he was so alarmed that he ran away, expecting the neighbourhood to be aroused. When all was silent, he went back and found Fowler standing over the old man's body. 'It's your fault, you cur!', snarled Fowler, 'for leaving a man on his own.' They then ransacked the house and opened the safe with a key found in the old man's trouser pocket. After that, they went and hid in the woods until dawn, then walked home, with Fowler wearing Milsom's overcoat to hide the blood on his clothes. Later that day, he called at Milsom's house and gave him £53 as his share of the loot.

As Fowler listened to all this, he lunged at Milsom and tried to get his hands around his throat; the policeman who also stood in the dock dragged them apart. Then Fowler gave his own version. The safe had contained £112, he said, and he had given Milsom £53 of it; was that likely if Milsom had been a mere onlooker? According to Fowler, Milsom had stood with his foot on the old man's neck until he was dead. And the judge himself was to point out that two pocket knives had been found by the body – knives that had been used to cut up the table-cloth that had been used to bind the victim; this showed conclusively that Milsom had helped to tie the old man, and had therefore been present when he was killed.

For the second time, Fowler tried to kill his companion; this time he succeeded in getting a grip on his throat and hurling him to the floor; police filled the dock and tried to drag them apart; the glass screen around the dock shattered and the dock itself swayed. Fowler struggled to his feet, lashing out at the police who held him and kicking at Milsom, who was still on the floor. Then handcuffs were snapped on his wrists, and he was dragged out of court, still roaring defiance. The fight had lasted 12 minutes.

He was returned to court when the jury filed in; in the ruins of the dock, they heard themselves sentenced to death. In his cell, Fowler made two attempts to kill himself, but was prevented by guards. The two of them were hanged at Newgate, together with a man named William Seaman who had murdered an old man called Levy and his housekeeper; it is said that, as he stood between them on the trapdoor, Seaman remarked: 'It's the first time I've ever been a bloody peace-maker.'

4

The year 1898 saw the publication of two massive works on the history of crime and crime detection: *Mysteries of Police and Crime* by Major Arthur Griffiths, and *Murder in All Ages* by Matthew Worth Pinkerton, who was then the head of the Pinkerton detective agency. Both are heroic attempts to write a world history of crime, and both are now as readable as when they were written. And, as befits skilled criminal investigators, both have a note of buoyant optimism about the future of crime detection. Griffiths rightly singles out 'the patient investigations of the medical expert, M. Bertillon of Paris', and 'the results obtained by Mr Francis Galton with the human finger prints' as the brightest hope for the next century. Pinkerton announces cheerfully that the increase in crime is only apparent, due to better 'transmission of news', and states his belief that 'a brighter era has dawned for mankind', due to the 'wider dissemination of knowledge' and 'the awakened conscience of thousands of men and women who are forgetting something of self that they may reclaim and elevate their fellows.' He would have been saddened to learn that he was living in the dawn of a new 'crime explosion'.

France, the country of Orfila, Lacassagne and Bertillon, undoubtedly led the world in scientific crime detection. Yet the recognition of their own pre-eminence could occasionally lure the French into truly monumental errors of judgement, which were sometime – as in the Dreyfus case – complicated by a refusal to acknowledge the error. Such was the incredible affair of the 'ogress of the Goutte d'Or'.

In the Goutte d'Or, a slum passageway in Montmartre, lived four brothers named Weber, one of whose wives, Jeanne Weber, had lost two of her three children, and consoled herself with cheap red wine. Just around the corner lived her brother-in-law Pierre and his wife. On 2 March 1905, Mme Pierre asked her sister-in-law if she would baby-sit with her two children, Suzanne and Georgette, while she went to the public *lavoir,* the 1905 equivalent of a launderette. Mme Pierre had been there only a short time when a neighbour rushed in and told her that 18-month-old Georgette was ill – she had heard her choking and gasping as she passed. The mother hurried home, and found her child on the bed, her face blue and with foam around her mouth; her aunt Jeanne was massaging the baby's chest. Mme Pierre took the child on her lap and rubbed her back until her breathing became easier, then went back to the launderette. But when she returned an hour later, with a basket of clean washing, Georgette was dead. The neighbour observed some red marks on the baby's throat, and pointed them out to the father, but he seems to have shrugged it off. Nobody felt any suspicion towards Jeanne Weber, who had behaved admirably and apparently done her best.

Nine days later, when both parents had to be away from home, they again asked Aunt Jeanne to baby-sit. Two-year-old Suzanne was dead when they returned, again with foam around her mouth. The doctor diagnosed the cause of death as convulsions. Aunt Jeanne appeared to be dazed with grief.

Two weeks later, on 25 March, Jeanne Weber went to visit another brother-in-law, Leon Weber, and was left with the seven-month-old daughter Germaine while her mother went shopping. The grandmother, who lived on the floor below, heard sudden cries, and hurried upstairs to find Germaine in 'convulsions', gasping for breath. After a few minutes of rubbing and patting, the baby recovered, and the grandmother returned to her own room. Minutes later, as she talked with a neighbour, she once more heard the child's cries. Again she hurried upstairs and found the baby choking. The neighbour who had accompanied her noticed red marks on the child's throat. When the parents returned, Germaine had recovered.

The following day, Jeanne Weber came to enquire after the baby. And, incredibly, the mother again left her baby-sitting. When she returned, her child was dead. The doctor diagnosed the cause as diphtheria.

Three days later, on the day of Germaine's funeral, Jeanne Weber stayed at home with her own child Marcel; he suffered the same convulsions, and was dead when the others returned.

A week later, on 5 April, Jeanne Weber invited to lunch the wife of Pierre Weber, and the wife of another brother-in-law, Charles. Mme Charles brought her ten-month-old son Maurice, a delicate child. After lunch, Jeanne baby-sat while her in-laws went shopping. When they returned, Maurice was lying on the bed, blue in the face, with foam around his lips, breathing with difficulty. The hysterical mother accused Jeanne of strangling him – there were marks on his throat – and she furiously denied it. So Mme Charles swept up her child in her arms, and hastened to the Hospital Brétonneau. She was sent immediately to the children's ward, where a Dr Saillant examined the marks on Maurice's throat. It certainly looked as if someone had tried to choke him. And when he heard the story of the other four deaths in the past month, Dr Saillant became even more suspicious. So was his colleague Dr Sevestre, and together they informed the police of this unusual case. Jeanne Weber was brought in for questioning, and Inspector Coiret began to look into her background. When he learned that all three of her children had died in convulsions, and that three years earlier, two other children – Lucie Alexandre and Marcel Poyatos – had died in the same mysterious way when in the care of Jeanne Weber, suspicion turned to certainty. The only thing that amazed him was that the Weber family had continued to ask her to baby-sit; they were either singularly fatalistic or criminally negligent. But then, the death of Jeanne's own son Marcel had dispelled any suspicions that might have been forming. When Examining Magistrate Leydet was informed of this, he found himself wondering whether this was precisely why Marcel had died.

The magistrate decided to call in a medical expert, and asked Dr Léon Henri Thoinot, one of Paris's most distinguished 'expert witnesses', second only to Paul Brouardel, the author of a classic book on strangulation and suffocation. Thoinot began by examining Maurice, who had now fully recovered. The child seemed perfectly healthy, and it was hard to see why he should have choked. Thoinot decided it could have been bronchitis. Next, the bodies of three of the dead children – Georgette, Suzanne and Germaine – were exhumed. Thoinot could find no traces of strangulation on their throats. Finally, Thoinot studied the body of Jeanne Weber's son Marcel; again he decided there was no evidence of strangulation – for example, the hyoid bone, which is easily broken by pressure on the throat, was intact.

The accusations of murder had caused a public sensation; Jeanne Weber was the most hated woman in France. The magistrate, Leydet, had no doubt whatsoever of her guilt. Yet at her trial on 29 January 1906, Thoinot once again stated his opinion that there was no evidence that the children had died by violence, while the defence lawyer Henri Robert – an unscrupulous man who had unsuccessfully defended Gabrielle Bompard – intimidated the prosecution witnesses until they contradicted themselves. The 'ogress of the Goutte d'Or' – as public opinion had christened her – was acquitted on all charges. The audience in the courtroom underwent a change of heart and cheered her. And Brouardel and Thoinot collaborated on an article in a medical journal in which they explained once again why Jeanne Weber had been innocent.

The public did not think so. Nor did her husband, who left her. Jeanne Weber decided that she had better move to some place where she was not known. She was a flabby, sallow-faced woman, who had little chance of attracting another male. And at that point, rescue arrived out of the blue. A man named Sylvain Bavouzet wrote to her from a place called Chambon – in the department of Indre – offering her a job as his housekeeper; it seemed he had been touched by her sad tale, and by the injustice that had almost condemned her to death. In the spring of 1907, Jeanne Weber – now calling herself by her unmarried name Moulinet – arrived at the farm of Sylvain Bavouzet, and understood that the offer had not been made entirely out of the goodness of his heart. It was a miserable, poverty-stricken place, and Bavouzet was a widower with three children, the eldest an ugly girl with a hare lip.

What he wanted was cheap labour and a female to share his bed. But at least it was a home.

A month later, on 16 April 1907, Bavouzet came home to find that his 9-year-old son Auguste was ill. He had recently eaten a large amount at a local wedding feast, so his discomfort could have been indigestion. The child's sister Louise was sent to the local town Villedieu to ask the doctor to call. But Dr Papazoglou gave her some indigestion mixture and sent her on her way. Hours later, Sylvain Bavouzet arrived, in a state of agitation, and said the boy was worse. When Papazoglou arrived, Auguste was dead, and the new housekeeper was standing by the bedside. The child was wearing a clean shirt, tightly buttoned at the collar, and when this was opened, the doctor saw a red mark around his neck. This led him to refuse a death certificate. The next day, the coroner, Charles Audiat, decided that, in spite of the red mark, Auguste's death was probably due to meningitis.

The dead boy's elder sister Germaine, the girl with the hare lip, hated the new housekeeper. She had overheard what 'Mme Moulinet' had told the doctor, and knew it was mostly lies. Her brother had not vomited just before his death – so requiring a change of shirt. Precisely how Germaine realized that Mme Moulinet was the accused murderess Jeanne Weber is not certain. One account of the case declares that she came upon Jeanne Weber's picture by chance in a magazine given to them by neighbours; another asserts that she searched the housekeeper's bag and found press cuttings about the case. What is certain is that she took her evidence to the police station in Villedieu and accused Mme Moulinet of murdering her brother.

An examining magistrate demanded a new autopsy, and this was performed by Dr Frédéric Bruneau. He concluded that there *was* evidence that Auguste had been strangled, possibly with a tourniquet. (Doctors had found a scarf wrapped around the throat of Maurice Weber, the child who had survived.) Jeanne Weber was arrested. The new accusation caused a sensation in Paris.

Understandably, Henri Robert, the man who had been responsible for her acquittal, felt that this reflected upon his professional integrity. Thoinot and Brouardel agreed. They decided that the unfortunate woman must once again be saved from public prejudice. Robert agreed to defend her for nothing, while Thoinot demanded another inquest. He carried it out three and half months after the child's death, by which time decay had made it impossible to determine whether Auguste Bavouzet had been strangled. Predictably, Thoinot decided that

Auguste had died of natural causes – intermittent fever. More doctors were called in. They agreed with Thoinot. The latter's prestige was such that Examining Magistrate Belleau decided to drop the charges against Jeanne Weber, although he was personally convinced of her guilt. Henri Robert addressed the Forensic Medicine Society and denounced the ignorance and stupidity of provincial doctors and magistrates. Jeanne Weber was free to kill again.

History repeated itself. A philanthropic doctor named Georges Bonjeau, president of the Society for the Protection of Children, offered her a job in the children's home in Orgeville. There she was caught trying to throttle a child and dismissed. But, like Thoinot and Henri Robert, Bonjeau did not believe in admitting his mistakes and he kept the matter to himself.

She became a tramp, living by prostitution. Arrested for vagrancy, she told M. Hamard, chief of the Sûreté, that she had been responsible for the deaths of her nieces. Then she withdrew the statement, and was sent to an asylum in Nanterre, from which she was quickly released as sane. A man named Joly offered her protection, and she lived with him at Lay-Saint-Remy, near Toul, until he grew tired of her and threw her out. Again she became a prostitute, and finally met a lime-burner named Émile Bouchery, who worked in the quarries of Euville, near Commercy. They lived in a room in a cheap inn run by a couple named Poirot. One evening, 'Mme Bouchery' told the Poirots that she was afraid that Bouchery meant to beat her up – as he did periodically when drunk – and asked them if their seven-year-old son Marcel could sleep in her bed. They agreed. At 10 o'clock that evening, a child's screams were heard, and the Poirots broke into Mme Bouchery's room. Marcel was dead, his mouth covered in bloodstained foam. Mme Bouchery was also covered in blood. A hastily summoned doctor realized that the child had been strangled, and had bitten his tongue in his agony. It was the police who discovered a letter from *maître* Henri Robert in Mme Bouchery's pocket, and realized that she was Jeanne Weber.

Once again, the reputations of Thoinot and Robert were at stake (Brouardel having escaped the public outcry by dying in 1906). Incredibly, both declined to admit their error. They agreed that the evidence proved unmistakably that Jeanne Weber had killed Marcel Poirot, but this, they insisted, was her first murder, brought about by the stress of years of persecution. It is unnecessary to say that the French Press poured scorn on this view. Yet such was the influence of Thoinot that Jeanne Weber was not brought to trial; instead she was moved out of the public gaze to an asylum on the island of Maré, off New Caledonia in the Pacific. There she died in convulsions two years later, her hands locked around her own throat.

5

At the time of Jeanne Weber's death, another French mass murderer had already embarked on the career that would end under the guillotine. But in 1910, Henri Desiré Landru was in prison for a series of pathetically amateurish frauds. The latest of these had involved advertising for a wife in a Lille newspaper, which led to an 'understanding' with a 40-year-old widow named Izoret. Landru handed her his 'deeds', and she handed over her cashbox, containing 20,000 francs. Then he vanished. In March 1910 Landru was sentenced to three years in prison, his fifth sentence in ten years. He was released in 1913, and within a year, had to flee from Paris to avoid prosecution for embezzlement.

In May 1918, the mayor of Gambais, a village about 40 kilometres south-west of Paris, received a letter from a Mlle Lacoste, a domestic servant, enquiring about her sister Mme Celestine Buisson, who had gone to live in Gambais with her fiancé, M. Fremyet, in the previous September. Since then, her family had heard nothing from her.

The mayor recalled that he had received a similar letter from Mme Pelat, enquiring about her sister Anna Collomb, who had also come to Gambais to live with her fiancé – a M. Dupont – and disappeared. As the mayor considered the two letters, he found himself wondering whether M. Fremyet and M. Dupont might conceivably be the same person. Mlle Lacoste had described the whereabouts of the villa – she had once visited her sister there – and it sounded to the mayor like the Villa Ermitage, owned by a M. Tric. He strolled out and inspected the villa – it was locked and shuttered. Then he spoke to the local shoemaker, who had given the keys to M. Dupont. It seemed that M. Dupont was a small, bald-headed man of 50 with a jutting beard, and he had been at the villa with many ladies. Since this villa was plainly the one described by Mlle Lacoste, it seemed clear that Dupont and Fremyet *were* the same person. Back at the town hall, the mayor dictated a reply, regretting that he was unable to help Mlle Lacoste, but mentioning that he had received a similar query from the Pelat family, and enclosing their address.

Mlle Lacoste hastened to contact the Pelat family, who were a step above her on the social scale. And when she described M. Fremyet – the bald head, the beard, the piercing eyes – Mme Pelat went pale and said: 'That is certainly Monsieur Dupont.'

On 6 April 1919, Commissioner Dautel of the Paris Préfecture of Police, summoned Inspector Jean Belin, and handed him the file of the disappearance of the two women. Belin soon established that M. Tric, the owner of the villa, had never met his tenant; Dupont had given an address in the rue Darnetal, in Rouen. But at the rue Darnetal, no one had ever heard of either Dupont or Fremyet.

Belin called on Mlle Lacoste, and was allowed to see her with some difficulty – servants were not allowed visitors. She was at first unwilling to speak to him but finally retold her story. In 1915, her sister, a widow of 44, had answered a matrimonial advertisement inserted by M. Fremyet, a rich land-owner; they met, she was fascinated, and became his mistress. But it was not until 1917 that she went to live with him at Gambais, and disappeared . . .

She could offer no further lead. Earnestly, Belin told her that if she happened to see M. Fremyet, she was to contact him immediately – he handed her his card. Then he went to call on Mme Collomb, mother of the missing Anna. When he returned to the Préfecture, he was convinced that he had a murder case on his hands; his colleagues ridiculed the idea. But that evening at seven o'clock, just as he was preparing to leave his office, he received an excited telephone call from Mlle Lacoste. 'Thank heavens you're still there. I've just seen him, in a china shop in the rue de Rivoli . . .'

Belin lost no time in joining her. She had, it seemed, been walking along the rue de Rivoli when she saw 'Fremyet' walking arm in arm with a young woman. She had followed him into a china shop, 'Lions de Faïence', and watched them choose a dinner service. He had paid a deposit and left his card. She had tried to follow them when they left the shop, but they had boarded a bus before she could reach them. Trying to jump on board, she had almost bumped into Fremyet, and he had looked straight into her eyes . . .

Belin's heart sank. Had he recognized her? If so, he may have already left his present lodgings. Belin hurried to the shop, and found that it had just closed. He obtained the manager's address from the night-watchman, and took a taxi there. It was out in the suburbs. The manager was unable to help him, but gave him the name of the assistant – he even offered to drive him there. The assistant was able to describe his customer – it was quite obviously Fremyet – but was unable to recall his name or address. Belin begged the manager and assistant to return with him to the shop. They searched for the invoice, and found it with the card attached. The man's name was Guillet, and his address was 76 rue de Rochechouart.

Belin had to tread delicately. He had no warrant for 'Guillet's' arrest; he had no proof that Guillet had been involved in any crime. Therefore he could not rush in and arrest him. Instead, Belin talked to the concierge, and was dismayed to learn that M. Guillet and his lady – a Mme Fernande Segret – had already left. They had not taken their belongings, but that meant nothing. If he knew he was being hunted, his quarry would lose no time in vanishing, preferably leaving no trace. Belin cursed his luck.

The next step was to get a warrant for Fremyet's arrest, in case he was traced. Then the house in rue Rochechouart was placed under round-the-clock surveillance. Since 'Fremyet' was given to advertising, he instituted a search of newspaper columns, looking for the name of Lucien Guillet. They soon found one – a M. Guillet had advertised a car for sale at Etampes.

Belin set about cultivating the concierge, and soon gained his confidence. Meanwhile, like Simenon's Maigret, he sat round in local bars and cafés, keeping his ears open. And while he was sitting over his glass of white wine one evening, the concierge hurried in and whispered frantically: 'He's back.'

Unfortunately, it was now after dark, and French law ordained that a search of a suspect's premises could not be conducted by night. So Belin stood outside Guillet's flat all night – at least the concierge allowed him into the building – and periodically placed his ear to the door. As the dawn broke, his colleague Inspector Riboulet tiptoed upstairs to join him.

At 9.30 he knocked on the door. There was no reply. Finally, a sleepy voice asked him what he wanted. Belin replied that he had come from Etampes about the car advertisement. The voice asked him to come back later. Belin said he couldn't. The key turned and the door opened a crack. Both men pushed it open, and grasped the small, dark-bearded man who stood there in his dressing-gown. He looked outraged. 'What is the meaning of this?' 'Police. We have a warrant for your arrest.' (Belin hoped the man would not ask to see it, for it was made out in the name of Fremyet, and Guillet could have thrown them out.) At the mention of police, there was a scream from the bedroom and a thud; the policemen followed Guillet through the door and saw a beautiful naked girl sprawled on the floor. They tactfully withdrew as Guillet comforted her and for a moment their eyes met. Neither was certain that Guillet was Fremyet and Dupont; this could all be a terrible mistake. But as Guillet prepared to leave, Belin began to experience a sense that all was well after all. Guillet was singing an aria from Massenet's *Manon:* 'Adieu notre petite table . . .', the air the lover sings before he is forced to abandon his mistress. It was not quite what one might expect from an innocent man who expected to clear up the misunderstanding in half and hour. And as Guillet left the lovely Fernande Segret, he kissed her long and tenderly, as if knowing that this was the last time.

As Guillet was being driven off to the Préfecture in charge of Riboulet and another policeman, Riboulet observed that he was cautiously trying to extract something from his pocket, obviously thinking of throwing it out of the open window. Riboulet seized his wrist and forced from the tightly clenched hand a small black notebook. 'I wonder why you were so anxious to get rid of this?' Riboulet asked as he slipped the book into his pocket.

Still in the flat in the rue Rochechouart, Belin was engaged in an illegal search (for he had no warrant). In an overcoat pocket, he came across an envelope addressed to 'Landru'. It aroused a flash of nostalgia, for he had once used that name himself when on a 'dirty weekend' with a mistress.

Back at the Préfecture, Belin glanced with interest at the small black notebook retrieved by Riboulet, and also at a smaller notebook found in Guillet's pocket. He glanced inside it, and saw two names that told him he had arrested the right suspect: they were Collomb and Buisson. But when asked about them, Guillet merely shrugged and said: 'I have nothing to say.' This man knew he was in a trap. He knew he would forfeit his head. His only hope was to refuse to admit anything, to leave it to the police to prove his guilt. Even at this early stage, Belin could sense this.

His next step was to search the files for a Landru. He found it without difficulty, and discovered to his delight that Landru was still wanted for a number of offences committed between 1913 and 1914. This was welcome news, for it meant he could hold Landru without a more up-to-date charge.

'Guillet' made no attempt to deny that he was Henri Desiré Landru, born in Paris in 1869; but when Belin mentioned murder, he shrugged and said that they would be unable to sustain that accusation.

Belin studied the black notebook. 'I see that on December 28, 1918, you bought a single and a return train ticket, costing 3.95 and 4.95 francs. I happen to knew that these are the fares from the Gare des Invalides to Houdan, the nearest station to Gambais. Why did you take a return for yourself and a single for your companion?'

Landru shrugged. 'It is too far back to remember.'

The police went on questioning him in relays. They had to admit to a certain grudging admiration for the man. He did not bluster or whine or plead; merely remained completely cool and detached. He behaved like a man who is quite sure that he can never be found guilty. That thought disturbed Belin.

He left another officer questioning Landru while he went through the papers he had taken from the flat. Among these was a rent receipt for a garage in Clichy. He went there and found that it was used as a storage place for all kinds of odds and ends – furniture; bedroom junk, women's underclothes, even false teeth. But in a corner there were documents that bore the names Buisson and Collomb, including marriage and birth certificates. They only confirmed what Belin knew: that these women were dead. The problem was to prove it – and, if possible, to discover the remains.

The following day, Landru was taken around the villa at Gambais. It was uncomfortable and badly furnished, hardly a 'love nest'. In one room there was a trunk with the intials 'C.L.'. Asked if it belonged to him, Landru said: 'Of course – C.L. stands for Charles Landru.'

'No. Your name is Henri Desiré Landru. This trunk belonged to Celestine Lacoste, or Madame Buisson – the label is from her home town of Bayonne. Where is she?'

Landru shrugged. 'I gave her a few hundred francs to get rid of her.'

'Where did she go?'

'I have no idea.'

And this continued to be Landru's answer to all questions about the list of names – ten of them – that appeared in his notebook. There were many others – amounting to nearly 300 – but these ten were names of women who had disappeared.

But all attempts to find bodies, or evidence of murder, were a failure. Various stains on mattresses, walls, clothes, were examined, but they proved not to be bloodstains. Ponds were drained or dragged, but nothing was found. The likeliest possibility was that Landru had burned his victims in a huge stove he had had installed at Gambais – Belin tried the experiment of burning a sheep's head, and it was consumed in a quarter of an hour. In the stove installed in his basement by H. H. Holmes, women's hair had been found in the chimney; in Landru's stove, the forensic experts could find nothing that suggested murder.

Belin began the long task of trying to trace the 283 women mentioned in Landru's notebook. Landru himself flatly declined to discuss any of them. But, little by little, Belin began to piece together Landru's career. From the little notebook *(carnet)* it seemed that Landru had decided to embark on a career of murder after his release in 1913. That was logical. Landru had tried his most ambitious swindle so far – absconding with Mme Izoret's dowry – and been caught because she had reported him to the police. If Mme Izoret had not been alive to report him, he might well have escaped . . . Now Landru was determined to continue to pursue his career of seduction combined with fraud – it was so much more enjoyable than mere fraud. It suited his romanticism, his vanity, and his intense sexual drive. So he continued to advertise for lonely widows. In 1914, he made the acquaintance of an attractive widow, Mme Jeanne Cuchet, who had a son of 17; she worked in a lingerie store. Landru introduced himself as Raymond Diard. In April 1914 they set up house together in the Paris suburb of Chantilly. Landru had introduced her to his two small daughters, but omitted to tell her that their mother Maria, whom he had married in 1893, was still alive; now, he claimed, he had sent the daughters to live with an aunt. He lost no time in transferring 5,000 francs of her money into his own account. Her relations instinctively disliked Landru. Endless delays in the marriage plans led her to storm out; Landru pursued her with love letters. Mme Cuchet asked her sister and brother-in-law to help smooth things over, and they went to the villa at Chantilly. It was empty; but in a box they found letters that revealed unmistakably that 'Diard' was a swindler and a seducer, as well as being already married. This should have been the end of the association. But Landru (she now knew this was his real name) presented himself at her door, told her he was unhappily married, and promised to get a divorce. Mme Cuchet and her son moved back to the villa in Chantilly. By the end of March 1915, both had vanished, and neighbours had noticed an unpleasant black smoke issuing from Landru's chimney. The local police were called; Landru protested he was merely burning rubbish, and asked the gendarme to return the next day when his wife would be home from visiting relatives. The next day he wrote to the police, explaining that he had been called away on urgent business, and would be in touch with them as soon as he returned. The matter was not pursued.

Landru had developed his basic method, and he now stuck to it. Victim number three was a Mme Laborde-Line, widow of a hotelier; she vanished about 26 June 1915, at his new villa at Vernouillet, only five days after she had moved in. Number four was a Mme Marie Guilli, who possessed 22,000 francs; she moved to Vernouillet in August; a few days later he was selling her bonds and furniture. Now he moved to Gambais, and there disposed of a 55-year-old widow named Mme Heon; she vanished in December. Anna Collomb, the cause of his ultimate downfall, already had a lover when she answered Landru's advertisement in May 1915; she moved to Gambais just after Christmas 1916, having presented Landru with most of her 8,000 francs. As usual, Landru bought a return ticket for himself and a single for her, saving 1 franc. In the *carnet,* Landru noted after her name: '4 o'clock'.

Victim number seven was a 19-year-old servant girl, Andrée Babelay, whom he picked up on a Metro platform when he noticed she was crying. She was poor and unemployed, so the motive was simply 'gallantry'. In two months he had tired of her, and on 29 March 1917, she accompanied him to Gambais on a one-way ticket. Victim number eight was Mme Celestine Buisson, whose sister's letter to the mayor of Gambais started the police enquiries; she died on 1 September, netting Landru a mere 1,000 francs. Next came Mme Barthélemey Louise Jaume, a highly religious woman whose demise in November 1917 brought Landru less than 2,000 francs. Number ten was a pretty divorcee named Anne-Marie Pascal who supplemented the income from her small dressmaker's business with prostitution. Like Andrée Babelay she was destitute, so Landru's motive must have been purely sexual. But the Pascal case offers one curious clue to Landru's method. After staying with him at Gambais, she rushed back to Paris, to pour out a strange story to her best friend. Landru had knelt at her feet and stared at her with such fixity that she had felt faint; she was unable to move, as though paralysed. She became unconscious, and rushed back to Paris the next morning. But a month later, on 4 April 1918, she went back, and this time failed to return. Landru wrote '17h.15' after her name.

The final victim was a Mlle Marchadier, another ex-prostitute who had run a small brothel and saved 8,000 francs. Landru offered to buy her furniture, and had to borrow the money from his wife. By

Christmas 1918, he was virtually destitute again, and persuaded her to sell her possessions and marry him. She moved to Gambais with her three dogs on 13 January 1919; on the following day, Landru paid several urgent debts. On the 18th, neighbours were disgusted by the stench of burning flesh issuing from the Villa Ermitage. The skeletons of the dogs were later found in the garden.

Ironically, Landru had by this time met the first woman whom he truly loved; Fernande Segret and a friend had been accosted by a 'funny old man' on a tramcar, and she agreed to meet him the next day. Soon she was living with him. And in April 1919, their idyll came to an end when Landru was arrested.

This was the story as it was gradually uncovered in court. The courtroom was always crowded with women, who found Landru fascinating; one day, when some of them were unable to find seats, Landru rose courteously in the dock and said: 'If one of you ladies would care to take my seat . . .' Yet the story that emerged was not of a demonic seducer but of a fool, a petty swindler who was permanently broke, and who made only about 3,000 francs per victim. Like so many mass murderers, he could have made far more at any honest occupation.

Landru's defence council, the fiery Corsican *maitre* de Moro-Giafferi, insisted that all the evidence against his client was entirely circumstantial, and he was undoubtedly correct. Many expected Landru to be acquitted, and if strictly legal rules had been applied, he might well have been. That he was, in fact, condemned to death may well have been due to his infuriating arrogance and cool disdain rather than to the evidence. There can be no doubt that if he had taken the precaution of destroying the *carnet*, the case against him would have collapsed. Fortunately, the *carnet* proved his guilt as certainly as 11 corpses would have done, and on 30 November 1921, he was sentenced to death.

The last act, on 25 February 1922, was described by a journalist named Webb Miller. Wearing a shirt from which the neck had been cut away, and a pair of cheap dark trousers, Landru was led out into the courtyard of the Versailles prison as the first streaks of dawn appeared in the sky. Since his condemnation, he had apparently lost interest in life, and spent hours gazing blankly at the ceiling.

On each side a gaoler held Landru by his arms, which were strapped behind him. They supported him and pulled him forward as fast as they could walk. His bare feet pattered on the cold cobblestones, and his knees seemed not be functioning. His face was pale and waxen, and as he caught sight of the ghastly machine, he went livid.

The two gaolers hastily pushed Landru face foremost against the upright board of the machine. It collapsed, and his body crumpled with it as they shoved him forward under the wooden block, which dropped down and clamped his neck beneath the suspended knife. In a split second the knife flicked down, and the head fell with a thud into a small basket. As an assistant lifted the hinged board and rolled the headless body into the big wicker basket, a hideous spurt of blood gushed out.

An attendant standing in front of the machine seized the basket containing the head, rolled it like a cabbage into a larger basket, and helped shove it hastily into a waiting van. The van doors slammed, and the horses were whipped into a gallop.

When Landru first appeared in the prison courtyard I had glanced at my wrist watch. Now I looked again. Only twenty six seconds had elapsed.

6

In France, the Landru case was the 'crime of the decade', just as the Brides in the Bath case had been in England a few years earlier. But then, the murderers of England and France were old-fashioned and conservative in their habits, and criminals in general behaved much as they had in the nineteenth century. One consequence was that the crime rate in both countries remained low. Across the Atlantic, it was quite different. Society was changing so fast that the criminals had to change with it. The big cities bred a new type of businessman and a new type of crook – in 1916, one ingenious swindler named Louis Enricht persuaded Henry Ford that he had invented a method of running an automobile on water instead of gasoline, and parted him from $10,000, then took another $100,000 from the inventor of the Maxim gun for the same 'discovery'; typically, Enricht stayed out of jail.

After the war, America made what was probably the greatest single mistake in its history and passed the Volstead Act outlawing alcohol; the result of Prohibition was an instant doubling of the crime rate, and it went on doubling every year or so. It enriched characters like Al Capone, Johnny Torrio and Dion O'Banion; by the time it was repealed in 1933, it was too late, and organized crime held America in a grip like an octopus. In any case, America was now in the throes of the great recession, and Capone and Torrio had been replaced as 'Public Enemy Number One' by men like John Dillinger, Baby Face Nelson, Clyde Barrow and Machine Gun Kelly. The latter, who specialized in bootlegging and kidnapping, liked to boast that he could write his name on the side of a barn in bullets.

Kidnapping was a relatively new crime; America's first case had occurred in July 1874, when four-year-old Charlie Ross was kidnapped from outside his home in Germantown, Philadelphia, and his father, a retired grocer, received a ransom demand for $20,000. But the ransom was never collected, and Charlie Ross was never recovered. In the December of that year, two burglars were shot down as they crept out of the home of a rich New York banker, and one of them gasped out a dying confession that he and his companion had kidnapped Charlie Ross. They were Joseph Douglass and William Mosher, and their corpses were later identified as the kidnappers by Charlie's brother; but Douglass had no time to say what they had done with Charlie before he died.

In the bootleg era, kidnapping became a major criminal undertaking; now most of the victims were rich businessmen. The gangsters realized that they were as easy to kidnap as a child, and that it aroused less public indignation. But the most horrific case of the 1920s concerned a child, 12-year-old Marian Parker, daughter of a Los Angeles banker; the $1,500 ransom demand was signed 'The Fox'. On 17 December 1927, Perry Parker took the money to a shadowy street; a masked man at the wheel of a car pointed a gun at him and demanded the money. When Parker asked where his daughter was, the man pointed to a child on the seat beside him; he took the money, and told Parker that he would let Marian out at the end of the street. The child proved to be dead, her hands and legs hacked off, her body' disembowelled, and the eyelids propped open with wire.

The following morning, a woman found a suitcase near the place where Marian had been left; it contained torn newspapers, towels, pieces of wire, and a writing pad, all soaked in blood. Laboratory examination established that the writing pad was the same one on which 'The Fox' had written his ransom demands, and fingerprints were found. The towels were traced to a nearby apartment building off Sunset Boulevard, and the manager thought that a tenant named Evans seemed to answer the description of the kidnapper. He had now left.

Milk bottles found in the apartment bore the same fingerprints as the notepaper, and laboratory analysis revealed spots of human blood on the bathroom floor; there were also traces of human flesh in the drain. A check with the criminal records revealed that the fingerprints were those of a young man jailed for forgery. His name was William Edward Hickman.

In Seattle a few days later, a haberdasher was struck by the strange, haunted eyes of a young man who came in to buy clothes, and offered a $20 bill in payment; he contacted the police, and discovered that the bill was one of those paid over in ransom. A garage attendant who had taken another of the ransom bills noted that the man was driving an olive-green Hudson. The car – a stolen one – was soon picked up, heading back towards Los Angeles, and Hickman was arrested. Psychiatric examination established that he was suffering from delusions and hearing voices; he had chosen Marian Parker because he believed that her father was responsible for his imprisonment for forgery. In spite of his obvious insanity, he was hanged on 4 February 1928.

Even without the $20 bills, Hickman would undoubtedly have been caught and convicted on the forensic evidence. In the most sensational kidnap case of the 1930s, forensic evidence was to play the crucial role in the conviction of the accused man.

March 1, 1932, was a rainy and windy day in Hopewell, New Jersey, and the family of the famous aviator Charles Lindbergh were all suffering from colds – which is why they had decided to delay their departure to the home of their in-laws by 24 hours. At 10 o'clock that evening, the nurse Betty Gow asked Ann Lindbergh if she had taken the baby from his cot. She said no, and they went to ask her husband if he had the baby. Then all three rushed up to the room where 19-month-old Charles jun. should have been asleep. On the windowsill was a note demanding $50,000 for the child's return.

There were few clues. Under the window the police found some smudged footprints; nearby there was a ladder in three sections and a chisel. The ladder, a crude home-made one, was broken where the top section joined the middle one. There were no fingerprints in the child's room.

The kidnapping caused a nation-wide sensation, and soon Hopewell was swarming with journalists – to Lindbergh's anger and embarrassment: he knew that the furore would make it more difficult for the kidnappers to make contact. Crooks all over the country had reason to curse the kidnappers as the police applied pressure. Meanwhile, the kidnappers were silent.

The note offered few clues. It had various spelling mistakes, like 'anyding' for 'anything', and a handwriting expert said that it had probably been written by a German with low educational qualifications. It was signed by two interlocking circles, one red, one blue.

A week after the kidnapping, a well-wisher named Dr John F. Condon sent a letter to his local newspaper in the Bronx offering $1,000 of his own money for the return of his child. The result was a letter addressed to Condon signed with two circles – a detail that had not been released to the public. It asked him to act as a go-between, and to place an advertisement reading 'Mony is Redy' when he was ready to hand it over.

Lindbergh was convinced by the evidence of the two circles; he instructed Condon to go ahead and place the advertisement. That evening, a man's deep voice spoke to Condon on the telephone – Condon could hear someone else speaking Italian in the background – and told him the gang would soon be in touch. A rendezvous was made at a cemetery; at the gates, a young man with a handkerchief over his face asked if Condon had brought the money; Condon said it was not yet ready. The man took fright and ran away; Condon caught up with him and assured him he could trust him. The man identified himself as 'John', and suddenly asked a strange question: 'Would I burn if the baby is dead?' Appalled, Condon asked: 'Is the baby dead?' The man assured him that the baby was alive, and said that he was now on a 'boad' (boat). As a token of good faith, he would send Condon the baby's sleeping suit. In fact, it arrived the following day, and the Lindberghs identified it as that of their son.

On 2 April 1932, Lindbergh himself accompanied Condon when he went to hand over the ransom money; he clearly heard the kidnapper's voice calling 'Hey, doctor!' But the baby was not returned. Lindbergh flew to look for a boat near Elizabeth Island, but failed to find it. And on 12 May, the decomposing body of a baby was found in a shallow grave in the woods near the Lindbergh home; he had been killed by a blow on the head – apparently on the night of the kidnapping.

The police investigation made no headway. The maid Betty Gow was widely suspected by the police of being an accomplice, but the Lindberghs had no doubt of her innocence. Suspicion transferred to another maid, Violet Sharpe, when she committed suicide with poison, but again there was no evidence.

Meanwhile, a wood technologist named Arthur Koehier was continuing his investigations into the ladder. He had written to Lindbergh offering to trace its wood, using the laboratory of the Forest Service in Wisconsin. Slivers of wood from the ladder had been sent to him for identification soon after the kidnapping. Now he spent four days studying the ladder microscopically, labelling every separate part. Three rails were of North Carolina yellow pine, four of Douglas fir, and ten of Ponderosa pine. The yellow pine rails contained nail holes, indicating that these pieces had been taken from elsewhere, and 'rail 16' had square nail holes, and differed from all the others in that it had obviously been planed down from something wider. The whole ladder was 'of poor workmanship', showing poor selection of wood and little skill in the use of tools. The microscope showed that the yellow pine rails had tiny grooves, which indicated that the lumber mill that had processed them had a defective knife in the planer. Koehler was aware that this was virtually a fingerprint; if he could find that planing machine, he would stand a good chance of finding what happened to this shipment of wood.

The investigation that followed has been called (in *The Trial of Richard Hauptmann)* 'one of the greatest feats of scientific detection of all time'. Koehier discovered that there were 1,598 lumber mills that handled yellow pine, and sent duplicated letters of enquiry to each of them. It took several months, but eventually he identified the mill as the Dorn Lumber Company in South Carolina. Between September 1929 and March 1932, they had shipped 47 car-loads of yellow pine to East Coast lumber yards; Koehler and Detective Lewis Bornmann spent 18 months visiting yard after yard, and finally had to admit defeat; most of them had long ago sold their consignments of yellow pine, and had no record of the customers. Yet for some reason, they decided to revisit the National Lumber and Millwork Company in the Bronx, and there found a wooden bin which had been constructed of some of the pine they were looking for, with its distinctive planing. Of course, that was no proof that the wood of the ladder had come from that particular lumber yard; it could have come from 29 others. But it was certainly a triumph of sheer persistence .

The ransom bills – which included 'gold certificates' which could be exchanged for gold – had all been marked (without Lindbergh's knowledge). Now banks were asked to look out for any of the bills, and in 1933 they began to turn up, mostly in New York, although some as far away as Chicago. This seemed to indicate that the kidnappers lived in

New York or thereabouts. In early September 1934, $10 gold certificates began to appear in northern New York and the Bronx. In May of that year, Roosevelt had abandoned the gold standard, and called in all gold certificates; but they continued to be accepted by bank – and, of course, shops.

On 15 September 1934, a dark-blue Dodge sedan drove into a garage in upper Manhattan, and the driver, who spoke with a German accent, paid for his fuel with a $10 gold certificate. Because these had ceased to be legal tender, the pump attendant noted the car's number on the back of the certificate. Four days later, a bank teller noticed that the certificate was part of the Lindbergh ransom money, and saw that it had a registration number on the back: 4U-13-41-NY. The police were informed. They quickly discovered that the vehicle was a dark-blue Dodge sedan belonging to Richard Bruno Hauptmann, a carpenter of 1279 East 222nd Street, the Bronx. It proved to be a small frame house, and that night, police surrounded it. The next morning, when a man stepped out of the door and drove off, police followed him and forced his car over to the kerb. Hauptmann, a lean, good-looking German in his mid-30s, made no resistance and was found to be unarmed. In his wallet, police found a $20 bill which proved to be from the ransom money. Concealed in his garage, they found a further hoard of Lindbergh money. Later, a further $860 of ransom money and a gun were found concealed in a plank in the garage.

The evidence seemed overwhelming – particularly when police discovered that Hauptmann bought his timber at the National Lumber Company in the Bronx located by Koehler and Bornmann. But Hauptmann protested his total innocence. The money, he explained, had been left in his care by a friend, Isidor Fisch, who had returned to Germany in December 1933, owing Hauptmann over $7,000, on a joint business deal. When Fisch had died of tuberculosis in March 1934, his friends in America – including Hauptmann – began looking into his business affairs, and realized that he had been a confidence trickster who had simply pocketed investments. Hauptmann and Fisch had been involved in a $20,000 deal in furs; now Hauptmann discovered that the warehouse did not even exist. In August 1934, said Hauptmann, he had noticed a shoe box which Fisch had given him for safe keeping before he left. It had been soaked by a leak, but proved to contain $14,600 in money and gold certificates. Feeling that at least half of it was his by right, Hauptmann dried it out and proceeded to spend it.

That was Hauptmann's story. It sounded too convenient to be true.

And when Hauptmann's trial opened in Flemington, New Jersey, on 2 January 1935, it was clear that no one believed it. But the most important piece of evidence was the ladder. Not only was there a clear possibility that some of its timber had been purchased at the Bronx yard where Hauptmann bought his timber, but one of the rungs (16) had been traced to Hauptmann's own attic: Detective Bornmann had noticed a missing board, and found what remained of it, with the 'rung' sawed out of it. The evidence could hardly have been more conclusive. Moreover, Condon's telephone number had been found pencilled on the back of a closet door in Hauptmann's house, together with the numbers of some bills.

It was true that there was nothing conclusive to connect Hauptmann with the kidnap itself. The footmarks found outside the child's bedroom window were not Hauptmann's size; none of Hauptmann's fingerprints were found on the ladder. But a man called Millard Whited, who lived near Lindbergh, identified Hauptmann as a man he had seen hanging around the Lindbergh home on two occasions. And Lindbergh himself declared in court that Hauptmann was the 'John' whose voice he had heard at the cemetery. All this, together with the ladder evidence, left the jury in no doubt whatsoever that Hauptmann was the kidnapper, and on 13 February 1935, he was sentenced to death. By October, the Court of Appeals had denied his appeal. But when the prison governor, Harold Hoffmann, interviewed Hauptmann in his cell in December, he emerged a puzzled man, feeling that Hauptmann's pleas of innocence rang true, and that the case deserved further investigation. The truth was that Hauptmann could easily have been 'framed'. Soon after her husband's arrest, Anna Hauptmann had made the supreme mistake of moving out of the house, leaving it empty for police and reporters to examine. It was after this that Bornmann had discovered the missing board in the attic. But was it likely that a carpenter, with plenty of wood at his disposal, would prise up a board in his attic and plane it down to size? Even the ladder itself gave rise to suspicion; as Koehier pointed out, it was crudely made, and showed poor judgement. But Hauptmann was a skilled carpenter . . .

For Lindbergh, Governor Hoffmann's attempts to prove Hauptmann innocent were the last straw. He was totally convinced that Hauptmann was guilty, and he felt that Hoffmann was seeking publicity. He and his wife sailed for England, and did not return for many years. He went to Germany, was impressed by Hitler's revolution, and became a frequent guest of the Nazis; later he tried hard to prevent America entering the war on the side of the British.

But Hoffmann's efforts were of no avail, and on 3 April 1936, Richard Hauptmann was finally electrocuted, still protesting his innocence.

Is it conceivable that Hauptmann was innocent? According to one investigator, Ludovic Kennedy, it is almost a certainty. In the early 1980s, Kennedy took the trouble to interview all witnesses who were still available, and to look closely into the evidence – that which was presented in court and that which was not. His book *The Airman and the Carpenter* (1985) makes one thing very clear; that if all this evidence *had* been presented in court, Hauptmann would have been acquitted. Hauptmann came to America as a stowaway in 1924; he had a minor police record for burglary during the black days of inflation. But in America he prospered; he and his wife worked hard, and by 1926 he was in a position to lend money and to buy a lunchroom; the day after the Wall Street crash he withdrew $2,800 from his account and began buying stocks and shares at rock bottom prices. Hauptmann had no need to kidnap the Lindbergh baby; by modern standards, he was very comfortably off in 1932.

Kennedy's investigations revealed that Hauptmann's story about his friend Isidor Fisch was true. Fisch *was* a confidence swindler; he and Hauptmann were in the fur business together, and Fisch *did* owe Hauptmann over $7,000. His swindles were uncovered only after his death in Leipzig in 1934.

Then how did Hauptmann – or Fisch come to be in possession of so much ransom money? The probable answer, Kennedy discovered, is that the Lindbergh ransom money was selling at a discount in New York's underworld – one convict bought some at 40 cents in the dollar. Nothing is more likely than that Fisch, with his underworld connections, bought a large quantity, and left it with Hauptmann when he sailed for Germany. Forensic examination of the money showed that it *had* been soaked and dried out, confirming Hauptmann's story that he had left it on a top shelf in a closet and forgotten about it.

But Kennedy's major discovery was that so much of the evidence against Hauptmann was fabricated. When arrested, he was asked to write out various sentences; the court was later told that Hauptmann's misspelling of various words had been exactly as in the ransom note. This was untrue; he had spelled correctly the first time, then been *told* to misspell various words – 'singature' for signature, 'were' for where, 'gut' for good. The court was also assured that handwriting experts had identified Hauptmann's writing as that of the ransom notes; Kennedy submitted the samples to two modern experts, who both said they were *not* written by the same man. Kennedy's investigation revealed that Millard Whited, the farmhand who identified Hauptmann as a man he had seen hanging around the Lindbergh property, had earlier flatly denied seeing anyone suspicious; he was later offered generous 'expenses', and changed his story. As to Lindbergh himself, he had been invited to sit quietly in a corner of the room in disguise when Hauptmann was brought in for questioning; he therefore knew him well when he identified him in court as 'John'. As to the writing in the closet, Kennedy established that it was made by a reporter, Tom Cassidy, who did it as a 'joke'. Hauptmann had no reason to write Condon's telephone number on the back of a door; he had no telephone, and in any case, the number was listed in the directory. The numbers of bills written on the door were not, in fact, those of Lindbergh ransom bills.

The most serious piece of evidence against Hauptmann was, of course, the ladder. This constituted the 'greatest feat of scientific detection of all time'. Examined closely, it is seen to be highly questionable. Koehier's efforts established that some of the yellow pine was sent to the Bronx timber yard, and it may have been from this consignment that the rungs of the ladder were made. But this was only one of thirty timber yards to which the same wood was sent; the man who made the ladder could have bought the wood at any of them. Hauptmann rightly pointed out in court that he was a skilled carpenter, and that the ladder was made by an amateur. If the jury registered this point, they may have felt that he had deliberately botched it to mislead investigators – for, after all, was there not the conclusive evidence of the sixteenth rung, whose wood was found in Hauptmann's attic?

But, as Kennedy points out, this plank was 'found' when Mrs Hauptmann had abandoned the house to the investigators. Was it likely that Hauptmann would go to the trouble of tearing up his attic floor, sawing out a piece of wood from the plank, then planing it down to size, when it would have been simpler to get another piece of wood? He was, after all, a professional carpenter. Kennedy quite clearly believes that rung 16 was concocted by Detective Bornmann or one of the other investigators – he refers to the whole story as 'Bornmann-in-Wonderland'.

So in retrospect, it seems clear that the 'greatest feat of scientific detection of all time' was based on false or suppressed evidence. The police firmly believed that Hauptmann was guilty, and they strengthened their case where necessary. Hauptmann may well have been guilty; but all the latest evidence points clearly to his innocence.

7

One result of the Lindbergh kidnapping was the 'Lindbergh law' enabling the FBI to enter a case if the victim had been taken across a state line; the death penalty was also introduced in certain cases. It made little difference. In June 1933, a gang led by bank robber Alvin ('Creepy') Karpis, and including two of the gangsters who had taken part in the St Valentine's Day Massacre, kidnapped a wealthy brewer named Hamm, of St Paul, Minnesota. They even took the precaution of having one of their men enrol in the local police force, in case treachery was attempted during the delivery of the ransom. Hamm was accosted outside his home and bundled into a car, driven by Karpis in chauffeur's uniform, then taken to the house of a postmaster in Bensenville, Illinois, where he was held. He was made to sign ransom notes demanding $100,000. When the police contact told the kidnappers that the police intended to hide a machine-gunner under the tarpaulin of the truck delivering the ransom, the instructions were changed. The $100,000 was duly collected, and sold to a dealer in 'hot money' for $95,000, which was then divided between the gang members. The gang got clean away. But Karpis was finally arrested by J. Edgar Hoover in 1936, and spent the next 33 years in jail; during his latter days, he became the friend and mentor of Charles Manson.

Thomas Thurmond, a Californian, was 24 years old when he decided to turn to crime; with a friend named John Holmes, he intercepted Brooke Hart, son of the owner of a department store, and drove him to the San Mateo-Hayward bridge across San Francisco Bay. Hart was then knocked unconscious, wired to a lump of concrete, and thrown into the bay. He woke up and began to scream; the kidnappers fired shots at him until he sank. That same evening – 9 November 1933 – Thurmond rang Hart's father, demanding a ransom of $40,000, and warning him not to call the police. Hart contacted the police immediately. When Thurmond rang up again on 15 November, his call was traced to a San Jose garage, and police arrested him while he was still arguing with Hart sen. about the pick-up point for the ransom.

When Brooke Hart's body was washed up nine days later, the enraged citizens of San Jose surrounded the jail – 15,000 of them. The police sprayed the mob with hoses and tear gas, but they battered down the gates. Holmes fought frenziedly for his life, and his eye was dangling from its socket when he was dragged out. Thurmond's cell seemed empty – until one of the searchers looked up and saw him hanging from the water pipes. Both men were lynched in the park. Governor Rolfe of California went on record saying that the lynch mob 'had proved the best lesson ever given to the country', and declaring that he would pardon any of them who were ever charged. No one ever was.

By 1933, Hoover had established what he called the 'kidnap line' – a direct line to his office, so that anyone in the United States could call him the moment a kidnap had occurred. This happened on Saturday 22 July 1933, and the call came from Oklahoma City. That evening, a millionaire named Charles F. Urschel had been sitting out on the porch of his home, playing an after-dinner game of bridge with his wife and two dinner guests, Mr and Mrs Walter Jarrett. Suddenly two men appeared on the porch, one carrying a sub-machine-gun. 'Which of you guys is Urschel?' When no one answered, the man said: 'OK, both you guys on your feet.' As the sound of the car died away, Mrs Urschel ran to the telephone and dialled the 'kidnap line' – a number that was familiar to most rich men in the country. A few hours later, as FBI agents were questioning the two women, Walter Jarrett walked in, looking exhausted. The gunman had halted ten miles outside town and taken their wallets; Urschel's visiting card had identified him. Jarrett had been ordered out, and had to walk back to town.

Four days later, a family friend received a ransom demand for $200,000, together with a letter from Urschel; Mrs Urschel was instructed to place an advertisement in the *Daily Oklahoman*, offering certain farm property for sale. She did so, and received instructions to send the courier with the money to Kansas City, where he was to check into a hotel and await further orders. In due course, the courier received a telephone call ordering him to walk west from the La Salle Hotel. There a man approached and told him that he would take the bag. The 'property deeds', he said, would be delivered within 12 hours. The next day, Charles Urschel returned home in a taxi.

For the investigators, Urschel proved to be a superb witness. He had paid minute attention to every waking moment of his captivity. In the car, his eyes had been taped, but the last thing he had seen before this was the power plant at Harrah. Through the open window – it was a hot night – he twice smelt the distinctive smell of freshly pumped oil and heard engines. He yawned and asked the time; one of his captors said it was 3.30.

The car halted, and he was made to get out and sit on the grass. Something bit his hand, and he caught an insect that was found in oil country. One of the men returned with a can of petrol, then they drove on for another hour. Dawn began to filter through the blindfold. The car stopped for a gate to be opened, then they drove into a garage or barn, where Urschel was transferred to another car; he smelt stable manure.

The drive continued for another 12 hours. Several times during the journey, it rained heavily. They pulled up for fuel at one point, and a woman with a shrill voice remarked that the rain was too late to save most of the crops, but might help the broom corn. When the car stopped again, he asked the time, and was told that it was 2.30. He was taken into a house, where he was handcuffed to a baby's high-chair and allowed to lie on a bed; a man and a woman talked, but one of his captors taped cotton wool over his ears. Then he was transferred to another house, about 20 minutes away, taken into a room with musty blankets on the floor, and left there. He could hear the sound of cows and guinea hens. He was given water in a handleless cup; it had a strong mineral taste, and came from a well on the north-west side of the house; when the bucket was drawn up, the windlass creaked.

He fell asleep, and when he woke up, he heard a plane overhead; he asked the time, and was told a quarter to ten. Later, he worked his blindfold loose enough to look at his watch. Later in the day, when another aeroplane passed over the house, it was 5.45. Thereafter, he noted the same aircraft at the same time every day, for eight days, except on Sunday. That day, there was a violent storm for most of the day. Later that day, he was told that his ransom had been paid, and he was free. The men drove him for hours to a town called Norman, gave him $10, and told him to catch a train home.

The investigators were delighted with this information. Urschel's observations indicated that he had been driven south, towards Texas. Reports from weather stations enabled them to check the route the kidnappers had taken. But the main clue was supplied by the aeroplane. Where in Texas was there a morning plane at 9.45, and an afternoon plane at 5.45? In 1933, there were not so many airfields. American Airlines had a flight from Fort Worth which left for Amarillo at 9.15 in the morning, and returned from Amarillo at 3.30 in the afternoon. At

9.45 and 5.45 the plane would be over a small town called Paradise, Texas.

An FBI team went to Paradise, posing as bankers willing to offer loans to local farmers, and toured the farms. At the farm of a man called R. G. Shannon, they found what they were looking for – the house with the creaking windlass to the north-west; when one of the 'bankers' mopped his brow and asked for a drink of water, it had a strong mineral taste.

Further checks on the weather confirmed that this was the right place. There *had* been a heavy rainstorm for most of the day on Sunday 30 July, so that the pilot had turned north to avoid it. Investigations into Shannon's background revealed that his stepdaughter was the wife of 'Machine Gun' Kelly, the bank robber, and that Shannon's son lived about a mile away – this sounded like the place where Urschel had been chained to a baby-chair. Urschel's description of the man who had handed him the $10 sounded like Machine Gun Kelly. Everything was falling into place.

At dawn on 12 August 1933, the police launched a raid and achieved complete surprise. Asleep in bed they found a gangster named Harvey Bailey, with a sub-machine-gun on the chair beside him. Urschel identified him as the man who had driven the car. Machine Gun Kelly's mother-in-law was among those arrested, and she mentioned that another gangster was involved in the kidnap plot, Albert L. Bates. Bates was later arrested in a brawl in Denver, Colorado, and found to be in possession of some of the kidnap money – whose numbers had been recorded. The home of Shannon's son Armon was also raided, and Urschel was able to see the baby-chair to which he had been handcuffed.

Eventually, 13 people were indicted for their parts in the kidnap plot, including a banker named Isadore Blumenfeld of Minneapolis, who was charged with 'laundering' the ransom money. (The indictment against him was dropped, but two of his men received five-year sentences.) But Kelly and his wife remained at large. When the trial began, Urschel received a threatening letter from Kelly, ending 'If the Shannons are convicted you can get another rich wife in hell, because that will be the only place you can use one.' Urschel ignored the threat and gave his crucial evidence. A week later, as the trial was still going on, newsboys outside shouted: 'Machine Gun Kelly captured!'

There was a curious story behind the arrest. In Memphis, Tennessee, a pretty 12-year-old girl named Geraldine Arnold confided to a playmate that she had some new parents; they had 'borrowed her' for the sake of appearances. The playmate talked to a friend whose father happened to be a policeman. Soon afterwards, the little girl was met by a friendly FBI agent who bought her candy and asked her questions about her new parents. Her answers convinced him that they were Machine Gun Kelly and his wife. There was a dawn raid on 26 September. Kelly heard the noise and threw open the bedroom door, a revolver in his hand; a policeman pointed a shotgun at his heart and said: 'Drop it Kelly.' Kelly remarked: 'I've been waiting for you all night.'

The version concocted by Hoover was that Kelly whined: 'Don't shoot, G-men', and that this is how the name 'G-men' originated. The local Memphis newspaper of the day shows that this is untrue. In fact, the term 'G-men' (meaning government agents) had been in use for some time.

Kelly and his wife received life imprisonment, and Kathryn Kelly was heard to murmur with disgust: 'In this court my Pekinese dog would have gotten a life sentence.' In fact, hers was well-deserved; it was she who had bullied the amiable but weak-willed Kelly into kidnapping Urschel, and she had tried hard to persuade him to kill the old man instead of allowing him to go free. Kelly's refusal cost him 20 years in Alcatraz, where he died of a heart attack in 1954; Kathryn Kelly was released in 1958.

8

There can be no doubt that detectives who have spent their lives hunting criminals finally develop an intuition that amounts to a 'sixth sense'. It was such an intuition that led Jean Belin, the man who arrested Landru, to the capture of his second mass murderer.

In 1937, the great International Exposition was held in Paris, and – like the Chicago World Fair, during which H. H. Holmes had flourished – it brought thousands of foreign visitors to the capital. One of these was a pretty American dance instructress named Jean de Koven, who was accompanied by her aunt, Mrs Ida Sackheim. It was in mid-August that Mrs Sackheim went to the police to report that her niece had vanished on 26 July. Two days before this, she had been sitting in the lounge of the Ambassador Hotel when she noticed a young man reading an English newspaper; when he put it down, she asked if she might look at it. The young man was handsome, and seemed to be rich; he called himself Bobby. Mrs Sackheim suspected that her niece had accepted an invitation to tea from Bobby, but she had no idea where this was to take place.

Belin, who was now the chief of the Mobile Brigade, sent his men enquiring after Bobby in the places where he had formerly been seen, but could find no trace of him. But two weeks after Jean de Koven's disappearance, her traveller's cheques were cashed by a young woman; the bank clerk had paid little attention to her, and could not say whether she was an American. Belin was inclined to believe that the charming Bobby was a confidence man, who had persuaded Jean de Koven to become his mistress for as long as her money lasted.

On 8 September 1937, the body of a private car hire driver was found near the Paris–Orléans road, shot in the back of the neck. He was Joseph Couffy, and his wife told the police that he had been hired by a man called Dushom to drive to the south of France via the Rhône valley. When Couffy had suggested taking a smaller car to save petrol, Dushom had said that he preferred comfort. The murderer had driven off in the car, and taken Couffy's money. Extensive police enquiries failed to find any trace of Dushom.

Five weeks later, a pedestrian in the rue des Graviers, in Neuilly, noticed that a car had been parked close to the cemetery for several days, and peered in through the window. In the back seat, he observed the naked body of a man, whose hands and wrists were tied. The victim proved to be a young businessman named Roger LeBlond, and he had also been shot in the back of the neck. It seemed that LeBlond wished to start a theatrical publicity agency, and had advertised for a 'sleeping partner' who would provide the money. A man named Pradier had come to see LeBlond at his apartment, and as they had left together, a servant had noticed that Pradier was returning his wallet to his pocket, and that LeBlond, who was accompanying him, looked well satisfied. It seemed that Pradier had driven to the cemetery with the young man, and had killed him – for what motive could not be ascertained.

Already, Belin noted the similarities between the three cases; a young man with a pleasant smile who seemed to have plenty of money But he refused to allow himself to speculate about whether 'Bobby', Dushom, and Pradier had all been the same man.

On 20 November 1937, the servant of an estate agent named Raymond Lesobre contacted the police to say that her employer had disappeared. All she could tell them was that Lesobre, who lived in St Cloud, had taken an English client to see a villa called Mon Plaisir, with a view to buying it. The police called at Mon Plaisir and found it locked. They forced an entry, and found Lesobre sprawled across the cellar steps, lying face downward, and shot in the back of the neck. This time the motive was clear: he had been robbed.

Now there was a massive manhunt for the killer who shot his victims in the back of the neck. The newspapers gave the case a great deal of publicity. Belin was aware that he could, in fact, be looking for two killers; LeBlond had been shot twice, with two different revolvers, and from different angles, suggesting a left-handed and a right-handed killer.

In frustration, Belin decided to look up some of his old underworld contacts, men who in the past had been willing to slip him titbits of information. But since he had been promoted to chief of the Mobile Brigade, these old contacts no longer trusted him; they excused themselves and hurried away. Meanwhile, the investigation was marking time. Belin's subordinates tried their own contacts in the Paris underworld, and also drew a blank. This was baffling. No one even seemed to be able to offer a suggestion about the identity of the killer. Could that be because he was an Englishman, in Paris for the Exposition? Jean de Koven's 'Bobby' had been reading an English newspaper; Lesobre had driven off with an 'Englishman'. Could that be why no one had heard of him?

One evening, Belin dropped into a bar near the Gare de l'Est to have a drink with a friend from early days, a policeman who was now in charge of that area. As they talked, two policemen who worked under Belin's friend came in. One of them, an Alsacien named Weber, was in an anxious mood. He explained that his nephew had not been seen for several days, and he was afraid that the young man had got himself into trouble. Belin asked why he thought so. Weber explained that his nephew, Fritz Frommer, had been in prison at Preugesheim, near Frankfurt, for his opposition to the Nazis, and that he had there made the acquaintance of a man named Siegfried Sauerbrey, who was in jail for robbery. When they were released, and returned to Paris, Fritz had continued to see Sauerbrey, although it was hardly appropriate for the nephew of a detective to mix with crooks.

Where does this Sauerbrey live? Belin wanted to know. Weber said that it was in a lonely house in the St Cloud forest . . .

Belin had one of his intuitive flashes. Lesobre, the dead estate agent, had lived in St Cloud. This Sauerbrey was a foreigner, just out of prison, and probably short of money. It was just possible . . .

'Do you have the address?'

'A villa called La Voulzie.'

Back at his office, Belin made some notes about the case. When he returned the next morning, it was to learn that his superiors had taken him off it, and assigned him to investigating some right-wing secret society, suspected of plotting a coup. But he handed the case to a subordinate, with a recommendation to investigate Sauerbrey at La Voulzie. On 8 December, two Sûreté plain-clothed men, Bourquin and Piognant, called at the villa, and found no one home. As they were calling a second time, a good-looking young man came out of a side street, playing with a dog. He asked the men if he could help them, and they told him they were from the rates office. Poignant had meanwhile taken out his wallet to offer his card, and then changed his mind; Bourquin could tell that the sharp-eyed young man had seen the inscription: Police. But he seemed perfectly at ease. Introducing himself as M. Karrer, he invited them inside. Bourquin now asked to see his papers, and Karrer reached casually into his pocket. A moment later, he was holding a gun, and his expression had changed to one of fury. 'Here are my papers, damn you!' The first bullet struck Poignant on the shoulder and knocked him onto the settee. Bourquin, who weighed 17 stone, grabbed hold of Karrer's wrist, but the man went on firing. One bullet grazed Bourquin's forehead, while another went through his hat. Karrer had now turned round in an effort to free himself, and was butting Bourquin with his backside. Bourquin saw a small hammer on the table, and hit the man with all his force. Karrer dropped to the carpet. He was quickly secured, and Bourquin telephoned the local police station. Inspector Poignant proved to be only slightly wounded, and helped Bourquin search the grounds. They soon noticed that the steps near the front door had been recently moved and replaced; when the police arrived, these were moved. Buried only a foot deep, the police found the body of Jean de Koven, fully clothed and even wearing gloves. Investigation of the cellar revealed the body of Weber's nephew Fritz Frommer. He had been shot in the back of the neck.

Back at the police station, the arrested man seemed as cool as Landru had been. With little prompting, he told Belin that his real name was Eugen Weidmann. Equally coolly, he admitted to murdering Jean de Koven – strangling her while she was drinking tea – Joseph Couffy, Roger LeBlond and Raymond Lesobre. In fact, the car in which

LeBlond's body had been found was the one stolen from Couffy; it had been repainted.

It gradually dawned upon Belin that he was talking to a psychopath; it was impossible otherwise to account for this absurd series of murders. Weidmann had been born in Frankfurt 28 years before, and had served his first term in reformatory for theft at the age of 14. His parents had sent him to Canada to make a fresh start – this is where he had learned his perfect English – but he was soon in jail again for theft. Back in Frankfurt, he had broken into a house and tied up two women; for this he had received a five-year sentence. It was during this sentence that he had met Fritz Frommer, who was a political prisoner. He had also met another two young Parisians named Roger Million – a slum boy – and Jean Blanc, son of a wealthy shopkeeper; they were serving time for currency fraud. Back in Paris, Weidmann, Million and Blanc had gone into partnership in crime. Their first project was to kidnap a wealthy American named Stein, and hold him for a $25,000 ransom. With money provided by Blanc, they rented the villa at St Cloud. But Stein became suspicious as Weidmann drove him back to St Cloud at 90 miles an hour, and insisted on getting out of the car.

After this came the murder of Jean de Koven; her traveller's cheques were cashed by Million's mistress, Colette Tricot. The murder of Couffy-also motivated by robbery – followed.

At this point in the questioning, Belin was interrupted by one of his subordinates. They had found a secret hiding-place in Weidmann's bedroom, and in it was a passport in the name of Jeannine Keller. Questioned about this, Weidmann admitted that she had been lured to Paris from Alsace with a promise of becoming a companion to an English girl who needed nursing. Weidmann had taken her for a walk in the woods near Fontainebleau and strangled her; then he and Million hid her body in a cave. (Weidmann led them to the cave, where the body was recovered.) The young man LeBlond had been shot by both Weidmann and Million, and according to Weidmann, Million had fired first. (Weidmann was the left-handed killer.)

Criminologically speaking, this is one of the most puzzling murder cases of the twentieth century. It seems clear that Weidmann fantasized about himself as a criminal genius and decided to form a gang consisting of men with whom he had been in prison; his aim was probably to dominate them entirely. (A curiously similar case had come to light in Stockholm the previous year, when a nerve specialist, Dr Sigward Thurnemann, had been exposed as the leader of a criminal gang whom he dominated by hypnosis and ordered to commit robberies and murders.*) In fact, Weidmann made so little from his six murders that it is tempting to look for some other motive. Was he, perhaps, a sadist like Peter Kürten, who derived sexual pleasure from strangling the woman and shooting men in the back of the neck? Unfortunately, there was no Professor Berg to study Weidmann as Kürten had been studied, so our knowledge is minimal. We know that Weidmann was bisexual, and that in the final year or so he had become entirely homosexual; this may explain why LeBlond was left naked. And it seem fairly certain that he tried to persuade Frommer to join the gang, and that Frommer was murdered when he refused. Otherwise, the case seems to belong to Locard's category of 'crimes sans cause'.

Weidmann was tried with his three companions – Million, Blanc and Colette Tricot. He and Million were sentenced to death; Blanc and Tricot were acquitted. Later, Million was reprieved, and it was Weidmann alone who went to the guillotine on 18 May 1939.

Belin was modest about the flash of intuition that led him to link the disappearance of Inspector Weber's nephew with the other murders. But it seems clear that, but for that inspired guess, Weidmann would have continued his strangely haphazard career of murder for a great deal longer. The psychopathic killer has always presented the greatest challenge to the craft of the manhunter.

9

Compared with California, the state of Oregon has a relatively low crime rate. But a case that occurred there in 1943 holds a unique place in the annals of crime detection.

On 21 June 1943, two fishermen discovered the body of a young girl, caught by the hair on a willow in the Willamette river; she proved to have died of drowning. But a bruise on her forehead suggested that she had been struck a blow which had knocked her unconscious, and had then been pushed into the river. The fact that one nylon stocking was missing, and the other dangling loose, indicated a sexual motive for the attack. This was confirmed by Dr Joseph Beeman, head of the Oregon State Crime Laboratory, who said that rape *had* been attempted – there were fragments of skin under the dead girl's nails – but not completed. Richard Layton, the police chief of Sweet Home, who was summoned

*See my *Criminal History of Mankind*, pp. 37–2.

by the fishermen, observed that the girl's hands were soft and well-manicured, and pointed out that she was probably from a comfortable middle-class home – a student rather than a farm girl. In which case, a report of her disappearance should not be long in reaching the police. What seemed strange is that her body had been in the icy water for about two weeks, and yet no missing person report had so far been filed.

Police Chief Layton was due to retire within a few days, so a team of investigators was sent from Portland; it was headed by Captain Walter Lansing of the Oregon State Police. Dr Beeman was able to tell Lansing that the girl had eaten a meal of beef soon before she died. When he returned to his laboratory, Beeman took the precaution of taking with him a sample of the girl's red-brown hair. Meanwhile, the corpse was moved to nearby Dallas, and newspaper publicity brought a stream of people to view it. And still no one was able to identify the pretty teenager. But as the body lay in the funeral parlour, Lansing observed two small marks on either side of the nose, indicating that she had worn glasses. A pair of glasses was placed on the dead face, and the girl photographed; but this still brought no identification.

The next problem was to try to find out where the girl had been killed. Captain Lansing and his assistant Sergeant C. D. Emahiser began to search both banks of the Willamette river further upstream. Five days later, they found a glade on the riverbank, littered with beer cans and debris which suggested that it was used as a drive-in for lovers. Here they found the girl's missing nylon stocking and a broken pair of rimless glasses. The fragments of glass were carefully gathered; they were hoping that an optician could determine their prescription, so it could be circulated to opticians.

The glade was painstakingly searched, but recent heavy rains had washed away tyre tracks or footprints. It ended in a steep drop to the river, and it seemed a fair assumption that the attacker had thrown the girl from there. As Sergeant Emahiser crawled among the pine needles, he found an unused bus ticket which had been issued on 7 June – two weeks before the body had been found. It would enable its holder to travel from Rickreall, a small town four miles east of Dallas, to Camp Adair, an army camp 20 miles to the south. Lansing contacted the Oregon Motor Stages Company, and had no difficulty in locating the man who had sold the ticket. He clearly recollected the girl, since she was friendly and talkative; she had mentioned that she was on her way to see a friend at Camp Adair. She had also mentioned that she had recently graduated from the high school at Independence, and was expecting to go to the University of Oregon in the fall.

The agent recollected something else. As they had been talking, a rancher named Ed Taylor had driven past, and recognized the girl; he was a friend, and offered to take her to Camp Adair. Since the ticket was already issued, it was too late to return her money; but the agent told her that if she mailed it to the bus company in Portland, they would give her a refund.

Lansing and Emahiser drove to the Independence high school. The students were on holiday, but the janitor was able to locate a copy of the school year-book. As soon as they turned to the senior class, they found the photograph of the girl who lay in the funeral parlour; her name was Ruth Hildebrand, and she was 17. School records also gave her home address on the outskirts of Dallas. Her mother, Martha Hildebrand, was badly shaken to learn that her daughter was the widely publicized 'sleeping beauty of Dallas' (as the newspapers had christened her). Ruth's father farmed near Camp Adair, and Ruth had gone off to see a schoolfriend at the army camp, saying that she would probably go on to visit her father. Mrs Hildebrand had assumed that this was where she was.

The next person to be questioned was the rancher Edgar Taylor. But all he could tell them was that he had driven Ruth Hildebrand to Camp Adair and dropped her there.

The two policemen drove to Camp Adair, and there talked to John Macdonald, an 18-year-old private. He was shattered to learn that Ruth was dead. But all he could tell them was that she had arrived at one o'clock on the afternoon of 7 June 1943, and left at 9.30 that evening; a few hours before she left, they had eaten a dinner of steak. When she left, she had not made up her mind whether to return home or to go to see her father – it depended upon whether a north- or south-bound bus was the first to arrive.

The girl's father verified what they had already guessed: that she had not gone there. And the bus driver whose vehicle had passed the camp at 10 o'clock that evening recognized her photograph as that of a girl he had taken back to Monmouth. The bus was not going all the way to Rickreall that day, but the girl had decided that she could catch a shuttle bus or take a taxi for the rest of the way.

If Ruth had caught a shuttle, she must have gone to the booking office. The ticket agent remembered her. She had been too late for the shuttle. But someone had offered her a lift home.

'Do you know who it was?'

'No. He was a big man with a moustache – about 30. He wore a sport shirt but no jacket. Ruth looked bothered when he first talked to her, but he pulled out his wallet and showed her something. Then she got into his car – it was a Ford or Chevrolet.'

The policemen called again on Ruth's mother and asked her if she knew anyone of that description. She shook her head. But she was quite certain that Ruth would never have accepted a lift from a stranger.

For the next few days, they questioned people throughout the area, asking if they knew a heavily built man who drove a Ford or Chevrolet; no one was able to help. Then one morning, as they sat eating breakfast in a Dallas café, Lansing suddenly gave an exclamation and pointed to an item in the *Portland Oregonian*.

'This had got be it. Richard Layton, former police chief of Sweet Home, has been given a six months sentence for attempted sexual assault on a cannery worker.'

Now, suddenly, the men knew what it was that the big man had shown to Ruth Hildebrand – it was his police identification card. That was why she had trusted a stranger.

The next stop was to interview the cannery worker who had been attacked; they obtained her name and address through the court that had sentenced Layton – it had been withheld in the news report. The girl told them she had accepted a lift on a hot day. Instead of taking her home, the driver had headed into the open country. The door had no handle, so it couldn't be opened from the inside. (In fact, both policemen had been in Layton's car when investigating the murder.) When he tried pulling off her clothes, she fought and scratched his face. In a fury, he went around to her side of the car and pulled her out. She clung to the seat, then let go, and he fell down. The girl jumped over a fence and ran into the woods. When she saw that the man was making no attempt to follow her, she crept back. As she expected, he turned his car and drove back the way he had come; as he passed, she was able to take down his licence number. That was why Richard Layton was now in jail.

Layton's car was towed to the Oregon State Crime Laboratory, and studied by Dr Joseph Beeman. His first interesting discovery was that the numbers on the engine block had been hammered out so they could not be read, but treatment with acid made them stand out. (Hammering the numbers would harden the metal, so it would become more resistant to acid than the metal around them, and would corrode less quickly.) The car proved to be one that had been stolen a year earlier.

With a small vacuum cleaner, Dr Beeman went over the car's interior. From the back of the front seat, it sucked up a chestnut hair. Beeman still had the hairs he had taken from Ruth Hildebrand's head. They proved to be identical with the hair found in the car.

In an identity parade, Layton was picked out by the ticket agent as the man who had offered Ruth Hildebrand a lift. When Layton was shown the matching photographs of the two hairs, he knew that denial was hopeless. He described how he had encountered the girl outside the bus depot, where he had gone hoping to make a pick-up. He had taken her to the glade by the river and tried to undress her. She fought back furiously, scratching his face. Layton only succeeded in stripping off one of her stockings. Then, as with the cannery worker, he had opened her door and pulled her out. She broke away and started to run – but made the mistake of running towards the river, where there was a six-foot drop. As she continued to fight back, Layton punched her in the face, breaking her glasses; she fell backwards into the river. It was in flood, and should have carried her down to the Columbia River and out to sea. But her hair caught in the branches of the willow tree several miles downstream. Ironically, it was close to the town of Sweet Home, and Layton was summoned to examine the corpse . . .

Richard Layton was found guilty of first degree murder; on 8 December 1944, he was executed in the gas chamber at Salem prison.

10

The crime rate always drops during wartime, for the obvious reason that most of the professional criminals are in the army. In England, it began its slow rise in 1946, as large numbers of ex-military personnel returned to the relative anticlimax of the drab post-war world. But this increase was confined mostly to cities such as London; in rural areas, serious crime remained a rarity.

On 23 June 1946, there was a violent exception in the peaceful city of Warwick. PC Arthur Collins was about to climb into bed after a late night shift when he heard the sound of breaking glass; it came from a warehouse on the other side of Theatre Street. He pulled on his boots, seized his truncheon, and hurried downstairs. His wife – who had been asleep – went to the open window to see what was happening.

In the moonlight she saw her husband being attacked by five men, and beaten to the ground. The sound of a police whistle was cut off as someone struck it from the constable's hand. Mrs Collins ran downstairs in her nightdress, and found her husband lying on the pavement, while a heavily built man leaned over him and struck him with his own truncheon. Mrs Collins grabbed him by the lapel and tried to pull him away; there was a sound of tearing cloth, and she was hit with the truncheon. Mrs Collins began to scream, and the attackers fled.

The police station was only 200 yards away, and her screams brought several policemen out to investigate; by the time they arrived, the men had gone. PC Collins was unconscious, and his pulse was so faint that it could hardly be detected.

The only clue was the piece of torn cloth. The following day it was shown to every tailor and clothing store in Warwick and Leamington. No one was able to identify it. Dustbins, rubbish tips and vacant lots were searched for the suit from which it had been torn, and after ten days, the Chief Constable of Warwick acknowledged that he needed the help of Scotland Yard.

The man who was sent was Detective Superintendent Robert Fabian, who was accompanied by his assistant, Detective Sergeant Arthur Veasey. The only clue the local police could offer was the piece of cloth. This proved to be most of a lapel, complete with buttonhole. Fabian had it photographed, and the pictures sent to every leading newspaper, with a request to publicize it. During all this time, Constable Collins still lay in hospital, and it seemed that the search might turn into a murder hunt at any moment.

Dozens of 'tips' poured in; few sounded promising. Police vehicles with loudspeakers toured the streets, asking locals to go and see if they recognized the cloth. Half-way through the afternoon, a bronzed man with a military moustache came in, glanced at the lapel, and said: 'I'm certain that's a bit of a demob suit.'

Fabian's heart sank. Demobilization suits had been handed out by the million. Yet this lapel had a distinctive pattern. Fabian and Veasey travelled to the nearest Ministry of Supply depot, which happened to be in Birmingham. There a Civil Servant produced a huge book of samples, and quickly matched the lapel. 'Pattern number DES 1012.' He turned to another file. 'Manufactured by Fox Brothers, Tone Dale Mills, Wellington, in Somerset.'

Fabian and Veasey drove overnight. The manager of Fox Brothers consulted his records, and told them that the pattern was made under contract for a Royal Ordance depot, and that 5,000 yards of the cloth had been woven. Most of this had been sent to Birmingham. But a small order of 900 yards had gone to a firm called Frazer Ross, in Glasgow.

Already, the case seemed hopeless. Many soldiers sold their demob suits to dealers waiting outside the gates, and they, in turn, sold them to cheap clothing stores. Nevertheless, Fabian went to call on the two Birmingham factories that had received the cloth. To his delight, neither of these had yet started to use their consignment. This left only the small order for Glasgow. Fabian and Veasey were on the next train. At the Frazer Ross factory, they spoke to the buyer. He told them that the cloth had already been made into suits, and took them into the workroom. There the supervisor studied the lapel and said: 'That's Mac's stitching.' He called: 'Mac, come here a moment.' A bent, elderly craftsman got up from his bench. 'Is that your stitching?'

Mac studied it and nodded. 'Aye, and there's nothin' amiss wi' it either.'

Fabian asked anxiously: 'I suppose you can't recall the suit it came from?' 'Aye. That lapel came from a suit specially made for a big man wi' a broad chest.'

The order book revealed that a suit had been made specially for a man who was six feet two and half inches tall, with a 45-inch chest. It had been ordered by the special-size department of the Central Ordnance Depot at Branston, Burton-on-Trent. A telephone call to the depot established that the suit had been despatched by registered mail on 10 January 1946 to Dominic Sutcliffe at an address in Birmingham.

By that evening, Fabian and Veasey were back in Birmingham and knocking on a door in a slum area. The big Irishman who opened it glared at them malevolently when they identified themselves as policemen. Fabian asked him what he had done with the demob suit despatched to him in January. Sutcliffe said he had sold it. When Fabian asked him who had bought it, he changed his mind and declared that he burned it. 'It was too small for me.'

Fabian shook his head. 'That can't be true. It was specially made to measure by a Scottish craftsman. I'd like you to accompany us to Warwick.'

Mrs Collins identified Sutcliffe as the man who had battered her husband to the ground – she had seen his face clearly in the moonlight. The four other men were soon tracked down, and stood beside him in the dock. Sutcliffe was sentenced to four years for grievous bodily harm, and the others to shorter terms. By that time – October 1946 – PC Collins was back on his feet, although still unable to resume his duties; Sutcliffe had only just escaped a murder charge.

11

Compared even with England, Japan had an exceptionally low crime rate; it seems typical that its Mafia – known as Yakuza – operate openly in buildings clearly labelled with their name, and that some citizens regard them as benefactors. When General Douglas MacArthur went to Japan in 1945 as the commander of the occupying forces, he expected to be received with hostility, perhaps with violence; instead, he was startled to be treated as a kind of father figure to whom the Japanese people owed respect and obedience.

This orderly and compliant aspect of the Japanese character is nowhere better illustrated than in the strange case of the poisoned teacups, whose solution, as we shall see, was also dependent on the typical Japanese virtues of efficiency and methodicalness.

At 3.20 on the afternoon of 26 January 1948, the Shinna-machi branch of Tokyo's Teikoku Bank was preparing to close its doors when a middle-aged man wearing an armband of the Welfare Department arrived and asked to see the manager. He was wearing a loose-fitting white cotton coat over a brown suit, and carrying a medical bag. The man's calling card was sent in to the manager, Takejiro Yoshida, and a moment later the Welfare official was ushered in. The card identified him as Dr Shigeru Matsui, and he explained that he had been sent from General MacArthur's headquarters, with orders to immunize the bank employees against an outbreak of amoebic dysentery.

In fact, Mr Yoshida was the acting manager that day because his superior had been stricken by a stomach ailment that morning, and had been forced to go home. He had also heard that one of the bank's customers was ill with dysentery. Therefore Mr Yoshida summoned the staff of the bank, and told them that they were all to be given medicine. At this point, Dr Matsui took over. Holding out an empty teacup, he explained that they would be required to take two drugs, one about a minute after the other. He then squirted liquid from a large syringe into each teacup, and handed out the teacups. At the command 'Dozo' (please), everyone raised his cup and drank. Many began to cough and complain that the liquid burned their throats. 'The second dose will make you feel better.' He refilled the syringe from a second bottle, and once again squirted liquid into the cups. Again, they all drank. Someone asked: 'May we gargle some water.' The doctor replied: 'Certainly'. But as they lined up at the water fountain, one female bank clerk collapsed. Then the accountant fell down. Within minutes, the entire bank staff was writhing on the ground. The doctor watched them calmly, then scooped up 164,400 yen in cash and a cheque for 17,405 yen – a total of about £350 or $600 – and walked out. It was an hour later that the alarm was given. By the time ambulances arrived, ten of the victims were dead; two died later. Only four people survived, including Mr Yoshida. When post-mortems were carried out, it was discovered that death was due to cyanide poisoning.

The totally ruthless nature of the crime indicated that the killer was completely self-centred, indifferent to the lives of others. And the fact that he was a middle-aged man suggested that he should already be a known criminal. Yet no known criminal seemed to fit the description. The survivors told Inspector Shigeki Horizaki, head of Tokyo's Homicide Squad, that the robber had a mole on his left cheek and a scar under his chin. That also failed to provide a lead. The most important clue seemed to be the calling card. In Japan, the exchange of calling cards is as common as a handshake. This card presented by the killer had belonged to a real Dr Shigeru Matsui, who lived in northern Honshu; but when Dr Matsui called at the Tokyo police headquarters, it was perfectly clear that he was not the wanted man. It followed that someone had used his calling card, and had probably given his own in exchange. Fortunately, Dr Matsui was a methodical man who filed all his cards. He recognized the card presented by the killer as one of a batch of 100, of which he had used 96, and taken 96 cards in exchange. The first task of the police was to interview every one of these persons.

Meanwhile, it was discovered that this was not the killer's first attempt. In the previous October, he had called at the Yasuda Bank in a Tokyo suburb and identified himself as Dr Matsui. And he had persuaded the employees to drink liquid from a teacup. No one had come to any harm, and the police suspected that this was intended as a dress rehearsal. But a week before the murders, he had called at the Nakai branch of the Mitsubishi Bank and handed over a card bearing the name 'Dr Jiro Yamaguchi' of the Welfare Ministry. When the manager asked to see more credentials, he had run away. Both cases had been reported to local police, but not to Tokyo's central police headquarters; the excuse was that, since no crime had been committed, it seemed unnecessary.

The day after the poisonings, the carelessness of a bank teller allowed the killer to escape again; he cashed the cheque for 17,405 yen at the Itabashi branch of the Yasuda bank by forging the endorsement.

One of the men assigned to the case was Sergeant Tamegoro Igii, who had been in the police force since before the war. Igii was something of an expert on calling cards – his colleagues even joked that he tried to foretell the future with them. He was among those whose task was to track down the 96 calling cards in Dr Matsui's file. Igii made a personal vow to track down the killer.

Among the cards in Dr Matsui's file was that of an artist called Sadamichi Hirasawa, who lived on Japan's northern island Hokkaido. His local police in Otaru had made a check on him, and reported that it was highly unlikely that he was the bank robber. He was a timid, gentlemanly sort of person in his 50s, and he had met Dr Matsui on the Hokkaido ferry. Matsui recollected that Hirasawa was carrying a picture which he was going to present to the Crown Prince. He had been impressed by Hirasawa's position in the art world, as it emerged from the artist's conversation. In fact, the investigators discovered that many critics regarded Hirasawa as second rate. And he had been twice under suspicion for arson – he had collected insurance after fires at his second home in Tokyo – but had so charmed the police that he had been allowed to go.

By April, the investigators had reached a standstill, and decided to study all the evidence a second time, in case they had missed something essential. Again Hirasawa was interviewed by his local police, and again they reported that their investigation had cleared him completely.

Igii was a persistent man. Although he and his colleagues had now interviewed almost 8,000 people, he decided to go back to the beginning. In June, he set out to interview all the possible suspects again. In due course, he came to Hirasawa's name. Apparently the artist had left Tokyo for Otaru because his parents were sick. Through the artist's brother, a dairyman, Igii arranged to meet Hirasawa. On their way to the house, he asked what Hirasawa was working on at present. The brother replied: 'Nothing'. But when he was ushered into the presence of the artist and his parents, Igii noticed that the sliding door into the next room was open, and that there was a painting on the easel and paint brushes nearby, as if they had just been laid down. Igii was observant enough to notice that both the canvas and the brushes seemed dry.

He concluded that Hirasawa wanted to give the impression of working hard.

Igii also noted that the parents seemed to be in the best of health, although Hirasawa had claimed they were both ill.

The first thing Igii noticed about Hirasawa was that he had a mole on his left cheek and a scar under his chin, and that he resembled the composite sketch that had been made of the bank robber. When he asked the artist what he had been doing on the day of the robbery, Hirasawa was able to offer an exceptionally full alibi. Igii pretended to be satisfied and took his leave. But a 'hunch' told him that this was the man he was seeking.

On his return journey, Igii invited the artist out for a meal. It was apparently a social call, and the two men treated one another with smiling Japanese courtesy. But when Igii asked Hirasawa for a photograph, the artist said he had none. That struck Igii as strange, and he insisted on taking a few snaps 'as souvenirs'.

When he asked about the meeting on the ferry between Hirasawa and Dr Matsui, Hirasawa remembered a detail that, if true, removed him from the list of suspects: he said that Dr Matsui had written his address on the back with a fountain pen. Igii asked if he could see the card; Hirasawa said that it had been stolen soon after when his wallet had been taken by a pickpocket.

One more thing made an impression on Igii; for an artist, Hirasawa seemed to have an unusually wide knowledge of chemicals .

Back in Tokyo, Igii checked with Dr Matsui about the writing on the back of the visiting card. Matsui denied it. 'In any case, I never carry a fountain pen.'

Igii felt certain that he had found his bank robber. He was therefore shattered by the news that his superiors had decided to suspend their enquiries into the case, which had apparently reached a dead end. Finally, they agreed to allow him to continue to work on his own, provided he did so discreetly. Igii even decided to mortgage his house to finance his investigation; fortunately, the police department came up with a small grant which would last for another ten weeks.

Igii interviewed Hirasawa's daughter and his wife. Now he discovered the interesting fact that, only two days before the bank robbery, Hirasawa had been unable to pay even the smallest bill, but that soon afterwards, he had given his wife nearly 70,000 yen (about $200). He also discovered that Hirasawa was keeping two mistresses, and that they were probably the recipients of the rest of the money.

Hirasawa suffered from a brain disease known as Korsakoff's syndrome, which involved amnesia relating to recent events; it was apparently the result of an anti-rabies injection. The disease had caused a deterioration in the artist's ability and a corresponding drop in income. But apparently he had told his family and mistresses that he had rich patrons and a large income – both statements being untrue. All this began to build up into a picture of a man driven into a corner by debt, who had decided to try and make a fortune with one desperate gamble. In fact, the robbery had brought only the equivalent of £350.

Igii's superiors agreed that there was now enough evidence to justify an arrest; on 20 August 1948, Igii journeyed to Otaru and charged Hirasawa with the Teikoku bank robbery. When the news got about, huge crowds waited at the railway stations to catch a glimpse of the suspected murderer of 12 people.

A search of Hirasawa's house revealed a brown suit and a loose-fitting white coat similar to those worn by the robber, as well as a leather case like a medical bag. Two of the survivors identified Hirasawa as the poisoner, although a third failed to recognize him.

Questioned about his income, Hirasawa told the story of rich patrons; but he was unable to name any of them. Asked about the money he had given his wife, Hirasawa claimed that he had received it from the sale of a painting to the president of a large industrial company the previous October; Igii, who had already checked this story, was able to state that the man had died in the previous August. Hirasawa looked shaken and admitted that he could not account for the discrepancy of his story.

Although the evidence against him seemed overwhelming, the artist continued to stick to his story, and to hint that Igii was 'framing' him. Many people believed in his innocence, and he began to accumulate a large number of supporters. In prison, he attempted suicide three times. After the third attempt, he confessed to being the bank murderer, declaring that the ghosts of the people he had killed were haunting him; he also asked to be executed with a dose of potassium cyanide. At his trial – which began in Tokyo on 10 December 1948 – his counsel insisted that the confession had been extracted from him under duress. But 15 months later, he was found guilty and sentenced to death. In fact, he was transferred to a prison cell to await execution, and remained there for the next 25 years, with many supporters attempting to obtain his release. Igii, who continued to have no doubt of Hirasawa's guilt, retired from the police force in 1964.

12

If Tamegoro Igii had an equivalent at Scotland Yard – a man who combined intuition with sheer persistence – it was Detective Superintendent John Capstick, known admiringly to the criminal fraternity as Charlie Artful. The Blackburn fingerprinting case (see p. 160) is an example of his persistence, but the case that best demonstrates the qualities that led to his nickname involved a double murder on a remote Welsh farm, and a killer who combined cunning and stupidity.

On 22 October 1953, the Carmarthen police received a report of the disappearance of a farmer and his wife. They were 63-year-old John Harries and his 54-year-old wife Phoebe; their farm, Derlwyn, was near the village of Llandinning. They had last been seen six days earlier, after attending a thanksgiving service for harvest; a neighbouring farmer, R. W. Morris, had walked home with them and gone in for a cup of tea. While he was there, a young man had also paid a call; he was Ronald Harries, the nephew of the couple, who worked on his father's farm near the same village. When Morris left, Ronald Harries was still talking to his uncle and aunt. But when a neighbour called at the farm the next morning, he found it deserted, the unmilked cattle lowing indignantly. He called again a fews hours later and found that the cattle had been milked, but the farm was still deserted. Meanwhile, Ronald Harries had been telling neighbours that his uncle and aunt had gone on holiday to London, and had asked him to look after the farm. It seemed strange that they had informed no one of their intention.

A local constable called at Derlwyn Farm, and there he discovered something that convinced him that John and Phoebe Harries had not gone to London: a joint in the oven, ready for cooking. No farmer's wife would waste a joint while she went on holiday, even if it had been a spur-of-the-moment decision.

Ronald Harries was questioned, and his story made the police even more suspicious. He claimed that he had driven his aunt and uncle into Carmarthen the previous Saturday to catch the London train. On the way, they had stopped at the Willow Café for tea, then gone to the station. But no one recalled seeing the trio, either at the café or at the station. Ronald Harries was now driving his uncle's car – although it had only third party insurance – and had transferred his uncle's cattle to his father's farm at Cadno, Pendine. The more the local police considered his story, the more suspicious they became. And the more they looked into the character and background of Harries – who was

£300 in debt – the more certain they became that he had murdered his uncle and aunt and concealed their bodies somewhere. But a careful search of both farms revealed no evidence of murder. When the Carmarthen police requested the assistance of Scotland Yard, Detective Superintendent John Capstick was sent down, together with his assistant Sergeant Bill Heddon.

Harries told Capstick the same story: that he had left his uncle talking to Farmer Morris – although Morris insisted that *he* had left first – and that the next morning he had driven them to the station, then returned to the farm to milk the cattle.

By this time, another damning piece of evidence had come to light: a cheque for £909, signed by John Harries and made out to Ronald Harries' father; this had been endorsed by Ronald Harries and paid into his own account. But John Harries had only £123 in his account; consequently the cheque 'bounced'. According to Ronald Harries, his uncle had handed him this cheque – to pay off debts – just before he caught the train on the 17th. Forensic examination of the cheque at the Home Office Laboratory showed that the original date had been 7 October, and that the digit had been added; the cheque itself had originally been for £9.0.9d. Here, then, was an obvious motive for murder. But where were the bodies?

Capstick searched Derlwyn Farm and the Cadno Farm owned by Harries' father. He was looking for newly disturbed earth, or the sinking that might indicate bodies; he found nothing. He asked local farmers to search their own fields for any such signs, and 300 of them combined their efforts, all to no avail. Local rumour had it that the bodies had been taken to the sinking sands at Pendine, where Ronald Harries lived with his wife and baby. If that was so, there was no hope of finding them, and no hope of arresting Ronald Harries for murder. The gravest charge on which he could be arrested was forgery. On a remote off-chance, Capstick used every available policeman and soldier to search a rocket site at Pendine, but again the results were negative.

Capstick was never one to be discouraged. He firmly dismissed from his mind the possibility that the bodies were in the sinking sands, and asked himself where else they might be. The obvious place was on the farm belonging to the missing couple – surely no murderer would want to transport the bodies farther than he had to? Ronald Harries *had* been at Derlwyn Farm when Morris left at 9.15. But at 10 o'clock he was due to collect his parents from friends. He had arrived half an hour late, claiming that he had towed a neighbour's car. The neighbour denied the towing incident. All this meant that Harries would have had time to take his aunt and uncle to his father's farm, murder them, then go and collect his parents.

Capstick decided that his only hope lay in persuading the murderer to show his hand. He and his sergeant were staying in a Carmarthen hotel, The Blue Boar, which was also jammed with reporters, so everything they did was under constant observation. But at three o'clock in the morning, he and his sergeant tiptoed downstairs, and slipped out of a window – by arrangement with the publican. They drove to Cadno Farm, and spent half an hour tying thin green thread across every gate. Then they turned on the car's headlights and started its engine. Dogs began to bark in the farmhouse. As they drove away, the policemen saw that a light had come on; it was in the room they knew to be used by Ronald Harries when he stayed with his parents. Early the next morning, Capstick hurried back to the farm and checked all the gates. Only one had its thread broken: the gate that led into a field of kale.

Once again Capstick enlisted the aid of the local police, all countrymen who were as familiar with the fields as with the streets of Carmarthen. A line of them walked slowly down the kale field, requested to report anything that struck them as unusual. Half-way down the field, a sergeant called to Capstick, and pointed out that the kale plants in front of him were slightly yellow in colour, and a few inches shorter than the rest; they looked as if they had been uprooted and replanted. Spades quickly uncovered the bodies of John and Phoebe Harries a few feet below the surface. Both had extensive injuries to the skull, suggesting blows from a hammer; John Harries also had a tear down his cheek, indicating that he had turned and fought before he was struck down.

Harries had so far been jauntily confident – one reporter described him as a 'bumptious, verbose, even jocular' young man. Now his demeanour was more subdued. When told he was being charged with murder, he merely repeated the story he had already told. But his clothes were sent to the laboratory for study, and on one jacket there were traces of human blood inside the sleeve – suggesting that it was the jacket he wore to strike the blows. On another, there was blood on the lapel and inside the lining; this was probably worn when, later that night, he buried the bodies and replanted the kale. A few days later, a careful search of Cadno Farm revealed a hammer hidden in a hedge –

a hammer that Harries had borrowed from a neighbour on the day of the murder, and later claimed that he had lost.

The trial was something of an anticlimax. Incredibly, Harries was convinced that he would be acquitted, and asked his parents to arrange a celebration party. The prosecution case was simple: that Ronald Harries had decided to solve the problem of his £300 bank overdraft – a large one for a farm labourer – by murdering his uncle and aunt. The idea had probably been suggested to him by the cheque made out to his father by John Harries ten days before the murder. On 16 October, he had gone to Derlwyn Farm with some story about his parents wanting to see his uncle and aunt. He had taken them to Cadno Farm, waited until their backs were turned, then struck them down with a hammer. The medical evidence – the size of the holes in the skulls – suggested that the hammer was the one found in the hedge.

Harries' line of defence was to make wild attacks on all the witnesses, declaring that one was guilty of rape, another was insane, another was in the habit of seducing maids. The real murderers, he said, had dumped the bodies inside his gate to put the blame on him. Yet in spite of the obvious absurdity of these accusations, he seemed genuinely shocked when the jury brought in a verdict of guilty. He continued to insist on his innocence to the moment he was hanged at Swansea jail on 28 April 1954.

10

The Soul of the Criminal

1

The biggest manhunt in New York's history began on 3 December 1956; on the previous evening, a bomb had exploded in the Brooklyn Paramount cinema, injuring seven people, one of them so badly that doctors spent the night trying to save his life. The man who planted it had been christened by the newspapers 'The Mad Bomber', and in the past 16 years he had planted 28 explosive devices in public places. Until the Brooklyn Paramount bomb, none of them had caused death, or even serious injury. But this was not because of any precaution on the bomber's part. In March 1951, a bomb had destroyed a telephone booth at Grand Central Station; anyone who had been making a call would have been blown to pieces. The same thing applied to a bomb that destroyed a telephone booth at the New York Public Library on Fifth Avenue a month later. During the next five years, there were explosions at the Radio City Music Hall, the Paramount Theatre, the Capitol Theatre, the Port Authority bus terminal, the Rockefeller Centre, and many other places, including the Consolidated Edison Plant on 19th Street.

To a Sherlock Holmes, the location of this latter might have presented a vital clue. For the first two bombs, both of them 'duds', had been planted at Consolidated Edison plants, the first in November 1940, the second nine years later. It was after this that the real epidemic of bombing began in 1951. But by 1956, these two earlier episodes had been forgotten.

The result of the Brooklyn cinema bomb, the first to involve serious injury, was a wave of panic, and a sudden drop in attendances at theatres, cinemas and museums. The police had few clues. On a few occasions, the Mad Bomber had tipped off the police by telephone, or by letters written in block capitals. But the voice was soft and anonymous, and the letters contained no fingerprints.

It was after the Brooklyn bomb that the editor of a New York newspaper, the *Journal-American,* decided to publish an open letter to the bomber. This appeared the day after Christmas 1956, and begged the bomber to give himself up, offering to give a full airing to his grievances. Two days later, a bomb was found in the Paramount Theatre, in an opening slashed in a seat; it was deactivated by a police bomb squad. Like the others, it was a home-made device consisting of a piece of piping with nuts at both ends. But on that same Friday afternoon, the *Journal-American* received a reply from the Mad Bomber. It was written in block capitals, and began:

> I read your paper of December 26 – placing myself in custody would be stupid – do not insult my intelligence – bring the Con Edison to justice – start working on Lehmann – Poletti – Andrews . . .

It was signed 'F.P.'

The men named were the former Governor of New York State, a former Lieutenant-Governor, and a former Industrial Commissioner. The bomber went on to promise a truce until mid-January, and to list 14 bombs he had planted in 1956, many of which had not so far been discovered. The police later found eight pipe-bombs, five dummies, but three still live and unexploded – the crude chemical detonating mechanism had failed to work.

Police Commissioner Stephen P. Kennedy asked the newspaper not to print the letter, in case it caused public panic; instead, the editor inserted an advertisement in the personal column:

> We received your letter. We appreciate truce. What were you deprived of? We want to hear your views and help you. We will keep our word. Contact us the same way as previously.

But other newspapers spotted the item, and the secret was out. The *Journal-American* decided to print most of the bomber's letter, together with yet another appeal.

The result was another letter from the bomber, promising a 'truce' until 1 March, and offering an important piece of information:

I was injured on a job at Consolidated Edison Plant – as a result I
am adjudged totally and permanently disabled. I did not receive
any aid of any kind from company – that I did not pay for myself
– while fighting for my life – section 28 came up.

Section 28 of the New York State Compensation Law limits the start
of any legal action to two years after the injury. The letter went on to
accuse the Edison company of blocking all his attempts to gain
compensation, and to criticize Lehmann, Poletti and Andrews for
ignoring his letters. Like the previous letter, this was signed 'F.P.'

Here, then, were clues that could lead to the bomber's identity. But
then, the Consolidated Edison company supplies New York with its
electric light, and has many power plants; if the bomber had been
injured before 1941 – the date of the first bomb – the chances were that
his records had been destroyed long ago or lost. The same problem
applied to Lehmann, Poletti and Andrews; they probably received a
hundred letters a day during their terms of office, and most of them
would have ended in the waste-paper basket. No politician files all his
crank letters.

The police decided on a curious expedient – to consult a psychiatrist
for his opinion on the bomber. This was the decision of Inspector
Howard F. Finney of the crime laboratory. The man he chose was Dr
James A. Brussel, who had been working for many years with the
criminally insane. Finney handed Brussel the file on the bomber,
together with the letters. Brussel studied the letters, and his first conclusion was that the bomber was not a native American; the letters
contained no Americanisms, while phrases like 'they will pay for their
dastardly deeds' suggested a member of the older generation.

The bomber, said Brussel, was obviously a paranoiac, a man far
gone in persecution mania. The paranoiac has allowed himself to
become locked into an inner world of hostility and resentment;
everyone is plotting against him and he trusts no one. But because he
is so close to the verge of insanity, he is careful, meticulous, highly
controlled – the block-capital letters were beautifully neat. Brussel's
experience of paranoia suggested that it most often develops in the
mid-30s. Since the first bomb was planted in 1940, this suggested that
he must now be in his mid-50s.

Brussel was a Freudian – like most psychiatrists of that period – and
he observed that the only letters that stood out from the others were the
W's, which were made up of two rounded U's, which looked like

breasts. From this Brussel deduced that the bomber was still a man with strong sex drives, and that he had probably had trouble with his mother. He also noted that the cinema bombs had been planted inside W-shaped slashes, and that these again had some sexual connotation. Brussel's final picture of the bomber was of a man in his 50s, Slavic in origin, neat and precise in his habits, who lived in some better part of New York with an elderly mother or female relative. He was – or had been – a good Catholic. He was of strong build. And finally, that he was the type who wore double-breasted suits. Some of these deductions were arrived at by study of the letters – the meticulousness, obsessive self-control – and others by a process of elimination: the bomber was not American, but the phrasing was not German, Italian or Spanish, so the likeliest alternative was a Slav. The majority of Slavs are Catholic, and the letters sometimes revealed a religious obsession . . .

Meanwhile, the *Journal-American* had printed a third appeal, this one promising that if the bomber gave further details of his grievances, the newspaper would do its best to reopen his case. This brought a typewritten reply that contained the requested details:

I was injured on September 5, 1931. There were over 12,000 danger signs in the plant, yet not even First Aid was available or rendered to me. I had to lay on cold concrete . . . Mr Reda and Mr Hooper wrote telling me that the $180 I got in sick benefits (that I was paying for) was ample for my illness.

Again, the signature was 'F.P.'

Now they had a date, all the clerical employees of the Consolidated Edison Company began searching the files. There was still no guarantee that a file dating back to 1931 would exist. But it was eventually located by a worker named Alice Kelly. The file concerned a man called George Metesky, born in 1904, who had been working as a generator wiper in 1931 at the Hell Gate power station of the United Electric and Power Company, later absorbed by Consolidated Edison. On 5 September 1931, Metesky had been caught in a boiler blowback and inhaled poisonous gases. These caused haemorrhages, and led to pneumonia and tuberculosis. He had been sent to Arizona to recuperate, but been forced to return to Waterbury – where he lived – because of lack of funds. He had received only $180 in sick benefits, and the file contained letters from the men called Reda and Hooper that he had mentioned . . .

The police lost no time in getting to Waterbury, taking a search warrant. The man who opened the door of the ramshackle four-storey house in an industrial area wore gold-framed glasses, and looked mildly at the policemen from a round, gentle face. He identified himself as George Metesky, and allowed the officers to come in. He lived in the 14-room house with two elderly half-sisters, May and Anna Milausky, daughters of his mother's previous marriage. On that matter, Brussel's 'guess' had been remarkably accurate.

A search of the house revealed nothing, but in the garage police found a workshop with a lathe, and a length of the pipe used in the bombs. In a bedroom there was a typewriter that would later be identified through forensic examination as the one that had written the letters. An hour later, at the police station, Metesky confessed that he was the 'Mad Bomber'. A photograph of him taken immediately after his arrest showed that, as Brussel had predicted, he wore a double-breasted suit. The initials 'F.P.' stood for 'fair play'.

Psychiatrists at Bellevue found Metesky to be insane and incapable of standing trial; he was committed to Matteawan State Hospital for the Criminally Insane, where he spent the remainder of his life.

2

The founding father of modern criminology – as noted earlier – was Cesare Lombroso, one of the most brilliant scientists of the nineteenth century. Born in Verona in 1835 into a Jewish family, Lombroso soon became an atheist and a materialist in reaction against the domination of the Catholic Church (Italy then being largely under the rule of the Catholic Austrians). After serving as an army surgeon in the war against the Austrians, he became Professor of Psychiatry at Pavia, as well as director of the lunatic asylum. He performed numerous dissections of the brains of madmen, hoping to establish some physical cause for insanity. This was unsuccessful, but in 1870 he was immensely excited when the German pathologist Rudolf Virchow announced that he had discovered certain 'atavistic' features in the skulls of criminals. Lombroso began studying criminals in Italian prisons, and was asked to perform the post-mortem of the body of the famous brigand Vilella. What he found seemed to confirm Virchow's observation: Vilella's brain had a depression in the place where the spine is normally found – a depression found in animals, particularly

fact, such 'alienated men' seldom turn to crime since, in spite of their alienation, their sense of fellow feeling is too strong. Yet the rise of the 'high IQ killer' since the 1960s – individuals like Ian Brady, Charles Manson and Ted Bundy – indicates that, in a civilization with a high level of technical achievement, 'alienation' becomes an increasingly important element in serious crime.

Goring's 'defective intelligence' theory certainly seems more convincing than Lombroso's cave-man theory, but it is open to a basic objection. When convicts in Sing Sing were tested, their average mental age was found to be 13, which appears to bear out Goring's theory. But when American soldiers were subjected to the same tests, their average mental age was found to be $13\frac{1}{2}$. And at the trial of the child-murderer John Thomas Straffen in 1952, Dr Alexander Leitch testified that, while Straffen's mental age was only $9\frac{1}{2}$, that of the average person is 15. And since only a tiny proportion of average people' are criminals, the defective intelligence theory has obvious drawbacks.

The connection between crime and sex received an interesting new emphasis in the researches of Professor Max Schlapp, a New York neuropathologist. One of his patients in the early 1920s was a wealthy woman who had a compulsion to steal handbags. Schlapp discovered that she had an abnormally high metabolic rate, and that her adrenal glands were hyperactive. Since these are closely associated with the sex glands, she was flooded with adrenalin whenever she began to menstruate. Under treatment with sedatives and gland extracts, her kleptomania vanished. Another patient, Arnold Anderson, was a member of a stable and religious family whose members were 'superior types', yet Anderson was a compulsive thief and burglar. Schlapp again discovered that he had overactive adrenals, which affected his sexuality. But Anderson grew tired of treatment and threw away his pills. In 1924, in the course of a burglary, he murdered a householder, and was sentenced to life imprisonment. Schlapp's book *The New Criminology* (1928) came at a time when enlightened prison governors were preaching reform of the harsh penal system. One of them, Thomas Mott Osborne, had actually got himself incarcerated in Auburn jail as a normal prisoner, and was horrified by what he found; as governor of Sing Sing, he instituted a humanitarian regime and an 'honour' system among the convicts which was immensely successful.

One of the most remarkable successes of this system came to light in the year *The New Criminology* appeared. One of the most violent and

ruthless criminals of the century, Carl Panzram, produced an autobiography which uncovered the motivations behind his life of robbery
and mass murder. Panzram had started life as an underprivileged child,
the son of a farmer who deserted his family, and he began committing
robberies as a kind of protest against his poverty. In prison he was
always violent and rebellious, and suffered endless beatings and
periods in solitary confinement – sometimes strung up by the hands
from the ceiling. There was nothing intelligent about his revolt; it was
motivated by resentment and sheer will-power. (Nietzsche would
certainly have admired him.) He was simply determined to continue to
fight back, and became one of the toughest trouble-makers the guards
had ever encountered. He burned down the prison workshop and
wrecked the kitchen with an axe. Then a new warden, Charles A.
Murphy, tried a new approach; he told Panzram that he would trust him
to walk out of the prison, and be back for supper-time. Panzram
promised – with every intention of breaking his word. Yet once
outside, he experienced a compulsion to keep his promise, and
returned. Murphy began to allow him increasing freedom – until one
night, Panzram got drunk and absconded. He was recaptured after a
gun battle and thrown into the punishment cell; Murphy's humanitarian
regime came to an end. Panzram realized that his own weakness was to
blame, and was plunged into an attitude of sullen defeatism. When he
escaped in the following year – 1918 – he began committing murders.
The motive was usually robbery and sex – he had acquired a taste for
sodomy in jail – but sometimes the crimes were motiveless, as when he
hired a canoe with six natives to take him on a trip in the Belgian
Congo, then shot them all in the back and threw them to the crocodiles.
Back in America he began raping and sodomizing boys – bringing the
number of his murders up to 20. Caught after a robbery, he was sent to
America's toughest prison, Dannemora, and the cycle of beating and
defiance began all over again.

At this point, a young Jewish guard, Henry Lesser, felt sorry for
Panzram, and after a particularly brutal bout of torture, sent him a
dollar by a 'trusty'. At first Panzram thought it was a joke; when he
realized it was a gesture of sympathy, his eyes filled with tears. He told
Lesser that if he would get him writing materials, he would write his
autobiography. The book, with its descriptions of rape and murder, was
far too horrifying to be published at the time; yet it revealed a man of
remarkable intelligence and honesty. As the book was shown to
American publishers and intellectuals, there was a movement to try to

get Panzram out of jail. He refused; he felt that he could never lose the habit of violence. Panzram finally murdered a guard, with the deliberate intention of getting himself sentenced to death; he succeeded, and was hanged in 1930, at the age of 38.

Perhaps one of the most significant episodes in Panzram's life was an occasion when Lesser went into his cell to check the bars, and turned his back on Panzram. Panzram was shocked: 'Don't ever do that again.' Lesser said: 'But you wouldn't harm me.' And Panzram replied: 'You're the one man I wouldn't want to kill. But I'm so erratic, I might do anything.' He was admitting that he had 'lost control'. He had become, in a sense, a wild animal – or rather, a part of him had become a wild animal that the human part could no longer control. This insight seems remarkably close to Lombroso's 'atavistic' theory, and makes us aware that Lombroso's basic intuition remains, in a sense, the foundation of all later criminology.

After the Second World War, criminological theories became increasingly 'liberal'. Dr Fredric Wertham, the man who had studied Albert Fish, wrote a number of influential books, including *Dark Legend* and *The Show of Violence*. *Dark Legend* is a study of an Italian boy, Gino, who murdered his mother with a breadknife, making an attempt to cut off her head. Wertham discovered that, after the death of the boy's father – when Gino was a child – the mother allowed the family to starve, and took a series of lovers. Wertham saw many parallels between Gino's crime and that of Orestes in Greek mythology, who murdered his mother because she had dishonoured his father. He also argues that Shakespeare is portraying the same symbolic situation in *Hamlet,* and that it is rooted in the child's incestuous desire for the mother. So Gino's crime becomes symbolic, like the Freudian Oedipus complex; in a sense, Gino is as much a victim as his mother. The same idea runs through *The Show of Violence* (1948) with its studies of murderers; these people are trapped in the tentacles of an invisible octopus. Like Lacassagne, Wertham feels that society gets the criminals it deserves, because 'in our society respect for human life is only a professed theoretical ideal'.

In 1961, another liberal American psychiatrist, Samuel Yochelson, decided to begin a programme of study of criminals in St Elizabeth's Hospital in Washington DC, starting out from 'the compassionate view that these people were the way they were because of deep-seated psychologic problems'. He worked with a younger colleague, Stanton E. Samenow. And the conclusions at which they began to arrive dismayed them both: that the central traits of the criminal personality were weakness, immaturity and self-delusion, mixed with a strong desire to deceive other people. Moreover, the rapists, murderers and child-molesters they studied seemed to have no *desire* to change; the moment they left the doctor's office, they went straight back to their previous criminal pattern. They had amazing skill in self-justification, and in appealing to the humanitarian sympathies of the doctors. They also had a 'shut-off mechanism' that enabled them to ignore or forget anything they preferred to ignore or forget; they might admit to something at one session, and then deny that they had ever said it at the next. They lacked self-discipline and were often cowards – for example, allowing their teeth to rot rather than face the pain of the dentist's drill. And 'the greatest fear of these criminals was that others would see some weakness in them'. They were hypersensitive to what was said to them and reacted very angrily when 'put down'. One of the few child-molesters who changed his pattern of behaviour did so 'because he applied choice, will and deterrence to a pattern that offended him' – in other words, because he suddenly developed the insight that his behaviour was simply the wrong way to achieve what he wanted to achieve. He was like a gambler who had adopted a 'system' that caused him to lose repeatedly, and who one day decided to abandon it and try another system.

Yochelson and Samenow recognized that what they wanted to achieve was something not unlike religious conversion: to activate a certain *insight* in the criminal, a desire to change himself. They realized, for example, that criminals were particularly susceptible to change when about to suffer a period of confinement for some offence, and when they were in a phase of inner conflict and self-disgust. Then they would be reminded that the three options open to a criminal are crime, suicide or change, and that it was up to them to choose.

Yochelson's view may be illustrated by an earlier case, that of Canada Blackie, described by Thomas Mott Osborne, the reforming governor of Sing Sing. Blackie was a bank robber, and his tendency to sudden violence alarmed the guards. After shooting a guard with a home-made gun, he was thrown into solitary confinement for a year and eight months, sleeping on the stone floor without covers. He contracted tuberculosis and went blind in one eye. Then he was placed in a normal cell, but still in solitary confinement, for several more years. When Canada Blackie heard about Osborne's reforms, he asked to see him. Then he drew out a tin containing a key to his cell, which he had filed, and a home-made knife. These he handed over to Osborne telling him: 'I want the Warden to know that he need have no further anxiety about me . . . I'm going straight.' Next day, Blackie was allowed out into the open air. Then he was made a 'trusty', and became assistant of the Mutual Welfare League, achieving immense popularity with the other prisoners because of his sufferings. When Osborne moved to Sing Sing, he took Blackie with him and gave him a comfortable bedroom overlooking the river instead of a cell. But Blackie was a sick man, and died in 1915, praying for three men who were to be electrocuted that day. What is clear is that Blackie's sufferings had made him ready to change, and that when the change came, it was basically a form of religious conversion. It all sounds like a story out of Dostoevsky's *House of the Dead,* and reminds us that that profound psychologist also understood that the springs of 'conversion' lie in man's recognition that he is free.

But perhaps the deepest insight into the criminal mentality was achieved by an American penologist named Dan MacDougald. MacDougald began, in fact, as a lawyer, and in the mid-1950s he was approached by farmers who wanted him to stop the Federal authorities in Georgia from overloading the Buford dam, which was flooding their land and drowning their cattle. Their case seemed so reasonable that MacDougald had no doubt it would be easily accomplished. To his astonishment, the authorities seemed literally deaf to his arguments, and it took three years and a cost of $46,000 to change things. Then one day, MacDougald heard of an experiment performed at Harvard by Dr Bernard Jouvet, and it seemed to throw a flood of light on the problem. Jouvet had connected a cat's aural nerve to an oscilloscope, so when a sharp click sounded in its ear, the oscilloscope registered the vibration. But if a jar with white mice was placed in front of the cat, it not only ignored the click, but the needle failed to move. This was preposterous, for even if the cat was too fascinated by the mice to hear the sound, it should nevertheless have travelled from its eardrum to the oscilloscope. The cat was somehow *cutting out* the sound at the eardrum, just as if it had put its paws over its ears. And this, MacDougald realized, was exactly what the Federal authorities had been doing. It struck MacDougald that this was also what criminals do. It was Yochelson's 'shut-off mechanism'. For example, when a swindler deliberately deceives someone, he keeps his human feelings in a separate compartment. To begin with, he may be two persons: a 'human being' with his wife and family, and a swindler with his dupes. But if he carries on long enough, he is bound to become less human with everyone. This is what H. H. Holmes meant when he said he had 'come to resemble the Evil One'.

According to MacDougald, the criminal is dominated by negative *attitudes* towards society; for example, he may feel that everyone is as dishonest as it suits them to be, that the basic law of life is 'Look after number one', and that society is a rat-race anyway. He literally *sees* things this way. He is blind and deaf to all things that contradict his negative view of existence. Dickens's Scrooge is an example of what MacDougald called 'negative blocking'. He has got himself into a state of general negativity and mistrust in which he has totally ceased to enjoy life. The three ghosts of Christmas cause him to *open up,* so he once again begins to appreciate life.

Now it is obvious that we are *all* in this condition, to some extent – for, as Wordsworth says, 'shades of the prison house' begin to close around us as we learn to 'cope' with the complexities of existence. So we are all in the position of the criminal. But criminals do it far more than most people – to such an extent that, when we read of a man like Holmes, we can suddenly *see* that he was an idiot to waste his own life and that of his victims. As strange as it sounds, studying criminality has much the same effect on most of us that the ghosts of Christmas had on Scrooge – of making us more widely aware of the reality we ignore. This is the ultimate justification of a book such as this.

MacDougald could see that his problem was to make criminals aware of their 'faulty blocking mechanisms', and cause them to 'open up'. If he could do this, they would cease to be criminals. MacDougald reasoned that the faulty blocking mechanism would become apparent if you studied the criminal's use of words, and got him to explain what he meant by certain words – such words as 'law', 'honesty', 'neighbour', 'love', 'self', and so on. The method he devised was basically Socratic: that is, the criminal was made to explain himself until he began to see where he was going wrong.

In 1967, Dr C. D. Warren, medical director of Georgia's maximum security prison near Reidesville, was told that he was going to be visited by MacDougald and another colleague from the 'Yonan Codex Foundation' – the name MacDougald had selected for his enterprise (he subsequently changed it to 'Emotional Maturity Instruction'), because they believed they had developed a method for rehabilitating 'hard-core psychopaths' in two or three months by 'specialized instruction'. Deeply sceptical to begin with, he was amazed by the success of the venture.

'Gentlemen, it worked. It worked so well it changed the attitudes of those ... in contact with the technique, and for the better ... You would not believe the results. In two weeks with the 22-man group, the constructive changes were impressive ... In eight weeks they had successfully rehabilitated 63 per cent of the men under instruction.' Moreover, the rehabilitated criminals became instructors to others, and showed the same rate of success. The 'unblocking' process had the effect of raising the subject's self-esteem, so he ceased to be a criminal – for MacDougald recognized that criminality is essentially an *undervaluation of oneself*. (We can see what he means in the case of Panzram, who hated himself as much as he hated everyone else, and whose self-hatred drove him virtually to suicide.) According to MacDougald, the New Testament invocation to love one's neighbour as much as oneself means that one *should* love oneself.

He gives an interesting example of what his method means in practice. One prisoner had come to hate another so much that he decided that, in order to live up to his code of honour, he had to kill him. He knew this meant life imprisonment, but he could see no alternative. So he stole a hacksaw blade from the prison workshop and fashioned himself a stiletto. But on the day he intended to use it, he attended one of MacDougald's sessions, and began to understand that his feeling that he had *no alternative* to murder was an example of what MacDougald meant by a faulty blocking mechanism. After the session, he saw his 'enemy' in the canteen, walked over to him, and offered to buy him a cup of coffee. The man looked astonished, but accepted, and the two became friends. The whole problem had dissolved away. In effect, he had seen his way out of the cul-de-sac that led Panzram to self-destruction.

The psychologist William Sheldon once remarked: 'To read Lombroso is to feel the strike of a powerful and dangerous game-fish. Lombroso hooked something of tremendous importance, but the tackle he had was insufficient to land it.' We can see that criminologists like Yochelson and MacDougald have begun to develop tackle that is strong enough to land it. We can also see that when MacDougald learned to diagnose the extent of a man's criminality from his 'word blindness', he was developing a technique that might also be as potentially useful as a lie-detector, and which could be compared with Dr Brussel's ability to form a clear picture of the Mad Bomber from his communications, or Dr David Canter's amazingly accurate assessment of the Railway Rapist from the crimes themselves – an assessment which actually led to the arrest of the rapist when Canter's 'portrait' was fed into the computer. This 'psychological dimension' is perhaps the most interesting development in crime detection in the second half of the twentieth century.

3

In November 1979, the New York police decided to ask the FBI for help in the case of a sex murder of a New York schoolteacher. On 12 October 1979, 26-year-old Francine Elveson, a graduate student at Fordham University, was on her way to work when she was accosted on the stairs of the apartment building – Pelham Parkway Houses, in the Bronx – and forced up to the roof at knifepoint. There she was stripped and raped, then strangled with the strap of her handbag. The police doctor discovered that she had been badly beaten about the face, and that her nipples had been cut off and placed on her chest. A pendant in the form of a Jewish good luck sign (Chai) was missing from around her neck, and her body had been spreadeagled in the form of the pendant. Her nylons had been tied around her wrists and ankles, and her knickers placed over her head. The ear-rings she had been wearing had been placed neatly and symmetrically on either side of her head. Her umbrella and a pen had been forced into her vagina, and a comb placed in her pubic hair. The words 'Fuck you' and 'You can't stop me' had been scrawled on her thighs and abdomen. There were clear teeth-marks on the victim's legs.

All the tenants of the building were interviewed, but there seemed to be no obvious clues, and after a few weeks, the investigation stalled; this was when it was referred to the FBI, who in turn referred it to their new 'psychological profiling team' at the FBI Academy in Quantico, Virginia. The team, consisting of nine men, was officially known as the Behavioural Science Unit, and its job was to try to apply the techniques originally developed by Dr James Brussel.

Agent John Douglas was able to make a number of immediate deductions from the scene-of-crime evidence. The ritualistic nature of the crime – the arrangement of the body in the form of a Chai, the neat arrangement of the ear-rings, the words scrawled on thighs and abdomen, the comb in the pubic hair – all these indicated a killer who was taking his time, and who was therefore relatively certain that he would not be disturbed. This in turn suggested that he knew the place well, and was therefore on his 'home territory'. So recommendation number one was: look for the killer in the building, or for someone who was thoroughly familiar with the building.

Douglas was also virtually certain that the killer was white. This was simply a matter of experience and statistics; in most mutilation murders, the victim is of the same race as the killer.

The face battering indicated to Douglas that the killer knew his victim. Again, this rule had emerged from a study of dozens of cases. The face of the stranger-victim is anonymous, so there is no point in battering it. But in the case of someone known to the killer, the same impulse that leads to the attack also leads to a desire to obliterate the *person;* the closer the relationship, the more violent the battering.

The killer's age, Douglas decided, was between 25 and the early 30s. Teenage killing tends to be violent and impulsive; this attack seemed measured and deliberate, a sign of an older man. Douglas ruled out the notion that the killer was a man in his late 30s or 40s, simply because such a man would probably be in prison. The urge to sexual attack manifests itself early – in some cases even before the rapist enters his teens – and when such men go on committing sex attacks, they usually get caught.

Douglas ventured another deduction based on experience: the killer would probably live alone; the crime had the characteristics of an alienated 'Outsider' type, not of someone integrated into a family. Moreover, the detailed nature of the ritual – the knickers covering the head, the umbrella in the vagina, and writing on the thigh – all indicated someone who fantasized a great deal about sex, and who therefore was an avid reader of pornography.

A clear picture was beginning to emerge – of someone who, assuming he was not actually a tenant, visited the building regularly, and often saw the schoolteacher; he had fantasized about attacking her for some time before doing so. He was also familiar with her movements, and had probably been waiting for her on the morning she was forced up to the roof.

Since the police had interviewed everyone in the area, it seemed fairly certain that they had already talked to the killer. Homicide detective Thomas Foley re-checked his list, and saw that the profile fitted an unemployed actor named Carmine Calabro, whose father had an apartment in the building. Calabro, who was 32, often visited his father, and must have known Francine Elveson. Foley had eliminated Calabro as a suspect because he had been in a mental hospital at the time of the murder. But further checks revealed that hospital security was lax enough to allow patients to come and go as they pleased. Calabro proved to be a high school dropout – as Douglas had predicted – and he shared a pornography collection with his father. Calabro was asked for his tooth-prints, and three dental experts testified that they matched those on the victim's legs. He was found guilty of the murder, and sentenced to 25 years in jail.

Douglas applied the same technique to a case involving the kidnapping and murder of a baby-sitter, Betty Shade, in Logan, Pennsylvania, in June 1979. Her mutilated body was found on a rubbish dump, and there was evidence that she had been raped after death. The injuries to her face convinced Douglas again that the killer knew the victim well, and had killed her in a fury of resentment; but the mutilations had been performed after death, suggesting that the killer was too frightened to inflict them while she was alive. This indicated a young and nervous killer. Yet the girl had been driven from her baby-sitting job to the dump in a car, requiring a degree of organization. The rape after death also suggested a killer who was taking his time. To Douglas, all this pointed unmistakably to two killers. Again, his 'profile' pointed the police in the right direction. The girl lived with her boyfriend, and it seemed unlikely that he would rape her after death, which is why he had originally been eliminated from the inquiry. But the boyfriend had an elder brother who owned a car. Both men were eventually convicted of the murder. The younger man had killed and mutilated her; the brother had raped her after death.

Such accuracy is the result of long experience. In the 1960s, 'psychological profiling' had been altogether more haphazard. Between June 1962 and January 1964, 13 women were strangled and raped in Boston, with the result that the killer became known as the Boston Strangler. The result was a police operation similar to that of the Jack the Ripper investigation in 1888, but far bigger. A psychiatric team which included Dr James Brussel was set up to try to create a 'profile' of the Strangler. Their conclusion was that there were two stranglers, one a man who lived alone and was probably a schoolteacher, one a homosexual with a hatred of women. On 4 January 1964, 19-year-old Mary Sullivan was strangled and raped; the killer bit her all over her body, masturbated on her face, and left her with a broom handle thrust into her vagina. But then, suddenly, the killings stopped. Rapes continued in the Boston area, but the rapist seemed to be a polite and gentle sort of person; he always apologized before he left, and if the woman seemed too distressed, even omitted the rape. The descriptions of this 'gentle rapist' reminded the police of an offender who had been jailed for two years in 1960. He had become known as 'the measuring man', because he talked his way into apartments, posing as an executive from a modelling agency, and persuaded young women to allow him to take their measurements. Occasionally he ventured a few indecent caresses. Some of the women allowed him to make love to them as a bribe – the modelling jobs, of course, never materialized. The 'measuring man' was a husky young ex-soldier named Albert DeSalvo, and he was sentenced for 'lewd and lascivious behaviour', as well as for attempted breaking and entry.

DeSalvo was identified by the rape victims, and sent to the Bridgewater mental institution for observation; there he was found to be schizophrenic and not competent to stand trial. Soon after his permanent committal to Bridgewater, DeSalvo confessed to a fellow patient that he was the Boston Strangler, and the patient informed his lawyer, who happened to be the controversial F. Lee Bailey. In taped interviews with Bailey, DeSalvo confessed in detail to the 13 murders in Boston; the police were at first inclined to be sceptical, but soon became convinced by DeSalvo's detailed knowledge of the crimes. As a result, DeSalvo was sentenced to life imprisonment; he had served only six years when he was found stabbed to death in his cell by a fellow prisoner who was never identified.

In fact, nothing about the 'psychological profile' corresponded to the real Albert DeSalvo. DeSalvo was not a homosexual, or a schoolteacher who lived alone; he was a married man with children. His real problem was hypersexuality – a sex drive so powerful that his wife complained that he often wanted intercourse six times a day. There was no Freudian hatred of his mother; on the contrary, he loved her deeply. His father had been a brutal man who ill-treated his mother – on one occasion he broke her fingers one by one – and who brought home prostitutes, with whom he had sex in front of the children. Albert DeSalvo had incestuous relations with his sisters. The DeSalvo home, like the Kürten home, was permeated with an overpowering atmosphere of sex. The real key to the Boston Strangler was not that he was a neurotic driven by a hatred of women, but a man who wanted sex with *every* woman he saw. Several of the murders should have given the investigators a clue, for the women were often raped more than once in a brief period. But then, when the police have dozens of possible suspects and hundreds of possible leads, it is often difficult to see the wood for the trees.

Even Brussel was hopelessly wrong about the Strangler. Misled by the fact that some of the victims had been elderly women, he theorized that the Strangler had an Oedipus complex, and was 'searching for his potency'. (We may note that the one part of Brussel's profile of the 'Mad Bomber' that was totally wrong was the Freudian part – W's shaped like breasts, etc.) In the early murders he had often assaulted the victims with bottles or broom handles – a confession of impotence. Then he had attacked a 20-year-old girl, Sophie Clark, and 'found his potency'. This was why the murders stopped; he was 'cured'. The simple truth was that, in spite of his manic sex drive, DeSalvo was basically a 'nice guy', and he later admitted that talking with his intended victims made it hard to go through with the killing. In the last case, Mary Sullivan, the girl had been so open and trusting that killing her produced a powerful revulsion; after that he went back to straight-forward rape. What seems to have misled Brussel – and all the other psychiatrists – about the Strangler was that his crimes seemed to be those of a madman; in fact, DeSalvo was not a psychotic, only a 'satyr', a man who can never get enough sex.

Fourteen years after the Strangler came the Son of Sam case. In July 1976, an unknown man began shooting couples in cars in the New York area, killing six and wounding seven. A letter addressed to the police captain in charge of the case declared 'I am the Son of Sam', and explained he liked to hunt women because they were 'tasty meat'. One year later, after shooting a courting couple in Brooklyn, the killer jumped into his car and drove away; but he had parked near a fire hydrant, and a policeman had stuck a parking ticket on his windscreen. A woman saw him drive off and reported the incident when she heard of the shootings – one victim died and the other was blinded – and the police checked on the four parking tickets that had been issued that night, and found that one of them bore the registration number of David Berkowitz, of Pine Street, Yonkers. Arrested three days later, Berkowitz proved to be a pudgy little man with a beaming smile, a paranoid schizophrenic who lived alone in a room lit by a naked light bulb, and slept on a bare mattress.

In the Berkowitz case, a team of 45 psychiatrists was assembled at Creedmore Hospital, but in a three-hour meeting all that emerged was that they all had their individual theories about the killer. But the final police theory was remarkably close to Berkowitz: describing him as neurotic, schizophrenic and paranoid, it continued: 'He is probably shy and odd, a loner, inept in establishing relationships, especially with women.' The major problem was that Berkowitz was not on any list of suspects, so a profile was of no practical value.

But the case made the police aware of the importance of learning as much as possible about such random killers. FBI agent Howard Teten, who taught a course in applied criminology at the Academy, seemed to have a natural talent for 'profiling' random killers, which he had been applying since the early 1970s. On one occasion, a Californian policeman had contacted him about a case in which a young woman had been stabbed to death by a frenzied killer. The frenzy suggested to Teten that the murderer was an inexperienced youth, and that this was probably his first crime, committed in a violently emotional state. And, as in the later case of the Bronx schoolteacher, Teten thought the evidence pointed to someone who lived close to the scene of the crime. He told the policeman that he should be looking for a teenager with acne, a loner, who would probably be feeling tremendous guilt and would be ready to confess. If they ran across such a person, the best approach would be just to look at him and say 'You know why I'm here'. In fact, the teenager who answered the door said: 'You got me' even before the policeman had time to speak.

With Teten as an adviser, the FBI Behavioural Science Unit was set up with a grant of $128,000 from the National Institute of Justice. It began by building a file of taped interviews with mass murderers and assassins, such as Charles Manson, Richard Speck – the killer of eight nurses in a Chicago hostel in 1966 – David Berkowitz, Sirhan Sirhan (assassin of Robert Kennedy) and the necrophile killer Ed Gein who ate parts of corpses from the local graveyard and made a waistcoat from the skin of one of them. It was a project that had been foreshadowed by Karl Berg's study of Peter Kürten in the early 1930s, but which, unfortunately, had never been folowed up. (I myself had been recommending such a study project since An Encyclopedia of Murder in 1960.) Now, with over 100 tapes of interviews with mass murderers and assassins, the FBI team began placing the similarities on computer. Some of this information could have been gathered from Berg's study of Kürten – for example, the discovery that when Son of Sam was unable to find a suitable victim, he went back to the scene of a previous murder and fantasized about it. They also discovered that Berkowitz, like the Yorkshire Ripper, thought that demons were urging him to kill.

The FBI's new insight into the mind of the killer and rapist began to pay dividends almost immediately. In 1979, a woman reported being raped in an east-coast city; the police realized that the *modus operandi* of the rapist was identical to that of seven other cases in the past two years. They approached the FBI unit with details of all the cases. The deliberation of the rapes seemed to indicate that the attacker was not a teenager or a man in his early 20s, but a man in his late 20s or early 30s. Other details indicated that he was divorced or separated from his wife, that he was a labourer whose education had not progressed beyond high school, that he had a poor self-image, and that he was probably a Peeping Tom. In all probability he had already been interviewed by police, since they had been questioning men wandering the streets in the early hours of the morning. This 'profile' led the police to shortlist 40 suspects living in the neighbourhood, and then gradually, using the profile, to narrow this list down to one. This man was arrested and found guilty of the rapes.

It soon became clear that psychological profiling could also help in the interrogation of suspects. The agency began a programme of instructing local policemen in interrogation techniques. Their value was soon demonstrated in a murder case of 1980. On 17 February the body of a girl was found in a dump area behind Daytona Beach Airport in Florida; she had been stabbed repeatedly, and the body was in a state of decomposition which indicated that she had been dead for a matter of weeks. The girl was fully dressed and panties and bra were apparently undisturbed; she had been partly covered with branches, and laid out neatly and ritualistically on her back, with her arms at her sides. The FBI team would immediately have said that this indicated a killer in his late 20s or early 30s. From missing persons reports, Detective Sergeant Paul Crowe identified her as Mary Carol Maher, a 20-year-old swimming star who had vanished at the end of January, more than two weeks previously. She had been in the habit of hitching lifts.

Towards the end of March, a local prostitute complained of being attacked by a customer who had picked her up in a red car. She had been high on drugs, so could not recollect the details of what caused the disagreement. Whatever it was, the man had pulled a knife and attacked her – one cut on her thigh required 27 stitches. She described her assailant as a heavily built man with glasses and a moustache, and the car as a red Gremlin with dark windows. She thought he had been a previous customer, and that he might live in or near the Derbyshire Apartments.

Near these apartments an investigating officer found a red Gremlin with dark windows; a check with the vehicle licensing department revealed that it was registered to a man called Gerald Stano. And the manager of the Derbyshire Apartments said that he used to have a tenant called Gerald Stano, who drove a red Gremlin with dark windows. A check revealed that Stano had a long record of arrests for attacking prostitutes, although no convictions; he apparently made a habit of picking up prostitutes who were hitch-hiking. A photograph of Stano was procured, and shown to the prostitute, who identified the man as her attacker.

It was at this point that Detective Crowe heard about the case, and reflected that Mary Carol Maher had also been in the habit of hitching lifts – she had been an athletic girl who was usually able to take care of herself. Crowe's observations at the crime scene told him that Mary Maher's killer had been a compulsively neat man; he was now curious to see Stano.

The suspect was located at an address in nearby Ormond Beach, and brought in for questioning. Crowe stood and watched as Stano was interrogated by a colleague, whom he had primed with certain questions. But his first encounter with Stano answered the question about compulsive neatness; Stano looked at him and told him that his moustache needed a little trimming on the right side.

What Crowe wanted to study was Stano's 'body language', which can be as revealing as a lie detector. And he soon discovered that Stano was an easy subject to 'read'. When telling the truth, he would pull his chair up to the desk or lean forward, rearranging the objects on the desk-top while talking. When lying, he would push back his chair and cross his legs, placing his left ankle on his right knee.

It was not difficult to get Stano to admit to the attack on the prostitute – he knew that she could identify him. Then Crowe took over, and explained that he was interested in the disappearance of Mary Carol Maher. He showed Stano the girl's photograph, and Stano immediately admitted to having given her a lift. 'She was with another girl', he said, pushing back his chair and placing his left ankle on his right knee. After more conversation – this time about the fact that Stano was an orphan – Crowe again asked what had happened with Mary Maher. Pushing his chair back and crossing his legs, Stano declared that he had driven her to a night-club called Fannie Farkel's – Crowe knew this was one of Mary's favourite haunts, a place frequented by the young set – but that she had not wanted to go in. Crowe knew that the truth was probably the opposite: Stano had not wanted to mix with a young crowd (he was 28). He asked Stano if he had tried to 'get inside her pants'. Stano pulled the chair up to the desk and growled 'Yeah'. 'But she didn't want to?' 'No!' Crowe recalled being told by Mary's mother that her daughter had, on one occasion, 'beaten the hell' out of two men who had tried to 'get fresh'. 'She could hit pretty hard, couldn't she?' 'You're goddam right she could', said Stano angrily. 'So you hit her?' Stano pushed back his chair and crossed his legs. 'No, I let her out. I haven't seen the bitch since.'

Crowe knew he now had the advantage. As he pressed Stano about the girl's resistance, it visibly revived the anger he had felt at the time. And when Crowe asked: 'You got pretty mad, didn't you?' Stano snorted: 'You're damn right I did. I got so goddam mad I stabbed her just as hard as I could.' Then he immediately pushed back his chair, crossed his legs, and withdrew his statement. But when Crowe pressed him to tell how he stabbed her, he pulled his chair forward again and described stabbing her back-handed in the chest, then, as she tried to scramble out of the door, slashing her thigh and stabbing her twice in the back – Crowe had already noted these injuries when he first examined the body. After this admission, Stano drove with Crowe to the dump behind the airport, and showed where he had hidden the body.

It was after Stano had signed a confession to killing Mary Carol Maher that one of Crowe's fellow detectives showed him a photograph of a missing black prostitute, Toni Van Haddocks, and asked: 'See if he knows anything about her.' When Crowe placed the photograph in front of Stano, Stano immediately sat back in his chair and placed his left ankle on his right knee. But he persisted in his denials of knowing the woman. Two weeks later, on 15 April 1980, a resident of Holly Hill, near Daytona Beach, found a skull in his back garden. Local policemen discovered the scene of the murder in a nearby wooded area – bones scattered around by animals. When Crowe went to visit the scene, he immediately noted that four low branches had been torn off pine trees surrounding the clearing, and recognized Stano's method.

Back at headquarters, he again showed Stano the photograph, asking: 'How often do you pick up black girls?' Stano pushed back his chair. 'I hate them bastards.' 'But you picked her up.' Stano stared at the photograph, his legs still crossed. 'That's the only one I ever picked up.' It was at this point that Crowe realized that he was talking to a multiple killer.

Stano persisted in denying that he had killed Toni Van Haddocks. Crowe stood up to leave the room. 'I know you did because you left your signature there.' Stano stared with amazement, then called Crowe back: 'Hey, wait. Did I really leave my name there?' Then, realizing that he had virtually admitted killing her, he went on to confess to the crime. But these two murders, he insisted, were the only ones he had ever committed.

Crowe did not believe him. Now he knew that Stano was a ritualistic killer, and that ritualistic killers often kill many times. There had been no more recent disappearances in Daytona Beach, so Crowe studied the missing persons files and records of past murders. He found many. In January 1976, the body of Nancy Heard, a hotel maid, had been discovered in Tomoka State Park, near Ormond Beach, where Stano lived. Reports said the death scene looked 'arranged'. She had last been seen alive hitch-hiking. Ramona Neal, an 18-year-old girl from Georgia, had been found in the same park in May 1976, her body concealed by branches. In Bradford County, 100 miles away, an unknown young woman was found concealed by tree branches, while in Titusville, to the south, another girl had been found under branches – a girl who had last been seen hitch-hiking on Atlantic Avenue in Daytona Beach.

When Stano had moved to Florida in 1973 – from New Jersey – he had lived in Stuart. A check with the Stuart police revealed that there had been several unsolved murders of girls there during the period of Stano's residence.

Stano's adoptive parents told Crowe that they had fostered Gerald Stano even after a New York child psychiatrist had labelled him 'unadoptable'. He had been taken away from his natural mother as a result of 'horrible neglect'. In all probability, Stano had never received even that minimum of affection in the first days of his life to form any kind of human bond. He had never shown any affection, and he had been compulsively dishonest from the beginning, stealing, cheating and lying. He preferred associating with younger children – a sign of low self-esteem – and preferred girls who were deformed or crippled – he had got a retarded girl pregnant once. He had married a compulsive over-eater, but the marriage quickly broke down.

Crowe traced Stano's wife, who was living with her parents in a house of spectacular untidiness – Crowe admitted that it reminded him of the home of the TV character Archie Bunker, who spends most of his time in his undervest. There Stano's ex-wife answered questions as she rested her huge breasts on the kitchen table. Stano's sexual demands had been normal, as was only to be expected 'with his itty-bitty penis'. But he *had* a peculiar habit of going out late at night, and returning, exhausted, in the early hours of the morning . . .

What had now emerged about Stano convinced Crowe of the need for more psychological 'profiling', and he called in an Ormond Beach psychologist, Dr Ann MacMillan, who had impressed police with her profile' of a mass killer called Carl Gregory (see p. 627). The result of tests on Stano revealed a psychological profile almost identical with those of Charles Manson and David Berkowitz; she believed that it meant that his crimes were virtually predictable – or, in other words, that he was one of Lombroso's 'born killers'.

Over many months, Crowe's interrogation of Stano continued. At some point, Stano realized that Crowe was 'reading' his physical 'signals', and changed them. But his compulsive nature made it inevitable that he developed new ones, and Crowe soon learned to read these. Eventually, Stano confessed to killing 34 women; then, typically, he declared that this had been a stratagem to make him appear insane. As with Peter Kürten, his memory of his crimes was remarkably detailed – for example, he was able to describe a prostitute whom he had picked up in Daytona Beach as wearing a brown leather jacket, brown shoes, and a shirt with an inscription: 'Do it in the dirt.' When he led them to the woman's skeleton – covered with branches – the police found that it was wearing precisely these clothes.

With plea-bargaining, Stano finally agreed to admit to six murders: Mary Maher, Toni Van Haddocks, Nancy Heard, Ramona Neal, Linda Hamilton, and an unidentified girl. On 2 September 1981, Stano was sentenced to three consecutive terms of 25 year – 75 years in all – and was taken to the Florida State prison. But a later trial resulted in a death sentence.

4

Lombroso may be regarded as the father of 'psychological profiling'. He noticed that when people tell lies, they often blush or lower their eyes. A good liar can disguise such reactions; even so, he becomes slightly more tense, so that blood pressure and pulse rate increase. And since doctors are able to detect blood pressure and pulse rate mechanically, should it not be possible to construct a machine that would detect lies? Lombroso designed a machine that would measure the pulse, and cause it to register as a line on a revolving drum; he called it the hydrosphygmograph. This consisted of a glass bulb filled with water, and the fist of the suspect, grasping a short rod, was sealed in by a rubber membrane. Pulsations of the heart visibly lowered and raised the water level in the bulb, and these fluctuations were transferred to a column of air in a graduated glass tube. Changes in the pulse rate could be clearly seen. An opportunity to try it out came when a thief named Bersone Pierre was arrested on a charge of robbing railway passengers of 20,000 francs. He was also found to be in possession of a passport belonging to a man named Torelli. Lombroso looked at Pierre and decided that he conformed to his 'criminal type'. He then connected him up to the machine and questioned him about the railway robbery. Pierre denied it, and his pulse remained steady. But when Lombroso questioned him about Torelli, the pulse revealed that Pierre was nervous. Lombroso reported that Pierre had nothing to do with the railway theft, but that he had almost certainly robbed the owner of the passport. The police later discovered both these assertions to be true.

It was at about this time (1905) that a young man named August Vollmer was appointed Town Marshall of Berkeley, in California; he was only 29 at the time, and the crooks dubbed him 'the boy marshall'. But, like Allan Pinkerton 40 years earlier, he proved to have a brilliant natural talent for detection and organization, as well as a bravery that made him widely respected. On one occasion, a call from Alameda told him that a murderer named Browne had escaped from the jail there, and was thought to be heading for Berkeley, where his father lived. Vollmer had the father's telephone tapped, and that night, Browne rang and arranged to meet him at the corner of 62nd Street and San Pablo Avenue at midnight. When Vollmer and some officers arrived, they saw that it was a well-lit spot. 'If I were a murderer I wouldn't wait here', said Vollmer, 'I'm going to take a look down that dark alley.' He had only walked a block when a man stepped out of the shadows and pointed a gun at him: 'Beat it quick, or I'll plug you.' Vollmer had his hands in his pockets, and he took the risk of walking straight towards the man. 'I just want to talk to you.' The man backed away. Then, as Vollmer came close, the man turned and ran. Vollmer pulled his gun, shouting 'Stop or I'll shoot.' Then, as the running man raised his gun, he pulled the trigger at the same moment the other fired. The man dropped, and the police came running up. Browne was dead, shot through the head. 'But I aimed at his legs' said Vollmer. An autopsy showed that Vollmer's bullet had gone through Browne's right leg, and that the bullet in his brain was from his own pistol.

Vollmer was the first man to introduce a signal system into police work. In the days before portable radios, there was no way of relaying messages to his men on the beat. Then he heard of a private detective in Los Angeles who had devised his own method of protecting a wealthy neighbourhood: to attach small telephone boxes to poles around the neighbourhood, each box being wired back to his own home. Vollmer went to see for himself, and accompanied the detective – a man named Foster – on his beat. A red light flashed, and Foster and Vollmer rode off on bicycles. Foster's wife had received a telephone call reporting a prowler. Within minutes, Foster and Vollmer had caught the prowler hiding in a large dustbin.

Vollmer was impressed, and decided to have similar red lights suspended at intersections throughout the town. His board of trustees vetoed the idea as too expensive – it would cost $25,000. Vollmer insisted on demanding a vote of all the citizens, and they supported him; the money was raised by a bond issue, and Vollmer now had a way of signalling to individual policemen to get to the nearest telephone and ring headquarters.

But Vollmer was not simply a good Chief of Police; he never ceased to ask *why* men became criminals. One of his best known remarks was: 'Attempting to make folks good by law is the height of imbecility. What we need is a study of the factors underlying delinquency rather than bigger, better laws.' This is why he created the first Crime Prevention Bureau, as well as the first Police School. And he kept Hans Gross's *Criminal Investigation* on his desk. It was when reading the chapter on liars in Gross's *Criminal Psychology* that Vollmer began to wonder whether it might not be possible to build a machine to detect lies. His curiosity finally led him to Lombroso's researches, and those of Lombroso's colleague Vittono Benussi. And in 1921, Vollmer read an article by William Marston, of Fordham University, in the Bronx, about his own researches into a lie detector. Marston and his colleague Father Walter Summers believed that the most significant thing about the liar is that his blood pressure rises, and they were working on a machine that would detect even small increases.

Vollmer sent for Sergeant John Larson, who happened to be a University of California graduate as well as a policeman, and explained the problem. Larson had already devised a better method of finger-printing. It took Larson some weeks to build his first model. It was a simple variation on the device doctors still use for testing blood pressure – an inflatable rubber tube wrapped around the arm where the pulse beats, and a needle that would register the pressure on a roll of paper. Vollmer was the first person on whom it was tried. Larson told him that he had to answer a simple yes or no to various questions, and began by asking if he had had lunch today. Vollmer said yes.

'Do you like to swim?'

'Yes.'

'Did you go to bed after midnight last night?'

'No.'

'Do you like roast beef?'

'No.'

'Do you like ice cream?'

'Yes.'

'Do you live on Bonita Street?'

'Yes.'

'Did you go to bed after midnight last night?'

'No.'

And at this point Vollmer could no longer contain his enthusiasm; he had been watching the needle tracing a line on the soot-blackened paper. 'It registered every time I lied – about not liking roast beef and about going to bed before midnight.'

Larson called his machine the cardio-pneumo-psychogram, but this ponderous label was soon dropped in favour of lie detector. Tramps were picked up in boxcars, and brought in for testing; the result was some confessions. Two youths were brought in for questioning regarding hold-ups on automobiles, and their nervousness soon convinced Larson that they were lying. Faced with this apparently omniscient machine, they broke down and admitted that they were members of a gang of eight, who had begun by frightening courting couples, and when they realized how easy it was, began robbing them at gunpoint. All eight were charged with a series of robberies.

The lie detector soon achieved wider publicity when it solved one of the most publicized cases of 1921. On the evening of 2 August, the house-keeper of Father Patrick E. Heslin answered an urgent knocking at the door of the priest's residence in Colma, just outside San Francisco, and found herself confronted by a man wearing motorists' goggles and a long overcoat with the collar turned up; his car was idling at the kerb behind him. The man explained that a friend had been badly injured in a motor accident, and that he wanted Father Heslin. The priest, a burly man of 60, lost no time in pulling on his own coat and clambering into the car. That was the last his housekeeper saw of him.

The housekeeper – Marie Wendel – decided to inform the archbishop, Edward J. Hanna. Soon after this telephone call, Hanna received a kidnap note demanding $6,500 for the return of Father Heslin. That afternoon, the newspaper headlines announced the kidnapping.

The note was partly handwritten, partly typewritten, and it declared that the priest was being held in a cellar. On the table there was a candle, and when this burned to the bottom, it would ignite a mass of chemicals that would fill the room with deadly poison gas. This candle would be lit when the kidnapper went to collect the ransom money, so there must be no attempt to trap him . . . A further message specifying the exact spot would be sent at nine o'clock that evening.

In fact, this letter never arrived; the kidnapper was obviously alarmed by the newspaper publicity. Mass searches were organized, but at the end of eight days, nothing had been found. A second ransom note reiterated the demand for $6,500, but again failed to specify how the money should be delivered.

On the afternoon of 10 August 1921, a reporter named George Lynn went to call on Archbishop Hanna, and as he waited for the door to be opened, a round-faced stranger walked up and stood beside him. A Filipino houseboy opened the door and asked them to come in and wait. And as the reporter and the stranger sat in the parlour, the stranger explained that his name was William A. Hightower, and that he thought he knew where the priest could be found. He had learned it via a prostitute named Dolly Mason, who had heard it from a client. A man who fries pancakes all the time was watching over him . . .

The reporter did not jump to the conclusion that Hightower was insane, for he knew that there was a vast billboard displaying just such a sign above Salada Beach. Further questioning elicited the explanation that Hightower had learned of a cache of bootleg liquor buried beneath the billboard, and had gone to dig it up; as he was digging, he had uncovered a black scarf, such as that which had been worn by the priest (according to the newspapers). So he was certain the priest would be buried there. 'And now', asked Hightower, 'do you think I'm eligible for the reward?'

A few hours later, policemen carrying shovels and lights accompanied Hightower to Salada Beach. The talkative Hightower had by now told them most of his life story – how he had once been a successful baker, but had gone bankrupt; how he had invented a machine-gun and a candied-fruit substitute . . . He was still talking as he pointed to the black scarf. 'Start digging there. . .' He seized a shovel and thrust it vigorously into the sand. 'Be careful', said Police Chief O'Brien, 'you might damage his face.' 'That's all right', said Hightower, 'I'm digging at his feet.' O'Brien stared at him. 'I thought you hadn't uncovered the body?' 'That's right' said Hightower, still digging. A moment later, one of the policemen said: 'I've found him.'

Father Heslin, it seemed, had been knocked unconscious by a tremendous blow which had crushed the back of his skull, then shot twice.

In the San Mateo county jail, Hightower stuck to his story that he had found the priest accidentally when looking for a cache of bootleg liquor. Nothing would shake his story, and he was obviously more interested in the reward than in answering questions. Chief O'Brien remembered Vollmer's lie detector, and telephoned the Berkeley headquarters. Within an hour, John Larson was on his way over with his lie detector.

Hightower submitted cheerfully to being attached to the machine. Then Larson began to question him about his story of the bootleg liquor. Again and again, the needle leapt upward, indicating a rise in systolic blood pressure. And Hightower, who could see this, began to look less euphoric. When the test was over, Larson was able to tell O'Brien with confidence that Hightower had murdered the priest.

Hightower's guilt was confirmed by other evidence. Handwriting experts said that his block-printing was identical with that of the kidnap note, while a typewriter in his hotel room matched the typed part.

Hightower was found guilty, but sentenced only to life imprisonment – probably because both judge and jury had strong doubts about his sanity. He spent the rest of his life in jail, where his megalomania flourished, and died in the early 1960s.

Another young recruit to the Berkeley police force, Leonarde Keeler, built a portable lie detector in 1923. This quickly proved its value when a girl in a sorority house was accused of thieving. She denied it, and Keeler's portable lie detector established that she was telling the truth. He tried it on all the other girls, and eliminated them from the inquiry. Then, in order to be thorough, he tested the woman who ran the place; the needle immediately began to jump wildly; the woman became increasingly confused, and finally confessed.

In 1926, Keeler decided to try a new idea. His machine already registered blood pressure, pulse and breathing rate; he decided to add a device for measuring skin resistance to electricity. The theory was that when a suspect lies, his pores exude tiny quantities of sweat, and his skin resistance drops. This proved to be the best idea so far, and the basic principle of the modern polygraph was established.

In 1930, a young recruit named Albert Riedel joined the Berkeley force, and became fascinated by the lie detector. Riedel soon realized the machine was far from foolproof. To begin with, a tired suspect would often cease to react when he told a lie; he had used up all his adrenalin. Riedel made it a rule never to question a suspect for more than three minutes without allowing him a break. He also realized that other kinds of tension – such as heat or the sound of a telephone – could confuse the issue, so he always insisted that a suspect should be questioned in a comfortable, well-lit, well-ventilated room, with no telephone and no one allowed to enter. He learned the importance of getting to know about the suspect's background and social standing, for these could offer important clues on how he should be handled. It was also of vital importance that a question should be quite unambiguous. Finally, Riedel made a habit of mixing relevant and irrelevant questions, so he could note the difference in response. His technique was taught at the Berkeley Police School, and finally became the standard method all over the world.

There were, nevertheless, still problems. A madman who was asked whether he was Napoleon said no, and the machine registered a lie. Clearly, the mind could influence the reading. And in 1935, a widely publicized murder caused a loss of confidence in the efficiency of the lie detector. On 17 June, the body of a girl was found in a ditch in the cemetery of Peoria, Illinois. She was identified as 19-year-old Mildred Hallmark, and her neck had been broken in the course of violent strangulation; lying near the body was underwear that had been cut off with a pair of scissors. As a result of newspaper publicity, 25 girls came forward to say that they had been raped by a man who was young, good-looking, and very strong.

Five days after the murder, another girl came to the police head-quarters with the same story. She had been waiting for a bus when a charming and clean-cut young man offered her a lift; he seemed so polite that she felt sure she could trust him. He chatted as they drove along, and he said that his name was Lee Bridges. But in a quiet lane, he stopped and grabbed her. She fought back and he hit her under the jaw again and again, holding her neck with the other hand; finally, when she was stunned and submissive, he raped her, cutting off her clothes with scissors. Sobbing, she told him that she would go to the police as soon as he released her; at this, Bridges dragged her in front of the car, threw her down on the road, turned on the headlights, and took photographs of her with a box camera. He told her that if she reported the rape, he would send copies to her friends and neighbours. Then he allowed her to dress in her torn clothes, and dropped her off a block from her home.

This was six months ago, and she had never reported the rape. But two months later, at a dance, she had been introduced to a man who looked just like the rapist. When she asked him if they had met before, he denied it, and gave his name as Jerry Thompson, and said that he lived with his grandparents in East Peoria. But the girl was sure he was the rapist. And now she had decided to come to the police.

The police called on Mildred Hallmark's father, who worked in a caterpillar tractor factory, and asked him if he knew a Lee Bridges or Jerry Thompson. 'Oh sure I know Jerry – I work next to him.' They asked him if Mildred also knew him. 'Yes, he used to live a couple of blocks away.'

The police lost no time in interviewing Gerald Thompson, a handsome, curly-haired man of 25. He flatly denied the rapes, even when the girl picked him out unhesitatingly in a line-up. Asked if he would take a polygraph test, Thompson agreed readily. Fred Imbau, the lie detector expert, wired him up to his machine. Asked if he had killed Mildred, Thompson replied 'No', and the needle remained steady, indicating that he was telling the truth.

But a search of the house where Thompson lived with his grandparents left no doubt of his guilt. The police not only found the photographs of naked girls that proved he was the Peoria rapist; they also found a bloodstained car cushion and bloodstained trousers. Tested in the laboratory, they proved to be of the same blood type as Mildred Hallmark. Faced with this evidence, Thompson finally confessed. He had offered Mildred a lift, and she had accepted because she knew him. When he took her to the cemetery where he had taken so many previous victims, she fought savagely, scratching his face – scratches he still bore when questioned. He had beaten and throttled her into submission, then realized that he had broken her neck. So he tossed the body into a ditch and drove off. When a collection was taken at the factory for the dead girl's funeral, Thompson gave generously.

Public outrage led the police to transfer Thompson out of town to prevent him from being lynched. On 30 July 1935, he was sentenced to death, and on 15 October, he was electrocuted. But before he died, he told how he had deceived the lie detector. When asked if he had murdered Mildred, he had simply thought of another Mildred, and the polygraph had registered that he was telling the truth . . .

In fact, Leonarde Keeler admitted that he had learned to deceive his own lie detector by various techniques. It demanded, obviously, a remarkable degree of self-control. But it could be done. (In 1960, a multiple killer named Chester Weger, who had murdered three women in a state park, passed lie detector tests twice by washing down aspirins with Coca Cola before he took the tests.) What was altogether more serious was that innocent suspects might well register as guilty because they were so nervous. This happened in the 1950s in the case of a suspect named Paul Altheide, convicted of murdering a tailor in Phoenix, Arizona, although he protested that he was in Texas at the time. His polygraph test so clearly proclaimed his guilt that the police did not bother to check his alibi. But a reporter named Gene McLain went to Texas, and discovered that the alibi was genuine; Altheide was released after serving four months of his sentence. Cases such as this led J. Edgar Hoover to denounce the lie detector as thoroughly unreliable, and after 1923 – when a man named Frye tried to introduce his polygraph test to prove his innocence of murder, and was refused – polygraph evidence became inadmissible in most American courts. (It can be used only if both sides agree, or the judge demands it.)

Chris Gugas, founder of the National Board of Polygraph Examiners, argues passionately that this is unfair. In *The Silent Witness* (1979), he points out that modern leaps in technology mean that the polygraph is now almost infallible; a study of 4,280 criminals in the 1950s revealed that the accuracy of the polygraph – provided it was used by a trained expert – was 95 per cent.

Gugas's casebook makes fascinating reading because it becomes clear that the lie detector is as important in the establishment of innocence as of guilt. He tells, for example, the story of a well-known actor who was charged with exposing himself to schoolgirls. The schoolgirls claimed that he had parked near their school – in Hollywood – opened the car door, and masturbated himself. The actor agreed that he had driven around the school that day, looking for the home of a friend. But he had not stopped the car. The police had shown the schoolgirls several photographs, including that of the actor, and two of them had immediately picked him out. There could be no doubt that it looked bad.

Gugas was approached by the actor's lawyer, and submitted him to a polygraph test. It showed him that the actor was telling the truth. He was, in fact, a rather prudish man, with almost Victorian morals, and this accusation had shattered him.

Gugas reasoned that the girls who had identified him had seen his face on the television or in movies; he was not a famous star, but one of those faces that everyone knows in secondary roles. And when Gugas learned that the actor always had to wear glasses when driving, he asked him to accompany him to the homes of the girls. At the first one, he introduced the actor as his associate, then questioned the young girl about the man who had exposed himself. Would she recognize him if she saw him again? She was emphatic: she would never forget that face . . . Gugas pointed to his associate. 'Was he anything like Mr Jones?' The girl shook her head. 'No. He was like that photograph the police showed me.' The photograph was without the driving glasses that the actor was now wearing.

The result at two more homes was the same; the girls failed to recognize Gugas' bespectacled associate as the 'flasher'. The fourth girl's mother refused to allow them to see her.

Gugas had recorded the interviews; when he played them to the public prosecutor the next day, the case was dropped.

Gugas makes it clear that the lie detector can do far more than detect lies. After the Second World War, he was sent to a Greek seaport to train local police in the new methods of crime detection (Gugas is Greek by birth). The Chief of Police was convinced that the lie detector was a waste of time. Gugas agreed to demonstrate, and set out to make it as dramatic as possible. He chose three men at random and told them that one of them was to play the part of a pickpocket and steal a wallet. Another three men were to agree privately on a certain colour. Finally, he told the police chief that the polygraph would tell him the name of his mother. Then Gugas left the room for five minutes. When he returned, he tested the first group of three, then the second – in this case simply running through a list of colours. In neither case did he reveal his results. Then he attached the machine to the police chief, and read out a list of the names of Greek women. He got a strong reaction on two names – although one was weaker than the other. When it was over, he pretended to be unsure of himself. The police chief chuckled. 'The Nazis could get nothing out of me. How could I be intimidated by a few knobs and wires? Now give us your results.'

Gugas pointed at one of the first group. 'You stole the wallet.' The man nodded. Gugas turned to the second group. 'The colour was red, wasn't it?' There was a murmur of superstitious astonishment as they admitted it. Then Gugas turned to the police chief. 'Your mother's name is Helena.' The chief stared with incredulity. Finally he said: 'But I thought only of the name of my grandmother.' 'Oh, I know that too. It was Maria, wasn't it?' He was right. After that, he encountered no more incredulity.

At the end of his term in the seaport, Gugas produced his most conclusive demonstration. A powerful local politician named Petroklos was making life difficult for the police because his wife had disappeared. Gugas learned, to his astonishment, that they had not even questioned the politician – the man was too powerful and respected. He persuaded some police officers to accompany him to Petroklos's house, where the man agreed to answer some innocuous questions about his wife's habits, but announced: 'The interview is at an end', when Gugas asked whether they had quarrelled.

Gugas learned that Petroklos had a mistress, and went to interview her. The result was an angry call from Petroklos's lawyer, and an interview with the American consul in which Gugas was warned to 'lay off'. He ignored the warning, and went on probing. When he learned that Petroklos's wife had owned a remote estate, now deserted, he sent police photographers out to take as many pictures as possible. Then he asked Petroklos's lawyer if he could interview his client again. The lawyer refused. But Petroklos finally came of his own accord when Gugas promised to get off the case. When Gugas held out the photographs, Petroklos tried to take them; Gugas refused, saying that he first wanted to connect him up to the polygraph. Petroklos finally agreed, on condition that he would be asked no questions. Gugas said he had no intention of asking questions. And when Petroklos was connected to the machine, he showed him the photographs one by one. When they came to the stable building, there was an unmistakable reaction. Gugas completed the test, shook Petrokios by the hand, and said he would be in touch when he had analysed his results. He restrained an impulse to say 'I think we have solved your wife's disappearance', sensing that this would be dangerous as well as reckless.

Hours later, the police were digging up the half-decomposed body in the stable. Petroklos was charged with the murder of his wife, and later convicted. Gugas kept in the background, allowing the full credit to go to the local police.

5

Gugas's evidence makes one thing very clear: that as an instrument of scientific crime detection, the polygraph is as important as the microscope or the spectroscope. It is not 100 per cent reliable; but then, as we have seen in the course of this book, neither is any other technique of forensic science. But a machine that, in the hands of a skilled operator, is 95 per cent reliable is as valuable – in the all-important department of labour saving – as the police computer or the fingerprint file.

There is, admittedly, a purely practical problem. Even in the mid-1970s, the cost of a lie detector from the Leonarde Keeler Institute in Chicago, and of training an operator to use it, was a minimum of $5,000; a decade later it had more than doubled. This is why, in the winter of 1972, Police Chief Raymond Beary of Winter Park, Florida, requested two of his lieutenants to attend a seminar which a Los Angeles hypnotist, Dr William Bryan, would be conducting in Tampa.

In deciding to send them, Beary was undoubtedly recalling a remarkable case of 1956 which had been solved by hypnosis. On 2 February, a patrolman in a radio car on Biscaya Island, near Miami Beach, saw a body on a vacant lot near the sea. It proved to be that of an attractive brunette in her late teens or early 20s; she wore a bright red dress, and had been stabbed repeatedly. The pathologist established that she had died at about 3 a.m., although she may have been stabbed much earlier, and slowly bled to death. The first problem was to identify the body, and this was solved when her fingerprints were found in the files; she had once been detained in connection with a stolen car. She was 22-year-old Ruth Downing, a divorcee who had come to Florida looking for work. But even this failed to help the investigators. Her friends knew of no one who might have killed her, no regular boyfriends. Recently released sexual deviates were interviewed as a matter of course, but still no lead developed.

Lieutenant T. A. Buchanan of the homicide squad suspected that the killer was a man who had become known as the 'kiss or kill murderer', because he had approached a pretty secretary standing at a bus stop and asked for a kiss; when she refused, he had stabbed her in the throat. The man was obviously a mental case, since the incident had occurred at a busy street corner. A man of the same description – young and unshaven – had raped a young mother in the Miami area.

For two months police visited bars with a photograph of

Ruth Downing. Finally, in April, a tavern employee recognized her. He had seen her leaving the bar with a young man some time around the night of the murder. The description of the youth reminded the officers of an occasional sex offender called Rudolph Valentino Herring, one of whose habits was to try to induce unwilling girls to fellate him. He was known to be mentally unbalanced. Suddenly, it struck Buchanan that Herring sounded exactly like the man they were looking for. The next problem was to find him, since he had no fixed address. It took days of old-fashioned sleuthing before he was finally located living in an abandoned shack. When asked if he had murdered Ruth Downing, he shrugged and replied that he did not remember. But this was not just an excuse. He insisted that his mind was a blank, and that if the police could help him to restore his memory, he would willingly tell them anything he knew. Buchanan asked if he was willing to be hypnotized, and Herring agreed.

The hypnotist chosen was Dr Julien Arroyo, head of the Arroyo Academy of Advanced Hypnosis. The following morning, Arroyo succeeded in hypnotizing Herring, who proved to be a co-operative patient. And under hypnosis, Herring readily admitted his murder of Ruth Downing, whom he knew as Renée. He had met the divorcee casually, and the two had done some drinking together. On the evening of the murder, they had left the bar where her photograph had been recognized, and gone out to the vacant lot, known as a 'lovers' lane'. The girl had obviously been willing to have normal sexual intercourse, but when Herring demanded fellatio, she refused indignantly; he had pulled out a knife and stabbed her, then hitch-hiked back home.

Herring went on to confess to the rape of the young mother, and to stabbing the secretary in the throat when she refused to kiss him. In fact, he admitted that he had committed between 30 and 40 rapes, and that he had an inexplicable hatred of women.

Herring had a long police record for burglary, robbery and attempted rape, and had been a patient in the Chattaboochee State Hospital. A month earlier, an attempt had been made to return him there, but a judge had decided he was mentally competent.

For the police, the chief problem was that, now they had a confession, they still had only half a case. Florida had no cases in which a confession had been obtained by hypnosis; like the lie detector, such evidence would probably be inadmissible in court. After all, it might be argued that Herring was simply highly suggestible, and had agreed to whatever the hypnotist had wanted him to say. The problem was eventually solved by having him examined by a panel of psychiatrists, who decided that his mental state warranted a re-committal to the Chattaboochee State Hospital.

Such a result was obviously unsatisfactory, and probably explained why there was no further attempt to use hypnosis in Florida until Dr William Bryan came to lecture in Tampa in 1972. Two police lieutenants, Avery and Aurbeck, were asked to attend. And, to Police Chief Beary's surprise, they returned in a state of enthusiasm. Bryan had lectured on the use of hypnosis to solve certain plane crashes; when the pilot and some passengers had been hypnotized, they had been able to provide vital information which had been blotted from their memories by the trauma of the crash. Bryan had also revealed that he had played a vital part in the case of the Boston Strangler. When a patient in the Bridgewater State Hospital had told a fellow patient that he was the Strangler, the authorities were dubious; they thought it could be fantasy. The fellow patient's lawyer, F. Lee Bailey, interviewed the self-confessed Strangler, Albert DeSalvo, and persuaded the hospital authorities to allow him to be hypnotized. Dr Bryan was the man chosen. Before an audience of psychiatrists and detectives, he had placed his hands gently on DeSalvo's powerful shoulders, and spoken softly and coaxingly, until DeSalvo's eyes closed. Then he had told him that, as soon as he entered the trance, his right arm would become rigid and lose all feeling. Suddenly, DeSalvo's arm stiffened, the outstretched fingers pointing at the ceiling. Bryan ran a needle into the flesh; DeSalvo did not flinch, and when the needle was withdrawn, no blood came out. That convinced the audience he was not shamming. Then Bryan began asking DeSalvo about the eleventh murder victim, 68-year-old Evelyn Corbin. DeSalvo described how he had entered the apartment by posing as a building superintendent sent to repair a broken bathroom fixture, how he had coaxed the woman onto the bed, how she had refused to allow him to have sexual intercourse, and how he had strangled her. After this, Dr Bryan took DeSalvo back to the beginning, and extracted a confession that was so full of detail that was unknown to the general public that his guilt was established beyond all doubt . . .

Police Lieutenants Avery and Aurbeck had no doubt that hypnosis could help to solve crime; Police Chief Beary was more sceptical; how could they be sure that a subject was under hypnosis and not shamming, how could they be sure that a 'confession' was not the result of suggestion? The lieutenants begged to try it out, and Ron

Avery began experimenting on his family and colleagues until everyone was sick of hearing about hypnosis. He attended a hypnosis training course in Orlando. And finally, he had a chance to try his skill. A young man had been arrested, accused of sexual assault on a 14-year-old girl. She claimed that she had been on her way to work in a local hamburger restaurant when the youth had forced her into his car, driven her to a remote spot, and forced her to perform fellatio. He had also beaten her and thrown her out of the car near her home. Her story was reinforced by the fact that she *had* been beaten.

The youth, who was 18, had a different story. He claimed that he knew the girl as a 'hot little number', and had offered her a lift when he saw her at a bus stop. They had driven to a quiet spot and engaged in heavy petting; but the girl had refused to allow him sexual intercourse, and slapped him when he offered her money. He had then hit her, and she began crying. Eventually, as he apologized and comforted her, she softened and they began petting again; this time she performed fellatio. When he dropped her off at home, she was worried that she had missed work and it was late; he advised her to invent some story.

Avery talked to the girl's mother, and asked her permission to hypnotize her daughter; the mother agreed. Then Avery placed her under hypnosis and asked her if she was a virgin; she said no. He asked how many times she had had intercourse, and she admitted she didn't know. When Avery went on to question her about the incident in the car, her story tallied exactly with that of the boy. She had invented the story about the rape to excuse her lateness and the fact that she had missed work. The result was that the boy received a six-month suspended sentence for intercourse with a minor, while the girl was subjected to stricter parental supervision.

6

Doubts about the use of hypnosis in criminal cases are understandable; for more than a century now, there has been a widespread belief that a person cannot be hypnotized to do something that he or she finds disagreeable. In that case, it seems obvious that a criminal could not be induced to confess 'against his will'. In fact, this notion is based on a failure to understand the nature of hypnosis. When a patient is hypnotized, a part of the mind goes to sleep, and so do certain inhibitory mechanisms. But normal 'defence mechanisms' remain active. A medical student who was a pupil of the great Charcot once placed a girl under hypnosis in front of a class, and ordered her to remove her clothes; she immediately came out of the trance. But if he had told her that she was in her bedroom, and ordered her to prepare herself for sleep, she would almost certainly have undressed. The hypnotist's problem is simply to find a way of slipping below the patient's 'threshold of resistance'. It has been proved repeatedly that a hypnotized subject can be induced to harm other people. In the mid-1930s, a crook named Franz Walter hypnotized a woman he met on a train, induced her to work for him as a prostitute, and finally ordered her to kill her husband by tampering with the brakes on his car. The husband became suspicious after her sixth attempt and went to the police. Dr Ludwig Mayer, a psychologist, placed the woman under hypnosis, and learned that the previous hypnotist had imposed certain 'blocks' to prevent her confessing. With skill and patience, he succeeded in slipping below this 'resistance threshold' and getting the full story; Walter was sentenced to ten years in jail.

The strangest of post-war murder cases began on 29 March 1951, when a young man in overalls entered a Copenhagen bank and in the course of a hold-up shot dead the cashier and manager; he then walked out and escaped on a bicycle. An alert youth leapt on his own bicycle and followed him; within an hour, the police had arrested a 29-year-old man named Palle Hardrup, who immediately confessed to the robbery, and insisted that he had acted completely alone. But the police soon received a tip-off to the effect that Hardrup was completely under the domination of an older man, Bjorn Nielsen, whom he had met in prison when Hardrup was serving a sentence as a Nazi collaborator. The police psychiatrist, Dr Max Schmidt, slowly came to the conclusion that Hardrup had been hypnotized, and the police learned that, while he was in jail, Nielsen could place him in a hypnotic trance simply by making an X-sign in chalk. When Nielsen was first brought in for questioning, the police made the mistake of putting both men in the same room; Nielsen leaned forward on the desk, crossing his forearms, whereupon Hardrup instantly went into a blank, passive state and confirmed everything that Nielsen said.

Little by little, the police accumulated evidence that Nielsen had planned the robbery, as well as a previous one in which Hardrup had walked out of a bank with $61,000. And in prison, Hardrup finally broke down and wrote a full confession revealing how Nielsen had achieved total hypnotic domination over him, and ordered him to commit the bank robberies – the profits of which went entirely to Nielsen. The task of studying the minds of both men was placed in the hands of Dr Paul I. Reiter, whose work on the subject, *Antisocial or Criminal Acts and Hypnosis* (1958) has become a classic of psychology. Nielsen was sentenced to life imprisonment, Hardrup to detention in a criminal lunatic asylum.

The science of psychology has still failed to achieve a full understanding of hypnosis; the only thing that seems to be clear is that the normal conscious ego – the 'you' – is lulled into a form of sleep, while normal physical actions – walking, talking, and so on – become mechanical. The phenomenon was first recognized in 1780, when Armand Chastenet, the Marquis de Puységur – who happened to be a disciple of the celebrated Dr Mesmer – was trying to cure a young peasant named Victor Race; he had tied him to a tree and was making passes with a magnet over his head (the theory being that Race's 'vital energies' needed to be moved around his body). Suddenly, Race's gaze became blank, then his eyes closed. Yet when Puységur ordered him to untie himself he did so. Puységur discovered that Race was an excellent hypnotic subject; moreover, when he was hypnotized, he would respond to Puységur's thoughts – for example, singing a song that Puységur was singing 'in his head'. This seemed to show that while hypnosis placed the conscious 'self' in a state of trance, it could enhance the powers of the unconscious part of the mind – for example, enabling the subject to retrieve forgotten memories.

This was the aspect of hypnosis that Police Lieutenant Ron Avery found most useful. In many rape cases, the trauma causes the victim to 'block out' the details, so that she may not even be able to recall how many men were involved. Avery discovered that, under hypnosis, rape victims could often supply precise descriptions of the attacker, as well as recalling small details that helped to identify him. A burglary victim was able to provide vital details about a burglar under hypnosis. Victims of car crashes were able to describe the cause of the crash in detail, although they had unconsciously repressed them. When a 17-year-old girl named Karen Chitwood was murdered in her apartment, Avery obtained precise descriptions of the suspected killer from witnesses under hypnosis, and as a result, was able to arrest Cecil Floyd, who confessed to the murder.

But it was not Avery, but two fellow investigators, who solved, by hypnosis, one of Florida's worst cases of mass murder. On 22 February 1972, two corpses were found in the cemetery at Wildwood, Florida, both victims of a violent knife attack. Detective Officers Don Plummer and Wayne Pierce – from Gainesville – were summoned to the scene. The victims lay near a parked car; the youth had been stabbed 43 times, the girl – who was naked from the waist down – had 31 knife wounds. The girl had apparently been stabbed on the nearby road, and had fled back to the car, chased by her attacker.

The girl was identified as a cashier and clerk in a truckers' overnight stop; her name was Shirley Whiddon, and she was 19. Her companion was an assistant truck driver named Roger Higgins. There seemed to be few clues. The man's trouser pocket had been ripped off, and the inside handle of the driver's door was bent. When the police tried to raise the bonnet of the car, it seemed to be stuck, and it took three men to raise it; they then discovered that it was held down by a home-made catch. The car tyres were also slashed badly, demonstrating that the killer had been in a kind of frenzy. Shirley Whiddon had taken a break at three o'clock that morning, and gone off with Roger Higgins, who was regarded as her boyfriend.

Three weeks later, Plummer had followed up every lead, and the investigation was at a standstill. At this point, he opened the morning's mail, and saw a wanted notice from Charlotte, North Carolina. The wanted man had murdered the man and woman with whom he was boarding, shooting them with a pistol. His name was Karl de Gregory, and he was believed to be living in Ormond Beach. What struck Plummer was that the killer had shown the same kind of maniacal frenzy in killing the Charlotte couple that the Wildwood cemetery murderer had displayed. Plummer drove to Ormond Beach, made enquiries, and finally located Karl de Gregory, a man of 27 who spoke with a French accent. He was a salesman for a chemical firm in Daytona Beach, a married man with a wife and two children. He flatly denied any knowledge of either the Charlotte crime or the Wildwood cemetery murders. Since he seemed a pleasant and open young man, Plummer was half-inclined to believe him.

But nine days after his arrest, de Gregory suddenly changed his mind. He admitted that he had killed the couple in the cemetery. According to de Gregory, he had left home after a quarrel with his wife, driven aimlessly for hours, and ended at the truck-stop at Wildwood. He saw a couple embracing in a corner of the building; then they climbed into a car and drove off. De Gregory followed them to the cemetery, and stabbed them both to death.

Plummer was not entirely happy about this story. There were some internal discrepancies. Could it be that de Gregory was *not* the murderer of the young couple, but was merely confessing to it for his own advantage? North Carolina law makes no allowance for 'temporary insanity', so the charge there could lead to life imprisonment or a death sentence. In Florida, he might succeed in getting himself committed to an institution for the criminally insane . . .

Plummer's first thought was the lie detector. The nearest one was in Tallahassee, and an expert came over to interview de Gregory. As he left the room he said: 'He's your man.' But lie detector evidence was inadmissible in court. Plummer called upon the Ormond Beach psychologist Dr Ann MacMillan – who was later to play an important part in the case of Gerald Stano – and asked her to examine de Gregory. She spent two hours talking to de Gregory, and when she left his cell, her face was pale. 'He's a killer all right. He may be guilty of as many as twenty-two murders.'

But for the moment, Plummer had no desire to get sidetracked into any other crimes de Gregory might have committed. He could think of only one solution: to try hypnosis. Dr Joe B. McCawley agreed to undertake the case. And in front of Don Plummer, Wayne Pierce and de Gregory's attorney, he set out to place the accused killer in a trance. The detectives knew he had succeeded when McCawley asked de Gregory his name. The voice that replied no longer had a French accent; instead, a deep southern drawl replied: 'Carl D. Gregory'. He went on to tell how he had run away from home at the age of 16, had taught himself French (although he was a high school dropout) and acquired forged papers which showed him to be a French national who was discharged from the American Air Force with the rank of captain; this had enabled him to obtain an excellent job with the Daytona Beach chemical company. He explained that he had shot the couple in Charlotte because the woman had kissed him, and that proved she was a 'bad woman'.

His description of the cemetery murder left Plummer in no doubt that Gregory was the killer. He described how he had halted at the truck-stop at Wudwood, left his car, and seen the young couple kissing. This, he said, proved that she was also a 'bad woman'. In fact, it seemed clear that he had followed them with the intention of playing the part of a Peeping Tom. It was, Gregory claimed, his 'brother' who took over when he went into a maniacal frenzy. He had watched the two kissing and 'fooling around', then pulled open the driver's door and started to stab the boy. As he dragged him out of the car, Higgins' pocket had caught on the inside handle, and bent it, tearing off the pocket – just as the detectives had observed. The girl had run away screaming, with Gregory stalking her. She ran back to the car, and, afraid that she might drive away, Gregory tried to raise the bonnet to disable the engine. It refused to move, so he decided to slash the tyres. After that, he chased the girl to the road, where he stabbed her repeatedly. Then he dragged her body back to the car, leaving it by the body of Roger Higgins.

Ann MacMillan had mentioned a possible 22 other murders. Under hypnosis, Gregory confessed to only three, but in such detail that there could be no doubt of his guilt. After all this, he was extradited back to North Carolina, where he was indicted for the double killing, and received two life sentences, to run consecutively. It was the first mass murder case in Florida history in which hypnosis had played a vital part.

7

Such cases make it clear that the modern detective is faced with a completely new type of problem. From Fielding to Bertillón, the criminal pursued his uncomplicated ends with uncomplicated animal cunning, and the problem of the detective was simplified by the straightforwardness of the motive. Until the late nineteenth century, most crimes were committed for profit – with the exception of the occasional *crime passionnel*. With the Jack the Ripper murders, this ceased to be true; the Whitechapel killer was the first of a new type of sadistic mass murderer. Fortunately, the Joseph Vachers, Earle Nelsons and Peter Kürtens remained a rarity; their victims comprised an insignificant percentage of the murder statistics. But in the 1970s, the American police suddenly became aware that this had ceased to be true. The proportion of random killings had risen from 6 per cent in the mid-1960s to 18 per cent in the mid-1970s, a total of more than 4,000 cases a year. Moreover, the solution rate for homicides, which had been about 90 per cent immediately after the Second World War, continued to fall until it was down to 76 per cent by 1983. This was not due to the inefficiency of the police, but to the fact that, as we have seen, a murder is solved by tracing a link between victim and the killer. If no such link exists, then the case can be solved only by chance. The rise in the rate of unsolved murders suggested an increasing number of crimes in which there was no connection between killer and victim.

It is difficult to name any specific case that alerted police to the existence of the new problem. The crimes of the Boston Strangler, the Manson family, 'Zodiac', John Linley Frazier and Herb Mullin were treated as the individual aberrations of 'weirdos'. But in 1973, the murder of a homosexual named Dean Corll by his 17-year-old lover Elmer Wayne Henley led to the discovery of the bodies of 27 teenage boys in Houston, Texas, and to the realization that Corll had been raping and murdering boys for the past three years. The sheer number of victims – more than 30 in all – suggested that for Dean Corll, murder had ceased to be a catharsis, a release of tension, and had become a *habit*, like smoking. And throughout the 1970s, it became clear that this applied to an increasing number of killers. In June 1972, a supermarket hold-up in Santa Barbara resulted in the arrest of a man named Sherman McCrary, his teenage son Danny and his son-in-law Carl Taylor; as police investigated the activities of this 'nomadic' family – which included McCrary's wife, daughter and three grandchildren – they realized that they had left a trail of at least 22 bodies from Texas to California, most of them shop assistants and waitresses who had been abducted in the course of robbery, then raped and murdered. A murderer who raped and mutilated more than 40 teenage boys, then dumped their bodies beside California highways, became known as the Freeway Killer; in December 1981, a man named William Bonin, who admitted that he 'threw away bodies like garbage', was sentenced to death. Randall Woodfield, known as the 'I.5 killer', raped and murdered an unknown number of girls as he travelled up and down the Interstate 5 highway between California, Oregon and Washington State. And in Chicago in 1978, police found the bodies of 27 teenage boys under the floors in the house of a contractor named John Wayne Gacy, who later confessed to murdering and raping 31 young men. Such killings were not confined to North America. In April 1980, a swollen river near Ambato, in Ecuador, overflowed its banks and uncovered the corpses of four pre-pubescent girls; a few days later, a 31-year-old vagrant named Pedro Alonzo Lopez was arrested when trying to abduct an 11-year-old girl; Lopez later confessed to the murder of about 350 girls between 1978 and 1980, most of them Indians. In 1983, discovery of decaying flesh in a drain in Muswell Hill, north London, led to the arrest of an employment officer named Dennis Nilsen, and to his confession to the murder and dismemberment of 16 young men in the past five years. In 1986, a Colombian named Daniel Camargo Barbosa was arrested in Quito, Ecuador, with blood on his clothing, and subsequently admitted to killing 72 pre-pubescent girls in the past year; he was sentenced to 16 years, the maximum penalty in Ecuador. At about the same time the Soviet news agency Tass announced that a Soviet man would go on trial for the murders of 33 women around the Byelorussian city of Vitebsk.

The case that made the American public aware of the existence of serial killers began in June 1983, when a preacher named Reuben Moore – who ran a small fundamentalist sect called the House of Prayer in Stoneberg, Texas – reported to the police that a member of his flock was in possession of a gun; since the man in question – Henry Lee Lucas – was an ex-convict, this was a felony. Lucas was an unprepossessing individual with a glass eye and a downturned mouth, who looked as if he had stepped out of a horror movie, and it was probably his appearance as much as his subsequent confession to 360 murders, that led to the widespread morbid interest in his career. In the following months he often retracted and then repeated his confession, leading to widespread doubts about the precise figure; but the recovery of several bodies at sites indicated by Lucas demonstrated that it was not entirely fantasy.

It became clear that, from the beginning, Lucas had been a 'loser'. The child of alcoholic parents, he was continually beaten and abused by his mother, a Chippewa Indian who was also a prostitute; she had once hit him so hard with a piece of wood that she caused brain damage. His father had lost both legs in a railway accident, and had subsequently been thrown out of his home and left to freeze to death. In 1960, when he was 23, Lucas had stabbed and raped his mother, then left her to die; for this he was sentenced to 40 years in prison. But he had committed his first murder at the age of 15, when he had tried to rape a 17-year-old girl at a bus stop, and strangled her when she resisted.

After several suicide attempts, Lucas was committed to a mental hospital; recommended for parole in 1970, he warned the prison authorities that he would go on killing after his release; they nevertheless discharged him. Lucas told them: 'I'll leave you a present on the doorstep'; and on the day he was released, he killed a woman in Jackson, only a few miles down the road – a murder that remained unsolved until his subsequent confession. For the next 13 years Lucas went on a killing spree – during the latter years accompanied by another vagrant named Ottis Elwood Toole, whose own sexual preference was for children, whom he raped, tortured and murdered; Lucas later claimed that he had crucified some victims and 'filleted others like a fish'. His statements about motive bring Carl Panzram to mind: 'I was bitter at the world', said Lucas, 'I had nothing but pure hatred. Killing someone is just like walking outdoors. If I wanted a victim, I'd just go get one.'

Newspaper accounts of Lucas and Toole led to a spate of publicity about 'serial killers', and one police officer speculated that there could be as many as 35 killers at large in America, and that the number could be increasing at the rate of one a month. In 1984 the FBI admitted that there was an 'epidemic' of serial murders in America. When a psychologist, Joel Norris, began to study the case of Wayne Williams, the black youth accused of 28 child murders in Atlanta, he realized that there were no fewer than six other less publicized cases of serial murder in Georgia alone, and dozens throughout America. And in a subsequent book on serial killers, Norris admitted that he could see no obvious solution to the problem. He noted that the majority of serial killers are 'physically and psychologically damaged people . . . Almost all of them had scars on their bodies, missing fingers, evidence of previous contusions and multiple abrasions on and around the head and neck area.' And he points out that demands for vengeance and retribution are counter-productive. 'Perversely, he wishes for death, and the threat of the gas chamber, the electric chair or the lethal injection is only an inducement to keep committing murders until he is caught and put to death.' For: 'he is suffering from a disease that is terminal, not only for his numerous victims but also for himself. He is his ultimate victim. On his own initiative, the serial killer can no more stop killing than a heroin addict can kick the habit.'

All this would seem to suggest that the problem of serial killers is virtually insoluble – at least, until some great social transformation has created a society in which there are no alcoholic parents or abused children. Yet Norris and his associates believe that 'most forms of episodic aggression – including serial murder – could be prevented through an organized programme of testing and diagnosis and intervention'. This is because 'as our understanding of the serial killer syndrome developed, we realized that these profiles could lead to the development of a diagnostic or prediction instrument that would identify individuals who might be at risk . . .' Many serial killers, he points out, have sustained severe head injuries (Earle Nelson is an obvious example); most have had emotionally traumatic childhoods, with lack of maternal affection; many are the unwanted children of alcoholic or drug-addicted parents. And, oddly enough, many have 'obvious physical and congenital defects such as webbed fingers, attached ear lobes, elongated limbs and other abnormalities', an interesting, if belated, confirmation of some of Lombroso's observations.

Yet Norris goes on to undermine his own theory by asking: 'Do all people who sustain head traumas become murderers? Do all people who hate women become murderers? Do all people who sustain chronic physical abuse as children become murderers?' The obvious answer is no. Then wherein lies the difference? Norris touches upon an important clue when he speaks of what he calls 'the mask of sanity', 'manifested through grandiosity or a belief in his own superhuman importance'. But this makes it sound as though such individuals are paranoiacs who suffer from delusions of grandeur. The truth is simpler: that many serial killers not only appear to be normal members of society, but even seem to be model citizens of more-than-average achievement. John Gacy was a highly successful building contractor who canvassed for the Democrats and was photographed shaking hands with Mrs Jimmy Carter. Wayne Williams ran his own advertising agency and was featured in local newspapers and television programmes. Gerald Schaefer, a Florida serial killer suspected of the murder of 28 girls, was a high school teacher, a deputy policeman and a member of the local golf club. And Ted Bundy, one of the most widely publicized serial killers of the 1970s, was a law student who had worked for the Crime Commission and the Office of Justice Planning, and had been a highly regarded volunteer on the staff of the local Democratic candidate. The Bundy case offers an important insight into this aspect of the psychology of the serial killer.

8

On 31 January 1974, a student at the University of Washington, in Seattle, Lynda Ann Healy, vanished from her room; the bedsheets were bloodstained, suggesting that she had been struck violently on the head. During the following March, April and May, three more girl students vanished; in June, two more. In July, two girls vanished on the same day. It happened at a popular picnic spot, Lake Sammanish; a number of people saw a good-looking young man, with his arm in a sling, accost a girl named Janice Ott and ask her to help him lift a boat onto the roof of his car; she walked away with him and did not return. Later, a girl named Denise Naslund was accosted by the same young man; she also vanished. He had been heard to introduce himself as 'Ted'.

In October 1974 the killings shifted to Salt Lake City; three girls disappeared in one month. In November, the police had their first break in the case: a girl named Carol DaRonch was accosted in a shopping centre by a young man who identified himself as a detective, and told her that there had been an attempt to break into her car; she agreed to accompany him to headquarters to view a suspect. In the car he snapped a handcuff on her wrist and pointed a gun at her head; she fought and screamed, and managed to jump from the car. That evening, a girl student vanished on her way to meet her brother. A handcuff key was found near the place from which she had been taken.

Meanwhile, the Seattle police had fixed on a young man named Ted Bundy as a main suspect. For the past six years, he had been involved in a close relationship with a divorcee named Meg Anders, but she had called off the marriage when she realized he was a habitual thief. After the Lake Sammanish disappearances, she had seen a photofit drawing of the wanted 'Ted' in the *Seattle Times* and thought it looked like Bundy; moreover, 'Ted' drove a Volkswagen like Bundy's. She had seen crutches and plaster of Paris in Bundy's room, and the coincidence seemed too great; with immense misgivings, she telephoned the police. They told her that they had already checked on Bundy; but at the suggestion of the Seattle police, Carol DaRonch was shown Bundy's photograph. She tentatively identified it as resembling the man who had tried to abduct her, but was obviously far from sure. (Bundy had been wearing a beard at the time.)

In January, March, April, July and August 1975, more girls vanished in Colorado. (Their bodies – or skeletons – were found later in remote spots.) On 16 August 1975, Bundy was arrested for the first time. As a police car was driving along a dark street in Salt Lake City, a parked Volkswagen launched into motion; the policeman followed, and it accelerated. He caught up with the car at a service station, and found in the car a pantyhose mask, a crow-bar, an icepick and various other tools; there was also a pair of handcuffs.

Bundy, 29 years old, seemed an unlikely burglar. He was a graduate of the University of Washington, and was in Utah to study law; he had worked as a political campaigner, and for the Crime Commission in Seattle. In his room there was nothing suspicious – except maps and brochures of Colorado, from which five girls had vanished that year. But strands of hair were found in the car, and they proved to be identical with those of Melissa Smith, daughter of the Midvale police chief, who had vanished in the previous October. Carol DaRonch had meanwhile identified Bundy in a police line-up as the fake policeman, and bloodspots on her clothes – where she had scratched her assailant – were of Bundy's group. Credit card receipts showed that Bundy had been close to various places from which girls had vanished in Colorado.

In theory, this should have been the end of the case – and if it had been, it would have been regarded as a typical triumph of scientific detection, beginning with the photofit drawing and concluding with the hair and blood evidence. The evidence was, admittedly, circumstantial, but taken all together, it formed a powerful case. The central objection to it became apparent as soon as Bundy walked into court. He looked so obviously decent and clean-cut that most people felt there must be some mistake. He was polite, well-spoken, articulate, charming, the kind of man who could have found himself a girlfriend for each night of the week. Why *should* such a man be a sex killer? In spite of which, the impression he made was of brilliance and plausibility rather than innocence. For example, he insisted that he had driven away from the police car because he was smoking marijuana, and that he had thrown the joint out of the window.

The case seemed to be balanced on a knife-edge – until the judge pronounced a sentence of guilty of kidnapping. Bundy sobbed and pleaded not to be sent to prison; but the judge sentenced him to a period between 1 and 15 years.

The Colorado authorities now charged him with the murder of a girl called Caryn Campbell, who had been abducted from a ski resort where Bundy had been seen by a witness. After a morning courtroom session in Aspen, Bundy succeeded in wandering into the library during the lunch recess, and jumping out of the window. He was recaptured eight days later, tired and hungry, and driving a stolen car.

Legal arguments dragged on for another six months – what evidence was admissible and what was not. And on 30 December 1977, Bundy escaped again, using a hacksaw blade to cut through an imperfectly welded steel plate above the light fixture in his cell. He made his way to Chicago, then south to Florida; there, near the Florida State University in Tallahassee, he took a room. A few days later, a man broke into a nearby sorority house and attacked four girls with a club, knocking them unconscious; one was strangled with her pantyhose and raped; another died on her way to hospital. One of the strangled girl's nipples had been almost bitten off, and she had a bite mark on her left buttock. An hour and a half later, a student woke up in another sorority house when she heard bangs next door, and a girl whimpering. She dialled the number of the room, and as the telephone rang, someone could be heard running out. Cheryl Thomas was found lying in bed, her skull fractured but still alive.

Three weeks later, on 6 February 1978, Bundy – who was calling himself Chris Hagen – stole a white Dodge van and left Tallahassee; he stayed in the Holiday Inn, using a stolen credit card. The following day a 12-year-old girl named Kimberley Leach walked out of her classroom in Lake City, Florida, and vanished. Bundy returned to Tallahassee to take a girl out for an expensive meal – paid for with a stolen credit card – then absconded via the fire escape, owing large arrears of rent. At 4 a.m. on 15 February, a police patrolman noticed an orange Volkswagen driving suspiciously slowly, and radioed for a check on its number; it proved to be stolen from Tallahassee. After a struggle and a chase, during which he tried to kill the policeman, Bundy was captured yet again. When the police learned his real name, and that he had just left a town in which five girls had been attacked, they suddenly understood the importance of their capture. Bundy seemed glad to be in custody, and began to unburden himself. He explained that 'his problem' had begun when he had seen a girl on a bicycle in Seattle, and 'had to have her'. He had followed her, but she escaped. 'Sometimes', he admitted, 'I feel like a vampire.'

On 7 April, a party of searchers along the Suwanee river found the body of Kimberley Leach in an abandoned hut; she had been strangled and sexually violated. Three weeks later, surrounded by hefty guards, Bundy allowed impressions of his teeth to be taken, for comparison with the marks on the buttocks of the dead student, Lisa Levy.

Bundy's lawyers persuaded him to enter into 'plea bargaining': in exchange for a guarantee of life imprisonment – rather than a death sentence – he would confess to the murders of Lisa Levy, Margaret Bowman and Kimberley Leach. But Bundy changed his mind at the last moment and decided to sack his lawyers.

Bundy's trial began on 25 June 1979, and the evidence against him was damning; a witness who had seen him leaving the sorority house after the attacks; a pantyhose mask found in the room of Cheryl Thomas, which resembled the one found in Bundy's car; but above all, the fact that Bundy's teeth matched the marks on Lisa Levy's buttocks. The highly compromising taped interview with the Pensacola police was judged inadmissible in court because his lawyer had not been present. Bundy again dismissed his defence and took it over himself; the general impression was that he was trying to be too clever. The jury took only six hours to find him guilty on all counts. Judge Ed Cowart pronounced sentence of death by electrocution, but evidently felt some sympathy for the good-looking young defendant. 'It's a tragedy for this court to see such a total waste of humanity. You're a bright young man. You'd have made a good lawyer. . . But you went the wrong way, partner. Take care of yourself . . .'

Bundy was taken to Raiford prison, Florida, where he was placed on Death Row. On 2 July 1986, when he was due to die a few hours before Gerald Stano, both were granted a stay of execution.

The Bundy case illustrates the immense problems faced by investigators of serial murders. When Meg Anders – Bundy's mistress – telephoned the police after the double murder near Lake Sammanish, Bundy's name had already been suggested by three people. But he was only one of 3,500 suspects. Later Bundy was added to the list of 100 'best suspects' which investigators constructed on grounds of age, occupation and past record. Two hundred thousand items were fed into computers, including the names of 41,000 Volkswagen owners, 5,000 men with a record of mental illness, every student who had taken classes with the dead girls, and all transfers from other colleges they had attended. All this was programmed into 37 categories, each using a different criterion to isolate the suspect. Asked to name anyone who came up on any three of these programs, the computer produced 16,000 names. When the number was raised to four, it was reduced to 600. Only when it was raised to 25 was it reduced to ten suspects, with Bundy seventh on the list. The police were still investigating number six when Bundy was detained in Salt Lake City with burgling tools in his car. Only after that did Bundy become suspect number one. And by that time, he had already committed a minimum of 17 murders. (There seems to be some doubt about the total, estimates varying between 20 and 40; Bundy himself told the Pensacola investigators that it ran into double figures.) Detective Robert Keppel, who worked on the case, is certain that Bundy would have been revealed as suspect number one even if he had not been arrested. But in 1982, Keppel and his team were presented with another mass killer in the Seattle area, the so-called Green River Killer, whose victims were mostly prostitutes picked up on the 'strip' in Seattle. Seven years later, in 1989, he has killed at least 49 women, and the computer has still failed to identify an obvious suspect number one.

The Bundy case is doubly baffling because he seems to contradict the basic assertions of every major criminologist from Lombroso to Yochelson. Bundy is not an obvious born criminal, with degenerate physical characteristics; there is (as far as is known) no history of insanity in his family; he was not a social derelict or a failure. In her book *The Stranger Beside Me,* his friend Ann Rule describes him as 'a man of unusual accomplishment'. How could the most subtle 'psychological profiling' target such a man as a serial killer?

The answer to the riddle emerged fairly late in the day, four years after Bundy had been sentenced to death. Before his conviction, Bundy had indicated his willingness to co-operate on a book about himself, and two journalists, Stephen G. Michaud and Hugh Aynesworth, went to interview him in prison. They discovered that Bundy had no wish to discuss guilt, except to deny it, and he actively discouraged them from investigating the case against him. He wanted them to produce a gossipy book focusing squarely on himself, like bestselling biographies of celebrities such as Frank Sinatra. Michaud and Aynesworth would have been happy to write a book demonstrating his innocence, but as they looked into the case, they found it impossible to accept this; instead, they concluded that he had killed at least 21 girls. When they began to probe, Bundy revealed the characteristics that Yochelson and Samenow had found to be so typical of criminals: hedging, lying, pleas of faulty memory, and self-justification: 'Intellectually, Ted seemed profoundly dissociative, a compartmentalizer, and thus a superb rationalizer.' Emotionally, he struck them as a severe case of arrested development: 'he might as well have been a twelve year old, and a precocious and bratty one at that. So extreme was his childishness that his pleas of innocence were of a character very similar to that of the little boy who'll deny wrongdoing in the face of overwhelming evidence to the contrary.' So Michaud had the ingenious idea of suggesting that Bundy should 'speculate on the nature of a person capable of doing what Ted had been accused (and convicted) of doing'. Bundy embraced this idea with enthusiasm, and talked for hours into a tape recorder. Soon Michaud became aware that there were, in effect, two 'Teds' – the analytical human being, and an entity inside him that Michaud came to call the 'hunchback'. (We have encountered this 'other person' – Mr Hyde – syndrome in many killers, from William Heirens and Peter Sutcliffe to Carl Gregory.)

After generalizing for some time about violence in modern society, the disintegration of the home, and so on, Bundy got down to specifics, and began to discuss his own development.

He had been an illegitimate child, born to a respectable young girl in Philadelphia. She moved to Seattle to escape the stigma, and married a cook in the Veterans' Hospital. Ted was an oversensitive and self-conscious child who had all the usual day-dreams of fame and wealth. And at an early stage he became a thief and something of a habitual liar – as many imaginative children do. But he seems to have been deeply upset by the discovery of his illegitimacy.

Bundy was not, in fact, a brilliant student. Although he struck his fellow students as witty and cultivated, his grades were usually Bs. In his late teens he became heavily infatuated with a fellow student, Stephanie Brooks, who was beautiful, sophisticated and came of a wealthy family. Oddly enough, she responded and they became 'engaged'. To impress her he went to Stanford University to study Chinese; but he felt lonely away from home, and his grades were poor. 'I found myself thinking about standards of success that I just didn't seem to be living up to.' Stephanie wearied of his immaturity, and threw him over – the severest blow so far. He became intensely moody. 'Dogged by feelings of worthlessness and failure', he took a job as a busboy in a hotel dining-room. And at this point, he began the drift that eventually turned him into a serial killer. He became friendly with a drug addict. One night, they entered a cliffside house that had been partly destroyed by a landslide, and stole whatever they could find. 'It was really thrilling.' He began shoplifting and stealing 'for thrills', once walking openly into someone's greenhouse, taking an eight-foot tree in a pot, and putting it in his car with the top sticking out of the sunroof.

He also became a full-time volunteer worker for Art Fletcher, the black Republican candidate for Lieutenant-Governor. He enjoyed the sense of being a 'somebody' and mixing with interesting people. But Fletcher lost, and Bundy became a salesman in a department store. He met Meg Anders in a college beer joint, and they became lovers – she had a gentle, easy-going nature, which brought out Bundy's protective side. But she was shocked by his kleptomania.

In fact, the criminal side – the 'hunchback' – was now developing fast. He acquired a taste for violent pornography – easy to buy openly in American shops. Once, walking round the university district, he saw a girl undressing in a lighted room. This was the turning point in his life. He began to devote hours to walking around, hoping to see more girls undressing. He was back at university, studying psychology, but his night prowling prevented him from making full use of his undoubted intellectual capacities. He obtained his degree in due course – this may tell us more about American university standards than about Bundy's abilities – and tried to find a law school that would take him. He failed all the aptitude tests and was repeatedly turned down. A year later, he was finally accepted – he worked for the Crime Commission for a month, as an assistant, and for the Office of Justice Planning. His self-confidence increased by leaps and bounds. When he flew to San Francisco to see Stephanie Brooks, the girl who had jilted him, she was deeply impressed, and willing to renew their affair. He was still having an affair with Meg Anders, and entered on this new career as a Don Juan with his usual enthusiasm. He and Stephanie spent Christmas together and became 'engaged'. Then he dumped her as she had dumped him.

By this time, he had committed his first murder. For years, he had been a pornography addict and a Peeping Tom. ('He approached it almost like a project, throwing himself into it, literally, for years.') Then the 'hunchback' had started to demand 'more active kinds of gratification'. He tried disabling women's cars, but the girls always had help on hand. He felt the need to indulge in this kind of behaviour after drinking had reduced his inhibitions. One evening, he stalked a girl from a bar, found a heavy piece of wood, and managed to get ahead of her and lie in wait. Before she reached the place where he was hiding, she stopped at her front door and went in. But the experience was like 'making a hole in a dam'. A few evenings later, as a woman was fumbling for her keys at her front door, he struck her on the head with a piece of wood. She collapsed, screaming, and he ran away. He was filled with remorse, and swore he would never do such a thing again. But six months later, he followed a woman home and peeped in as she undressed. He began to do this again and again. One day, when he knew the door was unlocked, he sneaked in, entered her bedroom, and jumped on her. She screamed and he ran away. Once again, there was a period of self-disgust and revulsion.

This was in the autumn of 1973. On 4 January 1974, he found a door that admitted him to the basement room of 18-year-old Sharon Clarke. Now, for the first time, he employed the technique he later used repeatedly, attacking her with a crow-bar until she was unconscious. Then he thrust a speculum, or vaginal probe, inside her, causing internal injuries. But he left her alive.

On the morning of 1 February 1974, he found an unlocked front door in a students' rooming-house and went in. He entered a bedroom at random; 21-year-old Lynda Healy was asleep in bed. He battered her unconscious, then carried the body out to his car. He drove to Taylor Mountain, 20 miles east of Seattle, made her remove her pyjamas, and raped her. When Bundy was later 'speculating' about this crime for Stephen Michaud's benefit, the interviewer asked: 'Was there any conversation?' Bundy replied: 'There'd be some. Since this girl in front of him represented not a person, but again the image of something desirable, the last thing we would expect him to want to do would be to personalize this person.

So Lynda Healy was bludgeoned to death; Bundy always insisted that he took no pleasure in violence, but that his chief desire was 'possession' of another person.

Now the 'hunchback' was in full control, and there were five more victims over the next five months. Three of the girls were taken to the same spot on Taylor Mountain and there raped and murdered – Bundy acknowledged that his sexual gratification would sometimes take hours. The four bodies were found together in the following year. On the day he abducted the two girls from Lake Sammanish, Bundy 'speculated' that he had taken the first, Janice Ott, to a nearby house and raped her, then returned to abduct the second girl, Denise Naslund, who was taken back to the same house and raped in view of the other girl; both were then killed, and taken to a remote spot four miles north-east of the park, where the bodies were dumped.

By the time he had reached this point in his 'confession', Bundy had no further secrets to reveal; everything was obvious. Rape had become a compulsion that dominated his life. When he moved to Salt Lake City and entered the law school there – he was a failure from the beginning as a law student – he must have known that if he began to rape and kill young girls there, he would be establishing himself as suspect number one. This made no difference; he had to continue. Even the unsuccessful kidnapping of Carol DaRonch, and the knowledge that someone could now identify him, made no difference. He merely switched his activities to Colorado. Following his arrest, conviction and escape, he moved to Florida, and the compulsive attacks continued, although by now he must have known that another series of murders in a town to which he had recently moved must reduce his habitual plea of 'coincidence' to an absurdity. It seems obvious that by this time he had lost the power of choice. In his last weeks of freedom, Bundy showed all the signs of weariness and self-disgust that had driven Carl Panzram to contrive his own execution.

Time finally ran out for Bundy on 24 January 1989. Long before this, he had recognized that his fatal mistake was to decline to enter into plea bargaining at his trial; the result was a death sentence instead of life imprisonment. In January 1989, his final appeal was turned down and the date of execution fixed. Bundy then made a last-minute attempt to save his life by offering to bargain murder confessions for a reprieve – against the advice of his attorney James Coleman, who warned him that this attempt to 'trade over the victims' bodies' would only create hostility that would militate against further stays of execution. In fact, Bundy went on to confess to eight Washington murders, and then to a dozen others. Detective Bob Keppel, who had led the investigation in Seattle, commented: 'The game-playing stuff cost him his life.' Instead of making a full confession, Bundy doled out information bit by bit. 'The whole thing was orchestrated', said Keppel, 'We were held hostage for three days.' And finally, when it was clear that there was no chance of further delay, Bundy confessed to the Chi Omega Sorority killings, admitting that he had been peeping through the window at girls undressing until he was carried away by desire and entered the building. He also mentioned pornography as being one of the factors that led him to murder. Newspaper columnists showed an inclination to doubt this, but Bundy's earlier confessions to Michaud leave no doubt that he was telling the truth.

At 7 a.m., Bundy was led into the execution chamber at Starke State prison, Florida; behind Plexiglass, an invited audience of 48 people sat waiting. As two warders attached his hands to the arms of the electric chair, Bundy recognized his attorney among the crowd; he smiled and nodded. Then straps were placed around his chest and over his mouth; the metal cap with electrodes was fastened onto his head with screws and the face was covered with a black hood. At 7.07 a.m. the executioner threw the switch; Bundy's body went stiff and rose fractionally from the chair. One minute later, as the power was switched off, the body slammed back into the chair. A doctor felt his pulse and pronounced him dead. Outside the prison, a mob carrying 'Fry Bundy!' banners cheered as the execution was announced.

9

The Bundy case makes it clear that, in one respect at least, the science of criminology needs updating.

It seems to be the general consensus among criminologists that the criminal is a social inadequate, and that the few exceptions only underscore the rule. Faced with difficulties that require courage and patience, he is inclined to run away. He lacks self-esteem; he tends to see himself as a loser, a failure. Crime is a 'short cut' to achieve something he believes he cannot achieve through his own merit. But everyone who reads this description must be aware that, to some extent, it fits himself. Being undermined by self-doubt is part of the human condition. Which of us, faced with problems, has not at some time chosen a judicious retreat?

The Bundy case underlines the point. Even as a schoolboy he was witty and amusing, and in his early 20s he developed a poise and confidence that were the envy of other males. Michaud quotes a fellow office worker: 'Frankly, he represented what it was that all young males ever wanted to be . . . I think half the people in the office were jealous of him . . . If there was any flaw in him it was that he was almost too perfect.'

If Yochelson and Samenow are right about the criminal personality, then Bundy should now have reached a point in his life when the criminal phase should have been left behind like a childhood ailment. According to them, criminality is closely connected to inadequacy, laziness and self-pity; it is another name for defeat-proneness. By the time he was in his mid-20s, Bundy had tasted enough success to stand outside this definition. Then what went wrong?

Ann Rule's book contains the vital clue. She comments that Bundy became violently upset if he telephoned Meg Anders from Salt Lake City – where his legal studies were foundering – and got no reply. 'Strangely, while he was being continuously unfaithful himself, he expected – demanded-that she be totally loyal to him.'

In 1954, the science fiction writer A. E. Van Vogt had encountered this same curious anomaly when he was studying male authoritarian behaviour for a novel called *The Violent Man*. He was intrigued by the number of divorce cases in which habitually unfaithful husbands had expected total fidelity from their wives; such a husband might flaunt his own infidelities, while erupting into murderous violence if his wife so much as smiled at another man. Such men obviously regarded women with deep hostility, as if they expected to be deceived or betrayed – this is why they chose to marry gentle and unaggressive women. Their 'conquests' were another form of aggression, the aim being to prove that they were masterful seducers who could have any woman they liked. Their whole unstable structure of self-esteem was founded upon this notion that women found them irresistible; so it was essential for the wife to behave like a slave in a harem. This also explained another characteristic of such men: that they could not bear to be contradicted or shown to be in the wrong; this also threatened their image of themselves as a kind of god or superman. If confronted with proof of their own fallibility, they would explode into violence rather than acknowledge that they had made a mistake. For this reason, Van Vogt labelled this type 'the Right Man' or 'the Violent Man'. To his colleagues at work he might appear perfectly normal and balanced; but his family knew him as a kind of paranoid dictator.

Only one thing could undermine this structure of self-delusion. If his wife walked out on him, she had demonstrated beyond all doubt that she rejected him; his tower of self-delusion was undermined, and often the result was mental breakdown, or even suicide.

Expressed in this way, it seems clear that the Right Man syndrome is a form of mild insanity. Yet it is alarmingly common; most of us know a Right Man, and some have the misfortune to have a Right Man for a husband or father. The syndrome obviously arises from the sheer competitiveness of the world we are born into. Every normal male has an urge to be a 'winner', yet he finds himself surrounded by people who seem better qualified for success. One common response is boasting to those who look as if they can be taken in – particularly women. Another is what the late Stephen Potter called 'One-upmanship', the attempt to make the other person feel inferior by a kind of cheating – or example, by pretending to know far more than you actually know. Another is to bully people over whom one happens to have authority. Many 'Right Men' are so successful in all these departments that they achieve a remarkably high level of self-esteem on remarkably slender talents. Once achieved, this self-esteem is like an addictive drug and any threat of withdrawal seems terrifying. Hence the violence with which he reacts to anything that challenges it.

It is obvious that the Right Man syndrome is a compensatory mechanism for profound self-doubt, and that its essence lies in convincing others of something he feels to be untrue; in other words, it is a form of confidence-trickery. It is, that is to say, a typically criminal form of 'shortcut', like cheating in an exam, or stealing something instead of saving up to buy it.

Now the basic characteristic of the criminal, and also of the Right Man, is a certain lack of self-control. Van Vogt writes that the Right Man 'makes the decision to be out of control' – that is, makes the decision to *lose* control at a certain point, exploding into violence rather than calling upon a more mature level of his personality. But he is adept at making excuses that place the blame for this lack of self-control on other people for provoking him. One British sex killer, Patrick Byrne, explained that he decided to terrorize women 'to get my own back on them for causing my nervous tension through sex'.

But the lack of self-control brings its own problems. Every time it happens he is, in effect, lowering his own bursting point. Carl Panzram told Henry Lesser never to turn his back on him: 'You're the one man I don't want to kill. But I'm so erratic I'm liable to do anything.' He is like a man who has trained an Alsatian dog to leap at people's throats, and finally realizes that the dog is stronger than he is. A 22-year-old sex killer named Stephen Judy begged the judge in Indianapolis to sentence him to death. He had been committing rapes and sex crimes since he was 12, and was on trial for killing a young mother and her three children. Aware that he would never be able to stop committing sex crimes, he told the jury: 'You'd better put me to death. Because next time it might be one of you or your daughter.' They agreed, and Judy was executed in 1981. Just before his death he told his stepmother that he had killed more women than he could remember, leaving a trail of bodies across the United States.

It should now be possible to see that the Right Man syndrome is the key to the serial killer, and that Bundy is a textbook case. From the beginning, he was obsessed by success: 'I found myself thinking about standards of success that I just didn't seem to be living up to.' The affair with Stephanie Brooks made it seem that success was within his grasp; he went to Stanford to study Chinese. But he lacked the application and self-confidence and she threw him over. This was the turning point; his brother commented: 'Stephanie screwed him up . . . I'd never seen him like this before. He'd always been in charge of his emotions.' It was after this rejection that Bundy became a klepto-maniac. This may seem a strange response to the end of a love affair. But stealing is a way of making a gesture of defiance at society. And this is what Bundy's thieving amounted to – as when he stole an eight-foot tree from a greenhouse and drove off with it sticking out of the roof of his car. It was essentially a symbolic gesture.

Seven years later, Bundy took his revenge on Stephanie Brooks. When she rang him to ask why he had not contacted her since their weekend together, he said coldly: 'I have no idea what you're talking about', and hung up on her. 'At length', says Ann Rule, 'she concluded that Ted's high-power courtship in the latter part of 1973 had been deliberately planned, that he had waited all these years to be in a position where he could make her fall in love with him, just so he could drop her, reject her as she had rejected him.' Stephanie Brooks wrote to a friend: 'I escaped by the skin of my teeth. When I think of his cold and calculating manner, I shudder.' The Right Man had escaped his feeling of vulnerability; he had established his dominance. Oddly enough, he committed his first violent sexual attack immediately after the weekend with Stephanie. He had proved that he was the conqueror; now, in this mood of exultation, he broke into the bedroom of a female student, battered her unconscious, and thrust a speculum into her vagina. Three weeks later he committed his first murder. It was also completely typical of the Right Man that, when eventually caught, he should continue to deny his guilt, even in the face of overwhelming evidence.

Henry Lee Lucas might seem an altogether less obvious example of a Right Man. But his confessions immediately make it clear that one of his most basic characteristics was 'the decision to be out of control'. He committed his first murder at the age of 15 – the 17-year-old girl he attacked at the bus stop. *She resisted;* so he killed her, raped her, then buried her. Resistance aroused all his violence. (Gerald Stano, we may recall, had the same characteristic; he killed only those girls who fought back.) In appearance, he was mild and self-effacing, one of society's losers. One middle-class couple trusted him sufficiently to pay him to look after the wife's 80-year-old mother, Kate Rich. But one evening, after an argument, Lucas stabbed her to death, raped her, then hid the body in a culvert. When anyone opposed him, he was like a striking snake.

The parents of his fellow murderer, Ottis Toole, also trusted him enough to appoint him the guardian of their two youngest children, Frank and Becky Powell. Becky was nine, and Lucas cared for her like a father, sent her to school, and taught her the craft of burglary. Inevitably, he began to have sex with her. They began to disagree when both joined the House of Prayer sect, and Becky announced her desire to return to Florida to serve out a period of juvenile detention; she was longing for a stable life. Lucas started to hitch-hike back to Florida with her, but one night they quarrelled, and she slapped his face. Without even thinking, he stabbed her to death. Then he dismembered her body and buried it. But he was overwhelmed by remorse, and from then on, ceased to show the instinct for self-preservation that had so far kept him out of the hands of the police. He was arrested nine months later, and almost immediately confessed. Becky's brother Frank had to be committed to a mental home.

Charles Manson provides another example of the apparently mild and self-effacing Right Man. In a prison interview, he told Joel Norris that he saw himself as the ultimate victim of society, and the impression he made on his disciples in the Haight-Ashbury district of San Francisco was of a gentle, slightly comic figure, a mixture of Christ and Charlie Chaplin. Most of these disciples were teenagers – Manson was in his mid-30s – and he became a father figure. As his success as a cult leader increased in 1968, disciples handed over money and property. One of his followers, Susan Atkins, declared that he was the king, the 'visible proof of God', and that his name meant 'son of man'. 'All he ever does is to give, and if you watched him you could see the love he suggests with everything he does' said another follower, Patricia Kienwinkel. Permanently high on psychedelic drugs, Manson was convinced that the confrontation between blacks and whites in the 1960s would finally lead to open warfare and mutual annihilation, a prospect he welcomed. Manson also played guitar and wrote songs, and believed that he could become as successful as the Beatles or Bob Dylan. He developed a murderous resentment for those he felt had slighted him or ignored his talent, and drew up a 'death list' that included Warren Beatty and Julie Christie, as well as Doris Day's son Terry Melcher, whom he believed responsible for causing a recording contract to fall through. And on the evening of 18 August 1969, Manson told his disciples that 'now was the time for Helter Skelter', his code-name for the war between blacks and whites, and four members of the gang went to the house in which Terry Melcher had lived, and murdered film star Sharon Tate and four other people, including a delivery boy. The following evening, Manson entered the nearby home of a couple called LaBianca, and tied them up at gunpoint; then his followers went in and killed them.

The solution of the case came through an unrelated piece of crime detection. In September 1969, rangers in the Death Valley National

Park discovered that someone had set fire to a skip-loader, a kind of bulldozer. They followed tyre tracks along the road, and some miles further on, found a wrecked car that had been driven into a tree. Its tyres corresponded to the tracks near the vandalized bulldozer; nearby were more tyre tracks from another car. This car was located in a valley, and was found to be a stolen Toyota. A man who lived nearby told the police about a family of 'hippies' who were living on a deserted ranch, and who were probably responsible for the theft and the destruction of the bulldozer. The police raided the ranch and arrested a crowd of hippies, including several girls.

It was one of these girls, Susan Atkins, who told a cell-mate that she had taken part in the Sharon Tate killings. Manson and his followers were interrogated, and eventually charged with the murders.

What was so strange about the trial was that Manson seemed determined to turn it into an indictment of the authorities. 'You make your children what they are . . . These children – everything they have done, they have done for the love of their brothers.' The jury found all this incomprehensible. Was Manson saying that his 'children' had not really committed the murders? When Susan Atkins was asked if she thought the murders of eight people were unimportant, she countered by asking if the killing of thousands of people with napalm was important, the implication being that two wrongs somehow made a right. What no one in the courtroom understood was that they were encountering the inverted logic of the Right Man, who is incapable of admitting that he is to blame. Eventually, Manson and four followers were sentenced to death, the sentences later being commuted to life imprisonment.

It should be clear by now that the Right Man syndrome is a mild form of insanity. The usual definition of insanity is a certain loss of contact with the real world, so that a person ceases to be able to distinguish between what is subjective and what is objective. In the case of Manson and many other serial killers (and it seems clear that the Manson family committed many more murders than those with which they were charged) this confusion was increased by drugs. The difference between the Right Man syndrome and clinical psychosis is that the psychotic is the victim of his delusions while the Right Man's separation from reality is to some extent voluntary; it is a form of self-deception. But when alcohol or drug abuse become involved, the dividing line becomes increasingly blurred. Van Vogt recognized that 'most Right Men deserve some sympathy, for they are struggling with an almost unbelievable inner horror . . .' It is as if a kind of inner dam threatened to collapse, leaving them at the mercy of all their worst fears. 'If they give way to the impulse to hit or choke', says Van Vogt, 'they are losing the battle, and are on the way to ultimate disaster.' But the serial killer *has* given way to his impulse to hit and choke. He is stranded in a kind of nightmare, faced with a deep, intuitive recognition that he has destroyed his potentialities as a human being and reached the end of the line. This explains why Panzram committed the murder that led to his execution, why Stephen Judy demanded to be electrocuted, and why so many serial killers have made obvious mistakes that led to their arrest.

10

A case of the mid-1980s provides a particularly clear example of this self-destructive mechanism. On 2 June 1985, a young Asian named Charles Ng tried to steal a vice from South City Lumber in San Francisco, but was caught after he had dropped it into the boot of his car. His companion, a man named Leonard Lake, offered to pay for the vice, but was told that the police were already on their way. Ng escaped, and a search of Lake's car revealed a hand-gun with a silencer. Taken to the police station, he asked for a glass of water, and swallowed a cyanide capsule. He died four days later without regaining consciousness. His car and identity papers were found to belong to a missing car salesman named Paul Cosner. When police searched a property belonging to Lake in Wilseyville, Calaveras County, they discovered an underground bunker with prison cells, and the remains of eight victims buried nearby. There were also two videotapes which made it clear that Lake and Ng tortured and raped their female victims. Ng was arrested a month later in Calgary, Canada, and sentenced to four and a half years for shoplifting; California applied for his extradition.

Lake had been a Vietnam veteran and a maker of pornographic films; his collection of videos was found to include 'snuff movies' with actual scenes of murder; he also kept photographs of his victims' bodies, which included seven men, three women and two children. Lake had apparently been inspired by a novel by John Fowles called *The Collector,* in which a man kidnaps a girl and holds her captive; Lake believed that a nuclear war was unavoidable, and had stockpiled food and weapons in his underground bunker. The cells were intended for 'sex slaves'.

The picture that began to emerge was of a man who spent most of his life living in a world of fantasy, a man who indulged in grandiose dreams of success without any realistic attempt to make them come true, and who boasted of imaginary heroic exploits in Vietnam. Like so many serial killers, he had been rejected by his parents at an early age, and brought up by a grandfather who imposed a military-style discipline. He was jealous of his younger brother Donald, who was favoured by their parents. But Donald himself was mentally disturbed, indulging in sadistic cruelty to animals – one of the basic characteristics of the serial killer – and attempting to have sexual intercourse with his younger sisters. (Lake obtained their sexual favours in exchange for protecting them from Donald – and eventually Donald was to become one of his victims.)

Lake also took nude photographs of his sisters and cousins – the beginning of a lifelong preoccupation that led him to make pornographic movies (starring his wife) and the 'snuff videos' of his victims. And in spite of his dominant role in relation to sisters and cousins, Lake had the Right Man's characteristic hatred and distrust of women, and the need for power over them. His fantasies were all about domination over women and their total submission to him.

So, as with so many Right Men, Lake's self-esteem was based on fantasies in which he was a kind of Haroun Al Raschid or Ivan the Terrible, with the power of life and death. He showed considerable skill at concealing his abnormality, teaching grade school, working as a volunteer fire-fighter, and donating his time to a company that provided free insulation in old people's homes. Slowly, the fantasies took over and he began to rape and kill. One video shows these fantasies in action. Eighteen-year-old Kathy Allen went searching for her boyfriend Michael Carroll, a drug dealer, and one of the many who made the fatal mistake of going to Lake's home to do business. The video shows Ng ordering her to undress, then shows Lake removing her handcuffs and clamping on leg irons. She is then ordered to take a shower. 'You'll wash for us, clean for us, fuck for us.' A later scene shows her strapped down to a bed, while Lake tells her that her boyfriend is dead.

The video cuts to another girl, Brenda O'Connor, who is handcuffed, and who asks about her baby. She is told that the baby is 'sound asleep like a rock', then offered the choice of being a 'sex slave' or dying. She agrees to co-operate. It emerges that Lake has invited the whole family – Brenda, common law husband, and two-year-old child – over for dinner, then has taken them prisoner. Brenda asks: 'Why do you guys do this?' and Lake replies: 'We don't like you. Would you like me to put it in writing?' 'You two are crazy.' 'The whole neighbourhood's crazy.' Ng starts to undress her saying: 'Let's see what we're buying.' 'Don't cut my bra off.' 'Nothing is yours now.' As she undresses she begs: 'Give my baby to me. I'll do anything you want. . .' 'You're going to do anything we want anyway.' 'He can't live without me.' 'He's gonna learn.' And the naked girl is made to enter the shower with Ng as a preliminary to becoming a 'sex slave' and then being killed.

What has happened is clear: Lake has taken the fatal step beyond most Right Men: he has decided he will *become* Haroun Al Raschid or Ivan the Terrible. But when fantasy comes into contact with reality, it melts away like fairy gold; the dreamer is left facing his own naked reality. Moreover, as Lake and Ng humiliate their victims, we sense that, in spite of the bravado and brutality ('Nothing is yours now'), they are still human enough to feel that they are outraging their own humanity. Like Panzram, Judy and Bundy, they have delivered themselves into the power of the 'hunchback', the killer Alsatian, and in so doing, have resigned from the human race. Lake admits in his diary that his dreams of success have eluded him and that his boasts of heroic deeds in Vietnam were delusions. He has become morally and spiritually bankrupt. Norris comments penetratingly: 'By the time he was arrested in San Francisco, Lake had reached the final stage of the serial murder syndrome: he realized that he had come to a dead end, with nothing but his own misery to show for it.' This is why Lake committed suicide when, if he had kept his head, he could probably have bluffed his way to freedom. His freedom had become meaningless.

11

It should be clear now that the Right Man syndrome is basically a matter of 'dominance'. This notion first came to general notice as a result of the work of students of animal behaviour like Konrad Lorenz and Niko Tinbergen, who noticed that the 'pecking order' of barnyard fowl has its counterpart in all human and animal societies. The psychologist Alfred Adler suggested that the 'will to power' is the basic human drive – and not, as Freud suggested, the sex urge. This was confirmed by Abraham Maslow when he was studying the behaviour of apes in the Bronx zoo in the 1930s; their activities made him at first conclude that their main interest in life was sex, since they spent all their time mounting one another; yet as he observed that females sometimes mounted males, and that both males and females mounted members of their own sex, it dawned on him that they were actually expressing dominance: the more aggressive apes asserted themselves by mounting the less aggressive ones, without regard to sex.

As a result of this observation Maslow decided, in 1936, to study dominance behaviour in human beings. Because he thought women tended to be more truthful about such matters, he began a series of interviews with college women, and soon made the interesting discovery that his subjects fell into three distinct dominance groups: high, medium and low. High dominance women tended to enjoy sex for its own sake – in a manner that is usually regarded as distinctly male – and to be sexually experimental. Medium dominance women enjoyed sex, but it had to be with someone with whom they were romantically involved; they were looking for 'Mr Right', the kind of man who would take them to restaurants with soft lights and present them with bouquets. Low dominance women thought sex was rather frightening and disgusting: they preferred the kind of man who would admire them from a distance for years without daring to speak. Maslow also made another interesting observation: that the high dominance females were exactly 5 per cent of the total – one in twenty. This also confirmed an observation already known to zoologists: that there is a 'dominant 5 per cent' in all animal groups. (Shaw once asked the explorer Stanley how many men could take over the leadership of his expedition if he himself fell ill; he replied: 'One in twenty.' 'Is that approximate or exact?' asked Shaw, and Stanley replied: 'Exact'.)

Maslow made another significant observation: for the most part, men and women form close relationships within their own dominance group. Highly dominant males preferred highly dominant females, and so on. A high dominance male *would* sleep with a medium dominance female, but there was nothing 'personal' about it; only in cases of 'sexual drought' would he form a permanent relation with such a woman. Maslow also noted that the male – female relation worked best in all groups if the male was slightly – but not too much – more dominant than the female.

It should now be clear that 'dominance' is the key to Right Man behaviour. Among apes, lions and bison, dominance is easily established: the two contenders simply fight one another. In human society, it is far more complex. The king is not necessarily more dominant than his prime minister, the colonel than the sergeant major, the manager than the foreman – he may not even be more intelligent or better qualified for the job. It can obviously be intensely frustrating for a high dominance individual to be the subordinate of someone of lower dominance – sometimes of dozens of people of lower dominance – particularly if the low dominance individual tries to make up for it by bullying. Some high dominance individuals, placed in this situation of subordination, attempt to express their dominance in the only way that is left open to them: the family situation. This is, in a sense, a confession of defeat: he has made fantasy a substitute for reality, and if something undermines the fantasy – such as the woman leaving him – the result may be suicidal despair.

It is impossible to grasp the motivations of a serial killer like Ted Bundy, Charles Manson or Leonard Lake without recognizing the basic role of dominance and fantasy-fulfilment. His crimes are fantasy-fulfilment, a substitute for the kind of real achievement to which he feels his dominance entitles him. The paradox is that the crimes cause the fulfilment to recede farther into the distance as if he is the victim of some magic spell.

One of the clearest examples is provided by the Moors murder case, which occurred in England in the mid-1960s; it also illustrates another curious aspect of the Right Man syndrome. Ian Brady, the illegitimate son of a waitress, was born in a tough Glasgow slum in 1938, and was farmed out to foster parents. He was intelligent and a good student; but at the age of 11 he won a scholarship to an expensive school where many of the students came from well-to-do families, and – like Panzram – he began to develop a fierce resentment of his own underprivileged position. He began committing burglaries, and at 13 was sentenced to two years' probation for housebreaking; as soon as this ended he was sentenced to another two years for ten burglaries. He also practised sadistic cruelty to animals. When his mother moved to Manchester with a new husband, he found a job in a brewery, but was dismissed for stealing, and sent to a Borstal institution. At 21, he became a clerk in Millwards, a chemical firm in Gorton, and began collecting books on the Nazis, and reading the Marquis de Sade.

Sade is virtually the patron saint of serial killers. His books give expression to their basic belief that the individual owes nothing to society, and has the right to live in it as a kind of outlaw – the philosophy of the fox in a poultry farm. Brady experienced a kind of religious conversion to these ideas. So far he had seen himself merely as a criminal; now – like Leonard Lake – he began to see himself as the heroic outcast, the scourge of society.

It was at about this point that Myra Hindley entered the story. She was a completely normal working-class girl, not bad-looking, inclined to go in for blonde hair-dos and bright lipstick, interested mainly in boys and dancing. She was a typical medium dominance female, who would have been perfectly content with a reasonably hard-working boy next door. When she came to work at Millwards, she was fascinated by Brady's sullen good looks and moody expression. But Brady was undoubtedly one of the dominant five per cent; he recognized her as a medium dominance type and ignored her; at the end of six months he had not even spoken to her. Without encouragement Myra filled her diary with declarations of love: 'I hope he loves me and will marry me some day.' Finally, Brady decided it would be a pity not to take advantage of the maidenhead that was being offered, and invited her out. Soon after this Myra surrendered her virginity on the divan bed in her gran's front room.

In the criminally inclined, the combination of high and medium dominance egos usually produces an explosive mixture – as can be seen, for example, in the Leopold and Loeb case. What seems to happen is that the high dominance partner finds himself regarded with admiration that acts as a kind of super-fertilizer on his ego; in no time at all he becomes a full-blown case of the Right Man syndrome. Brady found it intoxicating to have an audience; he talked to Myra enthusiastically about Hitler, and nicknamed her 'Hessie' after Myra Hess. He also paid her the high compliment of telling her that she looked like Irma Grese, the concentration camp guard. But her sexual submission was not enough; it only intensified his craving to be a 'somebody'. He announced that he was planning a series of payroll robberies, and induced her to join a local pistol club to gain access to guns. He also took photographs of her posing in the nude and, using a timing device, of the two of them having sexual intercourse. In some of the photographs – which Brady tried to sell – she has whip marks across her buttocks.

Some time in 1963 – when he was 25 and she 21 – he induced her to join with him in the murder of children. It is hard to understand how a typical medium dominance girl, who loved children and animals, allowed herself to be persuaded. But the answer undoubtedly lies in Brady's obsessive need to taste the delights of dominating another person, and in the sadism that had developed in him since childhood. The pleasure of completely dominating Myra aroused visions of dominating 'sex slaves'. Brady and Hindley kidnapped children by offering them lifts in Myra's car, then took them back to Myra's home, where they were subjected to bondage, sexual abuse and torture. They were photographed and their cries for mercy tape-recorded. Sixteen-year-old Pauline Reade, who knew Myra, was picked up on her way to a dance, taken up to the moor, and probably raped; then Brady cut her throat.

After four child murders – possibly more – Brady attempted to involve Myra Hindley's brother-in-law, a teenager named David Smith. He was still dreaming of bank robberies. On 6 October 1965, Brady picked up a teenage homosexual, Edward Evans, and took him back to the flat; then, with Smith looking on, he killed Evans with an axe. But he had overestimated Smith's callousness. (The FBI profiling team could have told him that a teenager would panic.) Smith lost no time in telling his wife what had happened, and together they telephoned the police. The corpse was still in the front room, wrapped in a polythene sheet, when Brady and Hindley were arrested the next day. Photographs of the graves led the police to uncover the bodies of a boy and a girl on Saddleworth Moor. In the typical manner of the Right Man, Brady refused to confess; to have done so would have been an admission that he was wrong. In May 1966, both were sentenced to life imprisonment.

12

The problem of the serial killer is one of the most perplexing and frightening that has so far confronted the criminologist. Yet our survey of the history of crime detection has at least shown us how to place it in perspective. We know that human beings have been murdering one another in various appalling ways for thousands of years. H. G. Wells defined the cause of the problem when he wrote:

Five hundred generations ago, human beings were brought together into a closeness of contact for which their past had not prepared them. The early civilisations were not slowly evolved and adapted *communities*. They were essentially jostling *crowds* in which quite unprecedented reactions were possible . . . With the first cities came the first slums, and ever since then the huge majority of mankind has been living in slums.*

These conditions, as Marx pointed out, produce 'alienation', a state in which human beings have no more fellow-feeling for one another than they have for the birds and animals they slaughter for sport. Plutarch speaks of a Greek brigand who used to make travellers jump off a high cliff, and describes the tyrant Alexander of Pherae who liked to bury men alive or watch them being torn to pieces by dogs. Every schoolboy has shuddered at the story of the Sicilian tyrant Phalaris who roasted men alive in a brazen bull. The Wallachian ruler Vlad the Impaler – the original Dracula – derived such pleasure from watching impaled victims dying in agony that he had pointed stakes set up in his dining-hall. Ivan the Terrible – another typical 'Right Man' – spent five weeks presiding over the torture of the inhabitants of Novgorod, taking special delight in torturing husbands and wives before one another. Gilles de Rais raped and dismembered more than 50 children. The Hungarian countess Elizabeth Bathory was tried in 1610 for murdering more than 80 servant girls in order to bathe in their blood. Clearly, then, cruelty has been with us down the ages, and the behaviour of the serial killer is no proof that our civilization is going to the dogs. What *is* unusual is that we are so shocked by cruelty. The present high regard for human life appeared only in the nineteenth century; before that, cruelty was accepted casually as one of the facts of life.

In the course of this book we have seen that it was not until the early nineteenth century that police forces became efficient enough to halt the more-or-less permanent crime waves that flourished in most major cities. And this was not due to some technological or sociological advance, but simply to the fact that men suddenly began to confront the problem in a new *spirit of optimism*. Instead of torturing men to make them confess, or crushing them under a series of 50 lb weights, the police began to pay attention to the importance of clues; they began to use reason and logic to understand the ways of criminals just as Isaac Newton had used reason and logic to understand the ways of the planets. The result was the rise of the science of crime detection – and prevention – as recounted in this book. Slowly, little by little, this turned the war between the police and the criminal into something like

*42 to '44, A Contemporary Memoir, Secker & Warburg, London, 1944, p. 15.

an equal battle. By the beginning of the twentieth century, prophets like H. G. Wells and Bernard Shaw could look forward to the day when crime would simply disappear, like all the other 'teething troubles of humanity'. The invention of the telephone meant that crimes could be reported so quickly that the burglar or the footpad could often be caught before he had time to escape. (We have seen how Police Chief August Vollmer used the latest scientific advances to bring law and order to the streets of Berkeley.) The 1920s and 1930s were the golden age of crime detection, when civilized countries had less unsolved crime than at any other point in history.

And then, it seemed, the situation changed overnight. The rise of the dictators made it seem that prophets like Wells had been far too optimistic about human nature. The invasion of Abyssinia, the Stalin show-trials, the Spanish Civil War, the Second World War, all seemed to demonstrate that civilization was no more than a veneer. Wells was so shocked by the atomic bomb and by the revelations of Buchenwald and Belsen that he wrote his most deeply pessimistic work, *Mind at the End of its Tether,* shortly before his death, prophesying some ultimate catastrophe that would bring an end to all life in the universe. And the steady rise in post-war crime seemed to justify his pessimism about human nature.

Yet such a view is hardly justified by the facts. It is true that the increase in drug abuse has caused a crime problem in the major cities. But modern London, Paris, Rome, New York or Los Angeles are oases of law and order compared with London and Paris in the early eighteenth century. What has happened is that man has realized that even the most intractable problems can be solved with the use of patience, reason and common sense. It was this new faith in reason and common sense that made all the difference between social chaos and social order. In 1750, most Londoners had come to accept that they had to live with footpads, pickpockets and highwaymen; at this point, Henry Fielding demonstrated that the problem could be brought under control with surprising ease by a fairly small number of dedicated men. The same general truth applies today, but with even greater force, since the police can now utilize the results of two centuries of scientific crime detection.

The problem of the serial killer – and the closely related problem of the sexual criminal – is a case in point. The examples discussed in the last two sections make it clear that the phenomenon is not as chaotic and unpredictable as it appears. On the contrary, the serial killer is a

recognizable type; in case after case, the same patterns repeat
themselves with almost monotonous regularity: deprivation of affection in childhood, sadism towards animals, fear and distrust of women,
alcohol and drug abuse, resentment towards society, high dominance,
and the tendency to escape into a world of fantasy. It is the combination of these last two that tends to produce the Right Man syndrome
which is so characteristic of serial killers. The main problem so far has
been that police and medical authorities have failed to recognize that
they are dealing with a clearly defined type. Yet as soon as Joel Norris
and his colleagues began to apply statistical methods to serial killers,
they recognized 'profiles that could lead to the development of a
diagnostic or prediction instrument'. Moreover, the recognition that the
serial killer is almost invariably a 'Right Man' adds a vitally important
element to the 'profile'. During his studies of dominance in women,
Maslow developed tests for determining the precise level of
dominance, and these would obviously be of use to psychologists
dealing with potential serial killers. It is true that the notion of a
'diagnostic or prediction instrument' tends to strike us as vague and
unrealistic; but it should be borne in mind that this is precisely how
Bertillon's proposals for a new system of identification struck *his*
contemporaries at the Sûreté.

In fact, there are altogether more down-to-earth possibilities for
solving the problem of the serial killer. A retired Los Angeles homicide
detective, Pierce Brooks, has created a programme known as VICAP,
the 'violent criminal apprehension programme'. He pointed out that
such killers as Sherman McCrary, Stephen Judy, Henry Lee Lucas and
Ted Bundy remained unapprehended for so long because they moved
on before state authorities had reason to suspect a multiple killer. But
this presents no problem to the computer, which can transmit information on 'unsolved homicides, violent or deviant sexual assaults, and
kidnappings or disappearances' to every other computer in the United
States, and alert police to the activities of habitual criminals. By simply
sending out questionnaires to imprisoned violent criminals (who, of
course, wished to improve their chance of parole by assisting the
authorities) the VICAP initiative soon built up a huge cross-section of
data about the habits, attitudes and motivations of society's most
dangerous citizens.

Indeed, the VICAP program soon provided police with a much more
powerful weapon against repeat criminals than they might ever have
dreamed, as it led directly to the development of the discipline known

as psychological profiling. VICAP showed that violent criminals (and, indeed, all people) run on patterns of behaviour that are both largely invisible to the untrained eye, yet are extremely predictable to those who know what to look for.

For example, an expert in profiling can tell, by studying a series of murders, if they were committed by the same killer or by different people. They can also tell whether a killer is a novice to murder or had become practiced at homicide. More importantly, a profiler, given enough evidence, can make strikingly accurate surmises as to the age, race, social background, marital status and even personal habits and attitudes of a murderer. This Sherlock Holmesian trick is based on the encyclopaedic knowledge of previous crimes provided by the VICAP program.

It has been shown, again and again, that even criminals with high IQ's follow typical patterns of behaviour and habit. A particular type of mutilation, a repeated method of dumping bodies, even a killer's choice of victims all provide the profiler with extensive insights into the criminal's life which, in turn, help investigating officers narrow their search.

As we saw in the chapter on the sexual criminal, psychological profiling was of key help in catching John Duffy, the London Railway Rapist. Dr David Canter's study of the series of rapes and murders brought up seventeen points he believed the police should look out for in their suspects, including apparently unrelated facts such as the killer being a semi-skilled worker with a bad relationship with his wife. Fed into a computer containing the names of thousands of possible suspects, Canter's seventeen points lead exclusively to John Duffy. Canter's analysis even suggested that Duffy had not acted alone on all the rape/murders – a fact not confirmed until 2001, when Duffy's evidence convicted his former school friend, David Mulcahy.

Over the last ten years, psychological profiling has become so highly refined and diversified that big businesses sometimes employ profilers to help when hiring key employees – aiming to find ideal personalities rather than habitual criminals, of course. There is even a new forensic technique, geographical profiling, that allows an expert to map the likely home area of a serial criminal.

Taken at its most simple level, geographical profiling is based on the idea that criminals have set 'prowling areas' – rather like hunting tigers. This area will not be too close to the criminal's home district, for fear that they might be recognized by an acquaintance. On the other hand, the prowling area will only stretch as far as the criminal has easy access – indicating further clues as to his method of transport and financial situation.

By running many varying factors thrown up by a case through a computer, a geographical profiler can offer the police a reasonably precise area from which to interview suspects. The technique is still in its infancy, but initial results have been positive.

For example, police in Lafayette, Louisiana, called in geographical profiler Kim Rossmo when they failed to catch a serial rapist who had attacked at least fifteen women over eleven years. Public response had been rather too helpful and the investigators had over two thousand tip-offs and over a thousand suspects to interview. Rossmo ran the profile program and highlighted a particular area in which the rapist was likely to live. Investigators targeted suspects in this area and soon, using traditional methods as well as DNA matching, caught the rapist: a sheriff's deputy called Randy Comeaux, who confessed and was sentenced to three life sentences.

The increased use of computer-enhanced forensic disciplines has had a major impact on most elements of law enforcement in the last decade. For example, the threatening phone caller might soon be a thing of the past, simply because all calls are completely traceable thanks to modern computerised exchanges. Even where a criminal might get around this problem – by, for example, using a stolen mobile phone or a public telephone – computer voice recognition programs are already capable of taking his 'vocal fingerprint.'

Even that Holy Grail for scene of crime officers – the taking of fingerprints from skin – is now available. This has always been thought an impossibility; fingerprints are made by the oils secreted by human skin, so any fingerprints on an area of skin would be made invisible by that skin's own oils. Now, however, it has been discovered that the evaporative staining of suspect areas of skin with fluorescent dyes, like iodine, can show-up fingerprints, which can then be read under certain types of medical laser or removed for permanent storage on plastic strips with a leuco crystal violet coating. What is more, this process will work on living as well as dead areas of skin, making not only murderers, but all types of physical attacker more likely to be identified.

At the time of writing, genetic fingerprinting offers the most important hope for the solution of serial killings and sex crimes. Most sexual criminals leave behind a sample of their sperm; many also leave samples of blood and skin under the fingernails of their victims. This means, in effect, that they have left behind a kind of visiting card, which has much the same value as a fingerprint or palmprint. If genetic fingerprinting had been known in the 1970s, Bundy would have been convicted as a multiple killer on the evidence of the bloodstains on Carol DaRonch, made during her fight to escape from his car – in which case, presumably, he would have been placed in a maximum security prison, and not allowed to escape to commit more murders. There seems no reason to doubt that the discovery of genetic finger-printing will prove as great a milestone in the history of crime detection as Henry's discovery of fingerprint classification in the 1890s.

In our present situation, it is tempting to dwell on the sociological causes of crime: boredom, alienation, psychological tensions, and the fact that deprived members of a consumer society feel that they deserve a share of its luxury goods. Seen in this perspective the problem seems insoluble, except in terms of some vague 'social revolution'. In fact, revolutions leave the problem untouched; they are too wholesale. If this book has taught us anything, it is that the problem has already been solved. It was solved in the eighteenth century, when a new type of 'detective' abandoned the old defeatist attitude towards crime, and began to treat the evidence as a witness that could be persuaded to tell its story. That change of attitude was more than a revolution in crime detection; it was a revolution in the history of the human mind.

Postscript

A book on crime detection seems hardly the place for philosophical reflections. But the last chapter should have demonstrated that even this grimly practical field can benefit from a wider intellectual perspective.

In the late 1930s, brain physiologists became aware that animal aggression seems to be associated with a part of the brain called the amygdala, or amygdaloid nucleus, an almond-shaped structure situated in the limbic system, the part of the brain that plays an important role in emotion and motivation. They discovered that if the amygdala of a highly aggressive ape is removed, it becomes good tempered and docile; when the amygdala of a sweet old lady was electrically stimulated, she became vituperative and aggressive.

But knowing the precise location of the 'aggression centre' fails to provide any real clue to the control of aggression. For it seems clear that the control of aggression depends largely upon whether a person *wants* to control it. Whether we like it or not, aggression depends, in the last resort, on 'free will'. Van Vogt says that the 'Violent Man' *makes the decision* to be out of control.

This question of decision is an interesting one. Try a simple experiment. Ask a child to stand in the centre of the room, then crawl towards him on all fours, making growling noises. His first reaction is amusement. As you get closer, the laughter develops a note of hysteria; at a certain distance, the child will turn and run – it is a good idea to have his mother sitting nearby so he can run into her arms. A more confident child may run at you, as if to prove this is only daddy. Now try the experiment yourself, getting a friend to crawl towards you growling; you will observe that you still feel a certain automatic alarm, which – being adult – you can easily control. It is an interesting demonstration that, although we consider ourselves to be rational creatures, there is still a part of us that stands outside our civilized conditioning.

It can, of course, be controlled. If you went on playing the game for half an hour, you would finally be able to watch your friend's approach without the slightest reaction. Moreover, if someone was rude to you within the next half hour, you would find that you had far less trouble than usual in controlling the rush of irritation.

It operates the other way around. If you respond to irritation by losing your temper, it becomes increasingly difficult to control your temper. The Panzram case is a classic illustration of how a man turns into a violent criminal simply by giving full rein to his resentment. At the same time, Panzram's rational self recognized that he was destroying the specifically human part of himself – after all, we use the word 'humanity' to mean decency and kindness.

In an article on aggressive epileptics,* Vernon H. Mark and Robert Neville suggest that brain surgery – on the amygdaloid nucleus – could solve the behaviour problems of many violent criminals. They go on to admit that this view will offend many humanitarians, who believe that violence is an expression of free will, and that brain surgery would have a 'degrading effect' on human dignity. But they then make the important comment: 'This view is particularly inappropriate, not because free will is to be denied, but because the quality of human life is to be prized. Many of the patients who come with focal brain disease associated with violent behaviour are so offended by their own actions that they have attempted suicide.' (This, of course, is what Panzram did.) They go on to argue that a brain operation could give a patient more rather than less control over his own behaviour, and therefore increase his ability to express free will.

Theirs, it seems to me, is the sensible view. Human violence cannot be explained either in terms of free will or of physiological reflexes. It can only be understood as a *combination* of these two. Human evolution depends upon increasing control of the reflexes. This is why 'the decision to be out of control' is always a mistake.

If we really wish to understand the issues involved, we must be prepared to consider them from a wider viewpoint than most scientists would allow themselves. In *A Criminal History of Mankind*, I suggested that they should be considered from the point of view of two opposing forces, which I suggest labelling Force T and Force C, the T

*In *Physiology of Aggression and Implications for Control*, edited by Kenneth Moyer, Raven Press, New York, 1976.

standing for tension, the C for control. When a man badly wants to urinate, he experiences increasing tension; his heartbeat and blood pressure increase, his temperature rises. When a man becomes deeply interested in some problem, the opposite occurs; he soothes his impatience, focuses his attention, damps down his energies, until he achieves a state of inner calm. Some mystics – Wordsworth, for example – can sink into such deep conditions of calm that they achieve an insight into 'unknown modes of being', and seem to grasp the workings of the universe. The criminal, with his tendency to lose control, has abandoned all possibility of such insights.

After publication of *An Encyclopedia of Murder,* many friends – and critics – expressed their perplexity about my interest in crime, which they seemed to feel indicated a streak of morbidity. One day when I was having dinner with the poet Ronald Duncan, and we were both in a pleasant state of alcoholic relaxation, he suddenly asked me: 'Why are you *really* interested in murder?' He was obviously hoping that I would admit to a secret compulsion to rape schoolgirls or disembowel animals. When I explained that I saw it as a symbolic representation of everything that is wrong with human consciousness, he shook his head wearily, evidently feeling that I was being evasive. But I was also aware that the fault lay partly in myself, for failing to explain what I meant.

But as I was writing the section on Dan MacDougald in the final chapter of this book, I suddenly became aware that I was succeeding in saying *precisely* why the study of crime seems to me as important as the study of philosophy or religion. It was in the passage where, after explaining that Dickens' Scrooge is an example of what MacDougald calls 'negative blocking', I go on:

Now it is obvious that we are *all* in this condition, to some extent – for, as Wordsworth says, 'shades of the prison house' begin to close around us as we learn to 'cope' with the complexities of existence. So we are all in the position of the criminal. But criminals do it far more than most people – to such an extent that, when we read of a man like H. H. Holmes, we can suddenly *see* that he was an idiot to waste his own life and that of his victims. As strange as it sounds, studying criminality has much the same effect on most of us that the ghosts of Christmas had on Scrooge – of making us more widely aware of the reality we ignore.

And there, I feel, I have succeeded in putting my finger squarely on the central problem – not only of criminal psychology, but of what I feel to be the essence of the human dilemma. This can be summarized in the statement that although human beings possess free will, they are usually unaware that they possess it. We *become* aware of it whenever we are in moods of happiness and excitement – what Maslow calls the peak experience. But under normal conditions, we are merely aware of the problems of everyday life, and these induce a feeling that we are fighting a purely defensive battle, like a man trying to prevent himself from drowning. Life seems to be an endless struggle, an endless series of problems and obstacles. And this condition produces a dangerous state of 'negative feedback'. As we contemplate the problems and obstacles, the heart sinks, and we lose all feeling of free will. And if our willpower is undermined, the obstacles seem twice as great. We *allow* the will to sink, until every problem produces a deep sense of discouragement.

On the other hand, when we are doing something we want to do, when we are carrying out some task with a deep sense of motivation, we are clearly aware of our freedom, and of our ability to 'summon energy' to surmount obstacles. This has the effect of revitalizing us and recharging our batteries, which in turn deepens our sense of motivation, so that we actually enjoy tackling obstacles. In this state, we often observe that things seem to go right', that obstacles seem to disappear of their own accord. This may or may not be true, but it certainly increases that feeling of zest and enthusiasm. We experience a kind of 'positive feedback'.

Now it obviously makes sense, on a purely logical level, to try to achieve these states of 'positive feedback'. No matter how serious the problems, it is obviously to our advantage to tackle them in a state of enthusiasm and optimism; it cannot possibly be to our advantage to sink into a state of discouragement. Unfortunately, we are not now dealing with a logical reaction, but with a purely instinctive one, like the child's desire to run away when you crawl towards him on all fours. And it is this negative reaction, this tendency to allow the will to collapse, and to seek the solution of the problem on a lower level, that constitutes the essence of criminal psychology.

Here is the paradox: that it is when we experience the feeling of helplessness, the sense that life has turned into a series of unfair frustrations and difficulties, that we are tempted to make 'the decision to be out of control', to *restore the sensation of free will* by doing something absurd or violent or even criminal. This is the time when we lose our temper, or give way to a fit of self-pity, or take some dangerous and unjustifiable risk, like overtaking on a bend. Graham Greene has described how, as a teenager, he reacted to depression by playing Russian roulette with his brother's revolver, and how, when there was only a 'click' on an empty chamber, he experienced a tremendous surge of joy; he had *become aware of his freedom*.

But this is only half the story. The mechanism can be studied even more clearly in Arthur Koestler's account of how he came to join the Communist Party. In *Arrow in the Blue,* he describes how he lost his money in a poker game, then got drunk at a party and discovered that the car radiator had frozen and the engine block had burst. He accepted the hospitality of a girl he disliked and spent the night in her bed. Waking up beside her with a hangover, he recalled that he had no money and no car, and felt the urge to 'do something desperate' which led to the decision to join the Communist Party. Here we can see that his misfortunes had induced a sense of non-freedom that led him to decide to renounce what freedom he felt he had left, and to take refuge in a crowd. (This is, of course, the basic mechanism of 'conversion'.)

We are all familiar with the same tendency. When our energies are low, our freedom seems non-existent, and everyday tasks and chores seem unutterably tiresome. Then we slip into the vicious circle of boredom and loss of motivation in which it seems self-evident that life is a long-drawn-out defeat. This state of mind tempts us to take 'short cuts'. And crime, of course, is a short cut. We can study the same mechanism in Carl Panzram, who became a killer after he had betrayed the trust of the prison governor and decided that he was 'worthless', and in Ted Bundy, who became a Peeping Tom after his girlfriend had jilted him.

In this respect at least, crime is closely related to mental illness. Maslow describes the case of a girl who had sunk into such a state of depression that she had even ceased to menstruate. He discovered that she had been a brilliant student of sociology, who had been forced by the Depression of the 1930s to accept a job in a chewing-gum factory. The boredom of the job had totally eroded her sense of freedom. Maslow advised her to study sociology at night school, and her problems soon vanished; her sense of freedom had been restored. Similarly, William James describes how, during a period of anxiety about his future prospects, he also fell into a state of depression. One day, entering a room at dusk, he recalled the face of an idiot he had seen in a mental home, staring in front of him with blank eyes, and was suddenly overwhelmed by the thought: 'If the hour should strike for me as it struck for him, *nothing* I possess could defend me from that fate.' 'There was . . . such a perception of my own merely momentary discrepancy from him, that it was as if something hitherto solid in my breast gave way, and I became a mass of quivering fear.'

We, of course, can see clearly that there was far more than a 'momentary discrepancy' between William James and an idiot suffering from catatonia; there was a vast difference in their capacity for freedom. But James had become *blind* to this difference because his depression had narrowed his senses. It is also significant that James began recovering from his period of mental illness when he came across a definition of free will by the philosopher Renouvier: that it is demonstrated by my capacity to *think one thing rather than another*. As soon as he became intellectually convinced that he possessed free will, he began to throw off his depression.

This is a point of central importance. Our free will is normally 'invisible' to us, as a candle flame is invisible in the sunlight. We only become aware of it when we are engaged in some purposeful activity. Maslow made the interesting observation that when his students began to discuss peak experiences amongst themselves, and recall past peak experiences, they began having peak experiences all the time. The reason is obvious. The peak experience is a sudden *recognition* that we possess free will. It might be compared to discovering that the candle flame *is* there by putting your finger near it. Once the students became *aware* that they possessed free will, they kept on 'recollecting' the fact with a shock of delight – the peak experience – like a man waking up in the middle of the night and remembering that he has inherited a fortune.

But *how* can we fall into this strange state of 'unawareness of freedom'? The answer lies in a concept I have called 'the robot'. We all have a kind of robot in our subconscious minds which makes life a great deal easier. I have to learn new skills – like typing, driving a car, speaking French – patiently and slowly; then the robot takes them over and does it far more quickly than I could do it consciously. The trouble is that the robot not only does the things I want him to do, like typing, but also the things I *don't* want him to do, like enjoying nature, listening to music, even love-making. When we are fired, the robot takes control, and we lose all sense of freedom. We feel that we are merely a part of the physical world, with little or no power to 'do'. We lose our sense of our own value, and decide that the answer lies in compromise and seeking short cuts.

If we possessed detailed biographies of every criminal, we should almost certainly discover that most of them became criminals after such a crisis of 'self-devaluation'. But it is also interesting to note that some of the worst criminals – Henry Lee Lucas is an example – undergo religious conversion after they have been caught, as if the attention focused on them has restored their sense of personal value, so that they now become appalled by what they have done.

There is no obvious and simple method of restoring a criminal's sense of personal value, or of preventing him from losing it in the first place. But it may be worth noting the lesson of William James and of Maslow's sociology student: that as soon as the will is put to active use, the sense of personal value returns automatically. I have often day-dreamed of the idea of a prison where, instead of receiving remission for good conduct – which is at best a negative virtue – prisoners receive it for creative activity: a month's remission for a good poem or painting, three months for a promising story or article, two years for a novel or symphony . . . The idea may be unworkable, but I have a feeling that the approach is along the right lines.

These reflections also lead me to the unfashionable view that the social philosophy promulgated by our educational institutions also deserves its share of the blame. The old religious philosophy of earlier centuries was authoritarian and repressive, but at least it assumed that man has an immortal soul, and that our task is to surmount the problems of everyday life by reminding ourselves of that fact. As far as Western civilization is concerned, the great change began after the year 1762, the year Rousseau's *Social Contract* appeared, with its famous words 'Man is born free but is everywhere in chains.' Unfortunately, this is a half-truth, which can be far more dangerous than a downright lie. Freedom is a quality of consciousness, not another name for a man's political rights. To confuse the two leads to intellectual chaos, which is the reverse of freedom. We all know people who ought to feel free because they have money and leisure, and yet who are miserable and neurotic. We all know people who ought to be miserable because they are poor and overworked, yet who remain remarkably cheerful. The very nature of freedom seems to be paradoxical.

As Rousseau's 'Man is born free . . .' became part of the conventional wisdom, it became a justification for crime, as we can see in the case of Lacenaire or Ravachol. If I believe that I *ought* to be free, and yet I do not feel free, then I look around for someone to blame. And if I allow Rousseau and Marx and Kropotkin to convince me that the blame should be placed squarely on the selfish philosophy of Capitalism, then I have found the ideal excuse for ignoring my own shortcomings and indulging in childish outbursts of self-pity. Lacenaire believed he was combating social injustice by stabbing a 'bourgeois' and pushing his body in the river. Charles Manson believed that society is so rotten that it is no crime to murder the 'pigs'. Carl Panzram went further and believed that life is so vile that to murder someone is to do him a favour.

We can see that this is merely unbelievably muddled thinking. But when so many academics and philosophers subscribe to it, we can hardly blame the criminals. Sartre is on record as describing the 'Free World' as 'that hell of misery and blood', and declaring that true progress lies in the attempt of the coloured races to liberate themselves through violence. This philosophy inspired Italian terrorists who burst into a university classroom and shot the professor in the legs, alleging that he was guilty of teaching his students to adapt to a fundamentally immoral society. The same philosophy could easily be adapted to defend the activities of the Mafia.

In the Introduction to the *Encyclopedia of Modern Murder,* I pointed out that Albert Camus' book *L'Homme revolt (The Rebel)* was designed as a final refutation of Rousseau. It sets out to demonstrate that all the philosophies of freedom and rebellion, from de Sade to Karl Marx, have led to tyranny and the destruction of freedom. The rising tide of violence in our society demonstrates that Camus was right and Rousseau wrong. And if Rousseau's idea could gain currency because a need for change was so urgent in the late eighteenth century, then the same applies to Camus' idea when there is an even more urgent need for change in the late twentieth century. That observation places the responsibility squarely on the shoulders of our educational institutions and on our 'intellectuals'. But this analysis of the nature of freedom should have made it clear that this is only part of the solution. The great 'metaphysical' problem of the human race is that we possess free will yet are usually unaware of it. We cease to be aware of it the moment we allow tiredness and pessimism to erode our sense of purpose. We *become* aware of it by flinging ourselves into purposeful activity. The real enemy is the pessimism that arises when we contemplate the problems – for example, the serial killers and 'motiveless murder' – in a defeatist frame of mind. For, as we have seen, it is that 'invisible' element of freedom that spells the difference between failure and success. And since the history of crime detection has been a history of optimism and logic, it would be a total absurdity to abandon our most powerful weapon at this point.

This had been for me the major 'lesson' of this book, and my justi-fication in writing it. But I trust I shall not be condemned as too 'metaphysical' if I also point out that is the general solution of the problem we all face every morning when we open our eyes. The problem of crime is the problem of human existence.

Select Bibliography

Angelella, Michael. *Trail of Blood – The Albert Fish Story*. New York: Bobbs-Merriil, 1979.

Bennett, Benjamin. *Famous South African Murders*. London: T. Werner Laurie, 1938.

Berg, Karl. *The Sadist*. London: Heinemann, 1945.

Block, Eugen B. *Famous Detectioes*. New York: Doubleday, 1967.

—— *Hypnosis: A New Tool in Crime Detection*. New York: David McKay, 1976.

Browne, Douglas G. and Alan Brock. *Fingerprints. Fifty Years of Scientific Crime Detection*. London: Harrap, 1953.

—— and F. V. Tullett. *Bernard Spilsbury. His Life and Cases*. London: Harrap, 1951.

Camps, Francis F., ed. *Gradwohl's Legal Medicine*. Bristol: John Wright & Sons, 1968.

—— *Medical and Scientific Investigations in the Christie Case*. London: Medical Publications, 1953.

Cantillon, Richard H. *In Defense of the Fox*. Atlanta: Droke House/Hallux, 1972.

Caputi, Jane Elizabeth. *The Age of Sex Crime*. Ann Arbor: University Microfilms International, 1982.

Cullen, Tom. *Crippen. The Mild Murderer*. London: The Bodley Head, 1977.

de River, J. Paul. *The Sexual Criminal*. Illinois: Charles C. Thomas, 1949.

Douthwaite, L. C. *Mass Murder*. London: John Long, 1928.

Dower, Alan. *Crime Chemist. The Life Story of Charles Anthony Taylor, Scientist for the Crown*. London: John Long, 1965.

Drzazga, John. *Sex Crimes*. Illinois: Charles C. Thomas, 1960.

Duke, Thomas S. *Celebrated Criminal Cases of America*. San Francisco: James H. Barry, 1910.

Dunning, John. *The Arbor House Treasury of True Crime*. New York: Arbor House, 1977.

Erskine, Addine G. *The Principles and Practice of Blood Grouping*. St Louis: C. V. Mosby, 1973.

Fayol, Amédée. La *Vie et l'oeuore d'Orfila*. Paris: Les Vies Authentiques, 1930.

Fletcher, Tony. *Memories of Murder*. London: Weidenfeld & Nicolson, 1986.

Frank, Gerold. *The Boston Strangler*. New York: The New American Library, 1966.

Franke, David. *The Torture Doctor*. New York: Hawthorn Books, 1975.

Furneaux, Rupert. *Famous Criminal Cases*. (7 Vols.) London: Allan Wingate, 1955–62.

—— *The Medical Murderer*. London: Elek Books, 1957.

—— *The Two Stranglers of Rillington Place*. London: Panther Books, 1961.

Gaddis, Thomas F., ed. *Killer. A Journal of Murder*. New York: Macmillan, 1970.

Gaute, J. H. H. and Robin Odell. *Murder 'Whatdunit'*. London: Harrap, 1982.

—— —— *Murder Whereabouts*. London: Harrap, 1986.

—— —— *The Murderers' Who's Who*. London: Harrap, 1979.

Glaister, John. *Medical Jurisprudence and Toxicology*. Edinburgh and London: Livingstone, 1953.

—— *The Power of Poison*. London: Christopher Johnson, 1954.

—— and James Couper Brash, eds. *Medico-legal Aspects of the Ruxton Case*. Edinburgh: Livingstone, 1937.

Goddard, Henry. *Memoirs of a Bow Street Runner*. London: Museum Press, 1956.

Gonzales, Thomas A. *et al. Legal Medicine. Pathology and Toxicology*. New York: Appleton-Century-Crofts, 1954.

Goodman, Jonathan, ed. *Trial of Ian Brady and Myra Hindley. The Moors Case*. Newton Abbot: David & Charles, 1973.

Grant, Michael, ed. *Cicero Murder Trials*. Harmondsworth: Penguin, 1973.

Griffiths, Arthur. *Mysteries of Police and Crime,* Vols I and II. London: Cassell, 1898

Hastings, Macdonald. *The Other Mr Churchill*. London: Harrap, 1963.

Haworth, Peter. *Before Scotland Yard*. Oxford: Basil Blackwell, 1927.

Heppenstall, Rayner. *Bluebeard and After*. London: Hamish Hamilton, 1972.

—— *French Crime in the Romantic Age*. London: Hamish Hamilton, 1970.

—— *A Little Pattern of French Crime*. London: Hamish Hamilton. 1969.

—— *Reflections on the Newgate Calendar*. London: W. H. Allen, 1975.

—— *The Sex War and Others*. London: Peter Owen, 1973.

Hibbert, Christopher. *The Roots of Evil*. London: Weidenfeld & Nicolson, 1963.

Higdon, Hal. *The Crime of the Century. The Leopold and Loeb Case*. New York: G. P. Putnam's Sons, 1975.

Horan, James. D. and Howard Swiggett. *The Pinkerton Story*. New York: G. P. Putnam's Sons, 1951.

Hoskins, Percy. *The Sound of Murder*. London: John Long, 1973.

Jackson, Robert. *The Crime Doctors*. London: Frederick Muller, 1966.

—— *Francis Camps. Famous Case Histories of the Most Celebrated Pathologist of our Time*. London: Hart-Davis, MacGibbon, 1975.

Jacobs, T. C. H. *Aspects of Murder*. London: Stanley Paul, 1956.

—— *Cavalcade of Murder*. London: Stanley Paul, 1955.

—— *Pageant of Murder*. London: Stanley Paul, 1956.

Kendall, Elizabeth. *The Phantom Prince. My Life With Ted Bundy*. Seattle: Madrona, 1981.

Kennedy, Ludovic. *The Airman and the Carpenter*. London: Fontana/Collins, 1985.

—— *Ten Rillington Place*. London: Gollancz, 1961.

Kind, Stuart. *The Scientific Investigation of Crime*. Harrogate: Forensic Science Services, 1987.

—— *et al. Science Against Crime*. London: Marshall Cavendish, 1982.

—— and Michael Overman. *Annual Report of the Director*. Home Office Forensic Science Service and Research Establishment, 1976.

—— —— *Science Against Crime*. London: Aldus Books, 1972.

Kunstler, William M. *The Minister and the Choir Singer. The Hall-Mills Murder Case*. London: Gollancz, 1964.

Larsen, Richard W. *Bundy: The Deliberate Stranger*. Englewood Cliffs: Prentice-Hall, 1980.

Lefebure, Molly. *Evidence for the Crown. Experiences of a Pathologist's Secretary*. London: Heinemann, 1955.

—— *Murder With a Difference. Studies of Haigh and Christie*. London: Heinemann, 1958.

Lewis, Alfred Allan and Herbert Leon MacDonell. *The Evidence Never Lies. The Casebook of a Modern Sherlock Holmes*. New York: A Laurel Trade Paperback, 1984.

Locard, Edmond. *Traite' de criminalistique*. (7 Vols.) Lyon: Joannès Desvigne et Ses Fils, 1931–39.

Lombroso, Cesare. *Criminal Man*. New York: G. P. Putnam's Sons, 1911.

Lunde, Donald T. *Murder and Madness*. San Francisco: San Francisco Press, 1975.

Mannheim, Hermann. *Comparative Criminology. A Text Book*. (2 Vols.) London: Routledge & Kegan Paul, 1965.

Mark, Robert and Peter D. Scott. *The Disease of Crime: Punishment or Treatment?* Beccles: William Clowes, 1972.

Messick, Hank and Burt Goldblatt. *Kidnapping. The Illustrated History*. New York: The Dial Press, 1974.

Michaud, Stephen G. and Hugh Aynesworth. *The Only Living Witness*. New York: Linden Press/Simon & Schuster, 1983.

Montarron, Marcel. *Histoire des crimes sexuals*. Paris: Plon, 1970.

Nash, Jay Robert. *Murder, America*. London: Harrap, 1981.

Norris, Joel. *Serial Killers*. New York: Doubleday, 1988.

Notable British Trials. (A series comprising 83 titles.)

Pascal, André. *Pranzini: The Crime in the Rue Montaigne*. London: Rich & Cowan, 1935.

Pelham, Camden. *The Chronicles of Crime; or The New Newgate Calendar*. (2 Vols.) London: Reeves and Turner, 1886.

Picton, Bernard. *Murder, Suicide or Accident*. London: Hale, 1971.

Pinkerton, Matthew Worth. *Murder in All Ages*. Chicago: A. F. Pinkerton & Co., 1898.

Pollard, H. B. C. *A History of Firearms*. London: Geoffrey Bles, 1926.

Rhodes, Henry T. F. *Clues and Crime*. London: John Murray, 1933.

—— *In the Tracks of Crime*. London: Turnstile Press, 1952.

Rule, Ann. *The Stranger Beside Me*. New York: W. W. Norton, 1980.

Sanders, Ed. *The Family. The Story of Charles Manson's Dune Buggy Attack Battalion*. London: Rupert Hart-Davis, 1972.

Scott, Harold, ed. *Crime and Criminals. The Concise Encyclopedia*. London: Andre Deutsch, 1961.

Sifakis, Carl. *The Encyclopedia of American Crime*. New York: Facts on File, 1982.

Simpson, Antony Eric. *Masculinity and Control: The Prosecution of Sex Offenses in Eighteenth-century London*. (2 Vols.) Ann Arbor: University Microfilms International, 1984.

Simpson, Keith. *Forty Years of Murder*. London: Harrap, 1978.

Smith, Fred J. *The Principles and Practice of Medical Jurisprudence*. (2 Vols.) London: J. & A. Churchill, 1905.

Smith, Sydney. *Mostly Murder*. London: Harrap, 1959.

Stead, Philip John. *The Memoirs of Lacenaire*. London and New York: Staples Press, 1952.

—— *Vidocq. A Biography*. London and New York: Staples Press, 1953.

Svensson, Arne and Otto Wendel. *Crime Detection*. London: Cleaver-Hume Press, 1954.

Taylerson, Anthony W. F. *The Revolver 1865–1888*. London: Herbert Jenkins, 1966.

—— *The Revolver 1889–1914*. London: Barrie & Jenkins, 1970.

Thompson, Charles J. S. *Poison Mysteries Unsolved*. London: Hutchinson, 1937.

—— *Poisons and Poisoners*. London: Harold Shaylor, 1931.

Thompson, John. *Crime Scientist*. London: Harrap, 1980.

Thorwald, Jürgen. *The Century of the Detective*. New York: Harcourt, Brace & World, 1964.

—— *Crime and Science. The New Frontier in Criminology*. New York: Harcourt, Brace & World, 1967.

Tullett, Tom. *Clues to Murder. Forensic Murder Investigations of Professor J. M. Cameron*. London: The Bodley Head, 1986.

Wagner, Margaret Seaton, *The Monster of Dusseldorf. The Life and Trial of Peter Kürten*. London: Faber & Faber, 1932.

Wailer, George. *Kidnap. The Story of the Lindbergh Case*. London: Hamish Hamilton, 1961.

Walls, H. J. *Expert Witness. My Thirty Years in Forensic Science*. London: John Long, 1972.

Whipple, Sidney B. *The Trial of Bruno Richard Hauptmann*. London: Heinemann, 1937.

Wilkinson, George Theodore. *The Newgate Calendar*. London: T. Werner Laurie, 1932.

Wilson, Colin. *A Casebook of Murder*. London: Leslie Frewin, 1969.

—— *Order of Assassins. A Psychology of Murder*. London: Rupert Hart-Davis, 1972.

—— and Robin Odell. *Jack the Ripper. Summing Up and Verdict*. London: Transworld, 1987.

—— and Patricia Pitman. *Encyclopedia of Murder*. New York: G. P. Putnam's Sons, 1962.

—— and Donald Seaman. *Encyclopedia of Modern Murder*. 1962–1982. London: Arthur Baker, 1983.

Yochelson, Samuel and Stanton F. Samenow. *The Criminal Personality*. (3 Vols.) New York: Jason Aronson, 1976–8.

Index